The Adventures of Tom Sawyer (1876) *The Adventures of Huckleberry Finn* (1885) ***The Man That Corrupted Hadleyburg*** (1900)	Mark Twain [S[illegible] (1[illegible]
Miss Ravenal's Conversion from Secession to Loyalty (1876)	John [illegible] Forest (1826-1906)
A Fool's Errand (1879)	Albion Winegar Tourgee (1838-1905)
Ben Hur (1880)	Gen. Lew Wallace (1827-1905)
Washington Square (1881) *The Ambassadors* (1903)	Henry James (1843-1916)
The Story of a Country Town (1883)	E. W. Howe (1853-1937)
Ramona (1884)	Helen Hunt Jackson (1831-1885)
The Rise of Silas Lapham (1885)	William Dean Howells (1837-1920)
East Angels (1886)	Constance Fenimore Woolson (1840-1894)
Looking Backward (1888)	Edward Bellamy (1850-1898)
In the Valley (1890) *The Damnation of Theron Ware* (1896)	Harold Frederic (1856-1898)
Colonel Carter of Cartersville (1891)	F. Hopkinson Smith (1838-1915)
The Cliff-Dwellers (1893)	Henry Blake Fuller (1857-1929)
Maggie: A Girl of the Streets (1893) *The Red Badge of Courage* (1895)	Stephen Crane (1871-1900)
A Kentucky Cardinal (1894)	James Lane Allen (1849-1925)
David Harum (1898)	Edward Noyes Westcott (1846-1898)
When Knighthood Was in Flower (1898)	Charles Major (1856-1913)
McTeague (1899)	Frank Norris (1870-1902)
To Have and to Hold (1899)	Mary Johnston (1870-1936)
Sister Carrie (1900) *An American Tragedy* (1925)	Theodore Dreiser (1871-1945)
The Virginian (1902)	Owen Wister (1860-1938)
The Sea Wolf (1904)	Jack London (1876-1916)
The Jungle (1906)	Upton Sinclair (1878-)
Melanctha (1909) *The Making of Americans* (1925)	Gertrude Stein (1874-1946)
Ethan Frome (1911)	Edith Wharton (1862-1937)
Westways (1913)	Dr. Silas Weir Mitchell (1829-1913)

See back cover for continuation of this chart.

AMERICAN SHORT NOVELS

Reader's Bookshelf of American Literature

American Drama, edited by Alan S. Downer

American Literary Essays, edited by Lewis Leary

American Poetry, edited by Karl Shapiro

American Short Novels, edited by R. P. Blackmur

American Short Stories, edited by Ray B. West, Jr.

GENERAL EDITOR: WILLIAM VAN O'CONNOR

American Short Novels

Edited by R. P. Blackmur

Thomas Y. Crowell Company · New York · Established 1834

Designed by Laurel Wagner
Library of Congress Catalog Card Number 60-6314
Manufactured in the United States of America
By Kingsport Press, Inc., Kingsport, Tennessee

Acknowledgments

Acknowledgment is gratefully made as follows for permission to reprint copyrighted novels.

Herman Melville, *Billy Budd.* Edited by Frederic Barron Freeman and corrected by Elizabeth Treeman. Cambridge, Mass.: Harvard University Press. Copyright, 1948, 1956 by the President and Fellows of Harvard College. Reprinted by permission of the publishers.

Gertrude Stein, *Melanctha.* From *Selected Writings of Gertrude Stein,* copyright 1909 and renewed 1936 by Gertrude Stein. Reprinted by permission of Random House, Inc.

Mark Twain, *The Man That Corrupted Hadleyburg.* Reprinted by permission of Harper & Brothers.

William Carlos Williams, *The Great American Novel.* Reprinted with the kind permission of the author.

Elinor Wylie, *The Venetian Glass Nephew.* Reprinted from *Collected Prose of Elinor Wylie* with permission of Alfred A. Knopf, Inc. Copyright 1925, 1933 by Alfred A. Knopf, Inc.

Contents

AMERICAN SHORT NOVELS

The Short Novel

Among forms, moreover, we had had, on dimensional ground—for length and breadth—our ideal, the beautiful and blest *nouvelle*, the generous, the enlightened hour for which appeared thus at last to shine. It was under the star of the *nouvelle* that, in other languages, a hundred interesting and charming results . . . all economically arrived at. . . . It had taken the blank misery of our Anglo-Saxon sense of such matters to organize, as might be said, the general indifference to this fine type of composition. In that dull view a "short story" was a "short story," and that was the end of it. Shades and differences, varieties and styles, the value above all of the idea happily *developed*, languished, to extinction, under the hard-and-fast rule of "from six to eight thousand words"—when, for one's benefit, the rigour was a little relaxed. For myself, I delighted in the shapely *nouvelle* —as, for that matter, I had from time to time and here and there been almost encouraged to show.

HENRY JAMES, Preface to *The Lesson of the Master*

Introduction

Fictions are what we make of ourselves, and they cannot help reflecting something of our character and forecasting something of our fate. One of the honest commonplaces of conversation is that knowledge of a strange country is better gained from its imaginative literature than from its guidebooks, history, and statistics. There is a sense in which it may be said that Greece wrote Homer, Rome Virgil, Italy Dante, Spain Cervantes, England Shakespeare, and Germany Goethe. (I myself found that the Mardrus-Mather *Arabian Nights,* read complete just before going to Cairo, made me at home there in an old-fashioned way, and the *Tale of Genji* was a considerable help in Tokyo, but I cannot say that the *Mahabharata* helped much in Delhi.) In the sense in which it is pertinent today this can be detached from the mass of impertinence: every writer is necessarily in some relation to his actual society and its culture when it has one, and the relation remains actual even when the writer lies, exaggerates or denies, or revolts against that society.

It was the French *ésprit* (mind taken with the effect of *spirit*) that inhabited Rousseau and assumed his romanticism, and it was made deliberately preposterous in Stendhal's wonderful almost autonomous lies. Great writers perhaps prophesy and enact the history and characters of great countries by giving their feelings form and their thought the special twist of idiom. The writers come, as each of the great masters named above came, at the time their countries reach a new stage of identity. Lesser writers perhaps reflect that identity, its lapses and recoveries, the hypocrisies and sincerities of custom and behavior by which it gets along. A new novel, or a novel newly read, is news from everywhere good every day, as if the best journalism were written ahead of time only waiting for behavior to catch up with its forms or to react against them. No matter what the lie, it is told in relation to the truth; no matter what the eccentricity, the center is at hand, and the end is missed or gained with respect to the means. Literature is the free will of the soul—as some say it is his words that make man conscious of his soul—circling about the will of things and the will of history. Literature has the great merit that it can be apt and false at once to the drift of truth, if only it knows how to say so. Thus it is we look for knowledge of a strange country to its tales and meditations about itself, and our own country is the strangest ever. But it is hard to generalize that intimate knowledge.

To an American who has not read his own serious literature for some time and who comes back to it (and I should suppose also to the unblemished reader who looks at it for the first time) its most striking general characteristic (aside from the recognition of detail and the authenticity of the idiom) is its steady habit of using the symbolic imagination, rather than the narrative or dramatic. The forest of symbols in it regards us with a frightening familiarity of glance, and we see at once we must find out what those symbols mean or would mean if we could put them together. We see the problematic quicker than we see the immediate, and indeed the immediate seems often to have been left out or to have become hidden in remote motions of the imagination. Action is just over the edge of vision, and its symbols draw us on. To D. H. Lawrence, and to other foreign writers, symbolism seemed inherent in the American literary character, or if not inherent seemed the result of an effort to make up for a defect in our culture. Either we write by nature more than we know or we will ourselves to write about what we cannot grasp except through symbolism. That is to say, if you like, religiously; but I would not like to say just that. Two other things, either one or both, seem more plausible to say. One derives from the notion that St. Thomas took about allegory: that it is the habit of so writing that words shall signify certain objects which in their turn signify something else. The other is that America has reached—indeed had reached it long ago—a stage of imagination singularly lacking in training in the unconscious skills which afford immediate body to the works of other cultures; less is present by nature in our words, therefore we must put more into them. The immense sophistication of the best American writing—Poe, Hawthorne, James, Melville, and Whitman (who wrote for the most sophisticated possible of audiences, the elite of sophisticated barbarians) was the effect of the need to put more into our words—in short, to invest them as symbols—than came with them at voting age. This is the live heart of Henry James's complaint on behalf of Hawthorne about the American lack of court and church and the various other external costumes of society.

Only the other day, according to the New York *Times,* Mr. Eisenhower's appearance at his dinner for Mr. Khrushchev was accompanied by a ruffle of drums; the president was in white tie but his chief guest, like the shade of Franklin, wore what is now called a dark business suit. The problem remains the same. Was it allegory in St. Thomas' sense? Was it sophistication grasping necessity? Only that great novel of American Culture, *The Education of Henry Adams,* could make any answer, and Adams' answer is now some fifty years stale in the writing and a full century in the reference. I mean especially the chapter called "The Perfection of Human Society"—a phrase detached from Charles Sumner, who made it of England in adulation, and applied by Adams as a weapon to the English "society" of the 1860's. Adams' own regular novels of the 80's, *Democracy* and *Esther,* pushed in both directions, *Democracy* for sophisticated symbolism and *Esther* which he said was written in blood, for that kind of allegory in which the originally signified objects go on creating forever.

The student of American literature who is intrigued by this problem, and who has himself a flexible mind, will turn from description to description of it in the fictions at hand, seeing himself first in one mirror then in another, but he is unlikely to reach any one position—let alone any solution—unless he arrests his powers of observation. As Henry Adams once said on one of his many returns from Europe to America, the American mind has never held that any one form of the good was *necessarily* superior to any other form; and this is also true of the forms of American imagination. It is only in his hysterias—his flashing manias, his occasional *idées fixes*—that the certainties of the American mind are absolute, and the hysterias change with the certainties. A freshman recently remarked in an examination on his abilities in English composition that he had no time to read because he spent all his time being civilized; which I suppose was his way of saying that every American has to make his culture for himself—which might be called the American Experiment. This is not true in itself; but there is certainly an effect of its being taken as if true in most of the leading American writers—especially when they make it out of some primitive culture, which is out of their own alien innocence; and perhaps most especially when they make it out of "European" culture, which is out of a borrowed guilt. We shall be saved neither by the Eskimo nor by any form whatever of the *ancien régime*, but the gestures of trying either are symbols of our hidden action. Whitman and Eliot, Melville and James, point our way. No wonder our writers have turned to allegory in one or another combination of its forms by which they could express what they had not achieved or could create what they did not yet know—like the morals in Faulkner's novels. (This differs from the works of those still inhabited by a culture: they create what they did not know, or only partly knew, that they knew—like the chorus of the women of Canterbury in Eliot's *Murder in the Cathedral.*) Many considerations arise from these notions. One feels the host at the back, and one seems about to see very far ahead into the possible drama of the American mind, till there is vertigo in the heart and blackness at the rim of vision. Stopping short of all that, which is the wound of incentive in the private sensibility, it is yet in the presence of these notions (and with a sense of their margins of possibility) that we can proceed to comment on some seven short American novels. But what we say will be affected by the forms of writing used.

Henry James is the only author on the list who was naturally a novelist in the old sense, earned between the time of Cervantes and that of Balzac—though Stephen Crane might have become so had he lived and found a positive talent. When you read the early James you can legitimately think of Scott and Dickens and Trollope, of Balzac, Flaubert, and Turgenev; his work is a continuous development and modification of the work of his predecessors as these were affected by his deepening sensibility and his increasing virtuosity in form and in language; but the sense of the story is never lost and the feeling for drama in the theatrical sense is everywhere cultivated. Thus *Washington Square* is both in the first and the last place a story in which the scene is more important that the episode. It was something written and something told pretty much without any external or over-riding ambition. James was already, in 1881, when he published the story, what thirty-odd years later he was to call himself in a letter to Henry Adams—he was already that "obstinate finality, the artist." He made life into stories and stories into life by skilled acts of nature. The role was perhaps not yet self-conscious, but it was there to play, not only when there was nothing else to play, but always—like what happens when you wake up—by a kind of second nature which had very nearly extinguished the first.

James, that is, was a professional author *tout court,* altogether, and at once. This is perhaps why so much of what he wrote hovers on the edge of disappearing into the mechanical forms which in his early years he borrowed and which later on he invented. Under his method a very little life could be very greatly felt. Whenever a man lives by method he seems to the outsider to live very little at all, even though, and possibly because, his every second is fatally occupied. James was impervious to every force to which he could not give a form, and what makes him a writer of great stature was the gradual deepening of the themes which beset him to find them form. The deepening was into the action of the human heart, and especially a heart deprived or frustrated which had in its own beat to make up for all that it had lost or had been kept from doing.

Without that deepening, James would have become, when his early freshness was lost, a popular, amusing, and forgotten writer. In his own later language he would have succumbed to "the platitude of mere statement." The deepening was what turned the struggle for money, for position, for prestige, for marriage, for all the goods of this world, into the contest of adverse wills. For James, the goods of this world expressed the desperate tangle of good and evil: of the innocence every creature has in inexhaustible reservoir and the encroaching tide of the evil that will be done to it, not so much by major motive as by the general shabbiness of our moral equipment. Our goods, his tales seem to say, are not adequate to express our needs, or to reach our ends; and yet the good, to repeat Aristotle, is what all things aim at. What then? what must be done? Nobody has ever been able to solve the problem of the good, except by offering bon-bons which sully the taste or apéritifs which replace appetite. In James the heroes and heroines offer no solutions, just as they reach no victories. Either they die, having recognized life as a Medusa, or they make renunciations as the nearest to a positive action they can take on behalf of life. Death leaves room for the next person, and renunciation seems to allow the momentum of life to take over. Death and renunciation are for these men and women the only available forms they can give to life when the goods of the world fall away. We think of Strether in *The Ambassadors,* of Isabelle in the *Portrait of a Lady,* or of Milly dead and Densher renouncing in *The Wings of the Dove.*

And so it is that we think of Catherine Sloper, at the end of *Washington Square,* in a limbo from which she will never be withdrawn where the quality of life is clear and its substance missing: the heiress of the human Psyche who has thrown away everything and insists she has lost nothing. It is a role very near and sharp to the romantic heart we have created for ourselves. We long for it against all our good sense, for we believe we could make ourselves meaningful if only we could sit still, if only we could keep the glory of our patience. Catherine is still and patient in her sitting room on a spring afternoon; it is sunny outside, but only a little way into the room the sun stops, and the light airs ruffle no more than the curtains. They belly against the sash. The sun is known by his shadows. Miss Sloper has a long time to live, and it will be longer, and more alive, because of what, on one mistake, she has given up.

Two facts are plain about the history of Catherine Sloper; its frame or scaffolding of convention is as melodramatic as *East Lynne* or *Crime and Punishment,* and its inner structure may be as properly related to Aristotle's *Poetics* as that of any work of modern Christian imagination. That is why the story was relatively popular when it appeared and perhaps also why it could be transformed into both a play and a movie without much formal loss. The strength was in the form of the action and in the familiarity and "natural" authority of the human types who make up its roll of persons; the reader or the spectator knew by long practice what to bring with him of immediate actuality to make the meaning and the motion of the meaning his own. The details did not matter so long as they were freshly observed, for the frame and the structure would lend force and identity to any details. We will know how to speak these lines when they are given us; the generalizations upon which they depend are already part of our private lives if not part of our culture. Melodrama is how we would like to live, if we did not know better; and Aristotle, looking at Sophocles, generalized the patterns by which we can look at life as melodrama even when we do know better. Not every scene can bring the house down, but every scene may lead to the idea of doing so. There is no sweeter vision than the world lying in ruins—while we, however ruined, remain steadfast in our purpose. That is why we distrust the good man; we know very well he sees us in ruins.

But to return to our facts. In *Washington Square,* we have the upright well-meaning father who wishes to protect his daughter from all possible worlds, especially from the wiles of her fortune-hunting lover and the follies of her aunt as well as from herself, and when she refuses to be protected threatens to disinherit her, and subsequently cuts her off with less than a fortune because she refuses to promise him not to marry her villainous lover. Thus she brings about her exclusion from the goods and evils of the world and alienates herself from her father, her aunt, and her lover—all by the exercise of her simpleton and obsessed will. This is melodrama that loses rather than that which wins. There is no true lover waiting against the folds of the portières, no posthumous disclosure of fatherly forgiveness; her melodrama has brought her house quite, quite down. There is instead an increasing distance of intimacy between Catherine Sloper and ourselves, and if we closed the distance the intimacy would be gone. Only one thing can this new-made maiden aunt treasure. Throughout her short life this plain and somewhat stupid girl has been tampered with—by her willful father, whose intelligence could not compass his daughter, by her silly aunt, and by her chosen lover. Now, after her reversal of roles and of fortune, and after her recognition that her lover did not love her even for his own sake let alone for hers, after all this one thinks she feels sure that however people may use her for the rest of her life, no one will ever again tamper with her. She turns from the window as the light fails, untouchable and faintly luminous; and to her changed heart even the movements of human affection had become an intolerable kind of tamperage. In James the social melodrama was translated into an allegory of the piercing virtue—Emily Dickinson's phrase—of renunciation. But the allegory is united with the story and needs no interpretation beyond the story, in much the same way that human behavior requires only confrontation and recognition.

James, then, wrote what we may call natural allegory, which is not to say primitive or willful, for it had lost the main part of its machinery and had become a skill in the blood of imagination whereby things put in motion could become their own meaning without losing, but increasing rather, their own identity. This is not at all the case with Melville's *Billy Budd,* which seems to have been the last thing Melville wrote, perhaps about 1891, though it was not published until 1924. Melville wrote Allegory in all the machinery of capital letters in the hope of finding—or creating—an absolute structure within which he could make a concert of the contrary powers of heaven and earth. Like Shakespeare, he had to make a concord out of discord, and especially out of the shifting discords of good and evil. His story could never be content to be a story, or its own meaning, but was compelled to assert a meaning which had not yet come to pass. The figures of Billy Budd, of Claggart, and of Captain Vere are something that has happened to the human, by human agency, against human interests. It is an example of Melville seeking, as he said Shakespeare did, what he must shun—but what, if you like, he must put up with all the more because he has sought it in the lonely places of the unmitigated and unaccommodated self. Though there is a story—a series of connected events—the story provides chiefly a frame for a series of meditations, and the story in the end would not hang together without the meditations which extract, which create, meaning from the series of events in the words of the mind as they are fused in the words of the senses. Consider, then, what takes place.

An impressed sailor in the British navy during the Napoleonic wars is falsely accused of mutiny by the master at arms. When confronted with his accuser by the captain, he is tongue-tied and strikes his accuser dead. The captain tries him by court-martial and he is hanged the following morning. There are only the antennae of human relations between the three figures concerned, and in any case the human relations are transformed by the accusation and the blow into official relations. It is as if the human and the official relations were warring forces, each of which was unstable from internal strife: the war we seek and shun.

Thus the facts reach immediately into a kind of form for all facts, their hidden and hideous form; and it is this form upon which Melville's meditations cast light, but we cannot say what it is except that we feel it as a unity. It is worth remembering that the great medieval masters of allegory *believed* in a unity of the world and of apprehension as already there, as a point of departure, and their allegories were intended only as interpretation, whereas most modern allegorists, such as Melville, believe increasingly in the fragmentary and the divisive out of which they wish to create a unity. This may account for the effect of strain and the air of hocus-pocus which seems to inhabit insistent and deliberate allegory as compared to the skilled ease of the older practice. Yet the two forms face what is at heart much the same situation; it is merely that God has turned his face to a fresh profile. We are, as we constantly hear, in defect of faith both of what we know and of what we do not know. There is at least a part of us, and perhaps our most energetic part, like those in Dante's limbo who had not the chance to worship God as he ought to be worshiped, since they lived in the other time and lacked baptism. "For such defects," says Virgil in *The Divine Comedy,* "and for no other fault, are we lost; and only insofar afflicted, that without hope we live in desire. *Senza speme vivemo in disio.*" Thomas Mann used this form to describe, in *Doctor Faustus,* the hell of the furious modern imagination, and Melville wrote from an earlier stage of the same condition, the stage of incredulous mutiny. It is possible that no man could mutiny against a unity in which he believed; but which of us is in belief all the time? There are moments when nothing is precious; others when belief falters. But any of us have the inner power to mutiny against either an imposed unity or a created unity, even when ourselves have created or imposed it.

In *Billy Budd* there was mutiny of several sorts. There was the mutiny of the evil against the good, as these entered human forms (as Judas mutinied against Jesus, and as Peter came near doing so, both in the line of Adam) as new creations. There was also the general perpetual possibility of mutiny against the imposed unity of the navy. The navy is always on the threshold of mutiny, no doubt because of the sharpness and clarity of its laws. Law cannot be just to the individual though the laws are themselves just and therefore command the sacrifice of the individual.

Just so we must sacrifice the good in order to put up with the evil. In his allegory of the mutinous human spirit Melville created his necessities: that the good is worth its death, where the evil merely deserves it, and I expect that something like this was what Captain Vere thought when he lay on his deathbed in Gibraltar muttering of Billy Budd; at any rate it was to such a thought that his actions had conformed. From the backward dream of the admirable there had emerged the scapegoat who must be sacrificed for the image of others' redemption, and to impose the sacrifice was the task of the rational and sensitive mind. One thinks of Brutus, in Shakespeare's play, just before the murder of Caesar:

The Genius and the mortal instruments
Are then in council, and the state of man
Like to a little kingdom suffers then
The nature of an insurrection.

But where Brutus acted upon the stage of history and in the dimensions of a hero, Captain Vere acted upon a kind of timeless stage, quite outside history, where men were mainly forces meaning things other than themselves, for their selves were incredible unless taken as gestures pointing, and beckoning, beyond. Billy Budd was an unstigmatized and unjustified saint, with a presence that put down quarrels, and made your ordinary villain love him. He was a child-man, whose "child's utter innocence is but its blank ignorance." His "simple-mindedness is unaffected by experience." He has "none of that intuitive knowledge of the bad which in natures not good or incompletely so foreruns experience." When he lies in irons and asleep the chaplain kisses the cheek of the innocent beauty. He could "in the nude . . . have passed for a statue of young Adam before the Fall." He was, so to speak, all of the good that is possible without experience.

That is a great deal too much for human nature to bear, and it is a relief for us to hear: "Baby Budd, *Jemmy Legs* is down on you." Claggart the ship's policeman is down on him, and his antipathy is called forth by Billy Budd's harmlessness. Claggart had "something defective or abnormal in the constitution and the blood," and he is altogether familiar to that part of the imagination which roves after images of pure evil in the smother of waking nightmare. He is "the direct reverse of a saint." Melville's phrases belong in the gothic dark at the end of every hall in the brain. "To pass from a normal nature to him one must cross 'the deadly space between' and this is best done by indirection. . . . a master of reason in the world, a riot of exemption in the heart. . . . With no power to annul the elemental evil in him, tho readily enough he could hide it; apprehending the good, but powerless to be it; a nature like Claggart's surcharged with energy as such natures almost invariably are, what recourse is left to it but to recoil upon itself and like the scorpion for which the Creator alone is responsible, act out to the end the part allotted to it. . . . Claggart's conscience being but the lawyer to his will." He is the incarnation of evil, and when the tongue-tied Billy Budd kills him, Captain Vere cries out: "Struck dead by an angel of God! Yet the angel must hang!"

As these symbolic figures clash and reverberate in Melville's meditations, one is struck with the possibility that whenever both good and evil are raised to their ideal force a permanent civil war is discovered in the nature that raises them, yet so to raise them is a regular temptation of our wills. When Billy Budd is hanged his last words are: "God bless Captain Vere!" These words are echoed by the crew, but a few moments later there is a rising mutter which makes a "sullen revocation" of that echo; and there is no longer any truth in the matter.

Some say that in this tale Melville recorded a final reconciliation with life and assented to society and nature, human and otherwise. I do not think so; I think rather he set loose one more set of images in a continuing allegory of how it is that we seek what we must shun. The truth, as Melville said, has ragged edges, whether or not uncompromisingly told, and it is the mutinous heart or the mutinous sea equally that shows those edges. The mutiny remains, and is the action of nature. In allegories of Melville's kind we make that action our own.

It is perhaps because we make these rash allegories, which then, like all allegories of damnation and salvation, imprison us in the action they engender, that another part of the spirit rebels in another way, and in the name of reality makes a burlesque both of our morals in action and of the allegories that appear to dominate them. Burlesque is how we tolerate reality when we cannot see visions, but we often do not give these names to what we are doing and would deny the names if they were offered to us. To repudiate categories is almost an act of nature, as to make them is another. Nevertheless or because of this it seems convenient to call such works as Stephen Crane's *Maggie* and Mark Twain's *The Man That Corrupted Hadleyburg* burlesque allegories of reality. Each was written in the hope that it would mean and be what it ought to mean and be, and each proceeded from prior generalizations to the instance in hand—as if a generalization could ever create an instance, or even mirror one, except cloudily. In art of the ambitious kind it is the generalizing power of the mind that seizes upon the instance and revitalizes itself; which is what Crane did in *The Open Boat* and Mark Twain in *Hucklebury Finn*. But art does not need to be so ambitious as all that, and the arbitrary content of the mind does very well for ordinary and familiar purposes. What we already know is quite enough for burlesque allegories, and needs only skill in handling the appropriate conventions of the form used.

"A very little boy stood upon a heap of gravel for the honor of Rum Alley. He was throwing stones at howling urchins from Devil's Row, who were circling madly about the heap and pelting him. His infantile countenance was livid with the fury of battle. His small body was writhing in the delivery of oaths."

This is the beginning paragraph of *Maggie: A Girl of the Streets*. Though no particular promise has been made, yet something has been promised—in the setting of the scene, in this first action under the subtitle, "A girl of the streets." We do not want to know precisely where and what we are, because we know quite enough to go on with; and we know it most from the diction, which is the diction of burlesque—the high language of low purpose. It is the diction which promises, and at the end of the tale it is the diction which rounds off the promise. In the beginning it is the brother who writhes "in the delivery of oaths"; in the end it is the mother who writhes in a burlesque of mourning.

"The mourner essayed to speak, but her voice gave way. She shook her great shoulders frantically, in an agony of grief. The tears seemed to scald her face. Finally her voice came and arose in a scream of pain. 'Oh, yes, I'll fergive her! I'll fergive her!' "

In between, Maggie, sister of the brute and daughter of the sot, had become a girl of the streets with no other equipment for the role than her circumstances, and had died as people die in the newspapers, after the brief—or long—illness of her life, in unconscious burlesque of her own possibilities. This is the allegory of evil forgiving evil by pushing it out of sight in brutality, seduction, drunkenness and prostitution, with the good pushed out of sight altogether without qualification, like blighted innocence pushed into the snowstorm which falls for that purpose. Everything happens at the perimeter of sensibility and is only known, where burlesque joins it, through a grossness of sentiment, to reality. What gives this fiction its force, and has led it to be called a realistic work, is that this is how many people make articulate their public, and indeed even their most private, reactions to life. The burlesque and the allegory are together what makes life seem tolerable when its momentum is not felt—when no events are felt astir—to these people who are "in" but not "of" the society where they find themselves.

The Man That Corrupted Hadleyburg exposes a different relation and a different psychology, that of an outsider who nevertheless participated in his society as one of the gods who make cruel sport of the fragile and preposterous structures of human virtue and its Siamese twin, human cant. But it is that curious outsider at work here who has the interests of natural virtue at heart. Like the elder Henry James, the father of the novelist, he understood the horror in the market place of flagrant morality, but unlike the novelist he never tried the broken steps on the moral staircase. One cannot think of Mark Twain wildly in air. He knew nothing of the perpetual disrepair in human institutions, and never groped for a missing handrail; his pessimism walked on solid if uneven ground. Hence his burlesque was nothing in the way of expression for the unwary and deluded, it was rather a castigation and a reduction of the canting form of the pretentious allegory whereby they managed their public relations. It is not a noble but it is a satisfying act to take revenge upon the cant one has suffered for a lifetime, even when one has oneself to masquerade in fraud and cant in order to do so. There is no escaping evil for the man who sets himself up to do good, and our fictions, which tamper with actions by giving them new constructions, make this almost as plain as our actions themselves do. It is the weakness of the human mind that it can get little help from its truths and must do the work of the world by its precious lies. Thus one trembles after every moment of sincerity. As in ourselves, it is the stranger within that corrupted Hadleyburg, and in telling his tale Mark Twain followed an old tradition. *Corruptio optima pessima,* which is a little nearer truth in Latin, because of compactness, than in English. In corruption the best is the worst.

"It was many years ago," Mark Twain begins reassuringly, and goes on with his fairy tale, so sonorous with his hatred of reality: "Hadleyburg was the most honest and upright town in all the region round about. It had kept that reputation unsmirched during three generations, and was prouder of it than of any other of its possessions. . . . Also, throughout the formative years temptations were kept out of the way of the young people, so that their honesty could have every chance to harden and solidify, and become a part of their very bone." Here again, as with *Maggie,* the title sets the course and promises a port, and the diction, so to speak, gives the weather of the voyage; so that it seems the fitting end of the sequence when, after all nineteen of Hadleyburg's leading citizens had "fallen a prey to the fiendish sack," the town changed its name by an act of the legislature and the motto on its seal by an omissive act of its own. Each of the nineteen had laid fraudulent claim to a unique act of virtue, eighteen of them flagrantly in open town meeting in a grand burlesque allegory of how unfortified virtue comes to a bad end. The nineteenth, who had been saved at the meeting by the cruel charity of Mr. Burgess, the clergyman who sat in the chair, made his claim in the agonized obloquy of a deathbed confession which was not believed and which renewed a wrong done many years earlier to the clergyman, whereby he had lost his cure of souls in Hadleyburg. The change of motto was the omission of the negative from a phrase in the Lord's Prayer so that it read: "Lead us into temptation." One wonders whether Mark Twain's might not have changed the next phrase of the prayer to read: "And deliver us unto evil," for it seems to be the meaning involved in the irony of the concluding sentence. "It is an honest town once more, and the man will rise early that catches it napping again."

It is perhaps a pity that the fiendish sack of false money should have provided the active motive for corruption when there are so many other darker temptations at hand. But Mark Twain was on sound *a priori* ground, that money is the root of all evil, which I suppose means that money is the most available agent and lever for converting the potency of evil into action—as we see in family quarrels about wills that are defective and can be broken. The point is that in Mark Twain's allegory the figure of the fiendish sack is immediately and universally believed, as is the probability that someone had made the remark, "You are far from being a bad man: Go, and reform." And if there were any that did not believe, there were none that did not delightedly and excitedly accept the burlesque excesses of the exposure that follows. What the reader believes is something else again. Perhaps he believes at a distance. Certainly what has happened in the tale does not work in him as Melville's *Billy Budd* does, nor does it hold the possibility of a personal role as Catharine Sloper does in *Washington Square;* yet what he sees is nearer to him than the accidents of circumstance in *Maggie*. What he sees is perhaps a parody of himself—he knows he is more and fears he is less than the parody shows. There ought to be an old saying, for it is everywhere illustrated, that no man is ever more than a parody of his best self.

On that sentiment we make a transition to Gertrude Stein and her story *Melanctha,* for she mined the deep possibilities of the self seen and created in parody as skillfully as any author of our time, especially in her early works, *The Making of Americans* and *Three Lives,* from which *Melanctha* is taken. What is meant by parody here is everything that goes with her best-known phrase, which so many have further parodied in quoting it: "A rose is a rose is a rose is a rose. . . ." Repetition and recurrence and periodicity in varying cycles produce changing patterns which are often astonishing, sometimes impenetrable, and occasionally full of *éclairissement* or completing enlightenment. As these patterns move they seem bound for infinity or one place short of it, and yet suggest simultaneously that at any moment they may be arrested by death, by collapse of interest, or by a willful boredom of sensibility—as if all the different clocks should stop ticking. There is no simpler figure for how her patterns are made and how they move than the kaleidoscope, where a small number of irregular pieces of colored glass are multiplied into changing patterns by a still smaller number of reflectors as the cylinder within which they are contained is little by little revolved: they shake, teeter, crash, or faintly modulate, securing novelty and affirming pattern—making prophecy and deriving from history—

as each precarious balance is succeeded by another. Thus we imitate the numerical mechanism of nature by mechanizing it a little further and by denaturalizing it (since we do not have the momentum or skill of nature) as little as may be. The chips of glass are substantive in nature and formal in their procession, color and translucence have a good deal to do with the effect of rearrangement, yet with each rearrangement a new force is precipitated, or sometimes aborted. So it is with Gertrude Stein; only her chips are not glass but fragments of human personality, emotion, action, and sensibility. Sometimes she changes the selection of the chips a little, and sometimes her creative presence intrudes to modify the tone. She cannot help trying to make up by her presence for what her method has compelled her to leave out. The method is not new; the Pindaric ode is the classical example; much Provençal poetry and the sestinas of Dante are another; what is new is the deliberate narrowness of scope in the selection of the chips and the repudiation, as far as possible, of the other and more rational modes of the mind in favor of the mode of intuition.

In Gertrude Stein intuition becomes a mode of abstraction, the thing itself is its own generalization, and the pattern of intuition takes on the obligations of rational imagination. It is as if for mastery one had to reject all help from what the mind has already learned from other minds. She is a beautiful but primitive example of Croce's aesthetic which says that poetry gives theoretic form to our intuitions of feeling; beautiful because she does so much, primitive because she ignores the further nature of the power with which she does it. It is allegory freed from all structure of belief, and imprisoned by what the solitary mind is capable of with the two helps of words and patterns. One of the things she is freed from is the plot which Aristotle called the soul—the form of forms—of the action, the shape of the myth by which we see human action rise, stretch itself upon experience, and reach its end. We can do without all that, she seems to say, and we must do without it; for it corrupts and twists and binds us, and we do not live like that. We must change our account of the world according to what we find in our natures as our unimpeded intuitions reveal them in words. Thus she is compelled to charge her words with their meanings by turning and returning them until their repetitions and modulations become a pattern. Luckily for her enterprise there is a common stock of both words and intuitions into which hers enter and to which we, the readers, can if we will bring ours; and so together we make a plot just the same.

Only, as our culture seems to desire, it is an unfinished plot. There is a shapiness to it but there is no final shape which can be repeated, perhaps changed a little, in the adventure of new experience. The mastery of life by intuition alone constitutes a surrender to it as experience; when we insist too much on our own meanings, things dwindle in their own meaningfulness. It is a sad delight to read *Melanctha,* for we are reminded as we watch her procession of gestures of every misgiving we have ever felt in our own self-confidence. The story of Melanctha Herbert caresses us as we see how she got blue and consumed away. First she tries to create love by asserting her intuitions upon reality. Reality rebelled against her, then imitated her intuitions when to her despair her lover wanted from her what she had wanted so long from him. Intuition here seems to create a world of persons who crush us because they cannot exist. As Dante says, in love things color as love wills, and only the angel of solicitude, which is reason made heavenly, can save us. Here there is no such solicitude, but there is the quick and truth of tenderness which may be the substance between people and which may also be injured between people, crucified in sentiment on the cross of loyalties.

One thinks of George Meredith, for whom tenderness in affection was the great gain and loss, and then one thinks of the difference there is in Gertrude Stein. Between Melanctha Herbert and Jeff Campbell there is not so much gain and loss as there is the positive torment of tenderness that goes with a relation without common enterprise outside and binding the relation. Melanctha wants relation for its own sake—as if the stakes could be won without a firm commitment. Indeed, Melanctha's life is a study of the intuitions of an unmoored romantic love—an illusion never more than on the verge of actuality, but which yet makes all other forms of life secondary and all other obligations nugatory. The soul dissipates in the blueness of that love in which one loves for one's own sake, that romantic love in which love creates its object and is jealous of its own creation. The losses, as Gertrude Stein says, are impossible to take up. "In tender hearted creatures, those that mostly never feel strong passion, suffering often comes to make them harder. When these do not know in themselves what it is to suffer, suffering is then very awful to them and they badly want to help everyone who has to suffer, and they have a deep reverence for anybody who knows really how to always suffer. But when it comes to them to really suffer, they soon begin to lose their fear and tenderness and wonder. Why it isn't so very much to suffer, when even I can bear to do it. It isn't very pleasant to be having all the time, to stand it, but they are not so much wiser after all, all the others just because they know too how to bear it." The ego is driven to new vanity by its losses, and this is what happens to Melanctha and Jeff in the allegory they make of love in action.

In each, love seizes on the autonomous in a world where there is no autonomy, and in each (one thinks a little of D. H. Lawrence) love then enters into the phase of anger—so near to reason, yet its opposite—for the last assertion of the self before it reaches isolation. This love is like conversion to a private religion which turns out to have no external object; and as faith cheats after its first deprivation, so does love. A conversion, when it disappears, leaves a real emptiness, and that emptiness is replaced, in Gertrude Stein's language, by a hot love, which neither Melanctha nor Jeff can accept in the other, since neither is in phase with the other's creation, whether in what happens to the sweetness of love or in what happens to real religion when these do not happen at the same time. Almost, this story seems to show, as its pattern widens, that real sweetness crossed by real sweetness comes to desolation, and that real religion comes to devastation. What Melanctha Herbert learned from love when she made it into religion was "new ways to be in trouble." So she consumed away and died—not because she was "in" society and not "of" it, but because at every critical point she found society was not in her, only trouble. This, I would suppose, is the kind of meaning that rises in "A rose is a rose is a rose," when it is said in the poignant parody which is sometimes all we have with which to greet a rose. Intuition is good only the first time; repeated, it leaves us defenseless and we wear away, seeing further and further into the beauty of what we have more and more lost in life.

Gertrude Stein had something to do with the perpetual process of self-creation, and she was mistress of the arts of giving revery effective form: her mode was the pattern of intuition, both her own and those her words yielded in repetition. William Carlos Williams has something to do with the perpetual alliance of our senses with the objects around us. His imagination makes a constant effort to see what forms objects will take when selected from the flux and put into words, and words for him are real objects too. He does not create from revery, for his business is to create everlastingly the immediate world in immediate words. I suppose he would assent in part to the medieval maxim that there is nothing in the mind that was not first in the senses, but I am not sure he would not go further and insist that what got into the live mind was the senses themselves, with words being taken as an extension of the senses. Like Gertrude Stein he is antirational in temper and desires no gifts but his own, especially nothing of the gift of old forms, old psychologies, old institutions. It is not that he is new, but that he is older than all that. He is rather like the image in his poem to the morning star:

It's a strange courage
you give me, ancient star:

Shine alone in the sunrise
towards which you lend no part!

Only you must think of the star as cranky, knowledgeable, and exact, as well as a light in itself, adding to what it shines on.

Put another way, Williams is an egregiously ebullient writer, as far as possible from sophistication. His allegory consists in seeing what will happen if he relates observations in the least rational order practicable. His observations become words which are names that as they move struggle with the fixed ideas and the fixed anti-ideas which irritate him in society. But he is of course never quite free of either, any more than the freshest sensation ever escapes its ancestry or fails to leave posterity. In his poetry he has no use for the sonnet, in his fiction no use for the plot, and the questions of unity of approach or the confusion of kinds would never seem to him valid. He speaks with the authority of sensation, not sentiment, yet his sensations achieve the form as they create the substance of emotions. Gertrude Stein wove according to pattern which as you get used to it is in part predictable. In Williams, as one of his poems says, the detail is all, and as the details are turned into words they end in a pattern: the pattern is how the words love him. He is as automatic as the lively intelligence can be; in his attendance on revery he is compelled to submit to his words, which insist on an order no matter what, and to the irregular intrusions of his rational predilections, which are almost as deep as his unconscious. Besides these, he submits with insistence and glee to the long order of the seasons and to the rougher order of the immediate weather.

In *The Great American Novel* and *In the American Grain,* written during the first part of the twenties, and which by some were called impressionistic essays, Williams began a long effort to write fictions wherein the rudiments of the American Psyche would make an allegory of themselves. He asks us to listen to a tumult of fragments, selected only because it is impossible to put everything that appears in lively revery into handy words, and given in minimum order only because everything looked at gains an order by the act of looking. Order is a human invention to account for what the senses perceive in sequence. Williams seems to hold that the best orders are the most fortuitous, least human, and those we can be most nearly careless of. For example in *The Great American Novel,* there is a running white water of likes and dislikes. He dislikes

England like a Chicago Irishman. He dislikes standard literature. And he dislikes the actual shift of one kind of order to another. On the other hand, he likes Esquimaus and the women of the Cumberland Mountains and yellow lady-slippers and all kinds of weather, and he is fascinated by certain shady aspects of history—especially Imperial Roman history—and archeology. But mostly he does not care whether he likes or dislikes a thing; his curiosity is equally intense, and his disinterestedness is a kind of animal recognition that something is happening or that something is there—who knows what?—namely itself. He is addicted to randomness and to identity which in combination fix and exhaust his attention.

At about the time he wrote *The Great American Novel,* and a little later, he used to call himself an Objectivist, a movement or point of view in which an intense subjectivity identifies itself with the random objects of the world. It is the practice of magpies made theoretic and fruitful; one takes title to and becomes rich in the random objects one collects. At least I suppose this to be what Williams means in the following sentences. "I know not a land except ours that has not to some small extent made its title clear. Translate this into ancient Greek and offer it to Harvard engraved on copper to be hung in the water-closets which freshmen use." It would be better if the sentiment were engraved in the language that cats and dogs can read—which Marianne Moore once said was plain American, and Williams' sentiment is very American indeed—assertive of vitality, muddled in mode, a little hysterical in tone, and quite unfair to the burden of its sentiment. Translated into something like the mode of Greek thought it might turn out roughly this way: If you insist too much on what you own, very few objects will seem appropriate to you, while in the piety of observation everything may yet come to be yours. I should like to think that at bottom this is the sort of thing that Williams meant. But he has been too restless, and in the heat of speech too eager for everything, to limit himself to saying so. Certainly it is what his poems and the best of his prose, whenever not argumentative, do say for him in great clarity. It is this clarity within his words that commands our attention even when we are bewildered by the confusion and the contrariety of their procession. Perhaps the burden is in this short paragraph.

"The sun has come back. The air is washed clean. Leaves lie plastered on the streets, against the tree trunks, upon the very house sides. The bird bath is filled to overflowing: a lame man is hurrying to the train." This is how observation, as the reader observes it again, makes itself into allegory: things which being themselves signify a further meaning. The observations are both exact and experimental.

There is more than this to say of *The Great American Novel.* Something about the First World War made many people think that America had come of age, or at least that she ought to have done so, and this thought raised a great deal of talk about the necessity for someone to write the great American novel to prove it. Writers as a class were held remiss for not producing it but it was felt that it would surely come in the next book one opened. It is impossible to recapture the tones of exhortation, prophecy, and annunciation with which article after article was written, and it is hard to remember how deeply public conversation and private ambition were infected—until one recaptures and remembers how in 1940 writers as a class and individually were held by their irresponsibility to have brought on the Second World War. However that may be, Williams' little book was an answer to the plea and a scheme for an example of what The Great American Novel must be. Hence

Williams' polemic and jingoistic tone. "We must first isolate ourselves. Free ourselves even more than we have. Let us learn the essentials of the American situation." And so on.

There is also in his book a paradigm, more individual in its elements than random—and altogether a product of Williams' own direct reading and observation—precisely of "the essentials of the American situation." Fact, fancy, and the documents of autobiography are mixed and rehearsed with the looseness and fragmentariness and enormous attractiveness of unsorted objects in a box. Anybody can add what he wants; everybody must put in what he can; everybody must take title to this fiction. For this is a fiction the reader must write as he reads. But it is a fiction, not an essay, at one of the extremities that fiction can reach: the extremity of expressionism which says that things mean whatever we would have them mean and that the structures we make will carry any weight we put upon them, even the weight of the real world. It is the sort of fiction that tugs at us to put our own reality in to see what will happen to it. After all, this is how most of us actually look at the world, and not alone in our daydreams, and there is every reason why there should be a form of fiction to correspond to a deep habit. We are all automatons until we use that part of the mind that puts things in order under public authority; Williams wants us to see the order things make for themselves in as near as possible their own waywardness and their own identity. It is as if, as it was with Gertrude Stein, things could be, when we are led to see them as their own selves, also their own generalizations beyond anything we can grasp, grasping us.

What Williams has no use for—which yet persists in use and possibility—is exemplified as well as anywhere in Elinor Wylie's *Venetian Glass Nephew.* Published in 1925, just two years after *The Great American Novel,* Elinor Wylie's book moves in every possible way opposite to the direction taken by Williams. Where Williams revolted by means of direct observation against the forms of art and the institutions of society, Elinor Wylie represents the double revolt of form and decorum against life and the further revolt which invents an artificial formality and fantasy whereby if we do not escape our compulsions we can at least criticize them and look at them in a different way. It is the sort of art Oscar Wilde had in mind when he said that nature imitates art; which is true to the degree that we believe in the art, and the calamity of collapse is no greater than that of most efforts of art to imitate nature. The creative mind is unequal to either task taken separately. Pygmalion is a pessimist at heart, but he does not discover it until Galatea turns out to have met only his known desires; yet those desires were very great, and the despair is earned in the gaps between the heart beats, and it is rightful to express it so long as one keeps to the mockery of good manners and polishes the details. We can polish the details only of what we ourselves invent out of forms and in fantasy, out of what has been received and in the mode of polite allegory.

Elinor Wylie made a pastoral allegory on a velvet lawn—perhaps our oldest formal tradition in the mode—but with no rough pasture of actual society behind her. She was the living flourish of those who were rootless in the New York and the Paris of the America of the twenties, and she made a great ado of liking it that way: why should she have roots since she had legs and great agility in moving them and a great skill in getting nowhere a long way off. In this case she got to the never-never land of Italy at the end of the eighteenth century, just before Stendhal and Byron got there with their flourishes of ingenuity and freedom, disdain and desperation, and what she found was a mixture of the gothic extravaganza of the late eighteenth century and the art-for-art's sake of the *Yellow Book* at the end of the nineteenth century. One thinks of Mrs. Radcliffe and Beckford, of Aubrey Beardsley and Oscar Wilde.

Out of such cross fertilization she made alchemy for fun and gave shape to the most archetypical of all daydreams, that in which we secure our immediate ends without human penalties, and in which the supernatural is at first on our side—until we realize that we have ourselves become inhuman and must make others become so if we are to survive. But it is a day dream with manners, elegance, verbal delicacy, and a feeling for hierarchy. Everything in the book is very "literary" in the sense that Virginia Woolf was; it could not have been written except in the presence and with the aid of the élite institutions of literature and the kind of culture that makes snobbery possible and enjoyable. It is, in short, a fairy tale written from above, a form not drawn from the depths but imposed upon them.

What do we have? An eighteenth-century Cardinal who has just found that it is intolerable to be without a nephew and secures one, perfect in every external detail, with the aid of alchemical magic and the glassmakers of Murano. He has then, a Pygmalion *manqué,* to preside over the life and loves of his creation. The nephew marries a paragon of youthful talent, beauty and spirit, and is of every service to her except those that go with exercise or any form of physical stamina. His hands splinter a little if too warmly grasped and he cannot for his life pursue his bride through the garden alleys; and she, for her part, would rather die than lose him. So the Cardinal arranges another creation, this time backwards. This infant Sappho, this Rosalba, must be turned into Sèvres porcelain that she may be proper wife to the Venetian Glass Nephew, an alchemy she is eager to experience: "It will not hurt me if I am not afraid."

To this the alchemist responds "in a terrible voice" with a classical allusion: "Non dolet"—words which a wife addressed to her coward husband as she hands him the knife with which she has stabbed herself: Non dolet—it doesn't hurt! (Martial's *Epigrams,* I, xiii is the best locus; it was once schoolboy Latin.) The scene continues with the poor Cardinal expressing the anxious hope that the transformation will require beneficent, or white, magic only.

"I can assure you of nothing so absurd, your Eminence," was the beginning of the reply. "The Deity may justly approve of the affair of Virginio; He cannot seriously object to the vivification of a few handfuls of Murano sand and a pipkin of holy water. But it is another and very different matter to deprive one of His creatures of the delights and powers bestowed upon her by Himself; we shall require the devil's aid in murdering Rosalba."

So begins the fable for frigidity with which the tale ends—though with luck and skill she will be in the simple biscuit state, without glaze. What fathers have done to their daughters out of envy, and husbands to their wives out of egotism or incapacity, this girl brings on herself out of romantic love. Thus the allegory of fantasy fastens itself upon reality with elegant iniquity; and if the result shocks us still it cannot very much surprise us, for the offense is within ourselves. If we are to succeed in romantic love we must be glass and porcelain and do without fear and pity—though we may arouse them. The allegory of fantasy will in meditation give rise to anything you like and much you dislike. But here is how the tale ends: "At any moment they may awake; Virginio will put on his pearl-coloured great-coat and wrap an ermine tippet about Rosalba's throat, and the season being winter and very clear and cold, they will hurry to a fashionable pastry cook's to eat whipped cream and wafers."

These remarks on seven American writers have repeated the word allegory so many times that its meaning must have become nearly obliterated, and it is to be hoped that a reading of the seven stories will make the word seem apt again, in different but related senses, for all of them. Our authors do not depend for the form in which their good things appear upon narrative, or drama, or the exhibition of character, anywhere near so much as they depend on allegory, and I think they do so because allegory is germane to their sensibility and appropriate to the culture they represent. Allegory is how they set the things of the mind in motion so as to make their words meaningful beyond themselves. As St. Thomas said, in allegory the words signify objects which themselves signify further. Some of the discriminations here made between the allegories in the different authors may seem unnecessary or trivial—if so the stories will repair the damage; but I hope none of them will seem forced, for they are meant only as provisional indications of the nature of American literature and the American psyche. Furthermore, for a last repetition, allegory is not taken here as a mode of interpretation, but as one of the great traditional creative modes of the mind, which it sometimes dominates.

Herman Melville

❊ 1819-1891

When Melville was eleven his family moved from New York City to Albany, where his father died in debt two years later. At the age of twenty he shipped on a merchantman for England. The following year he shipped on the Acushnet, *a whaler, to the South Seas. This voyage he later called "my Yale College and my Harvard." At Honolulu, in August of 1843, he was mustered into the United States Navy; he was discharged at Boston in October of 1844. This experience must have provided him with the background for* Billy Budd. *After his discharge he turned to writing.* Typee *appeared in 1846,* Omoo *in 1847,* Mardi *in 1849,* Redburn *in 1849,* White-Jacket *in 1850,* Moby Dick *in 1851,* Pierre *in 1853,* Israel Potter *in 1855, and* The Piazza Tales *in 1856. But as his work gained in richness and complexity Melville's public deserted him. The last volume of his fiction to be published during his lifetime was* The Confidence Man, *in 1857. For a number of years he supported his family by serving as Inspector of Customs in New York City. Melville continued to publish verses, but attempted no fiction until* Billy Budd, *written in the last three years of his life, and not published until 1924. It is possible that* Billy Budd *was inspired by the sudden death of Melville's son Malcolm at the age of 20.*

Billy Budd

PREFACE

The year 1797, the year of this narrative, belongs to a period which, as every thinker now feels, involved a crisis for Christendom not exceeded in its undetermined momentousness at the time by any other era whereof there is record. The opening proposition made by the Spirit of that Age involved rectification of the Old World's hereditary wrongs. In France, to some extent, this was bloodily effected. But what then? Straightway the Revolution itself became a wrongdoer, one more oppressive than the kings. Under Napoleon it enthroned upstart kings, and initiated that prolonged agony of continual war whose final throe was Waterloo. During those years not the wisest could have foreseen that the outcome of all would be what to some thinkers apparently it has since turned out to be—a political advance along nearly the whole line for Europeans.

Now, as elsewhere hinted, it was something caught from the Revolutionary Spirit that at Spithead emboldened the man-of-war's men to rise against real abuses, long-standing ones, and afterwards at the Nore to make inordinate and aggressive demands—successful resistance to which was confirmed only when the ringleaders were hung for an admonitory spectacle to the anchored fleet. Yet in a way analogous to the operation of the Revolution at large—the Great Mutiny, though by Englishmen naturally deemed monstrous at the time, doubtless gave the first latent prompting to most important reforms in the British navy.

1

In the time before steamships, or then more frequently than now, a stroller along the docks of any considerable seaport would occasionally have his attention arrested by a group of bronzed mariners, man-of-war's men or merchant-sailors in holiday attire ashore on liberty. In certain instances they would flank, or, like a body-guard quite surround some superior figure of their own class, moving along with them like Aldebaran among the lesser lights of his constellation. That signal object was the "Handsome Sailor" of the less prosaic time alike of the military and merchant navies. With no perceptible trace of the vainglorious about him, rather with the off-hand unaffectedness of natural regality, he seemed to accept the spontaneous homage of his shipmates. A somewhat remarkable instance recurs to me. In Liverpool, now half a century ago I saw under the shadow of the great dingy street-wall of Prince's Dock (an obstruction long since removed) a common sailor, so intensely black that he must needs have been a native African of the unadulterate blood of Ham. A symmetric figure much above the average height. The two ends of gay silk handkerchief thrown loose about the neck danced upon the displayed ebony of his chest; in his ears were big hoops of gold, and a Scotch Highland bonnet with a tartan band set off his shapely head.

It was a hot noon in July; and his face, lustrous with perspiration, beamed with barbaric good humor. In jovial sallies right and left[,] his white teeth flashing into view, he rollicked along, the centre of a company of his shipmates. These were made up of such an assortment of tribes and complexions as would have well fitted them to be marched up by Anacharsis Cloots before the bar of the first French Assembly as Representatives of the Human Race. At each spontaneous tribute rendered by the wayfarers to this black pagod of a fellow—the tribute of a pause and stare, and less frequent an exclamation,—the motley retinue showed that they took that sort of pride in the evoker of it which the Assyrian priests doubtless showed for their grand sculptured Bull when the faithful prostrated themselves.

To return.

If in some cases a bit of a nautical Murat in setting forth his person ashore, the handsome sailor of the period in question evinced nothing of the dandified Billy-be-Dam, an amusing character all but extinct now, but occasionally to be encountered, and in a form yet more amusing than the original, at the tiller of the boats on the tempestuous Erie Canal or, more likely, vaporing in the groggeries along the tow-path. Invariably a proficient in his perilous calling, he was also more or less of a mighty boxer or wrestler. It was strength and beauty. Tales of his prowess were recited. Ashore he was the champion; afloat the spokesman; on every suitable occasion always foremost. Close-reefing topstails in a gale, there he was, astride the weather yard-arm-end, foot in the Flemish horse as "stirrup," both hands tugging at the "ear-ring" as at a bridle, in very much the attitude of young Alexander curbing the fiery Bucephalus. A superb figure, tossed up as by the horns of Taurus against the thunderous sky, cheerily hallooing to the strenuous file along the spar.

The moral nature was seldom out of keeping with the physical make. Indeed, except as toned by the former, the comeliness and power, always attractive in masculine conjunction, hardly could have drawn the sort of honest homage the Handsome Sailor in some examples received from his less gifted associates.

Such a cynosure, at least in aspect, and something such too in nature, though with important variations made apparent as the story proceeds, was welkin-eyed Billy Budd, or Baby Budd as more familiarly under circumstances hereafter to be given he at last came to be called[,] aged twenty-one, a foretopman of the British fleet toward the close of the last decade of the eighteenth century. It was not very long prior to the time of the narration that follows that he had entered the King's Service, having been impressed on the Narrow Seas from a homeward-bound English merchantman into a seventy-four outward-bound, H.M.S. *Indomitable;* which ship, as was not unusual in those hurried days having been obliged to put to sea short of her proper complement of men. Plump upon Billy at first sight in the gangway the boarding officer Lieutenant Ratcliffe pounced, even before the merchantman's crew was formally mustered on the quarter-deck for his deliberate inspection. And him only he elected. For whether it was because the other men when ranged before him showed to ill advantage after Billy, or whether he had some scruples in view of the merchantman being rather short-handed, however it might be, the officer contented himself with his first spontaneous choice. To the surprise of the ship's company, though much to the Lieutenant's satisfaction Billy made no demur. But, indeed, any demur would have been as idle as the protest of a goldfinch popped into a cage.

Noting this uncomplaining acquiescence, all but cheerful one might say, the shipmates turned a surprised glance of silent reproach at the sailor. The shipmaster was one of those worthy mortals found in every vocation, even the humbler ones—the sort of person whom everybody agrees in calling "a respectable man." And—nor so strange to report as it may appear to be—though a ploughman of the troubled waters, life-long contending with the intractable elements, there was nothing this honest soul at heart loved better than simple peace and quiet. For the rest, he was fifty or thereabouts, a little inclined to corpulence, a prepossessing face, unwhiskered, and of an agreeable color—a rather full face, humanely intelligent in expression. On a fair day with a fair wind and all going well, a certain musical chime in his voice seemed to be the veritable unobstructed outcome of the innermost man. He had much prudence, much conscientiousness, and there were occasions when these virtues were the cause of overmuch disquietude in him. On a passage, so long as his craft was in any proximity to land, no sleep for Captain Graveling. He took to heart those serious responsibilities not so heavily borne by some shipmasters.

Now while Billy Budd was down in the forecastle getting his kit together, the *Indomitable's* lieutenant, burly and bluff, nowise disconcerted by Captain Graveling's omitting to proffer the customary hospitalities on an occasion so unwelcome to him, an omission simply caused by preoccupation of thought, unceremoniously invited himself into the cabin, and also to a flask from the spirit-locker, a receptacle which his experienced eye instantly discovered. In fact he was one of those sea-dogs in whom all the hardship and peril of naval life in the great prolonged wars of his time never impaired the natural instinct for sensuous enjoyment. His duty he always faithfully did; but duty is sometimes a dry obligation, and he was for irrigating its aridity, whensoever possible, with a fertilizing decoction of strong waters. For the cabin's proprietor there was nothing left but to play the part of the enforced host with whatever grace and alacrity were practicable. As necessary adjuncts to the flask, he silently placed tumbler and water-jug before the irrepressible guest. But excusing himself from partaking just then, [he] dismally watched the unembarrassed officer deliberately diluting his grog a little, then tossing it off in three swallows, pushing the empty tumbler away, yet not so far as to be beyond easy reach, at the same [time] settling himself in his seat and smacking his lips with high satisfaction, looking straight at the host.

These proceedings over, the Master broke the silence; and there lurked a rueful reproach in the tone of his voice:

"Lieutenant, you are going to take my best man from me, the jewel of 'em."

"Yes, I know" rejoined the other, immediately drawing back the tumbler preliminary to a replenishing; "Yes, I know. Sorry."

"Beg pardon, but you don't understand, Lieutenant. See here now. Before I shipped that young fellow, my forecastle was a rat-pit of quarrels. It was black times, I tell you, aboard the '*Rights*' here. I was worried to that degree my pipe had no comfort for me. But Billy came; and it was like a Catholic priest striking peace in an Irish shindy. Not that he preached to them or said or did anything in particular; but a virtue went out of him, sugaring the sour ones. They took to him like hornets to treacle; all but the buffer of the gang, the big shaggy chap with the fire-red whiskers. He indeed out of envy, perhaps, of the newcomer, and thinking such a 'sweet and pleasant fellow,' as he mockingly designated him to the others, could hardly have the spirit of a game-cock, must needs bestir himself in trying to get up an ugly row with him. Billy forebore with him and reasoned with him in a pleasant way—he is something like myself, lieutenant, to whom aught like a quarrel is hateful—but nothing served. So, in the second dog-watch one day the Red Whiskers in presence of the others, under pretence of showing Billy just whence a sirloin steak was cut—for the fellow had once been a butcher—insultingly gave him a dig under the ribs. Quick as lightning Billy let fly his arm. I dare say he never meant to do quite as much as he did, but anyhow he gave the burly fool a terrible drubbing. It took about half a minute, I should think. And, lord bless you, the lubber was astonished at the celerity. And will you believe it, Lieutenant, the Red Whiskers now really loves Billy—loves him, or is the biggest hypocrite that ever I heard of. But they all love him. Some of 'em do his washing, darn his old trousers for him; the carpenter is at odd times making a pretty little chest of drawers for him. Anybody will do anything for Billy Budd; and it's the happy family here. But now, Lieutenant, if that young fellow goes—I know how it will be aboard the '*Rights.*' Not again very soon shall I, coming up from dinner, lean over the capstan smoking a quiet pipe—no, not very soon again, I think. Ay, Lieutenant, you are going to take away the jewel of 'em; you are going to take away my peacemaker!" And with that the good soul had really some ado in checking a rising sob.

"Well," said the officer who had listened with amused interest to all this, and now waxing merry with his tipple; "Well, blessed are the peacemakers especially the fighting peacemakers! And such are the seventy-four beauties some of which you see poking their noses out of the port-holes of yonder war-ship lying-to for me" pointing thro' the cabin window at the *Indomitable*. "But courage! don't look so downhearted, man. Why, I pledge you in advance the royal approbation. Rest assured that His Majesty will be delighted to know that in a time when his hard tack is not sought for by sailors with such avidity as should be; a time also when some shipmasters privily resent the borrowing from them a tar or two for the service; His Majesty, I say, will be delighted to learn that *one* shipmaster at least cheerfully surrenders to the King, the flower of his flock, a sailor who with equal loyalty makes no dissent.—But where's my beauty? Ah," looking through the cabin's open door "Here he comes; and, by Jove—lugging along his chest—Apollo with his portmanteau!—My man," stepping out to him, "you can't take that big box aboard a warship. The boxes there are mostly shot-boxes. Put your duds in a bag, lad. Boot and saddle for the cavalryman, bag and hammock for the man-of-war's man."

The transfer from chest to bag was

made. And, after seeing his man into the cutter and then following him down, the lieutenant pushed off from the *Rights-of-Man.* That was the merchant-ship's name; tho' by her master and crew abbreviated in sailor fashion into *The Rights.* The hard-headed Dundee owner was a staunch admirer of Thomas Paine whose book in rejoinder to Burke's arraignment of the French Revolution had then been published for some time and had gone everywhere. In christening his vessel after the title of Paine's volume the man of Dundee was something like his contemporary shipowner, Stephen Girard of Philadelphia, whose sympathies, alike with his native land and its liberal philosophers, he evinced by naming his ships after Voltaire, Diderot, and so forth.

But now, when the boat swept under the merchant-man's stern, and officer and oarsmen were noting—some bitterly and others with a grin,—the name emblazoned there; just then it was that the new recruit jumped up from the bow where the coxswain had directed him to sit, and waving [his] hat to his silent shipmates sorrowfully looking over at him from the taffrail, bade the lads a genial good-bye. Then, making a salutation as to the ship herself, "And good-bye to you too, old *Rights of Man.*"

"Down, Sir!" roared the lieutenant, instantly assuming all the rigor of his rank, though with difficulty repressing a smile.

To be sure, Billy's action was a terrible breach of naval decorum. But in that decorum he had never been instructed; in consideration of which the lieutenant would hardly have been so energetic in reproof but for the concluding farewell to the ship. This he rather took as meant to convey a covert sally on the new recruit's part, a sly slur at impressment in general, and that of himself in especial. And yet, more likely, if satire it was in effect, it was hardly so by intention, for Billy tho' happily endowed with gayety of high health, youth, and a free heart, was yet by no means of a satirical turn. The will to it and the sinister dexterity were alike wanting. To deal in double meanings and insinuations of any sort was quite foreign to his nature.

As to his enforced enlistment, that he seemed to take pretty much as he was wont to take any vicissitude of weather. Like the animals, though no philosopher, he was, without knowing it, practically a fatalist. And, it may be, that he rather liked this adventurous turn in his affairs, which promised an opening into novel scenes and martial excitements.

Aboard the *Indomitable* our merchant-sailor was forthwith rated as an able-seaman and assigned to the starboard watch of the fore-top. He was soon at home in the service, not at all disliked for his unpretentious good looks and a sort of genial happy-go-lucky air. No merrier man in his mess: in marked contrast to certain other individuals included like himself among the impressed portion of the ship's company; for these when not actively employed were sometimes, and more particularly in the last dog-watch when the drawing near of twilight induced revery, apt to fall into a saddish mood which in some partook of sullenness. But they were not so young as our foretopman, and no few of them must have known a hearth of some sort, others may have had wives and children left, too probably, in uncertain circumstances, and hardly any but must have had acknowledged kith and kin, while for Billy, as will shortly be seen, his entire family was practically invested in himself.

2

Though our new-made foretopman was well received in the top and on the gun-decks, hardly here was he that cynosure he had previously been among those minor ship's companies of the merchant marine, with which companies only had he hitherto consorted.

He was young; and despite his all but fully developed frame in aspect looked even younger than he really was, owing to a lingering adolescent expression in the as yet smooth face all but feminine in purity of natural complexion but where, thanks to his seagoing, the lily was quite suppressed and the rose had some ado visibly to flush through the tan.

To one essentially such a novice in the complexities of factitious life, the abrupt transition from his former and simpler sphere to the ampler and more knowing world of a great warship; this might well have abashed him had there been any conceit or vanity in his composition. Among her miscellaneous multitude, the *Indomitable* mustered several individuals who however inferior in grade were of no common natural stamp, sailors more signally susceptive of that air which continuous martial discipline and repeated presence in battle can in some degree impart even to the average man. As the *handsome sailor* Billy Budd's position aboard the seventy-four was something analogous to that of a rustic beauty transplanted from the provinces and brought into competition with the high-born dames of the court. But this change of circumstances he scarce noted. As little did he observe that something about him provoked an ambiguous smile in one or two harder faces among the blue-jackets. Nor less unaware was he of the peculiar favorable effect his person and demeanor had upon the more intelligent gentlemen of the quarter-deck. Nor could this well have been otherwise. Cast in a mould peculiar to the finest physical examples of those Englishmen in whom the Saxon strain would seem not at all to partake of any Norman or other admixture, he showed in face that humane look of reposeful good nature which the Greek sculptor in some instances gave to his heroic strong man, Hercules. But this again was subtly modified by another and pervasive quality. The ear, small and shapely, the arch of the foot, the curve in mouth and nostril, even the indurated hand dyed to the orange-tawny of the toucan's bill, a hand telling alike of the halyards and tar-bucket; but, above all, something in the mobile expression, and every chance attitude and movement, something suggestive of a mother eminently favored by Love and the Graces; all this strangely indicated a lineage in direct contradiction to his lot. The mysteriousness here, became less mysterious through a matter-of-fact elicited when Billy at the capstan was being formally mustered into the service. Asked by the officer, a small brisk little gentleman as it chanced among other questions, his place of birth, he replied, "Please, Sir, I don't know."

"Don't know where you were born?—Who was your father?"

"God knows, Sir."

Struck by the straightforward simplicity of these replies, the officer next asked "Do you know anything about your beginning?"

"No, Sir. But I have heard that I was found in a pretty silk-lined basket hanging one morning from the knocker of a good man's door in Bristol[.]"

"*Found* say you? Well," throwing back his head and looking up and down the new recruit; "Well[,] it turns out to have been a pretty good find. Hope they'll find some more like you, my man; the fleet sadly needs them."

Yes, Billy Budd was a foundling, a presumable bye-blow, and, evidently, no ignoble one. Noble descent was as evident in him as in a blood horse.

For the rest, with little or no sharpness of faculty or any trace of the wisdom of the serpent, nor yet quite a dove, he possessed that kind and degree of intelligence going along with the unconventional rectitude of a sound human creature, one to whom not yet has been proffered the questionable apple of knowledge. He was illiterate; he could not read, but he could sing, and like the illiterate nightingale was sometimes the composer of his own song.

Of self-consciousness he seemed to have little or none, or about as much as we may reasonably impute to a dog of Saint Bernard's breed.

Habitually living with the elements and knowing little more of the land than as a beach, or, rather, that portion of the terraqueous globe providentially set apart for dance-hall doxies and tapsters, in short what sailors call a "fiddlers' green," his simple nature remained unsophisticated by those moral obliquities which are not in every case incompatible with that manufacturable thing known as respectability. But are sailors, frequenters of "fiddlers'-greens," without vices? No; but less often than with landsmen do their vices, so called, partake of crookedness of heart, seeming less to proceed from viciousness than exuberance of vitality after long constraint; frank manifestations in accordance with natural law. By his original constitution aided by the cooperating influences of his lot, Billy in many respects was little more than a sort of upright barbarian, much such perhaps as Adam presumably might have been ere the urbane Serpent wriggled himself into his company.

And here be it submitted that apparently going to corroborate the doctrine of man's fall, a doctrine now popularly ignored, it is observable that where certain virtues pristine and unadulterate peculiarly characterize anybody in the external uniform of civilization, they will upon scrutiny seem not to be derived from custom or convention, but rather to be out of keeping with these, as if indeed exceptionally transmitted from a period prior to Cain's city and citified man. The character marked by such qualities has to an unvitiated taste an untampered-with flavor like that of berries, while the man thoroughly civilized even in a fair specimen of the breed has to the same moral palate a questionable smack as of a compounded wine. To any stray inheritor of these primitive qualities found, like Caspar Hauser, wandering dazed in any Christian capital of our time the good-natured poet's famous invocation, near two thousand years ago, of the good rustic out of his latitude in the Rome of the Cesars, still appropriately holds:—

Honest and poor, faithful in word and thought
What has thee, Fabian, to the city brought.

Though our Handsome Sailor had as much of masculine beauty as one can expect anywhere to see; nevertheless, like the beautiful woman in one of Hawthorne's minor tales, there was just one thing amiss in him. No visible blemish indeed, as with the lady; no, but an occasional liability to a vocal defect. Though in the hour of elemental uproar or peril, he was everything that a sailor should be, yet under sudden provocation of strong heart-feeling his voice otherwise singularly musical, as if expressive of the harmony within, was apt to develop an organic hesitancy, in fact more or less of a stutter or even worse. In this particular Billy was a striking instance that the arch interferer, the envious marplot of Eden still has more or less to do with every human consignment to this planet of earth. In every case, one way or another he is sure to slip in his little card, as much as to remind us—I too have a hand here.

The avowal of such an imperfection in the Handsome Sailor should be evidence not alone that he is not presented as a conventional hero, but also that the story in which he is the main figure is no romance.

3

At the time of Billy Budd's arbitrary enlistment into the *Indomitable* that ship was on her way to join the Mediterranean fleet. No long time elapsed before the junction was effected. As one of that fleet the seventy-four participated in its movements, tho' at times on account of her superior sailing qualities, in the absence of frigates, despatched on separate duty as a scout and at times on less temporary service. But with all this the story has little concernment, restricted as it is to the inner life of one particular ship and the career of an individual sailor.

It was the summer of 1797. In the April of that year had occurred the commotion at Spithead followed in May by a second and yet more serious outbreak in the fleet at the Nore. The latter is known, and without exaggeration in the epithet, as the Great Mutiny. It was indeed a demonstration more menacing to England than the contemporary manifestoes and conquering and proselyting armies of the French Directory.

To the British Empire the Nore Mutiny was what a strike in the fire-brigade would be to London threatened by general arson. In a crisis when the kingdom might well have anticipated the famous signal that some years later published along the naval line of battle what it was that upon occasion England expected of Englishmen; *that* was the time when at the mast-heads of the three-deckers and seventy-fours moored in her own roadstead—a fleet, the right arm of a Power then all but the sole free conservative one of the Old World, the blue-jackets, to be numbered by thousands[,] ran up with huzzas the British colors with the union and cross wiped out; by that cancellation transmuting the flag of founded law and freedom defined, into the enemy's red meteor of unbridled and unbounded revolt. Reasonable discontent growing out of practical grievances in the fleet had been ignited into irrational combustion as by live cinders blown across the Channel from France in flames.

The event converted into irony for a time those spirited strains of Dibdin—as a song-writer no mean auxiliary to the English Government at the European conjuncture—strains celebrating, among other things, the patriotic devotion of the British tar:

And as for my life, 'tis the King's!

Such an episode in the Island's grand naval story her naval historians naturally abridge; one of them (G. P. R. James) candidly acknowledging that fain would he pass it over did not "impartiality forbid fastidiousness." And yet his mention is less a narration than a reference, having to do hardly at all with details. Nor are these readily to be found in the libraries. Like some other events in every age befalling states everywhere including America the Great Mutiny was of such character that national pride along with views of policy would fain shade it off into the historical background. Such events can not be ignored, but there is a considerate way of historically treating them. If a well-constituted individual refrains from blazoning aught amiss or calamitous in his family; a nation in the like circumstance may without reproach be equally discreet.

Though after parleyings between Government and the ringleaders, and concessions by the former as to some glaring abuses, the first uprising—that at Spithead—with difficulty was put down, or matters for the time pacified; yet at the Nore the unforeseen renewal of insurrection on a yet larger scale, and emphasized in the conferences that ensued by demands deemed by the authorities not only inadmissible but aggressively insolent, indicated—if the Red Flag did not sufficiently do so[—]what was the spirit animating the men. Final suppression, however, there was; but only made possible perhaps by the unswerving loyalty of the marine corps a[nd] voluntary resumption of loyalty among influential sections of the crews.

To some extent the Nore Mutiny may be regarded as analogous to the distempering irruption of contagious fever in a frame constitutionally sound, and which anon throws it off.

At all events, of these thousands of mutineers were some of the tars who not so very long afterwards—whether wholly prompted thereto by patriotism, or pugnacious instinct, or by both,—helped to win a coronet for Nelson at the Nile, and the naval crown of crowns for him at Trafalgar. To the mutineers those battles and especially Trafalgar were a plenary absolution and a grand one: For all that goes to make up scenic naval display, heroic magnificence in arms, those battles especially Trafalgar stand unmatched in human annals.

4

CONCERNING "THE GREATEST SAILOR SINCE THE WORLD BEGAN."

TENNYSON

In this matter of writing, resolve as one may to keep to the main road, some bypaths have an enticement not readily to be withstood. I am going to err into such a by-path. If the reader will keep me company I shall be glad. At the least we can promise ourselves that pleasure which is wickedly said to be in sinning, for a literary sin the divergence will be.

Very likely it is no new remark that the inventions of our time have at last brought about a change in sea-warfare in degree corresponding to the revolution in all warfare effected by the original introduction from China into Europe of gunpowder. The first European fire-arm, a clumsy contrivance, was, as is well known, scouted by no few of the knights as a base implement, good enough peradventure for weavers too craven to stand up crossing steel with steel in frank fight. But as ashore knightly valor tho' shorn of its blazonry did not cease with the knights, neither on the seas though nowadays in encounters there a certain kind of displayed gallantry be fallen out of date as hardly applicable under changed circumstances, did the nobler qualities of such naval magnates as Don John of Austria, Doria, Van Tromp, Jean Bart, the long line of British Admirals and the American Decaturs of 1812 become obsolete with their wooden walls.

Nevertheless, to anybody who can hold the Present at its worth without being inappreciative of the Past, it may be forgiven, if to such an one the solitary old hulk at Portsmouth, Nelson's *Victory*, seems to float there, not alone as the decaying monument of a fame incorruptible, but also as a poetic reproach, softened by its picturesqueness, to the *Monitors* and yet mightier hulls of the European iron-clads. And this not altogether because such craft are unsightly, unavoidably lacking the symmetry and grand lines of the old battle-ships, but equally for other reasons.

There are some, perhaps, who while not altogether inaccessible to that poetic reproach just alluded to, may yet on behalf of the new order, be disposed to parry it; and this to the extent of iconoclasm, if need be. For example, prompted by the sight of the star inserted in the *Victory's* quarter-deck designating the spot where the Great Sailor fell, these martial utilitarians may suggest considerations implying that Nelson's ornate publication of his person in battle was not only unnecessary, but not military, nay, savored of foolhardiness and vanity. They may add, too, that at Trafalgar it was in effect nothing less than a challenge to death; and death came; and that but for his bravado the victorious Admiral might possibly have survived the battle, and so, instead of having his sagacious dying injunctions overruled by his immediate successor in command he himself when the contest was decided might have brought his shattered fleet to anchor, a proceeding which might have averted the deplorable loss of life by shipwreck in the elemental tempest that followed the martial one.

Well, should we set aside the more disputable point whether for various reasons it was possible to anchor the fleet, then plausibly enough the Benthamites of war may urge the above.

But the *might-have-been* is but boggy ground to build on. And, certainly, in foresight as to the larger issue of an encounter, and anxious preparations for it—buoying the deadly way and mapping it out, as at Copenhagen—few commanders have been so painstakingly circumspect as this same reckless declarer of his person in fight.

Personal prudence even when dictated by quite other than selfish considerations surely is no special virtue in a military man; while an excessive love of glory, impassioning a less burning impulse, the honest sense of duty, is the first. If the name *Wellington* is not so much of a trumpet to the blood as the simpler name *Nelson,* the reason for this may perhaps be inferred from above. Alfred in his funeral ode on the victor of Waterloo ventures not to call him the greatest soldier of all time, tho' in the same ode he invokes Nelson as "the greatest sailor since the world began."

At Trafalgar Nelson on the brink of opening the fight sat down and wrote his last brief will and testament. If under the presentiment of the most magnificent of all victories to be crowned by his own glorious death, a sort of priestly motive led him to dress his person in the jewelled vouchers of his own shining deeds; if thus to have adorned himself for the altar and the sacrifice were indeed vainglory, then affectation and fustian is each more heroic line in the great epics and dramas, since in such lines the poet but embodies in verse those exaltations of sentiment that a nature like Nelson, the opportunity being given, vitalizes into acts.

5

Yes, the outbreak at the Nore was put down. But not every grievance was redressed. If the contractors, for example, were no longer permitted to ply some practices peculiar to their tribe everywhere, such as providing shoddy cloth, rations not sound, or false in the measure, not the less impressment, for one thing, went on. By custom sanctioned for centuries, and judicially maintained by a Lord Chancellor as late as Mansfield, that mode of manning the fleet, a mode now fallen into a sort of abeyance but never formally renounced, it was not practicable to give up in those years. Its abrogation would have crippled the indispensable fleet, one wholly under canvas, no steam-power, its innumerable sails and thousands of cannon, everything in short, worked by muscle alone; a fleet the more insatiate in demand for men, because then multiplying its ship[s] of all grades against contingencies present and to come of the convulsed Continent.

Discontent foreran the Two Mutinies, and more or less it lurkingly survived them. Hence it was not unreasonable to apprehend some return of trouble sporadic or general. One instance of such apprehensions: In the same year with this story, Nelson, then Vice Admiral Sir Horatio, being with the fleet off the Spanish coast, was directed by the Admiral in command to shift his pennant from the *Captain* to the *Theseus;* and for this reason: that the latter ship having newly arrived on the station from home where it had taken part in the Great Mutiny, danger was apprehended from the temper of the men; and it was thought that an officer like Nelson was the one, not indeed to terrorize the crew into base subjection, but to win them, by force of his mere presence back to an allegiance if not as enthusiastic as his own, yet as true. So it was that for a time on more than one quarter-deck anxiety did exist. At sea precautionary vigilance was strained against relapse. At short notice an engagement might come on. When it did, the lieutenants assigned to batteries felt it incumbent on them, in some instances, to stand with drawn swords behind the men working the guns.

6

But on board the seventy-four in which Billy now swung his hammock, very little in the manner of the men and nothing obvious in the demeanor of the officers would have suggested to an ordinary observer that the Great Mutiny was a recent event. In their general bearing and conduct the commissioned officers of a warship naturally take their tone from the commander, that is if he have that ascendancy of character that ought to be his.

Captain the Honorable Edward Fairfax Vere, to give his full title, was a bachelor of forty or thereabouts, a sailor of distinction even in a time prolific of renowned seamen. Though allied to the higher nobility his advancement had not been altogether owing to influences connected with that circumstance. He had seen much service, been in various engagements, always acquitting himself as an officer mindful of the welfare of his men, but never tolerating an infraction of discipline; thoroughly versed in the science of his profession, and intrepid to the verge of temerity, though never injudiciously so. For his gallantry in the West Indian waters as flag-lieutenant under Rodney in that Admiral's crowning victory over De Grass, he was made a post-captain.

Ashore in the garb of a civilian scarce anyone would have taken him for a sailor, more especially that he never garnished unprofessional talk with nautical terms, and grave in his bearing, evinced little appreciation of mere humor. It was not out of keeping with these traits that on a passage when nothing demanded his paramount action, he was the most undemonstrative of men. Any landsman observing this gentleman not conspicuous by his stature and wearing no pronounced insignia, emerging from his cabin to the open deck, and noting the silent deference of the officers retiring to leeward, might have taken him for the King's guest, a civilian aboard the King's-ship[,] some highly honorable discreet envoy on his way to an important post. But in fact this unobtrusiveness of demeanor may have proceeded from a certain unaffected modesty of manhood sometimes accompanying a resolute nature, a modesty evinced at all times not calling for pronounced action, and which shown in any rank of life suggests a virtue aristocratic in kind.

As with some others engaged in various departments of the world's more heroic activities, Captain Vere though practical enough upon occasion would at times betray a certain dreaminess of mood. Standing alone on the weather-side of the quarter deck, one hand holding by the rigging he would absently gaze off at the blank sea. At the presentation to him then of some minor matter interrupting the current of his thoughts he would show more or less irascibility; but instantly he would control it.

In the navy he was popularly known by the appellation—Starry Vere. How such a designation happened to fall upon one who whatever his sturdy qualities was without any brilliant ones was in this wise: A favorite kinsman, Lord Denton, a free-hearted fellow, had been the first to meet and congratulate him upon his return to England from his West Indian cruise; and but the day previous turning over a copy of Andrew Marvell's poems had lighted, not for the first time however, upon the lines entitled *Appleton House,* the name of one of the seats of their common ancestor, a hero in the German wars of the seventeenth century, in which poem occur the lines,

This 'tis to have been from the first
In a domestic heaven nursed,
Under the discipline severe
Of Fairfax and the starry Vere[.]

And so, upon embracing his cousin fresh from Rodney's great victory wherein he had played so gallant a part, brimming over with just family pride in the sailor of their house, he exuberantly exclaimed, "Give ye joy, Ed; give ye joy, my starry Vere!" This got currency, and the novel prefix serving in familiar parlance readily to distinguish the *Indomitable's* Captain from another Vere his senior, a distant relative an officer of like rank in the navy, it remained permanently attached to the surname.

7

In view of the part that the commander of the *Indomitable* plays in scenes shortly to follow, it may be well to fill out that sketch of him outlined in the previous chapter.

Aside from his qualities as a sea-officer Captain Vere was an exceptional character. Unlike no few of England's renowned sailors, long and arduous service with signal devotion to it, had not resulted in absorbing and *salting* the entire man. He had a marked leaning toward everything intellectual. He loved books, never going to sea without a newly replenished library, compact but of the best. The isolated leisure, in some cases so wearisome, falling at intervals to commanders even during a war-cruise, never was tedious to Captain Vere. With nothing of that literary taste which less heeds the thing conveyed than the vehicle, his bias was towards those books to which every serious mind of superior order occupying any active post of authority in the world, naturally inclines: books treating of actual men and events no matter of what era—history, biography and unconventional writers, who, free from cant and convention, like Montaigne, honestly and in the spirit of common sense philosophize upon realities.

In this line of reading he found confirmation of his own more reasoned thoughts—confirmation which he had vainly sought in social converse, so that as touching most fundamental topics, there had got to be established in him some positive convictions, which he forefelt would abide in him essentially unmodified so long as his intelligent part remained unimpaired. In view of the troubled period in which his lot was cast this was well for him. His settled convictions were as a dyke against those invading waters of novel opinion social political and otherwise, which carried away as in a torrent no few minds in those days, minds by nature not inferior to his own. While other members of that aristocracy to which by birth he belonged were incensed at the innovators mainly because their theories were inimical to the privileged classes, not alone Captain Vere disinterestedly opposed them because they seemed to him incapable of embodiment in lasting institutions, but at war with the peace of the world and the true welfare of mankind.

With minds less stored than his and less earnest, some officers of his rank, with whom at times he would necessarily consort, found him lacking in the companionable quality, a dry and bookish gentleman as they deemed. Upon any chance withdrawal from their company one would be apt to say to another, something like this: "Vere is a noble fellow, Starry Vere. Spite the gazettes, Sir Horatio["] meaning him with the Lord title ["]is at bottom scarce a better seaman or fighter. But between you and me now don't you think there is a queer streak of the pedantic running thro' him? Yes, like the King's yarn in a coil of navy-rope?["]

Some apparent ground there was for this sort of confidential criticism; since not only did the Captain's discourse never fall into the jocosely familiar, but in illustrating of any point touching the stirring personages and events of the time he would be as apt to cite some historic character or incident of antiquity as that he would cite from the moderns. He seemed unmindful of the circumstance that to his bluff company such remote allusions however pertinent they might really be were altogether alien to men whose reading was mainly confined to the journals. But considerateness in such matters is not easy to natures constituted like Captain Vere's. Their honesty prescribes to them directness, sometimes far-reaching like that of a migratory fowl that in its flight never heeds when it crosses a frontier.

8

The lieutenants and other commissioned gentlemen forming Captain Vere's staff it is not necessary here to particularize, nor needs it to make any mention of any of the warrant-officers. But among the petty-officers was one who having much to do with the story, may as well be forthwith introduced. His portrait I essay, but shall never hit it. This was John Claggart, the Master-at-arms. But that sea-title may to landsmen seem somewhat equivocal. Originally doubtless that petty-officer's function was the instruction of the men in the use of arms, sword or cutlas. But very long ago, owing to the advance in gunnery making hand-to-hand encounters less frequent and giving to nitre and sulphur the preeminence over steel, that function ceased; the master-at-arms of a great war-ship becoming a sort of Chief of Police charged among other matters with the duty of preserving order on the populous lower gun-decks.

Claggart was a man about five and thirty, somewhat spare and tall, yet of no ill figure upon the whole. His hand was too small and shapely to have been accustomed to hard toil. The face was a notable one; the features all except the chin cleanly cut as those on a Greek medallion; yet the chin, beardless as Tecumseh's, had something of strange protuberant heaviness in its make that recalled the prints of the Rev. Dr. Titus Oates, the historic deponent with the clerical drawl in the time of Charles II and the fraud of the alleged Popish Plot. It served Claggart in his office that his eye could cast a tutoring glance. His brow was of the sort phrenologically associated with more than average intellect; silken jet curls partly clustering over it, making a foil to the pallor below, a pallor tinged with a faint shade of amber akin to the hue of time-tinted marbles of old. This complexion, singularly contrasting with the red or deeply bronzed visages of the sailors, and in part the result of his official seclusion from the sunlight, tho it was not exactly displeasing, nevertheless seemed to hint of something defective or abnormal in the constitution and blood. But his general aspect and manner were so suggestive of an education and career incongruous with his naval function that when not actively engaged in it he looked like a man of high quality, social and moral, who for reasons of his own was keeping incog. Nothing was known of his former life. It might be that he was an Englishman; and yet there lurked a bit of accent in his speech suggesting that possibly he was not such by birth, but through naturalization in early childhood. Among certain grizzled sea-gossips of the gun-decks and forecastle went a rumor perdue that the master-at-arms was a *chevalier* who had volunteered into the King's navy by way of compounding for some mysterious swindle whereof he had been arraigned at the King's Bench. The fact that nobody could substantiate this report was, of course, nothing against its secret currency. Such a rumor once started on the gun-decks in reference to almost anyone below the rank of a commissioned officer would, during the period assigned to this narrative, have seemed not altogether wanting in credibility to the tarry old wiseacres of a man-of-war crew. And indeed a man of Claggart's accomplishments, without prior nautical experience entering the navy at mature life, as he did, and necessarily allotted at the start to the lowest grade in it; a man too who never made allusion to his previous life ashore; these were circumstances which in the dearth of exact knowledge as to his true antecedents opened to the invidious a vague field for unfavorable surmise.

But the sailors' dog-watch gossip concerning him derived a vague plausibility from the fact that now for some period the British Navy could so little afford to be squeamish in the matter of keeping up the muster-rolls, that not only were press-gangs notoriously abroad both afloat and ashore, but there was little or no secret about another matter, namely that the London police were at liberty to capture any able-bodied suspect, any questionable fellow at large and summarily ship him to the dockyard or fleet. Furthermore, even among voluntary enlistments there were instances where the motive thereto partook neither of patriotic impulse nor yet of a random desire to experience a bit of sea-life and martial adventure. Insolvent debtors of minor grade, together with the promiscuous lame ducks of morality found in the Navy a convenient and secure refuge. Secure, because once enlisted aboard a King's-Ship, they were as much in sanctuary, as the transgressor of the Middle Ages harboring himself under the shadow of the altar. Such sanctioned irregularities, which for obvious reasons the Government would hardly think to parade at the time and which consequently, and as affecting the least influential class of mankind, have all but dropped into oblivion, lend color to something for the truth whereof I do not vouch, and hence have some scruple in stating; something I remember having seen in print though the book I can not recall; but the same thing was personally communicated to me now more than forty years ago by an old pensioner in a cocked hat with whom I had a most interesting talk on the terrace at Greenwich, a Baltimore negro, a Trafalgar man. It was to this effect: In the case of a warship short of hands whose speedy sailing was imperative, the deficient quota in lack of any other way of making it good, would be eked out by draughts culled direct from the jails. For reasons previously suggested it would not perhaps be easy at the present day directly to prove or disprove the allegation. But allowed as a verity, how significant would it be of England's straits at the time confronted by those wars which like a flight of harpies rose shrieking from the din and dust of the fallen Bastille. That era appears measurably clear to us who look back at it, and but read of it. But to the grandfathers of us graybeards, the more thoughtful of them, the genius of it presented an aspect like that of Camoen's Spirit of the Cape, an eclipsing menace mysterious and prodigious. Not America was exempt from apprehension. At the height of Napoleon's unexampled conquests, there were Americans who had fought at Bunker Hill who looked forward to the possibility that the Atlantic might prove no barrier against the ultimate schemes of this French upstart from the Revolutionary chaos who seemed in act of fulfilling judgment prefigured in the Apocalypse.

But the less credence was to be given to the gun-deck talk touching Claggart, seeing that no man holding his office in a man-of-war can ever hope to be popular with the crew. Besides, in derogatory comments upon anyone against whom they have a grudge, or for any reason or no reason mislike, sailors are much like landsmen, they are apt to exaggerate or romance it.

About as much was really known to the *Indomitable's* tars of the master-at-arms' career before entering the service as an astronomer knows about a comet's travels prior to its first observable appearance in the sky. The verdict of the sea quidnuncs has been cited only by way of showing what sort of moral impression the man made upon rude uncultivated natures whose conceptions of human wickedness were necessarily of the narrowest, limited to ideas of vulgar rascality,—a thief among the swinging hammocks during a night-watch, or the man-brokers and land-sharks of the sea-ports.

It was no gossip, however, but fact, that though, as before hinted, Claggart upon his entrance into the navy was, as a novice, assigned to the least honorable section of a man-of-war's crew, embracing the drudgery, he did not long remain there.

The superior capacity he immediately evinced, his constitutional sobriety, ingratiating deference to superiors, together with a peculiar ferreting genius manifested on a singular occasion, all this capped by a certain austere patriotism abruptly advanced him to the position of master-at-arms.

Of this maritime Chief of Police the ship's-corporals, so called, were the immediate subordinates, and compliant ones; and this, as is to be noted in some business departments ashore, almost to a degree inconsistent with entire moral volition. His place put various converging wires of underground influence under the Chief's control, capable when astutely worked thro his understrappers of operating to the mysterious discomfort[,] if nothing worse, of any of the sea-commonalty.

9

Life in the fore-top well agreed with Billy Budd. There, when not actually engaged on the yards yet higher aloft, the topmen, who as such had been picked out for youth and activity, constituted an aerial club lounging at ease against the smaller stun'sails rolled up into cushions, spinning yarns like the lazy gods, and frequently amused with what was going on in the busy world of the decks below. No wonder then that a young fellow of Billy's disposition was well content in such society. Giving no cause of offence to anybody, he was always alert at a call. So in the merchant service it had been with him. But now such a punctiliousness in duty was shown that his topmates would sometimes good-naturedly laugh at him for it. This heightened alacrity had its cause, namely, the impression made upon him by the first formal gang-way-punishment he had ever witnessed, which befell the day following his impressment. It had been incurred by a little fellow, young, a novice[,] an after-guardsman absent from his assigned post when the ship was being put about; a dereliction resulting in a rather serious hitch to that manœuvre, one demanding instantaneous promptitude in letting go and making fast. When Billy saw the culprit's naked back under the scourge gridironed with red welts, and worse; when he marked the dire expression on the liberated man's face as with his woolen shirt flung over him by the executioner he rushed forward from the spot to bury himself in the crowd, Billy was horrified. He resolved that never through remissness would he make himself liable to such a visitation or do or omit aught that might merit even verbal reproof. What then was his surprise and concern when ultimately he found himself getting into petty trouble occasionally about such matters as the stowage of his bag or something amiss in his hammock, matters under the police oversight of the ship's-corporals of the lower decks, and which brought down on him a vague threat from one of them.

So heedful in all things as he was, how could this be? He could not understand it, and it more than vexed him. When he spoke to his young topmates about it they were either lightly incredulous or found something comical in his unconcealed anxiety. "Is it your bag, Billy?"

said one "well, sew yourself up in it, bully boy, and then you'll be sure to know if anybody meddles with it."

Now there was a veteran aboard who because his years began to disqualify him for more active work had been recently assigned duty as main-mast-man in his watch, looking to the gear belayed at the rail roundabout that great spar near the deck. At off-times the foretopman had picked up some acquaintance with him, and now in his trouble it occurred to him that he might be the sort of person to go to for wise counsel. He was an old Dansker long anglicized in the service, of few words, many wrinkles and some honorable scars. His wizened face, time-tinted and weather-stained to the complexion of an antique parchment, was here and there peppered blue by the chance explosion of a gun-cartridge in action. He was an *Agamemnon*-man; some two years prior to the time of this story having served under Nelson when but Sir Horatio in that ship immortal in naval memory, and which[,] dismantled and in part broken up to her bare ribs[,] is seen a grand skeleton in Haydon's etching. As one of a boarding-party from the *Agamemnon* he had received a cut slantwise along one temple and cheek leaving a long pale scar like a streak of dawn's light falling athwart the dark visage. It was on account of that scar and the affair in which it was known that he had received it, as well as from his blue-peppered complexion that the Dansker went among the *Indomitable's* crew by the name of "Board-her-in-the-smoke."

Now the first time that his small weazel-eyes happened to light on Billy Budd, a certain grim internal merriment set all his ancient wrinkles into antic play. Was it that his eccentric unsentimental old sapience primitive in its kind saw or thought it saw something which in contrast with the war-ship's environment looked oddly incongruous in the handsome sailor? But after slyly studying him at intervals, the old Merlin's equivocal merriment was modified; for now when the twain would meet, it would start in his face a quizzing sort of look, but it would be but momentary and sometimes replaced by an expression of speculative query as to what might eventually befall a nature like that, dropped into a world not without some man-traps and against whose subtleties simple courage lacking experience and address and without any touch of defensive ugliness, is of little avail; and where such innocence as man is capable of does yet in a moral emergency not always sharpen the faculties or enlighten the will.

However it was the Dansker in his ascetic way rather took to Billy. Nor was this only because of a certain philosophic interest in such a character. There was another cause. While the old man's eccentricities, sometimes bordering on the ursine, repelled the juniors, Billy, undeterred thereby, revering him as a salt hero would make advances, never passing the old Agamemnon-man without a salutation marked by that respect which is seldom lost on the aged however crabbed at times or whatever their station in life.

There was a vein of dry humor, or what not, in the mast-man; and, whether in freak of patriarchal irony touching Billy's youth and athletic frame, or for some other and more recondite reason, from the first in addressing him he always substituted Baby for Billy. The Dansker in fact being the originator of the name by which the foretopman eventually became known aboard ship.

Well then, in his mysterious little difficulty going in quest of the wrinkled one, Billy found him off duty in a dog-watch ruminating by himself seated on a shot-box of the upper gun-deck now and then surveying with a somewhat cynical regard certain of the more swaggering promenaders there. Billy recounted his trouble, again wondering how it all happened. The salt seer attentively listened, accompanying the foretopman's recital with queer twitchings of his wrinkles and problematical little sparkles of his small ferret eyes. Making an end of his story, the foretopman asked, "And now, Dansker, do tell me what you think of it."

The old man, shoving up the front of his tarpaulin and deliberately rubbing the long slant scar at the point where it entered the thin hair, laconically said, "Baby Budd, *Jemmy Legs*" (meaning the master-at-arms) "is down on you[.]"

"*Jemmy Legs!*" ejaculated Billy his welkin eyes expanding; "what for? Why he calls me *the sweet and pleasant young fellow,* they tell me."

"Does he so?" grinned the grizzled one; then said "Ay[,] Baby Lad[,] a sweet voice has *Jemmy Legs.*"

"No, not always. But to me he has. I seldom pass him but there comes a pleasant word."

"And that's because he's down upon you, Baby Budd."

Such reiteration along with the manner of it, incomprehensible to a novice, disturbed Billy almost as much as the mystery for which he had sought explanation. Something less unpleasingly oracular he tried to extract; but the old sea-Chiron thinking perhaps that for the nonce he had sufficiently instructed his young Achilles, pursed his lips, gathered all his wrinkles together and would commit himself to nothing further.

Years, and those experiences which befall certain shrewder men subordinated life-long to the will of superiors, all this had developed in the Dansker the pithy guarded cynicism that was his leading characteristic.

10

The next day an incident served to confirm Billy Budd in his incredulity as to the Dansker's strange summing up of the case submitted. The ship at noon going large before the wind was rolling on her course, and he below at dinner and engaged in some sportful talk with the members of his mess, chanced in a sudden lurch to spill the entire contents of his soup-pan upon the new scrubbed deck. Claggart, the Master-at-arms, official rattan in hand, happened to be passing along the battery in a bay of which the mess was lodged, and the greasy liquid streamed just across his path. Stepping over it, he was proceeding on his way without comment, since the matter was nothing to take notice of under the circumstances, when he happened to observe who it was that had done the spilling. His countenance changed. Pausing, he was about to ejaculate something hasty at the sailor, but checked himself, and pointing down to the streaming soup, playfully tapped him from behind with his rattan, saying in a low musical voice peculiar to him at times "Handsomely done, my lad! And handsome is as handsome did it too!" And with that passed on. Not noted by Billy as not coming within his view was the involuntary smile, or rather grimace, that accompanied Claggart's equivocal words. Aridly it drew down the thin corners of his shapely mouth. But everybody taking his remark as meant for humorous, and at which therefore as coming from a superior they were bound to laugh, "with counterfeited glee" acted accordingly; and Billy tickled, it may be, by the allusion to his being the handsome sailor, merrily joined in; then addressing his messmates exclaimed "There now, who says that Jemmy Legs is down on me!" "And who said he was, Beauty?" demanded one Donald with some surprise. Whereat the foretopman looked a little foolish recalling that it was only one person, Board-her-in-the-smoke who had suggested what to him was the smoky idea that this master-at-arms was in any peculiar way hostile to him. Meantime that functionary resuming his path must have momentarily worn some expression less guarded than that of the bitter smile, and usurping the face from the heart, some distorting expression perhaps, for a drummer-boy heedlessly frolicking along from the opposite direction and chancing to come into light collision with this person was strangely disconcerted by his aspect. Nor was the impression lessened when the official impulsively giving him a sharp cut with the rattan, vehemently exclaimed "Look where you go!"

11

What was the matter with the master-at-arms? And, be the matter what it might, how could it have direct relation to Billy Budd with whom prior to the affair of the spilled soup he had never come into any special contact official or otherwise? What indeed could the trouble have to do with one so little inclined to give offence as the merchant-ship's *peacemaker,* even him who in Claggart's own phrase was "the sweet and pleasant young fellow?["] Yes, why should *Jemmy Legs,* to borrow the Dansker's expression, be *down* on the Handsome Sailor? But, at heart and not for nothing, as the late chance encounter may indicate to the discerning, down on him, secretly down on him, he assuredly was.

Now to invent something touching the more private career of Claggart, something involving Billy Budd, of which something the latter should be wholly ignorant, some romantic incident implying that Claggart's knowledge of the young blue-jacket began at some period anterior to catching sight of him on board the seventy-four—all this, not so difficult to do, might avail in a way more or less interesting to account for whatever of enigma may appear to lurk in the case. But in fact there was nothing of the sort. And yet the cause, necessarily to be assumed as the sole one assignable, is in its very realism as much charged with that prime element of Radcliffian romance, *the mysterious,* as any that the ingenuity of the author of the *Mysteries of Udolpho* could devise. For what can more partake of the mysterious than an antipathy spontaneous and profound such as is evoked in certain exceptional mortals by the mere aspect of some other mortal, however harmless he may be? if not called forth by this very harmlessness itself.

Now there can exist no irritating juxtaposition of dissimilar personalities comparable to that which is possible aboard a great war-ship fully manned and at sea. There, every day among all ranks almost every man comes into more or less of contact with almost every other man. Wholly there to avoid even the sight of an aggravating object one must needs give it Jonah's toss or jump overboard himself. Imagine how all this might eventually operate on some peculiar human creature the direct reverse of a saint?

But for the adequate comprehending of Claggart by a normal nature these hints are insufficient. To pass from a normal nature to him one must cross "the deady space between." And this is best done by indirection.

Long ago an honest scholar my senior, said to me in reference to one who like himself is now no more, a man so unimpeachably respectable that against him nothing was ever openly said tho' among the few something was whispered, "Yes, X—— is a nut not to be cracked by the tap of a lady's fan. You are aware that I am the adherent of no organized religion much less of any philosophy built into a system. Well, for all that, I think that to try and get into X——, enter his labyrinth and get out again, without a clue derived from some source other than what is known as *knowledge of the world* —that were hardly possible, at least for me."

"Why" said I, "X—— however singular a study to some, is yet human, and knowledge of the world assuredly implies the knowledge of human nature, and in most of its varieties."

"Yes, but a superficial knowledge of it, serving ordinary purposes. But for anything deeper, I am not certain whether to know the world and to know human nature be not two distinct branches of knowledge, which while they may coexist in the same heart, yet either may exist with little or nothing of the other. Nay, in an average man of the world, his constant rubbing with it blunts that fine spiritual insight indispensable to the understanding of the essential in certain exceptional characters, whether evil ones or good. In a matter of some importance I have seen a girl wind an old lawyer about her little finger. Nor was it the dotage of senile love. Nothing of the sort. But he knew law better than he knew the girl's heart. Coke and Blackstone hardly shed so much light into obscure spiritual places as the Hebrew prophets. And who were they? Mostly recluses."

At the time my inexperience was such that I did not quite see the drift of all this. It may be that I see it now. And, indeed, if that lexicon which is based on Holy Writ were any longer popular, one might with less difficulty define and denominate certain phenomenal men. As it is, one must turn to some authority not liable to the charge of being tinctured with the Biblical element.

In a list of definitions included in the authentic translation of Plato, a list attributed to him, occurs this: "Natural Depravity: a depravity according to nature." A definition which tho' savoring of Calvinism, by no means involves Calvin's dogmas as to total mankind. Evidently its intent makes it applicable but to individuals. Not many are the examples of this depravity which the gallows and jail supply. At any rate for notable instances, since these have no vulgar alloy of the brute in them, but invariably are dominated by intellectuality, one must go elsewhere. Civilization, especially if of the austerer sort, is auspicious to it. It folds itself in the mantle of respectability. It has its certain negative virtues serving as silent auxiliaries. It never allows wine to get within its guard. It is not going too far to say that it is without vices or small sins. There is a phenomenal pride in it that excludes them from anything mercenary or avaricious. In short the depravity here meant partakes nothing of the sordid or sensual. It is serious, but free from acerbity. Though no flatterer of mankind it never speaks ill of it.

But the thing which in eminent instances signalizes so exceptional a nature is this: though the man's even temper and discreet bearing would seem to intimate a mind peculiarly subject to the law of reason, not the less in his heart he would seem to riot in complete exemption from that law[,] having apparently little to do with reason further than to employ it as an ambidexter implement for effecting the irrational. That is to say: Toward the accomplishment of an aim which in wantonness of malignity would seem to partake of the insane, he will direct a cool judgment sagacious and sound.

These men are true madmen, and of the most dangerous sort, for their lunacy is not continuous but occasional[,] evoked by some special object; it is probably secretive, which is as much to say it is self-contained; so that when moreover, most active[,] it is to the average mind not distinguishable from sanity, and for the reason above suggested that whatever its aims may be, and the aim is never declared—the method and the outward proceeding are always perfectly rational.

Now something such an one was Claggart, in whom was the mania of an evil nature, not engendered by vicious training or corrupting books or licentious living, but born with him and innate, in short "a depravity according to nature."

12

LAWYERS, EXPERTS, CLERGY: AN EPISODE

By the way, can it be the phenomenon, disowned or at least concealed, that in some criminal cases puzzles the courts? For this cause have our juries at times not only to endure the prolonged contentions of lawyers with their fees, but also the yet more perplexing strife of the medical experts with theirs?—But why leave it to them? why not subpoena as well the clerical proficients? Their vocation bringing them into peculiar contact with so many human beings, and sometimes in their least guarded hour, in interviews very much more confidential than those of physician and patient; this would seem to qualify them to know something about those intricacies involved in the question of moral responsibility; or whether in a given case, say, the crime proceeded from mania in the brain or rabies of the heart. As to any differences among themselves these clerical proficients might develop on the stand, these could hardly be greater than the direct contradictions exchanged between the remunerated medical experts.

Dark sayings are these, some will say. But why? Is it because they somewhat savor of Holy Writ in its phrase "mysteries of iniquity"? If they do, such savor was far from being intended for little will it commend these pages to many a reader of to-day.

The point of the present story turning on the hidden nature of the master-at-arms has necessitated this chapter. With an added hint or two in connection with the incident at the mess, the resumed narrative must be left to vindicate, as it may, its own credibility.

13

PALE IRE, ENVY AND DESPAIR

That Claggart's figure was not amiss, and his face, save the chin, well moulded, has already been said. Of these favorable points he seemed not insensible, for he was not only neat but careful in his dress. But the form of Billy Budd was heroic; and if his face was without the intellectual look of the pallid Claggart's, not the less was it lit, like his, from within, though from a different source. The bonfire in his heart made luminous the rose-tan in his cheek.

In view of the marked contrast between the persons of the twain, it is more than probable that when the master-at-arms in the scene last given applied to the sailor the proverb *Handsome is as handsome does;* he there let escape an ironic inkling, not caught by the young sailors who heard it, as to what it was that had first moved him against Billy, namely, his significant personal beauty.

Now envy and antipathy passions irreconcilable in reason, nevertheless in fact may spring conjoined like Chang and Eng in one birth. Is Envy then such a monster? Well, though many an arraigned mortal has in hopes of mitigated penalty pleaded guilty to horrible actions, did ever anybody seriously confess to envy? Something there is in it universally felt to be more shameful than even felonious crime. And not only does everybody disown it but the better sort are inclined to incredulity when it is in earnest imputed to an intelligent man. But since its lodgement is in the heart not the brain, no degree of intellect supplies a guarantee against it. But Claggart's was no vulgar form of the passion. Nor, as directed toward Billy Budd did it partake of that streak of apprehensive jealousy that marred Saul's visage perturbedly brooding on the comely young David.

Claggart's envy struck deeper. If askance he eyed the good looks, cheery health and frank enjoyment of young life in Billy Budd, it was because these [went] along with a nature that as Claggart magnetically felt, had in its simplicity never willed malice or experienced the reactionary bite of that serpent. To him, the spirit lodged within Billy, and looking out from his welkin eyes as from windows, that ineffability it was which made the dimple in his dyed cheek, suppled his joints, and dancing in his yellow curls made him preeminently the Handsome Sailor. One person excepted the master-at-arms was perhaps the only man in the ship intellectually capable of adequately appreciating the moral phenomenon presented in Billy Budd. And the insight but intensified his passion, which assuming various secret forms within him, at times assumed that of cynic disdain—disdain of innocence—To be nothing more than innocent! Yet in an æsthetic way he saw the charm of it, the courageous free-and-easy temper of it, and fain would have shared it, but he despaired of it.

With no power to annul the elemental evil in him, tho readily enough he could hide it; apprehending the good, but powerless to be it; a nature like Claggart's surcharged with energy as such natures almost invariably are, what recourse is left to it but to recoil upon itself and like the scorpion for which the Creator alone is responsible, act out to the end the part allotted it.

14

Passion, and passion in its profoundest, is not a thing demanding a palatial stage whereon to play its part. Down among the groundlings, among the beggars and rakers of the garbage, profound passion is enacted. And the circumstances that provoke it, however trivial or mean, are no measure of its power. In the present instance the stage is a scrubbed gun-deck, and one of the external provocations a man-of-war's-man's spilled soup.

Now when the Master-at-arms noticed whence came that greasy fluid streaming before his feet, he must have taken it—to some extent wilfully, perhaps—not for the mere accident it assuredly was, but for the sly escape of a spontaneous feeling on Billy's part more or less answering to the antipathy on his own. In effect a foolish demonstration he must have thought, and very harmless, like the futile kick of a heifer, which yet were the heifer a shod stallion, would not be so harmless. Even so was it that into the gall of Claggart's envy he infused the vitriol of his contempt. But the incident confirmed to him certain tell-tale reports purveyed to his ear by *Squeak*, one of his more cunning Corporals, a grizzled little man, so nicknamed by the sailors on account of his squeaky voice, and sharp visage ferreting about the dark corners of the lower decks after interlopers, satirically suggesting to them the idea of a rat in a cellar.

From his Chief's employing him as an implicit tool in laying little traps for the worriment of the Foretopman—for it was from the Master-at-arms that the petty persecutions heretofore adverted to had proceeded—the corporal having naturally enough concluded that his master could have no love for the sailor, made it his business, faithful understrapper that he was, to foment the ill blood by perverting to his Chief certain innocent frolics of the good natured Foretopman, besides inventing for his mouth sundry contumelious epithets he claimed to have overheard him let fall. The Master-at-arms never suspected the veracity of these reports, more especially as to the epithets, for he well knew how secretly unpopular may become a master-at-arms[,] at least a master-at-arms of those days zealous in his function, and how the blue-jackets shoot at him in private their raillery and wit; the nickname by which he goes among them (*Jemmy Legs*) implying under the form of merriment their cherished disrespect and dislike.

But in view of the greediness of hate for patrolmen it hardly needed a purveyor to feed Claggart's passion. An uncommon prudence is habitual with the subtler depravity, for it has everything to hide. And in case of an injury but suspected, its secretiveness voluntarily cuts it off from enlightenment or disillusion; and, not unreluctantly, action is taken upon surmise as upon certainty. And the retaliation is apt to be in monstrous disproportion to the supposed offence; for when in anybody was revenge in its exactions aught else but an inordinate usurer. But how with Claggart's conscience? For though consciences are unlike as foreheads, every intelligence, not excluding the Scriptural devils who "believe and tremble," has one. But Claggart's conscience being but the lawyer to his will, made ogres of trifles, probably arguing that the motive imputed to Billy in spilling the soup just when he did, together with the epithets alleged, these, if nothing more, made a strong case against him; nay, justified animosity into a sort of retributive righteousness. The Pharisee is the Guy Fawkes prowling in the hid chambers underlying the Claggarts. And they can really form no conception of an unreciprocated malice. Probably, the master-at-arms' clandestine persecution of Billy was started to try the temper of the man; but it had not developed any quality in him that enmity could make official use of or even pervert into plausible self-justification; so that the occurrence at the mess, petty if it were, was a welcome one to that peculiar conscience assigned to be the private mentor of Claggart; And, for the rest, not improbably it put him upon new experiments.

15

Not many days after the last incident narrated something befell Billy Budd that more gravelled him than aught that had previously occurred.

It was a warm night for the latitude; and the Foretopman, whose watch at the time was properly below, was dozing on the uppermost deck whither he had ascended from his hot hammock one of hundreds suspended so closely wedged together over a lower gun-deck that there was little or no swing to them. He lay as in the shadow of a hill-side, stretched under the lee of the booms, a piled ridge of spare spars amidships between foremast and mainmast and among which the ship's largest boat, the launch, was stowed. Alongside of three other slumberers from below, he lay near that end of the booms which approaches the foremast; his station aloft on duty as a foretopman being just over the deck-station of the forecastlemen, entitling him according to usage to make himself more or less at home in that neighborhood.

Presently he was stirred into semi-consciousness by somebody, who must have previously sounded the sleep of the others, touching his shoulder, and then as the Foretopman raised his head, breathing into his ear in a quick whisper, "Slip into the lee forechains, Billy; there is something in the wind. Don't speak. Quick, I will meet you there;" and disappeared.

Now Billy like sundry other essentially good-natured ones had some of the weaknesses inseparable from essential good nature; and among these was a reluctance, almost an incapacity of plumply saying *no* to an abrupt proposition not obviously absurd, on the face of it, nor obviously unfriendly, nor iniquitous. And being of warm blood he had not the phlegm tacitly to negative any proposition by unresponsive inaction. Like his sense of fear, his apprehension as to aught outside of the honest and natural was seldom very quick. Besides, upon the present occasion, the drowse from his sleep still hung upon him.

However it was, he mechanically rose, and sleepily wondering what could be in the wind, betook himself to the designated place, a narrow platform, one of six, outside of the high bulwarks and screened by the great dead-eyes and multiple columned lanyards of the shrouds and back-stays; and, in a great war-ship of that time, of dimensions commensurate [with the] hull's magnitude; a tarry balcony in short overhanging the sea, and so secluded that one mariner of the *Indomitable,* a non-conformist old tar of a serious turn, made it even in daytime his private oratory.

In this retired nook the stranger soon joined Billy Budd. There was no moon as yet; a haze obscured the star-light. He could not distinctly see the stranger's face. Yet from something in the outline and carriage, Billy took him to be, and correctly, for one of the afterguard.

"Hist! Billy," said the man in the same quick cautionary whisper as before; "You were impressed, weren't you? Well, so was I"; and he paused, as to mark the effect. But Billy not knowing exactly what to make of this said nothing. Then the other: "We are not the only impressed ones, Billy. There's a gang of us.—Couldn't you—help—at a pinch?["]

"What do you mean?["] demanded Billy here thoroughly shaking off his drowse.

"Hist, hist!["] the hurried whisper now growing husky, ["]see here"; and the man held up two small objects faintly twinkling in the nightlight; "see, they are yours, Billy, if you'll only—"

But Billy broke in, and in his resentful eagerness to deliver himself his vocal infirmity somewhat intruded: "D-D-Damme, I don't know what you are d-d-driving at, or what you mean, but you had better g-g-go where you belong!" For the moment the fellow, as confounded, did not stir; and Billy springing to his feet, said "If you d-don't start I'll t-t-toss you back over the r-rail!" There was no mistaking this and the mysterious emissary decamped disappearing in the direction of the mainmast in the shadow of the booms.

"Hallo, what's the matter?" here came growling from a forecastleman awakened from his deck-doze by Billy's raised voice. And as the foretopman reappeared and was recognized by him; "Ah, *Beauty,* is it you? Well, something must have been the matter for you st-st-stuttered."

"O," rejoined Billy, now mastering the impediment; "I found an afterguardsman in our part of the ship here and I bid him be off where he belongs."

"And is that all you did about it, foretopman?" gruffly demanded another, an irascible old fellow of brick-colored visage and hair, and who was known to his associate forecastlemen as *Red Pepper;* "Such sneaks I should like to marry to the gunner's daughter!" by that expression meaning that he would like to subject them to disciplinary castigation over a gun.

However, Billy's rendering of the matter satisfactorily accounted to these inquirers for the brief commotion, since of all the sections of a ship's company the forecastlemen, veterans for the most part and bigoted in their sea-prejudices, are the most jealous in resenting territorial encroachments, especially on the part of any of the afterguard, of whom they have but a sorry opinion, chiefly landsmen, never going aloft except to reef or furl the mainsail, and in no wise competent to handle a marlinspike or turn in a *dead-eye,* say.

16

This incident sorely puzzled Billy Budd. It was an entirely new experience; the first time in his life that he had ever been personally approached in underhand intriguing fashion. Prior to this encounter he had known nothing of the afterguardsman, the two men being stationed wide apart, one forward and aloft during his watch, the other on deck and aft.

What could it mean? And could they really be guineas, those two glittering objects the interloper had held up to his (Billy's) eyes? Where could the fellow get guineas? Why even buttons spare buttons are not so plentiful at sea. The more he turned the matter over, the more he was non-plussed, and made uneasy and discomforted. In his disgustful recoil from an overture which tho' he but ill comprehended he instinctively knew must involve evil of some sort, Billy Budd was like a young horse fresh from the pasture suddenly inhaling a vile whiff from some chemical factory and by repeated snortings tries to get it out of his nostrils and lungs. This frame of mind barred all desire of holding further parley with the fellow, even were it but for the purpose of gaining some enlightenment as to his design in approaching him. And yet he was not without natural curiosity to see how such a visitor in the dark would look in broad day.

He espied him the following afternoon in his first dog-watch below one of the smokers on that forward part of the upper gun deck allotted to the pipe. He recognized him by his general cut and build, more than by his round freckled face and glassy eyes of pale blue, veiled with lashes all but white. And yet Billy was a bit uncertain whether indeed it were he—yonder chap about his own age chatting and laughing in free-hearted way, leaning against a gun; a genial young fellow enough to look at, and something of a rattle-brain, to all appearance. Rather chubby too for a sailor even an afterguardsman. In short the last man in the world, one would think, to be overburthened with thoughts, especially those perilous thoughts that must needs belong to a conspirator in any serious project, or even to the underling of such a conspirator.

Altho' Billy was not aware of it, the fellow, with a side-long watchful glance had perceived Billy first, and then noting that Billy was looking at him, thereupon nodded a familiar sort of friendly recognition as to an old acquaintance, without interrupting the talk he was engaged in with the group of smokers. A day or two afterwards chancing in the evening promenade on a gun deck, to pass Billy, he offered a flying word of good-fellowship as it were, which by its unexpectedness, and equivocalness under the circumstances so embarrassed Billy that he knew not how to respond to it, and let it go unnoticed.

Billy was now left more at a loss than before. The ineffectual speculation into which he was led was so disturbingly alien to him that he did his best to smother [it]. It never entered his mind that here was a matter which from its extreme questionableness, it was his duty as a loyal blue-jacket to report in the proper quarter. And, probably, had such a step been suggested to him, he would have been deterred from taking it by the thought, one of novice-magnanimity, that it would savor overmuch of the dirty work of a tell-tale. He kept the thing to himself. Yet upon one occasion, he could not forbear a little disburthening himself to the old Dansker, tempted thereto perhaps by the influence of a balmy night when the ship lay becalmed; the twain, silent for the most part, sitting together on deck, their heads propped against the bulwarks. But it was only a partial and anonymous account that Billy gave, the unfounded scruples above referred to preventing full disclosure to anybody. Upon hearing Billy's version, the sage Dansker seemed to divine more than he was told; and after a little meditation during which his wrinkles were pursed as into a point, quite effacing for the time that quizzing expression his face sometimes wore,—"Didn't I say so, Baby Budd?"

"Say what?" demanded Billy.

"Why, *Jemmy Legs* is *down* on you."

"And what" rejoined Billy in amazement, "has *Jemmy Legs* to do with that cracked afterguardsman?"

"Ho, it was an afterguardsman then. A cat's-paw, a cat's-paw!" And with that exclamation, which, whether it had reference to a light puff of air just then coming over the calm sea, or subtler relation to the afterguardsman, there is no telling, the old Merlin gave a twisting wrench with his black teeth at his plug of tobacco, vouchsafing no reply to Billy's impetuous question, tho' now repeated, for it was his wont to relapse into grim silence when interrogated in skeptical sort as to any of his sententious oracles, not always very clear ones, rather partaking of that obscurity which invests most Delphic deliverances from any quarter.

Long experience had very likely brought this old man to that bitter prudence which never interferes in aught and never gives advice.

17

Yes, despite the Dansker's pithy insistence as to the Master-at-arms being at the bottom of these strange experiences of Billy on board the *Indomitable*, the young sailor was ready to ascribe them to almost anybody but the man who, to use Billy's own expression, "always had a pleasant word for him." This is to be wondered at. Yet not so much to be wondered at. In certain matters, some sailors even in mature life remain unsophisticated enough. But a young seafarer of the disposition of our athletic Foretopman, is much of a child-man. And yet a child's utter innocence is but its blank ignorance, and the innocence more or less wanes as intelligence waxes. But in Billy Budd intelligence, such as it was, had advanced, while yet his simple mindedness remained for the most part unaffected. Experience is a teacher indeed; yet did Billy's years make his experience small. Besides, he had none of that intuitive knowledge of the bad which in natures not good or incompletely so foreruns experience, and therefore may pertain, as in some instances it too clearly does pertain, even to youth.

And what could Billy know of man except of man as a mere sailor? And the old-fashioned sailor, the veritable man-before-the-mast, the sailor from boyhood up, he, tho' indeed of the same species as a landsman is in some respects singularly distinct from him. The sailor is frankness, the landsman is finesse. Life is not a game with the sailor, demanding the long head; no intricate game of chess where few moves are made in straightforwardness, and ends are attained by indirection; an oblique, tedious, barren game hardly worth that poor candle burnt out in playing it.

Yes, as a class, sailors are in character a juvenile race. Even their deviations are marked by juvenility. And this more especially holding true with the sailors of Billy's time. Then, too, certain things which apply to all sailors, do more pointedly operate here and there, upon the junior one. Every sailor, too is accustomed to obey orders without debating them; his life afloat is extremely ruled for him; he is not brought into that promiscuous commerce with mankind where unobstructed free agency on equal terms—equal superficially, at least—soon teaches one that unless upon occasion he exercise a distrust keen in proportion to the fairness of the appearance, some foul turn may be served him. A ruled undemonstrative distrustfulness is so habitual, not with business-men so much, as with men who know their kind in less shallow relations than business, namely, certain men-of-the-world, that they come at last to employ it all but unconsciously; and some of them would very likely feel real surprise at being charged with it as one of their general characteristics.

18

But after the little matter at the mess Billy Budd no more found himself in strange trouble at times about his hammock or his clothesbag or what not. While, as to that smile that occasionally sunned him, and the pleasant passing word, these were if not more frequent, yet if anything more pronounced than before.

But for all that, there were certain other demonstrations now. When Claggart's unobserved glance happened to light on belted Billy rolling along the upper gun-deck in the leisure of the second dog-watch exchanging passing broadsides of fun with other young promenaders in the crowd; that glance would follow the cheerful sea-Hyperion with a settled meditative and melancholy expression, his eyes strangely suffused with incipient feverish tears. Then would Claggart look like the man of sorrows. Yes, and sometimes the melancholy expression would have in it a touch of soft yearning, as if Claggart could even have loved Billy but for fate and ban. But this was an evanescence, and quickly repented of, as it were, by an immitigable look, pinching and shrivelling the visage into the momentary semblance of a wrinkled walnut. But sometimes catching sight in advance of the foretopman coming in his direction, he would, upon their nearing, step aside a little to let him pass, dwelling upon Billy for the moment with the glittering dental satire of a Guise. But upon any abrupt unforeseen encounter a red light would [flash] forth from his eye like a spark from an anvil in a dusk smithy. That quick fierce light was a strange one, darted from orbs which in repose were of a color nearest approaching a deeper violet, the softest of shades.

Tho' some of these caprices of the pit could not but be observed by their object, yet were they beyond the construing of such a nature. And the *thews* of Billy were hardly compatible with that sort of sensitive spiritual organisation which in some cases instinctively conveys to ignorant innocence an admonition of the proximity of the malign. He thought the Master-at-arms acted in a manner rather queer at times. That was all. But the occasional frank air and pleasant word went for what they purported to be, the young sailor never having heard as yet of the "too fair-spoken man."

Had the foretopman been conscious of having done or said anything to provoke the ill will of the official, it would have been different with him, and his sight might have been purged if not sharpened. As it was[,] innocence was his blinder.

So was it with him in yet another matter. Two minor officers—the Armorer and Captain of the Hold, with whom he had never exchanged a word, his position in the ship not bringing him into contact with them; these men now for the first began to cast upon Billy when they chanced to encounter him, that peculiar glance which evidences that the man from whom it comes has been some way tampered with and to the prejudice of him upon whom the glance lights. Never did it occur to Billy as a thing to be noted or a thing suspicious, tho' he well knew the fact, that the Armorer and Captain of the Hold, with the ship's-yeoman, apothecary, and others of that grade, were by naval usage, mess-mates of the master-at-arms, men with ears convenient to his confidential tongue.

But the general popularity that our *Handsome Sailor's* manly forwardness upon occasion, and [his] irresistible good nature[,] indicating no mental superiority tending to excite an invidious feeling; this good will on the part of most of his shipmates made him the less to concern himself about such mute aspects toward him as those whereto allusion has just been made.

As to the afterguardsman, tho' Billy for reasons already given necessarily saw little of him, yet when the two did happen to meet, invariably came the fellow's off-hand cheerful recognition, sometimes accompanied by a passing pleasant word or two. Whatever that equivocal young person's original design may really have been, or the design of which he might have been the deputy, certain it was from his manner upon these occasions, that he had wholly dropped it.

It was as if his precocity of crookedness (and every vulgar villain is precocious) had for once deceived him, and the man he had sought to entrap as a simpleton had, through his very simplicity ignorantly baffled him.

But shrewd ones may opine that it was hardly possible for Billy to refrain from going up to the afterguardsman and bluntly demanding to know his purpose in the initial interview, so abruptly closed in the fore-chains. Shrewd ones may also think it but natural in Billy to set about sounding some of the other impressed men of the ship in order to discover what basis, if any, there was for the emissary's obscure suggestions as to plotting disaffection aboard. Yes, [the] shrewd may so think. But something more, or rather, something else than mere shrewdness is perhaps needful for the due understanding of such a character as Billy Budd's.

As to Claggart, the monomania in the man—if that indeed it were—as involuntarily disclosed by starts in the manifestations detailed, yet in general covered over by his self-contained and rational demeanor; this, like a subterranean fire was eating its way deeper and deeper in him. Something decisive must come of it.

19

After the mysterious interview in the fore-chains, the one so abruptly ended there by Billy, nothing especially German to the story occurred until the events now about to be narrated.

Elsewhere it has been said that in the lack of frigates (of course better sailers than line-of-battle ships) in the English squadron up the Straits at that period, the *Indomitable* was occasionally employed not only as an available substitute for a scout, but at times on detached service of more important kind. This was not alone because of her sailing qualities, not common in a ship of her rate, but quite as much, probably, that the character of her commander, it was thought, specially adapted him for any duty where under unforeseen difficulties a prompt initiative might have to be taken in some matter demanding knowledge and ability in addition to those qualities implied in good seamanship. It was on an expedition of the latter sort, a somewhat distant one, and when the *Indomitable* was almost at her furthest remove from the fleet that in the latter part of an afternoon-watch she unexpectedly came in sight of a ship of the enemy. It proved to be a frigate. The latter perceiving thro' the glass that the weight of men and metal would be heavily against her, invoking her light heels crowded sail to get away. After a chase urged almost against hope and lasting until about the middle of the first dog-watch, she signally succeeded in effecting her escape.

Not long after the pursuit had been given up, and ere the excitement incident thereto had altogether waned away, the

Master-at-Arms ascending from his cavernous sphere made his appearance cap in hand by the mainmast respectfully waiting the notice of Captain Vere then solitary walking the weather-side of the quarter-deck, doubtless somewhat chafed at the failure of the pursuit. The spot where Claggart stood was the place allotted to men of lesser grades seeking some more particular interview either with the officer-of-the-deck or the Captain himself. But from the latter it was not often that a sailor or petty-officer of those days would seek a hearing; only some exceptional cause, would, according to established custom, have warranted that.

Presently, just as the Commander absorbed in his reflections was on the point of turning aft in his promenade, he became sensible of Claggart's presence, and saw the doffed cap held in deferential expectancy. Here be it said that Captain Vere's personal knowledge of this petty-officer had only begun at the time of the ship's last sailing from home, Claggart then for the first, in transfer from a ship detained for repairs, supplying on board the *Indomitable* the place of a previous master-at-arms disabled and ashore.

No sooner did the Commander observe who it was that now deferentially stood awaiting his notice, than a peculiar expression came over him. It was not unlike that which uncontrollably will flit across the countenance of one at unawares encountering a person who though known to him indeed has hardly been long enough known for thorough knowledge, but something in whose aspect nevertheless now for the first provokes a vaguely repellent distaste. But coming to a stand, and resuming much of his wonted official manner, save that a sort of impatience lurked in the intonation of the opening word, he said "Well? what is it, Master-at-Arms?"

With the air of a subordinate grieved at the necessity of being a messenger of ill tidings, and while conscientiously determined to be frank, yet equally resolved upon shunning overstatement, Claggart at this invitation or rather summons to disburthen, spoke up. What he said, conveyed in the language of no uneducated man, was to the effect following if not altogether in these words, namely, that during the chase and preparations for the possible encounter he had seen enough to convince him that at least one sailor aboard was a dangerous character in a ship mustering some who not only had taken a guilty part in the late serious troubles, but others also who, like the man in question, had entered His Majesty's service under another form than enlistment.

At this point Captain Vere with some impatience, interrupted him: "Be direct, man; say impressed men."

Claggart made a gesture of subservience, and proceeded.

Quite lately he (Claggart) had begun to suspect that on the gun-decks some sort of movement prompted by the sailor in question was covertly going on, but he had not thought himself warranted in reporting the suspicion so long as it remained indistinct. But from what he had that afternoon observed in the man referred to the suspicion of something clandestine going on had advanced to a point less removed from certainty. He deeply felt, he added, the serious responsibility assumed in making a report involving such possible consequences to the individual mainly concerned, besides tending to augment those natural anxieties which every naval commander must feel in view of extraordinary outbreaks so recent as those which, he sorrowfully said it, it needed not to name.

Now at the first broaching of the matter Captain Vere taken by surprise could not wholly dissemble his disquietude. But as Claggart went on, the former's aspect changed into restiveness under something in the witness' manner in giving his testimony. However, he refrained from interrupting him. And Claggart, continuing, concluded with this:

"God forbid, your honor, that the *Indomitable's* should be the experience of the—"

"Never mind that!" here peremptorily broke in the superior, his face altering with anger, instinctively divining the ship that the other was about to name, one in which the Nore Mutiny had assumed a singularly tragical character that for a time jeopardized the life of its commander. Under the circumstances he was indignant at the purposed allusion. When the commissioned officers themselves were on all occasions very heedful how they referred to the recent events, for a petty-officer unnecessarily to allude to them in the presence of his Captain, this struck him as a most immodest presumption. Besides, to his quick sense of self-respect, it even looked under the circumstances something like an attempt to alarm him. Nor at first was he without some surprise that one who so far as he had hitherto come under his notice had shown considerable tact in his function should in this particular evince such lack of it.

But these thoughts and kindred dubious ones flitting across his mind were suddenly replaced by an intuitional surmise which though as yet obscure in form served practically to affect his reception of the ill tidings. Certain it is, that long versed in everything pertaining to the complicated gun-deck life, which like every other form of life, has its secret mines and dubious side, the side popularly disclaimed, Captain Vere did not permit himself to be unduly disturbed by the general tenor of his subordinate's report. Furthermore, if in view of recent events prompt action should be taken at the first palpable sign of recurring insubordination, for all that, not judicious would it be, he thought, to keep the idea of lingering disaffection alive by undue forwardness in crediting an informer even if his own subordinate and charged among other things with police surveillance of the crew. This feeling would not perhaps have so prevailed with him were it not that upon a prior occasion the patriotic zeal officially evinced by Claggart had somewhat irritated him as appearing rather supersensible and strained. Furthermore, something even in the official's self-possessed and somewhat ostentatious manner in making his specifications strangely reminded him of a bandsman, a perjurous witness in a capital case before a court-martial ashore of which when a lieutenant he Captain Vere had been a member.

Now the peremptory check given to Claggart in the matter of the arrested allusion was quickly followed up by this: "You say that there is at least one dangerous man aboard. Name him."

"William Budd. A foretopman, your honor—"

"William Budd" repeated Captain Vere with unfeigned astonishment; "and mean you the man that Lieutenant Ratcliffe took from the merchantman not very long ago—the young fellow who seems to be so popular with the men—Billy, the Handsome Sailor, as they call him?[”]

"The same, your honor; but for all his youth and good looks, a deep one. Not for nothing does he insinuate himself into the good will of his shipmates, since at the least all hands will at a pinch say a good word for him at all hazards. Did Lieutenant Ratcliffe happen to tell your honor of that adroit fling of Budd's, jumping up in the cutter's bow under the merchantman's stern when he was being taken off? It is even masqued by that sort of good humored air that at heart he resents his impressment. You have but noted his fair cheek. A man-trap may be under his ruddy-tipped daisies."

Now the *Handsome Sailor* as a signal figure among the crew had naturally enough attracted the Captain's attention from the first. Tho' in general not very demonstrative to his officers, he had congratulated Lieutenant Ratcliffe upon his good fortune in lighting on such a fine specimen of the genus homo, who in the nude might have posed for a statue of young Adam before the Fall.

As to Billy's adieu to the ship *Rights-of-Man,* which the boarding lieutenant had indeed reported to him but in a deferential way more as a good story than aught else, Captain Vere[,] tho mistakenly understanding it as a satiric sally, had but thought so much the better of the impressed man for it; as a military sailor, admiring the spirit that could take an arbitrary enlistment so merrily and sensibly. The foretopman's conduct, too, so far as it had fallen under the Captain's notice had confirmed the first happy augury, while the new recruit's qualities as a *sailor-man* seemed to be such that he had thought of recommending him to the executive officer for promotion to a place that would more frequently bring him under his own observation, namely, the captaincy of the mizzen-top, replacing there in the starboard watch a man not so young whom partly for that reason he deemed less fitted for the post. Be it parenthesized here that since the mizzen-top-men having not to handle such breadths of heavy canvas as the lower sails on the main-mast and fore-mast, a young man if of the right stuff not only seems best adapted to duty there, but in fact is generally selected for the captaincy of that top, and the company under him are light hands and often but striplings. In sum, Captain Vere had from the beginning deemed Billy Budd to be what in the naval parlance of the time was called a "*King's bargain*[,]" that is to say, for His Britannic Majesty's navy a capital investment at small outlay or none at all.

After a brief pause during which the reminiscences above mentioned passed vividly through his mind and he weighed the import of Claggart's last suggestion conveyed in the phrase "pitfall under the clover," and the more he weighed it the less reliance he felt in the informer's good faith. Suddenly he turned upon him and in a low voice: "Do you come to me, master-at-arms[,] with so foggy a tale? As to Budd, cite me an act or spoken word of his confirmatory of what you in general charge against him. Stay," drawing nearer to him "heed what you speak. Just now, and in a case like this, there is a yard-arm-end for the false-witness."

"Ah, your honor!" sighed Claggart mildly shaking his shapely head as in sad deprecation of such unmerited severity of tone. Then, bridling—erecting himself as in virtuous self-assertion, he circumstantially alleged certain words and acts, which collectively, if credited, led to presumptions mortally inculpating Budd. And for some of these averments, he added, substantiating proof was not far.

With gray eyes impatient and distrustful essaying to fathom to the bottom Claggart's calm violet ones, Captain Vere again heard him out; then for the moment stood ruminating. The mood he evinced, Claggart—himself for the time liberated from the other's scrutiny—steadily regarded with a look difficult to render,—a look curious of the operation of his tactics, a look such as might have been that of the spokesman of the envious children of Jacob deceptively imposing upon the troubled patriarch the blood-dyed coat of young Joseph.

Though something exceptional in the moral quality of Captain Vere made him, in earnest encounter with a fellow-man, a veritable touch-stone of that man's essential nature, yet now as to Claggart and what was really going on in him his feeling partook less of intuitional conviction than of strong suspicion clogged by strange dubieties. The perplexity he evinced proceeded less from aught touching the man informed against —as Claggart doubtless opined—than from considerations how best to act in regard to the informer. At first indeed he was naturally for summoning that substantiation of his allegations which Claggart said was at hand. But such a proceeding would result in the matter at once getting abroad, which in the present stage of it, he thought, might undesirably affect the ship's company. If Claggart was a false witness,—that closed the affair. And therefore before trying the accusation, he would first practically test the accuser; and he thought this could be done in a quiet undemonstrative way.

The measure he determined upon involved a shifting of the scene, a transfer to a place less exposed to observation than the broad quarter-deck. For although the few gun-room officers there at the time had, in due observance of naval etiquette, withdrawn to leeward the moment Captain Vere had begun his promenade on the deck's weather-side; and tho' during the colloquy with Claggart they of course ventured not to diminish the distance; and though throughout the interview Captain Vere's voice was far from high, and Claggart's silvery and low; and the wind in the cordage and the wash of the sea helped the more to put them beyond ear-shot; nevertheless, the interview's continuance already had attracted observation from some topmen aloft and other sailors in the waist or further forward.

Having determined upon his measures, Captain Vere forthwith took action. Abruptly turning to Claggart he asked "Master-at-arms, it is now Budd's watch aloft?"

"No, your honor." Whereupon, "Mr. Wilkes!" summoning the nearest midshipman, "tell Albert to come to me." Albert was the Captain's hammock-boy, a sort of sea-valet in whose discretion and fidelity his master had much confidence. The lad appeared. "You know Budd the foretopman?"

"I do, Sir."

"Go find him. It is his watch off. Manage to tell him out of earshot that he is wanted aft. Contrive it that he speaks to nobody. Keep him in talk yourself. And not till you get well aft here, not till then let him know that the place where he is wanted is my cabin. You understand. Go.—Master-at-Arms, show yourself on the decks below, and when you think it time for Albert to be coming with his man, stand by quietly to follow the sailor in."

20

Now when the foretopman found himself closeted there, as it were, in the cabin with the Captain and Claggart, he was surprised enough. But it was a surprise unaccompanied by apprehension or distrust. To an immature nature essentially honest and humane, forewarning intimations of subtler danger from one's kind come tardily if at all. The only thing that took shape in the young sailor's mind was this: Yes, the Captain, I have always thought, looks kindly upon me. Wonder if he's going to make me his coxswain. I should like that. And maybe now he is going to ask the master-at-arms about me.

"Shut the door there, sentry," said the commander; "stand without, and let nobody come in.—Now, master-at-arms, tell this man to his face what you told of him to me;" and stood prepared to scrutinize the mutually confronting visages.

With the measured step and calm collected air of an asylum-physician approaching in the public hall some patient beginning to show indications of a coming paroxysm, Claggart deliberately advanced within short range of Billy, and mesmerically looking him in the eye, briefly recapitulated the accusation.

Not at first did Billy take it in. When

he did, the rose-tan of his cheek looked struck as by white leprosy. He stood like one impaled and gagged. Meanwhile the accuser's eyes removing not as yet from the blue dilated ones, underwent a phenomenal change, their wonted rich violet color blurring into a muddy purple. Those lights of human intelligence losing human expression, gelidly protruding like the alien eyes of certain uncatalogued creatures of the deep. The first mesmeric glance was one of serpent fascination; the last was as the hungry lurch of the torpedo-fish.

"Speak, man!" said Captain Vere to the transfixed one struck by his aspect even more than by Claggart's, "Speak! defend yourself." Which appeal caused but a strange dumb gesturing and gurgling in Billy; amazement at such an accusation so suddenly sprung on inexperienced nonage; this, and, it may be horror of the accuser, serving to bring out his lurking defect and in this instance for the time intensifying it into a convulsed tongue-tie; while the intent head and entire form straining forward in an agony of ineffectual eagerness to obey the injunction to speak and defend himself, gave an expression to the face like that of a condemned Vestal priestess in the moment of being buried alive, and in the first struggle against suffocation.

Though at the time Captain Vere was quite ignorant of Billy's liability to vocal impediment, he now immediately divined it, since vividly Billy's aspect recalled to him that of a bright young schoolmate of his whom he had once seen struck by much the same startling impotence in the act of eagerly rising in the class to be foremost in response to a testing question put to it by the master. Going close up to the young sailor, and laying a soothing hand on his shoulder, he said[:] "There is no hurry, my boy. Take your time, take your time." Contrary to the effect intended, these words so fatherly in tone, doubtless touching Billy's heart to the quick, prompted yet more violent efforts at utterance—efforts soon ending for the time in confirming the paralysis, and bringing to his face an expression which was as a crucifixion to behold. The next instant, quick as the flame from a discharged cannon at night, his right arm shot out, and Claggart dropped to the deck. Whether intentionally or but owing to the young athlete's superior height, the blow had taken effect full upon the forehead, so shapely and intellectual-looking a feature in the master-at-arms; so that the body fell over lengthwise, like a heavy plank tilted from erectness. A gasp or two, and he lay motionless.

"Fated boy," breathed Captain Vere in tone so low as to be almost a whisper, "what have you done! But here, help me."

The twain raised the felled one from the loins up into a sitting position. The spare form flexibly acquiesced, but inertly. It was like handling a dead snake. They lowered it back. Regaining erectness Captain Vere with one hand covering his face stood to all appearance as impassive as the object at his feet. Was he absorbed in taking in all the bearings of the event and what was best not only now at once to be done, but also in the sequel? Slowly he uncovered his face; and the effect was as if the moon emerging from eclipse should reappear with quite another aspect than that which had gone into hiding. The father in him, manifested towards Billy thus far in the scene, was replaced by the military disciplinarian. In his official tone he bade the foretopman retire to a state-room aft, (pointing it out) and there remain till thence summoned. This order Billy in silence mechanically obeyed. Then going to the cabin-door where it opened on the quarter-deck, Captain Vere said to the sentry without, "Tell somebody to send Albert here." When the lad appeared his master so contrived it that he should not catch sight of the prone one. "Albert," he said to him, "tell the Surgeon I wish to see him. You need not come back till called." When the Surgeon entered—a self-poised character of that grave sense and experience that hardly anything could take him aback,—Captain Vere advanced to meet him, thus unconsciously intercepting his view of Claggart and interrupting the other's wonted ceremonious salutation, said, "Nay, tell me how it is with yonder man," directing his attention to the prostrate one.

The Surgeon looked, and for all his self-command, somewhat started at the abrupt revelation. On Claggart's always pallid complexion, thick black blood was now oozing from nostril and ear. To the gazer's professional eye it was unmistakably no living man that he saw.

"Is it so then?["] said Captain Vere intently watching him. "I thought it. But verify it." Whereupon the customary tests confirmed the Surgeon's first glance, who now looking up in unfeigned concern, cast a look of intense inquisitiveness upon his superior. But Captain Vere, with one hand to his brow, was standing motionless. Suddenly, catching the Surgeon's arm convulsively, he exclaimed, pointing down to the body—"It is the divine judgment on Ananias! Look!"

Disturbed by the excited manner he had never before observed in the *Indomitable's* Captain, and as yet wholly ignorant of the affair, the prudent Surgeon nevertheless held his peace, only again looking at earnest interrogation as to what it was that had resulted in such a tragedy.

But Captain Vere was now again motionless standing absorbed in thought. But again starting, he vehemently exclaimed—"Struck dead by an angel of God! Yet the angel must hang![")]

At these passionate interjections, mere incoherences to the listener as yet unapprised of the antecedents, the Surgeon was profoundly discomposed. But now as recollecting himself, Captain Vere in less harsh tone briefly related the circumstances leading up to the event.

["]But come; we must despatch" he added. ["]Help me to remove him (meaning the body) to yonder compartment,["] designating one opposite that where the foretopman remained immured. Anew disturbed by a request that as implying a desire for secrecy, seemed unaccountably strange to him, there was nothing for the subordinate to do but comply.

"Go now" said Captain Vere with something of his wonted manner—["]Go now. I shall presently call a drum-head court. Tell the lieutenants what has happened, and tell Mr. Mordant," meaning the captain of marines, "and charge them to keep the matter to themselves."

21

Full of disquietude and misgiving the Surgeon left the cabin. Was Captain Vere suddenly affected in his mind, or was it but a transient excitement, brought about by so strange and extraordinary a happening? As to the drum-head court, it struck the Surgeon as impolitic, if nothing more. The thing to do, he thought, was to place Billy Budd in confinement and in a way dictated by usage, and postpone further action in so extraordinary a case, to such time as they should rejoin the squadron, and then refer it to the Admiral. He recalled the unwonted agitation of Captain Vere and his excited exclamations so at variance with his normal manner. Was he unhinged? But assuming that he is, it is not so susceptible of proof. What then can he do? No more trying situation is conceivable than that of an officer subordinate under a Captain whom he suspects to be, not mad indeed, but yet not quite unaffected in his intellect. To argue his order to him would be insolence. To resist him would be mutiny.

In obedience to Captain Vere he communicated what had happened to the lieutenants & captain of marines; saying nothing as to the Captain's state. They fully shared his own surprise and concern. Like him too they seemed to think that such a matter should be referred to the Admiral.

22

Who in the rainbow can draw the line where the violet tint ends and the orange tint begins? Distinctly we see the difference of the colors, but where exactly does the one first blendingly enter into the other? So with sanity and insanity. In pronounced cases there is no question about them. But in some supposed cases, in various degrees supposedly less pronounced, to draw the exact line of demarkation few will undertake tho for a fee some professional experts will. There is nothing namable but that some men will undertake to do it for pay.

Whether Captain Vere, as the Surgeon professionally and privately surmised, was really the sudden victim of any degree of aberration, one must determine for himself by such light as this narrative may afford.

[That] the unhappy event which has been narrated could not have happened at a worse juncture was but too true. For it was close on the heel of the suppressed insurrections, an aftertime very critical to naval authority, demanding from every English sea-commander two qualities not readily interfusable—prudence and rigor. Moreover there was something crucial in the case.

In the jugglery of circumstances preceding and attending the event on board the *Indomitable* and in the light of that martial code whereby it was formally to be judged, innocence and guilt personified in Claggart and Budd in effect changed places. In a legal view the apparent victim of the tragedy was he who had sought to victimize a man blameless; and the indisputable deed of the latter, navally regarded, constituted the most heinous of military crimes. Yet more. The essential right and wrong involved in the matter, the clearer that might be, so much the worst for the responsibility of a loyal sea-commander inasmuch as he was not authorized to determine the matter on that primitive basis.

Small wonder then that the *Indomitable's* Captain though in general a man of rapid decision, felt that circumspectness not less than promptitude was necessary. Until he could decide upon his course, and in each detail; and not only so, but until the concluding measure was upon the point of being enacted, he deemed it advisable, in view of all the circumstances to guard as much as possible against publicity. Here he may or may not have erred. Certain it is however that subsequently in the confidential talk of more than one or two gun-rooms and cabins he was not a little criticized by some officers, a fact imputed by his friends and vehemently by his cousin Jack Denton to professional jealousy of *Starry Vere*. Some imaginative ground for invidious comment there was. The maintenance of secrecy in the matter, the confining all knowledge of it for a time to the place where the homicide occurred, the quarter-deck cabin; in these particulars lurked some resemblance to the policy adopted in those tragedies of the palace which have occurred more than once in the capital founded by Peter the Barbarian.

The case indeed was such that fain would the *Indomitable's* captain have deferred taking any action whatever respecting it further than to keep the foretopman a close prisoner till the ship rejoined the squadron and then submitting the matter to the judgement of his Admiral.

But a true military officer is in one particular like a true monk. Not with more self-abnegation will the latter keep his vows of monastic obedience than the former his vows of allegiance to martial duty.

Feeling that unless quick action was taken on it, the deed of the foretopman, so soon as it should be known on the gun-decks would tend to awaken any slumbering embers of the Nore among the crew, a sense of the urgency of the case overruled in Captain Vere every other consideration. But tho' a conscientious disciplinarian he was no lover of authority for mere authority's sake. Very far was he from embracing opportunities for monopolizing to himself the perils of moral responsibility[,] not at least that could properly be referred to an official superior or shared with him by his official equals or even subordinates. So thinking[,] he was glad it would not be at variance with usage to turn the matter over to a summary court of his own officers, reserving to himself as the one on whom the ultimate accountability would rest, the right of maintaining a supervision of it, or formally or informally interposing at need. Accordingly a drumhead court was summarily convened, he electing the individuals composing it, the First Lieutenant, the Captain of marines, and the Sailing Master.

In associating an officer of marines with the sea-lieutenants in a case having to do with a sailor the Commander perhaps deviated from general custom. He was prompted thereto by the circumstance that he took that soldier to be a judicious person, thoughtful, and not altogether incapable of grappling with a difficult case unprecedented in his prior experience. Yet even as to him he was not without some latent misgiving, for withal he was an extremely good-natured man, an enjoyer of his dinner, a sound sleeper, and inclined to obesity. [A] man who tho' he would always maintain his manhood in battle might not prove altogether reliable in a moral dilemma involving aught of the tragic. As to the First Lieutenant and the Sailing Master Captain Vere could not but be aware that though honest natures, of approved gallantry upon occasion[,] their intelligence was mostly confined to the matter of active seamanship and the fighting demands of their profession. The court was held in the same cabin where the unfortunate affair had taken place. This cabin, the Commander's, embraced the entire area under the poop-deck. Aft, and on either side[,] was a small state-room[;] the one room temporarily a jail & the other a dead-house[,] and a yet smaller compartment leaving a space between, expanding forward into a goodly oblong of length coinciding with the ship's beam. A skylight of moderate dimension was overhead and at each end of the oblong space were two sashed port-hole windows easily convertible back into embrasures for short carronades.

All being quickly in readiness, Billy Budd was arraigned, Captain Vere necessarily appearing as the sole witness in the case, and as such temporarily sinking his rank, though singularly maintaining it in a matter apparently trivial, namely, that he testified from the ship's weather-side[,] with that object having caused the court to sit on the lee-side. Concisely he narrated all that had led up to the catastrophe, omitting nothing in Claggart's accusation and deposing as to the manner in which the prisoner had received it. At this testimony the three officers glanced with no little surprise at Billy Budd, the last man they would have suspected either of the mutinous design alleged by Claggart or the undeniable deed he himself had done.

The First Lieutenant[,] taking judicial primacy and turning toward the prisoner, said, "Captain Vere has spoken. Is it or is it not as Captain Vere says?" In response came syllables not so much impeded in the utterance as might have been anticipated. They were these: "Captain Vere tells the truth. It is just as Captain Vere says, but it is not as the Master-at-Arms said. I have eaten the King's bread and I am true to the King."

"I believe you, my man" said the witness[,] his voice indicating a suppressed emotion not otherwise betrayed.

"God will bless you for that, Your Honor!" not without stammering said Billy, and all but broke down. But immediately was recalled to self-control by another quesiton, to which with the same emotional difficulty of utterance he said "No, there was no malice between us. I never bore malice against the Master-at-arms. I am sorry that he is dead. I did not mean to kill him. Could I have used my tongue I would not have struck him. But he foully lied to my face and in presence of my Captain, and I had to say something, and I could only say it with a blow, God help me!"

In the impulsive above-board manner of the frank one[,] the court saw confirmed all that was implied in words that just previously had perplexed them[,] coming as they did from the testifier to the tragedy and promptly following Billy's impassioned disclaimer of mutinous intent—Captain Vere's words, "I believe you, my man."

Next it was asked of him whether he knew of or suspected aught savoring of incipient trouble (meaning mutiny, tho' the explicit term was avoided) going on in any section of the ship's company.

The reply lingered. This was naturally imputed by the court to the same vocal embarrassment which had retarded or obstructed previous answers. But in main it was otherwise here; the question immediately recalling to Billy's mind the interview with the afterguardsman in the fore-chains. But an innate repugnance to playing a part at all approaching that of an informer against one's own shipmates—the same erring sense of uninstructed honor which had stood in the way of his reporting the matter at the time though as a loyal man-of-war-man it was incumbent on him[,] and failure so to do if charged against him and proven, would have subjected him to the heaviest of penalties; this, with the blind feeling now his, that nothing really was being hatched, prevailed with him. When the answer came it was negative.

"One question more," said the officer of marines now first speaking and with a troubled earnestness, "You tell us that what the Master-at-arms said against you was a lie. Now why should he have so lied, so maliciously lied, since you declare there was no malice between you?"

At that question unintentionally touching on a spiritual sphere wholly obscure to Billy's thoughts, he was nonplussed, evincing a confusion indeed that some observers, such as can readily be imagined, would have construed into involuntary evidence of hidden guilt. Nevertheless he strove some way to answer, but all at once relinquished the vain endeavor, at the same time turning an appealing glance towards Captain Vere as deeming him his best helper and friend. Captain Vere who had been seated for a time rose to his feet, addressing the interrogator. "The question you put to him comes naturally enough. But how can he rightly answer it? or anybody else? unless indeed it be he who lies within there" designating the compartment where lay the corpse. "But the prone one there will not rise to our summons. In effect, tho', as it seems to me, the point you make is hardly material. Quite aside from any conceivable motive actuating the Master-at-arms, and irrespective of the provocation to the blow, a martial court must needs in the present case confine its attention to the blow's consequence, which consequence justly is to be deemed not otherwise than as the striker's deed."

This utterance the full significance of which it was not at all likely that Billy took in, nevertheless caused him to turn a wistful interrogative look toward the speaker, a look in its dumb expressiveness not unlike that which a dog of generous breed might turn upon his master seeking in his face some elucidation of a previous gesture ambiguous to the canine intelligence. Nor was the same utterance without marked effect upon the three officers, more especially the soldier. Couched in it seemed to them a meaning unanticipated, involving a prejudgment on the speaker's part. It served to augment a mental disturbance previously evident enough.

The soldier once more spoke; in a tone of suggestive dubiety addressing at once his associates and Captain Vere: "Nobody is present—none of the ship's company, I mean, who might shed lateral light, if any is to be had, upon what remains mysterious in this matter."

"That is thoughtfully put" said Captain Vere; "I see your drift. Ay, there is a mystery; but, to use a Scriptural phrase, it is 'a mystery of iniquity,' a matter for psychologic theologians to discuss. But what has a military court to do with it? Not to add that for us any possible investigation of it is cut off by the lasting tongue-tie of—him—in yonder," again designating the mortuary state-room ["]The prisoner's deed,—with that alone we have to do."

To this, and particularly the closing reiteration, the marine soldier knowing not how aptly to reply, sadly abstained from saying aught. The First Lieutenant who at the outset had not unnaturally assumed primacy in the court, now overrulingly instructed by a glance from Captain Vere, a glance more effective than words, resumed that primacy. Turning to the prisoner, "Budd," he said, and scarce in equable tones, "Budd, if you have aught further to say for yourself, say it now."

Upon this the young sailor turned another quick glance toward Captain Vere; then, as taking a hint from that aspect, a hint confirming his own instinct that silence was now best, replied to the Lieutenant "I have said all, Sir."

The marine—the same who had been the sentinel without the cabin-door at the time that the foretopman followed by the master-at-arms, entered it—he, standing by the sailor throughout these judicial proceedings, was now directed to take him back to the after compartment originally assigned to the prisoner and his custodian. As the twain disappeared from view, the three officers as partially liberated from some inward constraint associated with Billy's mere presence, simultaneously stirred in their seats. They exchanged looks of troubled indecision, yet feeling that decide they must and without long delay. As for Captain Vere, he for the time stood unconsciously with his back toward them, apparently in one of his absent fits, gazing out from a sashed port-hole to windward upon the monotonous blank of the twilight sea. But the court's silence continuing, broken only at moments by brief consultations in low earnest tones, this seemed to arm him and energize him. Turning, he to-and-fro paced the cabin athwart; in the returning ascent to windward, climbing the slant deck in the ship's lee roll; without knowing it symbolizing thus in his action a mind resolute to surmount difficulties even if against primitive instincts strong as the wind and the sea. Presently he came to a stand before the three. After scanning their faces he stood less as mustering his thoughts for expression, than as one inly deliberating how best to put them to well-meaning men not intellectually mature, men with whom it was necessary to demonstrate certain principles that were axioms to himself. Similar impatience as to talking is perhaps one reason that deters some minds from addressing any popular assemblies.

When speak he did, something both in the substance of what he said and his manner of saying it, showed the influence of unshared studies modifying and tempering the practical training of an active career. This, along with his phraseology now and then was suggestive of the grounds whereon rested that imputation of a certain pedantry socially alleged against him by certain naval men of wholly practical cast, captains who nevertheless would frankly concede that His Majesty's navy mustered no more efficient officer of their grade than *Starry Vere*.

What he said was to this effect: "Hitherto I have been but the witness, little more; and I should hardly think now to take another tone, that of your coadjutor, for the time, did I not perceive in you,—at the crisis too—a troubled hesitancy, proceeding, I doubt not from the clash of military duty with moral scruple—scruple vitalized by compassion. For the compassion how can I otherwise than share it. But, mindful of paramount obligations I strive against scruples that may tend to enervate decision. Not, gentlemen, that I hide from myself that the case is an exceptional one. Speculatively regarded, it well might be referred to a jury of casuists. But for us here acting not as casuists or moralists, it is a case practical, and under martial law practically to be dealt with.

"But your scruples: do they move as in a dusk? Challenge them. Make them advance and declare themselves. Come now: do they import something like this: If, mindless of palliating circumstances, we are bound to regard the death of the Master-at-arms as the prisoner's deed, then does that deed constitute a capital crime whereof the penalty is a mortal one. But in natural justice is nothing but the prisoner's overt act to be considered? How can we adjudge to summary and shameful death a fellow-creature innocent before God, and whom we feel to be so?—Does that state it aright? You sign sad assent. Well, I too feel that, the full force of that. It is Nature. But do these buttons that we wear attest that our allegiance is to Nature? No, to the King. Though the ocean, which is inviolate Nature primeval, tho' this be the element where we move and have our being as sailors, yet as the King's officers lies our duty in a sphere correspondingly natural? So little is that true, that in receiving our commissions we in the most important regards ceased to be natural free-agents. When war is declared are we the commissioned fighters previously consulted? We fight at command. If our judgements approve the war, that is but coincidence. So in other particulars. So now. For suppose condemnation to follow these present proceedings. Would it be so much we ourselves that would condemn as it would be martial law operating through us? For that law and the rigour of it, we are not responsible. Our vowed responsibility is in this: That however pitilessly that law may operate, we nevertheless adhere to it and administer it.

["]But the exceptional in the matter moves the hearts within you. Even so too is mine moved. But let not warm hearts betray heads that should be cool. Ashore in a criminal case will an upright judge allow himself off the bench to be waylaid by some tender kinswoman of the accused seeking to touch him with her tearful plea? Well the heart here denotes the feminine in man is as that piteous woman, and hard tho' it be[,] she must here be ruled out."

He paused, earnestly studying them for a moment; then resumed.

"But something in your aspect seems to urge that it is not solely the heart that moves in you, but also the conscience, the private conscience. But tell me whether or not, occupying the position we do, private conscience should not yield to that imperial one formulated in the code under which alone we officially proceed?"

Here the three men moved in their seats, less convinced than agitated by the course of an argument troubling but the more the spontaneous conflict within.

Perceiving which, the speaker paused for a moment; then abruptly changing his tone, went on.

"To steady us a bit, let us recur to the facts.—In war-time at sea a man-of-war's-man strikes his superior in grade, and the blow kills. Apart from its effect the blow itself is, according to the Articles of War, a capital crime. Furthermore—"

"Ay, Sir," emotionally broke in the officer of marines, "in one sense it was. But surely Budd purposed neither mutiny nor homicide."

"Surely not, my good man. And before a court less arbitrary and more merciful than a martial one, that plea would largely extenuate. At the Last Assizes it shall acquit. But how here? We proceed under the law of the Mutiny Act. In feature no child can resemble his father more than that Act resembles in spirit the thing from which it derives—War. In His Majesty['s] service—in this ship indeed—there are Englishmen forced to fight for the King against their will. Against their conscience, for aught we know. Tho' as their fellow-creatures some of us may appreciate their position, yet as navy officers, what reck we of it? Still less recks the enemy. Our impressed men he would fain cut down in the same swath with our volunteers. As regards the enemy's naval conscripts, some of whom may even share our own abhorrence of the regicidal French Directory, it is the same on our side. War looks but to the frontage, the appearance. And the Mutiny Act, War's child, takes after the father. Budd's intent or non-intent is nothing to the purpose.

["]But while, put to it by those anxieties in you which I can not but respect, I only repeat myself—while thus strangely we prolong proceedings that should be summary—the enemy may be sighted and an engagement result. We must do; and one of two things must we do—condemn or let go."

"Can we not convict and yet mitigate the penalty?" asked the junior Lieutenant here speaking, and falteringly, for the first.

"Lieutenant, were that clearly lawful for us under the circumstances consider the consequences of such clemency. The people" (meaning the ship's company) "have native-sense; most of them are familiar with our naval usage and tradition; and how would they take it? Even could you explain to them—which our official position forbids—they, long moulded by arbitrary discipline have not that kind of intelligent responsiveness that might qualify them to comprehend and discriminate. No, to the people the foretopman's deed however it be worded in the announcement will be plain homicide committed in a flagrant act of mutiny. What penalty for that should follow, they know. But it does not follow. *Why?* they will ruminate. You know what sailors are. Will they not revert to the recent outbreak at the Nore? Ay. They know the well-founded alarm—the panic it struck throughout England. Your clement sentence they would account pusillanimous. They would think that we flinch, that we are afraid of them—afraid of practising a lawful rigor singularly demanded at this juncture lest it should provoke new troubles. What shame to us such a conjecture on their part, and how deadly to discipline. You see then, whither prompted by duty and the law I steadfastly drive. But I beseech you, my friends, do not take me amiss. I feel as you do for this unfortunate boy. But did he know our hearts, I take him to be of that generous nature that he would feel even for us on whom in this military necessity so heavy a compulsion is laid."

With that, crossing the deck he resumed his place by the sashed port-hole, tacitly leaving the three to come to a decision. On the cabin's opposite side the troubled court sat silent. Loyal lieges, plain and practical, though at bottom they dissented from some points Captain Vere had put to them, they were without the faculty, hardly had the inclination to gainsay one whom they felt to be an earnest man, one too not less their superior in mind than in naval rank. But it is not improbable that even such of his words as were not without influence over them, less came home to them than his closing appeal to their instinct as sea-officers in the forethought he threw out as to the practical consequences to discipline, considering the unconfirmed tone of the fleet at the time, should a man-of-war's-man['s] violent killing at sea of a superior in grade be allowed to pass for aught else than a capital crime demanding prompt infliction of the penalty.

Not unlikely they were brought to something more or less akin to that harassed frame of mind which in the year 1842 actuated the commander of the U.S. brig-of-war *Somers* to resolve, under the so-called Articles of War, Articles modelled upon the English Mutiny Act, to resolve upon the execution at sea of a midshipman and two petty-officers as mutineers designing the seizure of the brig. Which resolution was carried out though in a time of peace and within not many days sail of home. An act vindicated by a naval court of inquiry subsequently convened ashore. History, and here cited without comment. True, the circumstances on board the *Somers* were different from those on board the *Indomitable*. But the urgency felt, well-warranted or otherwise, was much the same.

Says a writer whom few know, "Forty years after the battle it is easy for a non-combatant to reason about how it ought to have been fought. It is another thing personally and under fire to direct the fighting while involved in the obscuring smoke of it. Much so with respect to other emergencies involving considerations both practical and moral, and when it is imperative promptly to act. The greater the fog the more it imperils the steamer, and speed is put on tho' at the hazard of running somebody down. Little ween the snug card-players in the cabin of the responsibilities of the sleepless man on the bridge."

In brief, Billy Budd was formally convicted and sentenced to be hung at the yard-arm in the early morning-watch, it being now night. Otherwise, as is customary in such cases, the sentence would forthwith have been carried out. In war-time on the field or in the fleet, a mortal punishment decreed by a drum-head court—on the field sometimes decreed by but a nod from the General—follows without delay on the heel of conviction without appeal.

23

It was Captain Vere himself who of his own motion communicated the finding of the court to the prisoner; for that purpose going to the compartment where he was in custody and bidding the marine there to withdraw for the time.

Beyond the communication of the sentence what took place at this interview was never known. But in view of the character of the twain briefly closeted in that state-room, each radically sharing in the rarer qualities of our nature—so rare indeed as to be all but incredible to average minds however much cultivated—some conjectures may be ventured.

It would have been in consonance with the spirit of Captain Vere should he on this occasion have concealed nothing from the condemned one—should he indeed have frankly disclosed to him the part he himself had played in bringing about the decision, at the same time revealing his actuating motives. On Billy's side it is not improbable that such a confession would have been received in much the same spirit that prompted it.

Not without a sort of joy indeed he might have appreciated the brave opinion of him implied in his Captain making such a confidant of him. Nor, as to the sentence itself could he have been insensible that it was imparted to him as to one not afraid to die. Even more may have been. Captain Vere in [the] end may have developed the passion sometimes latent under a[n] exterior stoical or indifferent. He was old enough to have been Billy's father. The austere devotee of military duty letting himself melt back into what remains primeval in our formalized humanity may in [the] end have caught Billy to his heart even as Abraham may have caught young Isaac on the brink of resolutely offering him up in obedience to the exacting behest. But there is no telling the sacrament, seldom if in any case revealed to the gadding world wherever under circumstances at all akin to those here attempted to be set forth two of great Nature's nobler order embrace. There is privacy at the time, inviolable to the survivor, and holy oblivion the sequel to each diviner magnanimity, providentially covers all at last.

The first to encounter Captain Vere in act of leaving the compartment was the senior Lieutenant. The face he beheld, for the moment one expressive of the agony of the strong, was to that officer, tho' a man of fifty, a startling revelation. That the condemned one suffered less than he who mainly had effected the condemnation was apparently indicated by the former's exclamation in the scene soon perforce to be touched upon.

24

Of a series of incidents within a brief term rapidly following each other, the adequate narration may take up a term less brief, especially if explanation or comment here and there seem requisite to the better understanding of such incidents. Between the entrance into the cabin of him who never left it alive, and him who when he did leave it left it as one condemned to die; between this and the closeted interview just given less than an hour and a half had elapsed. It was an interval long enough however to awaken speculations among no few of the ship's company as to what it was that could be detaining in the cabin the master-at-arms and the sailor; for a rumor that both of them had been seen to enter it and neither of them had been seen to emerge, this rumor had got abroad upon the gun-decks and in the tops; the people of a great warship being in one respect like villagers taking microscopic note of every outward movement or non-movement going on. When therefore in weather not at all tempestuous all hands were called in the second dog-watch, a summons under such circumstances not usual in those hours, the crew were not wholly unprepared for some announcement extraordinary, one having connection too with the continued absence of the two men from their wonted haunts.

There was a moderate sea at the time; and the moon, newly risen and near to being at its full, silvered the white spar-deck wherever not blotted by the clear-cut shadows horizontally thrown of fixtures and moving men. On either side the quarter-deck the marine guard under arms was drawn up; and Captain Vere standing in his place surrounded by all the ward-room officers, addressed his men. In so doing his manner showed neither more nor less than that properly pertaining to his supreme position aboard his own ship. In clear terms and concise he told them what had taken place in the cabin; that the master-at-arms was dead; that he who had killed him had been already tried by a summary court and condemned to death; and that the execution would take place in the early morning watch. The word *mutiny* was not named in what he said. He refrained too from making the occasion an opportunity for any preachment as to the maintenance of discipline, thinking perhaps that under existing circumstances in the navy the consequence of violating discipline should be made to speak for itself.

Their captain's announcement was listed to by the throng of standing sailors in a dumbness like that of a seated congregation of believers in hell listening to the clergyman's announcement of his Calvinistic text.

At the close, however, a confused murmur went up. It began to wax. All but instantly, then, at a sign, it was pierced and suppressed by shrill whistles of the Boatswain and his Mates piping down one watch.

To be prepared for burial Claggart's body was delivered to certain petty-officers of his mess. And here, not to clog the sequel with lateral matters, it may be added that at a suitable hour, the Master-at-arms was committed to the sea with every funeral honor properly belonging to his naval grade.

In this proceeding as in every public one growing out of the tragedy strict adherence to usage was observed. Nor in any point could it have been at all deviated from, either with respect to Claggart or Billy Budd[,] without begetting undesirable speculations in the ship's company, sailors, and more particularly men-of-war's men, being of all men the greatest sticklers for usage.

For similar cause, all communication between Captain Vere and the condemned one ended with the closeted interview already given, the latter being now surrendered to the ordinary routine preliminary to the end. This transfer under guard from the Captain's quarters was effected without unusual precautions —at least no visible ones.

If possible not to let the men so much as surmise that their officers anticipate aught amiss from them is the tacit rule in a military ship. And the more that some sort of trouble should really be apprehended the more do the officers keep that apprehension to themselves; tho' not the less unostentatious vigilance may be augmented.

In the present instance the sentry placed over the prisoner had strict orders to let no one have communication with him but the Chaplain. And certain unobtrusive measures were taken absolutely to insure this point.

25

In a seventy-four of the old order the deck known as the upper gun-deck was the one covered over by the spar-deck which last though not without its armament was for the most part exposed to the weather. In general it was at all hours free from hammocks; those of the crew swinging on the lower gun-deck, and berth-deck, the latter being not only a dormitory but also the place for the stowing of the sailors' bags, and on both sides lined with the large chests or movable pantries of the many messes of the men.

On the starboard side of the *Indomitable's* upper gun-deck, behold Billy Budd under sentry lying prone in irons in one of the bays formed by the regular spacing of the guns comprising the batteries on either side. All these pieces were of the heavier calibre of that period. Mounted on lumbering wooden carriages they were hampered with cumbersome harness of breeching and strong side-tackles for running them out. Guns and carriages, together with the long rammers and shorter lintstocks lodged in loops overhead—all these, as customary, were painted black; and the heavy hempen breechings tarred to the same tint, wore the like livery of the undertakers. In contrast with the funereal hue of these surroundings the prone sailor's exterior apparel, white *jumper* and white duck trousers, each more or less soiled, dimly glimmered in the obscure light of the bay like a patch of discolored snow in early April lingering at some upland cave's black mouth. In effect he is already in his shroud or the garments that shall serve him in lieu of one. Over him but scarce illuminating him, two battle-lanterns swing from two massive beams of the deck above. Fed with the oil supplied by the war-contractors (whose gains, honest or otherwise, are in every land an anticipated portion of the harvest of death) with flickering splashes of dirty yellow light they pollute the pale moonshine[,] all but ineffectually struggling in obstructed flecks thro the open ports from which the tompioned cannon protrude. Other lanterns at intervals serve but to bring out somewhat the obscurer bays which like small confessionals or side-chapels in a cathedral branch from the long dim-vistaed broad aisle between the two batteries of that covered tier.

Such was the deck where now lay the Handsome Sailor. Through the rose-tan of his complexion, no pallor could have shown. It would have taken days of sequestration from the winds and the sun to have brought about the effacement of that. But the skeleton in the cheekbone at the point of its angle was just beginning delicately to be defined under the warm-tinted skin. In fervid hearts self-contained some brief experiences devour our human tissue as secret fire in a ship's hold consumes cotton in the bale.

But now lying between the two guns, as nipped in the vice of fate, Billy's agony, mainly proceeding from a generous young heart's virgin experience of the diabolical incarnate and effective in some men—the tension of that agony was over now. It survived not the something healing in the closeted interview with Captain Vere. Without movement, he lay as in a trance. That adolescent expression previously noted as his, taking on something akin to the look of a slumbering child in the cradle when the warm hearth-glow of the still chamber at night plays on the dimples that at whiles mysteriously form in the cheek, silently coming and going there. For now and then in the gyved one's trance a serene happy light born of some wandering reminiscence or dream would diffuse itself over his face, and then wane away only anew to return.

The Chaplain coming to see him and finding him thus, and perceiving no sign that he was conscious of his presence, attentively regarded him for a space, then slipping aside, withdrew for the time, peradventure feeling that even he the minister of Christ tho' receiving his stipend from Mars had no consolation to proffer which could result in a peace transcending that which he beheld. But in the small hours he came again. And the prisoner now awake to his surroundings noticed his approach and civilly, all but cheerfully, welcomed him. But it was to little purpose that in the interview following the good man sought to bring Billy Budd to some godly understanding that he must die, and at dawn. True, Billy himself freely referred to his death as a thing close at hand; but it was something in the way that children will refer to death in general, who yet among their other sports will play a funeral with hearse and mourners.

Not that like children Billy was incapable of conceiving what death really is. No, but he was wholly without irrational fear of it, a fear more prevalent in highly civilized communities than those so-called barbarous ones which in all respects stand nearer to unadulterate Nature. And, as elsewhere said, a barbarian Billy radically was; as much so, for all the costume, as his countrymen the British captives, living trophies, made to march in the Roman triumph of Germanicus. Quite as much so as those later barbarians, young men probably, and picked specimens among the earlier British converts to Christianity, at least nominally such and taken to Rome (as today converts from lesser isles of the sea may be taken to London) of whom the Pope at that time, admiring the strangeness of their personal beauty so unlike the Italian stamp, their clear ruddy complexion and curled flaxen locks, exclaimed, "Angles" (meaning *English* the modern derivative) "Angles do you call them? And is it because they look so like angels?" Had it been later in time one would think that the Pope had in mind Fra Angelico's seraphs some of whom, plucking apples in gardens of the Hesperides have the faint rose-bud complexion of the more beautiful English girls.

If in vain the good Chaplain sought to impress the young barbarian with ideas of death akin to those conveyed in the skull, dial, and crossbones on old tombstones; equally futile to all appearance were his efforts to bring home to him the thought of salvation and a Saviour. Billy listened, but less out of awe or reverence perhaps than from a certain natural politeness; doubtless at bottom regarding all that in much the same way that most mariners of his class take any discourse abstract or out of the common tone of the work-a-day world. And this sailor-way of taking clerical discourse is not wholly unlike the way in which the pioneer of Christianity full of transcendent miracles was received long ago on tropic isles by any superior *savage* so called—a Tahitian say of Captain Cook's time or shortly after that time. Out of natural courtesy he received, but did not appropriate. It was like a gift placed in the palm of an outstretched hand upon which the fingers do not close.

But the *Indomitable's* Chaplain was a discreet man possessing the good sense of a good heart. So he insisted not in his vocation here. At the instance of Captain Vere, a lieutenant had apprised him of pretty much everything as to Billy; and since he felt that innocence was even a better thing than religion wherewith to go to Judgement, he reluctantly withdrew; but in his emotion not without first performing an act strange enough in an Englishman, and under the circumstances yet more so in any regular priest. Stooping over, he kissed on the fair cheek his fellow-man, a felon in martial law, one who though on the confines of death he felt he could never convert to a dogma; nor for all that did he fear for his future.

Marvel not that having been made acquainted with the young sailor's essential innocence (an irruption of heretic thought hard to suppress) the worthy man lifted not a finger to avert the doom of such a martyr to martial discipline. So to do would not only have been as idle as invoking the desert, but would also have been an audacious transgression of the bounds of his function, one as exactly prescribed to him by military law as that of the boatswain or any other naval officer. Bluntly put, a chaplain is the minister of the Prince of Peace serving in the host of the God of War—Mars. As such, he is as incongruous as that musket of Blücher etc. at Christmas. Why then is he there? Because he indirectly subserves the purpose attested by the cannon; because too he lends the sanction of the religion of the meek to that which practically is the abrogation of everything but brute Force.

26

The night so luminous on the spar-deck but otherwise on the cavernous ones below, levels so like the tiered galleries in a coal-mine—the luminous night passed away. But, like the prophet in the chariot disappearing in heaven and dropping his mantle to Elisha, the withdrawing night transferred its pale robe to the breaking day. A meek shy light appeared in the East, where stretched a diaphanous fleece of white furrowed vapor. That light slowly waxed. Suddenly *eight bells* was struck aft, responded to by one louder metallic stroke from forward. It was four o'clock in the morning. Instantly the silver whistles were heard summoning all hands to witness punishment. Up through the great hatchways rimmed with racks of heavy shot, the watch below came pouring overspreading with the watch already on deck the space between the mainmast and foremast including that occupied by the capacious *launch* and the black booms tiered on either side of it, boat and booms making a summit of observation for the powder-boys and younger tars. A different group comprising one watch of topmen leaned over the rail of that sea-balcony, no small one in a seventy-four, looking down on the crowd below. Man or boy none spake but in whisper, and few spake at all. Captain Vere—as before, the central figure among the assembled commissioned officers—stood nigh the break of the poop-deck facing forward. Just below him on the quarter-deck the marines in full equipment were drawn up much as at the scene of the promulgated sentence.

At sea in the old time, the execution by halter of a military sailor was generally from the fore-yard. In the present instance, for special reasons the main-yard was assigned. Under an arm of that lee yard the prisoner was presently brought up, the Chaplain attending him. It was noted at the time and remarked upon afterwards, that in this final scene the good man evinced little or nothing of the perfunctory. Brief speech indeed he had with the condemned one, but the genuine Gospel was less on his tongue than in his aspect and manner towards him. The final preparations personal to the latter being speedily brought to an end by two boatswain's-mates, the consummation impended. Billy stood facing aft. At the penultimate moment, his words, his only ones, words wholly unobstructed in the utterance were these—"God bless Captain Vere!" Syllables so unanticipated coming from one with the ignominious hemp about his neck—a conventional felon's benediction directed aft towards the quarters of honor; syllables too delivered in the clear melody of a singing-bird on the point of launching from the twig, had a phenomenal effect, not unenhanced by the rare personal beauty of the young sailor spiritualized now thro' late experiences so poignantly profound.

Without volition as it were, as if indeed the ship's populace were but the vehicles of some vocal current electric, with one voice from alow and aloft came a resonant sympathetic echo—"God bless Captain Vere!" And yet at that instant Billy alone must have been in their hearts, even as he was in their eyes.

At the pronounced words and the spontaneous echo that voluminously rebounded them, Captain Vere, either thro stoic self-control or a sort of momentary paralysis induced by emotional shock, stood erectly rigid as a musket in the ship-armorer's rack.

The hull deliberately recovering from the periodic roll to leeward was just regaining an even keel, when the last signal[,] a preconcerted dumb one[,] was given. At the same moment it chanced that the vapory fleece hanging low in the East, was shot thro with a soft glory as of the fleece of the Lamb of God seen in mystical vision[,] and simultaneously therewith, watched by the wedged mass of upturned faces, Billy ascended; and, ascending, took the full rose of the dawn.

In the pinioned figure, arrived at the yard-end, to the wonder of all no motion was apparent[,] none save that created by the ship's motion, in moderate weather so majestic in a great ship ponderously cannoned.

27

A DIGRESSION

When some days afterward in reference to the singularity just mentioned, the Purser a rather ruddy rotund person more accurate as an accountant than profound as a philosopher, said at mess to the Surgeon, "What testimony to the force lodged in will-power" the latter—saturnine spare and tall, one in whom a discreet causticity went along with a manner less genial than polite, replied, "Your pardon, Mr. Purser. In a hanging scientifically conducted—and under special orders I myself directed how Budd's was to be effected—any movement following the completed suspension and originating in the body suspended, such movement indicates mechanical spasm in the muscular system. Hence the absence of that is no more attributable to will-power as you call it than to horse-power—begging your pardon."

"But this muscular spasm you speak of, is not that in a degree more or less invariable in these cases?["]

"Assuredly so, Mr. Purser."

"How then, my good sir, do you account for its absence in this instance?"

"Mr. Purser, it is clear that your sense of the singularity in this matter equals not mine. You account for it by what you call will-power a term not yet included in the lexicon of science. For me I do not, with my present knowledge pretend to account for it at all. Even should we assume the hypothesis that at the first touch of the halyards the action of Budd's heart, intensified by extraordinary emotion at its climax, abruptly stopt—much like a watch when in carelessly winding it up you strain at the finish, thus snapping the chain—even under that hypothesis how account for the phenomenon that followed."

"You admit then that the absence of spasmodic movement was phenomenal."

["]It was phenomenal, Mr. Purser, in the sense that it was an appearance the cause of which is not immediately to be assigned."

["]But tell me, my dear Sir,["] pertinaciously continued the other, "was the man's death effected by the halter, or was it a species of euthanasia?["]

"*Euthanasia,* Mr. Purser, is something like your *will-power:* I doubt its authenticity as a scientific term—begging your pardon again. It is at once imaginative and metaphysical,—in short, Greek. But" abruptly changing his tone "there is a case in the sick-bay that I do not care to leave to my assistants. Beg your pardon, but excuse me." And rising from the mess he formally withdrew.

28

The silence at the moment of execution and for a moment or two continuing thereafter, a silence but emphasized by the regular wash of the sea against the hull or the flutter of a sail caused by the helmsman's eyes being tempted astray, this emphasized silence was gradually disturbed by a sound not easily to be verbally rendered. Whoever has heard the freshet-wave of a torrent suddenly swelled by pouring showers in tropical mountains, showers not shared by the plain; whoever has heard the first muffled murmur of its sloping advance through precipitous woods, may form some conception of the sound now heard. The seeming remoteness of its source was because of its murmurous indistinctness since it came from close-by, even from the men massed on the ship's open deck. Being inarticulate, it was dubious in significance further than it seemed to indicate some capricious revulsion of thought or feeling such as mobs ashore are liable to, in the present instance possibly implying a sullen revocation on the men's part of their involuntary echoing of Billy's benediction. But ere the murmur had time to wax into clamor it was met by a strategic command, the more telling that it came with abrupt unexpectedness.

"Pipe down the starboard watch Boatswain, and see that they go."

Shrill as the shriek of the sea-hawk the whistles of the Boatswain and his Mates pierced that ominous low sound, dissipating it; and yielding to the mechanism of discipline the throng was thinned by one half. For the remainder most of them were set to temporary employments connected with trimming the yards and so forth, business readily to be got up to serve occasion by any officer-of-the-deck.

Now each proceeding that follows a mortal sentence pronounced at sea by a drum-head court is characterised by promptitude not perceptibly merging into hurry, tho bordering that. The hammock, the one which had been Billy's bed when alive, having already been ballasted with shot and otherwise prepared to serve for his canvas coffin, the last offices of the sea-undertakers, the Sail-Maker's Mates, were now speedily completed. When everything was in readiness a second call for all hands made necessary by the strategic movement before mentioned was sounded and now to witness burial.

The details of this closing formality it needs not to give. But when the tilted plank let slide its freight into the sea, a second strange human murmur was heard, blended now with another inarticulate sound proceeding from certain larger sea-fowl whose attention having been attracted by the peculiar commotion in the water resulting from the heavy sloped dive of the shotted hammock into the sea, flew screaming to the spot. So near the hull did they come, that the stridor or bony creak of their gaunt double-jointed pinions was audible. As the ship under light airs passed on, leaving the burial-spot astern, they still kept circling it low down with the moving shadow of their outstretched wings and the croaked requiem of their cries.

Upon sailors as superstitious as those of the age preceding ours, men-of-war's men too who had just beheld the prodigy of repose in the form suspended in air and now foundering in the deeps; to such mariners the action of the sea-fowl tho' dictated by mere animal greed for prey, was big with no prosaic significance. An uncertain movement began among them, in which some encroachment was made. It was tolerated but for a moment. For suddenly the drum beat to quarters, which familiar sound happening at least twice every day, had upon the present occasion a signal peremptoriness in it. True martial discipline long continued superinduces in average man a sort of impulse [of] docility whose operation at the official sound of command much resembles in its promptitude the effect of an instinct.

The drum-beat dissolved the multitude, distributing most of them along the batteries of the two covered gun-decks. There, as wont, the guns' crews stood by their respective cannon erect and silent. In due course the First Officer, sword under arm and standing in his place on the quarter-deck[,] formally received the successive reports of the sworded Lieutenants commanding the sections of batteries below; the last of which reports being made[,] the summed report he delivered with the customary salute to the Commander. All this occupied time, which in the present case, was the object of beating to quarters at an hour prior to the customary one. That such variance from usage was authorized by an officer like Captain Vere, a martinet as some deemed him, was evidence of the necessity for unusual action implied in what he deemed to be temporarily the mood of his men. "With mankind" he would say "forms, measured forms are everything; and that is the import couched in the story of Orpheus with his lyre spell-binding the wild denizens of the wood." And this he once applied to the disruption of forms going on across the Channel and the consequences thereof.

At this unwonted muster at quarters, all proceeded as at the regular hour. The band on the quarter-deck played a sacred air. After which the Chaplain went thro' the customary morning service. That done, the drum beat the retreat, and toned by music and religious rites subserving the discipline & purpose of war, the men in their wonted orderly manner, dispersed to the places allotted them when not at the guns.

And now it was full day. The fleece of low-hanging vapor had vanished, licked up by the sun that late had so glorified it. And the circumambient air in the clearness of its serenity was like smooth white marble in the polished block not yet removed from the marble-dealer's yard.

29

The symmetry of form attainable in pure fiction can not so readily be achieved in a narration essentially having less to do with fable than with fact. Truth uncompromisingly told will always have its ragged edges; hence the conclusion of such a narration is apt to be less finished than an architectural finial.

How it fared with the Handsome Sailor during the year of the Great Mutiny has been faithfully given. But tho' properly the story ends with his life, something in way of sequel will not be amiss. Three brief chapters will suffice.

In the general re-christening under the Directory of the craft originally forming the navy of the French monarchy, the *St. Louis* line-of-battle ship was named the *Athéiste.* Such a name, like some other substituted ones in the Revolutionary fleet while proclaiming the infidel audacity of the ruling power was yet, tho' not so intended to be, the aptest name, if one consider it, ever given to a war-ship; far more so indeed than the *Devastation,* the *Erebus* (the *Hell*) and similar names bestowed upon fighting-ships.

On the return-passage to the English fleet from the detached cruise during which occurred the events already recorded, the *Indomitable* fell in with the *Athéiste.* An engagement ensued; during which Captain Vere in the act of putting his ship alongside the enemy with a view of throwing his boarders across her bulwarks, was hit by a musket-ball from a port-hole of the enemy's main cabin. More than disabled he dropped to the deck and was carried below to the same cock-pit where some of his men already lay. The senior Lieutenant took command. Under him the enemy was finally captured and though much crippled was by rare good fortune successfully taken into Gibraltar, an English port not very distant from the scene of the fight. There, Captain Vere with the rest of the wounded was put ashore. He lingered for some days, but the end came. Unhappily he was cut off too early for the Nile and Trafalgar. The spirit that spite its philosophic austerity may yet have indulged in the most secret of all passions, ambition, never attained to the fulness of fame.

Not long before death while lying under the influence of that magical drug which soothing the physical frame mysteriously operates on the subtler element in man, he was heard to murmur words inexplicable to his attendant—"Billy Budd, Billy Budd." That these were not the accents of remorse, would seem clear from what the attendant said to the *Indomitable's* senior officer of marines who[,] as the most reluctant to condemn of the members of the drum-head court, too well knew[,] tho' here he kept the knowledge to himself, who Billy Budd was.

30

Some few weeks after the execution, among other matters under the head of *News from the Mediterranean,* there appeared in a naval chronicle of the time, an authorized weekly publication, an account of the affair. It was doubtless for the most part written in good faith, tho the medium, partly rumor, through which the facts must have reached the writer, served to deflect and in part falsify them. The account was as follows:—

"On the tenth of the last month a deplorable occurrence took place on board H.M.S. *Indomitable.* John Claggart, the ship's master-at-arms, discovering that some sort of plot was incipient among an inferior section of the ship's company, and that the ring-leader was one William Budd; he, Claggart in the act of arraigning the man before the Captain was vindictively stabbed to the heart by the suddenly drawn sheath-knife of Budd.

["]The deed and the implement employed, sufficiently suggest that tho' mustered into the service under an English name the assassin was no Englishman, but one of those aliens adopting English cognomens whom the present extraordinary necessities of the Service have caused to be admitted into it in considerable numbers.

["]The enormity of the crime and the extreme depravity of the criminal, appear the greater in view of the character of the victim, a middle-aged man respectable and discreet, belonging to that minor official grade, the petty-officers, upon whom, as none know better than the commissioned gentlemen, the efficiency of His Majesty's navy so largely depends. His function was a responsible one; at once onerous & thankless and his fidelity in it the greater because of his strong patriotic impulse. In this instance as in so many other instances in these days, the character of this unfortunate man signally refutes, if refutation were needed, that peevish saying attributed to the late Dr. Johnson, that patriotism is the last refuge of a scoundrel.

["]The criminal paid the penalty of his crime. The promptitude of the punishment has proved salutary. Nothing amiss is now apprehended aboard H.M.S. *Indomitable.*"

The above, appearing in a publication now long ago superannuated and forgotten[,] is all that hitherto has stood in human record to attest what manner of men respectively were John Claggart and Billy Budd[.]

31

Everything is for a term remarkable in navies. Any tangible object associated with some striking incident of the service is converted into a monument. The spar from which the Foretopman was suspended, was for some few years kept trace of by the bluejackets. Their knowledge followed it from ship to dock-yard and again from dock-yard to ship, still pursuing it even when at last reduced to a mere dock-yard boom. To them a chip of it was as a piece of the Cross. Ignorant tho' they were of the secret facts of the tragedy, and not thinking but that the penalty was somehow unavoidably inflicted from the naval point of view, for all that they instinctively felt that Billy was a sort of man as incapable of mutiny as of wilful murder. They recalled the fresh young image of the Handsome Sailor, that face never deformed by a sneer or subtler vile freak of the heart within. Their impression of him was doubtless deepened by the fact that he was gone, and in a measure mysteriously gone. At the time on the gun decks of the *Indomitable* the general estimate of his nature and its unconscious simplicity eventually found rude utterance from another foretopman[,] one of his own watch[,] gifted, as some sailors are, with an artless poetic temperament; the tarry hands made some lines which after circulating among the shipboard crew for a while, finally got rudely printed at Portsmouth as a ballad. The title given to it was the sailor's.

BILLY IN THE DARBIES

Good of the Chaplain to enter Lone Bay
And down on his marrow-bones here and pray
For the likes just o' me, Billy Budd.—But look:
Through the port comes the moon-shine astray!

It tips the guard's cutlas and silvers this nook;
But 'twill die in the dawning of Billy's last day.
A jewel-block they'll make of me tomorrow,
Pendant pearl from the yard-arm-end
Like the ear-drop I gave to Bristol Molly—
O, 'tis me, not the sentence they'll suspend.
Ay, Ay, all is up; and I must up too
Early in the morning, aloft from alow.
On an empty stomach, now, never it would do.
They'll give me a nibble—bit o' biscuit ere I go.
Sure, a messmate will reach me the last parting cup;
But, turning heads away from the hoist and the belay,
Heaven knows who will have the running of me up!
No pipe to those halyards.—But aren't it all sham?
A blur's in my eyes; it is dreaming that I am.
A hatchet to my hawser? all adrift to go?
The drum roll to grog, and Billy never know?
But Donald he has promised to stand by the plank;
So I'll shake a friendly hand ere I sink.
But—no! It is dead then I'll be, come to think.—
I remember Taff the Welshman when he sank.
And his cheek it was like the budding pink[.]
But me they'll lash me in hammock, drop me deep.
Fathoms down, fathoms down, how I'll dream fast asleep.
I feel it stealing now. Sentry, are you there?
Just ease this darbies at the wrist, and roll me over fair,
I am sleepy, and the oozy weeds about me twist.

END OF BOOK

Mark Twain

✻ 1835-1910

The boyhood of Mark Twain (the pen name of Samuel L. Clemens) was spent in Hannibal, Missouri, on the west bank of the Mississippi. He wrote later of this life: "I can call it back and make it as real as it ever was, and as blessed. I can call back the prairie and its loneliness and peace, and a vast hawk hanging motionless in the sky." After his father's death in 1847 he worked as printer's devil, as a steamboat pilot on the Mississippi, as a soldier, a miner, a journalist, and finally as an author. "The Celebrated Jumping Frog of Calaveras County," Mark Twain's version of a story he heard in a mining camp, won him wide acclaim as a humorist. Thereafter he brought out many books. His most well-known work, of course, is The Adventures of Huckleberry Finn, *which celebrates his early life on the Mississippi.* The Man That Corrupted Hadleyburg *appeared in 1900. Ludwig Lewisohn has said of Twain's humor that it "is directed against pretentiousness and falseness, against all 'putting on' of airs; its fairly constant intention is the discomfiture of the pretentious and false. . . . His sketches and stories are all written about a practical joke of some kind. But he is careful, unlike his predecessors, to be sure that the objects of the practical joke have justly lost the reader's moral sympathy.* The Man That Corrupted Hadleyburg *is an excellent illustration of the method."*

The Man That Corrupted Hadleyburg

1

It was many years ago. Hadleyburg was the most honest and upright town in all the region round about. It had kept that reputation unsmirched during three generations, and was prouder of it than of any other of its possessions. It was so proud of it, and so anxious to insure its perpetuation, that it began to teach the principles of honest dealing to its babies in the cradle, and made the like teachings the staple of their culture thenceforward through all the years devoted to their education. Also, throughout the formative years temptations were kept out of the way of the young people, so that their honesty could have every chance to harden and solidify, and become a part of their very bone. The neighboring towns were jealous of this honorable supremacy, and affected to sneer at Hadleyburg's pride in it and call it vanity; but all the same they were obliged to acknowledge that Hadleyburg was in reality an incorruptible town; and if pressed they would also acknowledge that the mere fact that a young man hailed from Hadleyburg was all the recommendation he needed when he went forth from his natal town to seek for responsible employment.

But at last, in the drift of time, Hadleyburg had the ill luck to offend a passing stranger—possibly without knowing it, certainly without caring, for Hadleyburg was sufficient unto itself, and cared not a rap for strangers or their opinions. Still, it would have been well to make an exception in this one's case, for he was a bitter man and revengeful. All through his wanderings during a whole year he kept his injury in mind, and gave all his leisure moments to trying to invent a compensating satisfaction for it. He contrived many plans, and all of them were good, but none of them was quite sweeping enough; the poorest of them would hurt a great many individuals, but what he wanted was a plan which would comprehend the entire town, and not let so much as one person escape unhurt. At last he had a fortunate idea, and when it fell into his brain it lit up his whole head with an evil joy. He began to form a plan at once, saying to himself, "That is the thing to do—I will corrupt the town."

Six months later he went to Hadleyburg, and arrived in a buggy at the house of the old cashier of the bank about ten at night. He got a sack out of the buggy, shouldered it, and staggered with it through the cottage yard, and knocked at the door. A woman's voice said "Come in," and he entered, and set his sack behind the stove in the parlor, saying politely to the old lady who sat reading the *Missionary Herald* by the lamp:

"Pray keep your seat, madam, I will not disturb you. There—now it is pretty well concealed; one would hardly know it was there. Can I see your husband a moment, madam?"

No, he was gone to Brixton, and might not return before morning.

"Very well, madam, it is no matter. I merely wanted to leave that sack in his care, to be delivered to the rightful owner when he shall be found. I am a stranger; he does not know me; I am merely passing through the town tonight to discharge a matter which has been long in my mind. My errand is now completed, and I go pleased and a little proud, and you will never see me again. There is a paper attached to the sack which will explain everything. Good-night, madam."

The old lady was afraid of the mysterious big stranger, and was glad to see him go. But her curiosity was roused, and she went straight to the sack and brought away the paper. It began as follows:

TO BE PUBLISHED; or, the right man sought out by private inquiry—either will answer. This sack contains gold coin weighing a hundred and sixty pounds four ounces—

"Mercy on us, and the door not locked!"

Mrs. Richards flew to it all in a tremble and locked it, then pulled down the window-shades and stood frightened, worried, and wondering if there was anything else she could do toward making herself and the money more safe. She listened awhile for burglars, then surrendered to curiosity and went back to the lamp and finished reading the paper:

I am a foreigner, and am presently going back to my own country, to remain there permanently. I am grateful to America for what I have received at her hands during my stay under her flag; and to one of her citizens—a citizen of Hadleyburg—I am especially grateful for a great kindness done me a year or two ago. Two great kindnesses; in fact. I will explain. I was a gambler. I say I WAS. I was a ruined gambler. I arrived in this village at night, hungry and without a penny. I asked for help—in the dark; I was ashamed to beg in the light. I begged of the right man. He gave me twenty dollars—that is to say, he gave me life, as I considered it. He also gave me fortune; for out of that money I have made myself rich at the gaming-table. And finally, a remark which he made to me has remained with me to this day, and has at last conquered me; and in conquering has saved the remnant of my morals; I shall gamble no more. Now I have no idea who that man was, but I want him found, and I want him to have this money, to give away, throw away or keep, as he pleases. It is merely my way of testifying my gratitude to him. If I could stay, I would find him myself; but no matter, he will be found. This is an honest town, an incorruptible town, and I know I can trust it without fear. This man can be identified by the remark which he made to me; I feel persuaded that he will remember it.

And now my plan is this: If you prefer to conduct the inquiry privately, do so. Tell the contents of this present writing to any one who is likely to be the right man. If he shall answer, "I am the man; the remark I made was so-and-so," apply the test—to wit: open the sack, and in it you will find a sealed envelope containing that remark. If the remark mentioned by the candidate tallies with it, give him the money, and ask no further questions, for he is certainly the right man.

But if you shall prefer a public inquiry, then publish this present writing in the local paper—with these instructions added, to wit: Thirty days from now, let the candidate appear at the town-hall at eight in the evening (Friday), and hand his remark, in a sealed envelope, to the Rev. Mr. Burgess (if he will be kind enough to act); and let Mr. Burgess there and then destroy the seals on the sack, open it, and see if the remark is correct; if correct, let the money be delivered, with my sincere gratitude, to my benefactor thus identified.

Mrs. Richards sat down, gently, quivering with excitement, and was soon lost in thinking—after this pattern: "What a strange thing it is! . . . And what a fortune for that kind man who set his bread afloat upon the waters! . . . If he had only been my husband that did it!—for we are so poor, so old and poor! . . ." Then, with a sigh—"But it was not my Edward; no, it was not he that gave the stranger twenty dollars. It is a pity too; I see it now. . . ." Then, with a shudder—"But it is *gambler's* money! the wages of sin: we couldn't take it; we couldn't touch it. I don't like to be near it; it seems a defilement." She moved to a farther chair. . . ." I wish Edward would come, and take it to the bank; a burglar might come at any moment; it is dreadful to be here all alone with it."

At eleven Mr. Richards arrived, and while his wife was saying, "I am *so* glad you've come!" he was saying, "I'm so tired—tired clear out; it is dreadful to be poor, and have to make these dismal journeys at my time of life. Always at the grind, grind, grind, on a salary—another man's slave, and he sitting at home in his slippers, rich and comfortable."

"I am so sorry for you, Edward, you know that; but be comforted; we have our livelihood; we have our good name—"

"Yes, Mary, and that is everything. Don't mind my talk—it's just a moment's irritation and doesn't mean anything. Kiss me—there, it's all gone now, and I am not complaining any more. What have you been getting? What's in the sack?"

Then his wife told him the great secret. It dazed him for a moment; then he said:

"It weighs a hundred and sixty pounds? Why, Mary, it's for-ty thou-sand dollars—think of it—a whole fortune! Not ten men in this village are worth that much. Give me the paper."

He skimmed through it and said:

"Isn't it an adventure! Why, it's a romance; it's like the impossible things one reads about in books, and never sees in life." He was well stirred up now; cheerful, even gleeful. He tapped his old wife on the cheek, and said, humorously, "Why, we're rich, Mary, rich; all we've got to do is to bury the money and burn the papers. If the gambler ever comes to inquire, we'll merely look coldly upon him and say: 'What is this nonsense you are talking? We have never heard of you and your sack of gold before;' and then he would look foolish, and—"

"And in the mean time, while you are running on with your jokes, the money is still here, and it is fast getting along toward burglar-time."

"True. Very well, what shall we do—make the inquiry private? No, not that: it would spoil the romance. The public method is better. Think what a noise it will make! And it will make all the other towns jealous; for no stranger would trust such a thing to any town but Hadleyburg, and they know it. It's a great card for us. I must get to the printing-office now, or I shall be too late."

"But stop—stop—don't leave me here alone with it, Edward!"

But he was gone. For only a little while, however. Not far from his own house he met the editor-proprietor of the paper, and gave him the document, and said, "Here is a good thing for you, Cox—put it in."

"It may be too late, Mr. Richards, but I'll see."

At home again he and his wife sat down to talk the charming mystery over; they were in no condition for sleep. The first question was, Who could the citizen have been who gave the stranger the twenty dollars? It seemed a simple one; both answered it in the same breath—

"Barclay Goodson."

"Yes," said Richards, "he could have done it, and it would have been like him, but there's not another in the town."

"Everybody will grant that, Edward—grant it privately, anyway. For six months, now, the village has been its own proper self once more—honest, narrow, self-righteous, and stingy."

"It is what he always called it, to the day of his death—said it right out publicly, too."

"Yes, and he was hated for it."

"Oh, of course; but he didn't care. I reckon he was the best-hated man among us, except the Reverend Burgess."

"Well, Burgess deserves it—he will never get another congregation here. Mean as the town is, it knows how to estimate *him*. Edward, doesn't it seem odd that the stranger should appoint Burgess to deliver the money?"

"Well, yes—it does. That is—that is—"

"Why so much that-*is*-ing? Would *you* select him?"

"Mary, maybe the stranger knows him better than this village does."

"Much *that* would help Burgess!"

The husband seemed perplexed for an answer; the wife kept a steady eye upon him, and waited. Finally Richards said, with the hesitancy of one who is making a statement which is likely to encounter doubt:

"Mary, Burgess is not a bad man."

His wife was certainly surprised.

"Nonsense!" she exclaimed.

"He is not a bad man. I know. The whole of his unpopularity had its foundation in that one thing—the thing that made so much noise."

"That 'one thing,' indeed! As if that 'one thing' wasn't enough, all by itself."

"Plenty. Plenty. Only he wasn't guilty of it."

"How you talk! Not guilty of it! Everybody knows he *was* guilty."

"Mary, I give you my word—he was innocent."

"I can't believe it, and I don't. How do you know?"

"It is a confession. I am ashamed, but I will make it. I was the only man who knew he was innocent. I could have saved him, and—and—well, you know how the town was wrought up—I hadn't the pluck to do it. It would have turned everybody against me. I felt mean, ever so mean; but I didn't dare; I hadn't the manliness to face that."

Mary looked troubled, and for a while was silent. Then she said, stammeringly:

"I—I don't think it would have done for you to—to—One must'nt—er—public opinion—one has to be so careful—so—" It was a difficult road, and she got mired; but after a little she got started again. "It was a great pity, but—Why, we couldn't afford it, Edward—we couldn't indeed. Oh, I wouldn't have had you do it for anything!"

"It would have lost us the good-will of so many people, Mary; and then—and then—"

"What troubles me now is, what *he* thinks of us, Edward."

"He? *He* doesn't suspect that I could have saved him."

"Oh," exclaimed the wife, in a tone of relief, "I'm glad of that. As long as he doesn't know that you could have saved him, he—he—well, that makes it a great deal better. Why, I might have known he didn't know, because he is always trying to be friendly with us, as little encouragement as we give him. More than once people have twitted me with it. There's the Wilsons, and the Wilcoxes, and the Harknesses, they take a mean pleasure in saying, '*Your friend* Burgess,' because they know it pesters me. I wish he wouldn't persist in liking us so; I can't think why he keeps it up."

"I can explain it. It's another confession. When the thing was new and hot, and the town made a plan to ride him on a rail, my conscience hurt me so that I couldn't stand it, and I went privately and gave him notice, and he got out of the town and staid out till it was safe to come back."

"Edward! If the town had found it out—"

"*Don't!* It scares me yet, to think of it. I repented of it the minute it was done; and I was even afraid to tell you, lest your face might betray it to somebody. I didn't sleep any that night, for worrying. But after a few days I saw that no one was going to suspect me, and after that I got to feeling glad I did it. And I feel glad yet, Mary—glad through and through."

"So do I, now, for it would have been a dreadful way to treat him. Yes, I'm glad; for really you did owe him that, you know. But, Edward, suppose it should come out yet, some day!"

"It won't."

"Why!"

"Because everybody thinks it was Goodson."

"Of course they would!"

"Certainly. And of course *he* didn't care. They persuaded poor old Sawlsberry to go and charge it on him, and he went blustering over there and did it. Goodson looked him over, like as if he was hunting for a place on him that he could despise the most, then he says, 'So you are the Committee of Inquiry, are you?' Sawlsberry said that was about what he was. 'Hm. Do they require particulars, or do you reckon a kind of a *general* answer will do?' 'If they require particulars, I will come back, Mr. Goodson; I will take the general answer first.' 'Very well, then, tell them to go to hell—I reckon that's general enough. And I'll give you some advice, Sawlsberry; when you come back for the particulars, fetch a basket to carry the relics of yourself home in.'"

"Just like Goodson; it's got all the marks. He had only vanity; he thought he could give advice better than any other person."

"It settled the business, and saved us, Mary. The subject was dropped."

"Bless you, I'm not doubting *that*."

Then they took up the gold-sack mystery again, with strong interest. Soon the conversation began to suffer breaks—interruptions caused by absorbed thinkings. The breaks grew more and more frequent. At last Richards lost himself wholly in thought. He sat long, gazing vacantly at the floor, and by-and-by he began to punctuate his thoughts with little nervous movements of his hands that seemed to indicate vexation. Meantime his wife too had relapsed into a thoughtful silence, and her movements were beginning to show a troubled discomfort. Finally Richards got up and strode aimlessly about the room, ploughing his hands through his hair, much as a somnambulist might do who was having a bad dream. Then he seemed to arrive at a definite purpose; and without a word he put on his hat and passed quickly out of the house. His wife sat brooding, with a drawn face, and did not seem to be aware that she was alone. Now and then she murmured, "Lead us not into t . . . but—but—we are so poor, so poor! . . . Lead us not into . . . Ah, who would be hurt by it?—and no one would ever know. . . . Lead us . . ." The voice died out in mumblings. After a little she glanced up and muttered in a half frightened, half-glad way—

"He is gone! But, oh dear, he may be too late—too late. . . . Maybe not—maybe there is still time." She rose and stood thinking, nervously clasping and unclasping her hands. A slight shudder shook her frame, and she said, out of a dry throat, "God forgive me—it's awful to think such things—but . . . Lord, how we are made—how strangely we are made!"

She turned the light low, and slipped stealthily over and kneeled down by the sack and felt of its ridgy sides with her hands, and fondled them lovingly; and there was a gloating light in her poor old eyes. She fell into fits of absence; and came half out of them at times to mutter, "If we had only waited!—oh, if we had only waited a little, and not been in such a hurry!"

Meantime Cox had gone home from his office and told his wife all about the strange thing that had happened, and they had talked it over eagerly, and guessed that the late Goodson was the only man in the town who could have helped a suffering stranger with so noble a sum as twenty dollars. Then there was a pause, and the two became thoughtful and silent. And by-and-by nervous and fidgety. At last the wife said, as if to herself:

"Nobody knows this secret but the Richardses . . . and us . . . nobody."

The husband came out of his thinkings with a slight start, and gazed wistfully at his wife, whose face was become very pale; then he hesitatingly rose, and glanced furtively at his hat, then at his wife—a sort of mute inquiry. Mrs. Cox swallowed once or twice, with her hand at her throat, then in place of speech she nodded her head. In a moment she was alone, and mumbling to herself.

And now Richards and Cox were hurrying through the deserted streets, from opposite directions. They met, panting, at the foot of the printing-office stairs; by the night-light there they read each other's face. Cox whispered:

"Nobody knows about this but us?"

The whispered answer was,

"Not a soul—on honor, not a soul!"

"If it isn't too late to—"

The men were starting up-stairs; at this moment they were overtaken by a boy, and Cox asked:

"Is that you, Johnny?"

"Yes, sir."

"You needn't ship the early mail—nor *any* mail; wait till I tell you."

"It's already gone, sir."

"Gone?" It had the sound of an unspeakable disappointment in it.

"Yes, sir. Time-table for Brixton and all the towns beyond changed to-day, sir—had to get the papers in twenty minutes earlier than common. I had to rush; if I had been two minutes later—"

The men turned and walked slowly away, not waiting to hear the rest. Neither of them spoke during ten minutes; then Cox said, in a vexed tone:

"What possessed you to be in such a hurry, *I* can't make out."

The answer was humble enough:

"I see it now, but somehow I never thought, you know, until it was too late. But the next time—"

"Next time be hanged! It won't come in a thousand years."

Then the friends separated without a good-night, and dragged themselves home with the gait of mortally stricken men. At their homes their wives sprang up with an eager "Well?"—then saw the answer with their eyes and sank down sorrowing, without waiting for it to come in words. In both houses a discussion followed of a heated sort—a new thing; there had been discussions before, but not heated ones, not ungentle ones. The discussions to-night were a sort of seeming plagarisms of each other. Mrs. Richards said,

"If you had only waited, Edward—if you had only stopped to think; but no, you must run straight to the printing-office and spread it all over the world."

"It *said* publish it."

"That is nothing; it also said do it privately, if you liked. There, now—is that true, or not?"

"Why, yes—yes, it is true; but when I thought what a stir it would make, and what a compliment it was to Hadleyburg that a stranger should trust it so—"

"Oh, certainly, I know all that; but if you had only stopped to think, you would have seen that you *couldn't* find the right man, because he is in his grave, and hasn't left chick nor child nor relation behind him; and as long as the money went to somebody that awfully needed it, and nobody would be hurt by it, and—and—"

She broke down, crying. Her husband tried to think of some comforting thing to say, and presently came out with this:

"But after all, Mary, it must be for the best—it *must* be; we know that. And we must remember that it was so ordered—"

"Ordered! Oh, everything's *ordered*, when a person has to find some way out when he has been stupid. Just the same, it was *ordered* that the money should come to us in this special way, and it was you that must take it on yourself to go meddling with the designs of Providence—and who gave you the right? It was wicked, that is what it was—just blasphemous presumption, and no more becoming to a meek and humble professor of—"

"But, Mary, you know how we have been trained all our lives long, like the whole village, till it is absolutely second nature to us to stop not a single moment to think when there's an honest thing to be done—"

"Oh, I know it, I know it—it's been one everlasting training and training and training in honesty—honesty shielded, from the very cradle, against every possible temptation, and so it's *artificial* honesty, and weak as water when temptation comes, as we have seen this night. God knows I never had shade nor shadow of a doubt of my petrified and indestructible honesty until now—and now, under the very first big and real temptation, I —Edward, it is my belief that this town's honesty is as rotten as mine; as rotten as yours is. It is a mean town, a hard, stingy town, and hasn't a virtue in the world but this honesty it is so celebrated for and so conceited about; and so help me, I do believe that if ever the day comes that its honesty falls under great temptation, its grand reputation will go to ruin like a house of cards. There, now, I've made confession, and I feel better; I am a humbug, and I've been one all my life, without knowing it. Let no man call me honest again—I will not have it."

"I—Well, Mary, I feel a good deal as you do; I certainly do. It seems strange, too, so strange. I never could have believed it—never."

A long silence followed; both were sunk in thought. At last the wife looked up and said:

"I know what you are thinking, Edward."

Richards had the embarrassed look of a person who is caught.

"I am ashamed to confess it, Mary, but—"

"It's no matter, Edward, I was thinking the same question myself."

"I hope so. State it."

"You were thinking, if a body could only guess out *what the remark was* that Goodson made to the stranger."

"It's perfectly true. I feel guilty and ashamed. And you?"

"I'm past it. Let us make a pallet here; we've got to stand watch till the bank vault opens in the morning and admits the sack. . . . Oh, dear, oh, dear—if we hadn't made the mistake!"

The pallet was made, and Mary said: "The open sesame—what could it have been? I do wonder what that remark could have been? But come; we will get to bed now."

"And sleep?"

"No; think."

"Yes, think."

By this time the Coxes too had completed their spat and their reconciliation, and were turning in—to think, to think, and toss, and fret, and worry over what the remark could possibly have been which Goodson made to the stranded derelict: that golden remark; that remark worth forty thousand dollars, cash.

The reason that the village telegraph-office was open later than usual that night was this: The foreman of Cox's paper was the local representative of the Associated Press. One might say its honorary representative, for it wasn't four times a year that he could furnish thirty words that would be accepted. But this time it was different. His despatch stating what he had caught got an instant answer:

Send the whole thing—all the details—twelve hundred words.

A colossal order! The foreman filled the bill; and he was the proudest man in the State. By breakfast-time the next morning the name of Hadleyburg the Incorruptible was on every lip in America, from Montreal to the Gulf, from the glaciers of Alaska to the orange-groves of Florida; and millions and millions of people were discussing the stranger and his money-sack, and wondering if the right man would be found, and hoping some more news about the matter would come soon—right away.

2

Hadleyburg village woke up world-celebrated—astonished—happy—vain. Vain beyond imagination. Its nineteen principal citizens and their wives went about shaking hands with each other, and beaming, and smiling, and congratulating, and saying *this* thing adds a new word to the dictionary—*Hadleyburg*, synonym for *incorruptible*—destined to live in dictionaries forever! And the minor and unimportant citizens and their wives went around acting in much the same way. Everybody ran to the bank to see the gold-sack; and before noon grieved and envious crowds began to flock in from Brixton and all the neighboring towns; and that afternoon and next day reporters began to arrive from everywhere to verify the sack and its history and write the whole thing up anew, and make dashing freehand pictures of the sack and of Richards's house, and the bank, and the Presbyterian church, and the Baptist church, and the public square, and the town-hall where the test would be applied and the money delivered; and damnable portraits of the Richardses, and Pinkerton the Banker, and Cox, and the foreman, and Reverend Burgess, and the postmaster—and even of Jack Halliday, who was the loafing, good-natured, no-account, irreverent fisherman, hunter, boys' friend, stray-dog's friend, typical "Sam Lawson" of the town. The little mean, smirking, oily Pinkerton showed the sack to all comers, and rubbed his sleek palms together pleasantly, and enlarged upon the town's fine old reputation for honesty and upon this wonderful endorsement of it, and hoped and believed that the example would now spread far and wide over the American world, and be epoch-making in the matter of moral regeneration. And so on, and so on.

By the end of a week things had quieted down again; the wild intoxication of pride and joy had sobered to a soft, sweet, silent delight—a sort of deep, nameless, unutterable content. All faces bore a look of peaceful, holy happiness.

Then a change came. It was a gradual change: so gradual that its beginnings were hardly noticed; maybe were not noticed at all, except by Jack Halliday, who always noticed everything; and always made fun of it, too, no matter what it was. He began to throw out chaffing remarks about people not looking quite so happy as they did a day or two ago; and next he claimed that the new aspect was deepening to positive sadness; next, that it was taking on a sick look; and finally he said that everybody was become so moody, thoughtful, and absent-minded that he could rob the meanest man in town of a cent out of the bottom of his breeches pocket and not disturb his revery.

At this stage—or at about this stage—a saying like this was dropped at bedtime—with a sigh, usually—by the head of each of the nineteen principal households: "Ah, what *could* have been the remark that Goodson made!"

And straightway—with a shudder—came this, from the man's wife:

"Oh, *don't!* What horrible thing are you mulling in your mind? Put it away from you, for God's sake!"

But that question was wrung from those men again the next night—and got the same retort. But weaker.

And the third night the men uttered the question yet again—with anguish, and absently. This time—and the following night—the wives fidgeted feebly, and tried to say something. But didn't.

And the night after that they found their tongues and responded—longingly, "Oh, if we *could* only guess!"

Halliday's comments grew daily more and more sparklingly disagreeable and disparaging. He went diligently about, laughing at the town, individually and in mass. But his laugh was the only one left in the village: it fell upon a hollow and mournful vacancy and emptiness. Not even a smile was findable anywhere. Halliday carried a cigar-box around on a tripod, playing that it was a camera, and halted all passers and aimed the thing and said, "Ready!—now look pleasant, please," but not even this capital joke could surprise the dreary faces into any softening.

So three weeks passed—one week was left. It was Saturday evening—after supper. Instead of the aforetime Saturday-evening flutter and bustle and shopping and larking, the streets were empty and desolate. Richards and his old wife sat apart in their little parlor—miserable and thinking. This was become their evening habit now: the life-long habit which had preceded it, of reading, knitting, and contented chat, or receiving or paying neighborly calls, was dead and gone and forgotten, ages ago—two or three weeks ago; nobody talked now, nobody read, nobody visited—the whole village sat at home, sighing, worrying, silent. Trying to guess out that remark.

The postman left a letter. Richards glanced listlessly at the superscription and the post-mark—unfamiliar, both—and tossed the letter on the table and resumed his might-have-beens and his hopeless dull miseries where he had left them off. Two or three hours later his wife got wearily up and was going away to bed without a good-night—custom now—but she stopped near the letter and eyed it awhile with a dead interest, then broke it open, and began to skim it over. Richards, sitting there with his chair tilted back against the wall and his chin between his knees, heard something fall. It was his wife. He sprang to her side, but she cried out:

"Leave me alone, I am too happy. Read the letter—read it!"

He did. He devoured it, his brain reeling. The letter was from a distant State, and it said:

I am a stranger to you, but no matter: I have something to tell. I have just arrived home from Mexico, and learned about that episode. Of course you do not know who made that remark, but I know, and I am the only person living who does know. It was GOODSON. I knew him well, many years ago. I passed through your village that very night, and was his guest till the midnight train came along. I overheard him make that remark to the stranger in the dark—it was in Hale Alley. He and I talked of it the rest of the way home, and while smoking in his house. He mentioned many of your villagers in the course of his talk—most of them in a very uncomplimentary way, but two or three favorably: among these latter yourself. I say "favorably"—nothing stronger. I remember his saying he did not actually LIKE any person in the town—not one; but that you—I THINK he said you—am almost sure, had done him a very great service once, possibly without knowing the full value of it, and he wished he had a fortune, he would leave it to you when he died, and a curse apiece for the rest of the citizens. Now, then, if it was you that did him that service, you are his legitimate heir, and entitled to the sack of gold. I know that I can trust to your honor and honesty, for in a citizen of Hadleyburg these virtues are an unfailing inheritance, and so I am going to reveal to you the remark, well satisfied that if you are not the right man you will seek and find the right one and see that poor Goodson's debt of gratitude for the service referred to is paid. This is the remark: "YOU ARE FAR FROM BEING A BAD MAN: GO, AND REFORM."

HOWARD L. STEPHENSON

"Oh, Edward, the money is ours, and I am so grateful, *oh*, so grateful—kiss me, dear, it's forever since we kissed—and we needed it so—the money—and now you are free of Pinkerton and his bank, and nobody's slave any more; it seems to me I could fly for joy."

It was a happy half-hour that the couple spent there on the settee caressing each other; it was the old days come again—days that had begun with their courtship and lasted without a break till the stranger brought the deadly money. By-and-by the wife said:

"Oh, Edward, how lucky it was you did him that grand service, poor Goodson! I never liked him, but I love him now. And it was fine and beautiful of you never to mention it or brag about it." Then, with a touch of reproach, "But you ought to have told *me*, Edward, you ought to have told your wife, you know."

"Well, I—er—well, Mary, you see——"

"Now stop hemming and hawing, and tell me about it, Edward. I always loved you, and now I'm proud of you. Everybody believes there was only one good generous soul in this village, and now it turns out that you—Edward, why don't you tell me?"

"Well—er—er— Why, Mary, I can't!"

"You *can't*? *Why* can't you?"

"You see, he—well, he—he made me promise I wouldn't."

The wife looked him over, and said, very slowly,

"Made—you—promise? Edward, what do you tell me that for?"

"Mary, do you think I would lie?"

She was troubled and silent for a moment, then she laid her hand within his and said:

"No . . . no. We have wandered far enough from our bearings—God spare us that! In all your life you have never uttered a lie. But now—now that the foundations of things seem to be crumbling from under us, we—we—" She lost her voice for a moment, then said, brokenly, "Lead us not into temptation. . . . I think you made the promise, Edward. Let it rest so. Let us keep away from that ground. Now—that is all gone by; let us be happy again; it is no time for clouds."

Edward found it something of an effort to comply, for his mind kept wandering—trying to remember what the service was that he had done Goodson.

The couple lay awake the most of the night, Mary happy and busy, Edward busy, but not so happy. Mary was planning what she would do with the money. Edward was trying to recall that service. At first his conscience was sore on account of the lie he had told Mary—if it was a lie. After much reflection—suppose it *was* a lie? What then? Was it such a great matter? Aren't we always *acting* lies? Then why not *tell* them? Look at Mary—look what she had done. While he was hurrying off on his honest errand, what was she doing? Lamenting because the papers hadn't been destroyed and the money kept! Is theft better than lying?

That point lost its sting—the lie dropped into the background and left comfort behind it. The next point came to the front: *had* he rendered that service? Well, here was Goodson's own evidence as reported in Stephenson's letter; there could be no better evidence than that—it was even *proof* that he had rendered it. Of course. So that point was settled. . . . No, not quite. He recalled with a wince that this unknown Mr. Stephenson was just a trifle unsure as to whether the performer of it was Richards or some other—and, oh dear, he had to put Richards on his honor! He must himself decide whither that money must go —and Mr. Stephenson was not doubting that if he was the wrong man he would go honorably and find the right one. Oh, it was odious to put a man in such a situation—ah, why couldn't Stephenson have left out that doubt! What did he want to intrude that for?

Further reflection. How did it happen that *Richards's* name remained in Stephenson's mind as indicating the right man, and not some other man's name? That looked good. Yes, that looked very good. In fact, it went on looking better and better, straight along—until by-and-by it grew into positive *proof*. And then Richards put the matter at once out of his mind, for he had a private instinct that a proof once established is better left so.

He was feeling reasonably comfortable now, but there was still one other detail that kept pushing itself on his notice: of course he had done that service—that was settled; but what *was* that service? He must recall it—he would not go to sleep till he had recalled it; it would make his peace of mind perfect. And so he thought and thought. He thought of a dozen things—possible services, even probable services—but none of them seemed adequate, none of them seemed large enough, none of them seemed worth the money—worth the fortune Goodson had wished he could leave in his will. And besides, he couldn't remember having done them, anyway. Now, then—now, then—what *kind* of a service would it be that would make a man so inordinately grateful? Ah—the saving of his soul! That must be it. Yes, he could remember, now, how he once set himself the task of converting Goodson, and labored at it as much as—he was going to say three months; but upon closer examination it shrunk to a month, then to a week, then to a day, then to nothing. Yes, he remembered now, and with unwelcome vividness, that Goodson had told him to go to thunder and mind his own business—*he* wasn't hankering to follow Hadleyburg to heaven!

So that solution was a failure—he hadn't saved Goodson's soul. Richards was discouraged. Then after a little came another idea: had he saved Goodson's property? No, that wouldn't do—he hadn't any. His life? This is it! Of course. Why, he might have thought of it before. This time he was on the right track, sure. His imagination was hard at work in a minute, now.

Thereafter during a stretch of two exhausting hours he was busy saving Goodson's life. He saved it in all kinds of difficult and perilous ways. In every case he got it saved satisfactorily up to a certain point; then, just as he was beginning to get well persuaded that it had really happened, a troublesome detail would turn up which made the whole thing impossible. As in the matter of drowning, for instance. In that case he had swum out and tugged Goodson ashore in an unconscious state with a great crowd looking on and applauding, but when he had got it all thought out and was just beginning to remember all about it a whole swarm of disqualifying details arrived on the ground: the town would have known of it, it would glare like a limelight in his own memory instead of being an inconspicuous service which he had possibly rendered "without knowing its full value." And at this point he remembered that he couldn't swim, anyway.

Ah—*there* was a point which he had been overlooking from the start: it had to be a service which he had rendered "possibly without knowing the full value of it." Why, really, that ought to be an easy hunt—much easier than those others. And sure enough, by-and-by he found it. Goodson, years and years ago, came near marrying a very sweet and pretty girl, named Nancy Hewitt, but in some way or other the match had been broken off; the girl died, Goodson remained a bachelor, and by-and-by became a soured one and a frank despiser of the human species. Soon after the girl's death the village found out, or thought it had found out, that she carried a spoonful of negro blood in her veins. Richards worked at these details a good while, and in the end he thought he remembered things concerning them which must have gotten mislaid in his memory through long neglect. He seemed to dimly remember that it was *he* that found out about the negro blood; that it was he that told the village; that the village told Goodson where they got it; that he thus saved Goodson from marrying the tainted girl; that he had done him this great service "without knowing the full value of it," in fact without knowing that he *was* doing it; but that Goodson knew the value of it, and what a narrow escape he had had, and so went to his grave grateful to his benefactor and wishing he had a fortune to leave him. It was all clear and simple now, and the more he went over it the more luminous and certain it grew; and at last, when he nestled to sleep satisfied and happy, he remembered the whole thing just as if it had been yesterday. In fact, he dimly remembered Goodson's *telling* him his gratitude once. Meantime Mary had spent six thousand dollars on a new house for herself and a pair of slippers for her pastor, and then had fallen peacefully to rest.

That same Saturday evening the postman had delivered a letter to each of the other principal citizens—nineteen letters in all. No two of the envelopes were alike, and no two of the superscriptions were in the same hand, but the letters inside were just like each other in every detail but one. They were exact copies of the letter received by Richards—handwriting and all—and were all signed by Stephenson, but in place of Richards's name each receiver's own name appeared.

All night long eighteen principal citizens did what their caste-brother Richards was doing at the same time—they put in their energies trying to remember what notable service it was that they had unconsciously done Barclay Goodson. In no case was it a holiday job; still they succeeded.

And while they were at this work, which was difficult, their wives put in the night spending the money, which was easy. During that one night the nineteen wives spent an average of seven thousand dollars each out of the forty thousand in the sack—a hundred and thirty-three thousand altogether.

Next day there was a surprise for Jack Halliday. He noticed that the faces of the nineteen chief citizens and their wives bore that expression of peaceful and holy happiness again. He could not understand it, neither was he able to invent any remarks about it that could damage it or disturb it. And so it was his turn to be dissatisfied with life. His private guesses at the reasons for the happiness failed in all instances, upon examination. When he met Mrs. Wilcox and noticed the placid ecstasy in her face, he said to himself. "Her cat has had kittens"—and went and asked the cook; it was not so; the cook had detected the happiness, but did not know the cause. When Halliday found the duplicate ecstasy in the face of "Shadbelly" Billson (village nickname), he was sure some neighbor of Billson's had broken his leg, but inquiry showed that this had not happened. The subdued ecstasy in Gregory Yates's face could mean but one thing—he was a mother-in-law short; it was another mistake. "And Pinkerton—Pinkerton—he has collected ten cents that he thought he was going to lose." And so on, and so on. In some cases the guesses had to remain in doubt, in the others they proved distinct errors. In the end Halliday said to himself, "Anyway, it foots up that there's nineteen Hadleyburg families temporarily in heaven: I don't know how it happened; I only know Providence is off duty today."

An architect and builder from the next State had lately ventured to set up a small business in this unpromising village, and his sign had now been hanging out a week. Not a customer yet; he was a discouraged man, and sorry he had come. But his weather changed suddenly now. First one and then another chief citizen's wife said to him privately:

"Come to my house Monday week—but say nothing about it for the present. We think of building."

He got eleven invitations that day. That night he wrote his daughter and broke off her match with her student. He said she could marry a mile higher than that.

Pinkerton the banker and two or three other well-to-do men planned country-seats—but waited. That kind don't count their chickens until they are hatched.

The Wilsons devised a grand new thing—a fancy-dress ball. They made no actual promises, but told all their acquaintanceship in confidence that they were thinking the matter over and thought they should give it—"And if we do, you will be invited, of course." People were surprised, and said, one to another, "Why, they are crazy, those poor Wilsons, they can't afford it." Several among the nineteen said privately to their husbands, "It is a good idea, we will keep still till their cheap thing is over, then *we* will give one that will make it sick."

The days drifted along, and the bill of future squanderings rose higher and higher, wilder and wilder, more and more foolish and reckless. It began to look as if every member of the nineteen would not only spend his whole forty thousand dollars before receiving-day, but be actually in debt by the time he got the money. In some cases light-headed people did not stop with planning to spend, they really spent—on credit. They bought land, mortgages, farms, speculative stocks, fine clothes, horses, and various other things, paid down the bonus, and made themselves liable for the rest—at ten days. Presently the sober second thought came, and Halliday noticed that a ghastly anxiety was beginning to show up in a good many faces. Again he was puzzled, and didn't know what to make of it. "The Wilcox kittens aren't dead, for they weren't born; nobody's broken a leg; there's no shrinkage in mother-in-laws; *nothing* has happened—it is an insolvable mystery."

There was another puzzled man, too—the Rev. Mr. Burgess. For days, wherever he went, people seemed to follow him or to be watching out for him; and if he ever found himself in a retired spot, a member of the nineteen would be sure to appear, thrust an envelope privately into his hand, whisper "To be opened at the town-hall Friday evening," then vanish away like a guilty thing. He was expecting that there might be one claimant for the sack—doubtful, however, Goodson being dead—but it never occurred to him that all this crowd might be claimants. When the great Friday came at last, he found that he had nineteen envelopes.

3

The town-hall had never looked finer. The platform at the end of it was backed by a showy draping of flags; at intervals along the walls were festoons of flags; the gallery fronts were clothed in flags; the supporting columns were swathed in flags; all this was to impress the stranger, for he would be there in considerable force, and in a large degree he would be connected with the press. The house was full. The 412 fixed seats were occupied; also the 68 extra chairs which had been packed into the aisles; the steps of the platform were occupied; some distinguished strangers were given seats on the platform; at the horseshoe of tables which fenced the front and sides of the platform sat a strong force of special correspondents who had come from everywhere. It was the best-dressed house the town had ever produced. There were some tolerably expensive toilets there, and in several cases the ladies who wore them had the look of being unfamiliar with that kind of clothes. At least the town thought they had that look, but the notion could have arisen from the town's knowledge of the fact that these ladies had never inhabited such clothes before.

The gold-sack stood on a little table at the front of the platform where all the house could see it. The bulk of the house gazed at it with a burning interest, a mouth-watering interest, a wistful and pathetic interest; a minority of nineteen couples gazed at it tenderly, lovingly, proprietarily, and the male half of this minority kept saying over to themselves the moving little impromptu speeches of thankfulness for the audience's applause and congratulations which they were presently going to get up and deliver. Every now and then one of these got a piece of paper out of his vest pocket and privately glanced at it to refresh his memory.

Of course there was a buzz of conversation going on—there always is; but at last when the Rev. Mr. Burgess rose and laid his hand on the sack he could hear his microbes gnaw, the place was so still. He related the curious history of the sack, then went on to speak in warm terms of Hadleyburg's old and well-earned reputation for spotless honesty, and of the town's just pride in this reputation. He said that this reputation was a treasure of priceless value; that under Providence its value had now become inestimably enhanced, for the recent episode had spread this fame far and wide, and thus had focussed the eyes of the American world upon this village, and made its name for all time, as he hoped and believed, a synonym for commercial incorruptibility. [*Applause.*] "And who is to be the guardian of this noble treasure—the community as a whole? No! The responsibility is individual, not communal. From this day forth each and every one of you is in his own person its special guardian and individually responsible that no harm shall come to it. Do you—does each of you—accept this great trust? [*Tumultuous assent.*] Then all is well. Transmit it to your children and to your children's children. To-day your purity is beyond reproach—see to it that it shall remain so. To-day there is not a person in your community who could be beguiled to touch a penny not his own—see to it that you abide in this grace. [*"We will! we will!"*] This is not the place to make comparisons between ourselves and other communities—some of them ungracious toward us; they have their ways, we have ours; let us be content. [*Applause.*] I am done. Under my hand, my friends, rests a stranger's eloquent recognition of what we are: through him the world will always henceforth know what we are. We do not know who he is, but in your name I utter your gratitude, and ask you to raise your voices in endorsement."

The house rose in a body and made the walls quake with the thunders of its thankfulness for the space of a long minute. Then it sat down, and Mr. Burgess took an envelope out of his pocket. The house held its breath while he slit the envelope open and took from it a slip of paper. He read its contents—slowly and impressively—the audience listening with tranced attention to this magic document, each of whose words stood for an ingot of gold:

"*'The remark which I made to the distressed stranger was this: "You are very far from being a bad man; go, and reform."'*" Then he continued: "We shall know in a moment now whether the remark here quoted corresponds with the one concealed in the sack; and if that shall prove to be so—and it undoubtedly will—this sack of gold belongs to a fellow-citizen who will henceforth stand before the nation as the symbol of the special virtue which has made our town famous throughout the land—Mr. Billson!"

The house had gotten itself all ready to burst into a proper tornado of applause; but instead of doing it, it seemed stricken with a paralysis; there was a deep hush for a moment or two, then a wave of whispered murmurs swept the place—of about this tenor: "*Billson!* oh, come, this is *too* thin! Twenty dollars to a stranger—or *anybody*—*Billson!* Tell it to the marines!" And now at this point the house caught its breath all of a sudden in a new access of astonishment, for it discovered that whereas in one part of the hall Deacon Billson was standing up with his head meekly bowed, in another part of it Lawyer Wilson was doing the same. There was a wondering silence now for a while. Everybody was puzzled, and nineteen couples were surprised and indignant.

Billson and Wilson turned and stared at each other. Billson asked, bitingly,

"Why do *you* rise, Mr. Wilson?"

"Because I have a right to. Perhaps you will be good enough to explain to the house why *you* rise?"

"With great pleasure. Because I wrote that paper."

"It is an impudent falsity! I wrote it myself."

It was Burgess's turn to be paralyzed. He stood looking vacantly at first one of the men and then the other, and did not seem to know what to do. The house was stupefied. Lawyer Wilson spoke up, now, and said,

"I ask the Chair to read the name signed to that paper."

That brought the Chair to itself, and it read out the name,

"'John Wharton *Billson.*'"

"There!" shouted Billson, "what have you got to say for yourself, now? And what kind of apology are you going to make to me and to this insulted house for the imposture which you have attempted to play here?"

"No apologies are due, sir; and as for the rest of it, I publicly charge you with pilfering my note from Mr. Burgess and substituting a copy of it signed with your own name. There is no other way by which you could have gotten hold of the test-remark; I alone, of living men, possessed the secret of its wording."

There was likely to be a scandalous state of things if this went on; everybody noticed with distress that the short-hand scribes were scribbling like mad; many people were crying "Chair, Chair! Order! order!" Burgess rapped with his gavel, and said:

"Let us not forget the proprieties due. There has evidently been a mistake somewhere, but surely that is all. If Mr. Wilson gave me an envelope—and I remembered now that he did—I still have it."

He took one out of his pocket, opened it, glanced at it, looked surprised and worried, and stood silent a few moments. Then he waved his hand in a wandering and mechanical way, and made an effort or two to say something, then gave it up, despondently. Several voices cried out:

"Read it! read it! What is it?"

So he began in a dazed and sleep-walker fashion:

"'*The remark which I made to the unhappy stranger was this: "You are far from being a bad man.* [The house gazed at him, marvelling.] *Go, and reform."'* [*Murmurs:* "Amazing! what can this mean?"] This one," said the Chair, "is signed Thurlow G. Wilson."

"There!" cried Wilson, "I reckon that settles it! I knew perfectly well my note was purloined."

"Purloined!" retorted Billson. "I'll let you know that neither you nor any man of your kidney must venture to—"

The Chair. "Order, gentlemen, order! Take your seats, both of you, please."

They obeyed, shaking their heads and grumbling angrily. The house was profoundly puzzled; it did not know what to do with this curious emergency. Presently Thompson got up. Thompson was the hatter. He would have liked to be a Nineteener; but such was not for him; his stock of hats was not considerable enough for the position. He said:

"Mr. Chairman, if I may be permitted to make a suggestion, can both of these gentlemen be right? I put it to you, sir, can both have happened to say the very same words to the stranger? It seems to me—"

The tanner got up and interrupted him. The tanner was a disgruntled man; he believed himself entitled to be a Nineteener, but he couldn't get recognition. It made him a little unpleasant in his ways and speech. Said he:

"Sho, *that's* not the point! *That* could happen—twice in a hundred years—but not the other thing. *Neither* of them gave the twenty dollars!" [*A ripple of applause.*]

Billson. "I did!"

Wilson. "I did!"

Then each accused the other of pilfering.

The Chair. "Order! Sit down, if you please—both of you. Neither of the notes has been out of my possession at any moment."

A Voice. "Good—that settles *that!*"

The Tanner. "Mr. Chairman, one thing is now plain: one of these men has been eavesdropping under the other one's bed, and filching family secrets. If it is not unparliamentary to suggest it, I will remark that both are equal to it. [*The Chair.* "Order! order!"] I withdraw the remark, sir, and will confine myself to suggesting that *if* one of them has overheard the other reveal the test-remark to his wife, we shall catch him now."

A Voice. "How?"

The Tanner. "Easily. The two have not quoted the remark in exactly the same words. You would have noticed that, if there hadn't been a considerable stretch of time and an exciting quarrel inserted between the two readings."

A Voice. "Name the difference."

The Tanner. "The word *very* is in Billson's note, and not in the other."

Many Voices. "That's so—he's right."

The Tanner. "And so, if the Chair will examine the test-remark in the sack, we shall know which of these two frauds—[*The Chair.* "Order!"]—which of these two adventurers—[*The Chair.* "Order! order!"]—which of these two gentlemen—[*laughter and applause*]—is entitled to wear the belt as being the first dishonest blatherskite ever bred in this town—which he has dishonored, and which will be a sultry place for him from now on!" [*Vigorous applause.*]

Many Voices. "Open it!—open the sack!"

Mr. Burgess made a slit in the sack, slid his hand in and brought out an envelope. In it were a couple of folded notes. He said:

"One of these is marked, 'Not to be examined until all written communications which have been addressed to the Chair—if any—shall have been read.' The other is marked *'The Test.'* Allow me. It is worded—to wit:

"I do not require that the first half of the remark which was made to me by my benefactor shall be quoted with exactness, for it was not striking, and could be forgotten; but its closing fifteen words are quite striking, and I think easily rememberable; unless *these* shall be accurately reproduced, let the applicant be regarded as an imposter. My benefactor began by saying he seldom gave advice to any one, but that it always bore the hall-mark of high value when he did give it. Then he said this—and it has never faded from my memory: *"You are far from being a bad man—"*' "

Fifty Voices. "That settles it—the money's Wilson's! Wilson! Wilson! Speech! Speech!"

People jumped up and crowded around Wilson, wringing his hand and congratulating fervently—meantime the Chair was hammering with the gavel and shouting:

"Order, gentlemen! Order! Order! Let me finish reading, please." When quiet was restored, the reading was resumed—as follows:

" ' "*Go, and reform—or, mark my words—some day, for your sins, you will die and go to hell or Hadleyburg—* TRY AND MAKE IT THE FORMER." ' "

A ghastly silence followed. First an angry cloud began to settle darkly upon the faces of the citizenship; after a pause the cloud began to rise, and a tickled expression tried to take its place; tried so hard that it was only kept under with great and painful difficulty; the reporters, the Brixtonites, and other strangers bent their heads down and shielded their faces with their hands, and managed to hold in by main strength and heroic courtesy. At this most inopportune time burst upon the stillness the roar of a solitary voice—Jack Halliday's:

"*That's* got the hall-mark on it!"

Then the house let go, strangers and all. Even Mr. Burgess's gravity broke down presently, then the audience considered itself officially absolved from all restraint, and it made the most of its privilege. It was a good long laugh, and a tempestuously wholehearted one, but it ceased at last—long enough for Mr. Burgess to try to resume, and for the people to get their eyes partially wiped; then it broke out again; and afterward yet again; then at last Burgess was able to get out these serious words:

"It is useless to try to disguise the fact—we find ourselves in the presence of a matter of grave import. It involves the honor of your town, it strikes at the town's good name. The difference of a single word between the test-remarks offered by Mr. Wilson and Mr. Billson was itself a serious thing, since it indicated that one or the other of these gentlemen had committed a theft—"

The two men were sitting limp, nerveless, crushed; but at these words both were electrified into movement, and started to get up—

"Sit down!" said the Chair, sharply, and they obeyed. "That, as I have said, was a serious thing. And it was—but for only one of them. But the matter has become graver; for the honor of *both* is now in formidable peril. Shall I go even further, and say in inextricable peril? *Both* left out the crucial fifteen words." He paused. During several moments he allowed the pervading stillness to gather and deepen its impressive effects, then added: "There would seem to be but one way whereby this could happen. I ask these gentlemen—Was there *collusion?—agreement?*"

A low murmur sifted through the house; its import was, "He's got them both."

Billson was not used to emergencies; he sat in a helpless collapse. But Wilson was a lawyer. He struggled to his feet, pale and worried, and said:

"I ask the indulgence of the house while I explain this most painful matter. I am sorry to say what I am about to say, since it must inflict irreparable injury upon Mr. Billson, whom I have always esteemed and respected until now, and in whose invulnerability to temptation I entirely believed—as did you all. But for the preservation of my own honor I must speak—and with frankness. I confess with shame—and I now beseech your pardon for it—that I said to the ruined stranger all of the words contained in the test-remark, including the disparaging fifteen. [*Sensation.*] When the late publication was made I recalled them, and I resolved to claim the sack of coin, for by every right I was entitled to it. Now I will ask you to consider this point, and weigh it well: that stranger's gratitude to me that night knew no bounds; he said himself that he could find no words for it that were adequate, and that if he should ever be able he would repay me a thousandfold. Now, then, I ask you this: could I expect—could I believe—could I even remotely imagine—that, feeling as he did, he would do so ungrateful a thing as to add those quite unnecessary fifteen words to his test?—set a trap for me?—expose me as a slanderer of my own town before my own people assembled in a public hall? It was preposterous; it was impossible. His test would contain only the kindly opening clause of my remark. Of that I had no shadow of doubt. You would have thought as I did. You would not have expected a base betrayal from one whom you had befriended and against whom you had committed no offence. And so, with perfect confidence, perfect trust, I wrote on a piece of paper the opening words—ending with 'Go, and reform,'—and signed it. When I was about to put it in an envelope I was called into my back office, and without thinking I left the paper lying open on my desk." He stopped, turned his head slowly toward Billson, waited a moment, then added: "I ask you to note this: when I returned, a little later, Mr. Billson was retiring by my street door." (*Sensation.*)

In a moment Billson was on his feet and shouting:

"It's a lie! It's an infamous lie!"

The Chair. "Be seated, sir! Mr. Wilson has the floor."

Billson's friends pulled him into his seat and quieted him, and Wilson went on:

"Those are the simple facts. My note was now lying in a different place on the table from where I had left it. I noticed that, but attached no importance to it, thinking a draught had blown it there. That Mr. Billson would read a private paper was a thing which could not occur to me; he was an honorable man, and he would be above that. If you will allow me to say it, I think his extra word *'very'* stands explained; it is attributable to a defect of memory. I was the only man in the world who could furnish here any detail of the test-mark—by *honorable* means. I have finished."

There is nothing in the world like a persuasive speech to fuddle the mental apparatus and upset the convictions and debauch the emotions of an audience not practised in the tricks and delusions of oratory. Wilson sat down victorious. The house submerged him in tides of approving applause; friends swarmed to him and shook him by the hand and congratulated him, and Billson was shouted down and not allowed to say a word. The Chair hammered and hammered with its gavel, and kept shouting:

"But let us proceed, gentlemen, let us proceed!"

At last there was a measurable degree of quiet, and the hatter said:

"But what is there to proceed with, sir, but to deliver the money?"

Voices. "That's it! That's it! Come forward, Wilson!"

The Hatter. "I move three cheers for Mr. Wilson, Symbol of the special virtue which—"

The cheers burst forth before he could finish; and in the midst of them—and in the midst of the clamor of the gavel also—some enthusiasts mounted Wilson on a big friend's shoulder and were going to fetch him in triumph to the platform. The Chair's voice now rose above the noise—

"Order! To your places! You forget that there is still a document to be read." When quiet had been restored he took up the document, and was going to read it, but laid it down again, saying, "I forgot; this is not to be read until all written communications received by me have first been read." He took an envelope out of his pocket, removed its enclosure, glanced at it—seemed astonished—held it out and gazed at it—stared at it.

Twenty or thirty voices cried out:

"What is it? Read it! read it!"

And he did—slowly, and wondering:

" 'The remark which I made to the stranger—[*Voices.* "Hello! how's this?"] —was this: "You are far from being a bad man. [*Voices.* "Great Scott!"] Go, and reform." ' [*Voice.* "Oh, saw my leg off!"] Signed by Mr. Pinkerton the banker."

The pandemonium of delight which turned itself loose now was of a sort to make the judicious weep. Those whose withers were unwrung laughed till the tears ran down; the reporters, in throes of laughter, set down disordered pothooks which would never in the world be decipherable; and a sleeping dog jumped up, scared out of its wits, and barked itself crazy at the turmoil. All manner of cries were scattered through the din: "We're getting rich—*two* Symbols of Incorruptibility!—without counting Billson!" "*Three!*—count Shadbelly in—we can't have too many!" "All right —Billson's elected!" "Alas, poor Wilson —victim of *two* thieves!"

A Powerful Voice. "Silence! The Chair's fished up something more out of its pocket."

Voices. "Hurrah! Is it something fresh? Read it! read! read!"

The Chair [*reading*]. " 'The remark which I made,' etc. 'You are far from being a bad man. Go,' etc. Signed, 'Gregory Yates.' "

Tornado of Voices. "Four Symbols!" " 'Rah for Yates!" "Fish again!"

The house was in a roaring humor now, and ready to get all the fun out of the occasion that might be in it. Several Nineteeners, looking pale and distressed, got up and began to work their way toward the aisles, but a score of shouts went up:

"The doors, the doors—close the

doors; no Incorruptible shall leave this place! Sit down, everybody!"

The mandate was obeyed.

"Fish again! Read! read!"

The Chair fished again, and once more the familiar words began to fall from its lips—" 'You are far from being a bad man—' "

"Name! name! What's his name?"

" 'L. Ingoldsby Sargent.' "

"Five elected! Pile up the Symbols! Go on, go on!"

" 'You are far from being a bad—' "

"Name! name!"

" 'Nicholas Whitworth.' "

"Hooray! hooray! it's a symbolical day!"

Somebody wailed in, and began to sing this rhyme (leaving out "it's") to the lovely "Mikado" tune of "When a man's afraid, a beautiful maid—"; the audience joined in, with joy; then, just in time, somebody contributed another

And don't you this forget——

The house roared it out. A third line was at once furnished—

Corruptibles far from Hadleyburg are——

The house roared that one too. As the last note died, Jack Halliday's voice rose high and clear, freighted with a final line—

But the Symbols are here, you bet!

That was sung, with booming enthusiasm. Then the happy house started in at the beginning and sang the four lines through twice, with immense swing and dash, and finished up with a crashing three-times-three and a tiger for "Hadleyburg the Incorruptible and all Symbols of it which we shall find worthy to receive the hall-mark to-night."

Then the shoutings at the Chair began again, all over the place:

"Go on! go on! Read! read some more! Read all you've got!"

"That's it—go on! We are winning eternal celebrity!"

A dozen men got up now and began to protest. They said that this farce was the work of some abandoned joker, and was an insult to the whole community. Without a doubt these signatures were all forgeries—

"Sit down! sit down! Shut up! You are confessing. We'll find *your* names in the lot."

"Mr. Chairman, how many of those envelopes have you got?"

The Chair counted.

"Together with those that have been already examined, there are nineteen."

A storm of derisive applause broke out.

"Perhaps they all contain the secret. I move that you open them all and read every signature that is attached to a note of that sort—and read also the first eight words of the note."

"Second the motion!"

It was put and carried—uproariously. Then poor old Richards got up, and his wife rose and stood at his side. Her head was bent down, so that none might see that she was crying. Her husband gave her his arm, and so supporting her, he began to speak in a quavering voice:

"My friends, you have known us two —Mary and me—all our lives, and I think you have liked us and respected us—"

The Chair interrupted him:

"Allow me. It is quite true—that which you are saying, Mr. Richards; this town *does* know you two; it *does* like you; it *does* respect you; more—it honors you and *loves* you—"

Halliday's voice rang out:

"That's the hall-marked truth, too! If the Chair is right, let the house speak up and say it. Rise! Now, then—hip! hip! hip!—all together!"

The house rose in mass, faced toward the old couple eagerly, filled the air with a snowstorm of waving handkerchiefs, and delivered the cheers with all its affectionate heart.

The Chair then continued:

"What I was going to say is this: We know your good heart, Mr. Richards, but this is not a time for the exercise of charity toward offenders. [Shouts of "Right! right!"] I see your generous purpose in your face, but I cannot allow you to plead for these men—"

"But I was going to—"

"Please take your seat, Mr. Richards. We must examine the rest of these notes —simple fairness to the men who have already been exposed requires this. As soon as that has been done—I give you my word for this—you shall be heard."

Many Voices. "Right!—the Chair is right—no interruption can be permitted at this stage! Go on!—the names! the names!—according to the terms of the motion!"

The old couple sat reluctantly down, and the husband whispered to the wife, "It is pitifully hard to have to wait; the shame will be greater than ever when they find we were only going to plead for *ourselves.*"

Straightway the jollity broke loose again with the reading of the names.

" 'You are far from being a bad man—' Signature, 'Robert J. Titmarsh.'

" 'You are far from being a bad man—' Signature, 'Eliphalet Weeks.'

" 'You are far from being a bad man—' Signature, 'Oscar B. Wilder.' "

At this point the house lit upon the idea of taking the eight words out of the Chairman's hands. He was not unthankful for that. Thenceforward he held up each note in its turn, and waited. The house droned out the eight words in a massed and measured and musical deep volume of sound (with a daringly close resemblance to a well-known church chant)—" 'You are f-a-r from being a b-a-a-a-d man.' " Then the Chair said, "Signature, 'Archibald Wilcox.' " And so on, and so on, name after name, and everybody had an increasingly and gloriously good time except the wretched Nineteen. Now and then, when a particularly shining name was called, the house made the Chair wait while it chanted the whole of the test-remark from the beginning to the closing words, "And go to hell or Hadleyburg—try and make it the for-or-m-e-r!" and in these special cases they added a grand and agonized and imposing "A-a-a-a-*men!*"

The list dwindled, dwindled, dwindled, poor old Richards keeping tally of the count, wincing when a name resembling his own was pronounced, and waiting in miserable suspense for the time to come when it would be his humiliating privilege to rise with Mary and finish his plea, which he was intending to word thus: ". . . for until now we have never done any wrong thing, but have gone our humble way unreproached. We are very poor, we are old, and have no chick nor child to help us; we were sorely tempted, and we fell. It was my purpose when I got up before to make confession and beg that my name might not be read out in this public place, for it seemed to us that we could not bear it; but I was prevented. It was just; it was our place to suffer with the rest. It has been hard for us. It is the first time we have ever heard our name fall from any one's lips —sullied. Be merciful—for the sake of the better days; make our shame as light to bear as in your charity you can." At this point in his revery Mary nudged him, perceiving that his mind was absent. The house was chanting. "You are f-a-r," etc.

"Be ready," Mary whispered. "Your name comes now; he has read eighteen."

The chant ended.

"Next! next! next!" came volleying from all over the house.

Burgess put his hand into his pocket.

The old couple, trembling, began to rise, Burgess fumbled a moment, then said,

"I find I have read them all."

Faint with joy and surprise, the couple sank into their seats, and Mary whispered:

"Oh, bless God, we are saved!—he has lost ours—I wouldn't give this for a hundred of those sacks!"

The house burst out with its "Mikado" travesty, and sang it three times with ever-increasing enthusiasm, rising to its feet when it reached for the third time the closing line—

But the Symbols are here, you bet!

and finished up with cheers and a tiger for "Hadleyburg purity and our eighteen immortal representatives of it."

Then Wingate, the saddler, got up and proposed cheers "for the cleanest man in town, the one solitary important citizen in it who didn't try to steal that money—Edward Richards."

They were given with great and moving heartiness; then somebody proposed that Richards be elected sole Guardian and Symbol of the now Sacred Hadleyburg Tradition, with power and right to stand up and look the whole sarcastic world in the face.

Passed, by acclamation; then they sang the "Mikado" again, and ended it with,

And there's *one* Symbol left, you bet!

There was a pause; then—

A Voice. "Now, then, who's to get the sack?"

The Tanner (*with bitter sarcasm*). "That's easy. The money has to be divided among the eighteen Incorruptibles. They gave the suffering stranger twenty dollars apiece—and that remark—each in his turn—it took twenty-two minutes for the procession to move past. Staked the stranger—total contribution, $360. All they want is just the loan back—and interest—forty thousand dollars altogether."

Many voices [*derisively*]. "That's it! Divvy! divvy! Be kind to the poor—don't keep them waiting!"

The Chair. "Order! I now offer the stranger's remaining document. It says: 'If no claimant shall appear [*grand chorus of groans*], I desire that you open the sack and count out the money to the principal citizens of your town, they to take it in trust [*Cries of "Oh! Oh! Oh!"*], and use it in such ways as to them shall seem best for the propagation and preservation of your community's noble reputation for incorruptible honesty [*more cries*]—a reputation to which their names and their efforts will add a new and far-reaching lustre.' [*Enthusiastic outburst of sarcastic applause.*] That seems to be all. No—here is a postscript:

"'P. S.—CITIZENS OF HADLEYBURG: There *is* no test-remark—nobody made one. [*Great sensation.*] There wasn't any pauper stranger, nor any twenty-dollar contribution, nor any accompanying benediction and compliment—these are all inventions. [*General buzz and hum of astonishment and delight.*] Allow me to tell my story—it will take but a word or two. I passed through your town at a certain time, and received a deep offense which I had not earned. Any other man would have been content to kill one or two of you and call it square, but to me that would have been a trivial revenge, and inadequate; for the dead do not *suffer*. Besides, I could not kill you all—and, anyway, made as I am, even that would not have satisfied me. I wanted to damage every man in the place, and every woman—and not in their bodies or in their estate, but in their vanity—the place where feeble and foolish people are most vulnerable. So I disguised myself and came back and studied you. You were easy game. You had an old and lofty reputation for honesty, and naturally you were proud of it—it was your treasure of treasures, the very apple of your eye. As soon as I found out that you carefully and vigilantly kept yourselves and your children *out of temptation,* I knew how to proceed. Why, you simple creatures, the weakest of all weak things is a virtue which has not been tested in the fire. I laid a plan, and gathered a list of names. My project was to corrupt Hadleyburg the incorruptible. My idea was to make liars and thieves of nearly half a hundred smirchless men and women who had never in their lives uttered a lie or stolen a penny. I was afraid of Goodson. He was neither born nor reared in Hadleyburg. I was afraid that if I started to operate my scheme by getting my letter laid before you, you would say to yourselves, "Goodson is the only man among us who would give away twenty dollars to a poor devil"—and then you might not bite at my bait. But Heaven took Goodson; then I knew I was safe, and I set my trap and baited it. It may be that I shall not catch all the men to whom I mailed the pretended test secret, but I shall catch the most of them, if I know Hadleyburg nature. [*Voices.* "Right—he got every last one of them."] I believe they will even steal ostensible *gamble*-money, rather than miss, poor, tempted, and mistrained fellows. I am hoping to eternally and everlastingly squelch your vanity and give Hadleyburg a new renown—one that will *stick*—and spread far. If I have succeeded, open the sack and summon the Committee on Propagation and Preservation of the Hadleyburg Reputation.' "

A Cyclone of Voices. "Open it! Open it! The Eighteen to the front! Committee on Propagation of the Tradition! Forward—the Incorruptibles!"

The Chair ripped the sack wide, and gathered up a handful of bright, broad, yellow coins, shook them together, then examined them—

"Friends, they are only gilded disks of lead!"

There was a crashing outbreak of delight over this news, and when the noise had subsided, the tanner called out:

"By right of apparent seniority in this business, Mr. Wilson is Chairman of the Committee on Propagation of the Tradition. I suggest that he step forward on behalf of his pals, and receive in trust the money."

A Hundred Voices. "Wilson! Wilson! Wilson! Speech! Speech!"

Wilson [*in a voice trembling with anger*]. "You will allow me to say, without apologies for my language, *damn* the money!"

A Voice. "Oh, and him a Baptist!"

A Voice. "Seventeen Symbols left! Step up, gentlemen, and assume your trust!"

There was a pause—no response.

The Saddler. "Mr. Chairman, we've got *one* clean man left, anyway, out of the late aristocracy; and he needs money, and deserves it. I move that you appoint Jack Halliday to get up there and auction off that sack of gilt twenty-dollar pieces, and give the result to the right man—the man whom Hadleyburg delights to honor—Edward Richards."

This was received with great enthusiasm, the dog taking a hand again; the saddler started the bids at a dollar, the Brixton folk and Barnum's representative fought hard for it, the people cheered every jump that the bids made, the excitement climbed moment by moment higher and higher, the bidders got on their mettle and grew steadily more and more daring, more and more determined, the jumps went from a dollar up to five, then to ten, then to twenty, then fifty, then to a hundred, then—

At the beginning of the auction Richards whispered in distress to his wife: "Oh, Mary, can we allow it? It—it—you see, it is an honor-reward, a testimonial to purity of character, and—and—can we allow it? Hadn't I better get up and—Oh, Mary, what ought we to do?—what do you think we—" [*Halliday's voice. "Fifteen I'm bid!—fifteen for the sack!—twenty!—ah, thanks!—thirty thanks again! Thirty, thirty, thirty!—do —I hear forty?—forty it is! Keep the ball rolling, gentlemen, keep it rolling!—fifty!—thanks, noble Roman!—going at fifty, fifty, fifty!—seventy!—ninety!—splendid!—a hundred!—pile it up, pile it up!—hundred and twenty—forty!—just in time!—hundred and fifty!—*TWO *hundred!—superb! Do I hear two h—thanks!—two hundred and fifty!——*"]

"It is another temptation, Edward—I'm all in a tremble—but, oh, we've escaped *one* temptation, and that ought to warn us, to—["*Six did I hear?—thanks! —six fifty, six f—*SEVEN *hundred!*"] And yet, Edward, when you think—nobody susp—["*Eight hundred dollars!—hurrah! —make it nine!—Mr. Parsons, did I hear you say—thanks!—nine!—this noble sack of virgin lead going at only nine hundred dollars, gilding and all—come! do I hear —a thousand!—gratefully yours!—did some one say eleven?—a sack which is going to be the most celebrated in the whole Uni——*"] Oh, Edward" (*beginning to sob*), "we are *so* poor!—but—but —do as you think best—do as you think best."

Edward fell—that is, he sat still; sat with a conscience which was not satisfied, but which was overpowered by circumstances.

Meanwhile a stranger, who looked like an amateur detective gotten up as an impossible English earl, had been watching the evening's proceedings with manifest interest, and with a contented expression in his face; and he had been privately commenting to himself. He was now soliloquizing somewhat like this: "None of the Eighteen are bidding; that is not satisfactory; I must change that—the dramatic unities require it; they must buy the sack they tried to steal; they must pay a heavy price, too—some of them are rich. And another thing, when I make a mistake in Hadleyburg nature the man that puts that error upon me is entitled to a high honorarium, and some one must pay it. This poor old Richards has brought my judgment to shame; he is an honest man;—I don't understand it, but I acknowledge it. Yes, he saw my deuces —*and* with a straight flush, and by rights the pot is his. And it shall be a jackpot, too, if I can manage it. He disappointed me, but let that pass."

He was watching the bidding. At a thousand, the market broke; the prices tumbled swiftly. He waited—and still watched. One competitor dropped out; then another, and another. He put in a bid or two, now. When the bids had sunk to ten dollars, he added a five; some one raised him a three; he waited a moment, then flung in a fifty-dollar jump, and the sack was his—at $1,282. The house broke out in cheers—then stopped; for he was on his feet and had lifted his hand. He began to speak.

"I desire to say a word, and ask a favor. I am a speculator in rarities, and I have dealings with persons interested in numismatics all over the world. I can make a profit on this purchase, just as it stands; but there is a way, if I can get your approval, whereby I can make every one of these leaden twenty-dollar pieces worth its face in gold, and perhaps more. Grant me that approval, and I will give part of my gains to your Mr. Richards, whose invulnerable probity you have so justly and so cordially recognized to-night; his share shall be ten thousand dollars, and I will hand him the money to-morrow. [*Great applause from the house.* But the "invulnerable probity" made the Richardses blush prettily; however, it went for modesty, and did no harm.] If you will pass my proposition by a good majority—I would like a two-thirds vote—I will regard that as the town's consent, and that is all I ask. Rarities are always helped by any device which will rouse curiosity and compel remark. Now if I may have your permission to stamp upon the faces of each of these ostensible coins the names of the eighteen gentlemen who—"

Nine-tenths of the audience were on their feet in a moment—dog and all—and the proposition was carried with a whirlwind of approving applause and laughter.

They sat down, and all the Symbols except "Dr." Clay Harkness got up, violently protesting against the proposed outrage, and threatening to—

"I beg you not to threaten me," said the stranger, calmly. "I know my legal rights, and am not accustomed to being frightened at bluster." [*Applause.*] He sat down. "Dr." Harkness saw an opportunity here. He was one of the two very rich men of the place, and Pinkerton was the other. Harkness was proprietor of a mint; that is to say, a popular patent medicine. He was running for the Legislature on one ticket, and Pinkerton on the other. It was a close race and a hot one, and getting hotter every day. Both had strong appetites for money; each had bought a great tract of land, with a purpose; there was going to be a new railway, and each wanted to be in the Legislature and help locate the route to his own advantage; a single vote might make the decision, and with it two or three fortunes. The stake was large, and Harkness was a daring speculator. He was sitting close to the stranger. He leaned over while one or another of the other Symbols was entertaining the house with protests and appeals, and asked, in a whisper,

"What is your price for the sack?"

"Forty thousand dollars."

"I'll give you twenty."

"No."

"Twenty-five."

"No."

"Say thirty."

"The price is forty thousand dollars; not a penny less."

"All right, I'll give it. I will come to the hotel at ten in the morning. I don't want it known; will see you privately."

"Very good." Then the stranger got up and said to the house:

"I find it late. The speeches of these gentlemen are not without merit, not without interest, not without grace; yet if I may be excused I will take my leave. I thank you for the great favor which you have shown me in granting my petition. I ask the Chair to keep the sack for me until to-morrow, and to hand these three five-hundred-dollar notes to Mr. Richards." They were passed up to the Chair. "At nine I will call for the sack, and at eleven will deliver the rest of the ten thousand to Mr. Richards in person, at his home. Good-night."

Then he slipped out, and left the audience making a vast noise, which was composed of a mixture of cheers, the "Mikado" song, dog-disapproval, and the chant, "you are f-a-r from being a b-a-a-d man—a-a-a-men!"

4

At home the Richardses had to endure congratulations and compliments until midnight. Then they were left to themselves. They looked a little sad, and they sat silent and thinking. Finally Mary sighed and said,

"Do you think we are to blame, Edward—*much* to blame?" and her eyes wandered to the accusing triplet of big bank-notes lying on the table, where the congratulators had been gloating over them and reverently fingering them. Edward did not answer at once; then he brought out a sigh and said, hesitatingly:

"We—we couldn't help it, Mary. It—well, it was ordered. *All* things are."

Mary glanced up and looked at him steadily, but he didn't return the look. Presently she said:

"I thought congratulations and praises always tasted good. But—it seems to me, now—Edward?"

"Well?"

"Are you going to stay in the bank?"

"N-no."

"Resign?"

"In the morning—by note."

"It does seem best."

Richards bowed his head in his hands and muttered:

"Before, I was not afraid to let oceans of people's money pour through my hands, but—Mary, I am so tired, so tired—"

"We will go to bed."

At nine in the morning the stranger called for the sack and took it to the hotel in a cab. At ten Harkness had a talk with him privately. The stranger asked for and got five checks on a metropolitan bank—drawn to "Bearer,"—four for $1,500 each, and one for $34,000. He put one of the former in his pocket-book, and the remainder, representing $38,500, he put in an envelope, and with these he added a note, which he wrote after Harkness was gone. At eleven he called at the Richards house and knocked. Mrs. Richards peeped through the shutters, then went and received the envelope, and the stranger disappeared without a word. She came back flushed and a little unsteady on her legs, and gasped out:

"I am sure I recognized him! Last night it seemed to me that maybe I had seen him somewhere before."

"He is the man that brought the sack here?"

"I am almost sure of it."

"Then he is the ostensible Stephenson too, and sold every important citizen in this town with his bogus secret. Now if he has sent checks instead of money, we are sold too, after we thought we had escaped. I was beginning to feel fairly comfortable once more, after my night's rest, but the look of that envelope makes me sick. It isn't fat enough; $8,500 in even the largest bank-notes makes more bulk than that."

"Edward, why do you object to checks?"

"Checks signed by Stephenson! I am resigned to take the $8,500 if it could come in bank-notes—for it does seem that it was so ordered, Mary—but I have never had much courage, and I have not the pluck to try to markct a check signed with that disastrous name. It would be a trap. That man tried to catch me; we escaped somehow or other; and now he is trying a new way. If it is checks——"

"Oh, Edward, it is *too* bad!" and she held up the checks and began to cry.

"Put them in the fire! quick! we mustn't be tempted. It is a trick to make the world laugh at *us*, along with the rest, and—Give them to *me*, since you can't do it!" He snatched them and tried to hold his grip till he could get to the stove; but he was human, he was a cashier, and he stopped a moment to make sure of the signature. Then he came near to fainting.

"Fan me, Mary, fan me! They are the same as gold!"

"Oh, how lovely, Edward! Why?"

"Signed by Harkness. What can the mystery of that be, Mary?"

"Edward, do you think——"

"Look here—look at this! Fifteen—fifteen—fifteen—thirty-four. Thirty-eight thousand five hundred! Mary, the sack isn't worth twelve dollars, and Harkness—apparently—has paid about par for it."

"And does it all come to us, do you think—instead of the ten thousand?"

"Why, it looks like it. And the checks are made to 'Bearer,' too."

"Is that good, Edward? What is it for?"

"A hint to collect them at some distant bank, I reckon. Perhaps Harkness doesn't want the matter known. What is that—a note?"

"Yes. It was with the checks."

It was in the "Stephenson" handwriting, but there was no signature. It said:

I am a disappointed man. Your honesty is beyond the reach of temptation. I had a different idea about it, but I wronged you in that, and I beg pardon, and do it sincerely. I honor you—and that is sincere, too. This town is not worthy to kiss the hem of your garment. Dear sir, I made a square bet with myself that there were nineteen debauchable men in your self-righteous community. I have lost. Take the whole pot, you are entitled to it.

Richards drew a deep sigh, and said: "It seems written with fire—it burns so. Mary—I am miserable again."

"I, too. Ah, dear, I wish——"

"To think, Mary—he *believes* in me."

"Oh, don't, Edward—I can't bear it."

"If those beautiful words were deserved, Mary—and God knows I believed I deserved them once—I think I could give the forty thousand dollars for them. And I would put that paper away, as representing more than gold and jewels, and keep it always. But now—We could not live in the shadow of its accusing presence, Mary."

He put it in the fire.

A messenger arrived and delivered an envelope. Richards took from it a note and read it; it was from Burgess.

You saved me, in a difficult time. I saved you last night. It was at cost of a lie, but I made the sacrifice freely, and out of grateful heart. None in this village knows so well as I know how brave and good and noble you are. At bottom you cannot respect me, knowing as you do of that matter of which I am accused, and by the general voice condemned; but I beg that you will at least believe that I am a grateful man; it will help me to bear my burden.

[*Signed*] BURGESS.

"Saved, once more. And on such terms!" He put the note in the fire. "I—I wish I were dead, Mary, I wish I were out of it all."

"Oh, these are bitter, bitter days, Edward. The stabs, through their very generosity, are so deep—and they come so fast!"

Three days before the election each of two thousand voters suddenly found himself in possession of a prized memento—one of the renowned bogus double-eagles. Around one of its faces was stamped these words: "THE REMARK I MADE TO THE POOR STRANGER WAS—" Around the other face was stamped these: "GO, AND REFORM. [SIGNED] PINKERTON." Thus the entire remaining refuse of the renowned joke was emptied upon a single head, and with calamitous effect. It revived the recent vast laugh and concentrated it upon Pinkerton; and Harkness's election was a walk-over.

Within twenty-four hours after the Richardses had received their checks their consciences were quieting down, discouraged; the old couple were learning to reconcile themselves to the sin which they had committed. But they were to learn, now, that a sin takes on new and real terrors when there seems a chance that it is going to be found out. This gives it a fresh and most substantial and important aspect. At church the morning sermon was of the usual pattern; it was the same old things said in the same old way; they had heard them a thousand times and found them innocuous, next to meaningless, and easy to sleep under; but now it was different: the sermon seemed to bristle with accusations; it seemed aimed straight and specially at people who were concealing deadly sins. After church they got away from the mob of congratulators as soon as they could, and hurried homeward, chilled to the bone at they did not know what—vague, shadowy, indefinite fears. And by chance they caught a glimpse of Mr. Burgess as he turned a corner. He paid no attention to their nod of recognition! He hadn't seen it; but they did not know that. What could his conduct mean? It might mean—it might mean—

oh, a dozen dreadful things. Was it possible that he knew that Richards could have cleared him of guilt in that bygone time, and had been silently waiting for a chance to even up accounts? At home, in their distress they got to imagining that their servant might have been in the next room listening when Richards revealed the secret to his wife that he knew of Burgess's innocence; next, Richards began to imagine that he had heard the swish of a gown in there at that time; next, he was sure he *had* heard it. They would call Sarah in, on a pretext, and watch her face: if she had been betraying them to Mr. Burgess, it would show in her manner. They asked her some questions—questions which were so random and incoherent and seemingly purposeless that the girl felt sure that the old people's mind had been affected by their sudden good fortune; the sharp and watchful gaze which they bent upon her frightened her, and that completed the business. She blushed, she became nervous and confused, and to the old people these were plain signs of guilt—guilt of some fearful sort or other—without doubt she was a spy and a traitor. When they were alone again they began to piece many unrelated things together and get horrible results out of the combination. When things had got about to the worst, Richards was delivered of a sudden gasp, and his wife asked:

"Oh, what is it?—what is it?"

"The note—Burgess's note! Its language was sarcastic, I see it now." He quoted: "'At bottom you cannot respect me, *knowing*, as you do, of *that matter* of which I am accused'—oh, it is perfectly plain, now, God help me! He knows that I know! You see the ingenuity of the phrasing. It was a trap—and like a fool, I walked into it. And Mary—?"

"Oh, it is dreadful—I know what you are going to say—he didn't return your transcript of the pretended test-remark."

"No—kept it to destroy us with. Mary, he has exposed us to some already. I know it—I know it well. I saw it in a dozen faces after church. Ah, he wouldn't answer our nod of recognition—*he* knew what he had been doing!"

In the night the doctor was called. The news went around in the morning that the old couple were rather seriously ill—prostrated by the exhausting excitement growing out of their great windfall, the congratulations, and the late hours, the doctor said. The town was sincerely distressed; for these old people were about all it had left to be proud of, now.

Two days later the news was worse. The old couple were delirious, and were doing strange things. By witness of the nurses, Richards had exhibited checks—for $8,500? No—for an amazing sum—$38,500! What could be the explanation of this gigantic piece of luck?

The following day the nurses had more news—and wonderful. They had concluded to hide the checks, lest harm come to them; but when they searched they were gone from under the patient's pillow—vanished away. The patient said:

"Let the pillow alone; what do you want?"

"We thought it best that the checks——"

"You will never see them again—they are destroyed. They came from Satan. I saw the hell-brand on them, and I knew they were sent to betray me to sin." Then he fell to gabbling strange and dreadful things which were not clearly understandable, and which the doctor admonished them to keep to themselves.

Richards was right; the checks were never seen again.

A nurse must have talked in her sleep, for within two days the forbidden gabblings were the property of the town; and they were of a surprising sort. They seemed to indicate that Richards had been a claimant for the sack himself, and that Burgess had concealed that fact and then maliciously betrayed it.

Burgess was taxed with this and stoutly denied it. And he said it was not fair to attach weight to the chatter of a sick old man who was out of his mind. Still, suspicion was in the air, and there was much talk.

After a day or two it was reported that Mrs. Richards's delirious deliveries were getting to be duplicates of her husband's. Suspicion flamed up into conviction, now, and the town's pride in the purity of its one undiscredited important citizen began to dim down and flicker toward extinction.

Six days passed, then came more news. The old couple were dying. Richards's mind cleared in his latest hour, and he sent for Burgess. Burgess said:

"Let the room be cleared. I think he wishes to say something in privacy."

"No!" said Richards; "I want witnesses. I want you all to hear my confession, so that I may die a man, and not a dog. I was clean—artificially—like the rest; and like the rest I fell when temptation came. I signed a lie, and claimed the miserable sack. Mr. Burgess remembered that I had done him a service, and in gratitude (and ignorance) he suppressed my claim and saved me. You know the thing that was charged against Burgess years ago. My testimony, and mine alone, could have cleared him, and I was a coward, and left him to suffer disgrace—"

"No—no—Mr. Richards, you—"

"My servant betrayed my secret to him—"

"No one has betrayed anything to me—"

—"and then he did a natural and justifiable thing, he repented of the saving kindness which he had done me, and he *exposed* me—as I deserved—"

"Never!—I make oath—"

"Out of my heart I forgive him."

Burgess's impassioned protestations fell upon deaf ears; the dying man passed away without knowing that once more he had done poor Burgess a wrong. The old wife died that night.

The last of the sacred Nineteen had fallen a prey to the fiendish sack; the town was stripped of the last rag of its ancient glory. Its mourning was not showy, but it was deep.

By act of the Legislature—upon prayer and petition—Hadleyburg was allowed to change its name to (never mind what—I will not give it away), and leave one word out of the motto that for many generations had graced the town's official seal.

It is an honest town once more, and the man will have to rise early that catches it napping again.

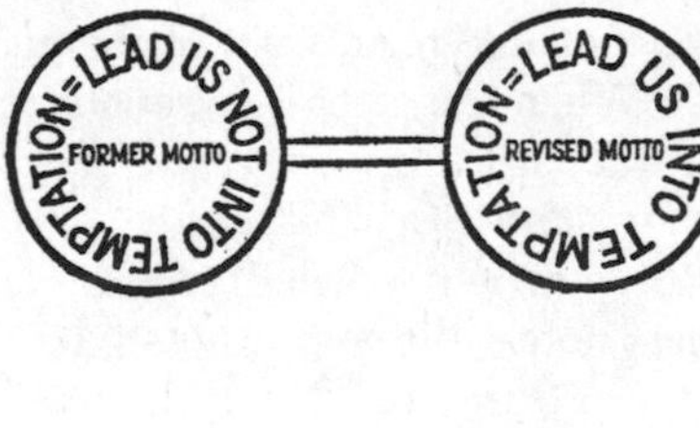

Stephen Crane

❋ 1871-1900

Crane died of tuberculosis at the age of 28—too young to become a truly great novelist. He was born in Newark, New Jersey, the fourteenth and youngest child of a Methodist preacher. In his short life there was little time for reading, but he studied briefly at both Lafayette College and at Syracuse University. In 1891 he went to New York City to become a newspaper reporter; later he served under shellfire as a war correspondent in Greece and Cuba. Toward the end of his life he lived in England. His fame rests on a few short stories, a few poems, and two short novels, Maggie: A Girl of the Streets *(1893) and* The Red Badge of Courage *(1895).* Maggie *pointed the way for the naturalists who followed Crane. It is remarkable for its break with the then prevalent "genteel tradition." Because its realistic treatment was considered sordid, Crane was unable to find a publisher for* Maggie, *but when the novel was privately printed it won for Crane the admiration and support of both Hamlin Garland and William Dean Howells.*

Maggie: A Girl of the Streets

1

A very little boy stood upon a heap of gravel for the honour of Rum Alley. He was throwing stones at howling urchins from Devil's Row, who were circling madly about the heap and pelting him. His infantile countenance was livid with the fury of battle. His small body was writhing in the delivery of oaths.

"Run, Jimmie, run! Dey'll git yehs!" screamed a retreating Rum Alley child.

"Naw," responded Jimmie with a valiant roar, "dese mugs can't make me run."

Howls of renewed wrath went up from Devil's Row throats. Tattered gamins on the right made a furious assault on the gravel-heap. On their small convulsed faces shone the grins of true assassins. As they charged, they threw stones and cursed in shrill chorus.

The little champion of Rum Alley stumbled precipitately down the other side. His coat had been torn to shreds in a scuffle, and his hat was gone. He had bruises on twenty parts of his body, and blood was dripping from a cut in his head. His wan features looked like those of a tiny insane demon. On the ground, children from Devil's Row closed in on their antagonist. He crooked his left arm defensively about his head and fought with madness. The little boys ran to and fro, dodging, hurling stones, and swearing in barbaric trebles.

From a window of an apartment-house that uprose from amid squat ignorant stables there leaned a curious woman. Some labourers, unloading a scow at a dock at the river, paused for a moment and regarded the fight. The engineer of a passive tugboat hung lazily over a railing and watched. Over on the island a worm of yellow convicts came from the shadow of a grey ominous building and crawled slowly along the river's bank.

A stone had smashed in Jimmie's mouth. Blood was bubbling over his chin and down upon his ragged shirt. Tears made furrows on his dirt-stained cheeks. His thin legs had begun to tremble and turn weak, causing his small body to reel. His roaring curses of the first part of the fight had changed to a blasphemous chatter. In the yells of the whirling mob of Devil's Row children there were notes of joy like songs of triumphant savagery. The little boys seemed to leer gloatingly at the blood upon the other child's face.

Down the avenue came boastfully sauntering a lad of sixteen years, although the chronic sneer of an ideal manhood already sat upon his lips. His hat was tipped over his eye with an air of challenge. Between his teeth a cigar-stump was tilted at the angle of defiance. He walked with a certain swing of the shoulders which appalled the timid. He glanced over into the vacant lot in which the little raving boys from Devil's Row seethed about the shrieking and tearful child from Rum Alley.

"Gee!" he murmured with interest, "a scrap. Gee!" He strode over to the cursing circle, swinging his shoulders in a manner which denoted that he held victory in his fists. He approached at the back of one of the most deeply engaged of the Devil's Row children. "Ah, what d' hell," he said, and smote the deeply engaged one on the back of the head.

The little boy fell to the ground and gave a tremendous howl. He scrambled to his feet, and perceiving, evidently, the size of his assailant, ran quickly off, shouting alarms. The entire Devil's Row party followed him. They came to a stand a short distance away and yelled taunting oaths at the boy with the chronic sneer.

The latter, momentarily, paid no attention to them. "What's wrong wi'che, Jimmie?" he asked of the small champion.

Jimmie wiped his blood-wet features with his sleeve. "Well, it was dis way, Pete, see? I was goin' teh lick dat Riley kid, an' dey all pitched on me."

Some Rum Alley children now came forward. The party stood for a moment exchanging vainglorious remarks with Devil's Row. A few stones were thrown at long distances, and words of challenge passed between small warriors. Then the Rum Alley contingent turned slowly in the direction of their home street. They began to give, each to each, distorted versions of the fight. Causes of retreat in particular cases were magnified. Blows dealt in the fight were enlarged to catapultian power, and stones thrown were alleged to have hurtled with infinite accuracy. Valour grew strong again, and the little boys began to brag with great spirit. "Ah, we blokies kin lick d' hull damn Row," said a child, swaggering.

Little Jimmie was trying to stanch the flow of blood from his cut lips. Scowling, he turned upon the speaker. "Ah, where was yehs when I was doin' all deh fightin'?" he demanded. "Youse kids makes me tired."

"Ah, go ahn!" replied the other argumentatively.

Jimmie replied with heavy contempt. "Ah, youse can't fight, Blue Billie! I kin lick yeh wid one han'."

"Ah, go ahn!" replied Billie again.

"Ah!" said Jimmie threateningly.

"Ah!" said the other in the same tone.

They struck at each other, clinched, and rolled over on the cobble-stones.

"Smash 'im, Jimmie, kick d' face off 'im!" yelled Pete, the lad with the chronic sneer, in tones of delight.

The small combatants pounded and kicked, scratched and tore. They began to weep, and their curses struggled in their throats with sobs. The other little boys clasped their hands and wriggled their legs in excitement. They formed a bobbing circle about the pair.

A tiny spectator was suddenly agitated. "Cheese it, Jimmie, cheese it! Here comes yer fader," he yelled.

The circle of little boys instantly parted. They drew away and waited in ecstatic awe for that which was about to happen. The two little boys, fighting in the modes of four thousand years ago, did not hear the warning.

Up the avenue there plodded slowly a man with sullen eyes. He was carrying a dinner-pail and smoking an applewood pipe. As he neared the spot where the little boys strove, he regarded them listlessly. But suddenly he roared an oath and advanced upon the rolling fighters. "Here, you Jim, git up, now, while I belt yer life out, yeh disorderly brat." He began to kick into the chaotic mass on the ground. The boy Billie felt a heavy boot strike his head. He made a furious effort and disentangled himself from Jimmie. He tottered away.

Jimmie arose painfully from the ground and, confronting his father, began to curse him. His parent kicked him. "Come home, now," he cried, "an' stop yer jawin' er I'll lam the everlasting head off yehs."

They departed. The man paced placidly along with the apple-wood emblem of serenity between his teeth. The boy followed a dozen feet in the rear. He swore luridly, for he felt that it was degradation for one who aimed to be some vague kind of soldier, or a man of blood with a sort of sublime licence, to be taken home by a father.

2

Eventually they entered a dark region where, from a careening building, a dozen gruesome doorways gave up loads of babies to the street and the gutter. A wind of early autumn raised yellow dust from the cobbles and swirled it against a hundred windows. Long streamers of garments fluttered from fire-escapes. In all unhandy places there were buckets, brooms, rags, and bottles. In the street infants played or fought with other infants or sat stupidly in the way of vehicles. Formidable women, with uncombed hair and disordered dress, gossiped while leaning on railings, or screamed in frantic quarrels. Withered persons, in curious postures of submission to something, sat smoking pipes in obscure corners. A thousand odours of cooking food came forth to the street. The building quivered and creaked from the weight of humanity stamping about in its bowels.

A small ragged girl dragged a red, bawling infant along the crowded ways. He was hanging back, baby-like, bracing his wrinkled, bare legs. The little girl cried out: "Ah, Tommie, come ahn. Dere's Jimmie and fader. Don't be a-pullin' me back." She jerked the baby's arm impatiently. He fell on his face, roaring. With a second jerk she pulled him to his feet, and they went on. With the obstinacy of his order, he protested against being dragged in a chosen direction. He made heroic endeavours to keep on his legs, denounced his sister, and consumed a bit of orange-peeling which he chewed between the times of his infantile orations.

As the sullen-eyed man, followed by the blood-covered boy, drew near, the little girl burst into reproachful cries. "Ah, Jimmie, youse bin fightin' agin."

The urchin swelled disdainfully. "Ah, what d' hell, Mag. See?"

The little girl upbraided him. "Youse allus fightin', Jimmie, an' yeh knows it puts mudder out when yehs come home half dead, an it's like we'll all get a poundin'." She began to weep. The babe threw back his head and roared at his prospects.

"Ah," cried Jimmie, "shut up er I'll smack yer mout'. See?" As his sister continued her lamentations, he suddenly struck her. The little girl reeled, and, recovering herself, burst into tears and quaveringly cursed him. As she slowly retreated, her brother advanced, dealing her cuffs.

The father heard, and turned about. "Stop that, Jim, d'yeh hear? Leave yer sister alone on the street. It's like I can never beat any sense into yer wooden head."

The urchin raised his voice in defiance to his parent, and continued his attacks. The babe bawled tremendously, protesting with great violence. During his sister's hasty manœuvres he was dragged by the arm.

Finally the procession plunged into one of the gruesome doorways. They crawled up dark stairways and along cold, gloomy halls. At last the father pushed open a door, and they entered a lighted room in which a large woman was rampant.

She stopped in a career from a seething stove to a pan-covered table. As the father and children filed in she peered at them. "Eh, what? Been fightin' agin!" She threw herself upon Jimmie. The urchin tried to dart behind the others, and in the scuffle the babe, Tommie, was knocked down. He protested with his usual vehemence because they had bruised his tender shins against a table leg.

The mother's massive shoulders heaved with anger. Grasping the urchin by the neck and shoulder she shook him until he rattled. She dragged him to an unholy sink, and, soaking a rag in water, began to scrub his lacerated face with it. Jimmie screamed in pain, and tried to twist his shoulders out of the clasp of the huge arms.

The babe sat on the floor watching the scene, his face in contortions like that of a woman at a tragedy. The father, with a newly ladened pipe in his mouth, sat in a backless chair near the stove. Jimmie's cries annoyed him. He turned about and bellowed at his wife. "Let the kid alone for a minute, will yeh, Mary? Yer allus poundin' 'im. When I come nights I can't get no rest 'cause yer allus poundin' a kid. Let up, d'yeh hear? Don't be allus poundin' a kid." The woman's operations on the urchin instantly increased in violence. At last she tossed him to a corner, where he limply lay weeping.

The wife put her immense hands on her hips, and with a chieftain-like stride approached her husband. "Ho!" she said, with a great grunt of contempt. "An' what in the devil are you stickin' your nose for?" The babe crawled under the table, and, turning, peered out cautiously. The ragged girl retreated, and the urchin in the corner drew his legs carefully beneath him.

The man puffed his pipe calmly and put his great muddied boots on the back part of the stove. "Go t' hell," he said tranquilly.

The woman screamed, and shook her fists before her husband's eyes. The rough yellow of her face and neck flared suddenly crimson. She began to howl.

He puffed imperturbably at his pipe for a time, but finally arose and went to look out the window into the darkening chaos of back yards. "You've been drinkin', Mary," he said. "You better let up on the bot', ol' woman, or you'll git done."

"You're a liar. I ain't had a drop," she roared in reply. They had a lurid altercation.

The babe was staring out from under the table, his small face working in his excitement. The ragged girl went stealthily over to the corner where the urchin lay. "Are yehs hurted much, Jimmie?" she whispered timidly.

"Not a little bit. See?" growled the little boy.

"Will I wash d' blood?"

"Naw!"

"Will I—"

"When I catch dat Riley kid I'll break 'is face! Dat's right! See?" He turned his face to the wall as if resolved grimly to bide him time.

In the quarrel between husband and wife the woman was victor. The man seized his hat and rushed from the room, apparently determined upon a vengeful drunk. She followed to the door and thundered at him as he made his way downstairs.

She returned and stirred up the room until her children were bobbing about like bubbles. "Git outa d' way," she bawled persistently, waving feet with their dishevelled shoes near the heads of her children. She shrouded herself, puffing and snorting, in a cloud of steam at the stove, and eventually extracted a frying-pan full of potatoes that hissed. She flourished it. "Come t' yer suppers, now," she cried with sudden exasperation. "Hurry up, now, er I'll help yeh!"

The children scrambled hastily. With prodigious clatter they arranged themselves at table. The babe sat with his feet dangling high from a precarious infant's chair and gorged his small stomach. Jimmie forced, with feverish rapidity, the grease-enveloped pieces between his wounded lips. Maggie, with side glances of fear of interruption, ate like a small pursued tigress.

The mother sat blinking at them. She delivered reproaches, swallowed potatoes, and drank from a yellow-brown bottle. After a time her mood changed, and she wept as she carried little Tommie into another room and laid him to sleep, with his fists doubled, in an old quilt of faded red-and-green grandeur. Then she came and moaned by the stove. She rocked to and fro upon a chair, shedding tears and crooning miserably to the two children about their "poor mother" and "yer fader, damn 'is soul."

The little girl plodded between the table and the chair with a dishpan on it. She tottered on her small legs beneath burdens of dishes. Jimmie sat nursing his various wounds. He cast furtive glances at his mother. His practised eye perceived her gradually emerge from a mist of muddled sentiment until her brain burned in drunken heat. He sat breathless.

Maggie broke a plate.

The mother started to her feet as if propelled. "Good Gawd!" she howled. Her glittering eyes fastened on her child with sudden hatred. The fervent red of her face turned almost to purple. The little boy ran to the halls, shrieking like a monk in an earthquake. He floundered about in darkness until he found the stairs. He stumbled, panic-stricken, to the next floor.

An old woman opened a door. A light behind her threw a flare on the urchin's face. "Eh, child, what is it dis time? Is yer fader beatin' yer mudder, or yer mudder beatin' ye fader?"

3

Jimmie and the old woman listened long in the hall. Above the muffled roar of conversation, the dismal wailings of babies at night, the thumping of feet in unseen corridors and rooms, and the sound of varied hoarse shoutings in the street and the rattling of wheels over cobbles, they heard the screams of the child and the roars of the mother die away to a feeble moaning and a subdued bass muttering.

The old woman was a gnarled and leathery personage who could don at will an expression of great virtue. She possessed a small music-box capable of one tune, and a collection of "God bless yeh's" pitched in assorted keys of fervency. Each day she took a position upon the stones of Fifth Avenue, where she crooked her legs under her and crouched, immovable and hideous, like an idol. She received daily a small sum in pennies. It was contributed, for the most part, by persons who did not make their homes in that vicinity. Once, when a lady had dropped her purse on the sidewalk, the gnarled woman had grabbed it and smuggled it with great dexterity beneath her cloak. When she was arrested she had cursed the lady into a partial swoon, and with her aged limbs, twisted from rheumatism, had kicked the breath out of a huge policeman whose conduct upon that occasion she referred to when she said, "The police, damn 'em!"

"Eh, Jimmie, it's a shame," she said. "Go, now, like a dear, an' buy me a can, an' if yer mudder raises 'ell all night yehs can sleep here." Jimmie took a tendered tin pail and seven pennies and departed. He passed into the side door of a saloon and went to the bar. Straining up on his toes he raised the pail and pennies as high as his arms would let him. He saw two hands thrust down to take them. Directly the same hands let down the filled pail, and he left.

In front of the gruesome doorway he met a lurching figure. It was his father, swaying about on uncertain legs. "Give me deh can. See?" said the man.

"Ah, come off! I got dis can fer dat ol' woman, an' it 'ud be dirt teh swipe it. See?" cried Jimmie.

The father wrenched the pail from the urchin. He grasped it in both hands and lifted it to his mouth. He glued his lips to the under edge and tilted his head. His throat swelled until it seemed to grow near his chin. There was a tremendous gulping movement and the beer was gone. The man caught his breath and laughed. He hit his son on the head with the empty pail.

As it rolled clanging into the street, Jimmie began to scream, and kicked repeatedly at his father's shins. "Look at deh dirt what yeh done me," he yelled. "Deh ol' woman 'll be t'rowin' fits." He retreated to the middle of the street, but the old man did not pursue. He staggered toward the door. "I'll paste yeh when I ketch yeh!" he shouted, and disappeared.

During the evening he had been standing against a bar drinking whiskies, and declaring to all comers confidentially: "My home reg'lar livin' hell! Why do I come an' drin' whisk' here thish way? 'Cause home reg'lar livin' hell!"

Jimmie waited a long time in the street and then crept warily up through the building. He passed with great caution the door of the gnarled woman, and finally stopped outside his home and listened. He could hear his mother moving heavily about among the furniture of the room. She was chanting in a mournful voice, occasionally interjecting bursts of volcanic wrath at the father, who, Jimmie judged, had sunk down on the floor or in a corner.

"Why deh blazes don' cher try teh keep Jim from fightin'? I'll break yer jaw!" she suddenly bellowed.

The man mumbled with drunken indifference. "Ah, w'at's bitin' yeh? Wa'a's odds? W'a'makes kick?"

"Because he tears 'is clothes, yeh fool!" cried the woman in supreme wrath.

The husband seemed to become aroused. "Go chase yerself!" he thundered fiercely in reply. There was a crash against the door, and something broke into clattering fragments. Jimmy partially suppressed a yell and darted down the stairway. Below he paused and listened. He heard howls and curses, groans and shrieks—a confused chorus as if a battle were raging. With it all there was the crash of splintering furniture. The eyes of the urchin glared in his fear that one of them would discover him.

Curious faces appeared in doorways, and whispered comments passed to and fro. "Ol' Johnson's playin' horse agin."

Jimmie stood until the noises ceased and the other inhabitants of the tenement had all yawned and shut their doors. Then he crawled upstairs with the caution of an invader of a panther's den. Sounds of laboured breathing came through the broken door-panels. He pushed the door open and entered, quaking.

A glow from the fire threw red hues over the bare floor, the cracked and soiled plastering, and the overturned and broken furniture. In the middle of the floor lay his mother asleep. In one corner of the room his father's limp body hung across the seat of a chair.

The urchin stole forward. He began to shiver in dread of awakening his parents. His mother's great chest was heaving painfully. Jimmy paused and looked down at her. Her face was inflamed and swollen from drinking. Her yellow brows shaded eyelids that had grown blue. Her tangled hair tossed in waves over her forehead. Her mouth was set in the same lines of vindictive hatred that it had, perhaps, borne during the fight. Her bare red arms were thrown out above her head in an attitude of exhaustion, something, mayhap, like that of a sated villain.

The urchin bent over his mother. He was fearful lest she should open her eyes, and the dread within him was so strong that he could not forbear to stare, but hung as if fascinated over the woman's grim face. Suddenly her eyes opened. The urchin found himself looking straight into an expression which, it would seem, had the power to change his blood to salt. He howled piercingly and fell backward.

The woman floundered for a moment, tossed her arms about her head as if in combat, and again began to snore. Jimmie crawled back into the shadows and waited. A noise in the next room had followed his cry at the discovery that his mother was awake. He grovelled in the gloom, his eyes riveted upon the intervening door. He heard it creak, and then the sound of a small voice came to him. "Jimmie! Jimmie! Are yehs dere?" it whispered. The urchin started. The thin white face of his sister looked at him from the doorway of the other room. She crept to him across the floor.

The father had not moved, but lay in the same death-like sleep. The mother writhed in an uneasy slumber, her chest wheezing as if she were in the agonies of strangulation. Out at the window a florid moon was peering over dark roofs, and in the distance the waters of a river glimmered pallidly.

The small frame of the ragged girl was quivering. Her features were haggard from weeping, and her eyes gleamed with fear. She grasped the urchin's arm in her little trembling hands and they huddled in a corner. The eyes of both were drawn, by some force, to stare at the woman's face, for they thought she need only to awake and all the fiends would come from below. They crouched until the ghost mists of dawn appeared at the window, drawing close to the panes, and looking in at the prostrate, heaving body of the mother.

4

The babe, Tommie, died. He went away in an insignificant coffin, his small waxen hand clutching a flower that the girl, Maggie, had stolen from an Italian.

She and Jimmie lived.

The inexperienced fibres of the boy's eyes were hardened at an early age. He became a young man of leather. He lived some red years without labouring. During that time his sneer became chronic. He studied human nature in the gutter, and found it no worse than he thought he had reason to believe it. He never conceived a respect for the world, because he had begun with no idols that it had smashed.

He clad his soul in armour by means of happening hilariously in at a mission church where a man composed his sermons of "you's." Once a philosopher asked this man why he did not say "we" instead of "you." The man replied, "What?" While they got warm at the stove he told his hearers just where he calculated they stood with the Lord. Many of the sinners were impatient over the pictured depths of their degradation. They were waiting for soup-tickets. A reader of the words of wind-demons might have been able to see the portions of a dialogue pass to and fro between the exhorter and his hearers. "You are damned," said the preacher. And the reader of sounds might have seen the reply go forth from the ragged people: "Where's our soup?" Jimmie and a companion sat in a rear seat and commented upon the things that didn't concern them, with all the freedom of English tourists. When they grew thirsty and went out, their minds confused the speaker with Christ.

Momentarily, Jimmie was sullen with thoughts of a hopeless altitude which grew fruit. His companion said that if he should ever go to heaven he would ask for a million dollars and a bottle of beer. Jimmie's occupation for a long time was to stand at street corners and watch the world go by, dreaming blood-red dreams at the passing of pretty women. He menaced mankind at the intersections of streets. At the corners he was in life and of life. The world was going on and he was there to perceive it.

He maintained a belligerent attitude toward all well-dressed men. To him fine raiment was allied to weakness, and all good coats covered faint hearts. He and his orders were kings, to a certain extent, over the men of untarnished clothes, because these latter dreaded, perhaps, to be either killed or laughed at. Above all things he despised obvious Christians and ciphers with the chrysanthemums of aristocracy in their buttonholes. He considered himself above both of these classes. He was afraid of nothing.

When he had a dollar in his pocket his satisfaction with existence was the greatest thing in the world. So, eventually, he felt obliged to work. His father died, and his mother's years were divided up into periods of thirty days.

He became a truck-driver. There was given to him the charge of a painstaking pair of horses and a large rattling truck. He invaded the turmoil and tumble of the downtown streets, and learned to breathe maledictory defiance at the police, who occasionally used to climb up, drag him from his perch, and punch him. In the lower part of the city he daily involved himself in hideous tangles. If he and his team chanced to be in the rear he preserved a demeanour of serenity, crossing his legs and bursting forth into yells when foot passengers took dangerous dives beneath the noses of his champing horses. He smoked his pipe calmly, for he knew that his pay was marching on. If his charge was in the front, and if it became the key-trunk of chaos, he entered terrifically into the quarrel that was raging to and fro among the drivers on their high seats, and sometimes roared oaths and violently got himself arrested.

After a time his sneer grew so that it turned its glare upon all things. He became so sharp that he believed in nothing. To him the police were always actuated by malignant impulses, and the rest of the world was composed, for the most part, of despicable creatures who were all trying to take advantage of him, and with whom, in defence, he was obliged to quarrel on all possible occasions. He himself occupied a downtrodden position, which had a private but distinct element of grandeur in its isolation.

The greatest cases of aggravated idiocy were, to his mind, rampant upon the front platforms of all the street-cars. At first his tongue strove with these beings, but he eventually became superior. In him grew a majestic contempt for those strings of street-cars that followed him like intent bugs. He fell into the habit, when starting on a long journey, of fixing his eye on a high and distant object, commanding his horses to start, and then going into a trance of oblivion. Multitudes of drivers might howl in his rear, and passengers might load him with opprobrium, but he would not awaken until some blue policeman turned red and began frenziedly to seize bridles and beat the soft noses of the responsible horses.

When he paused to contemplate the attitude of the police toward himself and his fellows, he believed that they were the only men in the city who had no rights. When driving about, he felt that he was held liable by the police for anything that might occur in the streets, and that he was the common prey of all energetic officials. In revenge, he resolved never to move out of the way of anything, until formidable circumstances or a much larger man than himself forced him to it.

Foot passengers were mere pestering flies with an insane disregard for their legs and his convenience. He could not comprehend their desire to cross the streets. Their madness smote him with eternal amazement. He was continually storming at them from his throne. He sat aloft and denounced their frantic leaps, plunges, dives, and straddles. When they would thrust at, or parry, the noses of his champing horses, making them swing their heads and move their feet, and thus disturbing a stolid, dreamy repose, he swore at the men as fools, for he himself could perceive that Providence had caused it to be clearly written that he and his team had the inalienable right to stand in the proper path of the sun-chariot and, if they so minded, to obstruct its mission or take a wheel off. And if the god driver had had a desire to step down, put up his flame-coloured fists, and manfully dispute the right of way, he would have probably been immediately opposed by a scowling mortal with two sets of hard knuckles.

It is possible, perhaps, that this young man would have derided, in an axle-wide alley, the approach of a flying ferryboat. Yet he achieved a respect for a fire-engine. As one charged toward his truck, he would drive fearfully upon a sidewalk, threatening untold people with annihilation. When an engine struck a mass of blocked trucks, splitting it into fragments as a blow annihilates a cake of ice, Jimmie's team could usually be observed high and safe, with whole wheels, on the sidewalk. The fearful coming of the engine could break up the most intricate muddle of heavy vehicles at which the police had been storming for half an hour. A fire-engine was enshrined in his heart as an appalling thing that he loved with a distant, dog-like devotion. It had been known to overturn a street-car. Those leaping horses, striking sparks from the cobbles in their forward lunge, were creatures to be ineffably admired. The clang of the gong pierced his breast like a noise of remembered war.

When Jimmie was a little boy he began to be arrested. Before he reached a great age, he had a fair record. He developed too great a tendency to climb down from his truck and fight with other drivers. He had been in quite a number of miscellaneous fights, and in some general barroom rows that had become known to the police. Once he had been arrested for assaulting a Chinaman. Two women in different parts of the city, and entirely unknown to each other, caused him considerable annoyance by breaking forth, simultaneously, at fateful intervals, into wailings about marriage and support and infants.

Nevertheless, he had, on a certain starlit evening, said wonderingly and quite reverently, "Deh moon looks like hell, don't it?"

5

The girl, Maggie, blossomed in a mud-puddle. She grew to be a most rare and wonderful production of a tenement district, a pretty girl. None of the dirt of Rum Alley seemed to be in her veins. The philosophers, upstairs, downstairs, and on the same floor, puzzled over it. When a child, playing and fighting with gamins in the street, dirt disgusted her. Attired in tatters and grime, she went unseen.

There came a time, however, when the young men of the vicinity said, "Dat Johnson goil is a putty good looker." About this period her brother remarked to her: "Mag, I'll tell yeh dis! See? Yeh've eeder got t'go on d' toif er go t' work!" Whereupon she went to work, having the feminine aversion to the alternative. By a chance, she got a position in an establishment where they made collars and cuffs. She received a stool and a machine in a room where sat twenty girls of various shades of yellow discontent. She perched on the stool and treadled at her machine all day, turning out collars with a name which might have been noted for its irrelevancy to anything connected with collars. At night she returned home to her mother.

Jimmie grew large enough to take the vague position of head of the family. As incumbent of that office, he stumbled upstairs late at night, as his father had done before him. He reeled about the room, swearing at his relations, or went to sleep on the floor.

The mother had gradually risen to such a degree of fame that she could bandy words with her acquaintances among the police justices. Court officials called her by her first name. When she appeared they pursued a course which had been theirs for months. They invariably grinned, and cried out, "Hello, Mary, you here again?" Her grey head wagged in many courts. She always besieged the bench with voluble excuses, explanations, apologies, and prayers. Her flaming face and rolling eyes were a familiar sight on the island. She measured time by means of sprees, and was swollen and dishevelled.

One day the young man Pete, who as a lad had smitten the Devil's Row urchin in the back of the head and put to flight the antagonists of his friend Jimmie, strutted upon the scene. He met Jimmie one day on the street, promised to take him to a boxing match in Williamsburg, and called for him in the evening.

Maggie observed Pete.

He sat on a table in the Johnson home, and dangled his checked legs with an enticing nonchalance. His hair was curled down over his forehead in an oiled bang. His pugged nose seemed to revolt from contact with a bristling moustache of short, wire-like hairs. His blue double-breasted coat, edged with black braid, was buttoned close to a red puff tie, and his patent leather shoes looked like weapons. His mannerisms stamped him as a man who had a correct sense of his personal superiority. There were valour and contempt for circumstances in the glance of his eye. He waved his hands like a man of the world who dismisses religion and philosophy, and says "Rats!" He had certainly seen everything, and with each curl of his lip he declared that it amounted to nothing. Maggie thought he must be a very "elegant" bartender.

He was telling tales to Jimmie. Maggie watched him furtively, with half-closed eyes lit with a vague interest.

"Hully gee! Dey makes me tired," he said. "Mos' e'ry day some farmer comes in an' tries t' run d' shop. See? But d' gits t'rowed right out. I jolt dem right out in d' street before dey knows where dey is. See?"

"Sure," said Jimmie.

"Dere was a mug come in d' place d' odder day wid an idear he was goin' t' own d' place. Hully gee! he was goin' t' own d' place. I see he had a still on, an' I didn' wanna giv' 'im no stuff, so I says, 'Git outa here an' don' make no trouble,' I says like dat. See? 'Git outa here an' don' make no trouble'; like dat. 'Git outa here,' I says. See?"

Jimmie nodded understandingly. Over his features played an eager desire to state the amount of his valour in a similar crisis, but the narrator proceeded.

"Well, deh blokie he says: 'T' blazes wid it! I ain' lookin' for no scrap,' he says —see?—'but,' he says, 'I'm 'spectable cit'zen an' I wanna drink, an' quick, too.' See? 'Aw, go ahn!' I says, like dat. 'Aw, go ahn,' I says. See? 'Don' make no trouble,' I says, like dat. 'Don' make no trouble.' See? Den d' mug, he squared off an' said he was fine as silk wid his dukes—see?—an' he wan'ed a drink—quick. Dat's what he said. See?"

"Sure," repeated Jimmie.

Pete continued. "Say, I jes' jumped d' bar, an' d' way I plunked dat blokie was outa sight. See? Dat's right! In d' jaw! See? Hully gee! he t'rowed a spittoon t'rough d' front windee. Say, I t'ought I'd drop dead. But d' boss, he comes in after, an' he says: 'Pete, yehs done jes' right! Yeh've gotta keep order, an' it's all right.' See? 'It's all right,' he says. Dat's what he said."

The two held a technical discussion.

"Dat bloke was a dandy," said Pete in conclusion, "but he hadn' outa made no trouble. Dat's what I says t' dem: 'Don' come in here an' make no trouble,' I says, like dat. 'Don't make no trouble.' See?"

As Jimmie and his friend exchanged tales descriptive of their prowess, Maggie leaned back in the shadow. Her eyes dwelt wonderingly and rather wistfully upon Pete's face. The broken furniture, grimy walls, and general disorder and dirt of her home of a sudden appeared before her and began to take a potential aspect. Pete's aristocratic person looked as if it might soil. She looked keenly at him, occasionally wondering if he was feeling contempt. But Pete seemed to be enveloped in reminiscence.

"Hully gee!" said he, "dose mugs can't feaze me. Dey knows I kin wipe up d' street wid any t'ree of dem."

When he said, "Ah, what d' hell!" his voice was burdened with disdain for the inevitable and contempt for anything that fate might compel him to endure.

Maggie perceived that here was the ideal man. Her dim thoughts were often searching for far-away lands where the little hills sing together in the morning. Under the trees of her dream-gardens there had always walked a lover.

6

Pete took note of Maggie. "Say, Mag, I'm stuck on yer shape. It's outa sight," he said parenthetically, with an affable grin.

As he became aware that she was listening closely, he grew still more eloquent in his description of various happenings in his career. It appeared that he was invincible in fights. "Why," he said, referring to a man with whom he had had a misunderstanding, "dat mug scrapped like a dago. Dat's right. He was dead easy. See? He t'ought he was a scrapper. But he foun' out diff'ent. Hully gee!"

He walked to and fro in the small room, which seemed then to grow even smaller and unfit to hold his dignity, the attribute of a supreme warrior. That swing of the shoulders which had frozen the timid when he was but a lad had increased with his growth and education in the ratio of ten to one. It, combined with the sneer upon his mouth, told mankind that there was nothing in space which could appal him. Maggie marvelled at him and surrounded him with greatness. She vaguely tried to calculate the altitude of the pinnacle from which he must have looked down upon her.

"I met a chump deh odder day way up in deh city," he said. "I was goin' teh see a frien' of mine. When I was a-crossin' deh street deh chump runned plump inteh me, an' den he turns aroun' an' says,

'Yer insolen' ruffin!' he says, like dat. 'Oh, gee!' I says, 'oh, gee! git off d' eart'!' I says, like dat. See? 'Git off d' eart'!' like dat. Den deh blokie he got wild. He says I was a contempt'ble scoun'el, er somethin' like dat, an' he says I was doom' teh everlastin' pe'dition, er somethin' like dat. 'Gee!' I says, 'gee! Yer joshin' me,' I says. 'Yer joshin' me.' An' den I slugged 'im. See?"

With Jimmie in his company, Pete departed in a sort of blaze of glory from the Johnson home. Maggie, leaning from the window, watched him as he walked down the street. Here was a formidable man who disdained the strength of a world full of fists. Here was one who had contempt for brass-clothed power; one whose knuckles could ring defiantly against the granite of law. He was a knight.

The two men went from under the glimmering street lamp and passed into shadows. Turning, Maggie contemplated the dark, dust-stained walls, and the scant and crude furniture of her home. A clock, in a splintered and battered oblong box of varnished wood, she suddenly regarded as an abomination. She noted that it ticked raspingly. The almost vanished flowers in the carpet pattern, she conceived to be newly hideous. Some faint attempts which she had made with blue ribbon to freshen the appearance of a dingy curtain, she now saw to be piteous.

She wondered what Pete dined on.

She reflected upon the collar-and-cuff factory. It began to appear to her mind as a dreary place of endless grinding. Pete's elegant occupation brought him, no doubt, into contact with people who had money and manners. It was probable that he had a large acquaintance with pretty girls. He must have great sums of money to spend.

To her the earth was composed of hardships and insults. She felt instant admiration for a man who openly defied it. She thought that if the grim angel of death should clutch his heart, Pete would shrug his shoulders and say, "Oh, ev'ryt'ing goes."

She anticipated that he would come again shortly. She spent some of her week's pay in the purchase of flowered cretonne for a lambrequin. She made it with infinite care, and hung it to the slightly careening mantel over the stove in the kitchen. She studied it with painful anxiety from different points in the room. She wanted it to look well on Sunday night when, perhaps, Jimmie's friend would come. On Sunday night, however, Pete did not appear. Afterward the girl looked at it with a sense of humiliation. She was now convinced that Pete was superior to admiration for lambrequins.

A few evenings later Pete entered with fascinating innovations in his apparel. As she had seen him twice and he wore a different suit each time, Maggie had a dim impression that his wardrobe was prodigious.

"Say, Mag," he said, "put on yer bes' duds Friday night an' I'll take yehs t' d' show. See?" He spent a few moments in flourishing his clothes, and then vanished without having glanced at the lambrequin.

Over the eternal collars and cuffs in the factory Maggie spent the most of three days in making imaginary sketches of Pete and his daily environment. She imagined some half-dozen women in love with him, and thought he must lean dangerously toward an indefinite one whom she pictured as endowed with great charms of person, but with an altogether contemptible disposition. She thought he must live in a blare of pleasure. He had friends and people who were afraid of him. She saw the golden glitter of the place where Pete was to take her. It would be an entertainment of many hues and many melodies, where she was afraid she might appear small and mouse-coloured.

Her mother drank whisky all Friday morning. With lurid face and tossing hair she cursed and destroyed furniture all Friday afternoon. When Maggie came home at half-past six her mother lay asleep amid the wreck of chairs and a table. Fragments of various household utensils were scattered about the floor. She had vented some phase of drunken fury upon the lambrequin. It lay in a bedraggled heap in the corner.

"Hah!" she snorted, sitting up suddenly, "where yeh been? Why don' yeh come home earlier? Been loafin' 'round d' streets. Yer gittin' t' be a reg'lar devil."

When Pete arrived, Maggie, in a worn black dress, was waiting for him in the midst of a floor strewn with wreckage. The curtain at the window had been pulled by a heavy hand and hung by one tack, dangling to and fro in the draught through the cracks at the sash. The knots of blue ribbons appeared like violated flowers. The fire in the stove had gone out. The displaced lids and open doors showed heaps of sullen grey ashes. The remnants of a meal, ghastly, lay in a corner. Maggie's mother, stretched on the floor, blasphemed, and gave her daughter a bad name.

7

An orchestra of yellow silk women and bald-headed men, on an elevated stage near the centre of a great green-hued hall, played a popular waltz. The place was crowded with people grouped about little tables. A battalion of waiters slid among the throng, carrying trays of beer-glasses, and making change from the inexhaustible vaults of their trousers pockets. Little boys, in the costumes of French chefs, paraded up and down the irregular aisles vending fancy cakes. There was a low rumble of conversation and a subdued clinking of glasses. Clouds of tobacco smoke rolled and wavered high in air above the dull gilt of the chandeliers.

The vast crowd had an air throughout of having just quitted labour. Men with calloused hands, and attired in garments that showed the wear of an endless drudging for a living, smoked their pipes contentedly and spent five, ten, or perhaps fifteen cents for beer. There was a mere sprinkling of men who smoked cigars purchased elsewhere. The great body of the crowd was composed of people who showed that all day they strove with their hands. Quiet Germans, with maybe their wives and two or three children, sat listening to the music, with the expressions of happy cows. An occasional party of sailors from a warship, their faces pictures of sturdy health, spent the earlier hours of the evening at the small round tables. Very infrequent tipsy men, swollen with the value of their opinions, engaged their companions in earnest and confidential conversation. In the balcony, and here and there below, shone the impassive faces of women. The nationalities of the Bowery beamed upon the stage from all directions.

Pete walked aggressively up a side aisle and took seats with Maggie at a table beneath the balcony. "Two beehs!" Leaning back, he regarded with eyes of superiority the scene before them. This attitude affected Maggie strongly. A man who could regard such a sight with indifference must be accustomed to very great things. It was obvious that Pete had visited this place many times before, and was very familiar with it. A knowledge of this fact made Maggie feel little and new.

He was extremely gracious and attentive. He displayed the consideration of a cultured gentleman who knew what was due. "Say, what's eatin' yeh? Bring d' lady a big glass! What use is dat pony?"

"Don't be fresh, now," said the waiter, with some warmth, as he departed.

"Ah, git off d' eart'!" said Pete, after the other's retreating form.

Maggie perceived that Pete brought forth all his elegance and all his knowledge of high-class customs for her benefit. Her heart warmed as she reflected upon his condescension.

The orchestra of yellow silk women and bald-headed men gave vent to a few bars of anticipatory music, and a girl, in a pink dress with short skirts, galloped upon the stage. She smiled upon the throng as if in acknowledgment of a warm welcome, and began to walk to and fro, making profuse gesticulations, and singing, in brazen soprano tones, a song the words of which were inaudible. When she broke into the swift rattling measures of a chorus some half-tipsy men near the stage joined in the rollicking refrain, and glasses were pounded rhythmically upon the tables. People leaned forward to watch her and to try to catch the words of the song. When she vanished there were long rollings of applause. Obedient to more anticipatory bars, she reappeared among the half-suppressed cheering of the tipsy men. The orchestra plunged into dance music, and the laces of the dancer fluttered and flew in the glare of gas-jets. She divulged the fact that she was attired in some half-dozen skirts. It was patent that any one of them would have proved adequate for the purpose for which skirts are intended. An occasional man bent forward, intent upon the pink stockings. Maggie wondered at the splendour of the costume and lost herself in calculations of the cost of the silks and laces.

The dancer's smile of enthusiasm was turned for ten minutes upon the faces of her audience. In the finale she fell into some of those grotesque attitudes which were at the time popular among the dancers in the theatres uptown, giving to the Bowery public the diversions of the aristocratic theatre-going public at reduced rates.

"Say, Pete," said Maggie, leaning forward, "dis is great."

"Sure!" said Pete, with proper complacence.

A ventriloquist followed the dancer. He held two fantastic dolls on his knees. He made them sing mournful ditties and say funny things about geography and Ireland.

"Do dose little men talk?" asked Maggie.

"Naw," said Pete, "it's some big jolly. See?"

Two girls, set down on the bills as sisters, came forth and sang a duet which is heard occasionally at concerts given under church auspices. They supplemented it with a dance, which, of course, can never be seen at concerts given under church auspices.

After they had retired, a woman of debatable age sang a negro melody. The chorus necessitated some grotesque waddlings supposed to be an imitation of a plantation darky, under the influence, probably, of music and the moon. The audience was just enthusiastic enough over it to make her return and sing a sorrowful lay, whose lines told of a mother's love, and a sweetheart who waited, and a young man who was lost at sea under harrowing circumstances. From the faces of a score or so in the crowd the self-contained look faded. Many heads were bent forward with eagerness and sympathy. As the last distressing sentiment of the piece was brought forth, it was greeted by the kind of applause which rings as sincere.

As a final effort, the singer rendered some verses which described a vision of Britain annihilated by America, and Ireland bursting her bonds. A carefully prepared climax was reached in the last line of the last verse, when the singer threw out her arms and cried, "The star-spangled banner." Instantly a great cheer swelled from the throats of this assemblage of the masses, most of them of foreign birth. There was a heavy rumble of booted feet thumping the floor. Eyes gleamed with sudden fire, and calloused hands waved frantically in the air.

After a few moments' rest, the orchestra played noisily, and a small fat man burst out upon the stage. He began to roar a song and to stamp back and forth before the footlights, wildly waving a silk hat and throwing leers broadcast. He made his face into fantastic grimaces until he looked like a devil on a Japanese kite. The crowd laughed gleefully. His short, fat legs were never still a moment. He shouted and roared and bobbed his shock of red wig until the audience broke out in excited applause.

Pete did not pay much attention to the progress of events upon the stage. He was drinking beer and watching Maggie. Her cheeks were blushing with excitement and her eyes were glistening. She drew deeps breaths of pleasure. No thoughts of the atmosphere of the collar-and-cuff factory came to her.

With the final crash of the orchestra they jostled their way to the sidewalk in the crowd. Pete took Maggie's arm and pushed a way for her, offering to fight with a man or two. They reached Maggie's home at a late hour and stood for a moment in front of the gruesome doorway.

"Say, Mag," said Pete, "give us a kiss for takin' yeh t' d' show, will yer?"

Maggie laughed, as if startled, and drew away from him. "Naw, Pete," she said, "dat wasn't in it."

"Ah, why wasn't it?" urged Pete.

The girl retreated nervously.

"Ah, go ahn!" repeated he.

Maggie darted into the hall and up the stairs. She turned and smiled at him, then disappeared.

Pete walked slowly down the street. He had something of an astonished expression upon his features. He paused under a lamp-post and breathed a low breath of surprise. "Gee!" he said, "I wonner if I've been played fer a duffer."

8

As thoughts of Pete came to Maggie's mind, she began to have an intense dislike for all of her dresses. "What ails yeh? What makes ye be allus fixin' and fussin'?" her mother would frequently roar at her. She began to note with more interest the well-dressed women she met on the avenues. She envied elegance and soft palms. She craved those adornments of person which she saw every day on the street, conceiving them to be allies of vast importance to women. Studying faces, she thought many of the women and girls she chanced to meet smiled with serenity as though for ever cherished and watched over by those they loved.

The air in the collar-and-cuff establishment strangled her. She knew she was gradually and surely shrivelling in the hot, stuffy room. The begrimed windows rattled incessantly from the passing of elevated trains. The place was filled with a whirl of noises and odours. She became lost in thought as she looked at some of the grizzled women in the room, mere mechanical contrivances sewing seams and grinding out, with heads bent over their work, tales of imagined or real girlhood happiness, or of past drunks, or the baby at home, and unpaid wages. She wondered how long her youth would endure. She began to see the bloom upon her cheeks as something of value. She imagined herself, in an exasperating future, as a scrawny woman with an eternal grievance. She thought Pete to be a very fastidious person concerning the appearance of women.

She felt that she should love to see somebody entangle their fingers in the oily beard of the fat foreigner who owned the establishment. He was a detestable character. He wore white socks with low shoes. He sat all day delivering orations in the depths of a cushioned chair. His pocket-book deprived them of the power of retort. "What do you sink I pie fife dolla a week for? Play? No, py tamn!"

Maggie was anxious for a friend to whom she could talk about Pete. She would have liked to discuss his admirable mannerisms with a reliable mutual friend. At home, she found her mother often drunk and always raving. It seemed that the world had treated this woman very badly, and she took a deep revenge upon such portions of it as came within her reach. She broke furniture as if she were at last getting her rights. She swelled with virtuous indignation as she carried the lighter articles of household use, one by one, under the shadows of the three gilt balls, where Hebrews chained them with chains of interest.

Jimmie came when he was obliged to by circumstances over which he had no control. His well-trained legs brought him staggering home and put him to bed some nights when he would rather have gone elsewhere.

Swaggering Pete loomed like a golden sun to Maggie. He took her to a dime museum, where rows of meek freaks astonished her. She contemplated their deformities with awe, and thought them a sort of chosen tribe. Pete, racking his brains for amusement, discovered the Central Park Menagerie and the Museum of Arts. Sunday afternoons would sometimes find them at these places. Pete did not appear to be particularly interested in what he saw. He stood around looking heavy, while Maggie giggled in glee.

Once at the menagerie he went into a trance of admiration before the spectacle of a very small monkey threatening to thrash a cageful because one of them had pulled his tail and he had not wheeled about quickly enough to discover who did it. Ever after Pete knew that monkey by sight, and winked at him, trying to induce him to fight with other and larger monkeys.

At the museum, Maggie said, "Dis is outa sight!"

"Aw, rats!" said Pete; "wait till next summer an' I'll take yehs to a picnic."

While the girl wandered in the vaulted rooms, Pete occupied himself in returning, stony stare for stony stare, the appalling scrutiny of the watch-dogs of the treasures. Occasionally he would remark in loud tones, "Dat jay has got glass eyes," and sentences of the sort. When he tired of this amusement he would go to the mummies and moralize over them.

Usually he submitted with silent dignity to all that he had to go through, but at times he was goaded into comment. "Aw!" he demanded once. "Look at all dese little jugs! Hundred jugs in a row! Ten rows in a case, an' 'bout a t'ousand cases! What d' blazes use is dem?"

In the evenings of week days he often took her to see plays in which the dazzling heroine was rescued from the palatial home of her treacherous guardian by the hero with the beautiful sentiments. The latter spent most of his time out at soak in pale-green snow-storms, busy with a nickel-plated revolver rescuing aged strangers from villains. Maggie lost herself in sympathy with the wanderers swooning in snow-storms beneath happy-hued church windows, while a choir within sang "Joy to the World." To Maggie and the rest of the audience this was transcendental realism. Joy always within, and they, like the actor, inevitably without. Viewing it, they hugged themselves in ecstatic pity of their imagined or real condition. The girl thought the arrogance and granite-heartedness of the magnate of the play were very accurately drawn. She echoed the maledictions that the occupants of the gallery showered on this individual when his lines compelled him to expose his extreme selfishness.

Shady persons in the audience revolted from the pictured villainy of the drama. With untiring zeal they hissed vice and applauded virtue. Unmistakably bad men evinced an apparently sincere admiration for virtue. The loud gallery was overwhelmingly with the unfortunate and the oppressed. They encouraged the struggling hero with cries, and jeered the villain, hooting and calling attention to his whiskers. When anybody died in the pale-green snowstorms, the gallery mourned. They sought out the painted misery and hugged it as akin.

In the hero's erratic march from poverty in the first act to wealth and triumph in the final one, in which he forgives all the enemies that he has left, he was assisted by the gallery, which applauded his generous and noble sentiments and confounded the speeches of his opponents by making irrelevant but very sharp remarks. Those actors who were cursed with the parts of villains were confronted at every turn by the gallery. If one of them rendered lines containing the most subtile distinctions between right and wrong, the gallery was immediately aware that the actor meant wickedness, and denounced him accordingly. The last act was a triumph for the hero, poor and of the masses, the representative of the audience, over the villain and the rich man, his pockets stuffed with bonds, his heart packed with tyrannical purposes, imperturbable amid suffering.

Maggie always departed with raised spirits from these melodramas. She rejoiced at the way in which the poor and virtuous eventually overcame the wealthy and wicked. The theatre made her think. She wondered if the culture and refinement she had seen imitated, perhaps grotesquely, by the heroine on the stage, could be acquired by a girl who lived in a tenement house and worked in a shirt factory.

9

A group of urchins were intent upon the side door of a saloon. Expectancy gleamed from their eyes. They were twisting their fingers in excitement. "Here she comes!" yelled one of them suddenly. The group of urchins burst instantly asunder and its individual fragments were spread in a wide, respectable half-circle about the point of interest. The saloon door opened with a crash, and the figure of a woman appeared upon the threshold. Her grey hair fell in knotted masses about her shoulders. Her face was crimsoned and wet with perspiration. Her eyes had a rolling glare. "Not a cent more of me money will yehs ever get—not a red! I spent me money here fer t'ree years, an' now yehs tells me yeh'll sell me no more stuff! Go fall on yerself, Johnnie Murckre! 'Disturbance'? Disturbance be blowed! Go fall on yerself, Johnnie—"

The door received a kick of exasperation from within, and the woman lurched heavily out on the sidewalk. The gamins in the half-circle became violently agitated. They began to dance about and hoot and yell and jeer. A wide dirty grin spread over each face.

The woman made a furious dash at a particularly outrageous cluster of little boys. They laughed delightedly, and scampered off a short distance, calling out to her over their shoulders. She stood tottering on the kerb-stone and thundered at them. "Yeh devil's kids!" she howled, shaking her fists. The little boys whooped in glee. As she started up the street they fell in behind and marched uproariously. Occasionally she wheeled about and made charges on them. They ran nimbly out of reach and taunted her.

In the frame of a gruesome doorway she stood for a moment cursing them. Her hair straggled, giving her red features a look of insanity. Her great fists quivered as she shook them madly in the air. The urchins made terrific noises until she turned and disappeared. Then they filed off quietly in the way they had come.

The woman floundered about in the lower hall of the tenement house, and finally stumbled up the stairs. On an upper hall a door was opened and a collection of heads peered curiously out, watching her. With a wrathful snort the woman confronted the door, but it was slammed hastily in her face and the key was turned.

She stood for a few minutes, delivering a frenzied challenge at the panels. "Come out in deh hall, Mary Murphy, if yehs want a scrap! Come ahn! yeh overgrown terrier, come ahn!" She began to kick the door. She shrilly defied the universe to appear and do battle. Her cursing trebles brought heads from all doors save the one she threatened. Her eyes glared in every direction. The air was full of her tossing fists. "Come ahn! deh hull gang of yehs, come ahn!" she roared at the spectators. An oath or two, catcalls, jeers, and bits of facetious advice were given in reply. Missiles clattered about her feet.

"What's wrong wi'che?" said a voice in the gathered gloom, and Jimmie came forward. He carried a tin dinner-pail in his hand and under his arm a truckman's brown apron done in a bundle. "What's wrong?" he demanded.

"Come out! all of yehs, come out," his mother was howling. "Come ahn an' I'll stamp yer faces t'rough d' floor."

"Shet yer face, an' come home, yeh old fool!" roared Jimmie at her. She strode up to him and twirled her fingers in his face. Her eyes were darting flames of unreasoning rage, and her frame trembled with eagerness for a fight.

"An' who are youse? I ain't givin' a snap of my fingers fer youse!" she bawled at him. She turned her huge back in tremendous disdain and climbed the stairs to the next floor.

Jimmie followed, and at the top of the flight he seized his mother's arm and started to drag her toward the door of their room. "Come home!" he gritted between his teeth.

"Take yer hands off me! Take yer hands off me!" shrieked his mother. She raised her arm and whirled her great fist at her son's face. Jimmie dodged his head, and the blow struck him in the back of the neck. "Come home!" he gritted again. He threw out his left hand and writhed his fingers about her middle arm. The mother and the son began to sway and struggle like gladiators.

"Whoop!" said the Rum Alley Tenement house. The hall filled with interested spectators. "Hi, ol' lady, dat was a dandy!" "T'ree t' one on d' red!" "Ah, quit yer scrappin'!"

The door of the Johnson home opened and Maggie looked out. Jimmie made a supreme cursing effort and hurled his mother into the room. He quickly followed and closed the door. The Rum Alley tenement swore disappointedly and retired.

The mother slowly gathered herself up from the floor. Her eyes glittered menacingly upon her children.

"Here now," said Jimmie, "we've had enough of dis. Sit down, an' don' make no trouble."

He grasped her arm and, twisting it, forced her into a creaking chair.

"Keep yer hands off me!" roared his mother again.

"Say, yeh ol' bat! Quit dat!" yelled Jimmie, madly. Maggie shrieked and ran into the other room. To her there came the sound of a storm of crashes and curses. There was a great final thump and Jimmie's voice cried: "Dere, now! Stay still." Maggie opened the door now, and went warily out. "Oh, Jimmie!"

He was leaning against the wall and swearing. Blood stood upon bruises on his knotty forearms where they had scraped against the floor or the walls in the scuffle. The mother lay screeching on the floor, the tears running down her furrowed face.

Maggie, standing in the middle of the room, gazed about her. The usual upheaval of the tables and chairs had taken place. Crockery was strewn broadcast in fragments. The stove had been disturbed on its legs, and now leaned idiotically to one side. A pail had been upset and water spread in all directions.

The door opened and Pete appeared. He shrugged his shoulders. "Oh, gee!" he observed. He walked over to Maggie and whispered in her ear: "Ah, what d' hell, Mag? Come ahn and we'll have a outa-sight time."

The mother in the corner upreared her head and shook her tangled locks. "Aw, yer bote no good, needer of yehs," she said, glowering at her daughter in the gloom. Her eyes seemed to burn balefully. "Yeh've gone t' d' devil, Mag Johnson, yehs knows yehs have gone t' d' devil. Yer a disgrace t' yer people. An' now, git out an' go ahn wid dat doe-faced jude of yours. Go wid him, curse yeh, an' a good riddance. Go, an' see how yeh likes it."

Maggie gazed long at her mother.

"Go now, an' see how yeh likes it. Git out. I won't have sech as youse in me house! Git out, d' yeh hear! Damn yeh, git out!"

The girl began to tremble.

At this instant Pete came forward. "Oh, what d' hell, Mag, see?" whispered he softly in her ear. "Dis all blows over. See? D' ol' woman'll be all right in d' mornin'. Come ahn out wid me! We'll have a outa-sight time."

The woman on the floor cursed. Jimmie was intent upon his bruised forearms. The girl cast a glance about the room filled with a chaotic mass of *débris*, and at the writhing body of her mother.

"Git th' devil outa here."

Maggie went.

10

Jimmie had an idea it wasn't common courtesy for a friend to come to one's home and ruin one's sister. But he was not sure how much Pete knew about the rules of politeness.

The following night he returned home from work at a rather late hour in the evening. In passing through the halls he came upon the gnarled and leathery old woman who possessed the music-box. She was grinning in the dim light that drifted through dust-stained panes. She beckoned to him with a smudged forefinger.

"Ah, Jimmie, what do yehs t'ink I tumbled to, las' night! It was deh funnies' t'ing I ever saw," she cried, coming close to him and leering. She was trembling with eagerness to tell her tale. "I was by me door las' night when yer sister and her jude feller came in late, oh, very late. An' she, the dear, she was a-cryin' as if her heart would break, she was. It was deh funnies' t'ing I ever saw. An' right out here by me door she asked him did he love her, did he. An' she was a-crying as if her heart would break, poor t'ing. An' him, I could see be deh way what he said it dat she had been askin' orften; he says, 'Oh, gee, yes,' he says, says he. 'Oh, gee, yes.'"

Storm-clouds swept over Jimmie's face, but he turned from the leathery old woman and plodded on upstairs.

"'Oh, gee, yes,'" she called after him. She laughed a laugh that was like a prophetic croak.

There was no one in at home. The rooms showed that attempts had been made at tidying them. Parts of the wreckage of the day before had been repaired by an unskilled hand. A chair or two and the table stood uncertainly upon legs. The floor had been newly swept. The blue ribbons had been restored to the curtains, and the lambrequin, with its immense sheaves of yellow wheat and red roses of equal size, had been returned, in a worn and sorry state, to its place at the mantel. Maggie's jacket and hat were gone from the nail behind the door.

Jimmie walked to the window and began to look through the blurred glass. It occurred to him to wonder vaguely, for an instant, if some of the women of his acquaintance had brothers.

Suddenly, however, he began to swear. "But he was me frien'! I brought 'im here! Dat's d' devil of it!" He fumed about the room, his anger gradually rising to the furious pitch. "I'll kill deh jay! Dat's what I'll do! I'll kill deh jay!"

He clutched his hat and sprang toward the door. But it opened, and his mother's great form blocked the passage. "What's d' matter wid yeh?" exclaimed she, coming into the rooms.

Jimmie gave vent to a sardonic curse and then laughed heavily. "Well, Maggie's gone teh d' devil! Dat's what! See?"

"Eh?" said his mother.

"Maggie's gone teh d' devil! Are yehs deaf?" roared Jimmie, impatiently.

"Aw, git out!" murmured the mother, astounded.

Jimmie grunted, and then began to stare out the window. His mother sat down in a chair, but a moment later sprang erect and delivered a maddened whirl of oaths. Her son turned to look at her as she reeled and swayed in the middle of the room, her fierce face convulsed with passion, her blotched arms raised high in imprecation.

"May she be cursed for ever!" she shrieked. "May she eat nothin' but stones and deh dirt in deh street. May she sleep in deh gutter an' never see deh sun shine again. D' bloomin'—"

"Here now," said her son. "Go fall on yerself, an' quit dat."

The mother raised lamenting eyes to the ceiling. "She's d' devil's own chil', Jimmie," she whispered. "Ah, who would t'ink such a bad girl could grow up in our fambly, Jimmie, me son. Many d' hour I've spent in talk wid dat girl an' tol' her if she ever went on d' streets I'd see her damned. An' after all her bringin'-up an' what I tol' her and talked wid her, she goes teh d' bad, like a duck teh water."

The tears rolled down her furrowed face. Her hands trembled. "An den when dat Sadie MacMallister next door to us was sent teh d' devil by dat feller what worked in d' soap factory, didn't I tell our Mag dat if she—"

"Ah, dat's anudder story," interrupted the brother. "Of course, dat Sadie was nice an' all dat—but—see?—it ain't dessame as if—well, Maggie was diff'ent—see?—she was diff'ent." He was trying to formulate a theory that he had always unconsciously held, that all sisters excepting his own could, advisedly, be ruined.

He suddenly broke out again. "I'll go t'ump d' mug what done her d' harm. I'll kill 'im! He t'inks he kin scrap, but when he gits me a-chasin' 'im he'll fin' out where he's wrong, d' big stiff! I'll wipe up d' street wid 'im." In a fury he plunged out the doorway.

As he vanished the mother raised her head and lifted both hands, entreating. "May she be cursed for ever!" she cried.

In the darkness of the hallway Jimmie discerned a knot of women talking volubly. When he strode by they paid no attention to him. "She allus was a bold thing," he heard one of them cry in an eager voice. "Dere wasn't a feller come teh deh house but she'd try teh mash 'im. My Annie says deh shameless t'ing tried teh ketch her feller, her own feller, what we useter know his fader."

"I could 'a' tol' yehs dis two years ago," said a woman, in a key of triumph. "Yes, sir, it was over two years ago dat I says teh my ol' man, I says, 'Dat Johnson girl ain't straight,' I says. 'Oh, rats!' he says. 'Oh, hell!' 'Dat's all right,' I says, 'but I know what I knows,' I says, 'an' it'll come out later. You wait an' see,' I says, 'you see.' "

"Anybody what had eyes could see dat dere was somethin' wrong wid dat girl. I didn't like her actions."

On the street Jimmie met a friend. "What's wrong?" asked the latter.

Jimmie explained. "An' I'll t'ump 'im till he can't stand."

"Oh, go ahn!" said the friend. "What's deh use! Yeh'll git pulled in! Every-body'ill be on to it! An' ten plunks! Gee!"

Jimmie was determined. "He t'inks he kin scrap, but he'll fin' out diff'ent."

"Gee!" remonstrated the friend, "what's d' use?"

11

On a corner a glass-fronted building shed a yellow glare upon the pavements. The open mouth of a saloon called seductively to passengers to enter and annihilate sorrow or create rage.

The interior of the place was papered in olive and bronze tints of imitation leather. A shining bar of counterfeit massiveness extended down the side of the room. Behind it a great mahogany-imitation sideboard reached the ceiling. Upon its shelves rested pyramids of shimmering glasses that were never disturbed. Mirrors set in the face of the sideboard multiplied them. Lemons, oranges, and paper napkins, arranged with mathematical precision, sat among the glasses. Many-hued decanters of liquor perched at regular intervals on the lower shelves. A nickel-plated cash-register occupied a place in the exact centre of the general effect. The elementary senses of it all seemed to be opulence and geometrical accuracy.

Across from the bar a smaller counter held a collection of plates upon which swarmed frayed fragments of crackers, slices of boiled ham, dishevelled bits of cheese, and pickles swimming in vinegar. An odour of grasping, begrimed hands and munching mouths pervaded all.

Pete, in a white jacket, was behind the bar bending expectantly toward a quiet stranger. "A beeh," said the man. Pete drew a foam-topped glassful, and set it dripping upon the bar.

At this moment the light bamboo doors at the entrance swung open and crashed against the wall. Jimmie and a companion entered. They swaggered unsteadily but belligerently toward the bar, and looked at Pete with bleared and blinking eyes.

"Gin," said Jimmie.

"Gin," said the companion.

Pete slid a bottle and two glasses along the bar. He bent his head sideways as he assiduously polished away with a napkin at the gleaming wood. He wore a look of watchfulness.

Jimmie and his companion kept their eyes upon the bartender and conversed loudly in tones of contempt.

"He's a dandy masher, ain't he?" laughed Jimmie.

"Well, ain't he!" said the companion, sneering. "He's great, he is. Git on to deh mug on deh blokie. Dat's enough to make a feller turn handsprings in 'is sleep."

The quiet stranger moved himself and his glass a trifle farther away and maintained an attitude of obliviousness.

"Gee! ain't he hot stuff?"

"Git on to his shape!"

"Hey!" cried Jimmie, in tones of command. Pete came along slowly, with a sullen dropping of the under lip.

"Well," he growled, "what's eatin' yehs?"

"Gin," said Jimmie.

"Gin," said the companion.

As Pete confronted them with the bottle and the glasses they laughed in his face. Jimmie's companion, evidently overcome with merriment, pointed a grimy forefinger in Pete's direction. "Say, Jimmie," demanded he, "what's dat behind d' bar?"

"Looks like some chump," replied Jimmie. They laughed loudly.

Pete put down a bottle with a bang and turned a formidable face toward them. He disclosed his teeth, and his shoulders heaved restlessly. "You fellers can't guy me," he said. "Drink yer stuff an' git out an' don' make no trouble."

Instantly the laughter faded from the faces of the two men, and expressions of offended dignity immediately came.

"Aw, who has said anyt'ing t' you?" cried they in the same breath.

The quiet stranger looked at the door calculatingly.

"Ah, come off," said Pete to the two men. "Don't pick me up fer no jay. Drink yer rum an' git out an' don' make no trouble."

"Aw, go ahn!" airly cried Jimmie.

"Aw, go ahn!" airly repeated his companion.

"We goes when we git ready! See?" continued Jimmie.

"Well," said Pete in a threatening voice, "don' make no trouble."

Jimmie suddenly leaned forward with his head on one side. He snarled like a wild animal. "Well, what if we does? See?" said he.

Hot blood flushed into Pete's face, and he shot a lurid glance at Jimmie. "Well, den we'll see who's d' bes' man, you or me," he said.

The quiet stranger moved modestly toward the door.

Jimmie began to swell with valour. "Don' pick me up fer no tenderfoot. When yeh tackles me yeh tackles one of d' bes' men in d' city. See? I'm a scrapper, I am. Ain't dat right, Billie?"

"Sure, Mike," responded his companion in tones of conviction.

"Aw!" said Pete, easily. "Go fall on yerself."

The two men again began to laugh.

"What is dat talking?" cried the companion.

"Don' ast me," replied Jimmie with exaggerated contempt.

Pete made a furious gesture. "Git outa here now, an' don' make no trouble. See? Youse fellers er lookin' fer a scrap, an' it's like yeh'll fin' one if yeh keeps on shootin' off yer mout's. I know yehs! See? I kin lick better men dan yehs ever saw in yer lifes. Dat's right! See? Don' pick me up fer no stiff, er yeh might be jolted out in d' street before yeh knows where yeh is. When I comes from behind dis bar, I t'rows yehs bote inteh d' street. See?"

"Ah, go ahn!" cried the two men in chorus.

The glare of a panther came into Pete's eyes. "Dat's what I said! Unnerstan'?"

He came through a passage at the end of the bar and swelled down upon the two men. They stepped promptly forward and crowded close to him. They bristled like three roosters. They moved their heads pugnaciously and kept their shoulders braced. The nervous muscles about each mouth twitched with a forced smile of mockery.

"Well, what yer goin' t' do?" gritted Jimmie.

Pete stepped warily back, waving his hands before him to keep the men from coming too near.

"Well, what yer goin' t' do?" repeated Jimmie's ally. They kept close to him, taunting and leering. They strove to make him attempt the initial blow.

"Keep back now! Don' crowd me," said Pete ominously.

Again they chorused in contempt. "Aw, go ahn!"

In a small, tossing group, the three men edged for positions like frigates contemplating battle.

"Well, why don' yeh try t' t'row us out?" cried Jimmie and his ally with copious sneers.

The bravery of bulldogs sat upon the faces of the men. Their clenched fists moved like eager weapons. The allied two jostled the bartender's elbows, glaring at him with feverish eyes and forcing him toward the wall.

Suddenly Pete swore furiously. The flash of action gleamed from his eyes. He threw back his arm and aimed a tremendous, lightning-like blow at Jimmie's face. His foot swung a step forward and the weight of his body was behind his fist. Jimmie ducked his head, Bowery-like, with the quickness of a cat. The fierce answering blows of Jimmie and his ally crushed on Pete's bowed head.

The quiet stranger vanished.

The arms of the combatants whirled in the air like flails. The faces of the men, at first flushed to flame-coloured anger, now began to fade to the pallor of warriors in the blood and heat of a battle. Their lips curled back and stretched tightly over the gums in ghoul-like grins. Through their white, gripped teeth struggled hoarse whisperings of oaths. Their eyes glittered with murderous fire.

Each head was huddled between its owner's shoulders, and arms were swinging with marvellous rapidity. Feet scraped to and fro with a loud scratching sound upon the sanded floor. Blows left crimson blotches upon the pale skin. The curses of the first quarter-minute of the fight died away. The breaths of the fighters came wheezing from their lips and the three chests were straining and heaving. Pete at intervals gave vent to low, laboured hisses, that sounded like a desire to kill. Jimmie's ally gibbered at times like a wounded maniac. Jimmie was silent, fighting with the face of a sacrificial priest. The rage of fear shone in all their eyes, and their blood-coloured fists whirled.

At a critical moment a blow from Pete's hand struck the ally, and he crashed to the floor. He wriggled instantly to his feet and, grasping the quiet stranger's beer-glass from the bar, hurled it at Pete's head.

High on the wall it burst like a bomb, shivering fragments flying in all directions. Then missiles came to every man's hand. The place had heretofore appeared free of things to throw, but suddenly glasses and bottles went singing through the air. They were thrown point-blank at bobbing heads. The pyramids of shimmering glasses, that had never been disturbed, changed to cascades as heavy bottles were flung into them. Mirrors splintered to nothing.

The three frothing creatures on the floor buried themselves in a frenzy for blood. There followed in the wake of missiles and fists some unknown prayers, perhaps for death.

The quiet stranger had sprawled very pyrotechnically out on the sidewalk. A laugh ran up and down the avenue for the half of a block. "Dey've t'rowed a bloke inteh deh street."

People heard the sound of breaking glass and shuffling feet within the saloon and came running. A small group, bending down to look under the bamboo doors, and watching the fall of glass and three pairs of violent legs, changed in a moment to a crowd. A policeman came charging down the sidewalk and bounced through the doors into the saloon. The crowd bent and surged in absorbing anxiety to see.

Jimmie caught the first sight of the oncoming interruption. On his feet he had the same regard for a policeman that, when on his truck, he had for a fire-engine. He howled and ran for the side door.

The officer made a terrific advance, club in hand. One comprehensive sweep of the long night-stick threw the ally to the floor and forced Pete to a corner. With his disengaged hand he made a furious effort at Jimmie's coattails. Then he regained his balance and paused. "Well, well, you are a pair of pictures. What have ye been up to?"

Jimmie, with his face drenched in blood, escaped up a side street, pursued a short distance by some of the more law-loving or excited individuals of the crowd.

Later, from a safe dark corner, he saw the policeman, the ally, and the bartender emerge from the saloon. Pete locked the doors and then followed up the avenue in the rear of the crowd-encompassed policeman and his charge.

At first Jimmie, with his heart throbbing at battle heat, started to go desperately to the rescue of his friend, but he halted. "Ah, what's d' use?" he demanded of himself.

12

In a hall of irregular shape sat Pete and Maggie drinking beer. A submissive orchestra dictated to by a spectacled man with frowsy hair and in soiled evening dress, industriously followed the bobs of his head and the waves of his baton. A ballad-singer, in a gown of flaming scarlet, sang in the inevitable voice of brass. When she vanished, men seated at the tables near the front applauded loudly, pounding the polished wood with their beer-glasses. She returned attired in less gown, and sang again. She received another enthusiastic encore. She reappeared in still less gown and danced. The deafening rumble of glasses and clapping of hands that followed her exit indicated an overwhelming desire to have her come on for the fourth time, but the curiosity of the audience was not gratified.

Maggie was pale. From her eyes had been plucked all look of self-reliance. She leaned with a dependent air toward her companion. She was timid, as if fearing his anger or displeasure. She seemed to beseech tenderness of him.

Pete's air of distinguished valour had grown upon him until it threatened to reach stupendous dimensions. He was infinitely gracious to the girl. It was apparent to her that his condescension was a marvel. He could appear to strut even while sitting still, and he showed that he was a lion of lordly characteristics by the air with which he spat.

With Maggie gazing at him wonderingly, he took pride in commanding the waiters, who were, however, indifferent or deaf. "Hi, you, git a russle on yehs! What yehs lookin' at? Two more beehs, d' yeh hear?" He leaned back and critically regarded the person of a girl with a straw-coloured wig who was flinging her heels about upon the stage in somewhat awkward imitation of a well-known *danseuse.*

At times Maggie told Pete long confidential tales of her former home life, dwelling upon the escapades of the other members of the family and the difficulties she had had to combat in order to obtain a degree of comfort. He responded in the accents of philanthropy. He pressed her arm with an air of reassuring proprietorship.

"Dey was cursed jays," he said, denouncing the mother and brother.

The sound of the music which, through the efforts of the frowsy-headed leader, drifted to her ears in the smoke-filled atmosphere, made the girl dream. She thought of her former Rum Alley environment and turned to regard Pete's strong protecting fists. She thought of a collar-and-cuff manufactory and the eternal moan of the proprietor: "What een hale do you sink I pie fife dolla a week for? Play? No, py tamn!" She contemplated Pete's man-subduing eyes and noted that wealth and prosperity were indicated by his clothes. She imagined a future rose-tinted because of its distance from all that she had experienced before.

As to the present she perceived only vague reasons to be miserable. Her life was Pete's, and she considered him worthy of the charge. She would be disturbed by no particular apprehensions so long as Pete adored her as he now said he did. She did not feel like a bad woman. To her knowledge she had never seen any better.

At times men at other tables regarded the girl furtively. Pete, aware of it, nodded at her and grinned. He felt proud. "Mag, yer a bloomin' good looker," he remarked, studying her face through the haze. The men made Maggie fear, but she blushed at Pete's words as it became apparent to her that she was the apple of his eye.

Grey-headed men, wonderfully pathetic in their dissipation, stared at her through clouds. Smooth-cheeked boys, some of them with faces of stone and mouths of sin, not nearly so pathetic as the grey heads, tried to find the girl's eyes in the smoke-wreaths. Maggie considered she was not what they thought her. She confined her glances to Pete and the stage.

The orchestra played negro melodies, and a versatile drummer pounded, whacked, clattered, and scratched on a dozen machines to make noise.

Those glances of the men, shot at Maggie from under half-closed lids, made her tremble. She thought them all to be worse men than Pete. "Come, let's go," she said.

As they went out Maggie perceived two women seated at a table with some men. They were painted, and their cheeks had lost their roundness. As she passed them the girl, with a shrinking movement, drew back her skirts.

13

Jimmie did not return home for a number of days after the fight with Pete in the saloon. When he did, he approached with extreme caution.

He found his mother raving. Maggie had not returned home. The parent continually wondered how her daughter could come to such a pass. She had never considered Maggie as a pearl dropped unstained into Rum Alley from Heaven, but she could not conceive how it was possible for her daughter to fall so low as to bring disgrace upon her family. She was terrific in denunciation of the girl's wickedness.

The fact that the neighbours talked of it maddened her. When women came in, and in the course of their conversation casually asked, "Where's Maggie dese days?" the mother shook her fuzzy head at them and appalled them with curses. Cunning hints inviting confidence she rebuffed with violence.

"An' wid all d' bringin'-up she had, how could she?" moaningly she asked of her son. "Wid all d' talkin' wid her I did an' d' t'ings I tol' her to remember. When a girl is bringed up d' way I bringed up Maggie, how kin she go teh d' devil?"

Jimmie was transfixed by these questions. He could not conceive how, under the circumstances, his mother's daughter and his sister could have been so wicked.

His mother took a drink from a bottle that sat on the table. She continued her lament. "She had a bad heart, dat girl did, Jimmie. She was wicked t' d' heart an' we never knowed it."

Jimmie nodded, admitting the fact.

"We lived in d' same house wid her an' I brought her up, an' we never knowed how bad she was."

Jimmie nodded again.

"Wid a home like dis an' a mudder like me, she went teh d' bad," cried the mother, raising her eyes.

One day Jimmie came home, sat down in a chair, and began to wriggle about with a new and strange nervousness. At last he spoke shamefacedly. "Well, look-a-here, dis t'ing queers us! See? We're queered! An' maybe it 'ud be better if I—well, I t'ink I kin look 'er up an'—maybe it 'ud be better if I fetched her home an'—"

The mother started from her chair and broke forth into a storm of passionate anger. "What! Let 'er come an' sleep under deh same roof wid her mudder agin? Oh, yes, I will, won't I! Sure! Shame on yehs, Jimmie Johnson, fer sayin' such a t'ing teh yer own mudder! Little did I t'ink when yehs was a baby playin' about me feet dat ye'd grow up teh say sech a t'ing teh yer mudder—yer own mudder. I never t'ought—"

Sobs choked her and interrupted her reproaches.

"Dere ain't nottin' teh make sech trouble about," said Jimmie. "I on'y says it 'ud be better if we keep dis t'ing dark, see? It queers us! See?"

His mother laughed a laugh that seemed to ring through the city and be echoed and re-echoed by countless other laughs. "Oh, yes, I will, won't I? Sure!"

"Well, yeh must take me fer a damn fool," said Jimmie, indignant at his mother for mocking him. "I didn't say we'd make 'er inteh a little tin angel, ner nottin', but deh way it is now she can queer us! Don'che see?"

"Ay, she'll git tired of deh life atter a while, an' den she'll wanna be a-comin' home, won' she, deh beast! I'll let 'er in den, won't I?"

"Well, I didn't mean none of dis prod'gal bus'ness anyway," explained Jimmie.

"It wa'n't no prod'gal daughter, yeh fool," said the mother. "It was prod'gal son, anyhow."

"I know dat," said Jimmie.

For a time they sat in silence. The mother's eyes gloated on the scene which her imagination called before her. Her lips were set in a vindictive smile. "Ay, she'll cry, won' she, an' carry on, an' tell how Pete, or some odder feller, beats 'er, an' she'll say she's sorry an' all dat, an' she ain't happy, she ain't, an' she wants to come home agin, she does." With grim humour the mother imitated the possible wailing notes of the daughter's voice. "Den I'll take 'er in, won't I? She kin cry 'er two eyes out on deh stones of deh street before I'll dirty d' place wid her. She abused an' ill-treated her own mudder—her own mudder what loved her, an' she'll never git anodder chance."

Jimmie thought he had a great idea of women's frailty, but he could not understand why any of his kin should be victims. "Curse her!" he said fervidly. Again he wondered vaguely if some of the women of his acquaintance had brothers. Nevertheless, his mind did not for an instant confuse himself with those brothers nor his sister with theirs.

After the mother had, with great difficulty, suppressed the neighbours, she went among them and proclaimed her grief. "May Heaven forgive dat girl," was her continual cry. To attentive ears she recited the whole length and breadth of her woes. "I bringed 'er up deh way a daughter oughta be bringed up, an' dis is how she served me! She went teh deh devil deh first chance she got! May Heaven forgive her."

When arrested for drunkenness she used the story of her daughter's downfall with telling effect upon the police justices. Finally one of them said to her, peering down over his spectacles: "Mary, the records of this and other courts show that you are the mother of forty-two daughters who have been ruined. The case is unparalleled in the annals of this court, and this court thinks—"

The mother went through life shedding large tears of sorrow. Her red face was a picture of agony.

Of course Jimmie publicly damned his sister that he might appear on a higher social plane. But, arguing with himself, stumbling about in ways that he knew not, he, once, almost came to a conclusion that his sister would have been more firmly good had she better known how. However, he felt that he could not hold such a view. He threw it hastily aside.

14

In a hilarious hall there were twenty-eight tables and twenty-eight women and a crowd of smoking men. Valiant noise was made on a stage at the end of the hall by an orchestra composed of men who looked as if they had just happened in. Soiled waiters ran to and fro, swooping down like hawks on the unwary in the throng; clattering along the aisles with trays covered with glasses; stumbling over women's skirts and charging two prices for everything but beer, all with a swiftness that blurred the view of the coconut palms and dusty monstrosities painted upon the walls of the room. A "bouncer," with an immense load of business upon his hands, plunged about in the crowd, dragging bashful strangers to prominent chairs, ordering waiters here and there, and quarreling furiously with men who wanted to sing with the orchestra.

The usual smoke-cloud was present, but so dense that heads and arms seemed entangled in it. The rumble of conversation was replaced by a roar. Plenteous oaths heaved through the air. The room rang with the shrill voices of women bubbling over with drink-laughter. The chief element in the music of the orchestra was speed. The musicians played in intent fury. A woman was singing and smiling upon the stage, but no one took notice of her. The rate at which the piano, cornet, and violins were going seemed to impart wildness to the half-drunken crowd. Beer-glasses were emptied at a gulp and conversation became a rapid chatter. The smoke eddied and swirled like a shadowy river hurrying toward some unseen falls. Pete and Maggie entered the hall and took chairs at a table near the door. The woman who was seated there made an attempt to occupy Pete's attention, and, failing, went away.

Three weeks had passed since the girl had left home. The air of spaniel-like dependence had been magnified and showed its direct effect in the peculiar off-handedness and ease of Pete's ways toward her. She followed Pete's eyes with hers, anticipating with smiles gracious looks from him.

A woman of brilliance and audacity, accompanied by a mere boy, came into the place and took a seat near them. At once Pete sprang to his feet, his face beaming with glad surprise. "Hully gee, dere's Nellie!" he cried. He went over to the table and held out an eager hand to the woman.

"Why, hello, Pete, me boy, how are you?" said she, giving him her fingers.

Maggie took instant note of the woman. She perceived that her black dress fitted her to perfection. Her linen collar and cuffs were spotless. Tan gloves were stretched over her well-shaped hands. A hat of a prevailing fashion perched jauntily upon her dark hair. She wore no jewellery and was painted with no apparent paint. She looked clear-eyed through the stares of the men.

"Sit down, and call your lady friend over," she said to Pete. At his beckoning Maggie came and sat between Pete and the mere boy.

"I t'ought yeh was gone away fer good," began Pete, at once. "When did yeh git back? How did dat Buff'lo business turn out?"

The woman shrugged her shoulders. "Well, he didn't have as many stamps as he tried to make out, so I shook him, that's all."

"Well, I'm glad teh see yehs back in deh city," said Pete, with gallantry. He and the woman entered into a long conversation, exchanging reminiscences of days together. Maggie sat still, unable to formulate an intelligent sentence as her addition to the conversation, and painfully aware of it.

She saw Pete's eyes sparkle as he gazed upon the handsome stranger. He listened smilingly to all she said. The woman was familiar with all his affairs, asked him about mutual friends, and knew the amount of his salary. She paid no attention to Maggie, looking toward her once or twice and apparently seeing the wall beyond.

The mere boy was sulky. In the beginning he had welcomed the additions with acclamations. "Let's all have a drink! What'll you take, Nell? And you, Miss

What's-your-name. Have a drink, Mr. —— you, I mean." He had shown a sprightly desire to do the talking for the company and tell all about his family. In a loud voice he declaimed on various topics. He assumed a patronizing air toward Pete. As Maggie was silent, he paid no attention to her. He made a great show of lavishing wealth upon the woman of brilliance and audacity.

"Do keep still, Freddie! You talk like a clock," said the woman to him. She turned away and devoted her attention to Pete. "We'll have many a good time together again, eh?"

"Sure, Mike," said Pete, enthusiastic at once.

"Say," whispered she, leaning forward, "let's go over to Billie's and have a time."

"Well, it's dis way! See?" said Pete. "I got dis lady frien' here."

"Oh, g'way with her," argued the woman.

Pete appeared disturbed.

"All right," said she, nodding her head at him. "All right for you! We'll see the next time you ask me to go anywheres with you."

Pete squirmed. "Say," he said, beseechingly, "come wid me a minute an' I'll tell yer why."

The woman waved her hand. "Oh, that's all right, you needn't explain, you know. You wouldn't come merely because you wouldn't come, that's all." To Pete's visible distress she turned to the mere boy, bringing him speedily out of a terrific rage. He had been debating whether it would be the part of a man to pick a quarrel with Pete, or would he be justified in striking him savagely with his beer-glass without warning. But he recovered himself when the woman turned to renew her smilings. He beamed upon her with an expression that was somewhat tipsy and inexpressibly tender.

"Say, shake that Bowery jay," requested he, in a loud whisper.

"Freddie, you are so funny," she replied.

Pete reached forward and touched the woman on the arm. "Come out a minute while I tells yeh why I can't go wid yer. Yer doin' me dirt, Nell! I never t'ought ye'd do me dirt, Nell. Come on, will yer?" He spoke in tones of injury.

"Why, I don't see why I should be interested in your explanations," said the woman, with a coldness that seemed to reduce Pete to a pulp.

His eyes pleaded with her. "Come out a minute while I tells yeh. On d' level, now."

The woman nodded slightly at Maggie and the mere boy, saying, " 'Scuse me."

The mere boy interrupted his loving smile and turned a shrivelling glare upon Pete. His boyish countenance flushed and he spoke in a whine to the woman: "Oh, I say, Nellie, this ain't a square deal, you know. You aren't goin' to leave me and go off with that duffer, are you? I should think—"

"Why, you dear boy, of course I'm not," cried the woman, affectionately. She bent over and whispered in his ear. He smiled again and settled in his chair as if resolved to wait patiently.

As the woman walked down between the rows of tables, Pete was at her shoulder talking earnestly, apparently in explanation. The woman waved her hands with studied airs of indifference. The doors swung behind them, leaving Maggie and the mere boy seated at the table.

Maggie was dazed. She could dimly perceive that something stupendous had happened. She wondered why Pete saw fit to remonstrate with the woman, pleading forgiveness with his eyes. She thought she noted an air of submission about her leonine Pete. She was astounded.

The mere boy occupied himself with cocktails and a cigar. He was tranquilly silent for half an hour. Then he bestirred himself and spoke. "Well," he said, sighing, "I knew this was the way it would be. They got cold feet." There was another stillness. The boy seemed to be musing. "She was pulling m' leg. That's the whole amount of it," he said, suddenly. "It's a bloomin' shame the way that girl does. Why, I've spent over two dollars in drinks to-night. And she goes off with that plug-ugly, who looks as if he had been hit in the face with a coin die. I call it rocky treatment for a fellah like me. Here, waiter, bring me a cocktail, and make it strong."

Maggie made no reply. She was watching the doors.

"It's a mean piece of business," complained the mere boy. He explained to her how amazing it was that anybody should treat him in such a manner. "But I'll get square with her, you bet. She won't get far ahead of yours truly, you know," he added, winking. "I'll tell her plainly that it was bloomin' mean business. And she won't come it over me with any of her 'now-Freddie-dear's.' She thinks my name is Freddie, you know, but of course it ain't. I always tell these people some name like that, because if they got on to your right name they might use it sometime. Understand? Oh, they don't fool me much."

Maggie was paying no attention, being intent upon the doors. The mere boy relapsed into a period of gloom, during which he exterminated a number of cocktails with a determined air, as if replying defiantly to fate. He occasionally broke forth into sentences composed of invectives joined together in a long chain.

The girl was still staring at the doors. After a time the mere boy began to see cobwebs just in front of his nose. He spurred himself into being agreeable and insisted upon her having a Charlotte Russe and a glass of beer.

"They's gone," he remarked, "they's gone." He looked at her through the smoke-wreaths. "Shay, lil' girl, we mightish well make bes' of it. You ain't such bad-lookin' girl, y'know. Not half bad. Can't come up to Nell, though. No, can't do it! Well, I should shay not! Nell finelookin' girl! F-i-n-ine. You look bad longsider her, but by y'self ain't so bad. Have to do, anyhow. Nell gone. O'ny you left. Not half bad, though."

Maggie stood up. "I'm going home," she said.

The mere boy started. "Eh? What? Home!" he cried, struck with amazement. "I beg pardon, did hear say home?"

"I'm going home," she repeated.

"Great heavens! what hav' a struck?" demanded the mere boy of himself, stupefied. In a semi-comatose state he conducted her on board an up-town car, ostentatiously paid her fare, leered kindly at her through the rear window, and fell off the steps.

15

A forlorn woman went along a lighted avenue. The street was filled with people desperately bound on missions. An endless crowd darted at the elevated station stairs, and the horse-cars were thronged with owners of bundles.

The pace of the forlorn woman was slow. She was apparently searching for some one. She loitered near the doors of saloons and watched men emerge from them. She furtively scanned the faces in the rushing stream of pedestrians. Hurrying men, bent on catching some boat or train, jostled her elbows, failing to notice her, their thoughts fixed on distant dinners.

The forlorn woman had a peculiar face. Her smile was no smile. But when in repose her features had a shadowy look that was like a sardonic grin, as if some one had sketched with cruel forefinger indelible lines about her mouth.

Jimmie came strolling up the avenue. The woman encountered him with an aggrieved air. "Oh, Jimmie, I've been lookin' all over for yehs—" she began.

Jimmie made an impatient gesture and quickened his pace. "Ah, don't bodder me!" he said, with the savageness of a man whose life is pestered.

The woman followed him along the sidewalk in somewhat the manner of a suppliant. "But, Jimmie," she said, "yehs told me yehs—"

Jimmie turned upon her fiercely as if resolved to make a last stand for comfort and peace. "Say, Hattie, don' foller me from one end of deh city ted deh odder. Let up, will yehs! Give me a minute's res', can't yehs? Yehs makes me tired, allus taggin' me. See? Ain' yehs got no sense? Do yehs want people teh get on to me? Go chase yerself."

The woman stepped closer and laid her fingers on his arm. "But, look a' here—"

Jimmie snarled. "Oh, go teh blazes!" He darted into the front door of a convenient saloon and a moment later came out into the shadows that surrounded the side door. On the brilliantly lighted avenue he perceived the forlorn woman dodging about like a scout. Jimmie laughed with an air of relief and went away.

When he returned home he found his mother clamouring. Maggie had returned. She stood shivering beneath the torrent of her mother's wrath.

"Well, I'm damned!" said Jimmie in greeting.

His mother, tottering about the room, pointed a quivering forefinger. "Look ut her, Jimmie, look ut her. Dere's yer sister, boy. Dere's yer sister. Look ut her! Look ut her!" She screamed at Maggie with scoffing laughter.

The girl stood in the middle of the room. She edged about as if unable to find a place on the floor to put her feet.

"Ha ha, ha!" bellowed the mother. "Dere she stands! Ain't she purty? Look ut her! Ain' she sweet, deh beast? Look ut her! Ha, ha! look ut her!" She lurched forward and put her red and seamed hands upon her daughter's face. She bent down and peered keenly up into the eyes of the girl. "Oh, she's jes dessame as she ever was, ain' she? She's her mudder's putty darlin' yit, ain' she? Look ut her, Jimmie. Come here and look ut her."

The loud, tremendous railing of the mother brought the denizens of the Rum Alley tenement to their doors. Women came in the hallways. Children scurried to and fro.

"What's up? Dat Johnson party on anudder tear?"

"Naw. Young Mag's come home!"

"Git out!"

Through the open doors curious eyes stared in at Maggie. Children ventured into the room and ogled her as if they formed the front row at a theatre. Women, without, bent toward each other and whispered, nodding their heads with airs of profound philosophy.

A baby, overcome with curiosity concerning this object at which all were looking, sidled forward and touched her dress, cautiously, as if investigating a red-hot stove. Its mother's voice rang out like a warning trumpet. She rushed forward and grabbed her child, casting a terrible look of indignation at the girl.

Maggie's mother paced to and fro, addressing the doorful of eyes, expounding like a glib showman. Her voice rang through the building. "Dere she stands," she cried, wheeling suddenly and pointing with dramatic finger. "Dere she stands! Look ut her! Ain' she a dandy? An' she was so good as to come home teh her mudder, she was! Ain' she a beaut'? Ain' she a dandy?"

The jeering cries ended in another burst of shrill laughter.

The girl seemed to awaken. "Jimmie—"

He drew hastily back from her. "Well, now, yer a t'ing, ain' yeh?" he said, his lips curling in scorn. Radiant virtue sat upon his brow, and his repelling hands expressed horror of contamination.

Maggie turned and went.

The crowd at the door fell back precipitately. A baby falling down in front of the door wrenched a scream like that of a wounded animal from its mother. Another woman sprang forward and picked it up with a chivalrous air, as if rescuing a human being from an oncoming express train.

As the girl passed down through the hall, she went before open doors framing more eyes strangely microscopic, and sending broad beams of inquisitive light into the darkness of her path. On the second floor she met the gnarled old woman who possessed the music-box.

"So," she cried, " 'ere yehs are back again, are yehs? An' dey've kicked yehs out? Well, come in an' stay wid me t'-night. I ain' got no moral standin'."

From above came an unceasing babble of tongues, over all of which rang the mother's derisive laughter.

16

Pete did not consider that he had ruined Maggie. If he had thought that her soul could never smile again, he would have believed the mother and brother, who were pyrotechnic over the affair, to be responsible for it. Besides, in his world, souls did not insist upon being able to smile. "What d' hell?"

He felt a trifle entangled. It distressed him. Revelations and scenes might bring upon him the wrath of the owner of the saloon, who insisted upon respectability of an advanced type. "What do dey wanna raise such a smoke about it fer?" demanded he of himself, disgusted with the attitude of the family. He saw no necessity that people should lose their equilibrium merely because their sister or daughter had stayed away from home. Searching about in his mind for possible reasons for their conduct, he came upon the conclusion that Maggie's motives were correct, but that the two others wished to snare him. He felt pursued.

The woman whom he had met in the hilarious hall showed a disposition to ridicule him. "A little pale thing with no spirit," she said. "Did you note the expression of her eyes? There was something in them about pumpkin pie and virtue. That is a peculiar way the left corner of her mouth has of twitching, isn't it? Dear, dear, Pete, what are you coming to?"

Pete asserted at once that he never was very much interested in the girl. The woman interrupted him, laughing. "Oh, it's not of the slightest consequence to me, my dear young man. You needn't draw maps for my benefit. Why should I be concerned about it?" But Pete continued with his explanations. If he was laughed at for his tastes in women, he felt obliged to say that they were only temporary or indifferent ones.

The morning after Maggie had departed from home Pete stood behind the bar. He was immaculate in white jacket and apron, and his hair was plastered over his brow with infinite correctness. No customers were in the place. Pete was twisting his napkined fist slowly in a beer-glass, softly whistling to himself, and occasionally holding the object of his attention between his eyes and a few weak beams of sunlight that found their way over the thick screens and into the shaded rooms.

With lingering thoughts of the woman of brilliance and audacity, the bartender raised his head and stared through the varying cracks between the swaying bamboo doors. Suddenly the whistling pucker faded from his lips. He saw Maggie walking slowly past. He gave a great start, fearing for the previously mentioned eminent respectability of the place.

He threw a swift, nervous glance about him, all at once feeling guilty. No one was in the room. He went hastily over to the side door. Opening it and looking out, he perceived Maggie standing, as if undecided, at the corner. She was searching the place with her eyes. As she turned her face toward him, Pete beckoned to her hurriedly, intent upon returning with speed to a position behind the bar, and to the atmosphere of respectability upon which the proprietor insisted.

Maggie came to him, the anxious look disappearing from her face and a smile wreathing her lips. "Oh, Pete—" she began brightly.

The bartender made a violent gesture of impatience. "Oh, say," cried he vehemently. "What d' yeh wanna hang aroun' here fer? Do yer wanna git me inteh trouble?" he demanded with an air of injury.

Astonishment swept over the girl's features. "Why, Pete! yehs tol' me—"

Pete's glance expressed profound irritation. His countenance reddened with the anger of a man whose respectability is being threatened. "Say, yehs makes me tired! See! What d' yeh wanna tag aroun' atter me fer? Yeh'll do me dirt wid' d' ol' man an' dey'll be trouble! If he sees a woman roun' here he'll go crazy an' I'll lose me job! See? Ain' yehs got no sense? Don' be allus bodderin' me. See? Yer brudder came in here an' made trouble an' d' ol' man hadda put up fer it! An' now I'm done! See? I'm done."

The girl's eyes stared into his face. "Pete, don' yeh remem—"

"Oh, go ahn!" interrupted Pete, anticipating.

The girl seemed to have a struggle with herself. She was apparently bewildered and could not find speech. Finally she asked in a low voice, "But where kin I go?"

The question exasperated Pete beyond the powers of endurance. It was a direct attempt to give him some responsibility in a matter that did not concern him. In his indignation he volunteered information. "Oh, go to hell!" cried he. He slammed the door furiously and returned, with an air of relief, to his respectability.

Maggie went away. She wandered aimlessly for several blocks. She stopped once and asked aloud a question of herself: "Who?" A man who was passing near her shoulder humorously took the questioning word as intended for him. "Eh! What? Who? Nobody! I didn't say anything," he laughingly said, and continued his way.

Soon the girl discovered that if she walked with such apparent aimlessness, some men looked at her with calculating eyes. She quickened her step, frightened. As a protection, she adopted a demeanour of intentness as if going somewhere.

After a time she left rattling avenues and passed between rows of houses with sternness and stolidity stamped upon their features. She hung her head, for she felt their eyes grimly upon her.

Suddenly she came upon a stout gentleman in a silk hat and a chaste black coat, whose decorous row of buttons reached from his chin to his knees. The girl had heard of the grace of God and she decided to approach this man. His beaming, chubby face was a picture of benevolence and kind-heartedness. His eyes shone good will.

But as the girl timidly accosted him he made a convulsive movement and saved his respectability by a vigorous side-step. He did not risk it to save a soul. For how was he to know that there was a soul before him that needed saving?

17

Upon a wet evening, several months later, two interminable rows of cars, pulled by slipping horses, jangled along a prominent side street. A dozen cabs, with coat-enshrouded drivers, clattered to and fro. Electric lights, whirring softly, shed a blurred radiance. A flower-dealer, his feet tapping impatiently, his nose and his wares glistening with raindrops, stood behind an array of roses and chrysanthemums. Two or three theatres emptied a crowd upon the stormswept sidewalks. Men pulled their hats over their eyebrows and raised their collars to their ears. Women shrugged impatient shoulders in their warm cloaks and stopped to arrange their skirts for a walk through the storm. People who had been constrained to comparative silence for two hours burst into a roar of conversation, their hearts still kindling from the glowings of the stage.

The sidewalks became tossing seas of umbrellas. Men stepped forth to hail cabs or cars, raising their fingers in varied forms of polite request or imperative demand. An endless procession wended toward elevated stations. An atmosphere of pleasure and prosperity seemed to hang over the throng, born, perhaps, of good clothes and of two hours in a place of forgetfulness.

In the mingled light and gloom of an adjacent park, a handful of wet wanderers, in attitudes of chronic dejection, were scattered among the benches.

A girl of the painted cohorts of the city went along the street. She threw changing glances at men who passed her, giving smiling invitations to those of rural or untaught pattern and usually seeming sedately unconscious of the men with a metropolitan seal upon their faces. Crossing glittering avenues, she went into the throng emerging from the places of forgetfulness. She hurried forward through the crowd as if intent upon reaching a distant home, bending forward in her handsome cloak, daintily lifting her skirts, and picking for her well-shod feet the dryer spots upon the sidewalks.

The restless doors of saloons, clashing to and fro, disclosed animated rows of men before bars and hurrying barkeepers. A concert-hall gave to the street faint sounds of swift, machine-like music, as if a group of phantom musicians were hastening.

A tall young man, smoking a cigarette with a sublime air, strolled near the girl. He had on evening dress, a moustache, a chrysanthemum, and a look of *ennui*, all of which he kept carefully under his eye. Seeing the girl walk on as if such a young man as he was not in existence, he looked back transfixed with interest. He stared glassily for a moment, but gave a slight convulsive start when he discerned that she was neither new, Parisian, nor theatrical. He wheeled about hastily and turned his stare into the air, like a sailor with a searchlight.

A stout gentleman, with pompous and philanthropic whiskers, went stolidly by, the broad of his back sneering at the girl. A belated man in business clothes, and in haste to catch a car, bounced against her shoulder. "Hi, there, Mary, I beg your pardon! Brace up, old girl." He grasped her arm to steady her, and then was away running down the middle of the street.

The girl walked on out of the realm of restaurants and saloons. She passed more glittering avenues and went into darker blocks than those where the crowd travelled.

A young man in light overcoat and Derby hat received a glance shot keenly from the eyes of the girl. He stopped and looked at her, thrusting his hands into his pockets and making a mocking smile curl his lips. "Come, now, old lady," he said, "you don't mean to tell me that you sized me up for a farmer?"

A labouring man marched along with bundles under his arms. To her remarks he replied, "It's a fine evenin', ain't it?"

She smiled squarely into the face of a boy who was hurrying by with his hands buried in his overcoat pockets, his blond locks bobbing on his youthful temples, and a cheery smile of unconcern upon his lips. He turned his head and smiled back at her, waving his hands. "Not this eve—some other eve."

A drunken man, reeling in her pathway, began to roar at her. "I ain' go' no money!" he shouted, in a dismal voice. He lurched on up the street, wailing to himself: "I ain' go' no money. Ba' luck. Ain' go' no more money."

The girl went into gloomy districts near the river, where the tall black factories shut in the street and only occasional broad beams of light fell across the sidewalks from saloons. In front of one of these places, whence came the sound of a violin vigorously scraped, the patter of feet on boards, and the ring of loud laughter, there stood a man with blotched features.

Farther on in the darkness she met a ragged being with shifting, bloodshot eyes and grimy hands.

She went into the blackness of the final block. The shutters of the tall buildings were closed like grim lips. The structures seemed to have eyes that looked over them, beyond them, at other things. Afar off the lights of the avenues glittered as if from an impossible distance. Streetcar bells jingled with a sound of merriment.

At the feet of the tall buildings appeared the deathly black hue of the river. Some hidden factory sent up a yellow glare, that lit for a moment the waters lapping oilily against timbers. The varied sounds of life, made joyous by distance and seeming unapproachables, came faintly and died away to a silence.

18

In a partitioned-off section of a saloon sat a man with a half-dozen women, gleefully laughing, hovering about him. The man had arrived at that stage of drunkenness where affection is felt for the universe. "I'm good f'ler, girls," he said, convincingly. "I'm good f'ler. An'body trea's me right, I allus trea's zem right! See?"

The women nodded their heads approvingly. "To be sure," they cried in hearty chorus. "You're the kind of a man we like, Pete. You're outa sight! What yeh goin' to buy this time, dear?"

"An't'ing yehs wants!" said the man in an abandonment of good will. His countenance shone with the true spirit of benevolence. He was in the proper mood of missionaries. He would have fraternized with obscure Hottentots. And above all he was overwhelmed in tenderness for his friends, who were all illustrious. "An't'ing yehs wants!" repeated he, waving his hands with beneficent recklessness. "I'm good f'ler, girls, an' if an'body trea's me right I—Here," called he through an open door to a waiter, "bring girls drinks. What 'ill yehs have, girls? An't'ing yehs want."

The waiter glanced in with the disgusted look of the man who serves intoxicants for the man who takes too much of them. He nodded his head shortly at the order from each individual, and went.

"W' 're havin' great time," said the man. "I like you girls! Yer right sort! See?" He spoke at length and with feeling concerning the excellences of his assembled friends. "Don' try pull man's leg, but have a good time! Dass right! Dass way teh do! Now, if I s'ought yehs tryin' work me fer drinks, wouldn' buy notting! But yer right sort! Yehs know how ter treat a f'ler, an' I stays by yehs till spen' las' cent! Dass right! I'm good f'ler an' I knows when an'body trea's me right!"

Between the times of the arrival and departure of the waiter, the man discoursed to the women on the tender regard he felt for all living things. He laid stress upon the purity of his motives in all dealings with men in the world, and spoke of the fervour of his friendship for those who were amiable. Tears welled slowly from his eyes. His voice quavered when he spoke to his companions.

Once when the waiter was about to depart with an empty tray, the man drew a coin from his pocket and held it forth. "Here," said he, quite magnificently, "here's quar'."

The waiter kept his hands on his tray. "I don't want yer money," he said.

The other put forth the coin with tearful insistence. "Here's quar'!" cried he, "take 't! Yer goo' f'ler an' I wan' yehs take 't!"

"Come, come, now," said the waiter, with the sullen air of a man who is forced into giving advice. "Put yer mon in yer pocket! Yer loaded an' yehs on'y makes a fool of yerself."

As the waiter passed out of the door the man turned pathetically to the women. "He don't know I'm goo' f'ler," cried he, dismally.

"Never you mind, Pete, dear," said the woman of brilliance and audacity, laying her hand with great affection upon his arm. "Never you mind, old boy! We'll stay by you, dear!"

"Dass ri'!" cried the man, his face lighting up at the soothing tones of the woman's voice. "Dass ri'; I'm goo' f'ler, an' w'en any one trea's me ri', I trea's zem ri'! Shee?"

"Sure!" cried the women. "And we're not goin' back on you, old man."

The man turned appealing eyes to the woman. He felt that if he could be convicted of a contemptible action he would die. "Shay, Nell, I allus trea's yehs shquare, didn' I? I allus been goo' f'ler wi' yehs, ain't I, Nell?"

"Sure you have, Pete," assented the woman. She delivered an oration to her companions. "Yessir, that's a fact. Pete's a square fellah, he is. He never goes back on a friend. He's the right kind an' we stay by him, don't we, girls?"

"Sure!" they exclaimed. Looking lovingly at him they raised their glasses and drank his health.

"Girlsh," said the man, beseechingly, "I allus trea's yehs ri', didn' I? I'm goo' f'ler, ain't I, girlsh?"

"Sure!" again they chorused.

"Well," said he finally, "le's have nozzer drink, zen."

"That's right," hailed a woman, "that's right. Ye no bloomin' jay! Yer spends yer money like a man. Dat's right."

The man pounded the table with his quivering fists. "Yessir," he cried, with deep earnestness, as if some one disputed him. "I'm goo' f'ler, an' w'en any one trea's me ri', I allus trea's—le's have nozzer drink." He began to beat the wood with his glass. "Shay!" howled he, growing suddenly impatient. As the waiter did not then come, the man swelled with wrath. "Shay!" howled he again. The waiter appeared at the door. "Bringsh drinksh," said the man.

The waiter disappeared with the orders.

"Zat f'ler fool!" cried the man. "He insul' me! I'm ge'man! Can' stan' be insul'! I'm goin' lick 'im when comes!"

"No, no!" cried the women, crowding about and trying to subdue him. "He's all right! He didn't mean anything! Let it go! He's a good fellah!"

"Di'n' he insul' me?" asked the man earnestly.

"No," said they. "Of course he didn't! He's all right!"

"Sure he didn' insul' me?" demanded the man, with deep anxiety in his voice.

"No, no! We know him! He's a good fellah. He didn't mean anything."

"Well, zen," said the man resolutely, "I'm go' 'pol'gize!"

When the waiter came, the man struggled to the middle of the floor. "Girlsh shed you insul' me! I shay—lie! I 'pol'gize!"

"All right," said the waiter.

The man sat down. He felt a sleepy but strong desire to straighten things out and have a perfect understanding with everybody. "Nell, I allus trea's yeh shquare, di'n' I? Yeh likes me, don' yehs, Nell? I'm goo' f'ler?"

"Sure!" said the woman.

"Yeh knows I'm stuck on yehs, don' yehs, Nell?"

"Sure!" she repeated carelessly.

Overwhelmed by a spasm of drunken adoration, he drew two or three bills from his pocket and, with the trembling fingers of an offering priest, laid them on the table before the woman. "Yehs knows yehs kin have all I got, 'cause I'm stuck on yehs, Nell, I—I'm stuck on yehs, Nell—buy drinksh—we're havin' grea' time—w'en any one trea's me ri'—I—Nell—we're havin' heluva—time."

Presently he went to sleep with his swollen face fallen forward on his chest.

The women drank and laughed, not heeding the slumbering man in the corner. Finally he lurched forward and fell groaning to the floor.

The women screamed in disgust and drew back their skirts.

"Come ahn!" cried one, starting up angrily, "let's get out of here."

The woman of brilliance and audacity stayed behind, taking up the bills and stuffing them into a deep, irregularly shaped pocket. A guttural snore from the recumbent man caused her to turn and look down at him. She laughed. "What a fool!" she said and went.

The smoke from the lamps settled heavily down in the little compartment, obscuring the way out. The smell of oil, stifling in its intensity, pervaded the air. The wine from an overturned glass dripped softly down upon the blotches on the man's neck.

19

In a room a woman sat at a table eating like a fat monk in a picture.

A soiled, unshaven man pushed open the door and entered. "Well," said he, "Mag's dead."

"What?" said the woman, her mouth filled with bread.

"Mag's dead," repeated the man.

"Deh blazes she is!" said the woman. She continued her meal.

When she finished her coffee she began to weep. "I kin remember when her two feet was no bigger dan yer t'umb, and she weared worsted boots," moaned she.

"Well, what a' dat?" said the man.

"I kin remember when she weared worsted boots," she cried.

The neighbours began to gather in the hall, staring in at the weeping woman as if watching the contortions of a dying dog. A dozen women entered and lamented with her. Under their busy hands the room took on that appalling appearance of neatness and order with which death is greeted.

Suddenly the door opened and a woman in a black gown rushed in with outstretched arms. "Ah, poor Mary!" she cried, and tenderly embraced the moaning one. "Ah, what ter'ble affliction is dis!" continued she. Her vocabulary was derived from mission churches. "Me poor Mary, how I feel fer yehs! Ah, what a ter'ble affliction is a disobed'ent chile." Her good, motherly face was wet with tears. She trembled in eagerness to express her sympathy.

The mourner sat with bowed head, rocking her body heavily to and fro, and crying out in a high, strained voice that sounded like a dirge on some forlorn pipe. "I kin remember when she weared worsted boots, an' her two feets was no bigger dan yer t'umb, an' she weared worsted boots, Miss Smith," she cried, raising her streaming eyes.

"Ah, me poor Mary!" sobbed the woman in black. With low, coddling cries, she sank on her knees by the mourner's chair, and put her arms about her. The other women began to groan in different keys.

"Yer poor misguided chil' is gone now, Mary, an' let us hope it's fer deh bes'. Yeh'll fergive her now, Mary, won't yehs, dear, all her disobed'ence? All her t'ankless behaviour to her mudder an' all her badness? She's gone where her ter'ble sins will be judged."

The woman in black raised her face and paused. The inevitable sunlight came streaming in at the window and shed a ghastly cheerfulness upon the faded hues of the room. Two or three of the spectators were sniffling, and one was weeping loudly.

The mourner arose and staggered into the other room. In a moment she emerged with a pair of faded baby shoes held in the hollow of her hand. "I kin remember when she used to wear dem!" cried she. The women burst anew into cries as if they had all been stabbed. The mourner turned to the soiled and unshaven man. "Jimmie, boy, go git yer sister! Go git yer sister an' we'll put deh boots on her feets!"

"Dey won't fit her now, yeh fool," said the man.

"Go git yer sister, Jimmie!" shrieked the woman, confronting him fiercely.

The man swore sullenly. He went over to a corner and slowly began to put on his coat. He took his hat and went out, with a dragging, reluctant step.

The woman in black came forward and again besought the mourner. "Yeh'll fergive her, Mary! Yeh'll fergive yer bad, bad chil'! Her life was a curse an' her days were black, an' yeh'll fergive yer bad girl? She's gone where her sins will be judged."

"She's gone where her sins will be judged!" cried the other women, like a choir at a funeral.

"Deh Lord gives and deh Lord takes away," said the woman in black, raising her eyes to the sunbeams.

"Deh Lord gives and deh Lord takes away," responded the others.

"Yeh'll fergive her, Mary?" pleaded the woman in black.

The mourner essayed to speak, but her voice gave way. She shook her great shoulders frantically, in an agony of grief. The tears seemed to scald her face. Finally her voice came and arose in a scream of pain. "Oh, yes, I'll fergive her! I'll fergive her!"

Henry James

✻ 1843-1916

James was born in New York City, the second son of Henry James, philosopher, theologian, and rebel intellectual. James's older brother William was Harvard's famous psychologist. During Henry's childhood and adolescence the family lived all over Europe and the Atlantic seaboard of the United States. His schooling was wide of range but unsystematic. James studied briefly at Harvard Law School, and then began to write criticism and stories. He continued to travel, and in 1876 he settled in England, where he stayed for the rest of his life. James's lifelong concern was the development and perfection of the writer's art. His veneration for his calling was extreme, and his constant analysis and reworking of his own fiction is recorded in his Notebooks. James published a prodigious number of works. The New York Edition of The Novels and Tales of Henry James *contains 26 volumes. On February 21, 1881, James recorded in his notebook an anecdote, told him the previous evening, which was the seed of* Washington Square, *published in the same year.*

Washington Square

1

During a portion of the first half of the present century, and more particularly during the latter part of it, there flourished and practised in the city of New York a physician who enjoyed perhaps an exceptional share of the consideration which, in the United States, has always been bestowed upon distinguished members of the medical profession. This profession in America has constantly been held in honor, and more successfully than elsewhere has put forward a claim to the epithet of "liberal." In a country in which, to play a social part, you must either earn your income or make believe that you earn it, the healing art has appeared in a high degree to combine two recognized sources of credit. It belongs to the realm of the practical, which in the United States is a great recommendation; and it is touched by the light of science—a merit appreciated in a community in which the love of knowledge has not always been accompanied by leisure and opportunity.

It was an element in Doctor Sloper's reputation that his learning and his skill were very evenly balanced; he was what you might call a scholarly doctor, and yet there was nothing abstract in his remedies—he always ordered you to take something. Though he was felt to be extremely thorough, he was not uncomfortably theoretic; and if he sometimes explained matters rather more minutely than might seem of use to the patient, he never went so far (like some practitioners one had heard of) as to trust to the explanation alone, but always left behind him an inscrutable prescription. There were some doctors that left the prescription without offering any explanation at all; and he did not belong to that class either, which was after all the most vulgar. It will be seen that I am describing a clever man; and this is really the reason why Doctor Sloper had become a local celebrity.

At the time at which we are chiefly

concerned with him he was some fifty years of age, and his popularity was at its height. He was very witty, and he passed in the best society of New York for a man of the world—which, indeed, he was, in a very sufficient degree. I hasten to add, to anticipate possible misconception, that he was not the least of a charlatan. He was a thoroughly honest man—honest in a degree of which he had perhaps lacked the opportunity to give the complete measure; and, putting aside the great good-nature of the circle in which he practised, which was rather fond of boasting that it possessed the "brightest" doctor in the country, he daily justified his claim to the talents attributed to him by the popular voice. He was an observer, even a philosopher, and to be bright was so natural to him, and (as the popular voice said) came so easily, that he never aimed at mere effect, and had none of the little tricks and pretensions of second-rate reputations. It must be confessed that fortune had favored him, and that he had found the path to prosperity very soft to his tread. He had married, at the age of twenty-seven, for love, a very charming girl, Miss Catherine Harrington, of New York, who, in addition to her charms, had brought him a solid dowry. Mrs. Sloper was amiable, graceful, accomplished, elegant, and in 1820 she had been one of the pretty girls of the small but promising capital which clustered about the Battery and overlooked the Bay, and of which the uppermost boundary was indicated by the grassy waysides of Canal Street. Even at the age of twenty-seven Austin Sloper had made his mark sufficiently to mitigate the anomaly of his having been chosen among a dozen suitors by a young woman of high fashion, who had ten thousand dollars of income and the most charming eyes in the island of Manhattan. These eyes, and some of their accompaniments, were for about five years a source of extreme satisfaction to the young physician, who was both a devoted and a very happy husband.

The fact of his having married a rich woman made no difference in the line he had traced for himself, and he cultivated his profession with as definite a purpose as if he still had no other resources than his fraction of the modest patrimony which, on his father's death, he had shared with his brothers and sisters. This purpose had not been preponderantly to make money—it had been rather to learn something and to do something. To learn something interesting, and to do something useful—this was, roughly speaking, the programme he had sketched, and of which the accident of his wife having an income appeared to him in no degree to modify the validity. He was fond of his practice, and of exercising a skill of which he was agreeably conscious, and it was so patent a truth that if he were not a doctor there was nothing else he could be, that a doctor he persisted in being, in the best possible conditions. Of course his easy domestic situation saved him a good deal of drudgery, and his wife's affiliation to the "best people" brought him a good many of those patients whose symptoms are, if not more interesting in themselves than those of the lower orders, at least more consistently displayed. He desired experience, and in the course of twenty years he got a great deal. It must be added that it came to him in some forms which, whatever might have been their intrinsic value, made it the reverse of welcome. His first child, a little boy of extraordinary promise, as the Doctor, who was not addicted to easy enthusiasm, firmly believed, died at three years of age, in spite of everything that the mother's tenderness and the father's science could invent to save him. Two years later Mrs. Sloper gave birth to a second infant—an infant of a sex which rendered the poor child, to the Doctor's sense, an inadequate substitute for his lamented first-born, of whom he had promised himself to make an admirable man. The little girl was a disappointment; but this was not the worst. A week after her birth the young mother, who, as the phrase is, had been doing well, suddenly betrayed alarming symptoms, and before another week had elapsed Austin Sloper was a widower.

For a man whose trade was to keep people alive he had certainly done poorly in his own family; and a bright doctor who within three years loses his wife and his little boy should perhaps be prepared to see either his skill or his affection impugned. Our friend, however, escaped criticism; that is, he escaped all criticism but his own, which was much the most competent and most formidable. He walked under the weight of this very private censure for the rest of his days, and bore forever the scars of a castigation to which the strongest hand he knew had treated him on the night that followed his wife's death. The world, which, as I have said, appreciated him, pitied him too much to be ironical; his misfortune made him more interesting, and even helped him to be the fashion. It was observed that even medical families cannot escape the more insidious forms of disease, and that, after all, Doctor Sloper had lost other patients besides the two I have mentioned; which constituted an honorable precedent. His little girl remained to him; and though she was not what he had desired, he proposed to himself to make the best of her. He had on hand a stock of unexpended authority, by which the child, in its early years, profited largely. She had been named, as a matter of course, after her poor mother, and even in her most diminutive babyhood the Doctor never called her anything but Catherine. She grew up a very robust and healthy child, and her father, as he looked at her, often said to himself that, such as she was, he at least need have no fear of losing her. I say "such as she was," because, to tell the truth— But this is a truth of which I will defer the telling.

2

When the child was about ten years old, he invited his sister, Mrs. Penniman, to come and stay with him. The Miss Slopers had been but two in number, and both of them had married early in life. The younger, Mrs. Almond by name, was the wife of a prosperous merchant and the mother of a blooming family. She bloomed herself, indeed, and was a comely, comfortable, reasonable woman, and a favorite with her clever brother, who, in the matter of women, even when they were nearly related to him, was a man of distinct preferences. He preferred Mrs. Almond to his sister Lavinia, who had married a poor clergyman, of a sickly constitution and a flowery style of eloquence, and then, at the age of thirty-three, had been left a widow—without children, without fortune—with nothing but the memory of Mr. Penniman's flowers of speech, a certain vague aroma of which hovered about her own conversation. Nevertheless, he had offered her a home under his own roof, which Lavinia accepted with the alacrity of a woman who had spent the ten years of her married life in the town of Poughkeepsie. The Doctor had not proposed to Mrs. Penniman to come and live with him indefinitely; he had suggested that she should make an asylum of his house while she looked about for unfurnished lodgings. It is uncertain whether Mrs. Penniman ever instituted a search for unfurnished lodgings, but it is beyond dispute that she never found them. She settled herself with her brother and never went away, and, when Catherine was twenty years old, her Aunt Lavinia was still one of the most striking features of her immediate *entourage*. Mrs. Penniman's own account of the matter was that she had remained to take charge of her niece's education. She had given this account, at least, to every one but the Doctor, who never asked for explanations which he could entertain himself any day with inventing. Mrs. Penniman, moreover, though she had a good deal of a certain sort of artificial assurance, shrunk, for indefinable reasons, from presenting herself to her brother as a fountain of instruction. She had not a high sense of humor, but she had enough to prevent her from making this mistake; and her brother, on his side, had enough to excuse her, in her situation, for laying him under contribution during a considerable part of a lifetime. He therefore assented tacitly to the proposition which Mrs. Penniman had tacitly laid down, that it was of importance that the poor motherless girl should have a brilliant woman near her. His assent could only be tacit, for he had never been dazzled by his sister's intellectual lustre. Save when he fell in love with Catherine Harrington, he had never been dazzled, indeed, by any feminine characteristics whatever; and though he was to a certain extent what is called a ladies' doctor, his private opinion of the more complicated sex was not exalted. He regarded its complications as more curious than edifying, and he had an idea of the beauty of *reason*, which was, on the whole, meagrely gratified by what he observed in his female patients. His wife had been a reasonable woman, but she was a bright exception; among several things that he was sure of, this was perhaps the principal. Such a conviction, of course, did little either to mitigate or to abbreviate his widowhood; and it set a limit to his recognition, at the best, of Catherine's possibilities and of Mrs. Penniman's ministrations. He nevertheless, at the end of six months, accepted his sister's permanent presence as an accomplished fact, and as Catherine grew older, perceived that there were in effect good reasons why she should have a companion of her own imperfect sex. He was extremely polite to Lavinia, scrupulously, formally polite; and she had never seen him in anger but once in her life, when he lost his temper in a theological discussion with her late husband. With her he never discussed theology, nor, indeed, discussed anything; he contented himself with making known, very distinctly, in the form of a lucid ultimatum, his wishes with regard to Catherine.

Once, when the girl was about twelve years old, he had said to her—

"Try and make a clever woman of her, Lavinia; I should like her to be a clever woman."

Mrs. Penniman, at this, looked thoughtful a moment. "My dear Austin," she then inquired, "do you think it is better to be clever than to be good?"

"Good for what?" asked the Doctor. "You are good for nothing unless you are clever."

From this assertion Mrs. Penniman saw no reason to dissent; she possibly reflected that her own great use in the world was owing to her aptitude for many things.

"Of course I wish Catherine to be good," the Doctor said next day; "but she won't be any the less virtuous for not being a fool. I am not afraid of her being wicked; she will never have the salt of malice in her character. She is 'as good as good bread,' as the French say; but six years hence I don't want to have to compare her to good bread-and-butter."

"Are you afraid she will be insipid? My dear brother, it is I who supply the butter; so you needn't fear!" said Mrs. Penniman, who had taken in hand the child's "accomplishments," overlooking her at the piano, where Catherine displayed a certain talent, and going with her to the dancing-class, where it must be confessed that she made but a modest figure.

Mrs. Penniman was a tall, thin, fair, rather faded woman, with a perfectly amiable disposition, a high standard of gentility, a taste for light literature, and a certain foolish indirectness and obliquity of character. She was romantic; she was sentimental; she had a passion for little secrets and mysteries—a very innocent passion, for her secrets had hitherto always been as unpractical as addled eggs. She was not absolutely veracious; but this defect was of no great consequence, for she had never had anything to conceal. She would have liked to have a lover, and to correspond with him under an assumed name, in letters left at a shop. I am bound to say that her imagination never carried the intimacy further than this. Mrs. Penniman had never had a lover, but her brother, who was very shrewd, understood her turn of mind. "When Catherine is about seventeen," he said to himself, "Lavinia will try and persuade her that some young man with a mustache is in love with her. It will be quite untrue; no young man, with a mustache or without, will ever be in love with Catherine. But Lavinia will take it up, and talk to her about it; perhaps, even, if her taste for clandestine operations doesn't prevail with her, she will talk to me about it. Catherine won't see it, and won't believe it, fortunately for her peace of mind; poor Catherine isn't romantic."

She was a healthy, well-grown child, without a trace of her mother's beauty. She was not ugly; she had simply a plain, dull, gentle countenance. The most that had ever been said for her was that she had a "nice" face; and, though she was an heiress, no one had ever thought of regarding her as a belle. Her father's opinion of her moral purity was abundantly justified; she was excellently, imperturbably good; affectionate, docile, obedient, and much addicted to speaking the truth. In her younger years she was a good deal of a romp, and, though it is an awkward confession to make about one's heroine, I must add that she was something of a glutton. She never, that I know of, stole raisins out of the pantry; but she devoted her pocket-money to the purchase of cream-cakes. As regards this, however, a critical attitude would be inconsistent with a candid reference to the early annals of any biographer. Catherine was decidedly not clever; she was not quick with her book, nor, indeed, with anything else. She was not abnormally deficient, and she mustered learning enough to acquit herself respectably in conversation with her contemporaries—among whom it must be avowed, however, that she occupied a secondary place. It is well known that in New York it is possible for a young girl to occupy a primary one. Catherine, who was extremely modest, had no desire to shine, and on most social occasions, as they are called, you would have found her lurking in the background. She was extremely fond of her father, and very much afraid of him; she thought him the cleverest and handsomest and most celebrated of men. The poor girl found her account so completely in the exercise of her affections that the little tremor of fear that mixed itself with her filial passion gave the thing an extra relish rather than blunted its edge. Her deepest desire was to please him, and her conception of happiness was to know that she had succeeded in pleasing him. She had never succeeded beyond a certain point. Though, on the whole, he was very kind to her, she was perfectly aware of this, and to go beyond the point in question seemed to her really something to live for. What she could not know, of course, was that she disappointed him, though on three or four occasions the Doctor had been almost frank about it. She grew up peacefully and prosperously; but at the age of eighteen Mrs. Penniman had not made a clever woman of her. Doctor Sloper would have liked to be proud of his daughter; but there was nothing to be proud of in poor Catherine. There was nothing, of course, to be ashamed of; but this was not enough for the Doctor, who was a proud man, and would have enjoyed being able to think of his daughter as an unusual girl. There would have been a fitness in her being pretty and graceful, intelligent and distinguished—for her mother had been the most charming woman of her little day—and as regards her father, of course he knew his own value. He had moments of irritation at having produced a commonplace child, and he even went so far at times as to take a certain satisfaction in the thought that his wife had not lived to find her out. He was naturally slow in making this discovery himself, and it was not till Catherine had become a young lady grown that he regarded the matter as settled. He gave her the benefit of a great many doubts; he was in no haste to conclude. Mrs. Penniman frequently assured him that his daughter had a delightful nature; but he knew how to interpret this assurance. It meant, to his sense, that Catherine was not wise enough to discover that her aunt was a goose—a limitation of mind that could not fail to be agreeable to Mrs. Penniman. Both she and her brother, however, exaggerated the young girl's limitations; for Catherine, though she was very fond of her aunt, and conscious of the gratitude she owed her, regarded her without a particle of that gentle dread which gave its stamp to her admiration of her father. To her mind there was nothing of the infinite about Mrs. Penniman; Catherine saw her all at once, as it were, and was not dazzled by the apparition; whereas her father's great faculties seemed, as they stretched away, to lose themselves in a sort of luminous vagueness, which indicated, not that they stopped, but that Catherine's own mind ceased to follow them.

It must not be supposed that Doctor Sloper visited his disappointment upon the poor girl, or ever let her suspect that she had played him a trick. On the contrary, for fear of being unjust to her, he did his duty with exemplary zeal, and recognized that she was a faithful and affectionate child. Besides, he was a philosopher: he smoked a good many cigars over his disappointment, and in the fulness of time he got used to it. He satisfied himself that he had expected nothing, though, indeed, with a certain oddity of reasoning. "I expect nothing," he said to himself; "so that, if she gives me a surprise, it will be all clear gain. If she doesn't, it will be no loss." This was about the time Catherine had reached her eighteenth year; so that it will be seen her father had not been precipitate. At this time she seemed not only incapable of giving surprises; it was almost a question whether she could have received one—she was so quiet and irresponsive. People who expressed themselves roughly called her stolid. But she was irresponsive because she was shy, uncomfortably, painfully shy. This was not always understood, and she sometimes produced an impression of insensibility. In reality, she was the softest creature in the world.

3

As a child she had promised to be tall; but when she was sixteen she ceased to grow, and her stature, like most other points in her composition, was not unusual. She was strong, however, and properly made, and, fortunately, her health was excellent. It has been noted that the Doctor was a philosopher, but I would not have answered for his philosophy if the poor girl had proved a sickly and suffering person. Her appearance of health constituted her principal claim to beauty; and her clear, fresh complexion, in which white and red were very equally distributed, was, indeed, an excellent thing to see. Her eye was small and quiet, her features were rather thick, her tresses brown and smooth. A dull, plain girl she was called by rigorous critics—a quiet, lady-like girl, by those of the more imaginative sort; but by neither class was she very elaborately discussed. When it had been duly impressed upon her that she was a young lady—it was a good while before she could believe it—she suddenly developed a lively taste for dress: a lively taste is quite the expression to use. I feel as if I ought to write it very small, her judgment in this matter was by no means infallible; it was liable to confusions and embarrassments. Her great indulgence of it was really the desire of a rather inarticulate nature to manifest itself; she sought to be eloquent in her garments, and to make up for her diffidence of speech by a fine frankness of costume. But if she expressed herself in her clothes, it is certain that people were not to blame for not thinking her a witty person. It must be added that, though she had the expectation of a fortune—Doctor Sloper for a long time had been making twenty thousand dollars a year by his profession, and laying aside the half of it—the amount of money at her disposal was not greater than the allowance made to many poorer girls. In those days, in New York, there were still a few altar-fires flickering in the temple of Republican simplicity, and Doctor Sloper would have been glad to see his daughter present herself, with a classic grace, as a priestess of this mild faith. It made him fairly grimace, in private, to think that a child of his should be both ugly and overdressed. For himself, he was fond of the good things of life, and he made a considerable use of them; but he had a dread of vulgarity, and even a theory that it was increasing in the society that surrounded him. Moreover, the standard of luxury in the United States thirty years ago was carried by no means so high as at present, and Catherine's clever father took the old-fashioned view of the education of young persons. He had no particular theory on the subject; it had scarcely as yet become a necessity of self-defence to have a collection of theories. It simply appeared to him proper and reasonable that a well-bred young woman should not carry half her fortune on her back. Catherine's back was a broad one, and would have carried a good deal; but to the weight of the paternal displeasure she never ventured to expose it, and our heroine was twenty years old before she treated herself, for evening wear, to a red satin gown trimmed with gold fringe; though this was an article which, for many years, she had coveted in secret. It made her look, when she sported it, like a woman of thirty; but oddly enough, in spite of her taste for fine clothes, she had not a grain of coquetry, and her anxiety when she put them on was as to whether they, and not she, would look well. It is a point on which history has not been explicit, but the assumption is warrantable; it was in the royal raiment just mentioned that she presented herself at a little entertainment given by her aunt, Mrs. Almond. The girl was at this time in her twenty-first year, and Mrs. Almond's party was the beginning of something very important.

Some three or four years before this, Doctor Sloper had moved his household gods up town, as they say in New York. He had been living ever since his marriage in an edifice of red brick, with granite copings and an enormous fan-light over the door, standing in a street within five minutes' walk of the City Hall, which saw its best days (from the social point of view) about 1820. After this, the tide of fashion began to set steadily northward, as, indeed, in New York, thanks to the narrow channel in which it flows, it is obliged to do, and the great hum of traffic rolled farther to the right and left of Broadway. By the time the Doctor changed his residence, the murmur of trade had become a mighty uproar, which was music in the ears of all good citizens interested in the commercial development, as they delighted to call it, of their fortunate isle. Doctor Sloper's interest in this phenomenon was only indirect—though, seeing that, as the years went on, half his patients came to be overworked men of business, it might have been more immediate—and when most of his neighbors' dwellings (also ornamented with granite copings and large fan-lights) had been converted into offices, warehouses, and shipping agencies, and otherwise applied to the base uses of commerce, he determined to look out for a quieter home. The ideal of quiet and of genteel retirement, in 1835, was found in Washington Square, where the Doctor built himself a handsome, modern, wide-fronted house, with a big balcony before the drawing-room windows, and a flight of white marble steps ascending to a portal which was also faced with white marble. This structure, and many of its neighbors, which it exactly resembled, were supposed, forty years ago, to embody the last results of architectural science, and they remain to this day very solid and honorable dwellings. In front of them was the square, containing a considerable quantity of inexpensive vegetation, enclosed by a wooden paling, which increased its rural and accessible appearance; and round the corner was the more august precinct of the Fifth Avenue, taking its origin at this point with a spacious and confident air which already marked it for high destinies. I know not whether it is owing to the tenderness of early associations, but this portion of New York appears to many persons the most delectable. It has a kind of established repose which is not of frequent occurrence in other quarters of the long, shrill city; it has a riper, richer, more honorable look than any of the upper ramifications of the great longitudinal thoroughfare—the look of having had something of a social history. It was here, as you might have been informed on good authority, that you had come into a world which appeared to offer a variety of sources of interest; it was here that your grandmother lived, in venerable solitude, and dispensed a hospitality which commended itself alike to the infant imagination and the infant palate; it was here that you took your first walks abroad, following the nursery-maid with unequal step, and sniffing up the strange odor of the ailanthus-trees which at that time formed the principal umbrage of the Square, and diffused an aroma that you were not yet critical enough to dislike as it deserved; it was here, finally, that your first school, kept by a broad-bosomed, broad-based old lady with a ferule, who was always having tea in a blue cup, with a saucer that didn't match, enlarged the circle both of your observations and your sensations. It was here, at any rate, that my heroine spent many years of her life; which is my excuse for this topographical parenthesis.

Mrs. Almond lived much farther up town, in an embryonic street, with a high number—a region where the extension of the city began to assume a theoretic air, where poplars grew beside the pavement (when there was one), and mingled their shade with the steep roofs of desultory Dutch houses, and where pigs and chickens disported themselves in the gutter. These elements of rural picturesqueness have now wholly departed from New York street scenery; but they were to be found within the memory of middle-aged persons in quarters which now would blush to be reminded of them. Catherine had a great many cousins, and with her Aunt Almond's children, who ended by being nine in number, she lived on terms of considerable intimacy. When she was younger they had been rather afraid of her; she was believed, as the phrase is, to be highly educated, and a person who lived in the intimacy of their Aunt Penniman had something of reflected grandeur. Mrs. Penniman, among the little Almonds, was an object of more admiration than sympathy. Her manners were strange and formidable, and her mourning robes—she dressed in black for twenty years after her husband's death, and then suddenly appeared, one morning, with pink roses in her cap—were complicated in odd, unexpected places with buckles, bugles, and pins, which discouraged familiarity. She took children too hard, both for good and for evil, and had an oppressive air of expecting subtle things of them; so that going to see her was a good deal like being taken to church and made to sit in a front pew. It was discovered after awhile, however, that Aunt Penniman was but an accident in Catherine's existence, and not a part of its essence, and that when the girl came to spend a Saturday with her cousins, she was available for "follow-my-master," and even for leap-frog. On this basis an understanding was easily arrived at, and for several years Catherine fraternized with her young kinsmen. I say young kinsmen, because seven of the little Almonds were boys, and Catherine had a preference for those games which are most conveniently played in trousers. By degrees, however, the little Almonds' trousers began to lengthen, and the wearers to disperse and settle themselves in life. The elder children were older than Catherine, and the boys were sent to college or placed in counting-rooms. Of the girls, one married very punctually, and the other as punctually became engaged. It was to celebrate this latter event that Mrs. Almond gave the little party I have mentioned. Her daughter was to marry a stout young stock-broker, a boy of twenty: it was thought a very good thing.

4

Mrs. Penniman, with more buckles and bangles than ever, came, of course, to the entertainment, accompanied by her niece; the Doctor, too, had promised to look in later in the evening. There was to be a good deal of dancing, and before it had gone very far Marian Almond came up to Catherine, in company with a tall young man. She introduced the young man as a person who had a great desire to make our heroine's acquaintance, and as a cousin of Arthur Townsend, her own intended.

Marian Almond was a pretty little person of seventeen, with a very small figure and a very big sash, to the elegance of whose manners matrimony had nothing to add. She already had all the airs of a hostess, receiving the company, shaking her fan, saying that with so many people to attend to she should have no time to dance. She made a long speech about Mr. Townsend's cousin, to whom she administered a tap with her fan before turning away to other cares. Catherine had not understood all that she said; her attention was given to enjoying Marian's ease of manner and flow of ideas, and to looking at the young man, who was remarkably handsome. She had succeeded, however, as she often failed to do when people were presented to her, in catching his name, which appeared to be the same as that of Marian's little stock-broker. Catherine was always agitated by an introduction; it seemed a difficult moment, and she wondered that some people—her new acquaintance at this moment, for instance—should mind it so little. She wondered what she ought to say, and what would be the consequences of her saying nothing. The consequences at present were very agreeable. Mr. Townsend, leaving her no time for embarrassment, began to talk to her with an easy smile, as if he had known her for a year.

"What a delightful party! What a charming house! What an interesting family! What a pretty girl your cousin is!"

These observations, in themselves of no great profundity, Mr. Townsend seemed to offer for what they were worth, and as a contribution to an acquaintance. He looked straight into Catherine's eyes. She answered nothing; she only listened, and looked at him; and he, as if he expected no particular reply, went on to say many other things in the same comfortable and natural manner. Catherine, though she felt tongue-tied, was conscious of no embarrassment; it seemed proper that he should talk, and that she should simply look at him. What made it natural was that he was so handsome, or, rather, as she phrased it to herself, so beautiful. The music had been silent for awhile, but it suddenly began again; and then he asked her, with a deeper, intenser smile, if she would do him the honor of dancing with him. Even to this inquiry she gave no audible assent; she simply let him put his arm round her waist—as she did so, it occurred to her more vividly than it had ever done before that this was a singular place for a gentleman's arm to be—and in a moment he was guiding her round the room in the harmonious rotation of the polka. When they paused, she felt that she was red; and then, for some moments, she stopped looking at him. She fanned herself, and looked at the flowers that were painted on her fan. He asked her if she would begin again, and she hesitated to answer, still looking at the flowers.

"Does it make you dizzy?" he asked, in a tone of great kindness.

Then Catherine looked up at him; he was certainly beautiful, and not at all red. "Yes," she said; she hardly knew why, for dancing had never made her dizzy.

"Ah, well, in that case," said Mr. Townsend, "we will sit still and talk. I will find a good place to sit."

He found a good place—a charming place; a little sofa that seemed meant only for two persons. The rooms by this time were very full; the dancers increased in number, and people stood close in front of them, turning their backs, so that Catherine and her companion seemed secluded and unobserved. "*We* will talk," the young man had said; but he still did all the talking. Catherine leaned back in her place, with her eyes fixed upon him, smiling, and thinking him very clever. He had features like young men in pictures; Catherine had never seen such features—so delicate, so chiselled and finished—among the young New Yorkers whom she passed in the streets and met at dancing-parties. He was tall and slim, but he looked extremely strong. Catherine thought he looked like a statue. But a statue would not talk like that, and, above all, would not have eyes of so rare a color. He had never been at Mrs. Almond's before; he felt very much like a stranger; and it was very kind of Catherine to take pity on him. He was Arthur Townsend's cousin —not very near; several times removed —and Arthur had brought him to present him to the family. In fact, he was a great stranger in New York. It was his native place; but he had not been there for many years. He had been knocking about the world, and living in queer corners; he had only come back a month or two before. New York was very pleasant, only he felt lonely.

"You see, people forget you," he said, smiling at Catherine with his delightful gaze, while he leaned forward obliquely, turning toward her, with his elbows on his knees.

It seemed to Catherine that no one who had once seen him would ever forget him; but though she made this reflection she kept it to herself, almost as you would keep something precious.

They sat there for some time. He was very amusing. He asked her about the people that were near them; he tried to guess who some of them were, and he made the most laughable mistakes. He criticised them very freely, in a positive, off-hand way. Catherine had never heard any one—especially any young man—talk just like that. It was the way a young man might talk in a novel; or, better still, in a play, on the stage, close before the foot-lights, looking at the audience, and with every one looking at him, so that you wondered at his presence of mind. And yet Mr. Townsend was not like an actor; he seemed so sincere, so natural. This was very interesting; but in the midst of it Marian Almond came pushing through the crowd, with a little ironical cry, when she found these young people still together, which made every one turn round, and cost Catherine a conscious blush. Marian broke up their talk, and told Mr. Townsend—whom she treated as if she were already married, and he had become her cousin—to run away to her mother, who had been wishing for the last half hour to introduce him to Mr. Almond.

"We shall meet again," he said to Catherine as he left her, and Catherine thought it a very original speech.

Her cousin took her by the arm, and made her walk about. "I needn't ask you what you think of Morris," the young girl exclaimed.

"Is that his name?"

"I don't ask you what you think of his name, but what you think of himself," said Marian.

"Oh, nothing particular," Catherine answered, dissembling for the first time in her life.

"I have half a mind to tell him that!" cried Marian. "It will do him good; he's so terribly conceited."

"Conceited?" said Catherine, staring.

"So Arthur says, and Arthur knows about him."

"Oh, don't tell him!" Catherine murmured, imploringly.

"Don't tell him he's conceited! I have told him so a dozen times."

At this profession of audacity Catherine looked down at her little companion in amazement. She supposed it was because Marian was going to be married that she took so much on herself; but she wondered too, whether, when she herself should become engaged, such exploits would be expected of her.

Half an hour later she saw her aunt Penniman sitting in the embrasure of a window, with her head a little on one side, and her gold eye-glass raised to her eyes, which were wandering about the room. In front of her was a gentleman, bending forward a little, with his back turned to Catherine. She knew his back immediately, though she had never seen it; for when he left her, at Marian's instigation, he had retreated in the best order, without turning round. Morris Townsend—the name had already become very familiar to her, as if some one had been repeating it in her ear for the last half hour—Morris Townsend was giving his impressions of the company to her aunt, as he had done to herself; he was saying clever things, and Mrs. Penniman was smiling, as if she approved of them. As soon as Catherine had perceived this she moved away; she would not have liked him to turn round and see her. But it gave her pleasure—the whole thing. That he should talk with Mrs. Penniman, with whom she lived and whom she saw and talked with every day—that seemed to keep him near her, and to make him even easier to contemplate than if she herself had been the object of his civilities; and that Aunt Lavinia should like him, should not be shocked or startled by what he said, this also appeared to the girl a personal gain; for Aunt Lavinia's standard was extremely high, planted as it was over the grave of her late husband, in which, as she had convinced every one, the very genius of conversation was buried. One of the Almond boys, as Catherine called them, invited our heroine to dance a quadrille, and for a quarter of an hour her feet at least were occupied. This time she was not dizzy; her head was very clear. Just when the dance was over, she found herself in the crowd face to face with her father. Doctor Sloper had usually a little smile, never a very big one, and with this little smile playing in his clear eyes and on his neatly-shaved lips, he looked at his daughter's crimson gown.

"Is it possible that this magnificent person is my child?" he said.

You would have surprised him if you had told him so; but it is a literal fact that he almost never addressed his daughter save in the ironical form. Whenever he addressed her he gave her pleasure; but she had to cut her pleasure out of the piece, as it were. There were portions left over, light remnants and snippets of irony, which she never knew what to do with, which seemed too delicate for her own use; and yet Catherine, lamenting the limitations of her understanding, felt that they were too valuable to waste, and had a belief that if they passed over her head they yet contributed to the general sum of human wisdom.

"I am not magnificent," she said, mildly, wishing that she had put on another dress.

"You are sumptuous, opulent, expensive," her father rejoined. "You look as if you had eighty thousand a year."

"Well, so long as I haven't—" said Catherine, illogically. Her conception of her prospective wealth was as yet very indefinite.

"So long as you haven't you shouldn't look as if you had. Have you enjoyed your party?"

Catherine hesitated a moment; and then, looking away, "I am rather tired," she murmured. I have said that this entertainment was the beginning of something important for Catherine. For the second time in her life she made an indirect answer; and the beginning of a period of dissimulation is certainly a significant date. Catherine was not so easily tired as that.

Nevertheless, in the carriage, as they drove home, she was as quiet as if fatigue had been her portion. Doctor Sloper's manner of addressing his sister Lavinia had a good deal of resemblance to the tone he had adopted toward Catherine.

"Who was the young man that was making love to you?" he presently asked.

"Oh, my good brother!" murmured Mrs. Penniman, in deprecation.

"He seemed uncommonly tender. Whenever I looked at you for half an hour, he had the most devoted air."

"The devotion was not to me," said Mrs. Penniman. "It was to Catherine; he talked to me of her."

Catherine had been listening with all her ears. "Oh, Aunt Penniman!" she exclaimed, faintly.

"He is very handsome; he is very clever; he expressed himself with a great deal—a great deal of felicity," her aunt went on.

"He is in love with this regal creature, then?" the Doctor inquired, humorously.

"Oh, father!" cried the girl, still more faintly, devoutly thankful the carriage was dark.

"I don't know that; but he admired her dress."

Catherine did not say to herself in the dark, "My dress only?" Mrs. Penniman's announcement struck her by its richness, not by its meagreness.

"You see," said her father, "he thinks you have eighty thousand a year."

"I don't believe he thinks of that," said Mrs. Penniman; "he is too refined."

"He must be tremendously refined not to think of that!"

"Well, he is!" Catherine exclaimed, before she knew it.

"I thought you had gone to sleep," her father answered. "The hour has come!" he added to himself. "Lavinia is going to get up a romance for Catherine. It's a shame to play such tricks on the girl. What is the gentleman's name?" he went on, aloud.

"I didn't catch it, and I didn't like to ask him. He asked to be introduced to me," said Mrs. Penniman, with a certain grandeur; "but you know how indistinctly Jefferson speaks." Jefferson was Mr. Almond. "Catherine, dear, what was the gentleman's name?"

For a minute, if it had not been for the rumbling of the carriage, you might have heard a pin drop.

"I don't know, Aunt Lavinia," said Catherine, very softly. And, with all his irony, her father believed her.

5

He learned what he had asked some three or four days later, after Morris Townsend, with his cousin, had called in Washington Square. Mrs. Penniman did not tell her brother, on the drive home, that she had intimated to this agreeable young man, whose name she did not know, that, with her niece, she should be very glad to see him; but she was greatly pleased, and even a little flattered, when, late on a Sunday afternoon, the two gentlemen made their appearance. His coming with Arthur Townsend made it more natural and easy; the latter young man was on the point of becoming connected with the family, and Mrs. Penniman had remarked to Catherine that, as he was going to marry Marian, it would be polite in him to call. These events came to pass late in the autumn, and Catherine and her aunt had been sitting together in the closing dusk, by the fire-light, in the high back-parlor.

Arthur Townsend fell to Catherine's portion, while his companion placed himself on the sofa beside Mrs. Penniman. Catherine had hitherto not been a harsh critic; she was easy to please—she liked to talk with young men. But Marian's betrothed, this evening, made her feel vaguely fastidious; he sat looking at the fire and rubbing his knees with his hands. As for Catherine, she scarcely even pretended to keep up the conversation; her attention had fixed itself on the other side of the room; she was listening to what went on between the other Mr. Townsend and her aunt. Every now and then he looked over at Catherine herself and smiled, as if to show that what he said was for her benefit too. Catherine would have liked to change her place, to go and sit near them, where she might see and hear him better. But she was afraid of seeming bold—of looking eager; and, besides, it would not have been polite to Marian's little suitor. She wondered why the other gentleman had picked out her aunt—how he came to have so much to say to Mrs. Penniman, to whom, usually, young men were not especially devoted. She was not at all jealous of Aunt Lavinia, but she was a little envious, and, above all, she wondered; for Morris Townsend was an object on which she found that her imagination could exercise itself indefinitely. His cousin had been describing a house that he had taken in view of his union with Marian, and the domestic conveniences he meant to introduce into it; how Marian wanted a larger one, and Mrs. Almond recommended a smaller one, and how he himself was convinced that he had got the neatest house in New York.

"It doesn't matter," he said; "it's only for three or four years. At the end of three or four years we'll move. That's the way to live in New York—to move every three or four years. Then you always get the last thing. It's because the city's growing so quick—you've got to keep up with it. It's going straight up town—that's where New York's going. If I wasn't afraid Marian would be lonely, I'd go up there—right up to the top—and wait for it. Only have to wait ten years—they'll all come up after you. But Marian says she wants some neighbors —she doesn't want to be a pioneer. She says that if she's got to be the first settler she had better go out to Minnesota. I guess we'll move up little by little; when we get tired of one street we'll go higher. So you see we'll always have a new house; it's a great advantage to have a new house; you get all the latest improvements. They invent everything all over again about every five years, and it's a great thing to keep up with the new things. I always try and keep up with the new things of every kind. Don't you think that's a good motto for a young couple—to keep 'going higher?' What's the name of that piece of poetry—what do they call it?—*Excelsior!*"

Catherine bestowed on her junior visitor only just enough attention to feel that this was not the way Mr. Morris Townsend had talked the other night, or that he was talking now to her fortunate aunt. But suddenly his aspiring kinsman became more interesting. He seemed to have become conscious that she was affected by his companion's presence, and he thought it proper to explain it.

"My cousin asked me to bring him, or I shouldn't have taken the liberty. He seemed to want very much to come; you know he's awfully sociable. I told him I wanted to ask you first, but he said Mrs. Penniman had invited him. He isn't particular what he says when he wants to come somewhere. But Mrs. Penniman seems to think it's all right."

"We are very glad to see him," said Catherine. And she wished to talk more about him, but she hardly knew what to say. "I never saw him before," she went on, presently.

Arthur Townsend stared.

"Why, he told me he talked with you for over half an hour the other night."

"I mean before the other night. That was the first time."

"Oh, he has been away from New York—he has been all round the world. He doesn't know many people here, but he's very sociable, and he wants to know every one."

"Every one?" said Catherine.

"Well, I mean all the good ones. All the pretty young ladies—like Mrs. Penniman!" And Arthur Townsend gave a private laugh.

"My aunt likes him very much," said Catherine.

"Most people like him—he's so brilliant."

"He's more like a foreigner," Catherine suggested.

"Well, I never knew a foreigner," said young Townsend, in a tone which seemed to indicate that his ignorance had been optional.

"Neither have I," Catherine confessed, with more humility. "They say they are generally brilliant," she added, vaguely.

"Well, the people of this city are clever enough for me. I know some of them that think they are too clever for me; but they ain't."

"I suppose you can't be too clever," said Catherine, still with humility.

"I don't know. I know some people that call my cousin too clever."

Catherine listened to this statement with extreme interest, and a feeling that if Morris Townsend had a fault it would naturally be that one. But she did not commit herself, and in a moment she asked, "Now that he has come back, will he stay here always?"

"Ah!" said Arthur, "if he can get something to do."

"Something to do?"

"Some place or other; some business."

"Hasn't he got any?" said Catherine, who had never heard of a young man—of the upper class—in this situation.

"No; he's looking round. But he can't find anything."

"I am very sorry," Catherine permitted herself to observe.

"Oh, he doesn't mind," said young Townsend. "He takes it easy—he isn't in a hurry. He is very particular."

Catherine thought he naturally would be, and gave herself up for some moments to the contemplation of this idea, in several of its bearings.

"Won't his father take him into his business—his office?" she at last inquired.

"He hasn't got any father—he has only got a sister. Your sister can't help you much."

It seemed to Catherine that if she were his sister she would disprove this axiom. "Is she—is she pleasant?" she asked in a moment.

"I don't know—I believe she's very respectable," said young Townsend. And then he looked across to his cousin and began to laugh. "I say, we are talking about you," he added.

Morris Townsend paused in his conversation with Mrs. Penniman, and stared, with a little smile. Then he got up, as if he were going.

"As far as you are concerned, I can't return the compliment," he said to Catherine's companion. "But as regards Miss Sloper, it's another affair."

Catherine thought this little speech wonderfully well turned; but she was embarrassed by it, and she also got up. Morris Townsend stood looking at her and smiling; he put out his hand for farewell. He was going, without having said anything to her; but even on these terms she was glad to have seen him.

"I will tell her what you have said —when you go!" said Mrs. Penniman, with a little significant laugh.

Catherine blushed, for she felt almost as if they were making sport of her. What in the world could this beautiful young man have said? He looked at her still, in spite of her blush, but very kindly and respectfully.

"I have had no talk with you," he said, "and that was what I came for. But it will be a good reason for coming another time; a little pretext—if I am obliged to give one. I am not afraid of what your aunt will say when I go."

With this the two young men took their departure; after which Catherine, with her blush still lingering, directed a serious and interrogative eye to Mrs. Penniman. She was incapable of elaborate artifice, and she resorted to no jocular device—to no affectation of the belief that she had been maligned—to learn what she desired.

"What did you say you would tell me?" she asked.

Mrs. Penniman came up to her, smiling and nodding a little, looked at her all over, and gave a twist to the knot of ribbon in her neck. "It's a great secret, my dear child; but he is coming a-courting!"

Catherine was serious still. "Is that what he told you?"

"He didn't say so exactly; but he left me to guess it. I'm a good guesser."

"Do you mean a-courting me?"

"Not me, certainly, miss; though I must say he is a hundred times more polite to a person who has no longer extreme youth to recommend her than most of the young men. He is thinking of some one else." And Mrs. Penniman gave her niece a delicate little kiss. "You must be very gracious to him."

Catherine stared—she was bewildered. "I don't understand you," she said; "he doesn't know me."

"Oh yes, he does; more than you think. I have told him all about you."

"Oh, Aunt Penniman!" murmured Catherine, as if this had been a breach of trust. "He is a perfect stranger—we don't know him." There was infinite modesty in the poor girl's "we."

Aunt Penniman, however, took no account of it; she spoke even with a touch of acrimony. "My dear Catherine, you know very well that you admire him."

"Oh, Aunt Penniman!" Catherine could only murmur again. It might very well be that she admired him—though this did not seem to her a thing to talk about. But that this brilliant stranger—this sudden apparition, who had barely heard the sound of her voice—took that sort of interest in her that was expressed by the romantic phrase of which Mrs. Penniman had just made use—this could only be a figment of the restless brain of Aunt Lavinia, whom every one knew to be a woman of powerful imagination.

6

Mrs. Penniman even took for granted at times that other people had as much imagination as herself; so that when, half an hour later, her brother came in, she addressed him quite on this principle.

"He has just been here, Austin; it's such a pity you missed him."

"Whom in the world have I missed?" asked the Doctor.

"Mr. Morris Townsend; he has made us such a delightful visit."

"And who in the world is Mr. Morris Townsend?"

"Aunt Penniman means the gentleman—the gentleman whose name I couldn't remember," said Catherine.

"The gentleman at Elizabeth's party who was so struck with Catherine," Mrs. Penniman added.

"Oh, his name is Morris Townsend, is it? And did he come here to propose to you?"

"Oh, father!" murmured the girl for an answer, turning away to the window, where the dusk had deepened to darkness.

"I hope he won't do that without your permission," said Mrs. Penniman, very graciously.

"After all, my dear, he seems to have yours," her brother answered.

Lavinia simpered, as if this might not be quite enough, and Catherine, with her forehead touching the window-panes, listened to this exchange of epigrams as reservedly as if they had not each been a pin-prick in her own destiny.

"The next time he comes," the Doctor added, "you had better call me. He might like to see me."

Morris Townsend came again some five days afterward; but Doctor Sloper was not called, as he was absent from home at the time. Catherine was with her aunt when the young man's name was brought in, and Mrs. Penniman, effacing herself and protesting, made a great point of her niece's going into the drawing-room alone.

"This time it's for you—for you only," she said. "Before, when he talked to me, it was only preliminary—it was to gain my confidence. Literally, my dear, I should not have the *courage* to show myself to-day."

And this was perfectly true. Mrs. Penniman was not a brave woman, and Morris Townsend had struck her as a young man of great force of character, and of remarkable powers of satire—a keen, resolute, brilliant nature, with which one must exercise a great deal of tact. She said to herself that he was "imperious," and she liked the word and the idea. She was not the least jealous of her niece, and she had been perfectly happy with Mr. Penniman, but in the bottom of her heart she permitted herself the observation, "That's the sort of husband I should have had!" He was certainly much more imperious—she ended by calling it imperial—than Mr. Penniman.

So Catherine saw Mr. Townsend alone, and her aunt did not come in even at the end of the visit. The visit was a long one; he sat there, in the front parlor, in the biggest arm-chair, for more than an hour. He seemed more at home this time—more familiar; lounging a little in the chair, slapping a cushion that was near him with his stick, and looking round the room a good deal, and at the objects it contained, as well as at Catherine; whom, however, he also contemplated freely. There was a smile of respectful devotion in his handsome eyes which seemed to Catherine almost solemnly beautiful; it made her think of a young knight in a poem. His talk, however, was not particularly knightly; it was light and easy and friendly; it took a practical turn, and he asked a number of questions about herself—what were her tastes—if she liked this and that—what were her habits. He said to her, with his charming smile, "Tell me about yourself; give me a little sketch." Catherine had very little to tell, and she had no talent for sketching; but before he went she had confided to him that she had a secret passion for the theatre, which had been but scantily gratified, and a taste for operatic music—that of Bellini and Donizetti, in especial (it must be remembered, in extenuation of this primitive young woman, that she held these opinions in an age of general darkness)—which she rarely had an occasion to hear, except on the hand-organ. She confessed that she was not particularly fond of literature. Morris Townsend agreed with her that books were tiresome things; only, as he said, you had to read a good many before you found it out. He had been to places that people had written books about, and they were not a bit like the descriptions. To see for yourself—that was the great thing; he always tried to see for himself. He had seen all the principal actors—he had been to all the best theatres in London and Paris. But the actors were always like the authors—they always exaggerated. He liked everything to be natural. Suddenly he stopped, looking at Catherine with his smile.

"That's what I like you for; you are so natural. Excuse me," he added; "you see I am natural myself."

And before she had time to think whether she excused him or not—which afterward, at leisure, she became conscious that she did—he began to talk about music, and to say that it was his greatest pleasure in life. He had heard all the great singers in Paris and London—Pasta and Rubini and Lablache—and when you had done that, you could say that you knew what singing was.

"I sing a little myself," he said; "some day I will show you. Not to-day, but some other time."

And then he got up to go. He had omitted, by accident, to say that he would sing to her if she would play to him. He thought of this after he got into the street; but he might have spared his compunction, for Catherine had not noticed the lapse. She was thinking only that "some other time" had a delightful sound; it seemed to spread itself over the future.

This was all the more reason, however, though she was ashamed and uncomfortable, why she should tell her father that Mr. Morris Townsend had called again. She announced the fact abruptly, almost violently, as soon as the Doctor came into the house; and having done so—it was her duty—she took measures to leave the room. But she could not leave it fast enough; her father stopped her just as she reached the door.

"Well, my dear, did he propose to you to-day?" the Doctor asked.

This was just what she had been afraid he would say; and yet she had no answer ready. Of course she would have liked to take it as a joke—as her father must have meant it; and yet she would have liked also, in denying it, to be a little positive, a little sharp, so that he would perhaps not ask the question again. She didn't like it—it made her unhappy. But Catherine could never be sharp; and for a moment she only stood, with her hand on the door-knob, looking at her satiric parent, and giving a little laugh.

"Decidedly," said the Doctor to himself, "my daughter is not brilliant!"

But he had no sooner made this reflection than Catherine found something; she had decided, on the whole, to take the thing as a joke.

"Perhaps he will do it the next time,"

she exclaimed, with a repetition of her laugh; and she quickly got out of the room.

The Doctor stood staring; he wondered whether his daughter were serious. Catherine went straight to her own room, and by the time she reached it she bethought herself that there was something else—something better—she might have said. She almost wished, now, that her father would ask his question again, so that she might reply, "Oh yes, Mr. Morris Townsend proposed to me, and I refused him."

The Doctor, however, began to put his questions elsewhere; it naturally having occurred to him that he ought to inform himself properly about this handsome young man, who had formed the habit of running in and out of his house. He addressed himself to the elder of his sisters, Mrs. Almond—not going to her for the purpose; there was no such hurry as that; but having made a note of the matter for the first opportunity. The Doctor was never eager, never impatient or nervous; but he made notes of everything, and he regularly consulted his notes. Among them the information he obtained from Mrs. Almond about Morris Townsend took its place.

"Lavinia has already been to ask me," she said. "Lavinia is most excited; I don't understand it. It's not, after all, Lavinia that the young man is supposed to have designs upon. She is very peculiar."

"Ah, my dear," the Doctor replied, "she has not lived with me these twelve years without my finding it out."

"She has got such an artificial mind," said Mrs. Almond, who always enjoyed an opportunity to discuss Lavinia's peculiarities with her brother. "She didn't want me to tell you that she had asked me about Mr. Townsend; but I told her I would. She always wants to conceal everything."

"And yet at moments no one blurts things out with such crudity. She is like a revolving lighthouse—pitch darkness alternating with a dazzling brilliancy! But what did you tell her?" the Doctor asked.

"What I tell you—that I know very little of him."

"Lavinia must have been disappointed at that," said the Doctor; "she would prefer him to have been guilty of some romantic crime. However, we must make the best of people. They tell me our gentleman is the cousin of the little boy to whom you are about to intrust the future of your little girl."

"Arthur is not a little boy; he is a very old man; you and I will never be so old! He is a distant relation of Lavinia's *protégé*. The name is the same, but I am given to understand that there are Townsends and Townsends. So Arthur's mother tells me; she talked about 'branches'—younger branches, elder branches, inferior branches—as if it were a royal house. Arthur, it appears, is of the reigning line, but poor Lavinia's young man is not. Beyond this, Arthur's mother knows very little about him; she has only a vague story that he has been 'wild.' But I know his sister a little, and she is a very nice woman. Her name is Mrs. Montgomery; she is a widow, with a little property and five children. She lives in the Second Avenue."

"What does Mrs. Montgomery say about him?"

"That he has talents by which he might distinguish himself."

"Only he is lazy, eh?"

"She doesn't say so."

"That's family pride," said the Doctor. "What is his profession?"

"He hasn't got any; he is looking for something. I believe he was once in the Navy."

"Once? What is his age?"

"I suppose he is upward of thirty. He must have gone into the Navy very young. I think Arthur told me that he inherited a small property—which was perhaps the cause of his leaving the Navy—and that he spent it all in a few years. He travelled all over the world, lived abroad, amused himself. I believe it was a kind of system, a theory he had. He has lately come back to America with the intention, as he tells Arthur, of beginning life in earnest."

"Is he in earnest about Catherine, then?"

"I don't see why you should be incredulous," said Mrs. Almond. "It seems to me that you have never done Catherine justice. You must remember that she has the prospect of thirty thousand a year."

The Doctor looked at his sister a moment, and then, with lightest touch of bitterness, "You at least appreciate her," he said.

Mrs. Almond blushed.

"I don't mean that is her only merit; I simply mean that it is a great one. A great many young men think so; and you appear to me never to have been properly aware of that. You have always had a little way of alluding to her as an unmarriageable girl."

"My allusions are as kind as yours, Elizabeth," said the Doctor, frankly. "How many suitors has Catherine had, with all her expectations—how much attention has she ever received? Catherine is not unmarriageable, but she is absolutely unattractive. What other reason is there for Lavinia being so charmed with the idea that there is a lover in the house? There has never been one before, and Lavinia, with her sensitive, sympathetic nature, is not used to the idea. It affects her imagination. I must do the young men of New York the justice to say that they strike me as very disinterested. They prefer pretty girls—lively girls—girls like your own. Catherine is neither pretty nor lively."

"Catherine does very well; she has a style of her own—which is more than my poor Marian has, who has no style at all," said Mrs. Almond. "The reason Catherine has received so little attention, is that she seems to all the young men to be older than themselves. She is so large, and she dresses so richly. They are rather afraid of her, I think; she looks as if she had been married already, and you know they don't like married women. And if our young men appear disinterested," the Doctor's wiser sister went on, "it is because they marry, as a general thing, so young—before twenty-five, at the age of innocence and sincerity—before the age of calculation. If they only waited a little, Catherine would fare better."

"As a calculation? Thank you very much," said the Doctor.

"Wait till some intelligent man of forty comes along, and he will be delighted with Catherine," Mrs. Almond continued.

"Mr. Townsend is not old enough, then? His motives may be pure."

"It is very possible that his motives are pure; I should be very sorry to take the contrary for granted. Lavinia is sure of it; and, as he is a very prepossessing youth, you might give him the benefit of the doubt."

Doctor Sloper reflected a moment.

"What are his present means of subsistence?"

"I have no idea. He lives, as I say, with his sister."

"A widow, with five children? Do you mean he lives *upon* her?"

Mrs. Almond got up, and with a certain impatience, "Had you not better ask Mrs. Montgomery herself?" she inquired.

"Perhaps I may come to that," said the Doctor. "Did you say the Second Avenue?" He made a note of the Second Avenue.

7

He was, however, by no means so much in earnest as this might seem to indicate; and, indeed, he was more than anything else amused with the whole situation. He was not in the least in a state of tension or of vigilance with regard to Catherine's prospects; he was even on his guard against the ridicule that might attach itself to the spectacle of a house thrown into agitation by its daughter and heiress receiving attentions unprecedented in its annals. More than this, he went so far as to promise himself some entertainment from the little drama—if drama it was—of which Mrs. Penniman desired to represent the ingenious Mr. Townsend as the hero. He had no intention, as yet, of regulating the *dénouement*. He was perfectly willing, as Elizabeth had suggested, to give the young man the benefit of every doubt. There was no great danger in it; for Catherine, at the age of twenty-two, was, after all, a rather mature blossom, such as could be plucked from the stem only by a vigorous jerk. The fact that Morris Townsend was poor, was not of necessity against him; the Doctor had never made up his mind that his daughter should marry a rich man. The fortune she would inherit struck him as a very sufficient provision for two reasonable persons, and if a penniless swain who could give a good account of himself should enter the lists, he should be judged quite upon his personal merits. There were other things besides. The Doctor thought it very vulgar to be precipitate in accusing people of mercenary motives, inasmuch as his door had as yet not been in the least besieged by fortune-hunters; and, lastly, he was very curious to see whether Catherine might really be loved for her moral worth. He smiled as he reflected that poor Mr. Townsend had been only twice to the house, and he said to Mrs. Penniman that the next time he should come she must ask him to dinner.

He came very soon again, and Mrs. Penniman had of course great pleasure in executing this mission. Morris Townsend accepted her invitation with equal good grace, and the dinner took place a few days later. The Doctor had said to himself, justly enough, that they must not have the young man alone; this would partake too much of the nature of encouragement. So two or three other persons were invited; but Morris Townsend, though he was by no means the ostensible, was the real occasion of the feast. There is every reason to suppose that he desired to make a good impression; and if he fell short of this result, it was not for want of a good deal of intelligent effort. The Doctor talked to him very little during dinner; but he observed him attentively, and after the ladies had gone out he pushed him the wine and asked him several questions. Morris was not a young man who needed to be pressed, and he found quite enough encouragement in the superior quality of the claret. The Doctor's wine was admirable, and it may be communicated to the reader that while he sipped it Morris reflected that a cellarful of good liquor—there was evidently a cellarful here—would be a most attractive idiosyncrasy in a father-in-law. The Doctor was struck with his appreciative guest; he saw that he was not a commonplace young man. "He has ability," said Catherine's father, "decided ability; he has a very good head if he chooses to use it. And he is uncommonly well turned out; quite the sort of figure that pleases the ladies; but I don't think I like him." The Doctor, however, kept his reflections to himself, and talked to his visitors about foreign lands, concerning which Morris offered him more information than he was ready, as he mentally phrased it, to swallow. Doctor Sloper had travelled but little, and he took the liberty of not believing everything that his talkative guest narrated. He prided himself on being something of a physiognomist; and while the young man, chatting with easy assurance, puffed his cigar and filled his glass again, the Doctor sat with his eyes quietly fixed on his bright, expressive face. "He has the assurance of the devil himself!" said Morris's host; "I don't think I ever saw such assurance. And his powers of invention are most remarkable. He is very knowing; they were not so knowing as that in my time. And a good head, did I say? I should think so—after a bottle of Madeira, and a bottle and a half of claret!"

After dinner Morris Townsend went and stood before Catherine, who was standing before the fire in her red satin gown.

"He doesn't like me—he doesn't like me at all," said the young man.

"Who doesn't like you?" asked Catherine.

"Your father; extraordinary man!"

"I don't see how you know," said Catherine, blushing.

"I feel; I am very quick to feel."

"Perhaps you are mistaken."

"Ah, well! you ask him, and you will see."

"I would rather not ask him, if there is any danger of his saying what you think."

Morris looked at her with an air of mock melancholy.

"It wouldn't give you any pleasure to contradict him?"

"I never contradict him," said Catherine.

"Will you hear me abused without opening your lips in my defence?"

"My father won't abuse you. He doesn't know you enough."

Morris Townsend gave a loud laugh, and Catherine began to blush again.

"I shall never mention you," she said, to take refuge from her confusion.

"That is very well; but it is not quite what I should have liked you to say. I should have liked you to say, 'If my father doesn't think well of you, what does it matter?' "

"Ah, but it would matter; I couldn't say that!" the girl exclaimed.

He looked at her for a moment, smiling a little; and the Doctor, if he had been watching him just then, would have seen a gleam of fine impatience in the sociable softness of his eye. But there was no impatience in his rejoinder —none, at least, save what was expressed in a little appealing sigh. "Ah, well! then I must not give up the hope of bringing him round."

He expressed it more frankly to Mrs. Penniman later in the evening. But before that he sang two or three songs at Catherine's timid request; not that he flattered himself that this would help to bring her father round. He had a sweet, light tenor voice, and, when he had finished, every one made some exclamation—every one, that is, save Catherine, who remained intensely silent. Mrs. Penniman declared that his manner of singing was "most artistic," and Doctor Sloper said it was "very taking—very taking, indeed"; speaking loudly and distinctly, but with a certain dryness.

"He doesn't like me—he doesn't like me at all," said Morris Townsend, addressing the aunt in the same manner as he had done the niece. "He thinks I am all wrong."

Unlike her niece, Mrs. Penniman asked for no explanation. She only smiled very sweetly, as if she understood everything; and, unlike Catherine too, she made no attempt to contradict him. "Pray, what does it matter?" she murmured, softly.

"Ah, you say the right thing!" said Morris, greatly to the gratification of Mrs. Penniman, who prided herself on always saying the right thing.

The Doctor, the next time he saw his sister Elizabeth, let her know that he had made the acquaintance of Lavinia's *protégé*.

"Physically," he said, "he's uncommonly well set up. As an anatomist, it is really a pleasure to me to see such a beautiful structure; although, if people were all like him, I suppose there would be very little need for doctors."

"Don't you see anything in people but their bones?" Mrs. Almond rejoined. "What do you think of him as a father?"

"As a father? Thank Heaven, I am not his father!"

"No; but you are Catherine's. Lavinia tells me she is in love."

"She must get over it. He is not a gentleman."

"Ah, take care! Remember that he is a branch of the Townsends."

"He is not what I call a gentleman; he has not the soul of one. He is extremely insinuating; but it's a vulgar nature. I saw through it in a minute. He is altogether too familiar;—I hate familiarity. He is a plausible coxcomb."

"Ah, well," said Mrs. Almond, "if you make up your mind so easily, it's a great advantage."

"I don't make up my mind easily. What I tell you is the result of thirty years of observation; and in order to be able to form that judgment in a single evening, I have had to spend a lifetime in study."

"Very possibly you are right. But the thing is for Catherine to see it."

"I will present her with a pair of spectacles!" said the Doctor.

8

If it were true that she was in love, she was certainly very quiet about it; but the Doctor was of course prepared to admit that her quietness might mean volumes. She had told Morris Townsend that she would not mention him to her father, and she saw no reason to retract this vow of discretion. It was no more than decently civil, of course, that, after having dined in Washington Square, Morris should call there again; and it was no more than natural that, having been kindly received on this occasion, he should continue to present himself. He had had plenty of leisure on his hands; and thirty years ago, in New York, a young man of leisure had reason to be thankful for aids to self-oblivion. Catherine said nothing to her father about these visits, though they had rapidly become the most important, the most absorbing thing in her life. The girl was very happy. She knew not as yet what would come of it; but the present had suddenly grown rich and solemn. If she had been told she was in love, she would have been a good deal surprised; for she had an idea that love was an eager and exacting passion, and her own heart was filled in these days with the impulse of self-effacement and sacrifice. Whenever Morris Townsend had left the house, her imagination projected itself, with all its strength, into the idea of his soon coming back; but if she had been told at such a moment that he would not return for a year, or even that he would never return, she would not have complained nor rebelled, but would have humbly accepted the decree, and sought for consolation in thinking over the times she had already seen him, the words he had spoken, the sound of his voice, of his tread, the expression of his face. Love demands certain things as a right; but Catherine had no sense of her rights; she had only a consciousness of immense and unexpected favors. Her very gratitude for these things had hushed itself; for it seemed to her that there would be something of impudence in making a festival of her secret. Her father suspected Morris Townsend's visits, and noted her reserve. She seemed to beg pardon for it; she looked at him constantly in silence, as if she meant to say that she said nothing because she was afraid of irritating him. But the poor girl's dumb eloquence irritated him more than anything else would have done, and he caught himself murmuring more than once that it was a grievous pity his only child was a simpleton. His murmurs, however, were inaudible; and for awhile he said nothing to any one. He would have liked to know exactly how often young Townsend came; but he had determined to ask no questions of the girl herself—to say nothing more to her that would show that he watched her. The Doctor had a great idea of being largely just: he wished to leave his daughter her liberty, and interfere only when the danger should be proved. It was not in his manner to obtain information by indirect methods, and it never even occurred to him to question the servants. As for Lavinia, he hated to talk to her about the matter; she annoyed him with her mock romanticism. But he had to come to this. Mrs. Penniman's convictions as regards the relations of her niece and the clever young visitor, who saved appearances by coming ostensibly for both the ladies—Mrs. Penniman's convictions had passed into a riper and richer phase. There was to be no crudity in Mrs. Penniman's treatment of the situation; she had become as uncommunicative as Catherine herself. She was tasting of the sweets of concealment; she had taken up the line of mystery. "She would be enchanted to be able to prove to herself that she is persecuted," said the Doctor; and when at last he questioned her, he was sure she would contrive to extract from his words a pretext for this belief.

"Be so good as to let me know what is going on in the house," he said to her, in a tone which, under the circumstances, he himself deemed genial.

"Going on, Austin?" Mrs. Penniman exclaimed. "Why, I am sure I don't know. I believe that last night the old gray cat had kittens."

"At her age?" said the Doctor. "The idea is startling—almost shocking. Be so good as to see that they are all drowned. But what else has happened?"

"Ah, the dear little kittens!" cried Mrs. Penniman. "I wouldn't have them drowned for the world!"

Her brother puffed his cigar a few moments in silence. "Your sympathy with kittens, Lavinia," he presently resumed, "arises from a feline element in your own character."

"Cats are very graceful, and very clean," said Mrs. Penniman, smiling.

"And very stealthy. You are the embodiment both of grace and of neatness; but you are wanting in frankness."

"You certainly are not, dear brother."

"I don't pretend to be graceful, though I try to be neat. Why haven't you let me know that Mr. Morris Townsend is coming to the house four times a week?"

Mrs. Penniman lifted her eyebrows. "Four times a week!"

"Three times, then, or five times, if you prefer it. I am away all day, and I see nothing. But when such things happen, you should let me know."

Mrs. Penniman, with her eyebrows still raised, reflected intently. "Dear Austin," she said at last, "I am incapable of betraying a confidence. I would rather suffer anything."

"Never fear; you shall not suffer. To whose confidence is it you allude? Has Catherine made you take a vow of eternal secrecy?"

"By no means. Catherine has not told me as much as she might. She has not been very trustful."

"It is the young man, then, who has made you his confidante? Allow me to say that it is extremely indiscreet of you to form secret alliances with young men; you don't know where they may lead you."

"I don't know what you mean by an alliance," said Mrs. Penniman. "I take a great interest in Mr. Townsend; I won't conceal that. But that's all."

"Under the circumstances, that is quite enough. What is the source of your interest in Mr. Townsend?"

"Why," said Mrs. Penniman, musing, and then breaking into her smile, "that he is so interesting!"

The Doctor felt that he had need of his patience. "And what makes him interesting?—his good looks?"

"His misfortunes, Austin."

"Ah, he has had misfortunes? That, of course, is always interesting. Are you at liberty to mention a few of Mr. Townsend's?"

"I don't know that he would like it," said Mrs. Penniman. "He has told me a great deal about himself—he has told me, in fact, his whole history. But I don't think I ought to repeat those things. He would tell them to you, I am sure, if he thought you would listen to him kindly. With kindness you may do anything with him."

The Doctor gave a laugh. "I shall request him very kindly, then, to leave Catherine alone."

"Ah!" said Mrs. Penniman, shaking her forefinger at her brother, with her little finger turned out, "Catherine has probably said something to him kinder than that!"

"Said that she loved him?—do you mean that?"

Mrs. Penniman fixed her eyes on the floor. "As I tell you, Austin, she doesn't confide in me."

"You have an opinion, I suppose, all the same. It is that I ask you for; though I don't conceal from you that I shall not regard it as conclusive."

Mrs. Penniman's gaze continued to rest on the carpet; but at last she lifted it, and then her brother thought it very expressive. "I think Catherine is very happy; that is all I can say."

"Townsend is trying to marry her—is that what you mean?"

"He is greatly interested in her."

"He finds her such an attractive girl?"

"Catherine has a lovely nature, Austin," said Mrs. Penniman, "and Mr. Townsend has had the intelligence to discover that."

"With a little help from you, I suppose. My dear Lavinia," cried the Doctor, "you are an admirable aunt!"

"So Mr. Townsend says," observed Lavinia, smiling.

"Do you think he is sincere?" asked her brother.

"In saying that?"

"No; that's of course. But in his admiration for Catherine?"

"Deeply sincere. He has said to me the most appreciative, the most charming things about her. He would say them to you, if he were sure you would listen to him—gently."

"I doubt whether I can undertake it. He appears to require a great deal of gentleness."

"He is a sympathetic, sensitive nature," said Mrs. Penniman.

Her brother puffed his cigar again in silence. "These delicate qualities have survived his vicissitudes, eh? All this while you haven't told me about his misfortunes."

"It is a long story," said Mrs. Penniman, "and I regard it as a sacred trust. But I suppose there is no objection to my saying that he has been wild—he frankly confesses that. But he has paid for it."

"That's what has impoverished him, eh?"

"I don't mean simply in money. He is very much alone in the world."

"Do you mean that he has behaved so badly that his friends have given him up?"

"He has had false friends, who have deceived and betrayed him."

"He seems to have some good ones too. He has a devoted sister, and half a dozen nephews and nieces."

Mrs. Penniman was silent a minute. "The nephews and nieces are children, and the sister is not a very attractive person."

"I hope he doesn't abuse her to you," said the Doctor; "for I am told he lives upon her."

"Lives upon her?"

"Lives with her, and does nothing for himself; it is about the same thing."

"He is looking for a position most earnestly," said Mrs. Penniman. "He hopes every day to find one."

"Precisely. He is looking for it here —over there in the front parlor. The position of husband of a weak-minded woman with a large fortune would suit him to perfection!"

Mrs. Penniman was truly amiable, but she now gave signs of temper. She rose with much animation, and stood for a moment looking at her brother. "My dear Austin," she remarked, "if you regard Catherine as a weak-minded woman you are particularly mistaken!" And with this she moved majestically away.

9

It was a regular custom with the family in Washington Square to go and spend Sunday evening at Mrs. Almond's. On the Sunday after the conversation I have just narrated this custom was not intermitted; and on this occasion, toward the middle of the evening, Doctor Sloper found reason to withdraw to the library with his brother-in-law, to talk over a matter of business. He was absent some twenty minutes, and when he came back into the circle, which was enlivened by the presence of several friends of the family, he saw that Morris Townsend had come in, and had lost as little time as possible in seating himself on a small sofa beside Catherine. In the large room, where several different groups had been formed, and the hum of voices and of laughter was loud, these two young persons might confabulate, as the Doctor phrased it to himself, without attracting attention. He saw in a moment, however, that his daughter was painfully conscious of his own observation. She sat motionless, with her eyes bent down, staring at her open fan, deeply flushed, shrinking together as if to minimize the indiscretion of which she confessed herself guilty.

The Doctor almost pitied her. Poor Catherine was not defiant; she had no genius for bravado, and as she felt that her father viewed her companion's attentions with an unsympathizing eye, there was nothing but discomfort for her in the accident of seeming to challenge him. The Doctor felt, indeed, so sorry for her that he turned away, to spare her the sense of being watched; and he was so intelligent a man that, in his thoughts, he rendered a sort of poetic justice to her situation.

"It must be deucedly pleasant for a plain, inanimate girl like that to have a beautiful young fellow come and sit down beside her, and whisper to her that he is her slave—if that is what this one whispers. No wonder she likes it, and that she thinks me a cruel tyrant; which of course she does, though she is afraid —she hasn't the animation necessary—to admit it to herself. Poor old Catherine!" mused the Doctor; "I verily believe she is capable of defending me when Townsend abuses me!"

And the force of this reflection, for the moment, was such in making him feel the natural opposition between his point of view and that of an infatuated child, that he said to himself that he was perhaps after all taking things too hard, and crying out before he was hurt. He must not condemn Morris Townsend unheard. He had a great aversion to taking things too hard; he thought that half the discomfort and many of the disappointments of life come from it; and for an instant he asked himself whether, possibly, he did not appear ridiculous to this intelligent young man, whose private perception of incongruities he suspected of being keen. At the end of a quarter of an hour Catherine had got rid of him, and

Townsend was now standing before the fireplace in conversation with Mrs. Almond.

"We will try him again," said the Doctor. And he crossed the room and joined his sister and her companion, making her a sign that she should leave the young man to him. She presently did so, while Morris looked at him, smiling, without a sign of evasiveness in his affable eye.

"He's amazingly conceited!" thought the Doctor; and then he said, aloud, "I am told you are looking out for a position."

"Oh, a position is more than I should presume to call it," Morris Townsend answered. "That sounds so fine. I should like some quiet work—something to turn an honest penny."

"What sort of thing should you prefer?"

"Do you mean what am I fit for? Very little, I am afraid. I have nothing but my good right arm, as they say in the melodramas."

"You are too modest," said the Doctor. "In addition to your good right arm you have your subtle brain. I know nothing of you but what I see; but I see by your physiognomy that you are extremely intelligent."

"Ah," Townsend murmured, "I don't know what to answer when you say that. You advise me, then, not to despair?"

And he looked at his interlocutor as if the question might have a double meaning. The Doctor caught the look and weighed it a moment before he replied. "I should be very sorry to admit that a robust and well-disposed young man need ever despair. If he doesn't succeed in one thing, he can try another. Only I should add, he should choose his line with discretion."

"Ah, yes, with discretion," Morris Townsend repeated, sympathetically. "Well, I have been indiscreet, formerly; but I think I have got over it. I am very steady now." And he stood a moment, looking down at his remarkably neat shoes. Then at last, "Were you kindly intending to propose something for my advantage?" he inquired, looking up and smiling.

"D—n his impudence!" the Doctor exclaimed, privately. But in a moment he reflected that he himself had, after all, touched first upon this delicate point, and that his words might have been construed as an offer of assistance. "I have no particular proposal to make," he presently said; "but it occurred to me to let you know that I have you in my mind. Sometimes one hears of opportunities. For instance, should you object to leaving New York—to going to a distance?"

"I am afraid I shouldn't be able to manage that. I must seek my fortune here or nowhere. You see," added Morris Townsend, "I have ties—I have responsibilities here. I have a sister, a widow, from whom I have been separated for a long time, and to whom I am almost everything. I shouldn't like to say to her that I must leave her. She rather depends upon me, you see."

"Ah, that's very proper; family feeling is very proper," said Doctor Sloper. "I often think there is not enough of it in our city. I think I have heard of your sister."

"It is possible, but I rather doubt it; she lives so very quietly."

"As quietly, you mean," the Doctor went on, with a short laugh, "as a lady may do who has several young children."

"Ah, my little nephews and nieces—that's the very point! I am helping to bring them up," said Morris Townsend. "I am a kind of amateur tutor; I give them lessons."

"That's very proper, as I say; but it is hardly a career."

"It won't make my fortune," the young man confessed.

"You must not be too much bent on a fortune," said the Doctor. "But I assure you I will keep you in mind; I won't lose sight of you."

"If my situation becomes desperate I shall perhaps take the liberty of reminding you," Morris rejoined, raising his voice a little, with a brighter smile, as his interlocutor turned away.

Before he left the house the Doctor had a few words with Mrs. Almond.

"I should like to see his sister," he said. "What do you call her—Mrs. Montgomery? I should like to have a little talk with her."

"I will try and manage it," Mrs. Almond responded. "I will take the first opportunity of inviting her, and you shall come and meet her; unless, indeed," Mrs. Almond added, "she first takes it into her head to be sick and to send for you."

"Ah no, not that; she must have trouble enough without that. But it would have its advantages, for then I should see the children. I should like very much to see the children."

"You are very thorough. Do you want to catechise them about their uncle?"

"Precisely. Their uncle tells me he has charge of their education, that he saves their mother the expense of school-bills. I should like to ask them a few questions in the commoner branches."

"He certainly has not the cut of a school-master," Mrs. Almond said to herself a short time afterward, as she saw Morris Townsend in a corner bending over her niece, who was seated.

And there was, indeed, nothing in the young man's discourse at this moment that savored of the pedagogue.

"Will you meet me somewhere tomorrow or next day?" he said, in a low tone, to Catherine.

"Meet you?" she asked, lifting her frightened eyes.

"I have something particular to say to you—very particular."

"Can't you come to the house? Can't you say it there?"

Townsend shook his head gloomily. "I can't enter your doors again."

"Oh, Mr. Townsend!" murmured Catherine. She trembled as she wondered what had happened—whether her father had forbidden it.

"I can't, in self-respect," said the young man. "Your father has insulted me."

"Insulted you?"

"He has taunted me with my poverty."

"Oh, you are mistaken—you misunderstood him!" Catherine spoke with energy, getting up from her chair.

"Perhaps I am too proud—too sensitive. But would you have me otherwise?" he asked, tenderly.

"Where my father is concerned, you must not be sure. He is full of goodness," said Catherine.

"He laughed at me for having no position. I took it quietly; but only because he belongs to you."

"I don't know," said Catherine—"I don't know what he thinks. I am sure he means to be kind. You must not be too proud."

"I will be proud only of you," Morris answered. "Will you meet in the Square in the afternoon?"

A great blush on Catherine's part had been the answer to the declaration I have just quoted. She turned away, heedless of his question.

"Will you meet me?" he repeated. "It is very quiet there—no one need see us —toward dusk."

"It is you who are unkind, it is you who laugh, when you say such things as that."

"My dear girl!" the young man murmured.

"You know how little there is in me to be proud of. I am ugly and stupid."

Morris greeted this remark with an ardent murmur, in which she recognized nothing articulate but an assurance that she was his own dearest.

But she went on. "I am not even—I am not even—" And she paused a moment.

"You are not what?"

"I am not even brave."

"Ah, then, if you are afraid, what shall we do?"

She hesitated awhile; then at last—"You must come to the house," she said; "I am not afraid of that."

"I would rather it were in the Square," the young man urged. "You know how empty it is, often. No one will see us."

"I don't care who sees us. But leave me now."

He left her resignedly; he had got what he wanted. Fortunately he was ignorant that half an hour later, going home with her father, and feeling him near, the poor girl, in spite of her sudden declaration of courage, began to tremble again. Her father said nothing; but she had an idea his eyes were fixed upon her in the darkness. Mrs. Penniman also was silent; Morris Townsend had told her that her niece preferred, unromantically, an interview in a chintz-covered parlor to a sentimental tryst beside a fountain sheeted with dead leaves, and she was lost in wonderment at the oddity—almost the perversity—of the choice.

10

Catherine received the young man the next day on the ground she had chosen—amidst the chaste upholstery of a New York drawing-room furnished in the fashion of fifty years ago. Morris had swallowed his pride, and made the effort necessary to cross the threshold of her too derisive parent—an act of magnanimity which could not fail to render him doubly interesting.

"We must settle something—we must take a line," he declared, passing his hand through his hair and giving a glance at the long, narrow mirror which adorned the space between the two windows, and which had at its base a little gilded bracket covered by a thin slab of white marble, supporting in its turn a backgammon-board folded together in the shape of two volumes—two shining folios inscribed, in greenish-gilt letters, *History of England*. If Morris had been pleased to describe the master of the house as a heartless scoffer, it is because he thought him too much on his guard, and this was the easiest way to express his own dissatisfaction—a dissatisfaction which he had made a point of concealing from the Doctor. It will probably seem to the reader, however, that the Doctor's vigilance was by no means excessive, and that these two young people had an open field. Their intimacy was now considerable, and it may appear that, for a shrinking and retiring person, our heroine had been liberal of her favors. The young man, within a few days, had made her listen to things for which she had not supposed that she was prepared; having a lively foreboding of difficulties, he proceeded to gain as much ground as possible in the present. He remembered that fortune favors the brave, and even if he had forgotten it, Mrs. Penniman would have remembered it for him. Mrs. Penniman delighted of all things in a drama, and she flattered herself that a drama would now be enacted. Combining as she did the zeal of the prompter with the impatience of the spectator, she had long since done her utmost to pull up the curtain. She, too, expected to figure in the performance—to be the confidante, the Chorus, to speak the epilogue. It may even be said that there were times when she lost sight altogether of the modest heroine of the play in the contemplation of certain great scenes which would naturally occur between the hero and herself.

What Morris had told Catherine at last was simply that he loved her, or rather adored her. Virtually, he had made known as much already—his visits had been a series of eloquent intimations of it. But now he had affirmed it in lover's vows, and, as a memorable sign of it, he had passed his arm round the girl's waist and taken a kiss. This happy certitude had come sooner than Catherine expected, and she had regarded it, very naturally, as a priceless treasure. It may even be doubted whether she had ever definitely expected to possess it; she had not been waiting for it, and she had never said to herself that at a given moment it must come. As I have tried to explain, she was not eager and exacting; she took what was given her from day to day; and if the delightful custom of her lover's visits, which yielded her a happiness in which confidence and timidity were strangely blended, had suddenly come to an end, she would not only not have spoken of herself as one of the forsaken, but she could not have thought of herself as one of the disappointed. After Morris had kissed her, the last time he was with her, as a ripe assurance of his devotion, she begged him to go away, to leave her alone, to let her think. Morris went away, taking another kiss first. But Catherine's meditations had lacked a certain coherence. She felt his kisses on her lips and on her cheeks for a long time afterward; the sensation was rather an obstacle than an aid to reflection. She would have liked to see her situation all clearly before her, to make up her mind what she should do if, as she feared, her father should tell her that he disapproved of Morris Townsend. But all that she could see with any vividness was that it was terribly strange that any one should disapprove of him; that there must in that case be some mistake, some mystery, which in a little while would be set at rest. She put off deciding and choosing; before the vision of a conflict with her father she dropped her eyes and sat motionless, holding her breath and waiting. It made her heart beat; it was intensely painful. When Morris kissed her and said these things—that also made her heart beat; but this was worse, and it frightened her. Nevertheless, to-day, when the young man spoke of settling something, taking a line, she felt that it was the truth, and she answered very simply and without hesitating.

"We must do our duty," she said; "we must speak to my father. I will do it to-night; you must do it to-morrow."

"It is very good of you to do it first," Morris answered. "The young man—the happy lover—generally does that. But just as you please."

It pleased Catherine to think that she should be brave for his sake, and in her satisfaction she even gave a little smile. "Women have more tact," she said; "they ought to do it first. They are more conciliating; they can persuade better."

"You will need all your powers of persuasion. But, after all," Morris added, "you are irresistible."

"Please don't speak that way—and promise me this: To-morrow, when you talk with father, you will be very gentle and respectful."

"As much so as possible," Morris promised. "It won't be much use, but I shall try. I certainly would rather have you easily than have to fight for you."

"Don't talk about fighting; we shall not fight."

"Ah, we must be prepared," Morris rejoined; "you especially, because for you it must come hardest. Do you know the first thing your father will say to you?"

"No, Morris; please tell me."

"He will tell you I am mercenary."

"Mercenary!"

"It's a big word, but it means a low thing. It means that I am after your money."

"Oh!" murmured Catherine, softly.

The exclamation was so deprecating

and touching that Morris indulged in another little demonstration of affection. "But he will be sure to say it," he added.

"It will be easy to be prepared for that," Catherine said. "I shall simply say that he is mistaken—that other men may be that way, but that you are not."

"You must make a great point of that, for it will be his own great point."

Catherine looked at her lover a minute, and then she said, "I shall persuade him. But I am glad we shall be rich," she added.

Morris turned away, looking into the crown of his hat. "No, it's a misfortune," he said at last. "It is from that our difficulty will come."

"Well, if it is the worst misfortune, we are not so unhappy. Many people would not think it so bad. I will persuade him, and after that we shall be very glad we have money."

Morris Townsend listened to this robust logic in silence. "I will leave my defence to you; it's a charge that a man has to stoop to defend himself from."

Catherine on her side was silent for awhile; she was looking at him while he looked, with a good deal of fixedness, out of the window. "Morris," she said, abruptly, "are you very sure you love me?"

He turned round, and in a moment he was bending over her. "My own dearest, can you doubt it?"

"I have only known it five days," she said; "but now it seems to me as if I could never do without it."

"You will never be called upon to try." And he gave a little tender, reassuring laugh. Then, in a moment he added, "There is something you must tell me, too." She had closed her eyes after the last words she uttered, and kept them closed; and at this she nodded her head, without opening them. "You must tell me," he went on, "that if your father is dead against me, if he absolutely forbids our marriage, you will still be faithful."

Catherine opened her eyes, gazing at him, and she could give no better promise than what he read there.

"You will cleave to me?" said Morris. "You know you are your own mistress —you are of age."

"Ah, Morris!" she murmured, for all answer; or rather not for all, for she put her hand into his own. He kept it awhile, and presently he kissed her again. This is all that need be recorded of their conversation; but Mrs. Penniman, if she had been present, would probably have admitted that it was as well it had not taken place beside the fountain in Washington Square.

11

Catherine listened for her father when he came in that evening, and she heard him go to his study. She sat quiet, though her heart was beating fast, for nearly half an hour; then she went and knocked at his door—a ceremony without which she never crossed the threshold of this apartment. On entering it now, she found him in his chair beside the fire, entertaining himself with a cigar and the evening paper.

"I have something to say to you," she began very gently; and she sat down in the first place that offered.

"I shall be very happy to hear it, my dear," said her father. He waited—waited, looking at her—while she stared, in a long silence, at the fire. He was curious and impatient, for he was sure she was going to speak of Morris Townsend; but he let her take her own time, for he was determined to be very mild.

"I am engaged to be married!" Catherine announced at last, still staring at the fire.

The Doctor was startled; the accomplished fact was more than he had expected; but he betrayed no surprise. "You do right to tell me," he simply said. "And who is the happy mortal whom you have honored with your choice?"

"Mr. Morris Townsend." And as she pronounced her lover's name Catherine looked at him. What she saw was her father's still gray eye and his clear-cut, definite smile. She contemplated these objects for a moment, and then she looked aback at the fire; it was much warmer.

"When was this arrangement made?" the Doctor asked.

"This afternoon—two hours ago."

"Was Mr. Townsend here?"

"Yes, father; in the front-parlor." She was very glad that she was not obliged to tell him that the ceremony of their betrothal had taken place out there under the bare ailanthus-trees.

"Is it serious?" said the Doctor.

"Very serious, father."

Her father was silent a moment. "Mr. Townsend ought to have told me."

"He means to tell you to-morrow."

"After I know all about it from you? He ought to have told me before. Does he think I didn't care, because I left you so much liberty?"

"Oh no," said Catherine; "he knew you would care. And we have been so much obliged to you for—for the liberty."

The Doctor gave a short laugh. "You might have made a better use of it, Catherine."

"Please don't say that, father!" the girl urged, softly, fixing her dull and gentle eyes upon him.

He puffed his cigar awhile, meditatively. "You have gone very fast," he said, at last.

"Yes," Catherine answered, simply; "I think we have."

Her father glanced at her an instant, removing his eyes from the fire. "I don't wonder Mr. Townsend likes you; you are so simple and so good."

"I don't know why it is; but he *does* like me. I am sure of that."

"And are you very fond of Mr. Townsend?"

"I like him very much, of course, or I shouldn't consent to marry him."

"But you have known him a very short time, my dear."

"Oh," said Catherine, with some eagerness, "it doesn't take long to like a person—when once you begin."

"You must have begun very quickly. Was it the first time you saw him—that night at your aunt's party?"

"I don't know, father," the girl answered. "I can't tell you about that."

"Of course; that's your own affair. You will have observed that I have acted on that principle. I have not interfered; I have left you your liberty; I have remembered that you are no longer a little girl—that you have arrived at years of discretion."

"I feel very old—and very wise," said Catherine, smiling faintly.

"I am afraid that before long you will feel older and wiser yet. I don't like your engagement."

"Ah!" Catherine exclaimed, softly, getting up from her chair.

"No, my dear. I am sorry to give you pain; but I don't like it. You should have consulted me before you settled it. I have been too easy with you, and I feel as if you had taken advantage of my indulgence. Most decidedly you should have spoken to me first."

Catherine hesitated a moment, and then—"It was because I was afraid you wouldn't like it," she confessed.

"Ah, there it is! You had a bad conscience."

"No, I have not a bad conscience, father!" the girl cried out, with considerable energy. "Please don't accuse me of anything so dreadful!" These words, in fact, represented to her imagination something very terrible indeed, something base and cruel, which she associated with malefactors and prisoners. "It was because I was afraid—afraid—" she went on.

"If you were afraid, it was because you had been foolish."

"I was afraid you didn't like Mr. Townsend."

"You were quite right. I don't like him."

"Dear father, you don't know him," said Catherine, in a voice so timidly argumentative that it might have touched him.

"Very true; I don't know him intimately. But I know him enough; I have my impression of him. You don't know him either."

She stood before the fire with her hands lightly clasped in front of her; and her father, leaning back in his chair and looking up at her, made this remark with a placidity that might have been irritating.

I doubt, however, whether Catherine was irritated, though she broke into a vehement protest. "I don't know him?" she cried. "Why, I know him—better than I have ever known any one!"

"You know a part of him—what he has chosen to show you. But you don't know the rest."

"The rest? What is the rest?"

"Whatever it may be, there is sure to be plenty of it."

"I know what you mean," said Catherine, remembering how Morris had forewarned her. "You mean that he is mercenary."

Her father looked up at her still, with his cold, quiet, reasonable eye. "If I meant it, my dear, I should say it! But there is an error I wish particularly to avoid—that of rendering Mr. Townsend more interesting to you by saying hard things about him."

"I won't think them hard if they are true," said Catherine.

"If you don't, you will be a remarkably sensible young woman!"

"They will be your reasons, at any rate, and you will want me to hear your reasons."

The Doctor smiled a little. "Very true. You have a perfect right to ask for them." And he puffed his cigar a few moments. "Very well, then; without accusing Mr. Townsend of being in love only with your fortune—and with the fortune that you justly expect—I will say that there is every reason to suppose that these good things have entered into his calculation more largely than a tender solicitude for your happiness strictly requires. There is, of course, nothing impossible in an intelligent young man entertaining a disinterested affection for you. You are an honest, amiable girl, and an intelligent young man might easily find it out. But the principal thing that we know about this young man—who is, indeed, very intelligent—leads us to suppose that, however much he may value your personal merits, he values your money more. The principal thing we know about him is that he has led a life of dissipation, and has spent a fortune of his own in doing so. That is enough for me, my dear. I wish you to marry a young man with other antecedents—a young man who could give positive guarantees. If Morris Townsend has spent his own fortune in amusing himself, there is every reason to believe that he would spend yours."

The Doctor delivered himself of these remarks slowly, deliberately, with occasional pauses and prolongations of accent, which made no great allowance for poor Catherine's suspense as to his conclusion. She sat down at last, with her head bent and her eyes still fixed upon him; and strangely enough—I hardly know how to tell it—even while she felt that what he said went so terribly against her, she admired his neatness and nobleness of expression. There was something hopeless and oppressive in having to argue with her father; but she too, on her side, must try to be clear. He was so quiet; he was not at all angry; and she, too, must be quiet. But her very effort to be quiet made her tremble.

"That is not the principal thing we know about him," she said; and there was a touch of her tremor in her voice. "There are other things—many other things. He has very high abilities—he wants so much to do something. He is kind, and generous, and true," said poor Catherine, who had not suspected hitherto the resources of her eloquence. "And his fortune—his fortune that he spent—was very small."

"All the more reason he shouldn't have spent it," cried the Doctor, getting up with a laugh. Then, as Catherine, who had also risen to her feet again, stood there in her rather angular earnestness, wishing so much and expressing so little, he drew her toward him and kissed her. "You won't think me cruel?" he said, holding her a moment.

This question was not reassuring; it seemed to Catherine, on the contrary, to suggest possibilities which made her feel sick. But she answered coherently enough, "No, dear father; because if you knew how I feel—and you must know, you know everything—you would be so kind, so gentle."

"Yes, I think I know how you feel," the Doctor said. "I will be very kind—be sure of that. And I will see Mr. Townsend to-morrow. Meanwhile, and for the present, be so good as to mention to no one that you are engaged."

12

On the morrow, in the afternoon, he stayed at home, awaiting Mr. Townsend's call—a proceeding by which it appeared to him (justly perhaps, for he was a very busy man) that he paid Catherine's suitor great honor, and gave both these young people so much the less to complain of. Morris presented himself with a countenance sufficiently serene—he appeared to have forgotten the "insult" for which he had solicited Catherine's sympathy two evenings before—and Doctor Sloper lost no time in letting him know that he had been prepared for his visit.

"Catherine told me yesterday what has been going on between you," he said. "You must allow me to say that it would have been becoming of you to give me notice of your intentions before they had gone so far."

"I should have done so," Morris answered, "if you had not had so much the appearance of leaving your daughter at liberty. She seems to me quite her own mistress."

"Literally, she is. But she has not emancipated herself morally quite so far, I trust, as to choose a husband without consulting me. I have left her at liberty, but I have not been in the least indifferent. The truth is, that your little affair has come to a head with a rapidity that surprises me. It was only the other day that Catherine made your acquaintance."

"It was not long ago, certainly," said Morris, with great gravity. "I admit that we have not been slow to—to arrive at an understanding. But that was very natural, from the moment we were sure of ourselves—and of each other. My interest in Miss Sloper began the first time I saw her."

"Did it not by chance precede your first meeting?" the Doctor asked.

Morris looked at him an instant. "I certainly had already heard that she was a charming girl."

"A charming girl—that's what you think her?"

"Assuredly. Otherwise I should not be sitting here."

The Doctor meditated a moment. "My dear young man," he said at last, "you must be very susceptible. As Catherine's father I have, I trust, a just and tender appreciation of her many good qualities;

but I don't mind telling you that I have never thought of her as a charming girl, and never expected any one else to do so."

Morris Townsend received this statement with a smile that was not wholly devoid of deference. "I don't know what I might think of her if I were her father. I can't put myself in that place. I speak from my own point of view."

"You speak very well," said the Doctor; "but that is not all that is necessary. I told Catherine yesterday that I disapproved of her engagement."

"She let me know as much, and I was very sorry to hear it. I am greatly disappointed." And Morris sat in silence awhile, looking at the floor.

"Did you really expect I would say I was delighted, and throw my daughter into your arms?"

"Oh no; I had an idea you didn't like me."

"What gave you the idea?"

"The fact that I am poor."

"That has a harsh sound," said the Doctor, "but it is about the truth—speaking of you strictly as a son-in-law. Your absence of means, of a profession, of visible resources or prospects, places you in a category from which it would be imprudent for me to select a husband for my daughter, who is a weak young woman with a large fortune. In any other capacity I am perfectly prepared to like you. As a son-in-law, I abominate you."

Morris Townsend listened respectfully. "I don't think Miss Sloper is a weak woman," he presently said.

"Of course you must defend her—it's the least you can do. But I have known my child twenty years, and you have known her six weeks. Even if she were not weak, however, you would still be a penniless man."

"Ah, yes; that is *my* weakness! And therefore, you mean, I am mercenary—I only want your daughter's money."

"I don't say that. I am not obliged to say it; and to say it, save under stress of compulsion, would be very bad taste. I say simply that you belong to the wrong category."

"But your daughter doesn't marry a category," Townsend urged, with his handsome smile. "She marries an individual—an individual whom she is so good as to say she loves."

"An individual who offers so little in return."

"Is it possible to offer more than the most tender affection and a life-long devotion?" the young man demanded.

"It depends how we take it. It is possible to offer a few other things besides, and not only is it possible, but it is the custom. A life-long devotion is measured after the fact; and meanwhile it is usual in these cases to give a few material securities. What are yours? A very handsome face and figure, and a very good manner. They are excellent as far as they go, but they don't go far enough."

"There is one thing you should add to them," said Morris—"the word of a gentleman."

"The word of a gentleman that you will always love Catherine? You must be a fine gentleman to be sure of that."

"The word of a gentleman that I am not mercenary; that my affection for Miss Sloper is as pure and disinterested a sentiment as was ever lodged in a human breast. I care no more for her fortune than for the ashes in that grate."

"I take note—I take note," said the Doctor. "But, having done so, I turn to our category again. Even with that solemn vow on your lips, you take your place in it. There is nothing against you but an accident, if you will; but, with my thirty years' medical practice, I have seen that accidents may have far-reaching consequences."

Morris smoothed his hat—it was already remarkably glossy—and continued to display a self-control which, as the Doctor was obliged to admit, was extremely creditable to him. But his disappointment was evidently keen.

"Is there nothing I can do to make you believe in me?"

"If there were, I should be sorry to suggest it, for—don't you see?—I don't want to believe in you," said the Doctor, smiling.

"I would go and dig in the fields."

"That would be foolish."

"I will take the first work that offers to-morrow."

"Do so by all means—but for your own sake, not for mine."

"I see; you think I am an idler!" Morris exclaimed, a little too much in the tone of a man who has made a discovery. But he saw his error immediately, and blushed.

"It doesn't matter what I think, when once I have told you I don't think of you as a son-in-law."

But Morris persisted: "You think I would squander her money?"

The Doctor smiled. "It doesn't matter, as I say; but I plead guilty to that."

"That's because I spent my own, I suppose," said Morris. "I frankly confess that. I have been wild; I have been foolish. I will tell you every crazy thing I ever did, if you like. There were some great follies among the number—I have never concealed that. But I have sown my wild-oats. Isn't there some proverb about a reformed rake? I was not a rake, but I assure you I have reformed. It is better to have amused one's self for awhile and have done with it. Your daughter would never care for a milksop; and I will take the liberty of saying that you would like one quite as little. Besides, between my money and hers there is a great difference. I spent my own; it was because it was my own that I spent it. And I made no debts; when it was gone I stopped. I don't owe a penny in the world."

"Allow me to inquire what you are living on now—though I admit," the Doctor added, "that the question, on my part, is inconsistent."

"I am living on the remnants of my property," said Morris Townsend.

"Thank you," the Doctor gravely replied.

Yes, certainly, Morris's self-control was laudable. "Even admitting I attach an undue importance to Miss Sloper's fortune," he went on, "would not that be in itself an assurance that I would take good care of it?"

"That you should take too much care would be quite as bad as that you should take too little. Catherine might suffer as much by your economy as by your extravagance."

"I think you are very unjust!" The young man made this declaration decently, civilly, without violence.

"It is your privilege to think so, and I surrender my reputation to you! I certainly don't flatter myself, I gratify you."

"Don't you care a little to gratify your daughter? Do you enjoy the idea of making her miserable?"

"I am perfectly resigned to her thinking me a tyrant for a twelvemonth."

"For a twelvemonth!" exclaimed Morris, with a laugh.

"For a lifetime, then. She may as well be miserable in that way as in the other."

Here at last Morris lost his temper. "Ah, you are not polite, sir!" he cried.

"You push me to it—you argue too much."

"I have a great deal at stake."

"Well, whatever it is," said the Doctor, "you have lost it."

"Are you sure of that?" asked Morris; "are you sure your daughter will give me up?"

"I mean, of course, you have lost it as far as I am concerned. As for Catherine's giving you up—no, I am not sure of it. But as I shall strongly recommend it, as I have a great fund of respect and affection in my daughter's mind to draw upon, and as she has the sentiment of duty developed in a very high degree, I think it extremely possible."

Morris Townsend began to smooth his hat again. "I, too, have a fund of affection to draw upon," he observed, at last.

The Doctor at this point showed his own first symptoms of irritation. "Do you mean to defy me?"

"Call it what you please, sir. I mean not to give your daughter up."

The Doctor shook his head. "I haven't the least fear of your pining away your life. You are made to enjoy it."

Morris gave a laugh. "Your opposition to my marriage is all the more cruel, then. Do you intend to forbid your daughter to see me again?"

"She is past the age at which people are forbidden, and I am not a father in an old-fashioned novel. But I shall strongly urge her to break with you."

"I don't think she will," said Morris Townsend.

"Perhaps not; but I shall have done what I could."

"She has gone too far—" Morris went on.

"To retreat? Then let her stop where she is."

"Too far to stop, I mean."

The Doctor looked at him a moment; Morris had his hand on the door. "There is a great deal of impertinence in your saying it."

"I will say no more, sir," Morris answered; and, making his bow, he left the room.

13

It may be thought the Doctor was too positive, and Mrs. Almond intimated as much. But, as he said, he had his impression; it seemed to him sufficient, and he had no wish to modify it. He had passed his life in estimating people (it was part of the medical trade), and in nineteen cases out of twenty he was right.

"Perhaps Mr. Townsend is the twentieth case," said Mrs. Almond.

"Perhaps he is, though he doesn't look to me at all like a twentieth case. But I will give him the benefit of the doubt, and, to make sure, I will go and talk with Mrs. Montgomery. She will almost certainly tell me I have done right; but it is just possible that she will prove to me that I have made the greatest mistake of my life. If she does, I will beg Mr. Townsend's pardon. You needn't invite her to meet me, as you kindly proposed; I will write her a frank letter, telling her how matters stand, and asking leave to come and see her."

"I am afraid the frankness will be chiefly on your side. The poor little woman will stand up for her brother, whatever he may be."

"Whatever he may be! I doubt that. People are not always so fond of their brothers."

"Ah," said Mrs. Almond, "when it's a question of thirty thousand a year coming into a family—"

"If she stands up for him on account of the money, she will be a humbug. If she is a humbug, I shall see it. If I see it, I won't waste time with her."

"She is not a humbug—she is an exemplary woman. She will not wish to play her brother a trick simply because he is selfish."

"If she is worth talking to, she will sooner play him a trick than that he should play Catherine one. Has she seen Catherine, by-the-way—does she know her?"

"Not to my knowledge. Mr. Townsend can have had no particular interest in bringing them together."

"If she is an exemplary woman, no. But we shall see to what extent she answers your description."

"I shall be curious to hear her description of you," said Mrs. Almond, with a laugh. "And, meanwhile, how is Catherine taking it?"

"As she takes everything—as a matter of course."

"Doesn't she make a noise? Hasn't she made a scene?"

"She is not scenic."

"I thought a lovelorn maiden was always scenic."

"A ridiculous widow is more so. Lavinia has made me a speech; she thinks me very arbitrary."

"She has a talent for being in the wrong," said Mrs. Almond. "But I am very sorry for Catherine, all the same."

"So am I. But she will get over it."

"You believe she will give him up?"

"I count upon it. She has such an admiration for her father."

"Oh, we know all about that. But it only makes me pity her the more. It makes her dilemma the more painful, and the effort of choosing between you and her lover almost impossible."

"If she can't choose, all the better."

"Yes; but he will stand there entreating her to choose, and Lavinia will pull on that side."

"I am glad she is not on my side; she is capable of ruining an excellent cause. The day Lavinia gets into your boat it capsizes. But she had better be careful," said the Doctor. "I will have no treason in my house."

"I suspect she will be careful; for she is at bottom very much afraid of you."

"They are both afraid of me, harmless as I am," the Doctor answered. "And it is on that that I build—on the salutary terror I inspire."

14

He wrote his frank letter to Mrs. Montgomery, who punctually answered it, mentioning an hour at which he might present himself in the Second Avenue. She lived in a neat little house of red brick, which had been freshly painted, with the edges of the bricks very sharply marked out in white. It has now disappeared, with its companions, to make room for a row of structures more majestic. There were green shutters upon the windows without slats, but pierced with little holes, arranged in groups; and before the house was a diminutive "yard," ornamented with a bush of mysterious character, and surrounded by a low wooden paling, painted in the same green as the shutters. The place looked like a magnified baby-house, and might have been taken down from a shelf in a toy-shop. Doctor Sloper, when he went to call, said to himself, as he glanced at the objects I have enumerated, that Mrs. Montgomery was evidently a thrifty and self-respecting little person—the modest proportions of her dwelling seemed to indicate that she was of small stature—who took a virtuous satisfaction in keeping herself tidy, and had resolved that, since she might not be splendid, she would at least be immaculate. She received him in a little parlor, which was precisely the parlor he had expected: a small unspeckled bower, ornamented with a desultory foliage of tissue-paper, and with clusters of glass drops, amidst which—to carry out the analogy—the temperature of the leafy season was maintained by means of a cast-iron stove, emitting a dry blue flame, and smelling strongly of varnish. The walls were embellished with engravings swathed in pink gauze, and the tables ornamented with volumes of extracts from the poets, usually bound in black cloth stamped with florid designs in jaundiced gilt. The Doctor had time to take cognizance of these details; for Mrs. Montgomery, whose conduct he pronounced under the circumstances inexcusable, kept him waiting some ten minutes before she appeared. At last, however, she rustled in, smoothing down a stiff poplin dress, with a little frightened flush in a gracefully rounded cheek.

She was a small, plump, fair woman, with a bright, clear eye, and an extraordinary air of neatness and briskness. But these qualities were evidently combined with an unaffected humility, and the Doctor gave her his esteem as soon as he had looked at her. A brave little person, with lively perceptions, and yet a disbelief in her own talent for social, as distinguished from practical, affairs—this was his rapid mental *résumé* of Mrs. Montgomery; who, as he saw, was flattered by what she regarded as the honor of his visit. Mrs. Montgomery, in her little red house in the Second Avenue, was a person for whom Dr. Sloper was one of the great men—one of the fine gentlemen of New York; and while she fixed her agitated eyes upon him, while she clasped her mittened hands together in her glossy poplin lap, she had the appearance of saying to herself that he quite answered her idea of what a distinguished guest would naturally be. She apologized for being late; but he interrupted her.

"It doesn't matter," he said; "for while I sat here I had time to think over what I wish to say to you, and to make up my mind how to begin."

"Oh, do begin!" murmured Mrs. Montgomery.

"It is not so easy," said the Doctor, smiling. "You will have gathered from my letter that I wish to ask you a few questions, and you may not find it very comfortable to answer them."

"Yes; I have thought what I should say. It is not very easy."

"But you must understand my situation—my state of mind. Your brother wishes to marry my daughter, and I wish to find out what sort of a young man he is. A good way to do so seemed to be to come and ask you, which I have proceeded to do."

Mrs. Montgomery evidently took the situation very seriously; she was in a state of extreme moral concentration. She kept her pretty eyes, which were illumined by a sort of brilliant modesty, attached to his own countenance, and evidently paid the most earnest attention to each of his words. Her expression indicated that she thought his idea of coming to see her a very superior conception, but that she was really afraid to have opinions on strange subjects.

"I am extremely glad to see you," she said, in a tone which seemed to admit, at the same time, that this had nothing to do with the question.

The Doctor took advantage of this admission. "I didn't come to see you for your pleasure; I came to make you say disagreeable things—and you can't like that. What sort of a gentleman is your brother?"

Mrs. Montgomery's illuminated gaze grew vague, and began to wander. She smiled a little, and for some time made no answer, so that the Doctor at last became impatient. And her answer, when it came, was not satisfactory. "It is difficult to talk about one's brother."

"Not when one is fond of him, and when one has plenty of good to say."

"Yes, even then, when a good deal depends on it," said Mrs. Montgomery.

"Nothing depends on it for you."

"I mean for—for—" and she hesitated.

"For your brother himself. I see."

"I mean for Miss Sloper," said Mrs. Montgomery.

The Doctor liked this; it had the accent of sincerity. "Exactly; that's the point. If my poor girl should marry your brother, everything—as regards her happiness—would depend on his being a good fellow. She is the best creature in the world, and she could never do him a grain of injury. He, on the other hand, if he should not be all that we desire, might make her very miserable. That is why I want you to throw some light upon his character, you know. Of course, you are not bound to do it. My daughter, whom you have never seen, is nothing to you; and I, possibly, am only an indiscreet and impertinent old man. It is perfectly open to you to tell me that my visit is in very bad taste, and that I had better go about my business. But I don't think you will do this; because I think we shall interest you—my poor girl and I. I am sure that if you were to see Catherine she would interest you very much. I don't mean because she is interesting in the usual sense of the word, but because you would feel sorry for her. She is so soft, so simple-minded, she would be such an easy victim! A bad husband would have remarkable facilities for making her miserable; for she would have neither the intelligence nor the resolution to get the better of him, and yet she would have an exaggerated power of suffering. I see," added the Doctor, with his most insinuating, his most professional laugh, "you are already interested."

"I have been interested from the moment he told me he was engaged," said Mrs. Montgomery.

"Ah! he says that—he calls it an engagement?"

"Oh, he has told me you didn't like it."

"Did he tell you that I don't like *him?*"

"Yes, he told me that too. I said I couldn't help it," added Mrs. Montgomery.

"Of course you can't. But what you can do is to tell me I am right—to give me an attestation, as it were." And the Doctor accompanied this remark with another professional smile.

Mrs. Montgomery, however, smiled not at all; it was obvious that she could not take the humorous view of his appeal. "That is a good deal to ask," she said, at last.

"There can be no doubt of that; and I must, in conscience, remind you of the advantages a young man marrying my daughter would enjoy. She has an income of ten thousand dollars in her own right, left her by her mother; if she marries a husband I approve, she will come into almost twice as much more at my death."

Mrs. Montgomery listened in great earnestness to this splendid financial statement; she had never heard thousands of dollars so familiarly talked about. She flushed a little with excitement. "Your daughter will be immensely rich," she said, softly.

"Precisely—that's the bother of it."

"And if Morris should marry her, he—he—" And she hesitated, timidly.

"He would be master of all that money? By no means. He would be master of the ten thousand a year that she has from her mother; but I should leave every penny of my own fortune, earned in the laborious exercise of my profession, to my nephews and nieces."

Mrs. Montgomery dropped her eyes at this, and sat for some time gazing at the straw matting which covered her floor.

"I suppose it seems to you," said the Doctor, laughing, "that in so doing I should play your brother a very shabby trick."

"Not at all. That is too much money to get possession of so easily by marrying. I don't think it would be right."

"It's right to get all one can. But in this case your brother wouldn't be able. If Catherine marries without my consent, she doesn't get a penny from my own pocket."

"Is that certain?" asked Mrs. Montgomery, looking up.

"As certain as that I sit here."

"Even if she should pine away?"

"Even if she should pine to a shadow, which isn't probable."

"Does Morris know this?"

"I shall be most happy to inform him," the Doctor exclaimed.

Mrs. Montgomery resumed her meditations; and her visitor, who was prepared to give time to the affair, asked himself whether, in spite of her little conscientious air, she was not playing into her brother's hands. At the same time he was half ashamed of the ordeal to which he had subjected her, and was touched by the gentleness with which she bore it. "If she were a humbug," he said, "she would get angry, unless she be very deep indeed. It is not probable that she is as deep as that."

"What makes you dislike Morris so much?" she presently asked, emerging from her reflections.

"I don't dislike him in the least as a friend, as a companion. He seems to me a charming fellow, and I should think he would be excellent company. I dislike him exclusively as a son-in-law. If the only office of a son-in-law were to dine at the paternal table, I should set a high value upon your brother: he dines capitally. But that is a small part of his function, which, in general, is to be a protector and care-taker of my child, who is singularly ill-adapted to take care of herself. It is there that he doesn't satisfy me. I confess I have nothing but my impression to go by; but I am in the habit of trusting my impression. Of course you are at liberty to contradict it flat. He strikes me as selfish and shallow."

Mrs. Montgomery's eyes expanded a little, and the Doctor fancied he saw the light of admiration in them. "I wonder you have discovered he is selfish," she exclaimed.

"Do you think he hides it so well?"

"Very well indeed," said Mrs. Montgomery. "And I think we are all rather selfish," she added, quickly.

"I think so too; but I have seen people hide it better than he. You see I am helped by a habit I have of dividing people into classes, into types. I may easily be mistaken about your brother as an individual, but his type is written on his whole person."

"He is very good-looking," said Mrs. Montgomery.

The Doctor eyed her a moment. "You women are all the same! But the type to which your brother belongs was made to be the ruin of you, and you were made to be its handmaids and victims. The sign of the type in question is the determination—sometimes terrible in its quiet intensity—to accept nothing of life but its pleasures, and to secure these pleasures chiefly by the aid of your complaisant sex. Young men of this class never do anything for themselves that they can get other people to do for them, and it is the infatuation, the devotion, the superstition of others that keeps them going. These others, in ninety-nine cases out of a hundred, are women. What our young friends chiefly insist upon is that some one else shall suffer for them; and women do that sort of thing, as you must know, wonderfully well." The Doctor paused a moment, and then he added, abruptly, "You have suffered immensely for your brother!"

This exclamation was abrupt, as I say, but it was also perfectly calculated. The Doctor had been rather disappointed at not finding his compact and comfortable little hostess surrounded in a more visible degree by the ravages of Morris Townsend's immorality; but he had said to himself that this was not because the young man had spared her, but because she had contrived to plaster up her wounds. They were aching there behind the varnished stove, the festooned engravings, beneath her own neat little poplin bosom; and if he could only touch the tender spot, she would make a movement that would betray her. The words I have just quoted were an attempt to put his finger suddenly upon the place, and they had some of the success that he looked for. The tears sprung for a moment to Mrs. Montgomery's eyes, and she indulged in a proud little jerk of the head.

"I don't know how you have found that out!" she exclaimed.

"By a philosophic trick—by what they call induction. You know you have always your option of contradicting me.

But kindly answer me a question: Don't you give your brother money? I think you ought to answer that."

"Yes, I have given him money," said Mrs. Montgomery.

"And you have not had much to give him?"

She was silent a moment. "If you ask me for a confession of poverty, that is easily made. I am very poor."

"One would never suppose it from your—your charming house," said the Doctor. "I learned from my sister that your income was moderate, and your family numerous."

"I have five children," Mrs. Montgomery observed; "but I am happy to say I can bring them up decently."

"Of course you can—accomplished and devoted as you are. But your brother has counted them over, I suppose?"

"Counted them over?"

"He knows there are five, I mean. He tells me it is he that brings them up."

Mrs. Montgomery stared a moment, and then quickly—"Oh yes; he teaches them—Spanish."

The Doctor laughed out. "That must take a great deal off your hands! Your brother also knows, of course, that you have very little money?"

"I have often told him so," Mrs. Montgomery exclaimed, more unreservedly than she had yet spoken. She was apparently taking some comfort in the Doctor's clairvoyance.

"Which means that you have often occasion to, and that he often sponges on you. Excuse the crudity of my language; I simply express a fact. I don't ask you how much of your money he has had, it is none of my business. I have ascertained what I suspected—what I wished." And the Doctor got up, gently smoothing his hat. "Your brother lives on you," he said, as he stood there.

Mrs. Montgomery quickly rose from her chair, following her visitor's movements with a look of fascination. But then, with a certain inconsequence—"I have never complained of him," she said.

"You needn't protest—you have not betrayed him. But I advise you not to give him any more money."

"Don't you see it is in my interest that he should marry a rich person?" she asked. "If, as you say, he lives on me, I can only wish to get rid of him; and to put obstacles in the way of his marrying is to increase my own difficulties."

"I wish very much you would come to me with your difficulties," said the Doctor. "Certainly, if I throw him back on your hands, the least I can do is to help you bear the burden. If you will allow me to say so, then, I shall take the liberty of placing in your hands, for the present, a certain fund for your brother's support."

Mrs. Montgomery stared; she evidently thought he was jesting; but she presently saw that he was not, and the complication of her feelings became painful. "It seems to me that I ought to be very much offended with you," she murmured.

"Because I have offered you money? That's a superstition," said the Doctor. "You must let me come and see you again, and we will talk about these things. I suppose that some of your children are girls?"

"I have two little girls," said Mrs. Montgomery.

"Well, when they grow up, and begin to think of taking husbands, you will see how anxious you will be about the moral character of these husbands. Then you will understand this visit of mine."

"Ah, you are not to believe that Morris's moral character is bad."

The Doctor looked at her a little, with folded arms. "There is something I should greatly like, as a moral satisfaction. I should like to hear you say, 'He is abominably selfish.' "

The words came out with the grave distinctness of his voice, and they seemed for an instant to create, to poor Mrs. Montgomery's troubled vision, a material image. She gazed at it an instant, and then she turned away. "You distress me, sir!" she exclaimed. "He is, after all, my brother; and his talents, his talents—" On these last words her voice quavered, and before he knew it she had burst into tears.

"His talents are first-rate," said the Doctor. "We must find the proper field for them." And he assured her most respectfully of his regret at having so greatly discomposed her. "It's all for my poor Catherine," he went on. "You must know her, and you will see."

Mrs. Montgomery brushed away her tears, and blushed at having shed them. "I should like to know your daughter," she answered; and then, in an instant—"Don't let her marry him!"

Doctor Sloper went away with the words gently humming in his ears—"Don't let her marry him!" They gave him the moral satisfaction of which he had just spoken, and their value was the greater that they had evidently cost a pang to poor little Mrs. Montgomery's family pride.

15

He had been puzzled by the way that Catherine carried herself; her attitude at this sentimental crisis seemed to him unnaturally passive. She had not spoken to him again after that scene in the library, the day before his interview with Morris; and a week had elapsed without making any change in her manner. There was nothing in it that appealed for pity, and he was even a little disappointed at her not giving him an opportunity to make up for his harshness by some manifestation of liberality which should operate as a compensation. He thought a little of offering to take her for a tour in Europe; but he was determined to do this only in case she should seem mutely to reproach him. He had an idea that she would display a talent for mute reproaches, and he was surprised at not finding himself exposed to these silent batteries. She said nothing, either tacitly or explicitly, and as she was never very talkative, there was now no especial eloquence in her reserve. And poor Catherine was not sulky—a style of behavior for which she had too little histrionic talent—she was simply very patient. Of course she was thinking over her situation, and she was apparently doing so in a deliberate and unimpassioned manner, with a view of making the best of it.

"She will do as I have bidden her," said the Doctor; and he made the further reflection that his daughter was not a woman of a great spirit.

I know not whether he had hoped for a little more resistance for the sake of a little more entertainment; but he said to himself, as he had said before, that though it might have its momentary alarms, paternity was, after all, not an exciting vocation.

Catherine meanwhile had made a discovery of a very different sort; it had become vivid to her that there was a great excitement in trying to be a good daughter. She had an entirely new feeling, which may be described as a state of expectant suspense about her own actions. She watched herself as she would have watched another person, and wondered what she would do. It was as if this other person, who was both herself and not herself, had suddenly sprung into being, inspiring her with a natural curiosity as to the performance of untested functions.

"I am glad I have such a good daughter," said her father, kissing her, after the lapse of several days.

"I am trying to be good," she answered, turning away, with a conscience not altogether clear.

"If there is anything you would like to say to me, you know you must not hesitate. You needn't feel obliged to be so quiet. I shouldn't care that Mr. Townsend should be a frequent topic of conversation, but whenever you have anything particular to say about him I shall be very glad to hear it."

"Thank you," said Catherine; "I have nothing particular at present."

He never asked her whether she had seen Morris again, because he was sure that if this had been the case she would tell him. She had, in fact, not seen him; she had only written him a long letter. The letter, at least, was long for her; and, it may be added, that it was long for Morris; it consisted of five pages, in a remarkably neat and handsome hand. Catherine's handwriting was beautiful, and she was even a little proud of it: she was extremely fond of copying, and possessed volumes of extracts which testified to this accomplishment, volumes which she had exhibited one day to her lover, when the bliss of feeling that she was important in his eyes was exceptionally keen. She told Morris, in writing, that her father had expressed the wish that she should not see him again, and that she begged he would not come to the house until she should have "made up her mind." Morris replied with a passionate epistle, in which he asked to what, in Heaven's name, she wished to make up her mind. Had not her mind been made up two weeks before, and could it be possible that she entertained the idea of throwing him off? Did she mean to break down at the very beginning of their ordeal, after all the promises of fidelity she had both given and extracted? And he gave an account of his own interview with her father—an account not identical at all points with that offered in these pages. "He was terribly violent," Morris wrote, "but you know my self-control. I have need of it all when I remember that I have it in my power to break in upon your cruel captivity." Catherine sent him, in answer to this, a note of three lines. "I am in great trouble; do not doubt of my affection, but let me wait a little and think." The idea of a struggle with her father, of setting up her will against his own, was heavy on her soul, and it kept her quiet, as a great physical weight keeps us motionless. It never entered into her mind to throw her lover off; but from the first she tried to assure herself that there would be a peaceful way out of their difficulty. The assurance was vague, for it contained no element of positive conviction that her father would change his mind. She only had an idea that if she should be very good, the situation would in some mysterious manner improve. To be good she must be patient, outwardly submissive, abstain from judging her father too harshly, and from committing any act of open defiance. He was perhaps right, after all, to think as he did; by which Catherine meant not in the least that his judgment of Morris's motives in seeking to marry her was perhaps a just one, but that it was probably natural and proper that conscientious parents should be suspicious and even unjust. There were probably people in the world as bad as her father supposed Morris to be, and if there were the slightest chance of Morris being one of these sinister persons, the Doctor was right in taking it into account. Of course he could not know what she knew—how the purest love and truth were seated in the young man's eyes; but Heaven, in its time, might appoint a way of bringing him to such knowledge. Catherine expected a good deal of Heaven, and referred to the skies the initiative, as the French say, in dealing with her dilemma. She could not imagine herself imparting any kind of knowledge to her father; there was something superior even in his injustice, and absolute in his mistakes. But she could at least be good, and if she were only good enough, Heaven would invent some way of reconciling all things—the dignity of her father's errors and the sweetness of her own confidence, the strict performance of her filial duties, and the enjoyment of Morris Townsend's affection.

Poor Catherine would have been glad to regard Mrs. Penniman as an illuminating agent, a part which this lady herself, indeed, was but imperfectly prepared to play. Mrs. Penniman took too much satisfaction in the sentimental shadows of this little drama to have, for the moment, any great interest in dissipating them. She wished the plot to thicken, and the advice that she gave her niece tended, in her own imagination, to produce this result. It was rather incoherent counsel, and from one day to another it contradicted itself; but it was pervaded by an earnest desire that Catherine should do something striking. "You must *act*, my dear; in your situation the great thing is to act," said Mrs. Penniman, who found her niece altogether beneath her opportunities. Mrs. Penniman's real hope was that the girl would make a secret marriage, at which she should officiate as brideswoman or duenna. She had a vision of this ceremony being performed in some subterranean chapel; subterranean chapels in New York were not frequent, but Mrs. Penniman's imagination was not chilled by trifles; and of the guilty couple—she liked to think of poor Catherine and her suitor as the guilty couple—being shuffled away in a fast-whirling vehicle to some obscure lodging in the suburbs, where she would pay them (in a thick veil) clandestine visits; where they would endure a period of romantic privation; and when ultimately, after she should have been their earthly providence, their intercessor, their advocate, and their world, they would be reconciled to her medium of communication with the brother in an artistic tableau, in which she herself should be somehow the central figure. She hesitated as yet to recommend this course to Catherine, but she attempted to draw an attractive picture of it to Morris Townsend. She was in daily communication with the young man, whom she kept informed by letters of the state of affairs in Washington Square. As he had been banished, as she said, from the house, she no longer saw him; but she ended by writing to him that she longed for an interview. This interview could take place only on neutral ground, and she bethought herself greatly before selecting a place of meeting. She had an inclination for Greenwood Cemetery, but she gave it up as too distant; she could not absent herself for so long, as she said, without exciting suspicion. Then she thought of the Battery, but that was rather cold and windy, besides one's being exposed to intrusion from the Irish emmigrants who at this point alight, with large appetites, in the New World; and at last she fixed upon an oyster saloon in the Seventh Avenue, kept by a negro—an establishment of which she knew nothing save that she had noticed it in passing. She made an appointment with Morris Townsend to meet him there, and she went to the tryst at dusk, enveloped in an impenetrable veil. He kept her waiting for half an hour—he had almost the whole width of the city to traverse—but she liked to wait, it seemed, to intensify the situation. She ordered a cup of tea, which proved excessively bad, and this gave her a sense that she was suffering in a romantic cause. When Morris at last arrived, they sat together for half an hour in the duskiest corner of the back shop; and it is hardly too much to say that this was the happiest half-hour that Mrs. Penniman had known for years. The situation was really thrilling, and it scarcely seemed to her a false note when her companion asked for an oyster stew, and proceeded to consume it before her eyes. Morris, indeed, needed all the satisfaction that stewed oysters could give him, for it may be intimated to the reader that he regarded Mrs. Penniman in the light of a fifth wheel to his coach.

He was in a state of irritation natural to a gentleman of fine parts who had been snubbed in a benevolent attempt to confer a distinction upon a young woman of inferior characteristics, and the insinuating sympathy of this somewhat desiccated matron appeared to offer him no practical relief. He thought her a humbug, and he judged of humbugs with a good deal of confidence. He had listened and made himself agreeable to her at first, in order to get a footing in Washington Square; and at present he needed all his self-command to be decently civil. It would have gratified him to tell her that she was a fantastic old woman, and that he would like to put her into an omnibus and send her home. We know, however, that Morris possessed the virtue of self-control, and he had moreover the constant habit of seeking to be agreeable; so that, although Mrs. Penniman's demeanor only exasperated his already unquiet nerves, he listened to her with a sombre deference in which she found much to admire.

16

They had of course immediately spoken of Catherine. "Did she send me a message,, or—or anything?" Morris asked. He appeared to think that she might have sent him a trinket or a lock of her hair.

Mrs. Penniman was slightly embarrassed, for she had not told her niece of her intended expedition. "Not exactly a message," she said: "I didn't ask her for one, because I was afraid to—to excite her."

"I am afraid she is not very excitable." And Morris gave a smile of some bitterness.

"She is better than that—she is steadfast, she is true."

"Do you think she will hold fast, then?"

"To the death!"

"Oh, I hope it won't come to that," said Morris.

"We must be prepared for the worst, and that is what I wish to speak to you about."

"What do you call the worst?"

"Well," said Mrs. Penniman, "my brother's hard, intellectual nature."

"Oh, the devil!"

"He is impervious to pity," Mrs. Penniman added, by way of explanation.

"Do you mean that he won't come round?"

"He will never be vanquished by argument. I have studied him. He will be vanquished only by the accomplished fact."

"The accomplished fact?"

"He will come round afterward," said Mrs. Penniman, with extreme significance. "He cares for nothing but facts—he must be met by facts."

"Well," rejoined Morris, "it is a fact that I wish to marry his daughter. I met him with that the other day, but he was not at all vanquished."

Mrs. Penniman was silent a little, and her smile beneath the shadow of her capacious bonnet, on the edge of which her black veil was arranged curtainwise, fixed itself upon Morris's face with a still more tender brilliancy. "Marry Catherine first, and meet himself afterward!" she exclaimed.

"Do you recommend that?" asked the young man, frowning heavily.

She was a little frightened, but she went on with considerable boldness. "That is the way I see it: a private marriage—a private marriage." She repeated the phrase because she liked it.

"Do you mean that I should carry Catherine off? What do they call it—elope with her?"

"It is not a crime when you are driven to it," said Mrs. Penniman. "My husband, as I have told you, was a distinguished clergyman—one of the most eloquent men of his day. He once married a young couple that had fled from the house of the young lady's father; he was so interested in their story. He had no hesitation, and everything came out beautifully. The father was afterward reconciled, and thought everything of the young man. Mr. Penniman married them in the evening, about seven o'clock. The church was so dark you could scarcely see, and Mr. Penniman was intensely agitated—he was so sympathetic. I don't believe he could have done it again."

"Unfortunately, Catherine and I have not Mr. Penniman to marry us," said Morris.

"No, but you have me!" rejoined Mrs. Penniman, expressively. "I can't perform the ceremony, but I can help you; I can watch!"

"The woman's an idiot!" thought Morris; but he was obliged to say something different. It was not, however, materially more civil. "Was it in order to tell me this that you requested I would meet you here?"

Mrs. Penniman had been conscious of a certain vagueness in her errand, and of not being able to offer him any very tangible reward for his long walk. "I thought perhaps you would like to see one who is so near to Catherine," she observed, with considerable majesty; "and also," she added, "that you would value an opportunity of sending her something."

Morris extended his empty hands with a melancholy smile. "I am greatly obliged to you, but I have nothing to send."

"Haven't you a *word*?" asked his companion, with her suggestive smile coming back.

Morris frowned again. "Tell her to hold fast," he said, rather curtly.

"That is a good word—a noble word: it will make her happy for many days. She is very touching, very brave," Mrs. Penniman went on, arranging her mantle and preparing to depart. While she was so engaged she had an inspiration; she found the phrase that she could boldly offer as a vindication of the step she had taken. "If you marry Catherine at all risks," she said, "you will give my brother a proof of your being what he pretends to doubt."

"What he pretends to doubt?"

"Don't you know what that is?" Mrs. Penniman asked, almost playfully.

"It does not concern me to know," said Morris, grandly.

"Of course it makes you angry."

"I despise it," Morris declared.

"Ah, you know what it is then?" said Mrs. Penniman, shaking her finger at him. "He pretends that you like—you like the money."

Morris hesitated a moment; and then, as if he spoke advisedly, "I *do* like the money!"

"Ah, but not—but not as he means it. You don't like it more than Catherine?"

He leaned his elbows on the table and buried his head in his hands. "You torture me!" he murmured. And, indeed, this was almost the effect of the poor lady's too importunate interest in his situation.

But she insisted in making her point. "If you marry her in spite of him, he will take for granted that you expect nothing of him, and are prepared to do without it; and so he will see that you are disinterested."

Morris raised his head a little, following this argument. "And what shall I gain by that?"

"Why, that he will see that he has been wrong in thinking that you wished to get his money."

"And seeing that I wish he would go to the deuce with it, he will leave it to a hospital. Is that what you mean?" asked Morris.

"No, I don't mean that; though that would be very grand," Mrs. Penniman quickly added. "I mean that, having done you such an injustice, he will think it his duty, at the end, to make some amends."

Morris shook his head, though it must be confessed he was a little struck with this idea. "Do you think he is so sentimental?"

"He is not sentimental," said Mrs. Penniman; "but, to be perfectly fair to him, I think he has, in his own narrow way, a certain sense of duty."

There passed through Morris Townsend's mind a rapid wonder as to what he might, even under a remote contingency, be indebted to from the action of this principle in Doctor Sloper's breast, and the inquiry exhausted itself in his sense of the ludicrous. "Your brother has no duties to me," he said presently, "and I none to him."

"Ah, but he has duties to Catherine."

"Yes; but you see, on that principle Catherine has duties to him as well."

Mrs. Penniman got up with a melancholy sigh, as if she thought him very unimaginative. "She has always performed them faithfully; and now do you think she has no duties to *you?*" Mrs. Penniman always, even in conversation, italicized her personal pronouns.

"It would sound harsh to say so. I am so grateful for her love," Morris added.

"I will tell her you said that. And now, remember that if you need me I am there." And Mrs. Penniman, who could think of nothing more to say, nodded vaguely in the direction of Washington Square.

Morris looked some moments at the sanded floor of the shop; he seemed to be disposed to linger a moment. At last, looking up with a certain abruptness, "It is your belief that if she marries me he will cut her off?" he asked.

Mrs. Penniman stared a little, and smiled. "Why, I have explained to you what I think would happen—that in the end it would be the best thing to do."

"You mean that, whatever she does, in the long-run she will get the money?"

"It doesn't depend upon her, but upon you. Venture to appear as disinterested as you are," said Mrs. Penniman, ingeniously. Morris dropped his eyes on the sanded floor again, pondering this, and she pursued: "Mr. Penniman and I had nothing, and we were very happy. Catherine, moreover, has her mother's fortune, which, at the time my sister-in-law married, was considered a very handsome one."

"Oh, don't speak of that!" said Morris; and indeed it was quite superfluous, for he had contemplated the fact in all its lights.

"Austin married a wife with money—why shouldn't you?"

"Ah! but your brother was a doctor," Morris objected.

"Well, all young men can't be doctors."

"I should think it an extremely loathsome profession," said Morris, with an air of intellectual independence; then, in a moment, he went on rather inconsequently, "Do you suppose there is a will already made in Catherine's favor?"

"I suppose so—even doctors must die; and perhaps a little in mine," Mrs. Penniman frankly added.

"And you believe he would certainly change it—as regards Catherine?"

"Yes; and then change it back again."

"Ah, but one can't depend on that," said Morris.

"Do you want to *depend* on it?" Mrs. Penniman asked.

Morris blushed a little. "Well, I am certainly afraid of being the cause of an injury to Catherine."

"Ah! you must not be afraid. Be afraid of nothing, and everything will go well."

And then Mrs. Penniman paid for her cup of tea, and Morris paid for his oyster stew, and they went out together into the dimly-lighted wilderness of the Seventh Avenue. The dusk had closed in completely, and the street lamps were separated by wide intervals of a pavement in which cavities and fissures played a disproportionate part. An omnibus, emblazoned with strange pictures, went tumbling over the dislocated cobblestones.

"How will you go home?" Morris asked, following this vehicle with an interested eye. Mrs. Penniman had taken his arm.

She hesitated a moment. "I think this manner would be pleasant," she said; and she continued to let him feel the value of his support.

So he walked with her through the devious ways of the west side of the town, and through the bustle of gathering nightfall in populous streets, to the quiet precinct of Washington Square. They lingered a moment at the foot of Doctor Sloper's white marble steps, above which a spotless white door, adorned with a glittering silver plate, seemed to figure for Morris the closed portal of happiness; and then Mrs. Penniman's companion rested a melancholy eye upon a lighted window in the upper part of the house.

"That is my room—my dear little room!" Mrs. Penniman remarked.

Morris started. "Then I needn't come walking round the Square to gaze at it."

"That's as you please. But Catherine's is behind; two noble windows on the second floor. I think you can see them from the other street."

"I don't want to see them, ma'am." And Morris turned his back to the house.

"I will tell her you have been *here*, at any rate," said Mrs. Penniman, pointing to the spot where they stood; "and I will give her your message—that she is to hold fast."

"Oh yes; of course. You know I write her all that."

"It seems to say more when it is spoken. And remember, if you need me, that I am *there*," and Mrs. Penniman glanced at the third floor.

On this they separated, and Morris, left to himself, stood looking at the house a moment; after which he turned away, and took a gloomy walk round the Square, on the opposite side, close to the wooden fence. Then he came back, and paused for a minute in front of Doctor Sloper's dwelling. His eyes travelled over it; they even rested on the ruddy windows of Mrs. Penniman's apartment. He thought it a devilish comfortable house.

17

Mrs. Penniman told Catherine that evening—the two ladies were sitting in the back-parlor—that she had had an interview with Morris Townsend; and on receiving this news the girl started with a sense of pain. She felt angry for the moment; it was almost the first time she had ever felt angry. It seemed to her that her aunt was meddlesome; and from this came a vague apprehension that she would spoil something.

"I don't see why you should have seen him. I don't think it was right," Catherine said.

"I was so sorry for him—it seemed to me some one ought to see him."

"No one but I," said Catherine, who felt as if she were making the most presumptuous speech of her life, and yet at the same time had an instinct that she was right in doing so.

"But you wouldn't, my dear," Aunt Lavinia rejoined; "and I didn't know what might have become of him."

"I have not seen him because my father has forbidden it," Catherine said, very simply.

There was a simplicity in this, indeed, which fairly vexed Mrs. Penniman. "If your father forbade you to go to sleep, I suppose you would keep awake!" she commented.

Catherine looked at her. "I don't understand you. You seem to me very strange."

"Well, my dear, you will understand me some day!" and Mrs. Penniman, who was reading the evening paper, which she perused daily from the first line to the last, resumed her occupation. She wrapped herself in silence; she was determined Catherine should ask her for an account of her interview with Morris. But Catherine was silent for so long that she almost lost patience; and she was on the point of remarking to her that she was very heartless, when the girl at last spoke.

"What did he say?" she asked.

"He said he is ready to marry you any day, in spite of everything."

Catherine made no answer to this, and Mrs. Penniman almost lost patience again; owing to which she at last volunteered the information that Morris looked very handsome, but terribly haggard.

"Did he seem sad?" asked her niece.

"He was dark under the eyes," said Mrs. Penniman. "So different from when I first saw him; though I am not sure that if I had seen him in this condition the first time, I should not have been even more struck with him. There is something brilliant in his very misery."

This was, to Catherine's sense, a vivid picture, and though she disapproved, she felt herself gazing at it. "Where did you see him?" she asked, presently.

"In—in the Bowery; at a confectioner's," said Mrs. Penniman, who had a general idea that she ought to dissemble a little.

"Whereabouts is the place?" Catherine inquired, after another pause.

"Do you wish to go there, my dear?" said her aunt.

"Oh no." And Catherine got up from her seat and went to the fire, where she stood looking awhile at the glowing coals.

"Why are you so dry, Catherine?" Mrs. Penniman said at last.

"So dry?"

"So cold—so irresponsive."

The girl turned very quickly. "Did *he* say that?"

Mrs. Penniman hesitated a moment. "I will tell you what he said. He said he feared only one thing—that you would be afraid."

"Afraid of what?"

"Afraid of your father."

Catherine turned back to the fire again, and then, after a pause, she said, "I *am* afraid of my father."

Mrs. Penniman got quickly up from her chair and approached her niece. "Do you mean to give him up, then?"

Catherine for some time never moved; she kept her eyes on the coals. At last she raised her head and looked at her aunt. "Why do you push me so?" she asked.

"I don't push you. When have I spoken to you before?"

"It seems to me that you have spoken to me several times."

"I am afraid it is necessary, then, Catherine," said Mrs. Penniman, with a good deal of solemnity. "I am afraid you don't feel the importance"—she paused a little; Catherine was looking at her—"the importance of not disappointing that gallant young heart!" And Mrs. Penniman went back to her chair by the lamp, and, with a little jerk, picked up the evening paper again.

Catherine stood there before the fire, with her hands behind her, looking at her aunt, to whom it seemed that the girl had never had just this dark fixedness in her gaze. "I don't think you understand or that you know me," she said.

"If I don't, it is not wonderful; you trust me so little."

Catherine made no attempt to deny this charge, and for some time more nothing was said. But Mrs. Penniman's imagination was restless, and the evening paper failed on this occasion to enchain it.

"If you succumb to the dread of your

father's wrath," she said, "I don't know what will become of us."

"Did *he* tell you to say these things to me?"

"He told me to use my influence."

"You must be mistaken," said Catherine. "He trusts me."

"I hope he may never repent of it!" And Mrs. Penniman gave a little sharp slap to her newspaper. She knew not what to make of her niece, who had suddenly become stern and contradictious.

This tendency on Catherine's part was presently even more apparent. "You had much better not make any more appointments with Mr. Townsend," she said. "I don't think it is right."

Mrs. Penniman rose with considerable majesty. "My poor child, are you jealous of me?" she inquired.

"Oh, Aunt Lavinia!" murmured Catherine, blushing.

"I don't think it is your place to teach me what is right."

On this point Catherine made no concession. "It can't be right to deceive."

"I certainly have not deceived *you!*"

"Yes; but I promised my father—"

"I have no doubt you promised your father. But I have promised him nothing."

Catherine had to admit this, and she did so in silence. "I don't believe Mr. Townsend himself likes it," she said, at last.

"Doesn't like meeting me?"

"Not in secret."

"It was not in secret; the place was full of people."

"But it was a secret place—away off in the Bowery."

Mrs. Penniman flinched a little. "Gentlemen enjoy such things," she remarked, presently. "I know what gentlemen like."

"My father wouldn't like it, if he knew."

"Pray, do you propose to inform him?" Mrs. Penniman inquired.

"No, Aunt Lavinia. But please don't do it again."

"If I do it again you will inform him—is that what you mean? I do not share your dread of my brother; I have always known how to defend my own position. But I shall certainly never again take any step on your behalf; you are much too thankless. I knew you were not a spontaneous nature, but I believed you were firm, and I told your father that he would find you so. I am disappointed, but your father will not be." And with this Mrs. Penniman offered her niece a brief good-night, and withdrew to her own apartment.

18

Catherine sat alone by the parlor fire—sat there for more than an hour, lost in her meditations. Her aunt seemed to her aggressive and foolish; and to see it so clearly—to judge Mrs. Penniman so positively—made her feel old and grave. She did not resent the imputation of weakness; it made no impression on her, for she had not the sense of weakness, and she was not hurt at not being appreciated. She had an immense respect for her father, and she felt that to displease him would be a misdemeanor analogous to an act of profanity in a great temple: but her purpose had slowly ripened, and she believed that her prayers had purified it of its violence. The evening advanced, and the lamp burnt dim without her noticing it; her eyes were fixed upon her terrible plan. She knew her father was in his study—that he had been there all the evening; from time to time she expected to hear him move. She thought he would perhaps come, as he sometimes came, into the parlor. At last the clock struck eleven, and the house was wrapped in silence; the servants had gone to bed. Catherine got up and went slowly to the door of the library, where she waited a moment, motionless. Then she knocked, and then she waited again. Her father had answered her, but she had not the courage to turn the latch. What she had said to her aunt was true enough—she was afraid of him; and in saying that she had no sense of weakness, she meant that she was not afraid of herself. She heard him move within, and he came and opened the door for her.

"What is the matter?" asked the Doctor. "You are standing there like a ghost!"

She went into the room, but it was some time before she contrived to say what she had come to say. Her father, who was in his dressing-gown and slippers, had been busy at his writing-table, and after looking at her for some moments, and waiting for her to speak, he went and seated himself at his papers again. His back was turned to her—she began to hear the scratching of his pen. She remained near the door, with her heart thumping beneath her bodice; and she was very glad that his back was turned, for it seemed to her that she could more easily address herself to this portion of his person than to his face. At last she began, watching it while she spoke:

"You told me that if I should have anything more to say about Mr. Townsend you would be glad to listen to it."

"Exactly, my dear," said the Doctor, not turning round, but stopping his pen.

Catherine wished it would go on, but she herself continued: "I thought I would tell you that I have not seen him again, but that I should like to do so."

"To bid him good-bye?" asked the Doctor.

The girl hesitated a moment. "He is not going away."

The Doctor wheeled slowly round in his chair, with a smile that seemed to accuse her of an epigram; but extremes meet, and Catherine had not intended one. "It is not to bid him good-bye, then?" her father said.

"No, father, not that; at least not forever. I have not seen him again, but I should like to see him," Catherine repeated.

The Doctor slowly rubbed his underlip with the feather of his quill.

"Have you written to him?"

"Yes, four times."

"You have not dismissed him, then. Once would have done that."

"No," said Catherine; "I have asked him—asked him to wait."

Her father sat looking at her, and she was afraid he was going to break out into wrath, his eyes were so fine and cold.

"You are a dear, faithful child," he said, at last. "Come here to your father." And he got up, holding out his hands toward her.

The words were a surprise, and they gave her an exquisite joy. She went to him, and he put his arm round her tenderly, soothingly; and then he kissed her. After this he said,

"Do you wish to make me very happy?"

"I should like to—but I am afraid I can't," Catherine answered.

"You can if you will. It all depends on your will."

"Is it to give him up?" said Catherine.

"Yes, it is to give him up."

And he held her still, with the same tenderness, looking into her face and resting his eyes on her averted eyes. There was a long silence; she wished he would release her.

"You are happier than I, father," she said, at last.

"I have no doubt you are unhappy just now. But it is better to be unhappy for three months and get over it, than for many years and never get over it."

"Yes, if that were so," said Catherine.

"It would be so; I am sure of that." She answered nothing, and he went on: "Have you no faith in my wisdom, in my tenderness, in my solicitude for your future?"

"Oh, father!" murmured the girl.

"Don't you suppose that I know something of men—their vices, their follies, their falsities?"

She detached herself, and turned upon him. "He is not vicious—he is not false!"

Her father kept looking at her with his sharp, pure eye. "You make nothing of my judgment, then?"

"I can't believe that!"

"I don't ask you to believe it, but to take it on trust."

Catherine was far from saying to herself that this was an ingenious sophism; but she met the appeal none the less squarely. "What has he done—what do you know?"

"He has never done anything—he is a selfish idler."

"Oh, father, don't abuse him!" she exclaimed, pleadingly.

"I don't mean to abuse him; it would be a great mistake. You may do as you choose," he added, turning away.

"I may see him again?"

"Just as you choose."

"Will you forgive me?"

"By no means."

"It will only be for once."

"I don't know what you mean by once. You must either give him up or continue the acquaintance."

"I wish to explain—to tell him to wait."

"To wait for what?"

"Till you know him better—till you consent."

"Don't tell him any such nonsense as that. I know him well enough, and I shall never consent."

"But we can wait a long time," said poor Catherine, in a tone which was meant to express the humblest conciliation, but which had upon her father's nerves the effect of an iteration not characterized by tact.

The Doctor answered however, quietly enough: "Of course; you can wait till I die, if you like."

Catherine gave a cry of natural horror.

"Your engagement will have one delightful effect upon you; it will make you extremely impatient for that event."

Catherine stood staring, and the Doctor enjoyed the point he had made. It came to Catherine with the force—or rather with the vague impressiveness—of a logical axiom which it was not in her province to controvert; and yet, though it was a scientific truth, she felt wholly unable to accept it.

"I would rather not marry, if that were true," she said.

"Give me a proof of it, then; for it is beyond a question that by engaging yourself to Morris Townsend you simply wait for my death."

She turned away, feeling sick and faint; and the Doctor went on: "And if you wait for it with impatience, judge, if you please, what *his* eagerness will be."

Catherine turned it over—her father's words had such an authority for her that her very thoughts were capable of obeying him. There was a dreadful ugliness in it, which seemed to glare at her through the interposing medium of her own feebler reason. Suddenly, however, she had an inspiration—she almost knew it to be an inspiration.

"If I don't marry before your death, I will not after," she said.

To her father, it must be admitted, this seemed only another epigram; and as obstinacy, in unaccomplished minds, does not usually select such a mode of expression, he was the more surprised at this wanton play of a fixed idea.

"Do you mean that for an impertinence?" he inquired; an inquiry of which, as he made it, he quite perceived the grossness.

"An impertinence? Oh, father, what terrible things you say!"

"If you don't wait for my death, you might as well marry immediately; there is nothing else to wait for."

For some time Catherine made no answer; but finally she said,

"I think Morris—little by little—might persuade you."

"I shall never let him speak to me again. I dislike him too much."

Catherine gave a long, low sigh; she tried to stifle it, for she had made up her mind that it was wrong to make a parade of her trouble, and to endeavor to act upon her father by the meretricious aid of emotion. Indeed, she even thought it wrong—in the sense of being inconsiderate—to attempt to act upon his feelings at all; her part was to effect some gentle, gradual change in his intellectual perception of poor Morris's character. But the means of effecting such a change were at present shrouded in mystery, and she felt miserably helpless and hopeless. She had exhausted all arguments, all replies. Her father might have pitied her, and in fact he did so; but he was sure he was right.

"There is one thing you can tell Mr. Townsend when you see him again," he said, "that if you marry without my consent, I don't leave you a farthing of money. That will interest him more than anything else you can tell him."

"That would be very right," Catherine answered. "I ought not in that case to have a farthing of your money."

"My dear child," the Doctor observed, laughing, "your simplicity is touching. Make that remark, in that tone, and with that expression of countenance, to Mr. Townsend, and take a note of his answer. It won't be polite—it will express irritation; and I shall be glad of that, as it will put me in the right; unless, indeed—which is perfectly possible—you should like him the better for being rude to you."

"He will never be rude to me," said Catherine, gently.

"Tell him what I say, all the same."

She looked at her father, and her quiet eyes filled with tears.

"I think I will see him, then," she murmured, in her timid voice.

"Exactly as you choose." And he went to the door and opened it for her to go out. The movement gave her a terrible sense of his turning her off.

"It will be only once, for the present," she added, lingering a moment.

"Exactly as you choose," he repeated, standing there with his hand on the door. "I have told you what I think. If you see him, you will be an ungrateful, cruel child; you will have given your old father the greatest pain of his life."

This was more than the poor girl could bear; her tears overflowed, and she moved toward her grimly consistent parent with a pitiful cry. Her hands were raised in supplication, but he sternly evaded this appeal. Instead of letting her sob out her misery on his shoulder, he simply took her by the arm and directed her course across the threshold, closing the door gently but firmly behind her. After he had done so, he remained listening. For a long time there was no sound; he knew that she was standing outside. He was sorry for her, as I have said; but he was so sure he was right. At last he heard her move away, and then her footstep creaked faintly upon the stairs.

The Doctor took several turns round his study, with his hands in his pockets, and a thin sparkle, possibly of irritation, but partly also of something like humor, in his eye. "By jove," he said to himself, "I believe she will stick—I believe she will stick!" And this idea of Catherine "sticking" appeared to have a comical side, and to offer a prospect of entertainment. He determined, as he said to himself, to see it out.

19

It was for reasons connected with this determination that on the morrow he sought a few words of private conversation with Mrs. Penniman. He sent for her to the library, and he there informed her that he hoped very much that, as regarded this affair of Catherine's, she would mind her *p's* and *q's*.

"I don't know what you mean by such an expression," said his sister. "You speak as if I were learning the alphabet."

"The alphabet of common-sense is something you will never learn," the Doctor permitted himself to respond.

"Have you called me here to insult me?" Mrs. Penniman inquired.

"Not at all. Simply to advise you. You have taken up young Townsend; that's your own affair. I have nothing to do with your sentiments, your fancies, your affections, your delusions; but what I request of you is that you will keep these things to yourself. I have explained my views to Catherine; she understands them perfectly, and anything that she does further in the way of encouraging Mr. Townsend's attentions will be in deliberate opposition to my wishes. Anything that you should do in the way of giving her aid and comfort will be—permit me the expression—distinctly treasonable. You know high-treason is a capital offence: take care how you incur the penalty."

Mrs. Penniman threw back her head, with a certain expansion of the eye which she occasionally practiced. "It seems to me that you talk like a great autocrat."

"I talk like my daughter's father."

"Not like your sister's brother," cried Lavinia.

"My dear Lavinia," said the Doctor. "I sometimes wonder whether I *am* your brother, we are so extremely different. In spite of differences, however, we can, at a pinch, understand each other; and that is the essential thing just now. Walk straight with regard to Mr. Townsend; that's all I ask. It is highly probable you have been corresponding with him for the last three weeks—perhaps even seeing him. I don't ask you—you needn't tell me." He had a moral conviction that she would contrive to tell a fib about the matter, which it would disgust him to listen to. "Whatever you have done, stop doing it; that's all I wish."

"Don't you wish also by chance to murder your child?" Mrs. Penniman inquired.

"On the contrary, I wish to make her live and be happy."

"You will kill her: she passed a dreadful night."

"She won't die of one dreadful night, nor of a dozen. Remember that I am a distinguished physician."

Mrs. Penniman hesitated a moment; then she risked her retort. "Your being a distinguished physician has not prevented you from already losing *two members* of your family."

She had risked it, but her brother gave her such a terribly incisive look—a look so like a surgeon's lancet—that she was frightened at her courage. And he answered her, in words that corresponded to the look, "It may not prevent me, either, from losing the society of still another."

Mrs. Penniman took herself off with whatever air of depreciated merit was at her command, and repaired to Catherine's room, where the poor girl was closeted. She knew all about her dreadful night, for the two had met again, the evening before, after Catherine left her father. Mrs. Penniman was on the landing of the second floor when her niece came upstairs; it was not remarkable that a person of so much subtlety should have discovered that Catherine had been shut up with the Doctor. It was still less remarkable that she should have felt an extreme curiosity to learn the result of this interview, and that this sentiment, combined with her great amiability and generosity, should have prompted her to regret the sharp words lately exchanged between her niece and herself. As the unhappy girl came into sight in the dusky corridor, she made a lively demonstration of sympathy. Catherine's bursting heart was equally oblivious; she only knew that her aunt was taking her into her arms. Mrs. Penniman drew her into Catherine's own room, and the two women sat there together far into the small hours, the younger one with her head on the other's lap, sobbing, and sobbing at first in a soundless, stifled manner, and then at last perfectly still. It gratified Mrs. Penniman to be able to feel conscientiously that this scene virtually removed the interdict which Catherine had placed upon her indulging in further communion with Morris Townsend. She was not gratified, however, when, in coming back to her niece's room before breakfast, she found that Catherine had risen and was preparing herself for this meal.

"You should not go to breakfast," she said; "you are not well enough, after your fearful night."

"Yes, I am very well, and I am only afraid of being late."

"I can't understand you," Mrs. Penniman cried. "You should stay in bed for three days."

"Oh, I could never do that," said Catherine, to whom this idea presented no attractions.

Mrs. Penniman was in despair; and she noted, with extreme annoyance, that the trace of the night's tears had completely vanished from Catherine's eyes. She had a most impracticable physique. "What effect do you expect to have upon your father," her aunt demanded, "if you come plumping down, without a vestige of any sort of feeling, as if nothing in the world had happened?"

"He would not like me to lie in bed," said Catherine, simply.

"All the more reason for your doing it. How else do you expect to move him?"

Catherine thought a little. "I don't know how; but not in that way. I wish to be just as usual." And she finished dressing—and, according to her aunt's expression, went plumping down into the paternal presence. She was really too modest for consistent pathos.

And yet it was perfectly true that she had had a dreadful night. Even after Mrs. Penniman left her she had had no sleep; she lay staring at the uncomforting gloom, with her eyes and ears filled with the movement with which her father had turned her out of his room, and of the words in which he had told her that she was a heartless daughter. Her heart was breaking; she had heart enough for that. At moments it seemed to her that she believed him, and that to do what she was doing a girl must indeed be bad. She *was* bad; but she couldn't help it. She would try to appear good, even if her heart were perverted; and from time to time she had a fancy that she might accomplish something by ingenious concessions to form, though she should persist in caring for Morris. Catherine's ingenuities were indefinite, and we are not called upon to expose their hollowness. The best of them, perhaps, showed itself in that freshness of aspect which was so discouraging to Mrs. Penniman, who was amazed at the absence of haggardness in a young woman who for a whole night had lain quivering beneath a father's curse. Poor Catherine was conscious of her freshness; it gave her a feeling about the future which rather added to the weight upon her mind. It seemed a proof that she was strong and solid and dense, and would live to a great age—longer than might be generally convenient; and this idea was pressing, for it appeared to saddle her with a pretension the more, just when the cultivation of any pretension was inconsistent with her doing right. She wrote that day to Morris Townsend, requesting him to come and see her on the morrow, using very few words, and explaining nothing. She would explain everything face to face.

20

On the morrow, in the afternoon, she heard his voice at the door, and his step in the hall. She received him in the big, bright front-parlor, and she instructed the servant that, if any one should call, she was particularly engaged. She was not afraid of her father's coming in, for at that hour he was always driving about town. When Morris stood there before her, the first thing that she was conscious of was that he was even more beautiful to look at than fond recollection had painted him; the next was that he had pressed her in his arms. When she was free again it appeared to her that she had now indeed thrown herself into the gulf of defiance, and even, for an instant, that she had been married to him.

He told her that she had been very cruel, and had made him very unhappy; and Catherine felt acutely the difficulty of her destiny, which forced her to give pain in such opposite quarters. But she wished that, instead of reproaches, however tender, he would give her help; he was certainly wise enough and clever enough to invent some issue from their troubles. She expressed this belief, and Morris received the assurance as if he thought it natural; but he interrogated at first—as was natural too—rather than committed himself to marking out a course.

"You should not have made me wait so long," he said. "I don't know how I have been living; every hour seemed like years. You should have decided sooner."

"Decided?" Catherine asked.

"Decided whether you would keep me or give me up."

"Oh, Morris," she cried, with a long, tender murmur, "I never thought of giving you up!"

"What, then, were you waiting for?" The young man was ardently logical.

"I thought my father might—might—" and she hesitated.

"Might see how unhappy you were?"

"Oh no. But that he might look at it differently."

"And now you have sent for me to tell me that at last he does so. Is that it?"

This hypothetical optimism gave the poor girl a pang. "No, Morris," she said, solemnly, "he looks at it still in the same way."

"Then why have you sent for me?"

"Because I wanted to see you," cried Catherine, piteously.

"That's an excellent reason, surely. But did you want to look at me only? Have you nothing to tell me?"

His beautiful persuasive eyes were fixed upon her face, and she wondered what answer would be noble enough to make to such a gaze as that. For a moment her own eyes took it in, and then—"I *did* want to look at you," she said, gently. But after this speech, most inconsistently, she hid her face.

Morris watched her for a moment attentively. "Will you marry me to-morrow?" he asked, suddenly.

"To-morrow?"

"Next week, then—any time within a month?"

"Isn't it better to wait?" said Catherine.

"To wait for what?"

She hardly knew for what; but this tremendous leap alarmed her. "Till we have thought about it a little more."

He shook his head sadly and reproachfully. "I thought you had been thinking about it these three weeks. Do you want to turn it over in your mind for five years? You have given me more than time enough. My poor girl," he added, in a moment, "you are not sincere."

Catherine colored from brow to chin, and her eyes filled with tears. "Oh, how can you say that?" she murmured.

"Why, you must take me or leave me," said Morris, very reasonably. "You can't please your father and me both; you must choose between us."

"I have chosen you," she said, passionately.

"Then marry me next week!"

She stood gazing at him. "Isn't there any other way?"

"None that I know of for arriving at the same result. If there is, I should be happy to hear of it."

Catherine could think of nothing of the kind, and Morris's luminosity seemed almost pitiless. The only thing she could think of was that her father might, after all, come round; and she articulated, with an awkward sense of her helplessness in doing so, a wish that this miracle might happen.

"Do you think it is in the least degree likely?" Morris asked.

"It would be, if he could only know you."

"He can know me if he will. What is to prevent it?"

"His ideas, his reasons," said Catherine. "They are so—so terribly strong." She trembled with the recollection of them yet.

"Strong!" cried Morris. "I would rather you should think them weak!"

"Oh, nothing about my father is weak," said the girl.

Morris turned away, walking to the window, where he stood looking out. "You are terribly afraid of him," he remarked at last.

She felt no impulse to deny it, because she had no shame in it; for, if it was no honor to herself, at least it was an honor to him. "I suppose I must be," she said, simply.

"Then you don't love me—not as I love you. If you fear your father more than you love me, then your love is not what I hoped it was."

"Ah, my friend!" she said, going to him.

"Do *I* fear anything?" he demanded, turning round on her. "For your sake what am I not ready to face?"

"You are noble—you are brave!" she answered, stopping short a distance that was almost respectful.

"Small good it does me, if you are so timid."

"I don't think I am—*really,*" said Catherine.

"I don't know what you mean by 'really.' It is really enough to make us miserable."

"I should be strong enough to wait—to wait a long time."

"And suppose after a long time your father should hate me worse than ever?"

"He wouldn't—he couldn't."

"He would be touched by my fidelity; is that what you mean? Is he is so easily touched, then why should you be afraid of him?"

This was much to the point, and Catherine was struck by it. "I will try not to be," she said. And she stood there submissively, the image, in advance, of a dutiful and responsible wife. This image could not fail to recommend itself to Morris Townsend, and he continued to give proof of the high estimation in which he held her. It could only have been at the prompting of such a sentiment that he presently mentioned to her that the course recommended by Mrs. Penniman was an immediate union, regardless of consequences.

"Yes, Aunt Penniman would like that," Catherine said, simply, and yet with a certain shrewdness. It must, however, have been in pure simplicity, and from motives quite untouched by sarcasm, that a few moments after she went on to say to Morris that her father had given her a message for him. It was quite on her conscience to deliver this message, and had the mission been ten times more painful, she would have as scrupulously performed it. "He told me to tell you—to tell you very distinctly, and directly from himself—that if I marry without his consent, I shall not inherit a penny of his fortune. He made a great point of this. He seemed to think—he seemed to think—"

Morris flushed, as any young man of spirit might have flushed at an imputation of baseness. "What did he seem to think?"

"That it would make a difference."

"It *will* make a difference—in many things. We shall be by many thousands of dollars the poorer; and that is a great difference. But it will make none in my affection."

"We shall not want the money," said Catherine; "for you know I have a good deal myself."

"Yes, my dear girl, I know you have something. And he can't touch that."

"He would never," said Catherine. "My mother left it to me."

Morris was silent awhile. "He was very positive about this, was he?" he asked at last. "He thought such a message would annoy me terribly, and make me throw off the mask, eh?"

"I don't know what he thought," said Catherine, sadly.

"Please tell him that I care for his message as much as for that!" and Morris snapped his fingers sonorously.

"I don't think I could tell him that."

"Do you know you sometimes disappoint me," said Morris.

"I should think I might. I disappoint every one—father and Aunt Penniman."

"Well, it doesn't matter with me, because I am fonder of you than they are."

"Yes, Morris," said the girl, with her imagination—what there was of it—swimming in this happy truth, which seemed, after all, invidious to no one.

"Is it your belief that he will stick to it—stick to it forever—to this idea of disinheriting you?—that your goodness and patience will never wear out his cruelty?"

"The trouble is that if I marry you he will think I am not good. He will think that a proof."

"Ah, then he will never forgive you!"

This idea, sharply expressed by Morris's handsome lips, renewed for a moment to the poor girl's temporarily pacified conscience all its dreadful vividness. "Oh, you must love me very much!" she cried.

"There is no doubt of that, my dear," her lover rejoined. "You don't like that word 'disinherited,'" he added, in a moment.

"It isn't the money; it is that he should—that he should feel so."

"I suppose it seems to you a kind of curse?" said Morris. "It must be very dismal. But don't you think," he went on, presently, "that if you were to try to be very clever, and to set rightly about it, you might in the end conjure it away? Don't you think," he continued further, in a tone of sympathetic speculation, "that a really clever woman, in your place, might bring him him round at last? Don't you think—"

Here, suddenly, Morris was interrupted; these ingenious inquiries had not reached Catherine's ears. The terrible word disinheritance, with all its impressive moral reprobation, was still ringing there—seemed, indeed, to gather force as it lingered. The mortal chill of her situation struck more deeply into her childlike heart, and she was overwhelmed by a feeling of loneliness and danger. But her refuge was there, close to her, and she put out her hands to grasp it. "Ah, Morris," she said, with a shudder, "I will marry you as soon as you please!" and she surrendered herself, leaning her head on his shoulder.

"My dear good girl!" he exclaimed, looking down at his prize. And then he looked up again, rather vaguely, with parted lips and lifted eyebrows.

21

Doctor Sloper very soon imparted his conviction to Mrs. Almond in the same terms in which he had announced it to himself. "She's going to stick, by Jove! she's going to stick."

"Do you mean that she is going to marry him?" Mrs. Almond inquired.

"I don't know that; but she is not going to break down. She is going to drag out the engagement, in the hope of making me relent."

"And shall you not relent?"

"Shall a geometrical proposition relent? I am not so superficial."

"Doesn't geometry treat of surfaces?" asked Mrs. Almond, who, as we know, was clever, smiling.

"Yes, but it treats of them profoundly. Catherine and her young man are my surfaces; I have taken their measure."

"You speak as if it surprised you."

"It is immense; there will be a great deal to observe."

"You are shockingly cold-blooded!" said Mrs. Almond.

"I need to be, with all this hot blood about me. Young Townsend, indeed, is cool; I must allow him that merit."

"I can't judge him," Mrs. Almond answered; "but I am not at all surprised at Catherine."

"I confess I am a little; she must have been so deucedly divided and bothered."

"Say it amuses you outright. I don't see why it should be such a joke that your daughter adores you."

"It is the point where the adoration stops that I find it interesting to fix."

"It stops where the other sentiment begins."

"Not at all; that would be simple enough. The two things are extremely mixed up, and the mixture is extremely odd. It will produce some third element, and that's what I'm waiting to see. I wait with suspense—with positive excitement; and that is a sort of emotion that I didn't suppose Catherine would ever provide for me. I am really very much obliged to her."

"She will cling," said Mrs. Almond; "she will certainly cling."

"Yes, as I say, she will stick."

"Cling is prettier. That's what those very simple natures always do, and nothing could be simpler than Catherine. She doesn't take many impressions; but when she takes one, she keeps it. She is like a copper kettle that receives a dent: you may polish up the kettle, but you can't efface the mark."

"We must try and polish up Catherine," said the Doctor. "I will take her to Europe!"

"She won't forget him in Europe."

"He will forget her, then."

Mrs. Almond looked grave. "Should you really like that?"

"Extremely," said the Doctor.

Mrs. Penniman, meanwhile, lost little time in putting herself again in communication with Morris Townsend. She requested him to favor her with another interview, but she did not on this occasion select an oyster saloon as the scene of their meeting. She proposed that he should join her at the door of a certain church after service on Sunday afternoon; and she was careful not to appoint the place of worship which she usually visited, and where, as she said, the congregation would have spied upon her. She picked out a less elegant resort, and on issuing from its portal at the hour she had fixed she saw the young man standing apart. She offered him no recognition until she had crossed the street, and he had followed her to some distance. Here, with a smile, "excuse my apparent want of cordiality," she said. "You know what to believe about that. Prudence before everything." And on his asking her in what direction they should walk, "Where we shall be least observed," she murmured.

Morris was not in good-humor and his response to this speech was not particularly gallant. "I don't flatter myself we shall be much observed anywhere." Then he turned recklessly toward the centre of the town. "I hope you have come to tell me that he has knocked under," he went on.

"I am afraid I am not altogether a harbinger of good; and yet, too, I am to a certain extent a messenger of peace. I have been thinking a great deal, Mr. Townsend," said Mrs. Penniman.

"You think too much."

"I suppose I do; but I can't help it, my mind is so terribly active. When I give myself, I give myself. I pay the penalty in my headaches, my famous headaches—a perfect circlet of pain! But I carry it as a queen carries her crown. Would you believe that I have one now? I wouldn't however, have missed our rendezvous for anything. I have something very important to tell you."

"Well, let's have it," said Morris.

"I was perhaps a little headlong the other day in advising you to marry immediately. I have been thinking it over, and now I see it just a little differently."

"You seem to have a great many different ways of seeing the same object."

"Their number is infinite!" said Mrs. Penniman, in a tone which seemed to suggest that this convenient faculty was one of her brightest attributes.

"I recommend you to take one way, and stick to it," Morris replied.

"Ah, but it isn't easy to choose. My imagination is never quiet, never satisfied. It makes me a bad adviser, perhaps, but it makes me a capital friend."

"A capital friend who gives bad advice!" said Morris.

"Not intentionally—and who hurries off, at every risk, to make the most humble excuses."

"Well, what do you advise me now?"

"To be very patient; to watch and wait."

"And it is that bad advice or good?"

"That is not for me to say," Mrs. Penniman rejoined, with some dignity. "I only claim it is sincere."

"And will you come to me next week and recommend something different and equally sincere?"

"I may come to you next week, and tell you that I am in the streets."

"In the streets?"

"I have had a terrible scene with my brother, and he threatens, if anything happens, to turn me out of the house. You know I am a poor woman."

Morris had a speculative idea that she had a little property; but he naturally did not press this.

"I should be very sorry to see you suffer martyrdom for me," he said. "But you make your brother out a regular Turk."

Mrs. Penniman hesitated a little.

"I certainly do not regard Austin as an orthodox Christian."

"And am I to wait till he is converted?"

"Wait at any rate till he is less violent. Bide your time, Mr. Townsend; remember the prize is great."

Morris walked along some time in silence, tapping the railings and gateposts very sharply with his stick.

"You certainly are devilish inconsistent!" he broke out at last. "I have already got Catherine to consent to a private marriage."

Mrs. Penniman was indeed inconsistent, for at this news she gave a little jump of gratification.

"Oh, when and where?" she cried. And then she stopped short.

Morris was a little vague about this.

"That isn't fixed; but she consents. It's deuced awkward now to back out."

Mrs. Penniman, as I say, had stopped short; and she stood there with her eyes fixed brilliantly on her companion.

"Mr. Townsend," she proceeded, "shall I tell you something. Catherine loves you so much that you may do anything."

This declaration was slightly ambiguous, and Morris opened his eyes.

"I am happy to hear it. But what do you mean by 'anything'?"

"You may postpone—you may change about; she won't think the worse of you."

Morris stood there still, with his raised

eyebrows; then he said, simply and rather dryly, "Ah!" After this he remarked to Mrs. Penniman that if she walked so slowly she would attract notice, and he succeeded, after a fashion, in hurrying her back to the domicile of which her tenure had become so insecure.

22

He had slightly misrepresented the matter in saying that Catherine had consented to take the great step. We left her just now declaring that she would burn her ships behind her; but Morris, after having elicited this declaration, had become conscious of good reasons for not taking it up. He avoided, gracefully enough, fixing a day, though he left her under the impression that he had his eye on one. Catherine may have had her difficulties; but those of her circumspect suitor are also worthy of consideration. The prize was certainly great; but it was only to be won by striking the happy mean between precipitancy and caution. It would be all very well to take one's jump and trust to Providence; Providence was more especially on the side of clever people, and clever people were known by an indisposition to risk their bones.

The ultimate reward of a union with a young woman who was both unattractive and impoverished ought to be connected with immediate disadvantages by some very palpable chain. Between the fear of losing Catherine and her possible fortune altogether, and the fear of taking her too soon and finding this possible fortune as void of actuality as a collection of emptied bottles, it was not comfortable for Morris Townsend to choose—a fact that should be remembered by readers disposed to judge harshly of a young man who may have struck them as making but an indifferently successful use of fine natural parts. He had not forgotten that in any event Catherine had her own ten thousand a year; he had devoted an abundance of meditation to this circumstance. But with his fine parts he rated himself high, and he had a perfectly definite appreciation of his value, which seemed to him inadequately represented by the sum I have mentioned. At the same time he reminded himself that this sum was considerable, that everything is relative, and that if a modest income is less desirable than a large one, the complete absence of revenue is nowhere accounted an advantage.

These reflections gave him plenty of occupation, and made it necessary that he should trim his sail. Doctor Sloper's opposition was the unknown quantity in the problem he had to work out. The natural way to work it out was by marrying Catherine; but in mathematics there are many short cuts, and Morris was not without a hope that he should yet discover one. When Catherine took him at his word, and consented to renounce the attempt to mollify her father, he drew back skilfully enough, as I have said, and kept the wedding-day still an open question. Her faith in his sincerity was so complete that she was incapable of suspecting that he was playing with her; her trouble just now was of another kind. The poor girl had an admirable sense of honor, and from the moment she had brought herself to the point of violating her father's wish, it seemed to her that she had no right to enjoy his protection. It was on her conscience that she ought to live under his roof only so long as she conformed to his wisdom. There was a great deal of glory in such a position, but poor Catherine felt that she had forfeited her claim to it. She had cast her lot with a young man against whom he had solemnly warned her, and broken the contract under which he provided her with a happy home. She could not give up the young man, so she must leave the home; and the sooner the object of her preference offered her another, the sooner her situation would lose its awkward twist. This was close reasoning; but it was commingled with an infinite amount of merely instinctive penitence. Catherine's days, at this time, were dismal, and the weight of some of her hours was almost more than she could bear. Her father never looked at her, never spoke to her. He knew perfectly what he was about, and this was part of a plan. She looked at him as much as she dared (for she was afraid of seeming to offer herself to his observation), and she pitied him for the sorrow she had brought upon him. She held up her head and busied her hands, and went about her daily occupations; and when the state of things in Washington Square seemed intolerable, she closed her eyes and indulged herself with an intellectual vision of the man for whose sake she had broken a sacred law.

Mrs. Penniman, of the three persons in Washington Square, had much the most of the manner that belongs to a great crisis. If Catherine was quiet, she was quietly quiet, as I may say, and her pathetic effects, which there was no one to notice, were entirely unstudied and unintended. If the Doctor was stiff and dry, and absolutely indifferent to the presence of his companions, it was so lightly, neatly, easily done, that you would have had to know him well to discover that, on the whole, he rather enjoyed having to be so disagreeable. But Mrs. Penniman was elaborately reserved and significantly silent; there was a richer rustle in the very deliberate movements to which she confined herself, and when she occasionally spoke, in connection with some very trivial event, she had the air of meaning something deeper than what she said. Between Catherine and her father nothing had passed since the evening she went to speak to him in his study. She had something to say to him—it seemed to her she ought to say it—but she kept it back for fear of irritating him. He also had something to say to her; but he was determined not to speak first. He was interested, as we know, in seeing how, if she were left to herself, she would "stick." At last she told him she had seen Morris Townsend again, and that their relations remained quite the same.

"I think we shall marry—before very long. And probably, meanwhile, I shall see him rather often; about once a week—not more."

The Doctor looked at her coldly from head to foot, as if she had been a stranger. It was the first time his eyes had rested on her for a week, which was fortunate, if that was to be their expression. "Why not three times a day?" he asked. "What prevents your meeting as often as you choose?"

She turned away a moment; there were tears in her eyes. Then she said, "It is better once a week."

"I don't see how it is better. It is as bad as it can be. If you flatter yourself that I care for little modifications of that sort, you are very much mistaken. It is as wrong of you to see him once a week as it would be to see him all day long. Not that it matters to me, however."

Catherine tried to follow these words, but they seemed to lead toward a vague horror from which she recoiled. "I think we shall marry pretty soon," she repeated, at last.

Her father gave her his dreadful look again, as if she were some one else. "Why do you tell me that? It's no concern of mine."

"Oh, father," she broke out, "don't you care, even if you do feel so?"

"Not a button. Once you marry, it's quite the same to me when, or where, or why you do it; and if you think to compound for your folly by hoisting your fly in this way, you may spare yourself the trouble."

With this he turned away. But the next day he spoke to her of his own accord, and his manner was somewhat changed. "Shall you be married within the next four or five months?" he asked.

"I don't know, father," said Catherine. "It is not very easy for us to make up our minds."

"Put it off, then, for six months, and in the mean time I will take you to Europe. I should like you very much to go."

It gave her such delight, after his words of the day before, to hear that he should "like" her to do something, and that he still had in his heart any of the tenderness of preference, that she gave a little exclamation of joy. But then she became conscious that Morris was not included in this proposal, and that—as regards really going—she would greatly prefer to remain at home with him. But she blushed none the less more comfortably than she had done of late. "It would be delightful to go to Europe," she remarked, with a sense that the idea was not original, and that her tone was not all it might be.

"Very well, then, we will go. Pack up your clothes."

"I had better tell Mr. Townsend," said Catherine.

Her father fixed his cold eyes upon her. "If you mean that you had better ask his leave, all that remains to me is to hope he will give it."

The girl was sharply touched by the pathetic ring of the words; it was the most calculated, the most dramatic little speech the Doctor had ever uttered. She felt that it was a great thing for her, under the circumstances, to have this fine opportunity of showing him her respect; and yet there was something else that she felt as well, and that she presently expressed. "I sometimes think that if I do what you dislike so much, I ought not to stay with you."

"To stay with me?"

"If I live with you, I ought to obey you."

"If that's your theory, it's certainly mine," said the Doctor, with a dry laugh.

"But if I don't obey you, I ought not to live with you—to enjoy your kindness and protection."

This striking argument gave the Doctor a sudden sense of having underestimated his daughter; it seemed even more than worthy of a young woman who had revealed the quality of unaggressive obstinacy. But it displeased him—displeased him deeply, and he signified as much. "That idea is in very bad taste," he said. "Did you get it from Mr. Townsend?"

"Oh no; it's my own," said Catherine, eagerly.

"Keep it to yourself, then," her father answered, more than ever determined she should go to Europe.

23

If Morris Townsend was not to be included in this journey, no more was Mrs. Penniman, who would have been thankful for an invitation, but who (to do her justice) bore her disappointment in a perfectly lady-like manner. "I should enjoy seeing the works of Raphael and the ruins—the ruins of the Pantheon," she said to Mrs. Almond; "but, on the other hand, I shall not be sorry to be alone and at peace for the next few months in Washington Square. I want rest; I have been through so much in the last four months." Mrs. Almond thought it rather cruel that her brother should not take poor Lavinia abroad; but she easily understood that, if the purpose of his expedition was to make Catherine forget her lover, it was not in his interest to give his daughter this young man's best friend as a companion. "If Lavinia had not been so foolish, she might visit the ruins of the Pantheon," she said to herself; and she continued to regret her sister's folly, even though the latter assured her that she had often heard the relics in question most satisfactorily described by Mr. Penniman. Mrs. Penniman was perfectly aware that her brother's motive in undertaking a foreign tour was to lay a trap for Catherine's constancy; and she imparted this conviction very frankly to her niece.

"He thinks it will make you forget Morris," she said (she always called the young man "Morris" now): "out of sight, out of mind, you know. He thinks that all the things you will see over there will drive him out of your thoughts."

Catherine looked greatly alarmed. "If he thinks that, I ought to tell him beforehand."

Mrs. Penniman shook her head. "Tell him afterward, my dear—after he has had all the trouble and expense. That's the way to serve him." And she added, in a softer key, that it must be delightful to think of those who love us among the ruins of the Pantheon.

Her father's displeasure had cost the girl, as we know, a great deal of deep-welling sorrow—sorrow of the purest and most generous kind, without a touch of resentment or rancor; but for the first time, after he had dismissed with such contemptuous brevity her apology for being a charge upon him, there was a spark of anger in her grief. She had felt his contempt; it had scorched her; that speech about her bad taste had made her ears burn for three days. During this period she was less considerate; she had an idea—a rather vague one, but it was agreeable to her sense of injury—that now she was absolved from penance, and might do what she chose. She chose to write to Morris Townsend to meet her in the Square and take her to walk about the town. If she were going to Europe out of respect to her father, she might at least give herself this satisfaction. She felt in every way at present more free and more resolute; there was a force that urged her. Now at last, completely and unreservedly, her passion possessed her.

Morris met her at last, and they took a long walk. She told him immediately what had happened; that her father wished to take her away—it would be for six months—to Europe; she would do absolutely what Morris should think best. She hoped inexpressibly that he would think it best she should stay at home. It was some time before he said what he thought; he asked, as they walked along, a great many questions. There was one that especially struck her; it seemed so incongruous.

"Should you like to see all those celebrated things over there?"

"Oh no, Morris!" said Catherine, quite deprecatingly.

"Gracious Heaven, what a dull woman!" Morris exclaimed to himself.

"He thinks I will forget you," said Catherine; "that all these things will drive you out of my mind."

"Well, my dear, perhaps they will."

"Please don't say that," Catherine answered, gently, as they walked along. "Poor father will be disappointed."

Morris gave a little laugh. "Yes, I verily believe that your poor father will be disappointed. But you will have seen Europe," he added, humorously. "What a take-in!"

"I don't care for seeing Europe," Catherine said.

"You ought to care, my dear; and it may mollify your father."

Catherine, conscious of her obstinacy, expected little of this, and could not rid herself of the idea that in going abroad and yet remaining firm, she should play her father a trick. "Don't you think it would be a kind of deception?" she asked.

"Doesn't he want to deceive you?" cried Morris. "It will serve him right. I really think you had better go."

"And not be married for so long?"

"Be married when you come back. You can buy your wedding-clothes in Paris." And then Morris, with great kindness of tone, explained his view of the matter. It would be a good thing that she should go; it would put them completely in the right. It would show they were reasonable, and willing to wait. Once they were so sure of each other, they could afford to wait—what had they to fear? If there was a particle of chance that her father would be favorably affected by her going, that ought to settle it; for, after all, Morris was very unwilling to be the cause of her being disinherited. It was not for himself, it was for her and for her children. He was willing to wait for her; it would be hard, but he could do it. And over there, among beautiful scenes and noble monuments, perhaps the old gentleman would be softened; such things were supposed to exert a humanizing influence. He might be touched by her gentleness, her patience, her willingness to make any sacrifice but *that* one; and if she should appeal to him some day, in some celebrated spot—in Italy, say, in the evening; in Venice, in a gondola, by moonlight—if she should be a little clever about it, and touch the right chord, perhaps he would fold her in his arms, and tell her that he forgave her. Catherine was immensely struck with this conception of the affair, which seemed eminently worthy of her lover's brilliant intellect, though she viewed it askance in so far as it depended upon her own powers of execution. The idea of being "clever" in a gondola by moonlight appeared to her to involve elements of which her grasp was not active. But it was settled between them that she should tell her father that she was ready to follow him obediently anywhere, making the mental reservation that she loved Morris Townsend more than ever.

She informed the Doctor she was ready to embark, and he made rapid arrangements for this event. Catherine had many farewells to make, but with only two of them are we actively concerned. Mrs. Penniman took a discriminating view of her niece's journey; it seemed to her very proper that Mr. Townsend's destined bride should wish to embellish her mind by a foreign tour.

"You leave him in good hands," she said, pressing her lips to Catherine's forehead. (She was very fond of kissing people's foreheads; it was an involuntary expression of sympathy with the intellectual part.) "I shall see him often; I shall feel like one of the vessels of old tending the sacred flame."

"You behave beautifully about not going with us," Catherine answered, not presuming to examine this analogy.

"It is my pride that keeps me up," said Mrs. Penniman, tapping the body of her dress, which always gave forth a sort of metallic ring.

Catherine's parting with her lover was short, and few words were exchanged.

"Shall I find you just the same when I come back?" she asked; though the question was not the fruit of skepticism.

"The same—only more so," said Morris, smiling.

It does not enter into our scheme to narrate in detail Doctor Sloper's proceedings in the Eastern hemisphere. He made the grand tour of Europe, travelled in considerable splendor, and (as was to have been expected in a man of his high cultivation) found so much in art and antiquity to interest him, that he remained abroad, not for six months, but for twelve. Mrs. Penniman, in Washington Square, accommodated herself to his absence. She enjoyed her uncontested dominion in the empty house, and flattered herself that she made it more attractive to their friends than when her brother was at home. To Morris Townsend, at least, it would have appeared that she made it singularly attractive. He was altogether her most frequent visitor, and Mrs. Penniman was very fond of asking him to tea. He had his chair—a very easy one—at the fireside in the back parlor (when the great mahogany sliding doors, with silver knobs and hinges, which divided this apartment from its more formal neighbor, were closed), and he used to smoke cigars in the Doctor's study, where he often spent an hour in turning over the curious collections of its absent proprietor. He thought Mrs. Penniman a goose, as we know; but he was no goose himself, and, as a young man of luxurious tastes and scanty resources, he found the house a perfect castle of indolence. It became for him a club with a single member. Mrs. Penniman saw much less of her sister than while the Doctor was at home; for Mrs. Almond had felt moved to tell her that she disapproved of her relations with Mr. Townsend. She had no business to be so friendly to a young man of whom their brother thought so meanly, and Mrs. Almond was surprised at her levity in foisting a most deplorable engagement upon Catherine.

"Deplorable!" cried Lavinia. "He will make her a lovely husband."

"I don't believe in lovely husbands," said Mrs. Almond; "I only believe in good ones. If he marries her, and she comes into Austin's money, they may get on. He will be an idle, amiable, selfish, and, doubtless, tolerably good-natured fellow. But if she doesn't get the money, and he finds himself tied to her, Heaven have mercy on her! He will have none. He will hate her for his disappointment, and take his revenge; he will be pitiless and cruel. Woe betide poor Catherine! I recommend you to talk a little with his sister; it's a pity Catherine can't marry *her!*"

Mrs. Penniman had no appetite whatever for conversation with Mrs. Montgomery, whose acquaintance she made no trouble to cultivate; and the effect of this alarming forecast of her niece's destiny was to make her think it indeed a thousand pities that Mr. Townsend's generous nature should be embittered. Bright enjoyment was his natural element, and how could he be comfortable if there should prove to be nothing to enjoy? It became a fixed idea with Mrs. Penniman that he should yet enjoy her brother's fortune, on which she had acuteness enough to perceive that her own claim was small.

"If he doesn't leave it to Catherine, it certainly won't be to leave it to me," she said.

24

The Doctor, during the first six months he was abroad, never spoke to his daughter of their little difference, partly on system, and partly because he had a great many other things to think about. It was idle to attempt to ascertain the state of her affections without direct inquiry, because if she had not had an expressive manner among the familiar influences of home, she failed to gather animation from the mountains of Switzerland or the monuments of Italy. She was always her father's docile and reasonable associate—going through their sight-seeing in deferential silence, never complaining of fatigue, always ready to start at the hour he had appointed overnight, making no foolish criticisms, and indulging in no refinements of appreciation. "She is about as intelligent as the bundle of shawls," the Doctor said, her main superiority being that, while the bundle of shawls sometimes got lost, or tumbled out of the carriage, Catherine was always at her post, and had a firm and ample seat. But her father had expected this, and he was not constrained to set down her intellectual limitations as a tourist to sentimental depression; she had completely divested herself of the characteristics of a victim, and during the whole time that they were abroad she never uttered an audible sigh. He supposed she was in correspondence with Morris Townsend, but he held his peace about it, for he never saw the young man's letters, and Catherine's own missives were always given to the courier to post. She heard from her lover with considerable regularity, but his letters came enclosed in Mrs. Penniman's; so that, whenever the Doctor handed her a packet addressed in his sister's hand, he was an involuntary instrument of the passion he condemned. Catherine made this reflection, and six months earlier she would have felt bound to give him warning; but now she deemed herself absolved. There was a sore spot in her heart that his own words had made when once she spoke to him as she thought honor prompted; she would try and please him as far as she could, but she would never speak that way again. She read her lover's letters in secret.

One day, at the end of the summer, the two travellers found themselves in a lonely valley of the Alps. They were crossing one of the passes, and on the long ascent they had got out of the carriage and had wandered much in advance. After awhile the Doctor descried a foot-path which, leading through a transverse valley, would bring them out, as he justly supposed, at a much higher point of the ascent. They followed this devious way, and finally lost the path; the valley proved very wild and rough, and their walk became rather a scramble. They were good walkers, however, and they took their adventure easily; from time to time they stopped, that Catherine might rest; and then she sat upon a stone and looked about her at the hard-featured rocks and the glowing sky. It was late in the afternoon, in the last of August; night was coming on, and as they had reached a great elevation the air was cold and sharp. In the west there was a great suffusion of cold red light, which made the sides of the little valley look only the more rugged and dusky. During one of their pauses her father left her and wandered away to some high place, at a distance, to get a view. He was out of sight; she sat there alone in the stillness, which was just touched by the vague murmur somewhere of a mountain brook. She thought of Morris Townsend, and the place was so desolate and lonely that he seemed very far away. Her father remained absent a long time; she began to wonder what had become of him. But at last he reappeared, coming toward her in the clear twilight, and she got up to go on. He made no motion to proceed, however, but came close to her, as if he had something to say. He stopped in front of her, and stood looking at her with eyes that had kept the light of the flushing snow-summits on which they had just been fixed. Then, abruptly, in a low tone, he asked her an unexpected question,

"Have you given him up?"

The question was unexpected, but Catherine was only superficially unprepared.

"No, father," she answered.

He looked at her again for some moments without speaking.

"Does he write to you?" he asked.

"Yes, about twice a month."

The Doctor looked up and down the valley, swinging his stick; then he said to her, in the same low tone,

"I am very angry."

She wondered what he meant—whether he wished to frighten her. If he did, the place was well chosen: this hard, melancholy dell, abandoned by the summer light, made her feel her loneliness. She looked around her, and her heart grew cold; for a moment her fear was great. But she could think of nothing to say, save to murmur, gently, "I am sorry."

"You try my patience," her father went on, "and you ought to know what I am. I am not a very good man. Though I am very smooth externally, at bottom I am very passionate; and I assure you I can be very hard."

She could not think why he told her these things. Had he brought her there on purpose, and was it part of a plan? What was the plan? Catherine asked herself. Was it to startle her suddenly into a retraction—to take advantage of her by dread? Dread of what? The place was ugly and lonely, but the place could do her no harm. There was a kind of still intensity about her father which made him dangerous, but Catherine hardly went so far as to say to herself that it might be part of his plan to fasten his hand—the neat, fine, supple hand of a distinguished physician—in her throat. Nevertheless, she receded a step. "I am sure you can be anything you please," she said; and it was her simple belief.

"I am very angry," he replied, more sharply.

"Why has it taken you so suddenly?"

"It has not taken me suddenly. I have been raging inwardly for the last six months. But just now this seemed a good place to flare out. It's so quiet, and we are alone."

"Yes, it's very quiet," said Catherine, vaguely looking about her. "Won't you come back to the carriage?"

"In a moment. Do you mean that in all this time you have not yielded an inch?"

"I would if I could, father; but I can't."

The Doctor looked round him too. "Should you like to be left in such a place as this, to starve?"

"What do you mean?" cried the girl.

"That will be your fate—that's how he will leave you."

He would not touch her, but he had touched Morris. The warmth came back to her heart. "That is not true, father," she broke out, "and you ought not to say it. It is not right, and it's not true."

He shook his head slowly. "No, it's not right, because you won't believe it. But it *is* true. Come back to the carriage."

He turned away, and she followed him; he went faster, and was presently much in advance. But from time to time he stopped, without turning round, to let her keep up with him, and she made her way forward with difficulty, her heart beating with the excitement of having for the first time spoken to him in violence. By this time it had grown almost dark, and she ended by losing sight of him. But she kept her course, and after a little, the valley making a sudden turn, she gained the road, where the carriage stood waiting. In it sat her father, rigid and silent; in silence, too, she took her place beside him.

It seemed to her, later, in looking back upon all this, that for days afterward not a word had been exchanged between them. The scene had been a strange one, but it had not permanently affected her feeling toward her father, for it was natural, after all, that he should occasionally make a scene of some kind, and he had let her alone for six months. The strangest part of it was that he had said he was not a good man; Catherine wondered a good deal what he had meant by that. The statement failed to appeal to her credence, and it was not grateful to any resentment that she entertained. Even in the utmost bitterness that she might feel, it would give her no satisfaction to think him less complete. Such a saying as that was a part of his great subtlety—men so clever as he might say anything and mean anything; and as to his being hard, that surely, in a man, was a virtue.

He let her alone for six months more—six months during which she accommodated herself without a protest to the extension of their tour. But he spoke again at the end of this time: it was at the very last, the night before they embarked for New York, in the hotel at Liverpool. They had been dining together in a great, dim, musty sitting-room; and then the cloth had been removed, and the Doctor walked slowly up and down. Catherine at last took her candle to go to bed, but her father motioned her to stay.

"What do you mean to do when you

get home?" he asked, while she stood there with her candle in her hand.

"Do you mean about Mr. Townsend?"

"About Mr. Townsend."

"We shall probably marry."

The Doctor took several turns again while she waited. "Do you hear from him as much as ever?"

"Yes, twice a month," said Catherine, promptly.

"And does he always talk about marriage?"

"Oh yes; that is, he talks about other things too, but he always says something about that."

"I am glad to hear he varies his subjects; his letters might otherwise be monotonous."

"He writes beautifully," said Catherine, who was very glad of a chance to say it.

"They always write beautifully. However, in a given case that doesn't diminish the merit. So, as soon as you arrive, you are going off with him?"

This seemed a rather gross way of putting it, and something that there was of dignity in Catherine resented it. "I cannot tell you till we arrive," she said.

"That's reasonable enough," her father answered. "That's all I ask of you—that you *do* tell me, that you give me definite notice. When a poor man is to lose his only child, he likes to have an inkling of it beforehand."

"Oh, father! you will not lose me," Catherine said, spilling her candle wax.

"Three days before will do," he went on, "if you are in a position to be positive then. He ought to be very thankful to me, do you know. I have done a mighty good thing for him in taking you abroad; your value is twice as great, with all the knowledge and taste that you have acquired. A year ago, you were perhaps a little limited—a little rustic; but now you have seen everything, and appreciated everything, and you will be a most entertaining companion. We have fattened the sheep for him before he kills it." Catherine turned away, and stood staring at the blank door. "Go to bed," said her father; "and as we don't go abroad till noon, you may sleep late. We shall probably have a most uncomfortable voyage."

25

The voyage was indeed uncomfortable, and Catherine, on arriving in New York, had not the compensation of "going off," in her father's phrase, with Morris Townsend. She saw him, however, the day after she landed; and in the mean time he formed a natural subject of conversation between our heroine and her Aunt Lavinia, with whom, the night she disembarked, the girl was closeted for a long time before either lady retired to rest.

"I have seen a great deal of him," said Mrs. Penniman. "He is not very easy to know. I suppose you think you know him; but you don't, my dear. You will some day; but it will only be after you have lived with him. I may almost say *I* have lived with him," Mrs. Penniman proceeded, while Catherine stared. "I think I know him now; I have had such remarkable opportunities. You will have the same—or, rather, you will have better"; and Aunt Lavinia smiled. "Then you will see what I mean. It's a wonderful character, full of passion and energy, and just as true."

Catherine listened with a mixture of interest and apprehension. Aunt Lavinia was intensely sympathetic, and Catherine, for the past year, while she wandered through foreign galleries and churches, and rolled over the smoothness of posting roads, nursing the thoughts that never passed her lips, had often longed for the company of some intelligent person of her own sex. To tell her story to some kind woman—at moments it seemed to her that this would give her comfort, and she had more than once been on the point of taking the landlady, or the nice young person from the dress-maker's, into her confidence. If a woman had been near her, she would on certain occasions have treated such a companion to a fit of weeping; and she had an apprehension that, on her return, this would form her response to Aunt Lavinia's first embrace. In fact, however, the two ladies had met, in Washington Square, without tears; and when they found themselves alone together a certain dryness fell upon the girl's emotion. It came over her with a greater force that Mrs. Penniman had enjoyed a whole year of her lover's society, and it was not a pleasure to her to hear her aunt explain and interpret the young man, speaking of him as if her own knowledge of him were supreme. It was not that Catherine was jealous; but her sense of Mrs. Penniman's innocent falsity, which had lain dormant, began to haunt her again, and she was glad that she was safely at home. With this, however, it was a blessing to be able to talk to Morris, to sound his name, to be with a person who was not unjust to him.

"You have been very kind to him," said Catherine. "He has written me that, often. I shall never forget that, Aunt Lavinia."

"I have done what I could; it has been very little. To let him come and talk to me, and give him his cup of tea—that was all. Your Aunt Almond thought it was too much, and used to scold me terribly; but she promised me, at least, not to betray me."

"To betray you?"

"Not to tell your father. He used to sit in your father's study," said Mrs. Penniman, with a little laugh.

Catherine was silent a moment. This idea was disagreeable to her, and she was reminded again, with pain, of her aunt's secretive habits. Morris, the reader may be informed, had had the tact not to tell her that he sat in her father's study. He had known her but for a few months, and her aunt had known her for fifteen years; and yet he would not have made the mistake of thinking that Catherine would see the joke of the thing. "I am sorry you made him go into father's room," she said, after a while.

"I didn't send him; he went himself. He liked to look at the books, and at all those things in the glass cases. He knows all about them; he knows all about everything."

Catherine was silent again; then, "I wish he had found some employment," she said.

"He has found some employment. It's beautiful news, and he told me to tell you as soon as you arrive. He has gone into partnership with a commission merchant. It was all settled, quite suddenly, a week ago."

This seemed to Catherine indeed beautiful news; it had a fine prosperous air. "Oh, I'm so glad!" she said; and now, for a moment, she was disposed to throw herself on Aunt Lavinia's neck.

"It's much better than being under some one; and he has never been used to that," Mrs. Penniman went on. "He is just as good as his partner—they are perfectly equal. You see how right he was to wait. I should like to know what your father can say now! They have got an office in Duane Street, and little printed cards; he brought me one to show me. I have got it in my room, and you shall see it to-morrow. That's what he said to me the last time he was here—'You see how right I was to wait.' He has got other people under him instead of being a subordinate. He could never be a subordinate; I have often told him I could never think of him in that way."

Catherine assented to this proposition, and was very happy to know that Morris was his own master; but she was deprived of the satisfaction of thinking that she might communicate this news in triumph to her father. Her father would care equally little whether Morris was established in business or transported for life. Her trunks had been brought into her room, and further reference to her lover was for a short time suspended, while she opened them and displayed to her aunt some of the spoils of foreign travel. These were rich and abundant; and Catherine had brought home a present to every one—to every one save Morris, to whom she had brought simply her undiverted heart. To Mrs. Penniman she had been lavishly generous, and Aunt Lavinia spent half an hour in unfolding and folding again, with little ejaculations of gratitude and taste. She marched about for some time in a splendid cashmere shawl, which Catherine had begged her to accept, settling it on her shoulders, and twisting down her head to see how low the point descended behind.

"I shall regard it only as a loan," she said. "I will leave it to you again when I die; or, rather," she added, kissing her niece again, "I will leave it to your first-born little girl." And draped in her shawl, she stood there smiling.

"You had better wait till she comes," said Catherine.

"I don't like the way you say that," Mrs. Penniman rejoined, in a moment. "Catherine, are you changed?"

"No; I am the same."

"You have not swerved a line?"

"I am exactly the same," Catherine repeated, wishing her aunt were a little less sympathetic.

"Well, I am glad"; and Mrs. Penniman surveyed her cashmere in the glass. Then, "How is your father?" she asked, in a moment, with her eyes on her niece. "Your letters were so meagre—I could never tell."

"Father is very well."

"Ah, you know what I mean," said Mrs. Penniman, with a dignity to which the cashmere gave a richer effect. "Is he still implacable?"

"Oh yes!"

"Quite unchanged?"

"He is, if possible, more firm."

Mrs. Penniman took off her great shawl, and slowly folded it up. "That is very bad. You had no success with your little project."

"What little project?"

"Morris told me all about it. The idea of turning the tables on him, in Europe; of watching him, when he was agreeably impressed by some celebrated sight—he pretends to be so artistic, you know—and then just pleading with him and bringing him round."

"I never tried it. It was Morris's idea; but if he had been with us in Europe, he would have seen that father was never impressed in that way. He *is* artistic—tremendously artistic; but the more celebrated places we visited, and the more he admired them, the less use it would have been to plead with him. They seemed only to make him more determined—more terrible," said poor Catherine. "I shall never bring him round, and I expect nothing now."

"Well, I must say," Mrs. Penniman answered, "I never supposed you were going to give it up."

"I have given it up. I don't care now."

"You have grown very brave," said Mrs. Penniman, with a short laugh. "I didn't advise you to sacrifice your property."

"Yes, I am braver than I was. You asked me if I had changed; I have changed in that way. Oh," the girl went on, "I have changed very much. And it isn't my property. If *he* doesn't care for it, why should I?"

Mrs. Penniman hesitated. "Perhaps he does care for it."

"He cares for it for my sake, because he doesn't want to injure me. But he will know—he knows already—how little he need be afraid about that. Besides," said Catherine, "I have got plenty of money of my own. We shall be very well off;

and now hasn't he got his business? I am delighted about that business." She went on talking, showing a good deal of excitement as she proceeded. Her aunt had never seen her with just this manner, and Mrs. Penniman, observing her, set it down to foreign travel, which had made her more positive, more mature. She thought also that Catherine had improved in appearance; she looked rather handsome. Mrs. Penniman wondered whether Morris Townsend would be struck with that. While she was engaged in this speculation, Catherine broke out, with a certain sharpness, "Why are you so contradictory, Aunt Penniman? You seem to think one thing at one time, and another at another. A year ago, before I went away, you wished me not to mind about displeasing father, and now you seem to recommend me to take another line. You change about so."

This attack was unexpected, for Mrs. Penniman was not used, in any discussion, to seeing the war carried into her own country—possibly because the enemy generally had doubts of finding subsistence there. To her own consciousness, the flowery fields of her reason had rarely been ravaged by a hostile force. It was perhaps on this account that in defending them she was majestic rather than agile.

"I don't know what you accuse me of, save of being too deeply interested in your happiness. It is the first time I have been told I am capricious. That fault is not what I am usually reproached with."

"You were angry last year that I wouldn't marry immediately, and now you talk about my winning my father over. You told me it would serve him right if he should take me to Europe for nothing. Well, he has taken me for nothing, and you ought to be satisfied. Nothing is changed—nothing but my feeling about father. I don't mind nearly so much now. I have been as good as I could, but he doesn't care. Now I don't care either. I don't know whether I have grown bad; perhaps I have. But I don't care for that. I have come home to be married—that's all I know. That ought to please you, unless you have taken up some new idea; you are so strange. You may do as you please, but you must never speak to me again about pleading with father. I shall never plead with him for anything; that is all over. He has put me off. I am come home to be married."

This was a more authoritative speech than she had ever heard on her niece's lips, and Mrs. Penniman was proportionately startled. She was, indeed, a little awe-struck, and the force of the girl's emotion and resolution left her nothing to reply. She was easily frightened, and she always carried off her discomfiture by a concession—a concession which was often accompanied, as in the present case, by a little nervous laugh.

26

If she had disturbed her niece's temper—she began from this moment forward to talk a good deal about Catherine's temper, an article which up to that time had never been mentioned in connection with our heroine—Catherine had opportunity on the morrow to recover her serenity. Mrs. Penniman had given her a message from Morris Townsend to the effect that he would come and welcome her home on the day after her arrival. He came in the afternoon; but, as may be imagined, he was not on this occasion made free of Doctor Sloper's study. He had been coming and going, for the past year, so comfortably and irresponsibly, that he had a certain sense of being wronged by finding himself reminded that he must now limit his horizon to the front parlor, which was Catherine's particular province.

"I am very glad you have come back," he said; "it makes me very happy to see you again." And he looked at her, smiling, from head to foot, though it did not appear afterward that he agreed with Mrs. Penniman (who, woman-like, went more into details) in thinking her embellished.

To Catherine he appeared resplendent; it was some time before she could believe again that this beautiful young man was her own exclusive property. They had a great deal of characteristic lovers' talk —a soft exchange of inquiries and assurances. In these matters Morris had an excellent grace, which flung a picturesque interest even over the account of his début in the commission business—a subject as to which his companion earnestly questioned him. From time to time he got up from the sofa where they sat together, and walked about the room; after which he came back, smiling and passing his hand through his hair. He was unquiet, as was natural in a young man who has just been reunited to a long-absent mistress, and Catherine made the reflection that she had never seen him so excited. It gave her pleasure, somehow, to note this fact. He asked her questions about her travels, to some of which she was unable to reply, for she had forgotten the names of places and the order of her father's journey. But for the moment she was so happy, so lifted up by the belief that her troubles at last were over, that she forgot to be ashamed of her meagre answers. It seemed to her now that she could marry him without the remnant of a scruple, or a single tremor save those that belonged to joy. Without waiting for him to ask, she told him that her father had come back in exactly the same state of mind—that he had not yielded an inch.

"We must not expect it now," she said, "and we must do without it."

Morris sat looking and smiling. "My poor, dear girl!" he exclaimed.

"You mustn't pity me," said Catherine. "I don't mind it now; I am used to it."

Morris continued to smile, and then he got up and walked about again. "You had better let me try him."

"Try to bring him over? You would only make him worse," Catherine answered, resolutely.

"You say that because I managed it so badly before. But I should manage it differently now. I am much wiser; I have had a year to think of it. I have more tact."

"Is that what you have been thinking of for a year?"

"Much of the time. You see, the idea sticks in my crop. I don't like to be beaten."

"How are you beaten if we marry?"

"Of course I am not beaten on the main issue; but I am, don't you see? on all the rest of it—on the question of my reputation, of my relations with your father, of my relations with my own children, if we should have any."

"We shall have enough for our children; we shall have enough for everything. Don't you expect to succeed in business?"

"Brilliantly, and we shall certainly be very comfortable. But it isn't of the mere material comfort I speak; it is of the moral comfort," said Morris—"of the intellectual satisfaction."

"I have great moral comfort now," Catherine declared, very simply.

"Of course you have. But with me it is different. I have staked my pride on proving to your father that he is wrong, and now that I am at the head of a flourishing business, I can deal with him as an equal. I have a capital plan—do let me go at him!"

He stood before her with his bright face, his jaunty air, his hands in his pockets; and she got up, with her eyes resting on his own. "Please don't, Morris; please don't," she said; and there was a certain mild, sad firmness in her tone which he heard for the first time. "We must ask no favors of him—we must ask nothing more. He won't relent, and nothing good will come of it. I know it now—I have a very good reason."

"And pray what is your reason?"

She hesitated to bring it out, but at last it came. "He is not very fond of me."

"Oh, bother!" cried Morris, angrily.

"I wouldn't say such a thing without being sure. I saw it, I felt it, in England, just before he came away. He talked to me one night—the last night—and then it came over me. You can tell when a person feels that way. I wouldn't accuse him if he hadn't made me feel that way. I don't accuse him; I just tell you that that's how it is. He can't help it; we can't govern our affections. Do I govern mine? Mightn't he say that to me? It's because he is so fond of my mother, whom we lost so long ago. She was beautiful, and very, very brilliant; he is always thinking of her. I am not at all like her; Aunt Penniman has told me that. Of course it isn't my fault; but neither is it his fault. All I mean is, it's true; and it's a stronger reason for his never being reconciled than simply his dislike for you."

" 'Simply?' " cried Morris, with a laugh. "I am much obliged for that."

"I don't mind about his disliking you now; I mind everything less. I feel differently; I feel separated from my father."

"Upon my word," said Morris, "you are a queer family."

"Don't say that—don't say anything unkind," the girl entreated. "You must be very kind to me now, because, Morris, because"—and she hesitated a moment —"because I have done a great deal for you."

"Oh, I know that, my dear."

She had spoken up to this moment without vehemence or outward sign of emotion, gently, reasoningly, only trying to explain. But her emotion had been ineffectually smothered, and it betrayed itself at last in the trembling of her voice. "It is a great thing to be separated like that from your father, when you have worshipped him before. It has made me very unhappy; or it would have made me so if I didn't love you. You can tell when a person speaks to you as if—as if—"

"As if what?"

"As if they despised you!" said Catherine, passionately. "He spoke that way the night before we sailed. It wasn't much, but it was enough, and I thought of it on the voyage all the time. Then I made up my mind. I will never ask him for anything again, or expect anything from him. It would not be natural now. We must be very happy together, and we must not seem to depend upon his forgiveness. And, Morris, Morris, you must never despise me!"

This was an easy promise to make, and Morris made it with fine effect. But for the moment he undertook nothing more onerous.

27

The Doctor, of course, on his return, had a good deal of talk with his sisters. He was at no great pains to narrate his travels or to communicate his impressions of distant lands to Mrs. Penniman, upon whom he contented himself with bestowing a memento of his enviable experience in the shape of a velvet gown. But he conversed with her at some length about matters nearer home, and lost no time in assuring her that he was still an inflexible father.

"I have no doubt you have seen a great deal of Mr. Townsend, and done your best to console him for Catherine's absence," he said. "I don't ask you, and you needn't deny it. I wouldn't put the question to you for the world, and expose you to the inconvenience of having to—a—excogitate an answer. No one has betrayed you, and there has been no spy upon your proceedings. Elizabeth has told no tales, and has never mentioned you except to praise your good looks and good spirits. The thing is simply an inference of my own—an induction, as the philosophers say. It seems to me likely that you would have offered an asylum to an interesting sufferer. Mr. Townsend has been a good deal in the house; there is something in the house that tells me so. We doctors, you know, end by acquiring fine perceptions, and it is impressed upon my sensorium that he has sat in these chairs, in a very easy attitude, and warmed himself at that fire. I don't grudge him the comfort of it; it is the only one he will ever enjoy at my expense. It seems likely, indeed, that I shall be able to economize at his own. I don't know what you may have said to him, or what you may say hereafter; but I should like you to know that if you have encouraged him to believe that he will gain anything by hanging on, or that I have budged a hair-breadth from the position I took up a year ago, you have played him a trick for which he may exact reparation. I'm not sure that he may not bring a suit against you. Of course you have done it conscientiously; you have made yourself believe that I can be tired out. This is the most baseless hallucination that ever visited the brain of a genial optimist. I am not in the least tired; I am as fresh as when I started; I am good for fifty years yet. Catherine appears not to have budged an inch either; she is equally fresh; so we are about where we were before. This, however, you know as well as I. What I wish is simply to give you notice of my own state of mind. Take it to heart, dear Lavinia. Beware of the just resentment of a deluded fortune-hunter!"

"I can't say I expected it," said Mrs. Penniman. "And I had a sort of foolish hope that you would come home without that odious ironical tone with which you treat the most sacred subjects."

"Don't undervalue irony; it is often of great use. It is not, however, always necessary, and I will show you how gracefully I can lay it aside. I should like to know whether you think Morris Townsend will hang on?"

"I will answer you with your own weapons," said Mrs. Penniman. "You had better wait and see."

"Do you call such a speech as that one of my own weapons? I never said anything so rough."

"He will hang on long enough to make you very uncomfortable, then."

"My dear Lavinia," exclaimed the Doctor, "do you call that irony? I call it pugilism."

Mrs. Penniman, however, in spite of her pugilism, was a good deal frightened, and she took counsel of her fears. Her brother meanwhile took counsel, with many reservations, of Mrs. Almond, to whom he was no less generous than to Lavinia, and a good deal more communicative.

"I suppose she has had him there all the while," he said. "I must look into the state of my wine. You needn't mind telling me now; I have already said all I mean to say to her on the subject."

"I believe he was in the house a good deal," Mrs. Almond answered. "But you must admit that your leaving Lavinia quite alone was a great change for her, and that it was natural she should want some society."

"I do admit that, and that is why I shall make no row about the wine; I shall set it down as compensation to Lavinia. She is capable of telling me that she drank it all herself. Think of the inconceivable bad taste, in the circumstances, of that fellow making free with the house—or coming there at all! If that doesn't describe him, he is indescribable."

"His plan is to get what he can. Lavinia will have supported him for a year," said Mrs. Almond. "It's so much gained."

"She will have to support him for the rest of his life, then," cried the Doctor; "but without wine, as they say at the *tables d'hôte*."

"Catherine tells me he has set up a business, and is making a great deal of money."

The Doctor stared. "She has not told me that—and Lavinia didn't deign. Ah!" he cried, "Catherine has given me up. Not that it matters, for all that the business amounts to."

"She has not given up Mr. Townsend," said Mrs. Almond; "I saw that in the first half-minute. She has come home exactly the same."

"Exactly the same; not a grain more intelligent. She didn't notice a stick or a stone all the while we were away—not a picture nor a view, not a statue nor a cathedral."

"How could she notice? She had other things to think of; they are never for an instant out of her mind. She touches me very much."

"She would touch me if she didn't irritate me. That's the effect she has upon me now. I have tried everything upon her; I really have been quite merciless. But it is of no use whatever; she is absolutely *glued*. I have passed, in consequence, into the exasperated stage. At first I had a good deal of a certain genial curiosity about it; I wanted to see if she really would stick. But, good Lord, one's curiosity is satisfied! I see she is capable of it, and now she can let go."

"She will never let go," said Mrs. Almond.

"Take care, or you will exasperate me too. If she doesn't let go, she will be shaken off—sent tumbling into the dust. That's a nice position for my daughter. She can't see that if you are going to be pushed, you had better jump. And then she will complain of her bruises."

"She will never complain," said Mrs. Almond.

"That I shall object to even more. But the deuce will be that I can't prevent anything."

"If she is to have a fall," said Mrs. Almond, with a gentle laugh, "we must spread as many carpets as we can." And she carried out this idea by showing a great deal of motherly kindness to the girl.

Mrs. Penniman immediately wrote to Morris Townsend. The intimacy between these two was by this time consummate, but I must content myself with noting but a few of its features. Mrs. Penniman's own share in it was a singular sentiment, which might have been misinterpreted, but which in itself was not discreditable to the poor lady. It was a romantic interest in this attractive and unfortunate young man, and yet it was not such an interest as Catherine might have been jealous of. Mrs. Penniman had not a particle of jealousy of her niece. For herself, she felt as if she were Morris's mother or sister—a mother or sister of an emotional temperament—and she had an absorbing desire to make him comfortable and happy. She had striven to do so during the year that her brother left her an open field, and her efforts had been attended with the success that has been pointed out. She had never had a child of her own, and Catherine, whom she had done her best to invest with the importance that would naturally belong to a youthful Penniman, had only partly rewarded her zeal. Catherine, as an object of affection and solicitude, had never had that picturesque charm which (as it seemed to her) would have been a natural attribute of her own progeny. Even the maternal passion in Mrs. Penniman would have been romantic and factitious, and Catherine was not constituted to inspire a romantic passion. Mrs. Penniman was as fond of her as ever, but she had grown to feel that with Catherine she lacked opportunity. Sentimentally speaking, therefore, she had (though she had not disinherited her niece) adopted Morris Townsend, who gave her opportunity in abundance. She would have been very happy to have a handsome and tyrannical son, and would have taken an extreme interest in his love affairs. This was the light in which she had come to regard Morris, who had conciliated her at first, and made his impression by his delicate and calculated deference—a sort of exhibition to which Mrs. Penniman was particularly sensitive. He had largely abated his deference afterward, for he economized his resources, but the impression was made, and the young man's very brutality came to have a sort of filial value. If Mrs. Penniman had had a son, she would probably have been afraid of him, and at this stage of our narrative she was certainly afraid of Morris Townsend. This was one of the results of his domestication in Washington Square. He took his ease with her—as, for that matter, he would certainly have done with his own mother.

28

The letter was a word of warning; it informed him that the Doctor had come home more impracticable than ever. She might have reflected that Catherine would supply him with all the information he needed on this point; but we know that Mrs. Penniman's reflections were rarely just; and, moreover, she felt that it was not for her to depend on what Catherine might do. She was to do her duty, quite irrespective of Catherine. I have said that her young friend took his ease with her, and it is an illustration of the fact that he made no answer to her letter. He took note of it amply; but he lighted his cigar with it, and he waited, in tranquil confidence that he should receive another. "His state of mind really freezes my blood," Mrs. Penniman had written, alluding to her brother; and it would have seemed that upon this statement she could hardly improve. Nevertheless, she wrote again, expressing herself with the aid of a different figure. "His hatred of you burns with a lurid flame—the flame that never dies," she wrote. "But it doesn't light up the darkness of your future. If my affection could do so, all the years of your life would be an eternal sunshine. I can extract nothing from C.; she is so terribly secretive, like her father. She seems to expect to be married very soon, and has evidently made preparations in Europe—quantities of clothing, ten pairs of shoes, etc. My dear friend, you cannot set up in married life simply with a few pairs of shoes, can you? Tell me what you think of this. I am intensely anxious to see you, I have so much to say. I miss you dreadfully; the house seems so empty without you. What is the news down town? Is the business extending?—that dear little business: I think it's so brave of you! Couldn't I come to your office?—just for three minutes? I might pass for a customer—is that what you call them? I might come in to buy something—some shares or some railroad things. *Tell me what you think of this plan.* I would carry a little reticule, like a woman of the people."

In spite of the suggestion about the reticule, Morris appeared to think poorly of the plan, for he gave Mrs. Penniman no encouragement whatever to visit his office, which he had already represented to her as a place peculiarly and unnaturally difficult to find. But as she persisted in desiring an interview—up to the last, after months of intimate colloquy, she called these meetings "interviews"—he agreed that they should take a walk together, and was even kind enough to leave his office for this purpose during the hours at which business might have been supposed to be liveliest. It was no surprise to him, when they met at a street corner, in a region of empty lots and undeveloped pavements (Mrs. Penniman being attired as much as possible like a "woman of the people"), to find that, in spite of her urgency, what she chiefly had to convey to him was the assurance of her sympathy. Of such assurances, however, he had already a voluminous collection, and it would not have been worth his while to forsake a fruitful avocation merely to hear Mrs. Penniman say, for the thousandth time, that she had made his cause her own. Morris had something of his own to say. It was not an easy thing to bring out, and while he turned it over, the difficulty made him acrimonious.

"Oh yes, I know perfectly that he combines the properties of a lump of ice and a red-hot coal," he observed. "Catherine has made it thoroughly clear, and you have told me so till I am sick of it. You needn't tell me again; I am perfectly satisfied. He will never give us a penny; I regard that as mathematically proved."

Mrs. Penniman at this point had an inspiration.

"Couldn't you bring a lawsuit against him?" She wondered that this simple expedient had never occurred to her before.

"I will bring a lawsuit against *you,*" said Morris, "if you ask me any more such aggravating questions. A man should know when he is beaten," he added, in a moment. "I must give her up!"

Mrs. Penniman received this declaration in silence, though it made her heart beat a little. It found her by no means unprepared, for she had accustomed herself to the thought that, if Morris should decidedly not be able to get her brother's money, it would not do for him to marry Catherine without it. "It would not do," was a vague way of putting the thing; but Mrs. Penniman's natural affection completed the idea, which, though it had not as yet been so crudely expressed between them as in the form that Morris had just given it, had nevertheless been implied so often, in certain easy intervals of talk, as he sat stretching his legs in the Doctor's well-stuffed arm-chairs, that she had grown first to regard it with an emotion which she flattered herself was philosophic, and then to have a secret tenderness for it. The fact that she kept her tenderness secret proves, of course, that she was ashamed of it; but she managed to blink her shame by reminding herself that she was, after all, the official protector of her niece's marriage. Her logic would scarcely have passed muster with the Doctor. In the first place, Morris *must* get the money, and she would help him to it. In the second, it was plain it would never come to him, and it would be a grievous pity he should marry without it—a young man who might so easily find something better. After her brother had delivered himself, on his return from Europe, of that incisive little address that has been quoted, Morris's cause seemed so hopeless that Mrs. Penniman fixed her attention exclusively upon the latter branch of her argument. If Morris had been her son, she would certainly have sacrificed Catherine to a superior conception of his future; and to be ready to do so, as the case stood, was therefore even a finer degree of devotion. Nevertheless, it checked her breath a little to have the sacrificial knife, as it were, suddenly thrust into her hand.

Morris walked along a moment, and then he repeated, harshly,

"I must give her up!"

"I think I understand you," said Mrs. Penniman, gently.

"I certainly say it distinctly enough—brutally and vulgarly enough."

He was ashamed of himself, and his shame was uncomfortable; and as he was extremely intolerant of discomfort, he felt vicious and cruel. He wanted to abuse somebody, and he began, cautiously—for he was always cautious—with himself.

"Couldn't you take her down a little?" he asked.

"Take her down?"

"Prepare her—try and ease me off."

Mrs. Penniman stopped, looking at him very solemnly.

"My poor Morris, do you know how much she loves you?"

"No, I don't. I don't want to know. I have always tried to keep from knowing. It would be too painful."

"She will suffer much," said Mrs. Penniman.

"You must console her. If you are as good a friend to me as you pretend to be, you will manage it."

Mrs. Penniman shook her head sadly.

"You talk of my 'pretending' to like you; but I can't pretend to hate you. I can only tell her I think very highly of you; and how will that console her for losing you?"

"The Doctor will help you. He will be delighted at the thing being broken off; and as he is a knowing fellow, he will invent something to comfort her."

"He will invent a new torture," cried Mrs. Penniman. "Heaven deliver her from her father's comfort! It will consist of his crowing over her, and saying, 'I always told you so!' "

Morris colored a most uncomfortable red.

"If you don't console her any better than you console me, you certainly won't be of much use. It's a damned disagreeable necessity; I feel it extremely, and you ought to make it easy for me."

"I will be your friend for life," Mrs. Penniman declared.

"Be my friend *now!*" and Morris walked on.

She went with him; she was almost trembling.

"Should you like me to tell her?" she asked.

"You mustn't tell her, but you can—you can—" And he hesitated, trying to think what Mrs. Penniman could do. "You can explain to her why it is. It's because I can't bring myself to step in between her and her father—to give him the pretext he grasps at so eagerly (it's a hideous sight!) for depriving her of her rights."

Mrs. Penniman felt with remarkable promptitude the charm of this formula.

"That's so like you," she said; "it's so finely felt."

Morris gave his stick an angry swing.

"Oh damnation!" he exclaimed, perversely.

Mrs. Penniman, however, was not discouraged.

"It may turn out better than you think. Catherine is, after all, so very peculiar." And she thought she might take it upon herself to assure him that, whatever happened, the girl would be very quiet—she wouldn't make a noise. They extended their walk, and while they proceeded Mrs. Penniman took upon herself other things besides, and ended by having assumed a considerable burden; Morris being ready enough, as may be imagined, to put everything off upon her. But he was not for a single instant the dupe of her blundering alacrity; he knew that of what she promised she was competent to perform but an insignificant fraction, and the more she professed her willingness to serve him, the greater fool he thought her.

"What will you do if you don't marry her?" she ventured to inquire in the course of this conversation.

"Something brilliant," said Morris. "Shouldn't you like me to do something brilliant?"

The idea gave Mrs. Penniman exceeding pleasure.

"I shall feel sadly taken in if you don't."

"I shall have to, to make up for this. This isn't at all brilliant, you know."

Mrs. Penniman mused a little, as if there might be some way of making out that it was; but she had to give up the attempt, and, to carry off the awkwardness of failure, she risked a new inquiry.

"Do you mean—do you mean another marriage?"

Morris greeted this question with a reflection which was hardly the less impudent from being inaudible. "Surely women are more crude than men!" And then he answered, audibly,

"Never in the world!"

Mrs. Penniman felt disappointed and snubbed, and she relieved herself in a little vaguely sarcastic cry. He was certainly perverse.

"I give her up, not for another woman, but for a wider career," Morris announced.

This was very grand; but still Mrs. Penniman, who felt that she had exposed herself, was faintly rancorous.

"Do you mean never to come to see her again?" she asked, with some sharpness.

"Oh no, I shall come again; but what is the use of dragging it out? I have been four times since she came back, and it's terribly awkward work. I can't keep it up indefinitely; she oughtn't to expect that, you know. A woman should never keep a man dangling," he added, finely.

"Ah, but you must have your last parting!" urged his companion, in whose imagination the idea of last partings occupied a place inferior in dignity only to that of first meetings.

29

He came again, without managing the last parting; and again and again, without finding that Mrs. Penniman had as yet done much to pave the path of retreat with flowers. It was devilish awkward, as he said, and he felt a lively animosity for Catherine's aunt, who, as he had now quite formed the habit of saying to himself, had dragged him into the mess, and was bound in the common charity to get him out of it. Mrs. Penniman, to tell the truth, had, in the seclusion of her own apartment—and, I may add, amid the suggestiveness of Catherine's, which wore in those days the appearance of that of a young lady laying out her *trousseau*—Mrs. Penniman had measured her responsibilities, and taken fright at their magnitude. The task of preparing Catherine and easing off Morris presented difficulties which increased in the execution, and even led the impulsive Lavinia to ask herself whether the modification of the young man's original project had been conceived in a happy spirit. A brilliant future, a wider career, a conscience exempt from the reproach of interference between a young lady and her natural rights—these excellent things might be too troublesomely purchased. From Catherine herself Mrs. Penniman received no assistance whatever; the poor girl was apparently without suspicion of her danger. She looked at her lover with eyes of undiminished trust, and though she had less confidence in her aunt than in a young man with whom she had exchanged so many tender vows, she gave her no handle for explaining or confessing. Mrs. Penniman, faltering and wavering, declared Catherine was very stupid, put off the great scene, as she would have called it, from day to day, and wandered about, very uncomfortably, with her own unexploded bomb in her hands. Morris's own scenes were very small ones just now; but even these were beyond his strength. He made his visits as brief as possible, and, while he sat with his mistress, found terribly little to talk about. She was waiting for him, in vulgar parlance, to name the day; and so long as he was unprepared to be explicit on this point, it seemed a mockery to pretend to talk about matters more abstract. She had no airs and no arts, she never attempted to disguise her expectancy. She was waiting on his good pleasure, and would wait modestly and patiently; his hanging back at this supreme time might appear strange, but of course he must have a good reason for it. Catherine would have made a wife of the gentle, old-fashioned pattern—regarding reasons as favors and windfalls, but no more expecting one every day than she would have expected a bouquet of camellias. During the period of her engagement, however, a young lady even of the most slender pretensions counts upon more bouquets than at other times; and there was a want of perfume in the air at this moment which at last excited the girl's alarm.

"Are you sick?" she asked of Morris. "You seem so restless, and you look pale."

"I am not at all well," said Morris; and it occurred to him that, if he could only make her pity him enough, he might get off.

"I am afraid you are overworked; you oughtn't to work so much."

"I must do that." And then he added, with a sort of calculated brutality, "I don't want to owe you everything."

"Ah, how can you say that?"

"I am too proud," said Morris.

"Yes—you are too proud."

"Well, you must take me as I am," he went on; "you can never change me."

"I don't want to change you," she said, gently; "I will take you as you are." And she stood looking at him.

"You know people talk tremendously about a man's marrying a rich girl," Morris remarked. "It's excessively disagreeable."

"But I am not rich," said Catherine.

"You are rich enough to make me talked about."

"Of course you are talked about. It's an honor."

"It's an honor I could easily dispense with."

She was on the point of asking him whether it was not a compensation for this annoyance that the poor girl who had the misfortune to bring it upon him loved him so dearly and believed in him so truly; but she hesitated, thinking that this would perhaps seem an exacting speech, and while she hesitated, he suddenly left her.

The next time he came, however, she brought it out, and she told him again that he was too proud. He repeated that he couldn't change, and this time she felt the impulse to say that with a little effort he might change.

Sometimes he thought that if he could only make a quarrel with her it might help him; but the question was how to quarrel with a young woman who had such treasures of concession. "I suppose you think the effort is all on your side," he broke out. "Don't you believe that I have my own effort to make?"

"It's all yours now," she said; "my effort is finished and done with."

"Well, mine is not."

"We must bear things together," said Catherine. "That's what we ought to do."

Morris attempted a natural smile. "There are some things which we can't very well bear together—for instance, separation."

"Why do you speak of separation?"

"Ah! you don't like it; I knew you wouldn't."

"Where are you going, Morris?" she suddenly asked.

He fixed his eye on her a moment, and for a part of that moment she was afraid of it. "Will you promise not to make a scene?"

"A scene!—do I make scenes?"

"All women do!" said Morris, with the tone of large experience.

"I don't. Where are you going?"

"If I should say I was going away on business, should you think it very strange?"

She wondered a moment, gazing at him. "Yes—no. Not if you will take me with you."

"Take you with me—on business?"

"What is your business? Your business is to be with me."

"I don't earn my living with you," said Morris. "Or, rather," he cried, with a sudden inspiration, "that's just what I do—or what the world says I do!"

This ought perhaps to have been a

great stroke, but it miscarried. "Where are you going?" Catherine simply repeated.

"To New Orleans—about buying some cotton."

"I am perfectly willing to go to New Orleans," Catherine said.

"Do you suppose I would take you to a nest of yellow-fever?" cried Morris. "Do you suppose I would expose you at such a time as this?"

"If there is yellow-fever, why should you go? Morris, you must not go."

"It is to make six thousand dollars," said Morris. "Do you grudge me that satisfaction?"

"We have no need of six thousand dollars. You think too much about money."

"You can afford to say that. This is a great chance; we heard of it last night." And he explained to her in what the chance consisted; and told her a long story, going over more than once several of the details, about the remarkable stroke of business which he and his partner had planned between them.

But Catherine's imagination, for reasons best known to herself, absolutely refused to be fired. "If you can go to New Orleans, I can go," she said. "Why shouldn't you catch yellow-fever quite as easily as I? I am every bit as strong as you, and not in the least afraid of any fever. When we were in Europe we were in very unhealthy places; my father used to make me take some pills. I never caught anything, and I never was nervous. What will be the use of six thousand dollars if you die of a fever? When persons are going to be married they oughtn't to think so much about business. You shouldn't think about cotton; you should think about me. You can go to New Orleans some other time—there will always be plenty of cotton. It isn't the moment to choose: we have waited too long already." She spoke more forcibly and volubly than he had ever heard her, and she held his arm in her two hands.

"You said you wouldn't make a scene," cried Morris. "I call this a scene."

"It's you that are making it. I have never asked you anything before. We have waited too long already." And it was a comfort to her to think that she had hitherto asked so little; it seemed to make her right to insist the greater now.

Morris bethought himself a little. "Very well, then; we won't talk about it any more. I will transact my business by letter." And he began to smooth his hat, as if to take leave.

"You won't go?" and she stood looking up at him.

He could not give up his idea of provoking a quarrel; it was so much the simplest way. He bent his eyes on her upturned face with the darkest frown he could achieve. "You are not discreet; you mustn't bully me."

But, as usual, she conceded everything. "No, I am not discreet; I know I am too pressing. But isn't it natural? It is only for a moment."

"In a moment you may do a great deal of harm. Try and be calmer the next time I come."

"When will you come?"

"Do you want to make conditions?" Morris asked. "I will come next Saturday."

"Come to-morrow," Catherine begged; "I want you to come to-morrow. I will be very quiet," she added; and her agitation had by this time become so great that the assurance was not unbecoming. A sudden fear had come over her; it was like the solid conjunction of a dozen disembodied doubts, and her imagination, at a single bound, had traversed an enormous distance. All her being, for the moment, was centred in the wish to keep him in the room.

Morris bent his head and kissed her forehead. "When you are quiet, you are perfection," he said; "but when you are violent, you are not in character."

It was Catherine's wish that there should be no violence about her save the beating of her heart, which she could not help; and she went on, as gently as possible, "Will you promise to come to-morrow?"

"I said Saturday!" Morris answered, smiling. He tried a frown at one moment, a smile at another; he was at his wit's end.

"Yes, Saturday too," she answered, trying to smile. "But to-morrow first." He was going to the door, and she went with him quickly. She leaned her shoulder against it; it seemed to her that she would do anything to keep him.

"If I am prevented from coming to-morrow, you will say I have deceived you," he said.

"How can you be prevented? You can come if you will."

"I am a busy man—I am not a dangler!" cried Morris, sternly.

His voice was so hard and unnatural that, with a helpless look at him, she turned away; and then he quickly laid his hand on the door-knob. He felt as if he were absolutely running away from her. But in an instant she was close to him again, and murmuring in a tone none the less penetrating for being low, "Morris, you are going to leave me."

"Yes, for a little while."

"For how long?"

"Till you are reasonable again."

"I shall never be reasonable, in that way." And she tried to keep him longer; it was almost a struggle. "Think of what I have done!" she broke out. "Morris, I have given up everything."

"You shall have everything back."

"You wouldn't say that if you didn't mean something. What is it?—what has happened?—what have I done?—what has changed you?"

"I will write to you—that is better," Morris stammered.

"Ah, you won't come back!" she cried, bursting into tears.

"Dear Catherine," he said, "don't believe that. I promise you that you shall see me again." And he managed to get away, and to close the door behind him.

30

It was almost the last outbreak of passion of her life; at least, she never indulged in another that the world knew anything about. But this one was long and terrible; she flung herself on the sofa and gave herself up to her grief. She hardly knew what had happened; ostensibly she had only had a difference with her lover, as other girls had had before, and the thing was not only not a rupture, but she was under no obligation to regard it even as a menace. Nevertheless, she felt a wound, even if he had not dealt it; it seemed to her that a mask had suddenly fallen from his face. He had wished to get away from her; he had been angry and cruel, and said strange things, with strange looks. She was smothered and stunned; she buried her head in the cushions, sobbing and talking to herself. But at last she raised herself, with the fear that either her father or Mrs. Penniman would come in; and then she sat there, staring before her, while the room grew darker. She said to herself that perhaps he would come back to tell her he had not meant what he said; and she listened for his ring at the door, trying to believe that this was probable. A long time passed, but Morris remained absent; the shadows gathered; the evening settled down on the meagre elegance of the light, clear-colored room; the fire went out. When it had grown dark, Catherine went to the window and looked out; she stood there for half an hour, on the mere chance that he would come up the steps. At last she turned away, for she saw her father come in. He had seen her at the window looking out, and he stopped a moment at the bottom of the white steps, and gravely, with an air of exaggerated courtesy, lifted his hat to her. The gesture was so incongruous to the condition she was in, this stately tribute of respect to a poor girl despised and forsaken was so out of place, that the thing gave her a kind of horror, and she hurried away to her room. It seemed to her that she had given Morris up.

She had to show herself half an hour later, and she was sustained at table by the immensity of her desire that her father should not perceive that anything had happened. This was a great help to her afterward, and it served her (though never as much as she supposed) from the first. On this occasion Doctor Sloper was rather talkative. He told a great many stories about a wonderful poodle that he had seen at the house of an old lady whom he visited professionally. Catherine not only tried to appear to listen to the anecdotes of the poodle, but she endeavored to interest herself in them, so as not to think of her scene with Morris. That perhaps was an hallucination; he was mistaken, she was jealous; people didn't change like that from one day to another. Then she knew that she had had doubts before—strange suspicions, that were at once vague and acute —and that he had been different ever since her return from Europe: whereupon she tried again to listen to her father, who told a story so remarkably well. Afterward she went straight to her own room; it was beyond her strength to undertake to spend the evening with her aunt. All the evening, alone, she questioned herself. Her trouble was terrible; but was it a thing of her imagination, engendered by an extravagant sensibility, or did it represent a clear-cut reality, and had the worst that was possible actually come to pass? Mrs. Penniman, with a degree of tact that was as unusual as it was commendable, took the line of leaving her alone. The truth is, that her suspicions having been aroused, she indulged a desire, natural to a timid person, that the explosion should be localized. So long as the air still vibrated she kept out of the way.

She passed and repassed Catherine's door several times in the course of the evening, as if she expected to hear a plaintive moan behind it. But the room remained perfectly still; and accordingly, the last thing before retiring to her own couch, she applied for admittance. Catherine was sitting up, and had a book that she pretended to be reading. She had no wish to go to bed, for she had no expectation of sleeping. After Mrs. Penniman had left her she sat up half the night, and she offered her visitor no inducement to remain. Her aunt came stealing in very gently, and approached her with great solemnity.

"I am afraid you are in trouble, my dear. Can I do anything to help you?"

"I am not in any trouble whatever, and do not need any help," said Catherine, fibbing roundly, and proving thereby that not only our faults, but our most involuntary misfortunes, tend to corrupt our morals.

"Has nothing happened to you?"

"Nothing whatever."

"Are you very sure, dear?"

"Perfectly sure."

"And can I really do nothing for you?"

"Nothing, aunt, but kindly leave me alone," said Catherine.

Mrs. Penniman, though she had been afraid of too warm a welcome before, was now disappointed at so cold a one; and in relating afterward, as she did to many persons, and with considerable variations of detail, the history of the termination of her niece's engagement, she was usually careful to mention that the young lady, on a certain occasion, had "hustled" her out of the room. It was characteristic of Mrs. Penniman that she related this fact, not in the least out of malignity to Catherine, whom she very sufficiently pitied, but simply from a natural disposition to embellish any subject that she touched.

Catherine, as I have said, sat up half the night, as if she still expected to hear Morris Townsend ring at the door. On the morrow this expectation was less unreasonable; but it was not gratified by the reappearance of the young man. Neither had he written; there was not a word of explanation or reassurance. Fortunately for Catherine, she could take refuge from her excitement, which had now become intense, in her determination that her father should see nothing of it. How well she deceived her father we shall have occasion to learn; but her innocent arts were of little avail before a person of the rare perspicacity of Mrs. Penniman. This lady easily saw that she was agitated, and if there was any agitation going forward, Mrs. Penniman was not a person to forfeit her natural share in it. She returned to the charge the next evening, and requested her niece to confide in her—to unburden her heart. Perhaps she should be able to explain certain things that now seemed dark, and that she knew more about than Catherine supposed. If Catherine had been frigid the night before, to-day she was haughty.

"You are completely mistaken, and I have not the least idea what you mean. I don't know what you are trying to fasten on me, and I have never had less need of any one's explanations in my life."

In this way the girl delivered herself, and from hour to hour kept her aunt at bay. From hour to hour Mrs. Penniman's curiosity grew. She would have given her little finger to know what Morris had said and done, what tone he had taken, what pretext he had found. She wrote to him, naturally, to request an interview; but she received, as naturally, no answer to her petition. Morris was not in a writing mood; for Catherine had addressed him two short notes which met with no acknowledgment. These notes were so brief that I may give them entire. "Won't you give me me some sign that you didn't mean to be so cruel as you seemed on Tuesday?"—that was the first; the other was a little longer. "If I was unreasonable or suspicious on Tuesday—if I annoyed you or troubled you in any way—I beg your forgiveness, and I promise never again to be so foolish. I am punished enough, and I don't understand. Dear Morris, you are killing me!" These notes were despatched on the Friday and Saturday; but Saturday and Sunday passed without bringing the poor girl the satisfaction she desired. Her punishment accumulated; she continued to bear it, however, with a good deal of superficial fortitude. On Saturday morning, the Doctor, who had been watching in silence, spoke to his sister Lavinia.

"The thing has happened—the scoundrel has backed out!"

"Never!" cried Mrs. Penniman, who had bethought herself what she should say to Catherine, but was not provided with a line of defence against her brother, so that indignant negation was the only weapon in her hands.

"He has begged for a reprieve, then, if you like that better!"

"It seems to make you very happy that your daughter's affections have been trifled with."

"It does," said the Doctor; "for I had foretold it! It's a great pleasure to be in the right."

"Your pleasures make one shudder!" his sister exclaimed.

Catherine went rigidly through her usual occupations; that is, up to the point of going with her aunt to church on Sunday morning. She generally went to afternoon service as well; but on this occasion her courage faltered, and she begged of Mrs. Penniman to go without her.

"I am sure you have a secret," said Mrs. Penniman, with great significance, looking at her rather grimly.

"If I have, I shall keep it!" Catherine answered, turning away.

Mrs. Penniman started for church; but before she had arrived, she stopped and turned back, and before twenty minutes had elapsed she re-entered the house, looked into the empty parlors, and then went up-stairs and knocked at Catherine's door. She got no answer; Catherine was not in her room, and Mrs. Penniman presently ascertained that she was not in the house. "She has gone to him! she has fled!" Lavinia cried, clasping her hands with admiration and envy. But she soon perceived that Catherine had taken nothing with her—all her personal property in her room was intact—and then she jumped at the hypothesis that the girl had gone forth, not in tenderness, but in resentment. "She has followed him to his own door! she has burst upon him in his own apartment!" It was in these terms that Mrs. Penniman depicted to herself her niece's errand, which, viewed in this light, gratified her sense of the picturesque only a shade less strongly than the idea of a clandestine marriage. To visit one's lover, with tears and reproaches, at his own residence, was an image so agreeable to Mrs. Penniman's mind that she felt a sort of æsthetic disappointment at its lacking, in this case, the harmonious accompaniments of darkness and storm. A quiet Sunday afternoon appeared an inadequate setting for it; and, indeed, Mrs. Penniman was quite out of humor with the conditions of the time, which passed very slowly as she sat in the front parlor, in her bonnet and her cashmere shawl, awaiting Catherine's return.

This event at last took place. She saw her—at the window—mount the steps, and she went to await her in the hall, where she pounced upon her as soon as she had entered the house, and drew her into the parlor, closing the door with solemnity. Catherine was flushed, and her eye was bright. Mrs. Penniman hardly knew what to think.

"May I venture to ask where you have been?" she demanded.

"I have been to take a walk," said Catherine. "I thought you had gone to church."

"I did go to church; but the service was shorter than usual. And pray where did you walk?"

"I don't know!" said Catherine.

"Your ignorance is most extraordinary! Dear Catherine, you can trust me."

"What am I to trust you with?"

"With your secret—your sorrow."

"I have no sorrow!" said Catherine, fiercely.

"My poor child," Mrs. Penniman insisted, "you can't deceive me. I know everything. I have been requested to—a—to converse with you."

"I don't want to converse!"

"It will relieve you. Don't you know Shakespeare's lines?—'The grief that does not speak!' My dear girl, it is better as it is!"

"What is better?" Catherine asked.

She was really too perverse. A certain amount of perversity was to be allowed for in a young lady whose lover had thrown her over; but not such an amount as would prove inconvenient to his apologists. "That you should be reasonable," said Mrs. Penniman, with some sternness; "that you should take counsel of worldly prudence, and submit to practical considerations; that you should agree to—a—separate."

Catherine had been ice up to this moment, but at this word she flamed up. "Separate? What do you know about our separating?"

Mrs. Penniman shook her head with a sadness in which there was almost a sense of injury. "Your pride is my pride, and your susceptibilities are mine. I see your side perfectly, but I also—" and she smiled with melancholy suggestiveness—"I also see the situation as a whole!"

This suggestiveness was lost upon Catherine, who repeated her violent inquiry. "Why do you talk about separation; what do you know about it?"

"We must study resignation," said Mrs. Penniman, hesitating, but sententious at a venture.

"Resignation to what?"

"To a change of—of our plans."

"My plans have not changed!" said Catherine, with a little laugh.

"Ah, but Mr. Townsend's have," her aunt answered, very gently.

"What do you mean?"

There was an imperious brevity in the tone of this inquiry, against which Mrs. Penniman felt bound to protest; the information with which she had undertaken to supply her niece was after all a favor. She had tried sharpness, and she had tried sternness; but neither would do; she was shocked at the girl's obstinacy. "Ah well," she said, "if he hasn't told you! . . ." and she turned away.

Catherine watched her a moment in silence; then she hurried after her, stopping her before she reached the door. "Told me what? What do you mean? What are you hinting at and threatening me with?"

"Isn't it broken off?" asked Mrs. Penniman.

"My engagement? Not in the least!"

"I beg your pardon in that case. I have spoken too soon!"

"Too soon? Soon or late," Catherine broke out, "you speak foolishly and cruelly!"

"What has happened between you then?" asked her aunt, struck by the sincerity of this cry; "for something certainly has happened."

"Nothing has happened but that I love him more and more!"

Mrs. Penniman was silent an instant. "I suppose that's the reason you went to see him this afternoon."

Catherine flushed as if she had been struck. "Yes, I did go to see him! But that's my own business."

"Very well, then; we won't talk about it." And Mrs. Penniman moved toward the door again; but she was stopped by a sudden imploring cry from the girl.

"Aunt Lavinia, *where* has he gone?"

"Ah, you admit then that he has gone away! Didn't they know at his house?"

"They said he had left town. I asked no more questions; I was ashamed," said Catherine, simply enough.

"You needn't have taken so compromising a step if you had had a little more confidence in me," Mrs. Penniman observed, with a good deal of grandeur.

"Is it to New Orleans?" Catherine went on, irrelevantly.

It was the first time Mrs. Penniman had heard of New Orleans in this connection; but she was averse to letting Catherine know that she was in the dark. She attempted to strike an illumination from the instructions she had received from Morris. "My dear Catherine," she said, "when a separation has been agreed upon, the farther he goes away the better."

"Agreed upon? Has he agreed upon it with you?" A consummate sense of her aunt's meddlesome folly had come over her during the last five minutes, and she was sickened at the thought that Mrs. Penniman had been let loose, as it were, upon her happiness.

"He certainly has sometimes advised with me," said Mrs. Penniman.

"Is it you, then, that has changed him and made him so unnatural?" Catherine cried. "Is it you that have worked on him and taken him from me? He doesn't belong to you, and I don't see how you have anything to do with what is between us! Is it you that have made this plot, and told him to leave me? How could you be so wicked, so cruel? What have I ever done to you? Why can't you leave me alone? I was afraid you would spoil everything; for you *do* spoil everything you touch! I was afraid of you all the time we were abroad; I had no rest when I thought that you were always talking to him." Catherine went on with growing vehemence, pouring out, in her bitterness and in the clairvoyance of her passion (which suddenly, jumping all processes, made her judge her aunt finally and without appeal), the uneasiness which had lain for so many months upon her heart.

Mrs. Penniman was scared and bewildered; she saw no prospect of introducing her little account of the purity of Morris's motives. "You are a most ungrateful girl!" she cried. "Do you scold me for talking with him? I'm sure we never talked of anything but you!"

"Yes; and that was the way you worried him; you made him tired of my very name! I wish you had never spoken of me to him; I never asked your help!"

"I am sure if it hadn't been for me he would never have come to the house, and you would never have known that he thought of you," Mrs. Penniman rejoined, with a good deal of justice.

"I wish he never had come to the house, and that I never had known it! That's better than this," said poor Catherine.

"You are a very ungrateful girl," Aunt Lavinia repeated.

Catherine's outbreak of anger and the sense of wrong gave her, while they lasted, the satisfaction that comes from all assertion of force; they hurried her along, and there is always a sort of pleasure in cleaving the air. But at bottom she hated to be violent, and she was conscious of no aptitude for organized resentment. She calmed herself with a great effort, but with great rapidity, and walked about the room a few moments, trying to say to herself that her aunt had meant everything for the best. She did not succeed in saying it with much conviction, but after a little she was able to speak quietly enough.

"I am not ungrateful, but I am very unhappy. It's hard to be grateful for that," she said. "Will you please tell me where he is?"

"I haven't the least idea; I am not in secret correspondence with him!" And Mrs. Penniman wished, indeed, that she were, so that she might let him know how Catherine abused her, after all she had done.

"Was it a plan of his, then, to break off—?" By this time Catherine had become completely quiet.

Mrs. Penniman began again to have a glimpse of her chance for explaining. "He shrunk—he shrunk," she said; "he lacked courage, but it was the courage to injure you! He couldn't bear to bring down on you your father's curse."

Catherine listened to this with her eyes fixed upon her aunt, and continued to gaze at her for some time afterward. "Did he tell you to say that?"

"He told me to say many things—all so delicate, so discriminating; and he told me to tell you he hoped you wouldn't despise him."

"I don't," said Catherine; and then she added, "And will he stay away forever?"

"Oh, forever is a long time. Your father, perhaps, won't live forever."

"Perhaps not."

"I am sure you appreciate—you understand—even though your heart bleeds," said Mrs. Penniman. "You doubtless think him too scrupulous. So do I, but I respect his scruples. What he asks of you is that you should do the same."

Catherine was still gazing at her aunt, but she spoke at last as if she had not heard or not understood her. "It has been a regular plan, then. He has broken it off deliberately; he has given me up."

"For the present, dear Catherine; he has put it off, only."

"He has left me alone," Catherine went on.

"Haven't you *me?*" asked Mrs. Penniman, with some solemnity.

Catherine shook her head slowly. "I don't believe it!" and she left the room.

31

Though she had forced herself to be calm, she preferred practising this virtue in private, and she forbore to show herself at tea—a repast which, on Sundays, at six o'clock, took the place of dinner. Doctor Sloper and his sister sat face to face, but Mrs. Penniman never met her brother's eye. Late in the evening she went with him, but without Catherine, to their sister Almond's, where, between the two ladies, Catherine's unhappy situation was discussed with a frankness that was conditioned by a good deal of mysterious reticence on Mrs. Penniman's part.

"I am delighted he is not to marry her," said Mrs. Almond, "but he ought to be horsewhipped all the same."

Mrs. Penniman, who was shocked at her sister's coarseness, replied that he had been actuated by the noblest of motives—the desire not to impoverish Catherine.

"I am very happy that Catherine is not to be impoverished—but I hope he may never have a penny too much! And what does the poor girl say to *you?*" Mrs. Almond asked.

"She says I have a genius for consolation," said Mrs. Penniman.

This was the account of the matter that she gave to her sister, and it was perhaps with the consciousness of genius that, on her return that evening to Washington Square, she again presented herself for admittance at Catherine's door. Catherine came and opened it; she was apparently very quiet.

"I only want to give you a little word of advice," she said. "If your father asks you, say that everything is going on."

Catherine stood there, with her hand on the knob, looking at her aunt, but not asking her to come in. "Do you think he will ask me?"

"I am sure he will. He asked me just now, on our way home from your aunt Elizabeth's. I explained the whole thing to your aunt Elizabeth. I said to your father I knew nothing about it."

"Do you think he will ask me, when he sees—when he sees—?" But here Catherine stopped.

"The more he sees, the more disagreeable he will be," said her aunt.

"He shall see as little as possible!" Catherine declared.

"Tell him you are to be married."

"So I am," said Catherine, softly; and she closed the door upon her aunt.

She could not have said this two days later—for instance, on Tuesday, when she at last received a letter from Morris Townsend. It was an epistle of considerable length, measuring five large square pages, and written at Philadelphia. It was an explanatory document, and it explained a great many things, chief among which were the considerations that had led the writer to take advantage of an urgent "professional" absence to try and banish from his mind the image of one whose path he had crossed only to scatter it with ruins. He ventured to expect but partial success in this attempt, but he could promise her that, whatever his failure, he would never again interpose between her generous heart and her brilliant prospects and filial duties. He closed with an intimation that his professional pursuits might compel him to travel for some months, and with the hope that when they should each have accommodated themselves to what was sternly involved in their respective positions—even should this result not be reached for years—they should meet as friends, as fellow-sufferers, as innocent but philosophic victims of a great social law. That her life should be peaceful and happy was the dearest wish of him who ventured still to subscribe himself her most obedient servant. The letter was beautifully written, and Catherine, who kept it for many years after this, was able, when her sense of the bitterness of its meaning and the hollowness of its tone had grown less acute, to admire its grace of expression. At present, for a long time after she received it, all she had to help her was the determination, daily more rigid, to make no appeal to the compassion of her father.

He suffered a week to elapse, and then one day, in the morning, at an hour at which she rarely saw him, he strolled into the back parlor. He had watched his time, and he found her alone. She was sitting with some work, and he came and stood in front of her. He was going out; he had on his hat, and was drawing on his gloves.

"It doesn't seem to me that you are treating me just now with all the consideration I deserve," he said in a moment.

"I don't know what I have done," Catherine answered, with her eyes on her work.

"You have apparently quite banished from your mind the request I made you at Liverpool before we sailed—the request that you would notify me in advance before leaving my house."

"I have not left your house," said Catherine.

"But you intend to leave it, and, by what you gave me to understand, your departure must be impending. In fact, though you are still here in body, you are already absent in spirit. Your mind has taken up its residence with your prospective husband, and you might quite as well be lodged under the conjugal roof for all the benefit we get from your society."

"I will try and be more cheerful," said Catherine.

"You certainly ought to be cheerful; you ask a great deal if you are not. To the pleasure of marrying a charming young man you add that of having your own way; you strike me as a very lucky young lady!"

Catherine got up; she was suffocating. But she folded her work deliberately and correctly, bending her burning face upon it. Her father stood where he had planted himself; she hoped he would go, but he smoothed and buttoned his gloves, and then he rested his hands upon his hips.

"It would be a convenience to me to know when I may expect to have an empty house," he went on. "When you go, your aunt marches."

She looked at him at last, with a long, silent gaze, which, in spite of her pride and her resolution, uttered part of the appeal she had tried not to make. Her father's cold gray eye sounded her own, and he insisted on his point.

"Is it to-morrow? Is it next week, or the week after?"

"I shall not go away!" said Catherine.

The Doctor raised his eyebrows. "Has he backed out?"

"I have broken off my engagement."

"Broken it off?"

"I have asked him to leave New York, and he has gone away for a long time."

The Doctor was both puzzled and disappointed, but he solved his perplexity by saying to himself that his daughter simply misrepresented—justifiably, if one would, but nevertheless, misrepresented—the facts; and he eased off his disappointment, which was that of a man losing a chance for a little triumph that he had rather counted on, by a few words that he uttered aloud.

"How does he take his dismissal?"

"I don't know!" said Catherine, less ingeniously than she had hitherto spoken.

"You mean you don't care? You are rather cruel, after encouraging him and playing with him for so long!"

The Doctor had his revenge, after all.

32

Our story has hitherto moved with very short steps, but as it approaches its termination it must take a long stride. As time went on, it might have appeared to the Doctor that his daughter's account of her rupture with Morris Townsend, mere bravado as he had deemed it, was in some degree justified by the sequel. Morris remained as rigidly and unremittingly absent as if he had died of a broken heart, and Catherine had apparently buried the memory of this fruitless episode as deep as if it had terminated by her own choice. We know that she had been deeply and incurably wounded, but the Doctor had no means of knowing it. He was certainly curious about it, and would have given a good deal to discover the exact truth; but it was his punishment that he never knew—his punishment, I mean, for the abuse of sarcasm in his relations with his daughter. There was a good deal of effective sarcasm in her keeping him in the dark, and the rest of the world conspired with her, in this sense, to be sarcastic. Mrs. Penniman told him nothing, partly because he never questioned her—he made too light of Mrs. Penniman for that—and partly because she flattered herself that a tormenting reserve, and a serene profession of ignorance, would avenge her for his theory that she had meddled in the matter. He went two or three times to see Mrs. Montgomery, but Mrs. Montgomery had nothing to impart. She simply knew that her brother's engagement was broken off; and now that Miss Sloper was out of danger, she preferred not to bear witness in any way against Morris. She had done so before—however unwillingly—because she was sorry for Miss Sloper; but she was not sorry for Miss Sloper now—not at all sorry. Morris had told her nothing about his relations with Miss Sloper at the time, and he had told her nothing since. He was always away, and he very seldom wrote to her; she believed he had gone to California. Mrs. Almond had, in her sister's phrase, "taken up" Catherine violently since the recent catastrophe; but, though the girl was very grateful to her for her kindness, she revealed no secrets, and the good lady could give the Doctor no satisfaction. Even, however, had she been able to narrate to him the private history of his daughter's unhappy love affair, it would have given her a certain comfort to leave him in ignorance; for Mrs. Almond was at this time not altogether in sympathy with her brother. She had guessed for herself that Catherine had been cruelly jilted—she knew nothing from Mrs. Penniman, for Mrs. Penniman had not ventured to lay the famous explanation of Morris's motives before Mrs. Almond, though she had thought it good enough for Catherine—and she pronounced her brother too consistently indifferent to what the poor creature must have suffered and must still be suffering. Doctor Sloper had his theory, and he rarely altered his theories. The marriage would have been an abominable one, and the girl had had a blessed escape. She was not to be pitied for that, and to pretend to condole with her would have been to make concessions to the idea that she had ever had a right to think of Morris.

"I put my foot on this idea from the first, and I keep it there now," said the Doctor. "I don't see any thing cruel in that; one can't keep it there too long." To this Mrs. Almond more than once replied that, if Catherine had got rid of her incongruous lover, she deserved the credit of it, and that to bring herself to her father's enlightened view of the matter must have cost her an effort that he was bound to appreciate.

"I am by no means sure she has got rid of him," the Doctor said. "There is not the smallest probability that, after having been as obstinate as a mule for two years, she suddenly became amenable to reason. It is infinitely more probable that he got rid of her."

"All the more reason you should be gentle with her."

"I *am* gentle with her. But I can't do the pathetic; I can't pump up tears, to look graceful, over the most fortunate thing that ever happened to her."

"You have no sympathy," said Mrs. Almond; "that was never your strong point. You have only to look at her to see that, right or wrong, and whether the rupture came from herself or from him, her poor little heart is grievously bruised."

"Handling bruises, and even dropping tears on them, doesn't make them any better! My business is to see she gets no more knocks, and that I shall carefully attend to. But I don't at all recognize your description of Catherine. She doesn't strike me in the least as a young woman going about in search of a moral poultice. In fact, she seems to me much better than while the fellow was hanging about. She is perfectly comfortable and blooming; she eats and sleeps, takes her usual exercise, and overloads herself, as usual, with finery. She is always knitting some purse or embroidering some handkerchief, and it seems to me she turns these articles out about as fast as ever. She hasn't much to say; but when had she anything to say? She had her little dance, and now she is sitting down to rest. I suspect that, on the whole, she enjoys it."

"She enjoys it as people enjoy getting rid of a leg that has been crushed. The state of mind after amputation is doubtless one of comparative repose."

"If your leg is a metaphor for young Townsend, I can assure you he has never been crushed. Crushed? Not he! He is alive and perfectly intact; and that's why I am not satisfied."

"Should you have liked to kill him?" asked Mrs. Almond.

"Yes, very much. I think it is quite possible that it is all a blind."

"A blind?"

"An arrangement between them. *Il fait le mort,* as they say in France; but he is looking out of the corner of his eye. You can depend upon it, he has not burnt his ships; he has kept one to come back in. When I am dead, he will set sail again, and then she will marry him."

"It is interesting to know that you accuse your only daughter of being the vilest of hypocrites," said Mrs. Almond.

"I don't see what difference her being my only daughter makes. It is better to accuse one than a dozen. But I don't accuse any one. There is not the smallest hypocrisy about Catherine, and I deny that she even pretends to be miserable."

The Doctor's idea that the thing was a "blind" had its intermissions and revivals; but it may be said, on the whole, to have increased as he grew older; together with his impressions of Catherine's blooming and comfortable condition. Naturally, if he had not found grounds for viewing her as a lovelorn maiden during the year or two that followed her great trouble, he found none at a time when she had completely recovered her self-possession. He was obliged to recognize the fact that, if the two young people were waiting for him to get out of the way, they were at least waiting very patiently. He had heard from time to time that Morris was in New York; but he never remained there long, and, to the best of the Doctor's belief, had no communication with Catherine. He was sure they never met, and he had reason to suspect that Morris never wrote to her. After the letter that has been mentioned, she heard from him twice again, at considerable intervals;

but on none of these occasions did she write herself. On the other hand, as the Doctor observed, she averted herself rigidly from the idea of marrying other people. Her opportunities for doing so were not numerous, but they occurred often enough to test her disposition. She refused a widower, a man with a genial temperament, a handsome fortune, and three little girls (he had heard that she was very fond of children, and he pointed to his own with some confidence); and she turned a deaf ear to the solicitations of a clever young lawyer, who, with the prospect of a great practice, and the reputation of a most agreeable man, had had the shrewdness, when he came to look about him for a wife, to believe that she would suit him better than several younger and prettier girls. Mr. Macalister, the widower, had desired to make a marriage of reason, and had chosen Catherine for what he supposed to be her latent matronly qualities; but John Ludlow, who was a year the girl's junior, and spoken of always as a young man who might have his "pick," was seriously in love with her. Catherine, however, would never look at him; she made it plain to him that she thought he came to see her too often. He afterward consoled himself, and married a very different person, little Miss Sturtevant, whose attractions were obvious to the dullest comprehension. Catherine, at the time of these events, had left her thirtieth year well behind her, and had quite taken her place as an old maid. Her father would have preferred she should marry, and he once told her that he hoped she would not be too fastidious. "I should like to see you an honest man's wife before I die," he said. This was after John Ludlow had been compelled to give it up, though the Doctor had advised him to persevere. The Doctor exercised no further pressure, and had the credit of not "worrying" at all over his daughter's singleness; in fact, he worried rather more than appeared, and there were considerable periods during which he felt sure that Morris Townsend was hidden behind some door. "If he is not, why doesn't she marry?" he asked himself. "Limited as her intelligence may be, she must understand perfectly well that she is made to do the usual thing." Catherine, however, became an admirable old maid. She formed habits, regulated her days upon a system of her own, interested herself in charitable institutions, asylums, hospitals, and aid societies; and went generally, with an even and noiseless step, about the rigid business of her life. This life had, however, a secret history as well as a public one—if I may talk of the public history of a mature and diffident spinster for whom publicity had always a combination of terrors. From her own point of view the great facts of her career were that Morris Townsend had trifled with her affection, and that her father had broken its spring. Nothing could ever alter these facts; they were always there, like her name, her age, her plain face. Nothing could ever undo the wrong or cure the pain that Morris had inflicted on her, and nothing could ever make her feel toward her father as she felt in her younger years. The was something dead in her life, and her duty was to try and fill the void. Catherine recognized this duty to the utmost; she had a great disapproval of brooding and moping. She had, of course, no faculty for quenching memory in dissipation; but she mingled freely in the usual gayeties of the town, and she became at last an inevitable figure at all respectable entertainments. She was greatly liked, and as time went on she grew to be a sort of kindly maiden-aunt to the younger portion of society. Young girls were apt to confide to her their love affairs (which they never did to Mrs. Penniman), and young men to be fond of her without knowing why. She developed a few harmless eccentricities; her habits, once formed, were rather stiffly maintained; her opinions, on all moral and social matters, were extremely conservative; and before she was forty she was regarded as an old-fashioned person, and an authority on customs that had passed away. Mrs. Penniman, in comparison, was quite a girlish figure; she grew younger as she advanced in life. She lost none of her relish for beauty and mystery, but she had little opportunity to exercise it. With Catherine's late wooers she failed to establish relations as intimate as those which had given her so many interesting hours in the society of Morris Townsend. These gentlemen had an indefinable mistrust of her good offices, and they never talked to her about Catherine's charms. Her ringlets, her buckles and bangles glistened more brightly with each succeeding year, and she remained quite the same officious and imaginative Mrs. Penniman, and the odd mixture of impetuosity and circumspection, that we have hitherto known. As regards one point, however, her circumspection prevailed, and she must be given due credit for it. For upward of seventeen years she never mentioned Morris Townsend's name to her niece. Catherine was grateful to her, but this consistent silence, so little in accord with her aunt's character, gave her a certain alarm, and she could never wholly rid herself of a suspicion that Mrs. Penniman sometimes had news of him.

33

Little by little Doctor Sloper had retired from his profession; he visited only those patients in whose symptoms he recognized a certain originality. He went again to Europe, and remained two years; Catherine went with him, and on this occasion Mrs. Penniman was of the party. Europe apparently had few surprises for Mrs. Penniman, who frequently remarked, in the most romantic sites, "You know I am very familiar with all this." It should be added that such remarks were usually not addressed to her brother, or yet to her niece, but to fellow-tourists who happened to be at hand, or even to the cicerone or the goatherd in the foreground.

One day, after his return from Europe, the Doctor said something to his daughter that made her start—it seemed to come from so far out of the past.

"I should like you to promise me something before I die."

"Why do you talk about your dying?" she asked.

"Because I am sixty-eight years old."

"I hope you will live a long time," said Catherine.

"I hope I shall! But some day I shall take a bad cold, and then it will not matter much what any one hopes. That will be the manner of my exit, and when it takes place, remember I told you so. Promise me not to marry Morris Townsend after I am gone."

This was what made Catherine start, as I have said; but her start was a silent one, and for some moments she said nothing. "Why do you speak of him?" she asked at last.

"You challenge everything I say. I speak of him because he's a topic, like any other. He's to be seen, like anyone else, and he is still looking for a wife—having had one and got rid of her, I don't know by what means. He has lately been in New York, and at your cousin Marian's house; your aunt Elizabeth saw him there."

"They neither of them told me," said Catherine.

"That's their merit; it's not yours. He has grown fat and bald, and he has not made his fortune. But I can't trust those facts alone to steel your heart against him, and that's why I ask your promise."

"Fat and bald"; these words presented a strange image to Catherine's mind, out of which the memory of the most beautiful young man in the world had never faded. "I don't think you understand," she said. "I very seldom think of Mr. Townsend."

"It will be very easy for you to go on, then. Promise me, after my death, to do the same."

Again, for some moments, Catherine was silent; her father's request deeply amazed her; it opened an old wound, and made it ache afresh. "I don't think I can promise that," she answered.

"It would be a great satisfaction," said her father.

"You don't understand. I can't promise that."

The Doctor was silent a minute. "I ask you for a particular reason. I am altering my will."

This reason failed to strike Catherine; and indeed she scarcely understood it. All her feelings were merged in the sense that he was trying to treat her as he had treated her years before. She had suffered from it then; and now all her experience, all her acquired tranquillity and rigidity protested. She had been so humble in her youth that she could now afford to have a little pride, and there was something in this request, and in her father's thinking himself so free to make it, that seemed an injury to her dignity. Poor Catherine's dignity was not aggressive; it never sat in state; but if you pushed far enough you could find it. Her father had pushed very far.

"I can't promise," she simply repeated.

"You are very obstinate," said the Doctor.

"I don't think you understand."

"Please explain, then."

"I can't explain," said Catherine; "and I can't promise."

"Upon my word," her father exclaimed, "I had no idea how obstinate you are!"

She knew herself that she was obstinate, and it gave her a certain joy. She was now a middle-aged woman.

About a year after this, the accident that the Doctor had spoken of occurred: he took a violent cold. Driving out to Bloomingdale one April day to see a patient of unsound mind, who was confined in a private aslyum for the insane, and whose family greatly desired a medical opinion from an eminent source, he was caught in a spring shower, and being in a buggy, without a hood, he found himself soaked to the skin. He came home with an ominous chill, and on the morrow he was seriously ill. "It is congestion of the lungs," he said to Catherine; "I shall need very good nursing. It will make no difference, for I shall not recover; but I wish everything to be done, to the smallest detail, as if I should. I hate an ill-conducted sick-room, and you will be so good as to nurse me, on the hypothesis that I shall get well." He told her which of his fellow-physicians to send for, and gave her a multitude of minute directions; it was quite on the optimistic hypothesis that she nursed him. But he had never been wrong in his life, and he was not wrong now. He was touching his seventieth year, and though he had a very well-tempered constitution, his hold upon life had lost its firmness. He died after three weeks' illness, during which Mrs. Penniman, as well as his daughter, had been assiduous at his bedside.

On his will being opened, after a decent interval, it was found to consist of two portions. The first of these dated from ten years back, and consisted of a series of dispositions by which he left the great mass of his property to his daughter, with becoming legacies to his two sisters. The second was a codicil, of recent origin, maintaining the annuities to Mrs. Penniman and Mrs. Almond, but reducing Catherine's share to a fifth of what he had first bequeathed to her. "She is amply provided for from her mother's side," the document ran, "never having spent more than a fraction of her income from this source; so that her fortune is already more than sufficient to attract those unscrupulous adventurers whom she has given me reason to believe that she persists in regarding as an interesting class." The large remainder of his property, therefore, Doctor Sloper had divided into seven unequal parts, which he left, as endowments, to as many different hospitals and schools of medicine in various cities of the Union.

To Mrs. Penniman it seemed monstrous that a man should play such tricks with other people's money; for after his death, of course, as she said, it was other people's. "Of course, you will immediately break the will," she remarked to Catherine.

"Oh no," Catherine answered. "I like it very much. Only I wish it had been expressed a little differently!"

34

It was her habit to remain in town very late in the summer; she preferred the house in Washington Square to any other habitation whatever, and it was under protest that she used to go to the sea-side for the month of August. At the sea she spent her month at an hotel. The year that her father died she intermitted this custom altogether, not thinking it consistent with deep mourning; and the year after that she put off her departure till so late that the middle of August found her still in the heated solitude of Washington Square. Mrs. Penniman, who was fond of a change, was usually eager for a visit to the country; but this year she appeared quite content with such rural impressions as she could gather at the parlor-window from the ailanthus-trees behind the wooden paling. The peculiar fragrance of this vegetation used to diffuse itself in the evening air, and Mrs. Penniman, on the warm nights of July, often sat at the open window and inhaled it. This was a happy moment for Mrs. Penniman; after the death of her brother she felt more free to obey her impulses. A vague oppression had disappeared from her life, and she enjoyed a sense of freedom of which she had not been conscious since the memorable time, so long ago, when the Doctor went abroad with Catherine and left her at home to entertain Morris Townsend. The year that had elapsed since her brother's death reminded her of that happy time, because, although Catherine, in growing older, had become a person to be reckoned with, yet her society was a very different thing, as Mrs. Penniman said, from that of a tank of cold water. The elder lady hardly knew what use to make of this larger margin of her life; she sat and looked at it very much as she had often sat, with her poised needle in her hand, before her tapestry-frame. She had confident hope, however, that her rich impulses, her talent for embroidery, would still find their application, and this confidence was justified before many months had elapsed.

Catherine continued to live in her father's house, in spite of its being represented to her that a maiden lady of quiet habits might find a more convenient abode in one of the smaller dwellings, with brown stone fronts, which had at this time begun to adorn the transverse thoroughfares in the upper part of the town. She liked the earlier structure—it had begun by this time to be called an "old" house—and proposed to herself to end her days in it. If it was too large for a pair of unpretending gentlewomen, this was better than the opposite fault; for Catherine had no desire to find herself in closer quarters with her aunt. She expected to spend the rest of her life in Washington Square, and to enjoy Mrs. Penniman's society for the whole of this period; as she had a conviction that, as long as she might live, her aunt would live as least at long, and always retain her brilliancy and activity. Mrs. Penniman suggested to her the idea of a rich vitality.

On one of those warm evenings in July of which mention has been made, the two ladies sat together at an open window, looking out on the quiet Square. It was too hot for lighted lamps, for reading, or for work; it might have appeared too hot even for conversation, Mrs. Penniman having long been speechless. She sat forward in the window, half on the balcony, humming a little song. Catherine was within the room, in a low rocking-chair, dressed in white, and slowly using a large palmetto fan. It was in this way, at this season, that the aunt and niece, after they had had tea, habitually spent their evenings.

"Catherine," said Mrs. Penniman at last, "I am going to say something that will surprise you."

"Pray do," Catherine answered; "I like surprises. And it is so quiet now."

"Well, then, I have seen Morris Townsend."

If Catherine was surprised, she checked the expression of it; she gave neither a start nor an exclamation. She remained, indeed, for some moments intensely still, and this may very well have been a symptom of emotion. "I hope he was well," she said at last.

"I don't know; he is a great deal changed. He would like very much to see you."

"I would rather not see him," said Catherine, quickly.

"I was afraid you would say that. But you don't seem surprised!"

"I am—very much."

"I met him at Marian's," said Mrs. Penniman. "He goes to Marian's, and they are so afraid you will meet him there. It's my belief that that's why he goes. He wants so much to see you." Catherine made no response to this, and Mrs. Penniman went on. "I didn't know him at first, he is so remarkably changed; but he knew me in a minute. He says I am not in the least changed. You know how polite he always was. He was coming away when I came, and we walked a little distance together. He is still very handsome, only of course he looks older, and he is not so—so animated as he used to be. There was a touch of sadness about him; but there was a touch of sadness about him before, especially when he went away. I am afraid he has not been very successful—that he has never got thoroughly established. I don't suppose he is sufficiently plodding, and that, after all, is what succeeds in this world." Mrs. Penniman had not mentioned Morris Townsend's name to her niece for upwards of the fifth of a century; but now that she had broken the spell, she seemed to wish to make up for lost time, as if there had been a sort of exhilaration in hearing herself talk of him. She proceeded, however, with considerable caution, pausing occasionally to let Catherine give some sign. Catherine gave no other sign than to stop the rocking of her chair and the swaying of her fan; she sat motionless and silent. "It was on Tuesday last," said Mrs. Penniman, "and I have been hesitating ever since about telling you. I didn't know how you might like it. At last I thought that it was so long ago that you would probably not have any particular feeling. I saw him again after meeting him at Marian's. I met him in the street, and he went a few steps with me. The first thing he said was about you; he asked ever so many questions. Marian didn't want me to speak to you; she didn't want you to know that they receive him. I told him I was sure that after all these years you couldn't have any feeling about that; you couldn't grudge him the hospitality of his own cousin's house. I said you would be bitter indeed if you did that. Marian has the most extraordinary ideas about what happened between you; she seems to think he behaved in some very unusual manner. I took the liberty of reminding her of the real facts, and placing the story in its true light. *He* has no bitterness, Catherine, I can assure you; and he might be excused for it, for things have not gone well with him. He has been all over the world, and tried to establish himself everywhere; but his evil star was against him. It is most interesting to hear him talk of his evil star. Everything failed; everything but his—you know, you remember—his proud, high spirit. I believe he married some lady somewhere in Europe. You know they marry in such a peculiar matter-of-course way in Europe; a marriage of reason they call it. She died soon afterward; as he said to me, she only flitted across his life. He has not been in New York for ten years; he came back a few days ago. The first thing he did was to ask me about you. He had heard you had never married; he seemed very much interested about that. He said you had been the real romance of his life."

Catherine had suffered her companion to proceed from point to point, and pause to pause, without interrupting her; she fixed her eyes on the ground and listened. But the last phrase I have quoted was followed by a pause of peculiar significance, and then, at last, Catherine spoke. It will be observed that before doing so she had received a good deal of information about Morris Townsend. "Please say no more; please don't follow up that subject."

"Doesn't it interest you?" asked Mrs. Penniman, with a certain timorous archness.

"It pains me," said Catherine.

"I was afraid you would say that. But don't you think you could get used to it? He wants so much to see you."

"Please don't, Aunt Lavinia," said Catherine, getting up from her seat. She moved quickly away, and went to the other window, which stood open to the balcony; and here, in the embrasure, concealed from her aunt by the white curtains, she remained a long time, looking out into the warm darkness. She had had a great shock; it was as if the gulf of the past had suddenly opened, and a spectral figure had risen out of it. There were some things she believed she had got over, some feelings that she had thought of as dead; but apparently there was a certain vitality in them still. Mrs. Penniman had made them stir themselves. It was but a momentary agitation, Catherine said to herself; it would presently pass away. She was trembling, and her heart was beating so that she could feel it; but this also would subside. Then suddenly, while she waited for a return of her calmness, she burst into tears. But her tears flowed very silently, so that Mrs. Penniman had no observation of them. It was perhaps, however, because Mrs. Penniman suspected them that she said no more that evening about Morris Townsend.

35

Her refreshed attention to this gentleman had not those limits of which Catherine desired, for herself, to be conscious; it lasted long enough to enable her to wait another week before speaking of him again. It was under the same circumstances that she once more attacked the subject. She had been sitting with her niece in the evening; only on this occasion, as the night was not so warm, the lamp had been lighted, and Catherine had placed herself near it with a morsel of fancy-work. Mrs. Penniman went and sat alone for half an hour on the balcony; then she came in, moving vaguely about the room. At last she sunk into a seat near Catherine, with clasped hands, and a little look of excitement.

"Shall you be angry if I speak to you again about *him?*" she asked.

Catherine looked up at her quietly. "Who is *he?*"

"He whom you once loved."

"I shall not be angry, but I shall not like it."

"He sent you a message," said Mrs. Penniman. "I promised him to deliver it, and I must keep my promise."

In all these years Catherine had had time to forget how little she had to thank her aunt for in the season of her misery; she had long ago forgiven Mrs. Penniman for taking too much upon herself. But for a moment this attitude of interposition and disinterestedness, this carrying of messages and redeeming of promises, brought back the sense that her companion was a dangerous woman. She had said she would not be angry; but for an instant she felt sore. "I don't care what you do with your promise!" she answered.

Mrs. Penniman, however, with her high conception of the sanctity of pledges, carried her point. "I have gone too far to retreat," she said, though precisely what this meant she was not at pains to explain. "Mr. Townsend wishes most particularly to see you, Catherine; he believes that if you knew how much, and why, he wishes it, you would consent to do so."

"There can be no reason," said Catherine; "no good reason."

"His happiness depends upon it. Is not that a good reason?" asked Mrs. Penniman, impressively.

"Not for me. My happiness does not."

"I think you will be happier after you have seen him. He is going away again—going to resume his wanderings. It is a very lonely, restless, joyless life. Before he goes he wishes to speak to you; it is a fixed idea with him—he is always thinking of it. He has something very important to say to you. He believes that you never understood him—that you never judged him rightly, and the belief has always weighed upon him terribly. He wishes to justify himself; he believes that in a very few words he could do so. He wishes to meet you as a friend."

Catherine listened to this wonderful speech without pausing in her work; she had now had several days to accustom herself to think of Morris Townsend again as an actuality. When it was over she said simply, "Please say to Mr. Townsend that I wish he would leave me alone."

She had hardly spoken when a sharp, firm ring at the door vibrated through the summer night. Catherine looked up at the clock; it marked a quarter past nine—a very late hour for visitors, especially in the empty condition of the town. Mrs. Penniman at the same moment gave a little start, and then Catherine's eyes turned quickly to her aunt. They met Mrs. Penniman's, and sounded them for a moment sharply. Mrs. Penniman was blushing; her look was a conscious one; it seemed to confess something. Catherine guessed its meaning, and rose quickly from her chair.

"Aunt Penniman," she said, in a tone that scared her companion, "have you taken *the liberty* . . . ?"

"My dearest Catherine," stammered Mrs. Penniman, "just wait till you see him!"

Catherine had frightened her aunt, but she was also frightened herself; she was on the point of rushing to give orders to the servant, who was passing to the door, to admit no one; but the fear of meeting her visitor checked her.

"Mr. Morris Townsend."

This was what she heard, vaguely but recognizably, articulated by the domestic, while she hesitated. She had her back turned to the door of the parlor, and for some moments she kept it turned, feeling that he had come in. He had not spoken, however, and at last she faced about. Then she saw a gentleman standing in the middle of the room, from which her aunt had discreetly retired.

She would never have known him. He

was forty-five years old, and his figure was not that of the straight, slim young man she remembered. But it was a very fine presence, and a fair and lustrous beard, spreading itself upon a well-presented chest, contributed to its effect. After a moment Catherine recognized the upper half of his face, which, though her visitor's clustering locks had grown thin, was still remarkably handsome. He stood in a deeply deferential attitude, with his eyes on her face. "I have ventured—I have ventured"; he said, and then he paused, looking about him, as if he expected her to ask him to sit down. It was the old voice; but it had not the old charm. Catherine, for a minute, was conscious of a distinct determination not to invite him to take a seat. Why had he come? It was wrong for him to come. Morris was embarrassed, but Catherine gave him no help. It was not that she was glad of his embarrassment; on the contrary, it excited all her own liabilities of this kind, and gave her great pain. But how could she welcome him when she felt so vividly that he ought not to have come? "I wanted so much—I was determined," Morris went on. But he stopped again; it was not easy. Catherine still said nothing, and he may well have recalled with apprehension her ancient faculty of silence. She continued to look at him, however, and as she did so she made the strangest observation. It seemed to be he, and yet not he; it was the man who had been everything, and yet this person was nothing. How long ago it was—how old she had grown—how much she had lived! She had lived on something that was connected with *him*, and she had consumed it in doing so. This person did not look unhappy. He was fair and well-preserved, perfectly dressed, mature and complete. As Catherine looked at him, the story of his life defined itself in his eyes; he had made himself comfortable, and he had never been caught. But even while her perception opened itself to this, she had no desire to catch him; his presence was painful to her, and she only wished he would go.

"Will you not sit down?" he asked.

"I think we had better not," said Catherine.

"I offend you by coming?" He was very grave; he spoke in a tone of the richest respect.

"I don't think you ought to have come."

"Did not Mrs. Penniman tell you—did she not give you my message?"

"She told me something, but I did not understand."

"I wish you would let *me* tell you—let me speak for myself."

"I don't think it is necessary," said Catherine.

"Not for you, perhaps, but for me. It would be a great satisfaction—and I have not many." He seemed to be coming nearer; Catherine turned away. "Can we not be friends again?" he asked.

"We are not enemies," said Catherine. "I have none but friendly feelings to you."

"Ah, I wonder whether you know the happiness it gives me to hear you say that!" Catherine uttered no intimation that she measured the influence of her words; and he presently went on, "You have not changed—the years have passed happily for you."

"They have passed very quietly," said Catherine.

"They have left no marks; you are admirably young." This time he succeeded in coming nearer—he was close to her; she saw his glossy perfumed beard, and his eyes above it looking strange and hard. It was very different from his old—from his young—face. If she had first seen him this way she would not have liked him. It seemed to her that he was smiling, or trying to smile. "Catherine," he said, lowering his voice, "I have never ceased to think of you."

"Please don't say these things," she answered.

"Do you hate me?"

"Oh no," said Catherine.

Something in her tone discouraged him, but in a moment he recovered himself. "Have you still some kindness for me, then?"

"I don't know why you have come here to ask me such things!" Catherine exclaimed.

"Because for many years it has been the desire of my life that we should be friends again."

"That is impossible."

"Why so? Not if you will allow it."

"I will not allow it," said Catherine.

He looked at her again in silence. "I see; my presence troubles you and pains you. I will go away; but you must give me leave to come again."

"Please don't come again," she said.

"Never?—never?"

She made a great effort; she wished to say something that would make it impossible he should ever again cross her threshold. "It is wrong of you. There is no propriety in it—no reason for it."

"Ah, dearest lady, you do me injustice!" cried Morris Townsend. "We have only waited, and now we are free."

"You treated me badly," said Catherine.

"Not if you think of it rightly. You had your quiet life with your father—which was just what I could not make up my mind to rob you of."

"Yes; I had that."

Morris felt it to be a considerable damage to his cause that he could not add that she had had something more besides; for it is needless to say that he had learned the contents of Doctor Sloper's will. He was, nevertheless, not at a loss. "There are worse fates than that!" he exclaimed, with expression; and he might have been supposed to refer to his own unprotected situation. Then he added, with a deeper tenderness, "Catherine, have you never forgiven me?"

"I forgave you years ago, but it is useless for us to attempt to be friends."

"Not if we forget the past. We have still a future, thank God!"

"I can't forget—I don't forget," said Catherine. "You treated me too badly. I felt it very much; I felt it for years." And then she went on, with her wish to show him that he must not come to her this way, "I can't begin again—I can't take it up. Everything is dead and buried. It was too serious; it made a great change in my life. I never expected to see you here."

"Ah, you are angry!" cried Morris, who wished immensely that he could extort some flash of passion from her calmness. In that case he might hope.

"No, I am not angry. Anger does not last that way for years. But there are other things. Impressions last, when they have been strong. But I can't talk."

Morris stood stroking his beard, with a clouded eye. "Why have you never married?" he asked, abruptly. "You have had opportunities."

"I didn't wish to marry."

"Yes, you are rich, you are free; you had nothing to gain."

"I had nothing to gain," said Catherine.

Morris looked vaguely round him, and gave a deep sigh. "Well, I was in hopes that we might still have been friends."

"I meant to tell you, by my aunt, in answer to your message—if you had waited for an answer—that it was unnecessary for you to come in that hope."

"Good-bye, then," said Morris. "Excuse my indiscretion."

He bowed, and she turned away—standing there, averted, with her eyes on the ground, for some moments after she had heard him close the door of the room.

In the hall he found Mrs. Penniman, fluttered and eager; she appeared to have been hovering there under the irreconcilable promptings of her curiosity and her dignity.

"That was a precious plan of yours!" said Morris, clapping on his hat.

"Is she so hard?" asked Mrs. Penniman.

"She doesn't care a button for me—with her confounded little dry manner."

"Was it very dry?" pursued Mrs. Penniman, with solicitude.

Morris took no notice of her question; he stood musing an instant, with his hat on. "But why the deuce, then, would she never marry?"

"Yes—why indeed?" sighed Mrs. Penniman. And then, as if from a sense of the inadequacy of this explanation, "But you will not despair—you will come back?"

"Come back? Damnation!" And Morris Townsend strode out of the house, leaving Mrs. Penniman staring.

Catherine, meanwhile, in the parlor, picking up her morsel of fancy-work, had seated herself with it again—for life, as it were.

Gertrude Stein

❊ 1874-1946

Gertrude Stein was born in Allegheny, Pennsylvania. The first years of her life were spent in Europe, and her girlhood in California. From 1893 to 1897 she studied at Radcliffe College. She specialized in psychology, and was a favorite pupil of William James. She then studied medicine for four years at Johns Hopkins University. In 1903, with her friend, companion, and secretary, Alice B. Toklas, she settled in France. Miss Stein returned to the United States only once, in 1934. In Paris she immersed herself in the theories, work, and society of "advance guard" artists such as Picasso, Bracque, and Matisse. She exerted a strong influence upon many younger writers, particularly Sherwood Anderson and Ernest Hemingway. Miss Stein's career was devoted to intense experimentation with language. Believing that "the business of art" is to live "in the complete actual present," she sought to achieve this end in prose. One of her techniques was the use of repetitive statements in such a way that each repetition added to the accumulating meaning. The work of Gertrude Stein has commonly been found to be difficult, and has aroused controversy for many years. But there is no question of her influence on the work of others. Her lecture at the University of Chicago, "How Writing Is Written," effectively sets forth her theories. Miss Stein died in the American Hospital at Neuilly, France, on July 27, 1946.

Melanctha

EACH ONE AS SHE MAY

Rose Johnson made it very hard to bring her baby to its birth.

Melanctha Herbert who was Rose Johnson's friend, did everything that any woman could. She tended Rose, and she was patient, submissive, soothing, and untiring, while the sullen, childish, cowardly, black Rosie grumbled and fussed and howled and made herself to be an abomination and like a simple beast.

The child though it was healthy after it was born, did not live long. Rose Johnson was careless and negligent and selfish, and when Melanctha had to leave for a few days, the baby died. Rose Johnson had liked the baby well enough and perhaps she just forgot it for awhile, anyway the child was dead and Rose and Sam her husband were very sorry but then these things came so often in the negro world in Bridgepoint, that they neither of them thought about it very long.

Rose Johnson and Melanctha Herbert had been friends now for some years. Rose had lately married Sam Johnson a decent honest kindly fellow, a deck hand on a coasting steamer.

Melanctha Herbert had not yet been really married.

Rose Johnson was a real black, tall, well built, sullen, stupid, childlike, good looking negress. She laughed when she was happy and grumbled and was sullen with everything that troubled.

Rose Johnson was a real black negress but she had been brought up quite like their own child by white folks.

Rose laughed when she was happy but she had not the wide, abandoned laughter that makes the warm broad glow of negro sunshine. Rose was never joyous with the earth-born, boundless joy of negroes. Hers was just ordinary, any sort of woman laughter.

Rose Johnson was careless and was

lazy, but she had been brought up by white folks and she needed decent comfort. Her white training had only made for habits, not for nature. Rose had the simple, promiscuous unmorality of the black people.

Rose Johnson and Melanctha Herbert like many of the twos with women were a curious pair to be such friends.

Melanctha Herbert was a graceful, pale yellow, intelligent, attractive negress. She had not been raised like Rose by white folks but then she had been half made with real white blood.

She and Rose Johnson were both of the better sort of negroes, there, in Bridgepoint.

"No, I ain't no common nigger," said Rose Johnson, "for I was raised by white folks, and Melanctha she is so bright and learned so much in school, she ain't no common nigger either, though she ain't got no husband to be married to like I am to Sam Johnson."

Why did the subtle, intelligent, attractive, half white girl Melanctha Herbert love and do for and demean herself in service to this coarse, decent, sullen, ordinary, black childish Rose, and why was this unmoral, promiscuous, shiftless Rose married, and that's not so common either, to a good man of the negroes, while Melanctha with her white blood and attraction and her desire for a right position had not yet been really married.

Sometimes the thought of how all her world was made, filled the complex, desiring Melanctha with despair. She wondered, often, how she could go on living when she was so blue.

Melanctha told Rose one day how a woman whom she knew had killed herself because she was so blue. Melanctha said, sometimes, she thought this was the best thing for her herself to do.

Rose Johnson did not see it the least bit that way.

"I don't see Melanctha why you should talk like you would kill yourself just because you're blue. I'd never kill myself Melanctha just 'cause I was blue. I'd maybe kill somebody else Melanctha 'cause I was blue, but I'd never kill myself. If I ever killed myself Melanctha it'd be by accident, and if I ever killed myself by accident Melanctha, I'd be awful sorry."

Rose Johnson and Melanctha Herbert had first met, one night, at church. Rose Johnson did not care much for religion. She had not enough emotion to be really roused by a revival. Melanctha Herbert had not come yet to know how to use religion. She was still too complex with desire. However, the two of them in negro fashion went very often to the negro church, along with all their friends, and they slowly came to know each other very well.

Rose Johnson had been raised not as a servant but quite like their own child by white folks. Her mother who had died when Rose was still a baby, had been a trusted servant in the family. Rose was a cute, attractive, good looking little black girl and these people had no children of their own and so they kept Rose in their house.

As Rose grew older she drifted from her white folks back to the colored people, and she gradually no longer lived in the old house. Then it happened that these people went away to some other town to live, and somehow Rose stayed behind in Bridgepoint. Her white folks left a little money to take care of Rose, and this money she got every little while.

Rose now in the easy fashion of the poor lived with one woman in her house, and then for no reason went and lived with some other woman in her house. All this time, too, Rose kept company, and was engaged, first to this colored man and then to that, and always she made sure she was engaged, for Rose had strong the sense of proper conduct.

"No, I ain't no common nigger just to go around with any man, nor you Melanctha shouldn't neither," she said one day when she was telling the complex and less sure Melanctha what was the right way for her to do. "No Melanctha, I ain't no common nigger to do so, for I was raised by white folks. You know very well Melanctha that I'se always been engaged to them."

And so Rose lived on, always comfortable and rather decent and very lazy and very well content.

After she had lived some time this way, Rose thought it would be nice and very good in her position to get regularly really married. She had lately met Sam Johnson somewhere, and she liked him and she knew he was a good man, and then he had a place where he worked every day and got good wages. Sam Johnson liked Rose very well and he was quite ready to be married. One day they had a grand real wedding and were married. Then with Melanctha Herbert's help to do the sewing and the nicer work, they furnished comfortably a little red brick house. Sam then went back to his work as deck hand on a coasting steamer, and Rose stayed home in her house and sat and bragged to all her friends how nice it was to be married really to a husband.

Life went on very smoothly with them all the year. Rose was lazy but not dirty and Sam was careful but not fussy, and then there was Melanctha to come in every day and help to keep things neat.

When Rose's baby was coming to be born, Rose came to stay in the house where Melanctha Herbert lived just then, with a big good natured colored woman who did washing.

Rose went there to stay, so that she might have the doctor from the hospital near by to help her have the baby, and then, too, Melanctha could attend to her while she was sick.

Here the baby was born, and here it died, and then Rose went back to her house again with Sam.

Melanctha Herbert had not made her life all simple like Rose Johnson. Melanctha had not found it easy with herself to make her wants and what she had, agree.

Melanctha Herbert was always losing what she had in wanting all the things she saw. Melanctha was always being left when she was not leaving others.

Melanctha Herbert always loved too hard and much too often. She was always full with mystery and subtle movements and denials and vague distrusts and complicated disillusions. Then Melanctha would be sudden and impulsive and unbounded in some faith, and then she would suffer and be strong in her repression.

Melanctha Herbert was always seeking rest and quiet, and always she could only find new ways to be in trouble.

Melanctha wondered often how it was she did not kill herself when she was so blue. Often she thought this would be really the best way for her to do.

Melanctha Herbert had been raised to be religious, by her mother. Melanctha had not liked her mother very well. This mother, "Mis" Herbert, as her neighbors called her, had been a sweet appearing and dignified and pleasant, pale yellow, colored woman. "Mis" Herbert had always been a little wandering and mysterious and uncertain in her ways.

Melanctha was pale yellow and mysterious and a little pleasant like her mother, but the real power in Melanctha's nature came through her robust and unpleasant and very unendurable black father.

Melanctha's father only used to come to where Melanctha and her mother lived, once in a while.

It was many years now that Melanctha had not heard or seen or known of anything her father did.

Melanctha Herbert almost always hated her black father, but she loved very well the power in herself that came through him. And so her feeling was really closer to her black coarse father, than her feeling had ever been toward her pale yellow, sweet-appearing mother. The things she had in her of her mother never made her feel respect.

Melanctha Herbert had not loved herself in childhood. All of her youth was bitter to remember.

Melanctha had not loved her father and her mother and they had found it very troublesome to have her.

Melanctha's mother and her father had been regularly married. Melanctha's father was a big black virile negro. He only came once in a while to where Melanctha and her mother lived, but always that pleasant, sweet-appearing, pale yellow woman, mysterious and uncertain and wandering in her ways, was close in sympathy and thinking to her big black virile husband.

James Herbert was a common, decent enough, colored workman, brutal and rough to his one daughter, but then she was a most disturbing child to manage.

The young Melanctha did not love her father and her mother, and she had a breakneck courage, and a tongue that could be very nasty. Then, too, Melanctha went to school and was very quick in all the learning, and she knew very well how to use this knowledge to annoy her parents who knew nothing.

Melanctha Herbert had always had a breakneck courage. Melanctha always loved to be with horses; she loved to do wild things, to ride the horses and to break and tame them.

Melanctha, when she was a little girl, had had a good chance to live with horses. Near where Melanctha and her mother lived was the stable of the Bishops, a rich family who always had fine horses.

John, the Bishops' coachman, liked Melanctha very well and he always let her do anything she wanted with the horses. John was a decent, vigorous mulatto with a prosperous house and wife and children. Melanctha Herbert was older than any of his children. She was now a well grown girl of twelve and just beginning as a woman.

James Herbert, Melanctha's father, knew this John, the Bishops' coachman very well.

One day James Herbert came to where his wife and daughter lived, and he was furious.

"Where's that Melanctha girl of yours," he said fiercely, "if she is to the Bishops' stables again, with that man John, I swear I kill her. Why don't you see to that girl better you, you're her mother."

James Herbert was a powerful, loose built, hard handed, black, angry negro. Herbert never was a joyous negro. Even when he drank with other men, and he did that very often, he was never really joyous. In the days when he had been most young and free and open, he had never had the wide abandoned laughter that gives the broad glow to negro sunshine.

His daughter, Melanctha Herbert, later always made a hard forced laughter. She was only strong and sweet and in her nature when she was really deep in trouble, when she was fighting so with all she really had, that she did not use her laughter. This was always true of poor Melanctha who was so certain that she hated trouble. Melanctha Herbert was always seeking peace and quiet, and she could always only find new ways to get excited.

James Herbert was often a very angry negro. He was fierce and serious, and he was very certain that he often had good reason to be angry with Melanctha, who knew so well how to be nasty, and to use her learning with a father who knew nothing.

James Herbert often drank with John, the Bishops' coachman. John in his good nature sometimes tried to soften Herbert's feeling toward Melanctha. Not that Melanctha ever complained to John of her home life or her father. It was never Melanctha's way, even in the midst of her worst trouble to complain to any one of what happened to her, but nevertheless somehow every one who knew Melanctha always knew how much she suffered. It was only while one really loved Melanctha that one understood how to forgive her, that she never once complained nor looked unhappy, and was always handsome and in spirits, and yet one always knew how much she suffered.

The father, James Herbert, never told his troubles either, and he was so fierce and serious that no one ever thought of asking.

"Mis" Herbert as her neighbors called her was never heard even to speak of her husband or her daughter. She was always pleasant, sweet-appearing, mysterious and uncertain, and a little wandering in her ways.

The Herberts were a silent family with their troubles, but somehow every one who knew them always knew everything that happened.

The morning of one day when in the evening Herbert and the coachman John were to meet to drink together, Melanctha had to come to the stable joyous and in the very best of humors. Her good friend John on this morning felt very firmly how good and sweet she was and how much she suffered.

John was a very decent colored coachman. When he thought about Melanctha it was as if she were the eldest of his children. Really he felt very strongly the power in her of a woman. John's wife always liked Melanctha and she always did all she could to make things pleasant. And Melanctha all her life loved and respected kind and good and considerate people. Melanctha always loved and wanted peace and gentleness and goodness and all her life for herself poor Melanctha could only find new ways to be in trouble.

This evening after John and Herbert had drunk awhile together, the good John began to tell the father what a fine girl he had for a daughter. Perhaps the good John had been drinking a good deal of liquor, perhaps there was a gleam of something softer than the feeling of a friendly elder in the way John then spoke of Melanctha. There had been a good deal of drinking and John certainly that very morning had felt strongly Melanctha's power as a woman. James Herbert was always a fierce, suspicious, serious negro, and drinking never made him feel more open. He looked very black and evil as he sat and listened while John grew more and more admiring as he talked half to himself, half to the father, of the virtues and the sweetness of Melanctha.

Suddenly between them there came a moment filled full with strong black curses, and then sharp razors flashed in the black hands, that held them flung backward in the negro fashion, and then for some minutes there was fierce slashing.

John was a decent, pleasant, good natured, light brown negro, but he knew how to use a razor to do bloody slashing.

When the two men were pulled apart by the other negroes who were in the room drinking, John had not been much wounded but James Herbert had gotten one good strong cut that went from his right shoulder down across the front of his whole body. Razor fighting does not wound very deeply, but it makes a cut that looks most nasty, for it is so very bloody.

Herbert was held by the other negroes until he was cleaned and plastered, and then he was put to bed to sleep off his drink and fighting.

The next day he came to where his wife and daughter lived and he was furious.

"Where's that Melanctha, of yours?" he said to his wife, when he saw her.

"If she is to the Bishops' stables now with that yellow John, I swear I kill her. A nice way she is going for a decent daughter. Why don't you see to that girl better you, ain't you her mother!"

Melanctha Herbert had always been old in all her ways and she knew very early how to use her power as a woman, and yet Melanctha with all her inborn intense wisdom was really very ignorant of evil. Melanctha had not yet come to understand what they meant, the things she so often heard around her, and which were just beginning to stir strongly in her.

Now when her father began fiercely to assail her, she did not really know what it was that he was so furious to force from her. In every way that he could think of in his anger, he tried to make her say a thing she did not really know. She held out and never answered anything he asked her, for Melanctha had a breakneck courage and she just then badly hated her black father.

When the excitement was all over, Melanctha began to know her power, the power she had so often felt stirring within her and which she now knew she could use to make her stronger.

James Herbert did not win this fight with his daughter. After awhile he forgot it as he soon forgot John and the cut of his sharp razor.

Melanctha almost forgot to hate her father, in her strong interest in the power she now knew she had within her.

Melanctha did not care much now, any longer, to see John or his wife or even the fine horses. This life was too quiet and accustomed and no longer stirred her to any interest or excitement.

Melanctha now really was beginning as a woman. She was ready, and she began to search in the streets and in dark corners to discover men and to learn their natures and their various ways of working.

In these next years Melanctha learned many ways that lead to wisdom. She learned the ways, and dimly in the distance she saw wisdom. These years of learning led very straight to trouble for Melanctha, though in these years Melanctha never did or meant anything that was really wrong.

Girls who are brought up with care and watching can always find moments to escape into the world, where they may learn the ways that lead to wisdom. For a girl raised like Melanctha Herbert, such escape was always very simple. Often she was alone, sometimes she was with a fellow seeker, and she strayed and stood, sometimes by railroad yards, sometimes on the docks or around new buildings where many men were working. Then when the darkness covered everything all over, she would begin to learn to know this man or that. She would advance, they would respond, and then she would withdraw a little, dimly, and always she did not know what it was that really held her. Sometimes she would almost go over, and then the strength in her of not really knowing, would stop the average man in his endeavor. It was a strange experience of ignorance and power and desire. Melanctha did not know what it was that she so badly wanted. She was afraid, and yet she did not understand that here she really was a coward.

Boys had never meant much to Melanctha. They had always been too young to content her. Melanctha had a strong respect for any kind of successful power. It was this that always kept Melanctha nearer, in her feeling toward her virile and unendurable black father, than she ever was in her feeling for her pale yellow, sweet-appearing mother. The things she had in her of her mother, never made her feel respect.

In these young days, it was only men that for Melanctha held anything there was of knowledge and power. It was not from men however that Melanctha learned to really understand this power.

From the time that Melanctha was twelve until she was sixteen she wandered, always seeking but never more than very dimly seeing wisdom. All this time Melanctha went on with her school learning; she went to school rather longer than do most of the colored children.

Melanctha's wanderings after wisdom she always had to do in secret and by snatches, for her mother was then still living and "Mis" Herbert always did some watching, and Melanctha with all her hard courage dreaded that there should be much telling to her father, who came now quite often to where Melanctha lived with her mother.

In these days Melanctha talked and stood and walked with many kinds of men, but she did not learn to know any of them very deeply. They all supposed her to have world knowledge and experience. They, believing that she knew all, told her nothing, and thinking that she was deciding with them, asked for nothing, and so though Melanctha wandered widely, she was really very safe with all the wandering.

It was a very wonderful experience this safety of Melanctha in these days of her attempted learning. Melanctha herself did not feel the wonder, she only knew that for her it all had no real value.

Melanctha all her life was very keen in her sense for real experience. She knew she was not getting what she so badly wanted, but with all her breakneck courage Melanctha here was a coward, and so she could not learn to really understand.

Melanctha liked to wander, and to stand by the railroad yard, and watch the men and the engines and the switches and everything that was busy there, working. Railroad yards are a ceaseless fascination. They satisfy every kind of nature. For the lazy man whose blood flows very slowly, it is a steady soothing world of motion which supplies him with the sense of a strong moving power. He need not work and yet he has it very deeply; he has it even better than the man who works in it or owns it. Then for natures that like to feel emotion without the trouble of having any suffering, it is very nice to get the swelling in the throat, and the fullness, and the heart beats, and all the flutter of excitement that comes as one watches the people come and go, and hears the engine pound and give a long drawn whistle. For a child watching through a hole in the fence above the yard, it is a wonder world of mystery and movement. The child loves all the noise, and then it loves the silence of the wind that comes before the full rush of the pounding train, that bursts out from the tunnel where it lost itself and all its noise in darkness, and the child loves all the smoke, that sometimes comes in rings, and always puffs with fire and blue color.

For Melanctha the yard was full of the excitement of many men, and perhaps a free and whirling future.

Melanctha came here very often and watched the men and all the things that were so busy working. The men always had time for, "Hullo sis, do you want to sit on my engine," and, "Hullo, that's a pretty lookin' yaller girl, do you want to come and see him cookin."

All the colored porters liked Melanctha. They often told her exciting things that had happened; how in the West they went through big tunnels where there was no air to breathe, and then out and winding around edges of great canyons on thin high spindling trestles, and sometimes cars, and sometimes whole trains fell from the narrow bridges, and always up from the dark places death and all kinds of queer devils looked up and laughed in their faces. And then they would tell how sometimes when the train went pounding down steep slippery mountains, great rocks would racket and roll down around them, and sometimes would smash in the car and kill men; and as the porters told these stories their round, black, shining faces would grow solemn, and their color would go grey beneath the greasy black, and their eyes would roll white in the fear and wonder of the things they could scare themselves by telling.

There was one, big, serious, melancholy, light brown porter who often told Melanctha stories, for he liked the way she had of listening with intelligence and sympathetic feeling, when he told how the white men in the far South tried to kill him because he made one of them who was drunk and called him a damned nigger, and who refused to pay money for his chair to a nigger, get off the train between stations. And then this porter had to give up going to that part of the Southern country, for all the white men swore that if he ever came there again they would surely kill him.

Melanctha liked this serious, melancholy light brown negro very well, and all her life Melanctha wanted and respected gentleness and goodness, and this man always gave her good advice and serious kindness, and Melanctha felt such things very deeply, but she could never let them help her or affect her to change the ways that always made her keep herself in trouble.

Melanctha spent many of the last hours of the daylight with the porters and with other men who worked hard, but when darkness came it was always different. Then Melanctha would find herself with the, for her, gentlemanly classes. A clerk, or a young express agent would begin to know her, and they would stand, or perhaps, walk a little while together.

Melanctha always made herself escape but often it was with an effort. She did not know what it was that she so badly wanted, but with all her courage Melanctha here was a coward, and so she could not learn to understand.

Melanctha and some man would stand in the evening and would talk together. Sometimes Melanctha would be with another girl and then it was much easier to stay or to escape, for then they could make way for themselves together, and by throwing words and laughter to each other, could keep a man from getting too strong in his attention.

But when Melanctha was alone, and she was so, very often, she would sometimes come very near to making a long step on the road that leads to wisdom. Some man would learn a good deal about her in the talk, never altogether truly, for Melanctha all her life did not know how to tell a story wholly. She always, and yet not with intention, managed to leave out big pieces which make a story very different, for when it came to what had happened and what she had said and what it was that she had really done, Melanctha never could remember right. The man would sometimes come a little nearer, would detain her, would hold her arm or make his jokes a little clearer, and then Melanctha would always make herself escape. The man thinking that she really had world wisdom would not make his meaning clear, and believing that she was deciding with him he never went so fast that he could stop her when at last she made herself escape.

And so Melanctha wandered on the edge of wisdom. "Say, Sis, why don't you when you come here stay a little longer?" they would all ask her, and they would hold her for an answer, and she would laugh, and sometimes she did stay longer, but always just in time she made herself escape.

Melanctha Herbert wanted very much to know and yet she feared the knowledge. As she grew older she often stayed a good deal longer, and sometimes it was almost a balanced struggle, but she always made herself escape.

Next to the railroad yard it was the shipping docks that Melanctha loved best when she wandered. Often she was alone, sometimes she was with some better kind of black girl, and she would stand a long time and watch the men working at unloading, and see the steamers do their coaling, and she would listen with full feeling to the yowling of the free swinging negroes, as they ran, with their powerful loose jointed bodies and their childish savage yelling, pushing, carrying, pulling great loads from the ships to the warehouses.

The men would call out, "Say, Sis, look out or we'll come and catch yer," or "Hi, there, you yaller girl, come here and we'll take you sailin'." And then, too, Melanctha would learn to know some of the serious foreign soldiers who told her all sorts of wonders, and a cook would sometimes take her and her friends over a ship and show where he made his messes and where the men slept, and where the shops were, and how everything was made by themselves, right there, on ship board.

Melanctha loved to see these dark and smelly places. She always loved to watch and talk and listen with men who worked hard. But it was never from these rougher people that Melanctha tried to learn the ways that lead to wisdom. In the daylight she always liked to talk with rough men and to listen to their lives and about their work and their various ways of doing, but when the darkness covered everything all over, Melanctha would meet, and stand, and talk with a clerk or a young shipping agent who had seen her watching, and so it was that she would try to learn to understand.

And then Melanctha was fond of watching men work on new buildings. She loved to see them hoisting, digging, sawing and stone cutting. Here, too, in the daylight, she aways learned to know the common workmen. "Heh, Sis, look out or that rock will fall on you and smash you all up into little pieces. Do you think you would make a nice jelly?" And then they would all laugh and feel that their jokes were very funny. And "Say, you pretty yaller girl, would it scare you bad to stand up here on top where I be? See if you've got grit and come up here where I can hold you. All you got to do is to sit still on that there rock that they're just hoistin', and then when you get here I'll hold you tight, don't you be scared Sis."

Sometimes Melanctha would do some of these things that had much danger, and always with such men, she showed her power and her breakneck courage. Once she slipped and fell from a high place. A workman caught her and so she was not killed, but her left arm was badly broken.

All the men crowded around her. They admired her boldness in doing and in bearing pain when her arm was broken. They all went along with her with great respect to the doctor, and then they took her home in triumph and all of them were bragging about her not squealing.

James Herbert was home where his wife lived, that day. He was furious when he saw the workmen and Melanctha. He drove the men away with curses so that they were all very nearly fighting, and he would not let a doctor come in to attend Melanctha. "Why don't you see to that girl better, you, you're her mother."

James Herbert did not fight things out now any more with his daughter. He feared her tongue, and her school learning, and the way she had of saying things that were very nasty to a brutal black man who knew nothing. And Melanctha just then hated him very badly in her suffering.

And so this was the way Melanctha lived the four years of her beginning as a woman. And many things happened to Melanctha, but she knew very well that none of them had led her on to the right way, that certain way that was to lead her to world wisdom.

Melanctha Herbert was sixteen when she first met Jane Harden. Jane was a negress, but she was so white that hardly any one could guess it. Jane had had a good deal of education. She had been two years at a colored college. She had had to leave because of her bad conduct. She taught Melanctha many things. She taught her how to go the ways that lead to wisdom.

Jane Harden was at this time twenty-three years old and she had had much experience. She was very much attracted by Melanctha, and Melanctha was very proud that this Jane would let her know her.

Jane Harden was not afraid to understand. Melanctha who had strong the sense for real experience, knew that here was a woman who had learned to understand.

Jane Harden had many bad habits. She drank a great deal, and she wandered widely. She was safe though now, when she wanted to be safe, in this wandering.

Melanctha Herbert soon always wandered with her. Melanctha tried the drinking and some of the other habits, but she did not find that she cared very much to do them. But every day she grew stronger in her desire to really understand.

It was now no longer, even in the daylight, the rougher men that these two learned to know in their wanderings, and for Melanctha the better classes were now a little higher. It was no longer express agents and clerks that she learned to know, but men in business, commercial travelers, and even men above these, and Jane and she would talk and walk and laugh and escape from them all very often. It was still the same, the knowing of them and the always just escaping, only now for Melanctha somehow it was different, for though it was always the same thing that happened it had a different flavor, for now Melanctha was with a woman who had wisdom, and dimly she began to see what it was that she should understand.

It was not from the men that Melanctha learned her wisdom. It was always Jane Harden herself who was making Melanctha begin to understand.

Jane was a roughened woman. She had power and she liked to use it, she had much white blood and that made her see clear, she liked drinking and that made her reckless. Her white blood was strong in her and she had grit and endurance and a vital courage. She was always game, however much she was in trouble. She liked Melanctha Herbert for the things that she had like her, and then Melanctha was young, and she had sweetness, and a way of listening with intelligence and sympathetic interest, to the stories that Jane Harden often told out of her experience.

Jane grew always fonder of Melanctha. Soon they began to wander, more to be together than to see men and learn their various ways of working. Then they began not to wander, and Melanctha would spend long hours with Jane in her room, sitting at her feet and listening to her stories, and feeling her strength and the power of her affection, and slowly she began to see clear before her one certain way that would be sure to lead to wisdom.

Before the end came, the end of the two years in which Melanctha spent all her time when she was not at school or in her home, with Jane Harden, before these two years were finished, Melanctha had come to see very clear, and she had come to be very certain, what it is that gives the world its wisdom.

Jane Harden always had a little money and she had a room in the lower part of the town. Jane had once taught in a colored school. She had had to leave that too on account of her bad conduct. It was her drinking that always made all the trouble for her, for that can never be really covered up.

Jane's drinking was always growing worse upon her. Melanctha had tried to do the drinking but it had no real attraction for her.

In the first year, between Jane Harden and Melanctha Herbert, Jane had been much the stronger. Jane loved Melanctha and she found her always intelligent and brave and sweet and docile, and Jane meant to, and before the year was over she had taught Melanctha what it is that gives many people in the world their wisdom.

Jane had many ways in which to do this teaching. She told Melanctha many things. She loved Melanctha hard and made Melanctha feel it very deeply. She would be with other people and with men and with Melanctha, and she would make Melanctha understand what everybody wanted, and what one did with power when one had it.

Melanctha sat at Jane's feet for many hours in these days and felt Jane's wisdom. She learned to love Jane and to have this feeling very deeply. She learned a little in these days to know joy, and she was taught too how very keenly she could suffer. It was very different this suffering from that Melanctha sometimes had from her mother and from her very unendurable black father. Then she was fighting and she could be strong and valiant in her suffering, but here with Jane Harden she was longing and she bent and pleaded with her suffering.

It was a very tumultuous, very mingled year, this time for Melanctha, but she certainly did begin to really understand.

In every way she got it from Jane Harden. There was nothing good or bad in doing, feeling, thinking or in talking, that Jane spared her. Sometimes the lesson came almost too strong for Melanctha, but somehow she always managed to endure it and so slowly, but always with increasing strength and feeling, Melanctha began to really understand.

Then slowly, between them, it began to be all different. Slowly now between them, it was Melanctha Herbert, who was stronger. Slowly now they began to drift apart from one another.

Melanctha Herbert never really lost her sense that it was Jane Harden who had taught her, but Jane did many things that Melanctha now no longer needed. And then, too, Melanctha never could remember right when it came to what she had done and what had happened. Melanctha now sometimes quarreled with Jane, and they no longer went about together, and sometimes Melanctha really forgot how much she owed to Jane Harden's teaching.

Melanctha began now to feel that she had always had world wisdom. She really knew of course, that it was Jane who had taught her, but all that began to be covered over by the trouble between them, that was now always getting stronger.

Jane Harden was a roughened woman. Once she had been very strong, but now she was weakened in all her kinds of strength by her drinking. Melanctha had tried the drinking but it had had no real attraction for her.

Jane's strong and roughened nature and her drinking made it always harder for her to forgive Melanctha, that now Melanctha did not really need her any longer. Now it was Melanctha who was stronger and it was Jane who was dependent on her.

Melanctha was now come to be about eighteen years old. She was a graceful, pale yellow, good looking, intelligent, attractive negress, a little mysterious sometimes in her ways, and always good and pleasant, and always ready to do things for people.

Melanctha from now on saw very little of Jane Harden. Jane did not like that very well and sometimes she abused Melanctha, but her drinking soon covered everything all over.

It was not in Melanctha's nature to really lose her sense for Jane Harden. Melanctha all her life was ready to help

Jane out in any of her trouble, and later, when Jane really went to pieces, Melanctha always did all that she could to help her.

But Melanctha Herbert was ready now herself to do teaching. Melanctha could do anything now that she wanted. Melanctha knew now what everybody wanted.

Melanctha had learned how she might stay a little longer; she had learned that she must decide when she wanted really to stay longer, and she had learned how when she wanted to, she could escape.

And so Melanctha began once more to wander. It was all now for her very different. It was never rougher men now that she talked to, and she did not care much now to know white men of the, for her, very better classes. It was now something realler that Melcantha wanted, something that would move her very deeply, something that would fill her fully with the wisdom that was planted now within her, and that she wanted badly, should really wholly fill her.

Melanctha these days wandered very widely. She was always alone now when she wandered. Melanctha did not need help now to know, or to stay longer, or when she wanted, to escape.

Melanctha tried a great many men, in these days before she was really suited. It was almost a year that she wandered and then she met with a young mulatto. He was a doctor who had just begun to practice. He would most likely do well in the future, but it was not this that concerned Melanctha. She found him good and strong and gentle and very intellectual, and all her life Melanctha liked and wanted good and considerate people, and then too he did not at first believe in Melanctha. He held off and did not know what it was that Melanctha wanted. Melanctha came to want him very badly. They began to know each other better. Things began to be very strong between them. Melanctha wanted him so badly that now she never wandered. She just gave herself to this experience.

Melanctha Herbert was now, all alone, in Bridgepoint. She lived now with this colored woman and now with that one, and she sewed, and sometimes she taught a little in a colored school as substitute for some teacher. Melanctha had now no home nor any regular employment. Life was just commencing for Melanctha. She had youth and had learned wisdom, and she was graceful and pale yellow and very pleasant, and always ready to do things for people, and she was mysterious in her ways and that only made belief in her more fervent.

During the year before she met Jefferson Campbell, Melanctha had tried many kinds of men but they had none of them interested Melanctha very deeply. She met them, she was much with them, she left them, she would think perhaps this next time it would be more exciting, and always she found that for her it all had no real meaning. She could now do everything she wanted, she knew now everything that everybody wanted, and yet it all had no excitement for her. With these men, she knew she could learn nothing. She wanted some one that could teach her very deeply and now at last she was sure that she had found him, yes she really had it, before she had thought to look if in this man she would find it.

During this year "Mis" Herbert as her neighbors called her, Melanctha's pale yellow mother was very sick, and in this year she died.

Melanctha's father during these last years did not come very often to the house where his wife lived and Melanctha. Melanctha was not sure that her father was now any longer here in Bridgepoint. It was Melanctha who was very good now to her mother. It was always Melanctha's way to be good to any one in trouble.

Melanctha took good care of her mother. She did everything that any woman could, she tended and soothed and helped her pale yellow mother, and she worked hard in every way to take care of her, and make her dying easy. But Melanctha did not in these days like her mother any better, and her mother never cared much for this daughter who was always a hard child to manage, and who had a tongue that always could be very nasty.

Melanctha did everything that any woman could, and at last her mother died, and Melanctha had her buried. Melanctha's father was not heard from, and Melanctha in all her life after, never saw or knew of anything that her father did.

It was the young doctor, Jefferson Campbell, who helped Melanctha toward the end, to take care of her sick mother. Jefferson Campbell had often before seen Melanctha Herbert, but he had never liked her very well, and he had never believed that she was any good. He had heard something about how she wandered. He knew a little too of Jane Harden, and he was sure that this Melanctha Herbert, who was her friend and who wandered, would never come to any good.

Dr. Jefferson Campbell was a serious, earnest, good young joyous doctor. He liked to take care of everybody and he loved his own colored people. He always found life very easy did Jeff Campbell, and everybody liked to have him with them. He was so good and sympathetic, and he was so earnest and so joyous. He sang when he was happy, and he laughed, and his was the free abandoned laughter that gives the warm broad glow to negro sunshine.

Jeff Campbell had never yet in his life had real trouble. Jefferson's father was a good, kind, serious, religious man. He was a very steady, very intelligent, and very dignified, light brown, grey haired negro. He was a butler and he had worked for the Campbell family many years, and his father and his mother before him had been in the service of this family as free people.

Jefferson Campbell's father and his mother had of course been regularly married. Jefferson's mother was a sweet, little, pale brown, gentle woman who reverenced and obeyed her good husband, and who worshipped and admired and loved hard her good, earnest, cheery, hard working doctor boy who was her only child.

Jeff Campbell had been raised religious by his people but religion had never interested Jeff very much. Jefferson was very good. He loved his people and he never hurt them, and he always did everything they wanted and that he could to please them, but he really loved best science and experimenting and to learn things, and he early wanted to be a doctor, and he was always very interested in the life of the colored people.

The Campbell family had been very good to him and had helped him on with his ambition. Jefferson studied hard, he went to a colored college, and then he learnt to be a doctor.

It was now two or three years, that he had started in to practice. Everybody liked Jeff Campbell, he was so strong and kindly and cheerful and understanding, and he laughed so with pure joy, and he always liked to help all his own colored people.

Dr. Jeff knew all about Jane Harden. He had taken care of her in some of her bad trouble. He knew about Melanctha too, though until her mother was taken sick he had never met her. Then he was called in to help Melanctha to take care of her sick mother. Dr. Campbell did not like Melanctha's ways and he did not think that she would ever come to any good.

Dr. Campbell had taken care of Jane Harden in some of her bad trouble. Jane sometimes had abused Melanctha to him. What right had that Melanctha Herbert who owed everything to her, Jane Harden, what right had a girl like that to go away to other men and leave her, but Melanctha Herbert never had any sense of how to act to anybody. Melanctha had a good mind, Jane never denied her that, but she never used it to do anything decent with it. But what could you expect when Melanctha had such a brute of a black nigger father, and Melanctha was always abusing her father and yet she was just like him, and really she admired him so much and he never had any sense of what he owed to anybody, and Melanctha was just like him and she was proud of it too, and it made Jane so tired to hear Melanctha talk all the time as if she wasn't. Jane Harden hated people who had good minds and didn't use them, and Melanctha always had that weakness, and wanting to keep in with people, and never really saying that she wanted to be like her father, and it was so silly of Melanctha to abuse her father, when she was so much like him and she really liked it. No, Jane Harden had no use for Melanctha. Oh yes, Melanctha always came around to be good to her. Melanctha was always sure to do that. She never really went away and left one. She didn't use her mind enough to do things straight out like that. Melanctha Herbert had a good mind, Jane never denied that to her, but she never wanted to see or hear about Melanctha Herbert any more, and she wished Melanctha wouldn't come in any more to see her. She didn't hate her, but she didn't want to hear about her father and all that talk Melanctha always made, and that just meant nothing to her. Jane Harden was very tired of all that now. She didn't have any use now any more for Melanctha, and if Dr. Campbell saw her he better tell her Jane didn't want to see her, and she could take her talk to somebody else, who was ready to believe her. And then Jane Harden would drop away and forget Melanctha and all her life before, and then she would begin to drink and so she would cover everything all over.

Jeff Campbell heard all this very often, but it did not interest him very deeply. He felt no desire to know more of this Melanctha. He heard her, once, talking to another girl outside of the house, when he was paying a visit to Jane Harden. He did not see much in the talk that he heard her do. He did not see much in the things Jane Harden said when she abused Melanctha to him. He was more interested in Jane herself than in anything he heard about Melanctha. He knew Jane Harden had a good mind, and she had had power, and she could really have done things, and now this drinking covered everything all over. Jeff Campbell was always very sorry when he had to see it. Jane Harden was a roughened woman, and yet Jeff found a great many strong good things in her, that still made him like her.

Jeff Campbell did everything he could for Jane Harden. He did not care much to hear about Melanctha. He had no feeling, much, about her. He did not find that he took any interest in her. Jane Harden was so much a stronger woman, and Jane really had had a good mind, and she had used it to do things with it, before this drinking business had taken such a hold upon her.

Dr. Campbell was helping Melanctha Herbert to take care of her sick mother. He saw Melanctha now for long times and very often, and they sometimes talked a good deal together, but Melanctha never said anything to him about Jane Harden. She never talked to him about anything that was not just general matters, or about medicine, or to tell him funny stories. She asked him many questions and always listened very well to all he told her, and she always remembered everything she heard him say about doctoring, and she always remembered everything that she had learned from all the others.

Jeff Campbell never found that all this talk interested him very deeply. He did not find that he liked Melanctha when he saw her so much, any better. He never found that he thought much about Melanctha. He never found that he believed much in her having a good mind, like Jane Harden. He found he liked Jane Harden always better, and that he wished very much that she had never begun that bad drinking.

Melanctha Herbert's mother was now getting sicker. Melanctha really did everything that any woman could. Melanctha's mother never liked her daughter any better. She never said much, did "Mis" Herbert, but anybody could see that she did not think much of this daughter.

Dr. Campbell now often had to stay a long time to take care of "Mis" Herbert. One day "Mis" Herbert was much sicker and Dr. Campbell thought that this night, she would surely die. He came back late to the house, as he had said he would, to sit up and watch "Mis" Herbert, and to help Melanctha, if she should need anybody to be with her. Melanctha Herbert and Jeff Campbell sat up all that night together. "Mis" Herbert did not die. The next day she was a little better.

This house where Melanctha had always lived with her mother was a little red brick, two story house. They had not much furniture to fill it and some of the windows were broken and not mended. Melanctha did not have much money to use now on the house, but with a colored woman, who was their neighbor and good natured and who had always helped them, Melanctha managed to take care of her mother and to keep the house fairly clean and neat.

Melanctha's mother was in bed in a room upstairs, and the steps from below led right up into it. There were just two rooms on this upstairs floor. Melanctha and Dr. Campbell sat down on the steps, that night they watched together, so that they could hear and see Melanctha's mother and yet the light would be shaded, and they could sit and read, if they wanted to, and talk low some, and yet not disturb "Mis" Herbert.

Dr. Campbell was always very fond of reading. Dr. Campbell had not brought a book with him that night. He had just forgotten it. He had meant to put something in his pocket to read, so that he could amuse himself, while he was sitting there and watching. When he was through with taking care of "Mis" Herbert, he came and sat down on the steps just above where Melanctha was sitting. He spoke about how he had forgotten to bring his book with him. Melanctha said there were some old papers in the house, perhaps Dr. Campbell could find something in them that would help pass the time for a while for him. All right, Dr. Campbell said, that would be better than just sitting there with nothing. Dr. Campbell began to read through the old papers that Melanctha gave him. When anything amused him in them, he read it out to Melanctha. Melanctha was now pretty silent, with him. Dr. Campbell began to feel a little, about how she responded to him. Dr. Campbell began to see a little that perhaps Melanctha had a good mind. Dr. Campbell was not sure yet that she had a good mind, but he began to think a little that perhaps she might have one.

Jefferson Campbell always liked to talk to everybody about the things he worked at and about his thinking about what he could do for the colored people. Melanctha Herbert never thought about these things the way that he did. Melanctha had never said much to Dr. Campbell about what she thought about them. Melanctha did not feel the same as he did about being good and regular in life, and not having excitements all the time, which was the way that Jefferson Campbell wanted that everybody should be, so that everybody would be wise and yet be happy. Melanctha always had strong the sense for real experience. Melanctha Herbert did not think much of this way of coming to real wisdom.

Dr. Campbell soon got through with his reading, in the old newspapers, and then somehow he began to talk along about the things he was always thinking. Dr. Campbell said he wanted to work so that he could understand what troubled people, and not to just have excitements, and he believed you ought to love your father and your mother and to be regular in all your life, and not to be always wanting new things and excitements, and to always know where you were, and what you wanted, and to always tell everything just as you meant it. That's the only kind of life he knew or believed in, Jeff Campbell repeated. "No I ain't got any use for all the time being in excitements and wanting to have all kinds of experience all the time. I got plenty of experience just living regular and quiet and with my family, and doing my work, and taking care of people, and trying to understand it. I don't believe much in this running around business and I don't want to see the colored people do it. I am a colored man and I ain't sorry, and I want to see the colored people like what is good and what I want them to have, and that's to live regular and work hard and understand things, and that's enough to keep any decent man excited." Jeff Campbell spoke now with some anger. Not to Melanctha, he did not think of her at all when he was talking. It was the life he wanted that he spoke to, and the way he wanted things to be with the colored people.

But Melanctha Herbert had listened to him say all this. She knew he meant it, but it did not mean much to her, and she was sure some day he would find out, that it was not all, of real wisdom. Melanctha knew very well what it was to have real wisdom. "But how about Jane Harden?" said Melanctha to Jeff Campbell, "seems to me Dr. Campbell you find her to have something in her, and you go there very often, and you talk to her much more than you do to the nice girls that stay at home with their people, the kind you say you are really wanting. It don't seem to me Dr. Campbell, that what you say and what you do seem to have much to do with each other. And about your being so good Dr. Campbell," went on Melanctha, "You don't care about going to church much yourself, and yet you always are saying you believe so much in things like that, for people. It seems to me, Dr. Campbell you want to have a good time just like all us others, and then you just keep on saying that it's right to be good and you ought not to have excitements, and yet you really don't want to do it Dr. Campbell, no more than me or Jane Harden. No, Dr. Campbell, it certainly does seem to me you don't know very well yourself, what you mean, when you are talking."

Jefferson had been talking right along, the way he always did when he got started, and now Melanctha's answer only made him talk a little harder. He laughed a little, too, but very low, so as not to disturb "Mis" Herbert who was sleeping very nicely, and he looked brightly at Melanctha to enjoy her, and then he settled himself down to answer.

"Yes," he began, "it certainly does sound a little like I didn't know very well what I do mean, when you put it like that to me, Miss Melanctha, but that's just because you don't understand enough about what I meant, by what I was just saying to you. I don't say, never, I don't want to know all kinds of people, Miss Melanctha, and I don't say there ain't many kinds of people, and I don't say ever, that I don't find some like Jane Harden very good to know and talk to, but it's the strong things I like in Jane Harden, not all her excitements. I don't admire the bad things she does, Miss Melanctha, but Jane Harden is a strong woman and I always respect that in her. No I know you don't believe what I say, Miss Melanctha, but I mean it, and it's all just because you don't understand it when I say it. And as for religion, that just ain't my way of being good, Miss Melanctha, but it's a good way for many people to be good and regular in their way of living, and if they believe it, it helps them to be good, and if they're honest in it, I like to see them have it. No, what I don't like, Miss Melanctha, is this what I see so much with the colored people, their always wanting new things just to get excited."

Jefferson Campbell here stopped himself in this talking. Melanctha Herbert did not make any answer. They both sat there very quiet.

Jeff Campbell then began again on the old papers. He sat there on the steps just above where Melanctha was sitting, and he went on with his reading, and his head went moving up and down, and sometimes he was reading, and sometimes he was thinking about all the things he wanted to be doing, and then he would rub the back of his dark hand over his mouth, and in between he would be frowning with his thinking, and sometimes he would be rubbing his head hard to help his thinking. And Melanctha just sat still and watched the lamp burning, and sometimes she turned it down a little, when the wind caught it and it would begin to get to smoking.

And so Jeff Campbell and Melanctha Herbert sat there on the steps, very quiet, a long time, and they didn't seem to think much, that they were together. They sat there so, for about an hour, and then it came to Jefferson very slowly and as a strong feeling that he was sitting there on the steps, alone, with Melanctha. He did not know if Melanctha Herbert was feeling very much about their being there alone together. Jefferson began to wonder about it a little. Slowly he felt that surely they must both have this feeling. It was so important that he knew that she must have it. They both sat there, very quiet, a long time.

At last Jefferson began to talk about how the lamp was smelling. Jefferson began to explain what it is that makes a lamp get to smelling. Melanctha let him talk. She did not answer, and then he stopped in his talking. Soon Melanctha began to sit up straighter and then she started in to question.

"About what you was just saying Dr. Campbell about living regular and all that, I certainly don't understand what you meant by what you was just saying. You ain't a bit like good people Dr. Campbell, like the good people you are always saying are just like you. I know good people Dr. Campbell, and you ain't a bit like men who are good and got religion. You are just as free and easy as any man can be Dr. Campbell, and you always like to be with Jane Harden, and she is a pretty bad one and you don't look down on her and you never tell her she is a bad one. I know you like her just like a friend Dr. Campbell, and so I certainly don't understand just what it is you mean by all that you was just saying to me. I know you mean honest Dr. Campbell, and I am always trying to believe you, but I can't say as I see just what you mean when you say you want to be good and real pious, because I am very certain Dr. Campbell that you ain't that kind of a man at all, and you ain't never ashamed to be with queer folks Dr. Campbell, and you seem to be thinking what you are doing is just like what you are always saying, and Dr. Campbell, I certainly don't just see what you mean by what you say."

Dr. Campbell almost laughed loud enough to wake "Mis" Herbert. He did enjoy the way Melanctha said these things to him. He began to feel very strongly about it that perhaps Melanctha really had a good mind. He was very free now in his laughing, but not so as to make Melanctha angry. He was very friendly with her in his laughing, and then he made his face get serious, and he rubbed his head to help him in his thinking.

"I know Miss Melanctha" he began, "It ain't very easy for you to understand what I was meaning by what I was just saying to you, and perhaps some of the good people I like so wouldn't think very much, any more than you do, Miss Melanctha, about the ways I have to be good. But that's no matter Miss Melanctha. What I mean Miss Melanctha by what I was just saying to you is, that I don't, no, never, believe in doing things just to get excited. You see Miss Melanctha I mean the way so many of the colored people do it. Instead of just working hard and caring about their working and living regular with their families and saving up all their money, so they will have some to bring up their children better, instead of living regular and doing like that and getting all their new ways from just decent living, the colored people just keep running around and perhaps drinking and doing everything bad they can ever think of, and not just because they like all those bad things that they are always doing, but only just because they want to get excited. No Miss Melanctha, you see I am a colored man myself and I ain't sorry, and I want to see the colored people being good and careful and always honest and living always just as regular as can be, and I am sure, Miss Melanctha, that that way everybody can have a good time, and be happy and keep right and be busy, and not always have to be doing bad things for new ways to get excited. Yes Miss Melanctha, I certainly do like everything to be good, and quiet, and I certainly do think that is the best way for all us colored people. No, Miss Melanctha too, I don't mean this except only just the way I say it. I ain't got any other meaning Miss Melanctha, and it's that what I mean when I am saying about being really good. It ain't Miss Melanctha to be pious and not liking every kind of people, and I don't say ever Miss Melanctha that when other kind of people come regular into your life you shouldn't want to know them always. What I mean Miss Melanctha by what I am always saying is, you shouldn't try to know everybody just to run around and get excited. It's that kind of way of doing that I hate so always Miss Melanctha, and that is so bad for all us colored people. I don't know as you understand now any better what I mean by what I was just saying to you. But you certainly do know now Miss Melanctha, that I always mean it what I say when I am talking."

"Yes I certainly do understand you when you talk so Dr. Campbell. I certainly do understand now what you mean by what you was always saying to me. I certainly do understand Dr. Campbell that you mean you don't believe it's right to love anybody." "Why sure no, yes I do Miss Melanctha, I certainly do believe strong in loving, and in being good to everybody, and trying to understand what they all need, to help them." "Oh I know all about that way of doing Dr. Campbell, but that certainly ain't the kind of love I mean when I am talking. I mean real, strong, hot love Dr. Campbell, that makes you do anything for somebody that loves you." "I don't know much about that kind of love yet Miss Melanctha. You see it's this way with me always Miss Melanctha. I am always so busy with my thinking about my work I am doing and so I don't have time for just fooling, and then too, you see Miss Melanctha, I really certainly don't ever like to get excited, and that kind of loving hard does seem always to mean just getting all the time excited. That certainly is what I always think from what I see of them that have it bad

Miss Melanctha, and that certainly would never suit a man like me. You see Miss Melanctha I am a very quiet kind of fellow, and I believe in a quiet life for all the colored people. No Miss Melanctha I certainly never have mixed myself up in that kind of trouble."

"Yes I certainly do see that very clear Dr. Campbell," said Melanctha, "I see that's certainly what it is always made me not know right about you and that's certainly what it is that makes you really mean what you was always saying. You certainly are just too scared Dr. Campbell to really feel things way down in you. All you are always wanting Dr. Campbell, is just to talk about being good, and to play with people just to have a good time, and yet always to certainly keep yourself out of trouble. It don't seem to me Dr. Campbell that I admire that way to do things very much. It certainly ain't really to me being very good. It certainly ain't any more to me Dr. Campbell, but that you certainly are awful scared about really feeling things way down in you, and that's certainly the only way Dr. Campbell I can see that you can mean, by what it is that you are always saying to me."

"I don't know about that Miss Melanctha, I certainly don't think I can't feel things very deep in me, though I do say I certainly do like to have things nice and quiet, but I don't see harm in keeping out of danger Miss Melanctha, when a man knows he certainly don't want to get killed in it, and I don't know anything that's more awful dangerous Miss Melanctha than being strong in love with somebody. I don't mind sickness or real trouble Miss Melanctha, and I don't want to be talking about what I can do in real trouble, but you know something about that Miss Melanctha, but I certainly don't see much in mixing up just to get excited, in that awful kind of danger. No Miss Melanctha I certainly do only know just two kinds of ways of loving. One kind of loving seems to me, is like one has a good quiet feeling in a family when one does his work, and is always living good and being regular, and then the other way of loving is just like having it like any animal that's low in the streets together, and that don't seem to me very good Miss Melanctha, though I don't say ever that it's not all right when anybody likes it, and that's all the kinds of love I know Miss Melanctha, and I certainly don't care very much to get mixed up in that kind of a way just to be in trouble."

Jefferson stopped and Melanctha thought a little.

"That certainly does explain to me Dr. Campbell what I been thinking about you this long time. I certainly did wonder how you could be so live, and knowing everything, and everybody, and talking so big always about everything, and everybody always liking you so much, and you always looking as if you was thinking, and yet you really was never knowing about anybody and certainly not being really very understanding. It certainly is all Dr. Campbell because you is so afraid you will be losing being good so easy, and it certainly do seem to me Dr. Campbell that it certainly don't amount to very much that kind of goodness."

"Perhaps you are right Miss Melanctha," Jefferson answered. "I don't say never, perhaps you ain't right Miss Melanctha. Perhaps I ought to know more about such ways Miss Melanctha. Perhaps it would help me some, taking care of the colored people, Miss Melanctha. I don't say, no, never, but perhaps I could learn a whole lot about women the right way, if I had a real good teacher."

"Mis" Herbert just then stirred a little in her sleep. Melanctha went up the steps to the bed to attend her. Dr. Campbell got up too and went to help her. "Mis" Herbert woke up and was a little better. Now it was morning and Dr. Campbell gave his directions to Melanctha, and then left her.

Melanctha Herbert all her life long, loved and wanted good, kind and considerate people. Jefferson Campbell was all the things that Melanctha had ever wanted. Jefferson was a strong, well built, good looking, cheery, intelligent and good mulatto. And then at first he had not cared to know Melanctha, and when he did begin to know her he had not liked her very well, and he had not thought that she would ever come to any good. And then Jefferson Campbell was so very gentle. Jefferson never did some things like other men, things that now were beginning to be ugly, for Melanctha. And then too Jefferson Campbell did not seem to know very well what it was that Melanctha really wanted, and all this was making Melanctha feel his power with her always getting stronger.

Dr. Campbell came in every day to see "Mis" Herbert. "Mis" Herbert, after that night they watched together, did get a little better, but "Mis" Herbert was really very sick, and soon it was pretty sure that she would have to die. Melanctha certainly did everything, all the time, that any woman could. Jefferson never thought much better of Melanctha while she did it. It was not her being good, he wanted to find in her. He knew very well Jane Harden was right, when she said Melanctha was always being good to everybody but that that did not make Melanctha any better for her. Then too, "Mis" Herbert never liked Melanctha any better, even on the last day of her living, and so Jefferson really never thought much of Melanctha's always being good to her mother.

Jefferson and Melanctha now saw each other, very often. They now always liked to be with each other, and they always now had a good time when they talked to one another. They, mostly in their talking to each other, still just talked about outside things and what they were thinking. Except just in little moments, and not those very often, they never said anything about their feeling. Sometimes Melanctha would tease Jefferson a little just to show she had not forgotten, but mostly she listened to his talking, for Jefferson still always liked to talk along about the things he believed in. Melanctha was liking Jefferson Campbell better every day, and Jefferson was beginning to know that Melanctha certainly had a good mind, and he was beginning to feel a little her real sweetness. Not in her being good to "Mis" Herbert, that never seemed to Jefferson to mean much in her, but there was a strong kind of sweetness in Melanctha's nature that Jefferson began now to feel when he was with her.

"Mis" Herbert was now always getting sicker. One night again Dr. Campbell felt very certain that before it was morning she would surely die. Dr. Campbell said he would come back to help Melanctha watch her, and to do anything he could to make "Mis" Herbert's dying more easy for her. Dr. Campbell came back that evening, after he was through with his other patients, and then he made "Mis" Herbert easy, and then he came and sat down on the steps just above where Melanctha was sitting with the lamp, and looking very tired. Dr. Campbell was pretty tired too, and they both sat there very quiet.

"You look awful tired to-night, Dr. Campbell," Melanctha said at last, with her voice low and very gentle, "Don't you want to go lie down and sleep a little? You're always being much too good to everybody, Dr. Campbell. I like to have you stay here watching to-night with me, but it don't seem right you ought to stay here when you got so much always to do for everybody. You are certainly very kind to come back, Dr. Campbell, but I can certainly get along to-night without you. I can get help next door sure if I need it. You just go 'long home to bed, Dr. Campbell. You certainly do look as if you need it."

Jefferson was silent for some time, and always he was looking very gently at Melanctha.

"I certainly never did think, Miss Melanctha, I would find you to be so sweet and thinking, with me." "Dr. Campbell" said Melanctha, still more gentle, "I certainly never did think that you would ever feel it good to like me. I certainly never did think you would want to see for yourself if I had sweet ways in me."

They both sat there very tired, very gentle, very quiet, a long time. At last Melanctha in a low, even tone began to talk to Jefferson Campbell.

"You are certainly a very good man, Dr. Campbell, I certainly do feel that more every day I see you. Dr. Campbell, I sure do want to be friends with a good man like you, now I know you. You certainly, Dr. Campbell, never do things like other men, that's always ugly for me. Tell me true, Dr. Campbell, how you feel about being always friends with me. I certainly do know, Dr. Campbell, you are a good man, and if you say you will be friends with me, you certainly never will go back on me, the way so many kinds of them do to every girl they ever get to like them. Tell me for true, Dr. Campbell, will you be friends with me."

"Why, Miss Melanctha," said Campbell slowly, "why you see I just can't say that right out that way to you. Why sure you know Miss Melanctha, I will be very glad if it comes by and by that we are always friends together, but you see, Miss Melanctha, I certainly am a very slow-minded quiet kind of fellow though I do say quick things all the time to everybody, and when I certainly do want to mean it what I am saying to you, I can't say things like that right out to everybody till I know really more for certain all about you, and how I like you, and what I really mean to do better for you. You certainly do see what I mean, Miss Melanctha." "I certainly do admire you for talking honest to me, Jeff Campbell," said Melanctha. "Oh, I am always honest, Miss Melanctha. It's easy enough for me always to be honest, Miss Melanctha. All I got to do is always just to say right out what I am thinking. I certainly never have got any real reason for not saying it right out like that to anybody."

They sat together, very silent. "I certainly do wonder, Miss Melanctha," at last began Jeff Campbell, "I certainly do wonder, if we know very right, you and me, what each other is really thinking. I certainly do wonder, Miss Melanctha, if we know at all really what each other means by what we are always saying." "That certainly do mean, by what you say, that you think I am a bad one, Jeff Campbell," flashed out Melanctha. "Why no, Miss Melanctha, why sure I don't mean anything like that at all, by what I am saying to you. You know well as I do, Miss Melanctha, I think better of you every day I see you, and I like to talk with you all the time now, Miss Melanctha, and I certainly do think we both like it very well when we are together, and it seems to me always more, you are very good and sweet always to everybody. It only is, I am really so slow-minded in my ways, Miss Melanctha, for all I talk so quick to everybody, and I don't like to say to you what I don't know for very sure, and I certainly don't know for sure I know just all what you mean by what you are always saying to me. And you see, Miss Melanctha, that's what makes me say what I was just saying to you when you asked me."

"I certainly do thank you again for being honest to me, Dr. Campbell," said Melanctha. "I guess I leave you now, Dr. Campbell. I think I go in the other room and rest a little. I leave you here, so perhaps if I ain't here you will maybe sleep and rest yourself a little. Good night now, Dr. Campbell, I call you if I need you later to help me, Dr. Campbell, I hope you rest well, Dr. Campbell."

Jeff Campbell, when Melanctha left him, sat there and he was very quiet and just wondered. He did not know very well just what Melanctha meant by what she was always saying to him. He did not know very well how much he really knew about Melanctha Herbert. He wondered if he should go on being so much all the time with her. He began to think about what he should do now with her. Jefferson Campbell was a man who liked everybody and many people liked very much to be with him. Women liked him, he was so strong, and good, and understanding, and innocent, and firm, and gentle. Sometimes they seemed to want very much he should be with them. When they got so, they always had made Campbell very tired. Sometimes he would play a little with them, but he never had had any strong feeling for them. Now with Melanctha Herbert everything seemed different. Jefferson was not sure that he knew here just what he wanted. He was not sure he knew just what it was that Melanctha wanted. He knew if it was only play, with Melanctha, that he did not want to do it. But he remembered always how she had told him he never knew how to feel things very deeply. He remembered how she told him he was afraid to let himself ever know real feeling, and then too, most of all to him, she had told him he was not very understanding. That always troubled Jefferson very keenly, he wanted very badly to be really understanding. If Jefferson only knew better just what Melanctha meant by what she said. Jefferson always had thought he knew something about women. Now he found that really he knew nothing. He did not know the least bit about Melanctha. He did not know what it was right that he should do about it. He wondered if it was just a little play that they were doing. If it was a play he did not want to go on playing, but if it was really that he was not very understanding, and that with Melanctha Herbert he could learn to really understand, then he was very certain he did not want to be a coward. It was very hard for him to know what he wanted. He thought and thought, and always he did not seem to know any better what he wanted. At last he gave up this thinking. He felt sure it was only play with Melanctha. "No, I certainly won't go on fooling with her any more this way," he said at last out loud to himself, when he was through with this thinking. "I certainly will stop fooling, and begin to go on with my thinking about my work and what's the matter with people like 'Mis' Herbert," and Jefferson took out his book from his pocket, and drew near to the lamp, and began with some hard scientific reading.

Jefferson sat there for about an hour reading, and he had really forgotten all about his trouble with Melanctha's meaning. Then "Mis" Herbert had some trouble with her breathing. She woke up and was gasping. Dr. Campbell went to her and gave her something that would help her. Melanctha came out from the other room and did things as he told her. They together made "Mis" Herbert more comfortable and easy, and soon she was again in her deep sleep.

Dr. Campbell went back to the steps where he had been sitting. Melanctha came and stood a little while beside him, and then she sat down and watched him reading. By and by they began with their talking. Jeff Campbell began to feel that perhaps it was all different. Perhaps it was not just play, with Melanctha. Anyway he liked it very well that she was with him. He began to tell her about the book he was just reading.

Melanctha was very intelligent always in her questions. Jefferson knew now very well that she had a good mind. They were having a very good time, talking there together. And then they began again to get quiet.

"It certainly was very good in you to come back and talk to me Miss Melanctha," Jefferson said at last to her, for now he was almost certain, it was no game she was playing. Melanctha really was a good woman, and she had a good mind, and she had a real, strong sweetness, and she could surely really teach him. "Oh I always like to talk to you Dr. Campbell" said Melanctha, "And then you was only just honest to me, and I always like it when a man is really honest to me." Then they were again very silent, sitting there together, with the lamp between them, that was always smoking. Melanctha began to lean a little more toward Dr. Campbell, where he was sitting, and then she took his hand between her two and pressed it hard, but she said nothing to him. She let it go then and leaned a little nearer to him. Jefferson moved a little but did not do anything in answer. At last, "Well," said Melanctha sharply to him. "I was just thinking" began Dr. Campbell slowly, "I was just wondering," he was beginning to get ready to go on with his talking. "Don't you ever stop with your thinking long enough ever to have any feeling Jeff Campbell," said Melanctha a little sadly. "I don't know," said Jeff Campbell slowly, "I don't know Miss Melanctha much about that. No, I don't stop thinking much Miss Melanctha and if I can't ever feel without stopping thinking, I certainly am very much afraid Miss Melanctha that I never will do much with that kind of feeling. Sure you ain't worried Miss Melanctha, about my really not feeling very much all the time. I certainly do think I feel some, Miss Melanctha, even though I always do it without ever knowing how to stop with my thinking." "I am certainly afraid I don't think much of your kind of feeling Dr. Campbell." "Why I think you certainly are wrong Miss Melanctha I certainly do think I feel as much for you Miss Melanctha, as you ever feel about me, sure I do. I don't think you know me right when you talk like that to me. Tell me just straight out how much do you care about me, Miss Melanctha." "Care about you Jeff Campbell," said Melanctha slowly. "I certainly do care for you Jeff Campbell less than you are always thinking and much more than you are ever knowing."

Jeff Campbell paused on this, and he was silent with the power of Melanctha's meaning. They sat there together very silent, a long time. "Well Jeff Campbell," said Melanctha. "Oh," said Dr. Campbell and he moved himself a little, and then they were very silent a long time. "Haven't you got nothing to say to me Jeff Campbell?" said Melanctha. "Why yes, what was it we were just saying about to one another. You see Miss Melanctha I am a very quiet, slow minded kind of fellow, and I am never sure I know just exactly what you mean by all that you are always saying to me. But I do like you very much Miss Melanctha and I am very sure you got very good things in you all the time. You sure do believe what I am saying to you Miss Melanctha." "Yes I believe it when you say it to me, Jeff Campbell," said Melanctha, and then she was silent and there was much sadness in it. "I guess I go in and lie down again Dr. Campbell," said Melanctha. "Don't go leave me Miss Melanctha," said Jeff Campbell quickly. "Why not, what you want of me Jeff Campbell?" said Melanctha. "Why," said Jeff Campbell slowly, "I just want to go on talking with you. I certainly do like talking about all kinds of things with you. You certainly know that all right, Miss Melanctha." "I guess I go lie down again and leave you here with your thinking," said Melanctha gently. "I certainly am very tired to night Dr. Campbell. Good night I hope you rest well Dr. Campbell." Melanctha stooped over him, where he was sitting, to say this good night, and then, very quick and sudden, she kissed him and then, very quick again, she went away and left him.

Dr. Campbell sat there very quiet, with only a little thinking and sometimes a beginning feeling, and he was alone until it began to be morning, and then he went, and Melanctha helped him, and he made "Mis" Herbert more easy in her dying. "Mis" Herbert lingered on till about ten o'clock the next morning, and then slowly and without much pain she died away. Jeff Campbell staid till the last moment, with Melanctha, to make her mother's dying easy for her. When it was over he sent in the colored woman from next door to help Melanctha fix things, and then he went away to take care of his other patients. He came back very soon to Melanctha. He helped her to have a funeral for her mother. Melanctha then went to live with the good natured woman, who had been her neighbor. Melanctha still saw Jeff Campbell very often. Things began to be very strong between them.

Melanctha now never wandered, unless she was with Jeff Campbell. Sometimes she and he wandered a good deal together. Jeff Campbell had not got over his way of talking to her all the time about all the things he was always thinking. Melanctha never talked much, now, when they were together. Sometimes Jeff Campbell teased her about her not talking to him. "I certainly did think Melanctha you was a great talker from the way Jane Harden and everybody said things to me, and from the way I heard you talk so much when I first met you. Tell me true Melanctha, why don't you talk more now to me, perhaps it is I talk so much I don't give you any chance to say things to me, or perhaps it is you hear me talk so much you don't think so much now of a whole lot of talking. Tell me honest Melanctha, why don't you talk more to me." "You know very well Jeff Campbell," said Melanctha "You certainly do know very well Jeff, you don't think really much, of my talking. You think a whole lot more about everything than I do Jeff, and you don't care much what I got to say about it. You know that's true what I am saying Jeff, if you want to be real honest, the way you always are when I like you so much." Jeff laughed and looked fondly at her. "I don't say ever I know, you ain't right, when you say things like that to me, Melanctha. You see you always like to be talking just what you think everybody wants to be hearing from you, and when you are like that, Melanctha, honest, I certainly don't care very much to hear you, but sometimes you say something that is what you are really thinking, and then I like a whole lot to hear you talking." Melanctha smiled, with her strong sweetness, on him, and she felt her power very deeply. "I certainly never do talk very much when I like anybody really, Jeff. You see, Jeff, it ain't much use to talk about what a woman is really feeling in her. You see all that, Jeff, better, by and by, when you get to really feeling. You won't be so ready then always with your talking. You see, Jeff, if it don't come true what I am saying." "I don't ever say you ain't always right, Melanctha," said Jeff Campbell. "Perhaps what I call my thinking ain't really so very understanding. I don't say, no never now any more, you ain't right, Melanctha, when you really say things to me. Perhaps I see it all to be very different when I come to really see what you mean by what you are always saying to me." "You is very sweet and good to me always, Jeff Campbell," said Melanctha. "'Deed I certainly am not good to you, Melanctha. Don't I bother you all the time with my talking, but I really do like you a whole lot, Melanctha." "And I like you, Jeff Campbell, and you certainly are mother, and father, and brother, and sister, and child and everything, always to me. I can't say much about how good you been to me, Jeff Campbell, I never knew any man who was good and didn't do things ugly, before I met you to take care of me, Jeff Campbell. Good-by, Jeff, come see me to-morrow, when you get through with your working." "Sure Melanctha, you know that already," said Jeff Campbell, and then he went away and left her.

These months had been an uncertain time for Jeff Campbell. He never knew how much he really knew about Melanctha. He saw her now for long times and very often. He was beginning always more and more to like her. But he did not seem to himself to know very much about her. He was beginning to feel he could almost trust the goodness in her. But then, always, really, he was not very sure about her. Melanctha always had ways that made him feel uncertain with her, and yet he was so near, in his feeling for her. He now never thought about all this in real words any more. He was always letting it fight itself out in him. He was now never taking any part in this fighting that was always going on inside him.

Jeff always loved now to be with Melanctha and yet he always hated to go to her. Somehow he was always afraid when he was to go to her, and yet he had made himself very certain that here he would not be a coward. He never felt any of this being afraid, when he was with her. Then they always were very true, and near to one another. But always when he was going to her, Jeff would like anything that could happen that would keep him a little longer from her.

It was a very uncertain time, all these months, for Jeff Campbell. He did not know very well what it was that he really wanted. He was very certain that he did not know very well what it was that Melanctha wanted. Jeff Campbell had always all his life loved to be with people, and he had loved all his life always to be thinking, but he was still only a great boy, was Jeff Campbell, and he had never before had any of this funny kind of feeling. Now, this evening, when he was free to go and see Melanctha, he talked to anybody he could find who would detain him, and so it was very late when at last he came to the house where Melanctha was waiting to receive him.

Jeff came in to where Melanctha was waiting for him, and he took off his hat and heavy coat, and then drew up a chair and sat down by the fire. It was very cold that night, and Jeff sat there, and rubbed his hands and tried to warm them. He had only said "How do you do" to Melanctha, he had not yet begun to talk to her. Melanctha sat there, by the fire, very quiet. The heat gave a pretty pink glow to her pale yellow and attractive face. Melanctha sat in a low chair, her hands, with their long, fluttering fingers, always ready to show her strong feeling, were lying quiet in her lap. Melanctha was very tired with her waiting for Jeff Campbell. She sat there very quiet and just watching. Jeff was a robust, dark, healthy, cheery negro. His hands were firm and kindly and unimpassioned. He touched women always with his big hands, like a brother. He always had a warm broad glow, like southern sunshine. He never had anything mysterious in him. He was open, he was pleasant, he was cheery, and always he wanted, as Melanctha once had wanted, always now he too wanted really to understand.

Jeff sat there this evening in his chair and was silent a long time, warming himself with the pleasant fire. He did not look at Melanctha who was watching. He sat there and just looked into the fire. At first his dark, open face was smiling, and he was rubbing the back of his black-brown hand over his mouth to help him in his smiling. Then he was thinking, and he frowned and rubbed his head hard, to help him in his thinking. Then he smiled again, but now his smiling was not very pleasant. His smile was now wavering on the edge of scorning. His smile changed more and more, and then he had a look as if he were deeply down, all disgusted. Now his face was darker, and he was bitter in his smiling, and he began, without looking from the fire, to talk to Melanctha, who was now very tense with her watching.

"Melanctha Herbert," began Jeff Campbell, "I certainly after all this time I know you, I certainly do know little, real about you. You see, Melanctha, it's like this way with me"; Jeff was frowning, with his thinking and looking very hard into the fire, "You see it's just this way, with me now, Melanctha. Sometimes you seem like one kind of a girl to me, and sometimes you are like a girl that is all different to me, and the two kinds of girls is certainly very different to each other, and I can't see any way they seem to have much to do, to be together in you. They certainly don't seem to be made much like as if they could have anything really to do with each other. Sometimes you are a girl to me I certainly never would be trusting, and you got a laugh then so hard, it just rattles, and you got ways so bad, I can't believe you mean them hardly, and yet all that I just been saying is certainly you one way I often see you, and it's what your mother and Jane Harden always found you, and it's what makes me hate so, to come near you. And then certainly sometimes, Melanctha, you certainly is all a different creature, and sometimes then there comes out in you what is certainly a thing, like a real beauty. I certainly, Melanctha, never can tell just how it is that it comes so lovely. Seems to me when it comes it's got a real sweetness, that is more wonderful than a pure flower, and a gentleness, that is more tender than the sunshine, and a kindness, that makes one feel like summer, and then a way to know, that makes everything all over, and all that, and it does certainly seem to be real for the little while it's lasting, for the little while that I can surely see it, and it gives me to feel like I certainly had got real religion. And then when I got rich with such a feeling, comes all that other girl, and then that seems more likely that that is really you what's honest, and then I certainly do get awful afraid to come to you, and I certainly never do feel I could be very trusting with you. And then I certainly don't know anything at all about you, and I certainly don't know which is a real Melanctha Herbert, and I certainly don't feel no longer, I ever want to talk to you. Tell me honest, Melanctha, which is the way that is you really, when you are alone, and real, and all honest. Tell me, Melanctha, for I certainly do want to know it."

Melanctha did not make him any answer, and Jeff, without looking at her, after a little while, went on with his talking. "And then, Melanctha, sometimes you certainly do seem sort of cruel, and not to care about people being hurt or in trouble, something so hard about you it makes me sometimes real nervous, sometimes somehow like you always, like your being, with 'Mis' Herbert. You sure did do everything that any woman could, Melanctha, I certainly never did see anybody do things any better, and yet, I don't know how to say just what I mean, Melanctha, but there was something awful hard about your feeling, so different from the way I'm always used to see good people feeling, and so it was the way Jane Harden and 'Mis' Herbert talked when they felt strong to talk about you, and yet, Melanctha, somehow I feel so really near to you, and you certainly have got an awful wonderful, strong kind of sweetness. I certainly would like to know for sure, Melanctha, whether I got really anything to be afraid for. I certainly did think once, Melanctha, I knew something about all kinds of women. I certainly know now really, how I don't know anything sure at all about you, Melanctha, though I been with you so long, and so many times for whole hours with you, and I like so awful much to be with you, and I can always say anything I am thinking to you. I certainly do awful wish, Melanctha, I really was more understanding. I certainly do that same, Melanctha."

Jeff stopped now and looked harder than before into the fire. His face changed from his thinking back into that look that was so like as if he was all through and through him, disgusted with what he had been thinking. He sat there a long time, very quiet, and then slowly, somehow, it came strongly to him that Melanctha Herbert, there beside him, was trembling and feeling it all to be very bitter. "Why, Melanctha," cried Jeff Campbell, and he got up and put his arm around her like a brother. "I stood it just so long as I could bear it, Jeff," sobbed Melanctha, and then she gave herself away, to her misery, "I was awful ready, Jeff, to let you say anything you liked that gave you any pleasure. You could say all about me what you wanted, Jeff, and I would try to stand it, so as you would be sure to be liking it, Jeff, but you was too cruel to me. When you do that kind of seeing how much you can make a woman suffer, you ought to give her a little rest, once sometimes, Jeff. They can't any of us stand it so for always, Jeff. I certainly did stand it just as long as I could, so you would like it, but I, —oh Jeff, you went on too long to-night Jeff. I couldn't stand it not a minute longer the way you was doing of it, Jeff. When you want to be seeing how the way a woman is really made of, Jeff, you shouldn't never be so cruel, never to be thinking how much she can stand, the strong way you always do it, Jeff." "Why, Melanctha," cried Jeff Campbell, in his horror, and then he was very tender to her, and like a good, strong, gentle brother in his soothing of her, "Why Melanctha dear, I certainly don't now see what it is you mean by what you was just saying to me. Why Melanctha, you poor little girl, you certainly never did believe I ever knew I was giving you real suffering. Why, Melanctha, how could you ever like me if you thought I ever could be so like a red Indian?" "I didn't just know, Jeff," and Melanctha nestled to him, "I certainly never did know just what it was you wanted to be doing with me, but I certainly wanted you should do anything you liked, you wanted, to make me more understanding for you. I tried awful hard to stand it, Jeff, so as you could do anything you wanted with me." "Good Lord and Jesus Christ, Melanctha!" cried Jeff Campbell. "I certainly never can know anything about you real, Melanctha, you poor little girl," and Jeff drew her closer to him, "But I certainly do admire and trust you a whole lot now, Melanctha. I certainly do, for I certainly never did think I was hurting you at all, Melanctha, by the things I always been saying to you. Melanctha, you poor little, sweet, trembling baby now, be good, Melanctha. I certainly can't ever tell you how awful sorry I am to hurt you so, Melanctha. I do anything I can to show you how I never did mean to hurt you, Melanctha." "I know, I know," murmured Melanctha, clinging to him. "I know you are a good man, Jeff. I always know that, no matter how much you can hurt me." "I sure don't see how you can think so, Melanctha, if you certainly did think I was trying so hard just to hurt you." "Hush, you are only a great big boy, Jeff Campbell, and you don't know nothing yet about real hurting," said Melanctha, smiling up through her crying, at him. "You see, Jeff, I never knew anybody I could know real well and yet keep on always respecting, till I came to know you real well, Jeff." "I sure don't understand that very well, Melanctha. I ain't a bit better than just lots of others of the colored people. You certainly have been unlucky with the kind you met before me, that's all, Melanctha. I certainly ain't very good, Melanctha." "Hush, Jeff, you don't know nothing at all about what you are," said Melanctha. "Perhaps you are right, Melanctha. I don't say ever any more, you ain't right, when you say things to me, Melanctha," and Jefferson sighed, and then he smiled, and then they were quiet a long time together, and then after some more kindness, it was late, and then Jeff left her.

Jeff Campbell, all these months, had never told his good mother anything about Melanctha Herbert. Somehow he always kept his seeing her so much now, to himself. Melanctha too had never had any of her other friends meet him. They always acted together, these two, as if their being so much together was a secret, but really there was no one who would have made it any harder for them. Jeff Campbell did not really know how it had happened that they were so secret. He did not know if it was what Melanctha wanted. Jeff had never spoken to her at all about it. It just seemed as if it were well understood between them that nobody should know that they were so much together. It was as if it were agreed between them, that they should be alone by themselves always, and so they would work out together what they meant by what they were always saying to each other.

Jefferson often spoke to Melanctha about his good mother. He never said anything about whether Melanctha would want to meet her. Jefferson never quite understood why all this had happened so, in secret. He never really knew what it was that Melanctha really wanted. In all these ways he just, by his nature, did, what he sort of felt Melanctha wanted. And so they continued to be alone and much together, and now it had come to be the spring time, and now they had all out-doors to wander.

They had many days now when they were very happy. Jeff every day found that he really liked Melanctha better. Now surely he was beginning to have real, deep feeling in him. And still he loved to talk himself out to Melanctha, and he loved to tell her how good it all was to him, and how he always loved to be with her, and to tell her always all about it. One day, now Jeff arranged, that Sunday they would go out and have a happy, long day in the bright fields, and they would be all day just alone together. The day before, Jeff was called in to see Jane Harden.

Jane Harden was very sick almost all day and Jeff Campbell did everything he could to make her better. After a while Jane became more easy and then she began to talk to Jeff about Melanctha. Jane did not know how much Jeff was now seeing of Melanctha. Jane these days never saw Melanctha. Jane began to talk of the time when she first knew Melanctha. Jane began to tell how in these days Melanctha had very little understanding. She was young then and she had a good mind. Jane Harden never would say Melanctha never had a good mind, but in those days Melanctha certainly had not been very understanding. Jane began to explain to Jeff Campbell how in every way, she Jane, had taught Melanctha. Jane then began to explain how eager Melanctha always had been for all that kind of learning. Jane Harden began to tell how they had wandered. Jane began to tell how Melanctha once had loved her, Jane Harden. Jane began to tell Jeff of all the bad ways Melanctha had used with her. Jane began to tell all she knew of the way Melanctha had gone on, after she had left her. Jane began to tell all about the different men, white ones and blacks, Melanctha never was particular about things like that, Jane Harden said in passing, not that Melanctha was a bad one, and she had a good mind, Jane Harden never would say that she hadn't, but

Melanctha always liked to use all the understanding ways that Jane had taught her, and so she wanted to know everything, always, that they knew how to teach her.

Jane was beginning to make Jeff Campbell see much clearer. Jane Harden did not know what it was that she was really doing with all this talking. Jane did not know what Jeff was feeling. Jane was always honest when she was talking, and now it just happened she had started talking about her old times with Melanctha Herbert. Jeff understood very well that it was all true what Jane was saying. Jeff Campbell was beginning now to see very clearly. He was beginning to feel very sick inside him. He knew now many things Melanctha had not yet taught him. He felt very sick and his heart was very heavy, and Melanctha certainly did seem very ugly to him. Jeff was at last beginning to know what it was to have deep feeling. He took care a little longer of Jane Harden, and then he went to his other patients, and then he went home to his room, and he sat down and at last he had stopped thinking. He was very sick and his heart was very heavy in him. He was very tired and all the world was very dreary to him, and he knew very well now at last, he was really feeling. He knew it now from the way it hurt him. He knew very well that now at last he was beginning to really have understanding. The next day he had arranged to spend, long and happy, all alone in the spring fields with Melanctha, wandering. He wrote her a note and said he could not go, he had a sick patient and would have to stay home with him. For three days after, he made no sign to Melanctha. He was very sick all these days, and his heart was very heavy in him, and he knew very well that now at last he had learned what it was to have deep feeling.

At last one day he got a letter from Melanctha. "I certainly don't rightly understand what you are doing now to me Jeff Campbell," wrote Melanctha Herbert. "I certainly don't rightly understand Jeff Campbell why you ain't all these days been near me, but I certainly do suppose it's just another one of the queer kind of ways you have to be good, and repenting of yourself all of a sudden. I certainly don't say to you Jeff Campbell I admire very much the way you take to be good Jeff Campbell. I am sorry Dr. Campbell, but I certainly am afraid I can't stand it no more from you the way you have been just acting. I certainly can't stand it any more the way you act when you have been as if you thought I was always good enough for anybody to have with them, and then you act as if I was a bad one and you always just despise me. I certainly am afraid Dr. Campbell I can't stand it any more like that. I certainly can't stand it any more the way you are always changing. I certainly am afraid Dr. Campbell you ain't man enough to deserve to have anybody care so much to be always with you. I certainly am awful afraid Dr. Campbell I don't ever any more want to really see you. Good-by Dr. Campbell I wish you always to be real happy."

Jeff Campbell sat in his room, very quiet, a long time, after he got through reading this letter. He sat very still and first he was very angry. As if he, too, did not know very badly what it was to suffer keenly. As if he had not been very strong to stay with Melanctha when he never knew what it was that she really wanted. He knew he was very right to be angry, he knew he really had not been a coward. He knew Melanctha had done many things it was very hard for him to forgive her. He knew very well he had done his best to be kind, and to trust her, and to be loyal to her, and now;—and then Jeff suddenly remembered how one night Melanctha had been so strong to suffer, and he felt come back to him the sweetness in her, and then Jeff knew that really, he always forgave her, and that really, it all was that he was so sorry he had hurt her, and he wanted to go straight away and be a comfort to her. Jeff knew very well, that what Jane Harden had told him about Melanctha and her bad ways, had been a true story, and yet he wanted very badly to be with Melanctha. Perhaps she could teach him to really understand it better. Perhaps she could teach him how it could be all true, and yet how he could be right to believe in her and to trust her.

Jeff sat down and began his answer to her. "Dear Melanctha," Jeff wrote to her. "I certainly don't think you got it all just right in the letter, I just been reading, that you just wrote me. I certainly don't think you are just fair or very understanding to all I have to suffer to keep straight on to really always to believe in you and trust you. I certainly don't think you always are fair to remember right how hard it is for a man, who thinks like I was always thinking, not to think you do things very bad very often. I certainly don't think, Melanctha, I ain't right when I was so angry when I got your letter to me. I know very well, Melanctha, that with you, I never have been a coward. I find it very hard, and I never said it any different, it is hard to me to be understanding, and to know really what it is you wanted, and what it is you are meaning by what you are always saying to me. I don't say ever, it ain't very hard for you to be standing that I ain't very quick to be following whichever way that you are always leading. You know very well, Melanctha, it hurts me very bad and way inside me when I have to hurt you, but I always got to be real honest with you. There ain't no other way for me to be, with you, and I know very well it hurts me too, a whole lot, when I can't follow so quick as you would have me. I don't like to be a coward to you, Melanctha, and I don't like to say what I ain't meaning to you. And if you don't want me to do things honest, Melanctha, why I can't ever talk to you, and you are right when you say, you never again want to see me, but if you got any real sense of what I always been feeling with you, and if you got any right sense, Melanctha, of how hard I been trying to think and to feel right for you, I will be very glad to come and see you, and to begin again with you. I don't say anything now, Melanctha, about how bad I been this week, since I saw you, Melanctha. It don't ever do any good to talk such things over. All I know is I do my best, Melanctha, to you, and I don't say, no, never, I can do any different than just to be honest and come as fast as I think it's right for me to be going in the ways you teach me to be really understanding. So don't talk any more foolishness, Melanctha, about my always changing. I don't change, never, and I got to do what I think is right and honest to me, and I never told you any different, and you always knew it very well that I always would do just so. If you like me to come and see you tomorrow, and go out with you, I will be very glad to, Melanctha. Let me know right away, what it is you want me to be doing for you, Melanctha.

Very truly yours,
JEFFERSON CAMPBELL

"Please come to me, Jeff." Melanctha wrote back for her answer. Jeff went very slowly to Melanctha, glad as he was, still to be going to her. Melanctha came, very quick, to meet him, when she saw him from where she had been watching for him. They went into the house together. They were very glad to be together. They were very good to one another.

"I certainly did think, Melanctha, this time almost really, you never did want me to come to you at all any more to see you," said Jeff Campbell to her, when they had begun again with their talking to each other. "You certainly did make me think, perhaps really this time, Melanctha, it was all over, my being with you ever, and I was very mad, and very sorry, too, Melanctha."

"Well you certainly was very bad to me, Jeff Campbell," said Melanctha, fondly.

"I certainly never do say any more you ain't always right, Melanctha," Jeff answered and he was very ready now with cheerful laughing, "I certainly never do say that any more, Melanctha, if I know it, but still, really, Melanctha, honest, I think perhaps I wasn't real bad to you any more than you just needed from me."

Jeff held Melanctha in his arms and kissed her. He sighed then and was very silent with her. "Well, Melanctha," he said at last, with some more laughing, "well, Melanctha, any way you can't say ever it ain't, if we are ever friends good and really, you can't say, no, never, but that we certainly have worked right hard to get both of us together for it, so we shall sure deserve it then, if we can ever really get it." "We certainly have worked real hard, Jeff, I can't say that ain't all right the way you say it," said Melanctha. "I certainly never can deny it, Jeff, when I feel so worn with all the trouble you been making for me, you bad boy, Jeff," and then Melanctha smiled and then she sighed, and then she was very silent with him.

At last Jeff was to go away. They stood there on the steps for a long time trying to say good-by to each other. At last Jeff made himself really say it. At last he made himself, that he went down the steps and went away.

On the next Sunday they arranged, they were to have the long happy day of wandering that they had lost last time by Jane Harden's talking. Not that Melanctha Herbert had heard yet of Jane Harden's talking.

Jeff saw Melanctha every day now. Jeff was a little uncertain all this time inside him, for he had never yet told to Melanctha what it was that had so nearly made him really want to leave her. Jeff knew that for him, it was not right he should not tell her. He knew they could only have real peace between them when he had been honest, and had really told her. On this long Sunday Jeff was certain that he would really tell her.

They were very happy all that day in their wandering. They had taken things along to eat together. They sat in the bright fields and they were happy, they wandered in the woods and they were happy. Jeff always loved in this way to wander. Jeff always loved to watch everything as it was growing, and he loved all the colors in the trees and on the ground, and the little, new, bright colored bugs he found in the moist ground and in the grass he loved to lie on and in which he was always so busy searching. Jeff loved everything that moved and that was still, and that had color, and beauty, and real being.

Jeff loved very much this day while they were wandering. He almost forgot that he had any trouble with him still inside him. Jeff loved to be there with Melanctha Herbert. She was always so sympathetic to him for the way she listened to everything he found and told her, the way she felt his joy in all this being, the way she never said she wanted anything different from the way they had it. It was certainly a busy and a happy day, this their first long day of really wandering.

Later they were tired, and Melanctha sat down on the ground, and Jeff threw himself his full length beside her. Jeff lay there, very quiet, and then he pressed her hand and kissed it and murmured to her, "You certainly are very good to me, Melanctha." Melanctha felt it very deep and did not answer. Jeff lay there a long time, looking up above him. He was counting all the little leaves he saw above him. He was following all the little clouds with his eyes as they sailed past him. He watched all the birds that flew high beyond him, and all the time Jeff knew he must tell to Melanctha what it was he knew now, that which Jane Harden, just a week ago, had told him. He knew very well that for him it was certain that he had to say it. It was hard, but for Jeff Campbell the only way to lose it was to say it, the only way to know Melanctha really, was to tell her all the struggle he had made to know her, to tell her so she could help him to understand his trouble better, to help him so that never again he could have any way to doubt her.

Jeff lay there a long time, very quiet, always looking up above him, and yet feeling very close now to Melanctha. At last he turned a little toward her, took her hands closer in his to make him feel it stronger, and then very slowly, for the words came very hard for him, slowly he began his talk to her.

"Melanctha," began Jeff, very slowly, "Melanctha, it ain't right I shouldn't tell you why I went away last week and almost never got the chance again to see you. Jane Harden was sick, and I went in to take care of her. She began to tell everything she ever knew about you. She didn't know how well now I know you. I didn't tell her not to go on talking. I listened while she told me everything about you. I certainly found it very hard with what she told me. I know she was talking truth in everything she said about you. I knew you had been free in your ways, Melanctha, I knew you liked to get excitement the way I always hate to see the colored people take it. I didn't know, till I heard Jane Harden say it, you had done things so bad, Melanctha. When Jane Harden told me, I got very sick, Melanctha. I couldn't bear hardly, to think, perhaps I was just another like them to you, Melanctha. I was wrong not to trust you perhaps, Melanctha, but it did make things very ugly to me. I try to be honest to you, Melanctha, the way you say you really want it from me."

Melanctha drew her hands from Jeff Campbell. She sat there, and there was deep scorn in her anger.

"If you wasn't all through just selfish and nothing else, Jeff Campbell, you would take care you wouldn't have to tell me things like this, Jeff Campbell."

Jeff was silent a little, and he waited before he gave his answer. It was not the power of Melanctha's words that held him, for, for them, he had his answer, it was the power of the mood that filled Melanctha, and for that he had no answer. At last he broke through this awe, with his slow fighting resolution, and he began to give his answer.

"I don't say ever, Melanctha," he began, "it wouldn't have been more right for me to stop Jane Harden in her talking and to come to you to have you tell me what you were when I never knew you. I don't say it, no never to you, that that would not have been the right way for me to do, Melanctha. But I certainly am without any kind of doubting, I certainly do know for sure, I had a good right to know about what you were and your ways and your trying to use your understanding, every kind of way you could to get your learning. I certainly did have a right to know things like that about you, Melanctha. I don't say it ever, Melanctha, and I say it very often, I don't say ever I shouldn't have stopped Jane Harden in her talking and come to you and asked you yourself to tell me all about it, but I guess I wanted to keep myself from how much it would hurt me more, to have you yourself say it to me. Perhaps it was I wanted to keep you from having it hurt you so much more, having you to have to tell it to me. I don't know, I don't say it was to help you from being hurt most, or to help me. Perhaps I was a coward to let Jane Harden tell me 'stead of coming straight to you, to have you tell me, but I certainly am sure, Melanctha, I certainly had a right to know such things about you. I don't say it ever, ever, Melanctha, I hadn't the just right to know those things about you." Melanctha laughed her harsh laugh. "You needn't have been under no kind of worry, Jeff Campbell, about whether you should have asked me. You could have asked, it wouldn't have hurt nothing. I certainly never would have told you nothing." "I am not so sure of that, Melanctha," said Jeff Campbell. "I certainly do think you would have told me. I certainly do think I could make you feel it right to tell me. I certainly do think all I did wrong was to let Jane Harden tell me. I certainly do know I never did wrong, to learn what she told me. I certainly know very well, Melanctha, if I had come here to you, you would have told it all to me, Melanctha."

He was silent, and this struggle lay there, strong, between them. It was a struggle, sure to be going on always between them. It was a struggle that was as sure always to be going on between them, as their minds and hearts always were to have different ways of working.

At last Melanctha took his hand, leaned over him and kissed him. "I sure am very fond of you, Jeff Campbell," Melanctha whispered to him.

Now for a little time there was not any kind of trouble between Jeff Campbell and Melanctha Herbert. They were always together now for long times, and very often. They got much joy now, both of them, from being all the time together.

It was summer now, and they had warm sunshine to wander. It was summer now, and Jeff Campbell had more time to wander, for colored people never get sick so much in summer. It was summer now, and there was a lovely silence everywhere, and all the noises, too, that they heard around them were lovely ones, and added to the joy, in these warm days, they loved so much to be together.

They talked some to each other in these days, did Jeff Campbell and Melanctha Herbert, but always in these days their talking more and more was like it always is with real lovers. Jeff did not talk so much now about what he before always had been thinking. Sometimes Jeff would be, as if he was just waking from himself to be with Melanctha, and then he would find he had been really all the long time with her, and he had really never needed to be doing any thinking.

It was sometimes pure joy Jeff would be talking to Melanctha, in these warm days he loved so much to wander with her. Sometimes Jeff would lose all himself in a strong feeling. Very often now, and always with more joy in his feeling, he would find himself, he did not know how or what it was he had been thinking. And Melanctha always loved very well to make him feel it. She always now laughed a little at him, and went back a little in him to his before, always thinking, and she teased him with his always now being so good with her in his feeling, and then she would so well and freely, and with her pure, strong ways of reaching, she would give him all the love she knew now very well, how much he always wanted to be sure he really had it.

And Jeff took it straight now, and he loved it, and he felt, strong, the joy of all this being, and it swelled out full inside him, and he poured it all out back to her in freedom, in tender kindness, and in joy, and in gentle brother fondling. And Melanctha loved him for it always, her Jeff Campbell now, who never did things ugly, for her, like all the men she always knew before always had been doing to her. And they loved it always, more and more, together, with this new feeling they had now, in these long summer days so warm; they, always together now, just these two so dear, more and more to each other always, and the summer evenings when they wandered, and the noises in the full streets, and the music of the organs, and the dancing, and the warm smell of the people, and of dogs and of the horses, and all the joy of the strong, sweet pungent, dirty, moist, warm negro southern summer.

Every day now, Jeff seemed to be coming nearer, to be really loving. Every day now, Melanctha poured it all out to him, with more freedom. Every day now, they seemed to be having more and more, both together, of this strong, right feeling. More and more every day now they seemed to know more really, what it was each other one was always feeling. More and more now every day Jeff found in himself, he felt more trusting. More and more every day now, he did not think anything in words about what he was always doing. Every day now more and more Melanctha would let out to Jeff her real, strong feeling.

One day there had been much joy between them, more than they ever yet had had with their new feeling. All the day they had lost themselves in warm wandering. Now they were lying there and resting, with a green, bright, light-flecked world around them.

What was it that now really happened to them? What was it that Melanctha did, that made everything get all ugly for them? What was it that Melanctha felt then, that made Jeff remember all the feeling he had had in him when Jane Harden told him how Melanctha had learned to be so very understanding? Jeff did not know how it was that it had happened to him. It was all green, and warm, and very lovely to him, and now Melanctha somehow had made it all so ugly for him. What was it Melanctha was now doing with him? What was it he used to be thinking was the right way for him and all the colored people to be always trying to make it right, the way they should be always living? Why was Melanctha Herbert now all so ugly for him?

Melanctha Herbert somehow had made him feel deeply just then, what very more it was that she wanted from him. Jeff Campbell now felt in him what everybody always had needed to make them really understanding, to him. Jeff felt a strong disgust inside him; not for Melanctha herself, to him, not for himself really, in him, not for what it was that everybody wanted, in them; he only had disgust because he never could know really in him, what it was he wanted, to be really right in understanding, for him, he only had disgust because he never could know really what it was really right to him to be always doing, in the things he had before believed in, the things he before had believed in for himself and for all the colored people, the living regular, and the never wanting to be always having new things, just to keep on, always being in excitements. All the old thinking now came up very strong inside him. He sort of turned away then, and threw Melanctha from him.

Jeff never, even now, knew what it was that moved him. He never, even now, was ever sure, he really knew what Melanctha was, when she was real herself, and honest. He thought he knew, and then there came to him some moment, just like this one, when she really woke him up to be strong in him. Then he really knew he could know nothing. He knew then, he never could know what it was she really wanted with him. He knew then he never could know really what it was he felt inside him. It was all so mixed up inside him. All he knew was he wanted very badly Melanctha should be there beside him, and he wanted very badly, too, always to throw her from him. What was it really that Melanctha wanted with him? What was it really, he, Jeff Campbell, wanted she should give him? "I certainly did think now," Jeff Campbell groaned inside him, "I certainly did think now I really was knowing all right, what I wanted. I certainly did really think now I was knowing how to be trusting with Melanctha. I certainly did think it was like that now with me sure, after all I've been through all this time with her. And now I certainly do know I don't know anything that's very real about her. Oh the good Lord help and keep me!" and Jeff groaned hard inside him, and he buried his face deep in the green grass underneath him, and Melanctha Herbert was very silent there beside him.

Then Jeff turned to look and see her. She was lying very still there by him, and the bitter water on her face was biting. Jeff was so very sorry then, all over and inside him, the way he always was when Melanctha had been deep hurt by him. "I didn't mean to be so bad again to you, Melanctha, dear one," and he was very tender to her. "I certainly didn't never mean to go to be so bad to you, Melanctha, darling. I certainly don't know, Melanctha, darling, what it is makes me act so to you sometimes, when I certainly ain't meaning anything like I want to hurt you. I certainly don't mean to be so bad, Melanctha, only it comes so quick on me before I know what I am acting to you. I certainly am all sorry, hard, to be so bad to you, Melanctha, darling." "I suppose, Jeff," said Melanctha, very low and bitter, "I suppose you are always thinking, Jeff, somebody had ought to be ashamed with us two together, and you certainly do think you don't see any way to it, Jeff, for me to be feeling that way ever, so you certainly don't see any way to it, only to do it just so often for me. That certainly is the way always with you, Jeff Campbell, if I understand you right the way you are always acting to me. That certainly is right the way I am saying it to you now, Jeff Campbell. You certainly didn't anyway trust me now no more, did you, when you just acted so bad to me. I certainly am right the way I say it Jeff now to you. I certainly am right when I ask you for it now, to tell me what I ask you, about not trusting me more then again, Jeff, just like you never really knew me. You certainly never did trust me just then, Jeff, you hear me?" "Yes, Melanctha," Jeff answered slowly. Melanctha paused. "I guess I certainly never can forgive you this time, Jeff Campbell," she said firmly. Jeff paused too, and thought a little. "I certainly am afraid you never can no more now again, Melanctha," he said sadly.

They lay there very quiet now a long time, each one thinking very hard on their own trouble. At last Jeff began again to tell Melanctha what it was he was always thinking with her. "I certainly do know, Melanctha, you certainly now don't want any more to be hearing me just talking, but you see, Melanctha, really, it's just like this way always with me. You see, Melanctha, its like this way now all the time with me. You remember, Melanctha, what I was once telling to you, when I didn't know you very long together, about how I certainly never did know more than just two kinds of ways of loving, one way the way it is good to be in families and the other kind of way, like animals are all the time just with each other, and how I didn't ever like that last kind of way much for any of the colored people. You see Melanctha, it's like this way with me. I got a new feeling now, you been teaching to me, just like I told you once, just like a new religion to me, and I see perhaps what really loving is like, like really having everything together, new things, little pieces all different, like I always before been thinking was bad to be having, all go together like, to make one good big feeling. You see, Melanctha, it's certainly like that you make me been seeing, like I never know before any way there was of all kinds of loving to come together to make one way really truly lovely. I see that now, sometimes, the way you certainly been teaching me, Melanctha, really, and then I love you those times, Melanctha, like a real religion, and then it comes over me all sudden, I don't know anything real about you Melanctha, dear one, and then it comes over me sudden, perhaps I certainly am wrong now, thinking all this way so lovely, and not thinking now any more the old way I always before was always thinking, about what was the right way for me, to live regular and all the colored people, and then I think, perhaps, Melanctha you are really just a bad one, and I think, perhaps I certainly am doing it so because I just am too anxious to be just having all the time excitements, like I don't ever like really to be doing when I know it, and then I always get so bad to you, Melanctha, and I can't help it with myself then, never, for I want to be always right really in the ways, I have to do them. I certainly do very badly want to be right, Melanctha, the only way I know is right Melanctha really, and I don't know any way, Melanctha, to find out really, whether my old way, the way I always used to be thinking, or the new way, you make so like a real religion to me sometimes, Melanctha, which way certainly is the real right way for me to be always thinking, and then I certainly am awful good and sorry, Melanctha, I always give you so much trouble, hurting you with the bad ways I am acting. Can't you help me to any way, to make it all straight for me, Melanctha, so I know right and real what it is I should be acting. You see, Melanctha, I don't want always to be a coward with you, if I only could know certain what was the right way for me to be acting. I certainly am real sure, Melanctha, that would be the way I would be acting, if I only knew it sure for certain now, Melanctha. Can't you help me any way to find out real and true, Melanctha, dear one. I certainly do badly want to know always, the way I should be acting."

"No, Jeff, dear, I certainly can't help you much in that kind of trouble you are always having. All I can do now, Jeff, is to just keep certainly with my believing you are good always, Jeff, and though you certainly do hurt me bad, I always got strong faith in you, Jeff, more in you certainly, than you seem to be having in your acting to me, always so bad, Jeff."

"You certainly are very good to me, Melanctha, dear one," Jeff said, after a long, tender silence. "You certainly are very good to me, Melanctha, darling, and me so bad to you always, in my acting. Do you love me good, and right, Melanctha, always?" "Always and always, you be sure of that now you have me. Oh you Jeff, you always be so stupid." "I certainly never can say now you ain't right, when you say that to me so, Melanctha," Jeff answered. "Oh, Jeff dear, I love you always, you know that now, all right, for certain. If you don't know it right now, Jeff, really, I prove it to you now, for good and always." And they lay there a long time in their loving, and then Jeff began again with his happy free enjoying.

"I sure am a good boy to be learning all the time the right way you are teaching me, Melanctha, darling," began Jeff Campbell, laughing, "You can't say no, never, I ain't a good scholar for you to be teaching now, Melanctha, and I am always so ready to come to you every day, and never playing hooky ever from you. You can't say ever, Melanctha, now can you, I ain't a real good boy to be always studying to be learning to be real bright, just like my teacher. You can't say ever to me, I ain't a good boy to you now, Melanctha." "Not near so good, Jeff Campbell, as such a good, patient kind of teacher, like me, who never teaches any ways it ain't good her scholars should be knowing, ought to be really having, Jeff, you hear me? I certainly don't think I am right for you, to be forgiving always, when you are so bad, and I so patient, with all this hard teaching always." "But you do forgive me always, sure, Melanctha, always?" "Always and always, you be sure Jeff, and I certainly am afraid I never can stop with my forgiving, you always are going to be so bad to me, and I always going to have to be so good with my forgiving." "Oh! Oh!" cried Jeff Campbell, laughing, "I ain't going to be so bad for always, sure I ain't, Melanctha, my own darling. And sure you do forgive me really, and sure you love me true and really, sure, Melanctha?" "Sure, sure, Jeff, boy, sure now and always, sure now you believe me, sure you do, Jeff, always." "I sure hope I does, with all my heart, Melanctha, darling." "I sure do that same, Jeff, dear boy, now you really know what it is to be loving, and I prove it to you now so, Jeff, you never can be forgetting. You see now, Jeff, good and certain, what I always before been saying to you, Jeff, now." "Yes, Melanctha, darling," murmured Jeff, and he was very happy in it, and so the two of them now in the warm air of the sultry, southern, negro sunshine, lay there for a long time just resting.

And now for a real long time there was no open trouble any more between Jeff Campbell and Melanctha Herbert. Then it came that Jeff knew he could not say out any more, what it was he wanted, he could not say out any more, what it was, he wanted to know about, what Melanctha wanted.

Melanctha sometimes now, when she was tired with being all the time so much excited, when Jeff would talk a long time to her about what was right for them both to be always doing, would be, as if she gave way in her head, and lost herself in a bad feeling. Sometimes when they had been strong in their loving, and Jeff would have rise inside him some strange feeling, and Melanctha felt it in him as it would soon be coming, she would lose herself then in this bad feeling that made her head act as if she never knew what it was they were doing. And slowly now, Jeff soon always came to be feeling that his Melanctha would be hurt very much in her head in the ways he never liked to think of, if she would ever now again have to listen to his trouble, when he was telling about what it was he still was wanting to make things for himself really understanding.

Now Jeff began to have always a strong feeling that Melanctha could no longer stand it, with all her bad suffering, to let him fight out with himself what was right for him to be doing. Now he felt he must not, when she was there with him, keep on, with this kind of fighting that was always going on inside him. Jeff Campbell never knew yet, what he thought was the right way, for himself and for all the colored people to be living. Jeff was coming always each time closer to be really understanding, but now Melanctha was so bad in her suffering with him, that he knew she could not any longer have him with her while he was always showing that he never really yet was sure what it was, the right way, for them to be really loving.

Jeff saw now he had to go so fast, so that Melanctha never would have to wait any to get from him always all that she ever wanted. He never could be honest now, he never could be now, any more, trying to be really understanding, for always every moment now he felt it to be a strong thing in him, how very much it was Melanctha Herbert always suffered.

Jeff did not know very well these days, what it was, was really happening to him. All he knew every now and then, when they were getting strong to get excited, the way they used to when he gave his feeling out so that he could be always honest, that Melanctha somehow never seemed to hear him, she just looked at him and looked as if her head hurt with him, and then Jeff had to keep himself from being honest, and he had to go so fast, and to do everything Melanctha ever wanted from him.

Jeff did not like it very well these days, in his true feeling. He knew now very well Melanctha was not strong enough inside her to stand any more of his slow way of doing. And yet now he knew he was not honest in his feeling. Now he always had to show more to Melanctha than he was ever feeling. Now she made him go so fast, and he knew it was not real with his feeling, and yet he could not make her suffer so any more because he always was so slow with his feeling.

It was very hard for Jeff Campbell to make all this way of doing, right, inside him. If Jeff Campbell could not be straight out, and real honest, he never could be very strong inside him. Now Melanctha, with her making him feel, always, how good she was and how very much she suffered in him, made him always go so fast then, he could not be strong then, to feel things out straight then inside him. Always now when he was with her, he was being more, than he could already yet, be feeling for her. Always now, with her, he had something inside him always holding in him, always now, with her, he was far ahead of his own feeling.

Jeff Campbell never knew very well these days what it was that was going on inside him. All he knew was, he was uneasy now always to be with Melanctha. All he knew was, that he was always uneasy when he was with Melanctha, not the way he used to be from just not being very understanding, but now, because he never could be honest with her, because he was now always feeling her strong suffering, in her, because he knew now he was having a straight, good feeling with her, but she went so fast, and he was so slow to her; Jeff knew his right feeling never got a chance to show itself as strong, to her.

All this was always getting harder for Jeff Campbell. He was very proud to hold himself to be strong, was Jeff Campbell. He was very tender not to hurt Melanctha, when he knew she would be sure to feel it badly in her head a long time after, he hated that he could not now be honest with her, he wanted to stay away to work it out all alone, without her, he was afraid she would feel it to suffer, if he kept away now from her. He was uneasy always, with her, he was uneasy when he thought about her, he knew now he had a good, straight, strong feeling of right loving for her, and yet now he never could use it to be good and honest with her.

Jeff Campbell did not know, these days, anything he could do to make it better for her. He did not know anything he could do, to set himself really right in his acting and his thinking toward her. She pulled him so fast with her, and he did not dare to hurt her, and he could not come right, so fast, the way she always needed he should be doing it now, for her.

These days were not very joyful ones now any more, to Jeff Campbell, with Melanctha. He did not think it out to himself now, in words, about her. He did not know enough, what was his real trouble, with her.

Sometimes now and again with them, and with all this trouble for a little while well forgotten by him, Jeff, and Melanctha with him, would be very happy in a strong, sweet loving. Sometimes then, Jeff would find himself to be soaring very high in his true loving. Sometimes Jeff would find then, in his loving, his soul swelling out full inside him. Always Jeff felt now in himself, deep feeling.

Always now Jeff had to go so much faster than was real with his feeling. Yet always Jeff knew now he had a right, strong feeling. Always now when Jeff was wondering, it was Melanctha he was doubting, in the loving. Now he would often ask her, was she real now to him, in her loving. He would ask her often, feeling something queer about it all inside him, though yet he was never really strong in his doubting, and always Melanctha would answer to him, "Yes Jeff, sure, you know it, always," and always Jeff felt a doubt now, in her loving.

Always now Jeff felt in himself, deep loving. Always now he did not know really, if Melanctha was true in her loving.

All these days Jeff was uncertain in him, and he was uneasy about which way he should act so as not to be wrong and put them both into bad trouble. Always now he was, as if he must feel deep into Melanctha to see if it was real loving he would find she now had in her, and always he would stop himself, with her, for always he was afraid now that he might badly hurt her.

Always now he liked it better when he was detained when he had to go and see her. Always now he never liked to go to be with her, although he never wanted really, not to be always with her. Always now he never felt really at ease with her, even when they were good friends together. Always now he felt, with her, he could not be really honest to her. And Jeff never could be happy with her when he could not feel strong to tell all his feeling to her. Always now every day he found it harder to make the time pass, with her, and not let his feeling come so that he would quarrel with her.

And so one evening, late, he was to go to her. He waited a little long, before he went to her. He was afraid, in himself, to-night, he would surely hurt her. He never wanted to go when he might quarrel with her.

Melanctha sat there looking very angry, when he came in to her. Jeff took off his hat and coat and then sat down by the fire with her.

"If you come in much later to me just now, Jeff Campbell, I certainly never would have seen you no more never to speak to you, 'thout your apologising real humble to me." "Apologising Melanctha," and Jeff laughed and was scornful to her, "Apologising, Melanctha, I ain't proud that kind of way, Melanctha, I don't mind apologising to you, Melanctha, all I mind, Melanctha is to be doing of things wrong, to you." "That's easy, to say things that way, Jeff to me. But you never was very proud Jeff, to be courageous to me." "I don't know about that Melanctha. I got courage to say some things hard, when I mean them, to you." "Oh, yes, Jeff, I know all about that, Jeff, to me. But I mean real courage, to run around and not care nothing about what happens, and always to be game in any kind of trouble. That's what I mean by real courage, to me, Jeff, if you want to know it." "Oh, yes, Melanctha, I know all that kind of courage. I see plenty of it all the time with some kinds of colored men and with some girls like you Melanctha, and Jane Harden. I know all about how you are always making a fuss to be proud because you don't holler so much when you run in to where you ain't got any business to be, and so you get hurt, the way you ought to. And then, you kind of people are very brave then, sure, with all your kinds of suffering, but the way I see it, going round with all my patients, that kind of courage makes all kind of trouble, for them who ain't so noble with their courage, and then they got it, always to be bearing it, when the end comes, to be hurt the hardest. It's like running around and being game to spend all your money always, and then a man's wife and children are the ones do all the starving and they don't ever get a name for being brave, and they don't ever want to be doing all that suffering, and they got to stand it and say nothing. That's the way I see it a good deal now with all that kind of braveness in some of the colored people. They always make a lot of noise to show they are so brave not to holler, when they got so much suffering they always bring all on themselves, just by doing things they got no business to be doing. I don't say, never, Melanctha, they ain't got good courage not to holler, but I never did see much in looking for that kind of trouble just to show you ain't going to holler. No its all right being brave every day, just living regular and not having new ways all the time just to get excitements, the way I hate to see it in all the colored people. No I don't see much, Melanctha, in being brave just to get it good, where you've got no business. I ain't ashamed Melanctha, right here to tell you, I ain't ashamed ever to say I ain't got no longing to be brave, just to go around and look for trouble." "Yes that's just like you always, Jeff, you never understand things right, the way you are always feeling in you. You ain't got no way to understand right, how it depends what way somebody goes to look for new things, the way it makes it right for them to get excited." "No Melanctha, I certainly never do say I understand much anybody's got a right to think they won't have real bad trouble, if they go and look hard where they are certain sure to find it. No Melanctha, it certainly does sound very pretty all this talking about danger and being game and never hollering, and all that way of talking, but when two men are just fighting, the strong man mostly gets on top with doing good hard pounding, and the man that's getting all that pounding, he mostly never likes it so far as I have been able yet to see it, and I don't see much difference what kind of noble way they are made of when they ain't got any kind of business to get together there to be fighting. That certainly is the only way I ever see it happen right, Melanctha, whenever I happen to be anywhere I can be looking." "That's because you never can see anything that ain't just so simple, Jeff, with everybody, the way you always think it. It do make all the difference the kind of way anybody is made to do things game Jeff Campbell." "Maybe Melanctha, I certainly never say no you ain't right, Melanctha. I just been telling it to you all straight, Melanctha, the way I always see it. Perhaps if you run around where you ain't got any business, and you stand up very straight and say, I am so brave, nothing can ever ever hurt me, maybe nothing will ever hurt you then Melanctha. I never have seen it do so. I never can say truly any differently to you Melanctha, but I always am ready to be learning from you, Melanctha. And perhaps when somebody cuts into you real hard, with a brick he is throwing, perhaps you never will do any hollering then, Melanctha. I certainly don't ever say no, Melanctha to you, I only say that ain't the way yet I ever see it happen when I had a chance to be there looking."

They sat there together, quiet by the fire, and they did not seem to feel very loving.

"I certainly do wonder," Melanctha said dreamily, at last breaking into their long unloving silence. "I certainly do wonder why always it happens to me I care for anybody who ain't no ways good enough for me ever to be thinking to respect him."

Jeff looked at Melanctha. Jeff got up then and walked a little up and down the room, and then he came back, and his face was set and dark and he was very quiet to her.

"Oh dear, Jeff, sure, why you look so solemn now to me. Sure Jeff I never am meaning anything real by what I just been saying. What was I just been saying Jeff to you. I only certainly was just thinking how everything always was just happening to me."

Jeff Campbell sat very still and dark, and made no answer.

"Seems to me, Jeff you might be good to me a little tonight when my head hurts so, and I am so tired with all the hard work I have been doing, thinking, and I always got so many things to be a trouble to me, living like I do with nobody ever who can help me. Seems to me you might be good to me Jeff tonight, and not get angry, every little thing I am ever saying to you."

"I certainly would not get angry ever with you, Melanctha, just because you say things to me. But now I certainly been thinking you really mean what you have been just then saying to me." "But you say all the time to me Jeff, you ain't no ways good enough in your loving to me, you certainly say to me all the time you ain't no ways good or understanding to me." "That certainly is what I say to you always, just the way I feel it to you Melanctha always, and I got it right in me to say it, and I have got a right in me to be very strong and feel it, and to be always sure to believe it, but it ain't right for you Melanctha to feel it. When you feel it so Melanctha, it does certainly make everything all wrong with our loving. It makes it so I certainly never can bear to have it."

They sat there then a long time by the fire, very silent, and not loving, and never looking to each other for it. Melanctha was moving and twitching herself and very nervous with it. Jeff was heavy and sullen and dark and very serious in it.

"Oh why can't you forget I said it to you Jeff now, and I certainly am so tired, and my head and all now with it."

Jeff stirred, "All right Melanctha, don't you go make yourself sick now in your head, feeling so bad with it," and Jeff made himself do it, and he was a patient doctor again now with Melanctha when he felt her really having her head hurt with it. "It's all right now Melanctha darling, sure it is now I tell you. You just lie down now a little, dear one, and I sit here by the fire and just read awhile and just watch with you so I will be here ready, if you need me to give you something to help you resting." And then Jeff was a good doctor to her, and very sweet and tender with her, and Melanctha loved him to be there to help her, and then Melanctha fell asleep a little, and Jeff waited there beside her until he saw she was really sleeping, and then he went back and sat down by the fire.

And Jeff tried to begin again with his thinking, and he could not make it come clear to himself, with all his thinking, and he felt everything all thick and heavy and bad, now inside him, everything that he could not understand right, with all the hard work he made, with his thinking. And then he moved himself a little, and took a book to forget his thinking, and then as always, he loved it when he was reading, and then very soon he was deep in his reading, and so he forgot now for a little while that he never could seem to be very understanding.

And so Jeff forgot himself for awhile in his reading, and Melanctha was sleeping. And then Melanctha woke up and she was screaming. "Oh, Jeff, I thought you gone away for always from me. Oh, Jeff, never now go away no more from me. Oh, Jeff, sure, sure, always be just so good to me."

There was a weight in Jeff Campbell from now on, always with him, that he could never lift out from him, to feel easy. He always was trying not to have it in him and he always was trying not to let Melanctha feel it, with him, but it was always there inside him. Now Jeff Campbell always was serious, and dark, and heavy, and sullen, and he would often sit a long time with Melanctha without moving.

"You certainly never have forgiven to me, what I said to you that night, Jeff, now have you?" Melanctha asked him after a long silence, late one evening with him. "It ain't ever with me a question like forgiving, Melanctha, I got in me. It's just only what you are feeling for me, makes any difference to me. I ain't ever seen anything since in you, makes me think you didn't mean it right, what you said about not thinking now any more I was good, to make it right for you to be really caring so very much to love me."

"I certainly never did see no man like you, Jeff. You always wanting to have it all clear out in words always, what everybody is always feeling. I certainly don't see a reason, why I should always be explaining to you what I mean by what I am just saying. And you ain't got no feeling ever for me, to ask me what I meant, by what I was saying when I was so tired, that night. I never know anything right I was saying." "But you don't ever tell me now, Melanctha, so I really hear you say it, you don't mean it the same way, the way you said it to me." "Oh Jeff, you so stupid always to me and always just bothering with your always asking to me. And I don't never any way remember ever anything I been saying to you, and I am always my head, so it hurts me it half kills me, and my heart jumps so, sometimes I think I die so when it hurts me, and I am so blue always, I think sometimes I take something to just kill me, and I got so much to bother thinking always and doing, and I got so much to worry, and all that, and then you come and ask me what I mean by what I was just saying to you. I certainly don't know, Jeff, when you ask me. Seems to me, Jeff, sometimes you might have some kind of a right feeling to be careful to me." "You ain't got no right Melanctha Herbert," flashed out Jeff through his dark, frowning anger, "you certainly ain't got no right always to be using your being hurt and being sick, and having pain, like a weapon, so as to make me do things it ain't never right for me to be doing for you. You certainly ain't got no right to be always holding your pain out to show me." "What do you mean by them words, Jeff Campbell." "I certainly do mean them just like I am saying them, Melanctha. You act always, like I been responsible all myself for all our loving one another. And if its anything anyway that ever hurts you, you act like as if it was me made you just begin it all with me. I ain't no coward, you hear me, Melanctha? I never put my trouble back on anybody, thinking that they made me. I certainly am right ready always, Melanctha, you certainly had ought to know me, to stand all my own trouble for me, but I tell you straight now, the way I think it Melanctha, I ain't going to be as if I was the reason why you wanted to be loving, and to be suffering so now with me." "But ain't you certainly ought to be feeling it so, to be right, Jeff Campbell. Did I ever do anything but just let you do everything you wanted to me. Did I ever try to make you be loving to me. Did I ever do nothing except just sit there ready to endure your loving with me. But I certainly never, Jeff Campbell, did make any kind of way as if I wanted really to be having you for me."

Jeff stared at Melanctha. "So that's the way you say it when you are thinking right about it all, Melanctha. Well I certainly ain't got a word to say ever to you any more, Melanctha, if that's the way its straight out to you now, Melanctha." And Jeff almost laughed out to her, and he turned to take his hat and coat, and go away now forever from her.

Melanctha dropped her head on her arms, and she trembled all over and inside her. Jeff stopped a little and looked very sadly at her. Jeff could not so quickly make it right for himself, to leave her.

"Oh, I certainly shall go crazy now, I certainly know that," Melanctha moaned as she sat there, all fallen and miserable and weak together.

Jeff came and took her in his arms, and held her. Jeff was very good then to her, but they neither of them felt inside all right, as they once did, to be together.

From now on, Jeff had real torment in him.

Was it true what Melanctha had said that night to him? Was it true that he was the one had made all his trouble for them? Was it true, he was the only one, who always had had wrong ways in him? Waking or sleeping Jeff now always had this torment going on inside him.

Jeff did not know any more, what to

feel within him. He did not know how to begin thinking out this trouble that must always now be bad inside him. He just felt a confused struggle and resentment always in him, a knowing, no, Melanctha was not right in what she had said that night to him, and then a feeling, perhaps he always had been wrong in the way he never could be understanding. And then would come strong to him, a sense of the deep sweetness in Melanctha's loving and a hating the cold slow way he always had to feel things in him.

Always Jeff knew, sure, Melanctha was wrong in what she had said that night to him, but always Melanctha had had deep feeling with him, always he was poor and slow in the only way he knew how to have any feeling. Jeff knew Melanctha was wrong, and yet he always had a deep doubt in him. What could he know, who had such slow feeling in him? What could he ever know, who always had to find his way with just thinking. What could he know, who had to be taught such a long time to learn about what was really loving? Jeff now always had this torment in him.

Melanctha was now always making him feel her way, strong whenever she was with him. Did she go on to do it just to show him, did she do it so now because she was no longer loving, did she do it so because that was her way to make him be really loving. Jeff never did know how it was that it all happened so to him.

Melanctha acted now the way she had said it always had been with them. Now it was always Jeff who had to do the asking. Now it was always Jeff who had to ask when would be the next time he should come to see her. Now always she was good and patient to him, and now always she was kind and loving with him, and always Jeff felt it was, that she was good to give him anything he ever asked or wanted, but never now any more for her own sake to make her happy in him. Now she did these things, as if it was just to please her Jeff Campbell who needed she should now have kindness for him. Always now he was the beggar, with them. Always now Melanctha gave it, not of her need, but from her bounty to him. Always now Jeff found it getting harder for him.

Sometimes Jeff wanted to tear things away from before him, always now he wanted to fight things and be angry with them, and always now Melanctha was so patient to him.

Now, deep inside him, there was always a doubt with Jeff, of Melanctha's loving. It was not a doubt yet to make him really doubting, for with that, Jeff never could be really loving, but always now he knew that something, and that not in him, something was wrong with their loving. Jeff Campbell could not know any right way to think out what was inside Melanctha with her loving, he could not use any way now to reach inside her to find if she was true in her loving, but now something had gone wrong between them, and now he never felt sure in him, the way once she had made him, that now at last he really had got to be understanding.

Melanctha was too many for him. He was helpless to find out the way she really felt now for him. Often Jeff would ask her, did she really love him. Always she said, "Yes Jeff, sure, you know that," and now instead of a full sweet strong love with it, Jeff only felt a patient, kind endurance in it.

Jeff did not know. If he was right in such a feeling, he certainly never any more did want to have Melanctha Herbert with him. Jeff Campbell hated badly to think Melanctha ever would give him love, just for his sake, and not because she needed it herself, to be with him. Such a way of loving would be very hard for Jeff to be enduring.

"Jeff what makes you act so funny to

me. Jeff you certainly now are jealous to me. Sure Jeff, now I don't see ever why you be so foolish to look so to me." "Don't you ever think I can be jealous of anybody ever Melanctha, you hear me. It's just, you certainly don't ever understand me. It's just this way with me always now Melanctha. You love me, and I don't care anything what you do or what you ever been to anybody. You don't love me, then I don't care any more about what you ever do or what you ever be to anybody. But I never want you to be being good Melanctha to me, when it ain't your loving makes you need it. I certainly don't ever want to be having any of your kind of kindness to me. If you don't love me, I can stand it. All I never want to have is your being good to me from kindness. If you don't love me, then you and I certainly do quit right here Melanctha, all strong feeling, to be always living to each other. It certainly never is anybody I ever am thinking about when I am thinking with you Melanctha darling. That's the true way I am telling you Melanctha, always. It's only your loving me ever gives me anything to bother me Melanctha, so all you got to do, if you don't really love me, is just certainly to say so to me. I won't bother you more then than I can help to keep from it Melanctha. You certainly need never to be in any worry, never, about me Melanctha. You just tell me straight out Melanctha, real, the way you feel it. I certainly can stand it all right, I tell you true Melanctha. And I never will care to know why or nothing Melanctha. Loving is just living Melanctha to me, and if you don't really feel it now Melanctha to me, there ain't ever nothing between us then Melanctha, is there? That's straight and honest just the way I always feel it to you now Melanctha. Oh Melanctha, darling, do you love me? Oh Melanctha, please, please, tell me honest, tell me, do you really love me?"

"Oh you so stupid Jeff boy, of course I always love you. Always and always Jeff and I always just so good to you. Oh, you so stupid Jeff and don't know when you got it good with me. Oh dear, Jeff I certainly am so tired Jeff to-night, don't you go be a bother to me. Yes I love you Jeff, how often you want me to tell you. Oh you so stupid Jeff, but yes I love you. Now I won't say it no more now tonight Jeff, you hear me. You just be good Jeff now to me or else I certainly get awful angry with you. Yes I love you, sure, Jeff, though you don't any way deserve it from me. Yes, yes I love you. Yes Jeff I say it till I certainly am very sleepy. Yes I love you now Jeff, and you certainly must stop asking me to tell you. Oh you great silly boy Jeff Campbell, sure I love you, oh you silly stupid, my own boy Jeff Campbell. Yes I love you and I certainly never won't say it one more time to-night Jeff, now you hear me."

Yes Jeff Campbell heard her, and he tried hard to believe her. He did not really doubt her but somehow it was wrong now, the way Melanctha said it. Jeff always now felt baffled with Melanctha. Something, he knew, was not right now in her. Something in her always now was making stronger the torment that was tearing every minute at the joy he once always had had with her.

Always now Jeff wondered did Melanctha love him. Always now he was wondering, was Melanctha right when she said, it was he had made all their beginning. Was Melanctha right when she said, it was he had the real responsibility for all the trouble they had and still were having now between them. If she was right, what a brute he always had been in his acting. If she was right, how good she had been to endure the pain he had made so bad so often for her. But no, surely she had made herself to bear it, for her own sake, not for his to make him happy. Surely he was not so twisted in all his long thinking.

Surely he could remember right what it was had happened every day in their long loving. Surely he was not so poor a coward as Melanctha always seemed to be thinking. Surely, surely, and then the torment would get worse every minute in him.

One night Jeff Campbell was lying in his bed with his thinking, and night after night now he could not do any sleeping for his thinking. To-night suddenly he sat up in his bed, and it all came clear to him, and he pounded his pillow with his fist, and he almost shouted out alone there to him, "I ain't a brute the way Melanctha has been saying. Its all wrong the way I been worried thinking. We did begin fair, each not for the other but for ourselves, what we were wanting. Melanctha Herbert did it just like I did it, because she liked it bad enough to want to stand it. It's all wrong in me to think it any way except the way we really did it. I certainly don't know now whether she is now real and true in her loving. I ain't got any way ever to find out if she is real and true now always to me. All I know is I didn't ever make her to begin to be with me. Melanctha has got to stand for her own trouble, just like I got to stand for my own trouble. Each man has got to do it for himself when he is in real trouble. Melanctha, she certainly don't remember right when she says I made her begin and then I made her trouble. No by God, I ain't no coward nor a brute either ever to her. I been the way I felt it honest, and that certainly is all about it now between us, and everybody always has just got to stand for their own trouble. I certainly am right this time the way I see it." And Jeff lay down now, at last in comfort, and he slept, and he was free from his long doubting torment.

"You know Melanctha," Jeff Campbell began, the next time he was alone to talk a long time to Melanctha. "You know Melanctha, sometimes I think a whole lot about what you like to say so much about being game and never doing any hollering. Seems to me Melanctha, I certainly don't understand right what you mean by not hollering. Seems to me it certainly ain't only what comes right away when one is hit, that counts to be brave to be bearing, but all that comes later from your getting sick from the shock of being hurt once in a fight, and all that, and all the being taken care of for years after, and the suffering of your family, and all that, you certainly must stand and not holler, to be certainly really brave the way I understand it." "What you mean Jeff by your talking." "I mean, seems to me really not to holler, is to be strong not to show you ever have been hurt. Seems to me, to get your head hurt from your trouble and to show it, ain't certainly no braver than to say, oh, oh, how bad you hurt me, please don't hurt me mister. It just certainly seems to me, like many people think themselves so game just to stand what we all of us always just got to be standing, and everybody stands it, and we don't certainly none of us like it, and yet we don't ever most of us think we are so much being game, just because we got to stand it."

"I know what you mean now by what you are saying to me now Jeff Campbell. You make a fuss now to me, because I certainly just have stopped standing and everything you like to be always doing so cruel to me. But that's just the way always with you Jeff Campbell, if you want to know it. You ain't got no kind of right feeling for all I always been forgiving to you." "I said it once for fun, Melanctha, but now I certainly do mean it, you think you got a right to go where you got no business, and you say, I am so brave nothing can hurt me, and then something, like always, it happens to hurt you, and you show your hurt always so everybody can see it, and you say, I am so brave nothing did hurt me except he certainly didn't have any right to, and see how bad I suffer, but you never hear me make a holler, though certainly anybody got any feeling, to see me suffer, would certainly never touch me except to take good care of me. Sometimes I certainly don't rightly see Melanctha, how much more game that is than just the ordinary kind of holler." "No, Jeff Campbell, and made the way you is you certainly ain't likely ever to be much more understanding." "No, Melanctha, nor you neither. You think always, you are the only one who ever can do any way to really suffer." "Well, and ain't I certainly always been the only person knows how to bear it. No, Jeff Campbell, I certainly be glad to love anybody really worthy, but I made so, I never seem to be able in this world to find him." "No, and your kind of way of thinking, you certainly Melanctha never going to any way be able ever to be finding of him. Can't you understand Melanctha, ever, how no man certainly ever really can hold your love for long times together. You certainly Melanctha, you ain't got down deep loyal feeling, true inside you, and when you ain't just that moment quick with feeling, then you certainly ain't ever got anything more there to keep you. You see Melanctha, it certainly is this way with you, it is, that you ain't ever got any way to remember right what you been doing, or anybody else that has been feeling with you. You certainly Melanctha, never can remember right, when it comes what you have done and what you think happens to you." "It certainly is all easy for you Jeff Campbell to be talking. You remember right, because you don't remember nothing till you get home with your thinking everything all over, but I certainly don't think much ever of that kind of way of remembering right, Jeff Campbell. I certainly do call it remembering right Jeff Campbell, to remember right just when it happens to you, so you have a right kind of feeling not to act the way you always been doing to me, and then you go home Jeff Campbell, and you begin with your thinking, and then it certainly is very easy for you to be good and forgiving with it. No, that ain't to me, the way of remembering Jeff Campbell, not as I can see it not to make people always suffer, waiting for you certainly to get to do it. Seems to me like Jeff Campbell, I never could feel so like a man was low and to be scorning of him, like that day in the summer, when you threw me off just because you got one of those fits of your remembering. No, Jeff Campbell, its real feeling every moment when its needed, that certainly does seem to me like real remembering. And that way, certainly, you don't never know nothing like what should be right Jeff Campbell. No Jeff, it's me that always certainly has had to bear it with you. It's always me that certainly has had to suffer, while you go home to remember. No you certainly ain't got no sense yet Jeff, what you need to make you really feeling. No, it certainly is me Jeff Campbell, that always has got to be remembering for us both, always. That's what's the true way with us Jeff Campbell, if you want to know what it is I am always thinking." "You is certainly real modest Melanctha, when you do this kind of talking, you sure is Melanctha," said Jeff Campbell laughing. "I think sometimes Melanctha I am certainly awful conceited, when I think sometimes I am all out doors, and I think I certainly am so bright, and better than most everybody I ever got anything now to do with, but when I hear you talk this way Melanctha, I certainly do think I am a real modest kind of fellow." "Modest!" said Melanctha, angry, "Modest, that certainly is a queer thing for you Jeff to be calling yourself even when you are laughing." "Well it certainly does depend a whole lot what you are thinking with," said Jeff Campbell. "I never did use to think I was so much on being real modest Melanctha, but now I know really I am, when I hear you talking. I see all the time there are many people living just as good as I am, though they are a little different to me. Now with you Melanctha if I understand you right what you are talking, you don't think that way of no other one that you are ever knowing." "I certainly could be real modest too, Jeff Campbell," said Melanctha, "If I could meet somebody once I could keep right on respecting when I got so I was really knowing with them. But I certainly never met anybody like that yet, Jeff Campbell, if you want to know it." "No, Melanctha, and with the way you got of thinking, it certainly don't look like as if you ever will Melanctha, with your never remembering anything only what you just then are feeling in you, and you not understanding what anyone else is ever feeling, if they don't holler just the way you are doing. No Melanctha, I certainly don't see any ways you are likely ever to meet one, so good as you are always thinking you be." "No, Jeff Campbell, it certainly ain't that way with me at all the way you say it. It's because I am always knowing what it is I am wanting, when I get it. I certainly don't never have to wait till I have it, and then throw away what I got in me, and then come back and say, that's a mistake I just been making, it ain't that never at all like I understood it, I want to have, bad, what I didn't think it was I wanted. It's that way of knowing right what I am wanting, makes me feel nobody can come right with me, when I am feeling things, Jeff Campbell. I certainly do say Jeff Campbell, I certainly don't think much of the way you always do it, always never knowing what it is you are ever really wanting and everybody always got to suffer. No Jeff, I don't certainly think there is much doubting which is better and the stronger with us two, Jeff Campbell."

"As you will, Melanctha Herbert," cried Jeff Campbell, and he rose up, and he thundered out a black oath, and he was fierce to leave her now forever, and then with the same movement, he took her in his arms and held her.

"What a silly goose boy you are, Jeff Campbell," Melanctha whispered to him fondly.

"Oh yes," said Jeff, very dreary. "I never could keep really mad with anybody, not when I was a little boy and playing. I used most to cry sometimes, I couldn't get real mad and keep on a long time with it, the way everybody always did it. It's certainly no use to me Melanctha, I certainly can't ever keep mad with you Melanctha, my dear one. But don't you ever be thinking it's because I think you right in what you been just saying to me. I don't Melanctha really think it that way, honest, though I certainly can't get mad the way I ought to. No Melanctha, little girl, really truly, you ain't right the way you think it. I certainly do know that Melanctha, honest. You certainly don't do me right Melanctha, the way you say you are thinking. Good-bye Melanctha, though you certainly is my own little girl for always." And then they were very good a little to each other, and then Jeff went away for that evening, from her.

Melanctha had begun now once more to wander. Melanctha did not yet always wander, but a little now she needed to begin to look for others. Now Melanctha Herbert began again to be with some of the better kind of black girls, and with them she sometimes wandered. Melanctha had not yet come again to need to be alone, when she wandered.

Jeff Campbell did not know that Melanctha had begun again to wander. All Jeff knew, was that now he could not be so often with her.

Jeff never knew how it had come to happen to him, but now he never thought to go to see Melanctha Herbert, until he had before, asked her if she could be going to have time then to have him with her. Then Melanctha would think a little, and then she would say to him, "Let me see Jeff, to-morrow, you was just saying to me. I certainly am awful busy you know Jeff just now. It certainly does seem to me this week Jeff, I can't anyways fix it. Sure I want to see you soon Jeff. I certainly Jeff got to do a little more now, I been giving so much time, when I had no business, just to be with you when you asked me. Now I guess Jeff, I certainly can't see you no more this week Jeff, the way I got to do things." "All right Melanctha," Jeff would answer and he would be very angry. "I want to come only just certainly as you want me now Melanctha." "Now Jeff you know I certainly can't be neglecting always to be with everybody just to see you. You come see me next week Tuesday Jeff, you hear me. I don't think Jeff I certainly be so busy, Tuesday." Jeff Campbell would then go away and leave her, and he would be hurt and very angry, for it was hard for a man with a great pride in himself, like Jeff Campbell, to feel himself no better than a beggar. And yet he always came as she said he should, on the day she had fixed for him, and always Jeff Campbell was not sure yet that he really understood what it was Melanctha wanted. Always Melanctha said to him, yes she loved him, sure he knew that. Always Melanctha said to him, she certainly did love him just the same as always, only sure he knew now she certainly did seem to be right busy with all she certainly now had to be doing.

Jeff never knew what Melanctha had to do now, that made her always be so busy, but Jeff Campbell never cared to ask Melanctha such a question. Besides Jeff knew Melanctha Herbert would never, in such a matter, give him any kind of a real answer. Jeff did not know whether it was that Melanctha did not know how to give a simple answer. And then how could he, Jeff, know what was important to her. Jeff Campbell always felt strongly in him, he had no right to interfere with Melanctha in any practical kind of a matter. There they had always, never asked each other any kind of question. There they had felt always in each other, not any right to take care of one another. And Jeff Campbell now felt less than he had ever, any right to claim to know what Melanctha thought it right that she should do in any of her ways of living. All Jeff felt a right in himself to question, was her loving.

Jeff learned every day now, more and more, how much it was that he could really suffer. Sometimes it hurt so in him, when he was alone, it would force some slow tears from him. But every day, now that Jeff Campbell, knew more how it could hurt him, he lost his feeling of deep awe that he once always had had for Melanctha's feeling. Suffering was not so much after all, thought Jeff Campbell, if even he could feel it so it hurt him. It hurt him bad, just the way he knew he once had hurt Melanctha, and yet he too could have it and not make any kind of a loud holler with it.

In tender hearted natures, those that mostly never feel strong passion, suffering often comes to make them harder. When these do not know in themselves what it is to suffer, suffering is then very awful to them and they badly want to help everyone who ever has to suffer, and they have a deep reverence for anybody who knows really how to always suffer. But when it comes to them to really suffer, they soon begin to lose their fear and tenderness and wonder. Why it isn't so very much to suffer, when even I can bear to do it. It isn't very pleasant to be having all the time, to stand it, but they are not so much wiser after all, all the others just because they know too how to bear it.

Passionate natures who have always made themselves, to suffer, that is all the kind of people who have emotions that come to them as sharp as a sensation, they always get more tender-hearted when they suffer, and it always does them good to suffer. Tender-hearted, unpassionate, and comfortable natures always get much harder when they suffer, for so they lose the fear and reverence and wonder they once had for everybody who ever has to suffer, for now they know themselves what it is to suffer and it is not so awful any longer to them when they know too, just as well as all the others, how to have it.

And so it came in these days to Jeff Campbell. Jeff knew now always, way inside him, what it is to really suffer, and now every day with it, he knew how to understand Melanctha better. Jeff Campbell still loved Melanctha Herbert and he still had a real trust in her and he still had a little hope that some day they would once more get together, but slowly, every day, this hope in him would keep growing always weaker. They still were a good deal of time together, but now they never any more were really trusting with each other. In the days when they used to be together, Jeff had felt he did not know much what was inside Melanctha, but he knew very well, how very deep always was his trust in her; now he knew Melanctha Herbert better, but now he never felt a deep trust in her. Now Jeff never could be really honest with her. He never doubted yet, that she was steady only to him, but somehow he could not believe much really in Melanctha's loving.

Melanctha Herbert was a little angry now when Jeff asked her, "I never give nobody before Jeff, ever more than one chance with me, and I certainly been giving you most a hundred Jeff, you hear me." "And why shouldn't you Melanctha, give me a million, if you really love me!" Jeff flashed out very angry. "I certainly don't know as you deserve that anyways from me, Jeff Campbell." "It ain't deserving, I am ever talking about to you, Melanctha. Its loving, and if you are really loving to me you won't certainly never any ways call them chances." "Deed Jeff, you certainly are getting awful wise Jeff now, ain't you, to me." "No I ain't Melanctha, and I ain't jealous either to you. I just am doubting from the way you are always acting to me." "Oh yes Jeff, that's what they all say, the same way, when they certainly got jealousy all through them. You ain't got no cause to be jealous with me Jeff, and I am awful tired of all this talking now, you hear me."

Jeff Campbell never asked Melanctha any more if she loved him. Now things were always getting worse between them. Now Jeff was always very silent with Melanctha. Now Jeff never wanted to be honest to her, and now Jeff never had much to say to her.

Now when they were together, it was Melanctha always did most of the talking. Now she often had other girls there with her. Melanctha was always kind to Jeff Campbell but she never seemed to need to be alone now with him. She always treated Jeff, like her best friend, and she always spoke so to him and yet she never seemed now to very often want to see him.

Every day it was getting harder for Jeff Campbell. It was as if now, when he had learned to really love Melanctha, she did not need any more to have him. Jeff began to know this very well inside him.

Jeff Campbell did not know yet that Melanctha had begun again to wander. Jeff was not very quick to suspect Melanctha. All Jeff knew was, that he did not trust her to be now really loving to him.

Jeff was no longer now in any doubt inside him. He knew very well now he really loved Melanctha. He knew now very well she was not any more a real religion to him. Jeff Campbell knew very well too now inside him, he did not really want Melanctha, now if he could no longer trust her, though he loved her hard and really knew now what it was to suffer.

Every day Melanctha Herbert was less and less near to him. She always was very pleasant in her talk and to be with him, but somehow now it never was any comfort to him.

Melanctha Herbert now always had a lot of friends around her. Jeff Campbell never wanted to be with them. Now Melanctha began to find it, she said it often to him, always harder to arrange to be alone now with him. Sometimes she would be late for him. Then Jeff always would try to be patient in his waiting, for Jeff Campbell knew very well how to remember, and he knew it was only right that he should now endure this from her.

Then Melanctha began to manage often not to see him, and once she went away when she had promised to be there to meet him.

Then Jeff Campbell was really filled up with his anger. Now he knew he could never really want her. Now he knew he never any more could really trust her.

Jeff Campbell never knew why Melanctha had not come to meet him. Jeff had heard a little talking now, about how Melanctha Herbert had commenced once more to wander. Jeff Campbell still sometimes saw Jane Harden, who always needed a doctor to be often there to help her. Jane Harden always knew very well what happened to Melanctha. Jeff Campbell never would talk to Jane Harden anything about Melanctha. Jeff was always loyal to Melanctha. Jeff never let Jane Harden say much to him about Melanctha, though he never let her know that now he loved her. But somehow Jeff did know now about Melanctha, and he knew about some men that Melanctha met with Rose Johnson very often.

Jeff Campbell would not let himself really doubt Melanctha, but Jeff began to know now very well, he did not want her. Melanctha Herbert did not love him ever, Jeff knew it now, the way he once had thought that she could feel it. Once she had been greater for him than he had thought he could ever know how to feel it. Now Jeff had come to where he could understand Melanctha Herbert. Jeff was not bitter to her because she could not really love him, he was bitter only that he had let himself have a real illusion in him. He was a little bitter too, that he had lost now, what he had always felt real in the world, that had made it for him always full of beauty, and now he had not got this new religion really, and he had lost what he before had to know what was good and had real beauty.

Jeff Campbell was so angry now in him, because he had begged Melanctha always to be honest to him. Jeff could stand it in her not to love him, he could not stand it in her not to be honest to him.

Jeff Campbell went home from where Melanctha had not met him, and he was sore and full of anger in him.

Jeff Campbell could not be sure what to do, to make it right inside him. Surely he must be strong now and cast this loving from him, and yet, was he sure he now had real wisdom in him. Was he sure that Melanctha Herbert never had had a real deep loving for him. Was he sure Melanctha Herbert never had deserved a reverence from him. Always now Jeff had this torment in him, but always now he felt more that Melanctha never had real greatness for him.

Jeff waited to see if Melanctha would send any word to him. Melanctha Herbert never sent a line to him.

At last Jeff wrote his letter to Melanctha. "Dear Melanctha, I certainly do know you ain't been any way sick this last week when you never met me right the way you promised, and never sent me any word to say why you acted a way you certainly never could think was the right way you should do it to me. Jane Harden said she saw you that day and you went out walking with some people you like now to be with. Don't be misunderstanding me now any more Melanctha. I love you now because that's my slow way to learn what you been teaching, but I know now you certainly never had what seems to me real kind of feeling. I don't love you Melanctha any more now like a real religion, because now I know you are just made like all us others. I know now no man can ever really hold you because no man can ever be real to trust in you, because you mean right Melanctha, but you never can remember, and so you certainly never have got any way to be honest. So please you understand me right now Melanctha, it never is I don't know how to love you. I do know now how to love you, Melanctha, really. You sure do know that, Melanctha, in me. You certainly always can trust me. And so now Melanctha, I can say to you certainly real honest with you, I am better than you are in my right kind of feeling. And so Melanctha, I don't never any more want to be a trouble to you. You certainly make me see things Melanctha, I never any other way could be knowing. You been very good and patient to me, when I was certainly below you in my right feeling. I certainly never have been near so good and patient to you ever any way Melanctha, I certainly know that Melanctha. But Melanctha, with me, it certainly is, always to be good together, two people certainly must be thinking each one as good as the other, to be really loving right Melanctha. And it certainly must never be any kind of feeling, of one only taking, and one only just giving, Melanctha, to me. I know you certainly don't really ever understand me now Melanctha, but that's no matter. I certainly do know what I am feeling now with you real Melanctha. And so good-bye now for good Melanctha. I say I can never ever really trust you real Melanctha, that's only just certainly from your way of not being ever equal in your feeling to anybody real, Melanctha, and your way never to know right how to remember. Many ways I really trust you deep Melanctha, and I certainly do feel deep all the good sweetness you certainly got real in you Melanctha. Its only just in your loving me Melanctha. You never can be equal to me and that way I certainly never can bear any more to have it. And so now Melanctha, I always be your friend, if you need me, and now we never see each other any more to talk to."

And then Jeff Campbell thought and thought, and he could never make any way for him now, to see it different, and so at last he sent this letter to Melanctha.

And now surely it was all over in Jeff Campbell. Surely now he never any more could know Melanctha. And yet, perhaps Melanctha really loved him. And then she would know how much it hurt him never any more, any way, to see her, and perhaps she would write a line to tell him. But that was a foolish way for Jeff ever to be thinking. Of course Melanctha never would write a word to him. It was all over now for always, everything between them, and Jeff felt it a real relief to him.

For many days now Jeff Campbell only felt it as a relief in him. Jeff was all locked up and quiet now inside him. It was all settling down heavy in him, and these days when it was sinking so deep in him, it was only the rest and quiet of not fighting that he could really feel inside him. Jeff Campbell could not think now, or feel anything else in him. He had no beauty nor any goodness to see around him. It was a dull, pleasant kind of quiet he now had inside him. Jeff almost began to love this dull quiet in him, for it was more nearly being free for him than anything he had known in him since Melanctha Herbert first had moved him. He did not find it a real rest yet for him, he had not really conquered what had been working so long in him, he had not learned to see beauty and real goodness yet in what had happened to him, but it was rest even if he was sodden now all through him. Jeff Campbell liked it very well, not to have fighting always going on inside him.

And so Jeff went on every day, and he was quiet, and he began again to watch himself in his working; and he did not see any beauty now around him, and it was dull and heavy always now inside him, and yet he was content to have gone so far in keeping steady to what he knew was the right way for him to come back to, to be regular, and see beauty in every kind of quiet way of living, the way he had always wanted it for himself and for all the colored people. He knew he had lost the sense he once had of joy all through him, but he could work, and perhaps he would bring some real belief back into him about the beauty that he could not now any more see around him.

And so Jeff Campbell went on with his working, and he staid home every evening, and he began again with his reading, and he did not do much talking, and he did not seem to himself to have any kind of feeling.

And one day Jeff thought perhaps he really was forgetting, one day he thought he could soon come back and be happy in his old way of regular and quiet living.

Jeff Campbell had never talked to any one of what had been going on inside him. Jeff Campbell liked to talk and he was honest, but it never came out from him, anything he was ever really feeling, it only came out from him, what it was that he was always thinking. Jeff Campbell always was very proud to hide what he was really feeling. Always he blushed hot to think things he had been feeling. Only to Melanctha Herbert, had it ever come to him, to tell what it was that he was feeling.

And so Jeff Campbell went on with this dull and sodden, heavy, quiet always in him, and he never seemed to be able to have any feeling. Only sometimes he shivered hot with shame when he remembered some things he once had been feeling. And then one day it all woke up, and was sharp in him.

Dr. Campbell was just then staying long times with a sick man who might soon be dying. One day the sick man was resting. Dr. Campbell went to the window to look out a little, while he was waiting. It was very early now in the southern springtime. The trees were just beginning to get the little zigzag crinkles in them, which the young buds always give them. The air was soft and moist and pleasant to them. The earth was wet and rich and smelling for them. The birds were making sharp fresh noises all around them. The wind was very gentle and yet urgent to them. And the buds and the long earthworms, and the negroes, and all the kinds of children, were coming out every minute farther into the new spring, watery, southern sunshine.

Jeff Campbell too began to feel a little his old joy inside him. The sodden quiet began to break up in him. He leaned far out of the window to mix it all up with him. His heart went sharp and then it almost stopped inside him. Was it Melanctha Herbert he had just seen passing by him? Was it Melanctha, or was it just some other girl, who made him feel so bad inside him? Well, it was no matter, Melanctha was there in the world around him, he did certainly always know that in him. Melanctha Herbert was always in the same town with him, and he could never any more feel her near him. What a fool he was to throw her from him. Did he know she did not really love him. Suppose Melanctha was now suffering through him. Suppose she really would be glad to see him. And did anything else he did, really mean anything now to him? What a fool he was to cast her from him. And yet did Melanctha Herbert want him, was she honest to him, had Melanctha ever loved him, and did Melanctha now suffer by him? Oh! Oh! Oh! and the bitter water once more rose up in him.

All that long day, with the warm moist young spring stirring in him, Jeff Campbell worked, and thought, and beat his breast, and wandered, and spoke aloud, and was silent, and was certain, and then in doubt and then keen to surely feel, and then all sodden in him; and he walked, and he sometimes ran fast to lose himself in his rushing, and he bit his nails to pain and bleeding, and he tore his hair so that he could be sure he was really feeling, and he never could know what it was right, he now should be doing. And then late that night he wrote it all out to Melanctha Herbert, and he made himself quickly send it without giving himself any time to change it.

"It has come to me strong to-day Melanctha, perhaps I am wrong the way I now am thinking. Perhaps you do want me badly to be with you. Perhaps I have hurt you once again the way I used to. I certainly Melanctha, if I ever think that really, I certainly do want bad not to be wrong now ever any more to you. If you do feel the way to-day it came to me strong may-be you are feeling, then say so Melanctha to me, and I come again to see you. If not, don't say anything any more ever to me. I don't want ever to be bad to you Melanctha, really. I never want ever to be a bother to you. I never can stand it to think I am wrong; really, thinking you don't want me to come to you. Tell me Melanctha, tell me honest to me, shall I come now any more to see you." "Yes" came the answer from Melanctha, "I be home Jeff to-night to see you."

Jeff Campbell went that evening late to see Melanctha Herbert. As Jeff came nearer to her, he doubted that he wanted really to be with her, he felt that he did not know what it was he now wanted from her. Jeff Campbell knew very well now, way inside him, that they could never talk their trouble out between them. What was it Jeff wanted now to tell Melanctha Herbert? What was it that Jeff Campbell now could tell her? Surely he never now could learn to trust her. Surely Jeff knew very well all that Melanctha always had inside her. And yet it was awful, never any more to see her.

Jeff Campbell went in to Melanctha, and he kissed her, and he held her, and then he went away from her and he stood still and looked at her. "Well Jeff!" "Yes Melanctha!" "Jeff what was it made you act so to me?" "You know very well Melanctha, it's always I am thinking you don't love me, and you are acting to me good out of kindness, and then Melanctha you certainly never did say anything to me why you never came to meet me, as you certainly did promise to me you would that day I never saw you!" "Jeff don't you really know for certain, I always love you?" "No Melanctha, deed I don't know it in me. Deed and certain sure Melanctha, if I only know that in me, I certainly never would give you any bother." "Jeff, I certainly do love you more seems to me always, you certainly had ought to feel that in you." "Sure Melanctha?" "Sure Jeff boy, you know that." "But then Melanctha why did you act so to me?" "Oh Jeff you certainly been such a bother to me. I just had to go away that day Jeff, and I certainly didn't mean not to tell you, and then that letter you wrote came to me and something happened to me. I don't know right what it was Jeff, I just kind of fainted, and what could I do Jeff, you said you certainly never any more wanted to come and see me!" "And no matter Melanctha, even if you knew, it was just killing me to act so to you, you never would have said nothing to me?" "No of course, how could I Jeff when you wrote that way to me. I know how you was feeling Jeff to me, but I certainly couldn't say nothing to you." "Well Melanctha, I certainly know I am right proud too in me, but I certainly never could act so to you Melanctha, if I ever knew any way at all you ever really loved me. No Melanctha darling, you and me certainly don't feel much the same way ever. Any way Melanctha, I certainly do love you true Melanctha." "And I love you too Jeff, even though you don't never certainly seem to believe me." "No I certainly don't any way believe you Melanctha, even when you say it to me. I don't know Melanctha how, but sure I certainly do trust you, only I don't believe now ever in your really being loving to me. I certainly do know you trust me always Melanctha, only somehow it ain't ever all right to me. I certainly don't know any way otherwise Melanctha, how I can say it to you." "Well I certainly can't help you no ways any more Jeff Campbell, though you certainly say it right when you say I trust you Jeff now always. You certainly is the best man Jeff Campbell, I ever can know, to me. I never been anyways thinking it can be ever different to me." "Well you trust me then Melanctha, and I certainly love you Melanctha, and seems like to me Melanctha, you and me had ought to be a little better than we certainly ever are doing now to be together. You certainly do think that way, too, Melanctha to me. But may be you do really love me. Tell me, please, real honest now Melanctha darling, tell me so I really always know it in me, do you really truly love me?" "Oh you stupid, stupid boy, Jeff Campbell. Love you, what do you think makes me always to forgive you. If I certainly didn't always love you Jeff, I certainly never would let you be always being all the time such a bother to me the way you certainly Jeff always are to me. Now don't you dass ever any more say words like that ever to me. You hear me now Jeff, or I do something real bad sometime, so I really hurt you. Now Jeff you just be good to me. You know Jeff how bad I need it, now you should always be good to me!"

Jeff Campbell could not make an answer to Melanctha. What was it he should now say to her? What words could help him to make their feeling any better? Jeff Campbell knew that he had learned to love deeply, that, he always knew very well now in him, Melanctha had learned to be strong to be always trusting, that he knew too now inside him, but Melanctha did not really love him, that he felt always too strong for him. That fact always was there in him, and it always thrust itself firm, between them. And so this talk did not make things really better for them.

Jeff Campbell was never any more a torment to Melanctha, he was only silent to her. Jeff often saw Melanctha and he was very friendly with her and he never any more was a bother to her. Jeff never any more now had much chance to be loving with her. Melanctha never was alone now when he saw her.

Melanctha Herbert had just been getting thick in her trouble with Jeff Campbell, when she went to that church where she first met Rose, who later was married regularly to Sam Johnson. Rose was a good-looking, better kind of black girl, and had been brought up quite like their own child by white folks. Rose was living now with colored people. Rose was staying just then with a colored woman, who had known "Mis" Herbert and her black husband and this girl Melanctha.

Rose soon got to like Melanctha Herbert and Melanctha now always wanted to be with Rose, whenever she could do it. Melanctha Herbert always was doing everything for Rose that she could think of that Rose ever wanted. Rose always liked to be with nice people who would do things for her. Rose had strong common sense and she was lazy. Rose liked Melanctha Herbert, she had such kind of fine ways in her. Then, too, Rose had it in her to be sorry for the subtle, sweet-natured, docile, intelligent Melanctha Herbert who always was so blue sometimes, and always had had so much trouble. Then, too, Rose could scold Melanctha, for Melanctha Herbert never could know how to keep herself from trouble, and Rose was always strong to keep straight, with her simple selfish wisdom.

But why did the subtle, intelligent, attractive, half white girl Melanctha Herbert, with her sweetness and her power and her wisdom, demean herself to do for and to flatter and to be scolded, by this lazy, stupid, ordinary, selfish black girl. This was a queer thing in Melanctha Herbert.

And so now in these new spring days, it was with Rose that Melanctha began again to wander. Rose always knew very well in herself what was the right way to do when you wandered. Rose knew very well, she was not just any common kind of black girl, for she had been raised by white folks, and Rose always saw to it that she was engaged to him when she had any one man with whom she ever always wandered. Rose always had strong in her the sense for proper conduct. Rose always was telling the complex and less sure Melanctha, what was the right way she should do when she wandered.

Rose never knew much about Jeff Campbell with Melanctha Herbert. Rose had not known about Melanctha Herbert when she had been almost all her time with Dr. Campbell.

Jeff Campbell did not like Rose when he saw her with Melanctha. Jeff would never, when he could help it, meet her. Rose did not think much about Dr. Campbell. Melanctha never talked much about him to her. He was not important now to be with her.

Rose did not like Melanctha's old friend Jane Harden when she saw her. Jane despised Rose for an ordinary, stupid, sullen black girl. Jane could not see what Melanctha could find in that black girl, to endure her. It made Jane sick to see her. But then Melanctha had a good mind, but she certainly never did care much to really use it. Jane Harden now really never cared any more to see Melanctha, though Melanctha still always tried to be good to her. And Rose, she hated that stuck up, mean speaking, nasty, drunk thing, Jane Harden. Rose did not see how Melanctha could bear to ever see her, but Melanctha always was so good to everybody, she never would know how to act to people the way they deserved that she should do it.

Rose did not know much about Melanctha, and Jeff Campbell and Jane Harden. All Rose knew about Melanctha was her old life with her mother and her father. Rose was always glad to be good to poor Melanctha, who had had such an awful time with her mother and her father, and now she was alone and had nobody who could help her. "He was a awful black man to you Melanctha, I like to get my hands on him so he certainly could feel it. I just would Melanctha, now you hear me."

Perhaps it was this simple faith and simple anger and simple moral way of doing in Rose, that Melanctha now found such a comfort to her. Rose was selfish and was stupid and was lazy, but she was decent and knew always what was the right way she should do, and what she wanted, and she certainly did admire how bright was her friend Melanctha Herbert, and she certainly did feel how very much it was she always suffered and she scolded her to keep her from more trouble, and she never was angry when she found some of the different ways Melanctha Herbert sometimes had to do it.

And so always Rose and Melanctha

were more and more together, and Jeff Campbell could now hardly ever any more be alone with Melanctha.

Once Jeff had to go away to another town to see a sick man. "When I come back Monday Melanctha, I come Monday evening to see you. You be home alone once Melanctha to see me." "Sure Jeff, I be glad to see you."

When Jeff Campbell came to his house on Monday there was a note there from Melanctha. Could Jeff come day after to-morrow, Wednesday? Melanctha was so sorry she had to go out that evening. She was awful sorry and she hoped Jeff would not be angry.

Jeff was angry and he swore a little, and then he laughed, and then he sighed. "Poor Melanctha, she don't know any way to be real honest, but no matter, I sure do love her and I be good if only she will let me."

Jeff Campbell went Wednesday night to see Melanctha. Jeff Campbell took her in his arms and kissed her. "I certainly am awful sorry not to see you Jeff Monday, the way I promised, but I just couldn't Jeff, no way I could fix it." Jeff looked at her and then he laughed a little at her. "You want me to believe that really now Melanctha. All right I believe it if you want me to Melanctha. I certainly be good to you to-night the way you like it. I believe you certainly did want to see me Melanctha, and there was no way you could fix it." "Oh Jeff dear," said Melanctha, "I sure was wrong to act so to you. It's awful hard for me ever to say it to you, I have been wrong in my acting to you, but I certainly was bad this time Jeff to you. It do certainly come hard to me to say it Jeff, but I certainly was wrong to go away from you the way I did it. Only you always certainly been so bad Jeff, and such a bother to me, and making everything always so hard for me, and I certainly got some way to do it to make it come back sometimes to you. You bad boy Jeff, now you hear me, and this certainly is the first time Jeff I ever yet said it to anybody, I ever been wrong, Jeff, you hear me!" "All right Melanctha, I sure do forgive you, cause it's certainly the first time I ever heard you say you ever did anything wrong the way you shouldn't," and Jeff Campbell laughed and kissed her, and Melanctha laughed and loved him, and they really were happy now for a little time together.

And now they were very happy in each other and then they were silent and then they became a little sadder and then they were very quiet once more with each other.

"Yes I certainly do love you Jeff!" Melanctha said and she was very dreamy. "Sure, Melanctha." "Yes Jeff sure, but not the way you are now ever thinking. I love you more and more seems to me Jeff always, and I certainly do trust you more and more always to me when I know you. I do love you Jeff, sure yes, but not the kind of way of loving you are ever thinking it now Jeff with me. I ain't got certainly no hot passion any more now in me. You certainly have killed all that kind of feeling now Jeff in me. You certainly do know that Jeff, now the way I am always, when I am loving with you. You certainly do know that Jeff, and that's the way you certainly do like it now in me. You certainly don't mind now Jeff, to hear me say this to you."

Jeff Campbell was hurt so that it almost killed him. Yes he certainly did know now what it was to have real hot love in him, and yet Melanctha certainly was right, he did not deserve she should ever give it to him. "All right Melanctha I ain't ever kicking. I always will give you certainly always everything you want that I got in me. I take anything you want now to give me. I don't say never Melanctha it don't hurt me, but I certainly don't say ever Melanctha it ought ever to be any different to me."

And the bitter tears rose up in Jeff Campbell, and they came and choked his voice to be silent, and he held himself hard to keep from breaking.

"Good-night Melanctha," and Jeff was very humble to her. "Good-night Jeff, I certainly never did mean any way to hurt you. I do love you, sure Jeff every day more and more, all the time I know you." "I know Melanctha, I know, it's never nothing to me. You can't help it, anybody ever the way they are feeling. It's all right now Melanctha, you believe me, good-night now Melanctha, I got now to leave you, good-by Melanctha, sure don't look so worried to me, sure Melanctha I come again soon to see you." And then Jeff stumbled down the steps, and he went away fast to leave her.

And now the pain came hard and harder in Jeff Campbell, and he groaned, and it hurt him so, he could not bear it. And the tears came, and his heart beat, and he was hot and worn and bitter in him.

Now Jeff knew very well what it was to love Melanctha. Now Jeff Campbell knew he was really understanding. Now Jeff knew what it was to be good to Melanctha. Now Jeff was good to her always.

Slowly Jeff felt it a comfort in him to have it hurt so, and to be good to Melanctha always. Now there was no way Melanctha ever had had to bear things from him, worse than he now had it in him. Now Jeff was strong inside him. Now with all the pain there was peace in him. Now he knew he was understanding, now he knew he had a hot love in him, and he was good always to Melanctha Herbert who was the one had made him have it. Now he knew he could be good, and not cry out for help to her to teach him how to bear it. Every day Jeff felt himself more a strong man, the way he once had thought was his real self, the way he knew it. Now Jeff Campbell had real wisdom in him, and it did not make him bitter when it hurt him, for Jeff knew now all through him that he was really strong to bear it.

And so now Jeff Campbell could see Melanctha often, and he was patient, and always very friendly to her, and every day Jeff Campbell understood Melanctha Herbert better. And always Jeff saw Melanctha could not love him the way he needed she should do it. Melanctha Herbert had no way she ever really could remember.

And now Jeff knew there was a man Melanctha met very often, and perhaps she wanted to try to have this man to be good, for her. Jeff Campbell never saw the man Melanctha Herbert perhaps now wanted. Jeff Campbell only knew very well that there was one. Then there was Rose that Melanctha now always had with her when she wandered.

Jeff Campbell was very quiet to Melanctha. He said to her, now he thought he did not want to come any more especially to see her. When they met, he always would be glad to see her, but now he never would go anywhere any more to meet her. Sure he knew she always would have a deep love in him for her. Sure she knew that. "Yes Jeff, I always trust you Jeff, I certainly do know that all right." Jeff Campbell said, all right he never could say anything to reproach her. She knew always that he really had learned all through him how to love her. "Yes, Jeff, I certainly do know that." She knew now she could always trust him. Jeff always would be loyal to her though now she never was any more to him like a religion, but he never could forget the real sweetness in her. That Jeff must remember always, though now he never can trust her to be really loving to any man for always, she never did have any way she ever could remember. If she ever needed anybody to be good to her, Jeff Campbell always would do anything he could to help her. He never can forget the things she taught him so he could be really understanding, but he never any more wants to see her. He be like a brother to her always, when she needs it, and he always will be a good friend to her. Jeff Campbell certainly was sorry never any more to see her, but it was good that they now knew each other really. "Good-by Jeff you always been very good always to me." "Good-by Melanctha you know you always can trust yourself to me." "Yes, I know, I know Jeff, really." "I certainly got to go now Melanctha, from you. I go this time, Melanctha really," and Jeff Campbell went away and this time he never looked back to her. This time Jeff Campbell just broke away and left her.

Jeff Campbell loved to think now he was strong again to be quiet, and to live regular, and to do everything the way he wanted it to be right for himself and all the colored people. Jeff went away for a little while to another town to work there, and he worked hard, and he was very sad inside him, and sometimes the tears would rise up in him, and then he would work hard, and then he would begin once more to see some beauty in the world around him. Jeff had behaved right and he had learned to have a real love in him. That was very good to have inside him.

Jeff Campbell never could forget the sweetness in Melanctha Herbert, and he was always very friendly to her, but they never any more came close to one another. More and more Jeff Campbell and Melanctha fell away from all knowing of each other, but Jeff never could forget Melanctha. Jeff never could forget the real sweetness she had in her, but Jeff never any more had the sense of a real religion for her. Jeff always had strong in him the meaning of all the new kind of beauty Melanctha Herbert once had shown him, and always more and more it helped him with his working for himself and for all the colored people.

Melanctha Herbert, now that she was all through with Jeff Campbell, was free to be with Rose and the new men she met now.

Rose was always now with Melanctha Herbert. Rose never found any way to get excited. Rose always was telling Melanctha Herbert the right way she should do, so that she would not always be in trouble. But Melanctha Herbert could not help it, always she would find new ways to get excited.

Melanctha was all ready now to find new ways to be in trouble. And yet Melanctha Herbert never wanted not to do right. Always Melanctha Herbert wanted peace and quiet, and always she could only find new ways to get excited.

"Melanctha," Rose would say to her, "Melanctha, I certainly have got to tell you, you ain't right to act so with that kind of feller. You better just had stick to black men now, Melanctha, you hear me what I tell you, just the way you always see me do it. They're real bad men, now I tell you Melanctha true, and you better had hear to me. I been raised by real nice kind of white folks, Melanctha, and I certainly knows awful well, soon as ever I can see 'em acting, what is a white man will act decent to you and the kind it ain't never no good to a colored girl to ever go with. Now you know real Melanctha how I always mean right good to you, and you ain't got no way like me Melanctha, what was raised by white folks, to know right what is the way you should be acting with men. I don't never want to see you have bad trouble come hard to you now Melanctha, and so you just hear to me now Melanctha, what I tell you, for I knows it. I don't say never certainly to you Melanctha, you never had ought to have nothing to do ever with no white men, though it ain't never to me Melanctha, the best kind of a way a colored girl can have to be acting, no I never do say to you Melanctha, you hadn't never ought to be with white men, though it ain't never the way I feel it ever real right for a decent colored girl to be always doing, but not never Melanctha, now you hear me, no not never no kind of white men like you been with always now Melanctha when I see you. You just hear to me Melanctha, you certainly had ought to hear to me Melanctha, I say it just like I knows it awful well, Melanctha, and I knows you don't know no better, Melanctha, how to act so, the ways I seen it with them kind of white fellers, them as never can know what to do right by a decent girl they have ever got to be with them. Now you hear to me Melanctha, what I tell you."

And so it was Melanctha Herbert found new ways to be in trouble. But it was not very bad this trouble, for these white men Rose never wanted she should be with, never meant very much to Melanctha. It was only that she liked it to be with them, and they knew all about fine horses, and it was just good to Melanctha, now a little, to feel real reckless with them. But mostly it was Rose and other better kind of colored girls and colored men with whom Melanctha Herbert now always wandered.

It was summer now and the colored people came out into the sunshine, full blown with the flowers. And they shone in the streets and in the fields with their warm joy, and they glistened in their black heat, and they flung themselves free in their wide abandonment of shouting laughter.

It was very pleasant in some ways, the life Melanctha Herbert now led with Rose and all the others. It was not always that Rose had to scold her.

There was not anybody of all these colored people, excepting only Rose, who ever meant much to Melanctha Herbert. But they all liked Melanctha, and the men all liked to see her do things, she was so game always to do anything anybody ever could do, and then she was good and sweet to do anything anybody ever wanted from her.

These were pleasant days then, in the hot southern negro sunshine, with many simple jokes and always wide abandonment of laughter. "Just look at that Melanctha there a running. Don't she just go like a bird when she is flying. Hey Melanctha there, I come and catch you, hey Melanctha, I put salt on your tail to catch you," and then the man would try to catch her, and he would fall full on the earth and roll in an agony of wide-mouthed shouting laughter. And this was the kind of way Rose always liked to have Melanctha do it, to be engaged to him, and to have a good warm nigger time with colored men, not to go about with that kind of white man, never could know how to act right, to any decent kind of girl they could ever get to be with them.

Rose, always more and more, liked Melanctha Herbert better. Rose often had to scold Melanctha Herbert, but that only made her like Melanctha better. And then Melanctha always listened to her, and always acted every way she could to please her. And then Rose was so sorry for Melanctha, when she was so blue sometimes, and wanted somebody should come and kill her.

And Melanctha Herbert clung to Rose in the hope that Rose could save her. Melanctha felt the power of Rose's selfish, decent kind of nature. It was so solid, simple, certain to her. Melanctha clung to Rose, she loved to have her scold her, she always wanted to be with her. She always felt a solid safety in her. Rose always was, in her way, very good to let Melanctha be loving to her. Melanctha never had any way she could really be a trouble to her. Melanctha never had any way that she could ever get real power, to come close inside to her. Melanctha was always very humble to her. Melanctha was always ready to do anything Rose wanted from her. Melanctha needed badly to have Rose always willing to let Melanctha cling to her. Rose was a simple, sullen, selfish, black girl, but she had a solid power in her. Rose had strong the sense of decent conduct, she had strong the sense for decent comfort. Rose always knew very well what it was she wanted, and she knew very well what was the right way to do to get everything she wanted, and she never had any kind of trouble to perplex her. And so the subtle intelligent attractive half white girl Melanctha Herbert loved and did for, and demeaned herself in service to this coarse, decent, sullen, ordinary, black, childish Rose and now this unmoral promiscuous shiftless Rose was to be married to a good man of the negroes, while Melanctha Herbert with her white blood and attraction and her desire for a right position was perhaps never to be really regularly married. Sometimes the thought of how all her world was made filled the complex, desiring Melanctha with despair. She wondered often how she could go on living when she was so blue. Sometimes Melanctha thought she would just kill herself, for sometimes she thought this would be really the best thing for her to do.

Rose was now to be married to a decent good man of the negroes. His name was Sam Johnson, and he worked as a deck-hand on a coasting steamer, and he was very steady, and he got good wages.

Rose first met Sam Johnson at church, the same place where she had met Melanctha Herbert. Rose liked Sam when she saw him, she knew he was a good man and worked hard and got good wages, and Rose thought it would be very nice and very good now in her position to get really, regularly married.

Sam Johnson liked Rose very well and he always was ready to do anything she wanted. Sam was a tall, square shouldered, decent, a serious, straightforward, simple, kindly, colored workman. They got on very well together, Sam and Rose, when they were married. Rose was lazy, but not dirty, and Sam was careful but not fussy. Sam was a kindly, simple, earnest, steady workman, and Rose had good common decent sense in her, of how to live regular, and not to have excitements, and to be saving so you could be always sure to have money, so as to have everything you wanted.

It was not very long that Rose knew Sam Johnson, before they were regularly married. Sometimes Sam went into the country with all the other young church people, and then he would be a great deal with Rose and with her Melanctha Herbert. Sam did not care much about Melanctha Herbert. He liked Rose's ways of doing, always better. Melanctha's mystery had no charm for Sam ever. Sam wanted a nice little house to come to when he was tired from his working, and a little baby all his own he could be good to. Sam Johnson was ready to marry as soon as ever Rose wanted he should do it. And so Sam Johnson and Rose one day had a grand real wedding and were married. Then they furnished completely, a little red brick house and then Sam went back to his work as deck hand on a coasting steamer.

Rose had often talked to Sam about how good Melanctha was and how much she always suffered. Sam Johnson never really cared about Melanctha Herbert, but he always did almost everything Rose ever wanted, and he was a gentle, kindly creature, and so he was very good to Rose's friend Melanctha. Melanctha Herbert knew very well Sam did not like her, and so she was very quiet, and always let Rose do the talking for her. She only was very good to always help Rose, and to do anything she ever wanted from her, and to be very good and listen and be quiet whenever Sam had anything to say to her. Melanctha liked Sam Johnson, and all her life Melanctha loved and wanted good and kind and considerate people, and always Melanctha loved and wanted people to be gentle to her, and always she wanted to be regular, and to have peace and quiet in her, and always Melanctha could only find new ways to be in trouble. And Melanctha needed badly to have Rose, to believe her, and to let her cling to her. Rose was the only steady thing Melanctha had to cling to and so Melanctha demeaned herself to be like a servant, to wait on, and always to be scolded, by this ordinary, sullen, black, stupid, childish woman.

Rose was always telling Sam he must be good to poor Melanctha. "You know Sam," Rose said very often to him, "You certainly had ought to be very good to poor Melanctha, she always do have so much trouble with her. You know Sam how I told you she had such a bad time always with that father, and he was awful mean to her always that awful black man, and he never took no kind of care ever to her, and he never helped her when her mother died so hard, that poor Melanctha. Melanctha's ma you know Sam, always was just real religious. One day Melanctha was real little, and she heard her ma say to her pa, it was awful sad to her, Melanctha had not been the one the Lord had took from them stead of the little brother who was dead in the house there from fever. That hurt Melanctha awful when she heard her ma say it. She never could feel it right, and I don't no ways blame Melanctha, Sam, for not feeling better to her ma always after, though Melanctha, just like always she is, always was real good to her ma after, when she was so sick, and died so hard, and nobody never to help Melanctha do it, and she just all alone to do everything without no help come to her no way, and that ugly awful black man she have for a father never all the time come near her. But that's always the way Melanctha is just doing Sam, the way I been telling to you. She always is being just so good to everybody and nobody ever there to thank her for it. I never did see nobody ever Sam, have such bad luck, seems to me always with them, like that poor Melanctha always has it, and she always so good with it, and never no murmur in her, and never no complaining from her, and just never saying nothing with it. You be real good to her Sam, now you hear me, now you and me is married right together. He certainly was an awful black man to her Sam, that father she had, acting always just like a brute to her and she so game and never to tell anybody how it hurt her. And she so sweet and good always to do anything anybody ever can be wanting. I don't see Sam how some men can be to act so awful. I told you Sam, how once Melanctha broke her arm bad and she was so sick and it hurt her awful and he never would let no doctor come near to her and he do some things so awful to her, she don't never want to tell nobody how bad he hurt her. That's just the way Sam with Melanctha always, you never can know how bad it is, it hurts her. You hear me Sam, you always be real good to her now you and me is married right to each other."

And so Rose and Sam Johnson were regularly married, and Rose sat at home and bragged to all her friends how nice it was to married really to a husband.

Rose did not have Melanctha to live with her, now Rose was married. Melanctha was with Rose almost as much as ever but it was a little different now their being together.

Rose Johnson never asked Melanctha to live with her in the house, now Rose was married. Rose liked to have Melanctha come all the time to help her, Rose liked Melanctha to be almost always with her, but Rose was shrewd in her simple selfish nature, she did not ever think to ask Melanctha to live with her.

Rose was hard headed, she was decent, and she always knew what it was she needed. Rose needed Melanctha to be with her, she liked to have her help her, the quick, good Melanctha to do for the slow, lazy, selfish, black girl, but Rose could have Melanctha to do for her and she did not need her to live with her.

Sam never asked Rose why she did not have her. Sam always took what Rose wanted should be done for Melanctha, as the right way he should act toward her.

It could never come to Melanctha to ask Rose to let her. It never could come to Melanctha to think that Rose would ask her. It would never ever come to Melanctha to want it, if Rose should ask her, but Melanctha would have done it for the safety she always felt when she was near her. Melanctha Herbert wanted badly to be safe now, but this living with her, that, Rose would never give her. Rose had strong the sense for decent comfort, Rose had strong the sense for proper conduct, Rose had strong the sense to get straight always what she wanted, and she always knew what was the best thing she needed, and always Rose got what she wanted.

And so Rose had Melanctha Herbert always there to help her, and she sat and was lazy and she bragged and she complained a little and she told Melanctha how she ought to do, to get good what she wanted like she Rose always did it, and always Melanctha was doing everything Rose ever needed. "Don't you bother so, doing that Melanctha, I do it or Sam when he comes home to help me. Sure you don't mind lifting it Melanctha? You is very good Melanctha to do it, and when you go out Melanctha, you stop and get some rice to bring me tomorrow when you come in. Sure you won't forget Melanctha. I never see anybody like you Melanctha to always do things so nice for me." And then Melanctha would do some more for Rose, and then very late Melanctha would go home to the colored woman where she lived now.

And so though Melanctha still was so much with Rose Johnson, she had times when she could not stay there. Melanctha now could not really cling there. Rose had Sam, and Melanctha more and more lost the hold she had had there.

Melanctha Herbert began to feel she must begin again to look and see if she could find what it was she had always wanted. Now Rose Johnson could no longer help her.

And so Melanctha Herbert began once more to wander and with men Rose never thought it was right she should be with.

One day Melanctha had been very busy with the different kinds of ways she wandered. It was a pleasant late afternoon at the end of a long summer. Melanctha was walking along, and she was free and excited. Melanctha had just parted from a white man and she had a bunch of flowers he had left with her. A young buck, a mulatto, passed by and snatched them from her. "It certainly is real sweet in you sister, to be giving me them pretty flowers," he said to her.

"I don't see no way it can make them sweeter to have with you," said Melanctha. "What one man gives, another man had certainly just as much good right to be taking." "Keep your old flowers then, I certainly don't never want to have them." Melanctha Herbert laughed at him and took them. "No, I didn't nohow think you really did want to have them. Thank you kindly mister, for them. I certainly always do admire to see a man always so kind of real polite to people." The man laughed, "You ain't nobody's fool I can say for you, but you certainly are a damned pretty kind of girl, now I look at you. Want men to be polite to you? All right, I can love you, that's real polite now, want to see me try it." "I certainly ain't got no time this evening just only left to thank you. I certainly got to be real busy now, but I certainly always will admire to see you." The man tried to catch and stop her, Melanctha Herbert laughed and dodged so that he could not touch her. Melanctha went quickly down a side street near her and so the man for that time lost her.

For some days Melanctha did not see any more of her mulatto. One day Melanctha was with a white man and they saw him. The white man stopped to speak to him. Afterwards Melanctha left the white man and she then soon met him. Melanctha stopped to talk to him. Melanctha Herbert soon began to like him.

Jem Richards, the new man Melanctha had begun to know now, was a dashing kind of fellow, who had to do with fine horses and with racing. Sometimes Jem Richards would be betting and would be good and lucky, and be making lots of money. Sometimes Jem would be betting badly, and then he would not be having any money.

Jem Richards was a straight man. Jem Richards always knew that by and by he would win again and pay it, and so Jem mostly did win again, and then he always paid it.

Jem Richards was a man other men always trusted. Men gave him money when he lost all his, for they all knew Jem Richards would win again, and when he did win they knew, and they were right, that he would pay it.

Melanctha Herbert all her life had always loved to be with horses. Melanctha liked it that Jem knew all about fine horses. He was a reckless man was Jem Richards. He knew how to win out, and always all her life, Melanctha Herbert loved successful power.

Melanctha Herbert always liked Jem Richards better. Things soon began to be very strong between them.

Jem was more game even than Melanctha. Jem always had known what it was to have real wisdom. Jem had always all his life been understanding.

Jem Richards made Melanctha Herbert come fast with him. He never gave her any time with waiting. Soon Melanctha always had Jem with her. Melanctha did not want anything better. Now in Jem Richards, Melanctha found everything she had ever needed to content her.

Melanctha was now less and less with Rose Johnson. Rose did not think much of the way Melanctha now was going. Jem Richards was all right, only Melanctha never had no sense of the right kind of way she should be doing. Rose often was telling Sam now, she did not like the fast way Melanctha was going. Rose told it to Sam, and to all the girls and men, when she saw them. But Rose was nothing just then to Melanctha. Melanctha Herbert now only needed Jem Richards to be with her.

And things were always getting stronger between Jem Richards and Melanctha Herbert. Jem Richards began to talk now as if he wanted to get married to her. Jem was deep in his love now for her. And as for Melanctha, Jem was all the world now to her. And so Jem gave her a ring, like white folks, to show he was engaged to her, and would by and by be married to her. And Melanctha was filled with joy to have Jem so good to her.

Melanctha always loved to go with Jem to the races. Jem had been lucky lately with his betting, and he had a swell turn-out to drive in, and Melanctha looked very handsome there beside him.

Melanctha was very proud to have Jem Richards want her. Melanctha loved it the way Jem knew how to do it. Melanctha loved Jem and loved that he should want her. She loved it too, that he wanted to be married to her. Jem Richards was a straight decent man, whom other men always looked up to and trusted. Melanctha needed badly a man to content her.

Melanctha's joy made her foolish. Melanctha told everybody about how Jem Richards, that swell man who owned all those fine horses and was so game, nothing ever scared him, was engaged to be married to her, and that was the ring he gave her.

Melanctha let out her joy very often to Rose Johnson. Melanctha had begun again now to go there.

Melanctha's love for Jem made her foolish. Melanctha had to have some one always now to talk to and so she went often to Rose Johnson.

Melanctha put all herself into Jem Richards. She was mad and foolish in the joy she had there.

Rose never liked the way Melanctha did it. "No Sam I don't say never Melanctha ain't engaged to Jem Richards the way she always says it, and Jem he is all right for that kind of a man he is, though he do think himself so smart and like he owns the earth and everything he can get with it, and he sure gave Melanctha a ring like he really meant he should be married right soon with it, only Sam, I don't ever like it the way Melanctha is going. When she is engaged to him Sam, she ain't not right to take on so excited. That ain't no decent kind of a way a girl ever should be acting. There ain't no kind of a man going stand that, not like I knows men Sam, and I sure does know them. I knows them white and I knows them colored, for I was raised by white folks, and they don't none of them like a girl to act so. That's all right to be so when you is just only loving, but it ain't no ways right to be acting so when you is engaged to him, and when he says, all right he get really regularly married to you. You see Sam I am right like I am always and I knows it. Jem Richards, he ain't going to the last to get real married, not if I knows it right, the way Melanctha now is acting to him. Rings or anything ain't nothing to them, and they don't never do no good for them, when a girl acts foolish like Melanctha always now is acting. I certainly will be right sorry Sam, if Melanctha has real bad trouble come now to her, but I certainly don't no ways like it Sam the kind of way Melanctha is acting to him. I don't never say nothing to her Sam. I just listens to what she is saying always, and I thinks it out like I am telling to you Sam but I don't never say nothing no more now to Melanctha. Melanctha didn't say nothing to me about that Jem Richards till she was all like finished with him, and I never did like it Sam, much, the way she was acting, not coming here never when she first ran with those men and met him. And I didn't never say nothing to her, Sam, about it, and it ain't nothing ever to me, only I don't never no more want to say nothing to her, so I just listens to what she got to tell like she wants it. No Sam, I don't never want to say nothing to her. Melanctha just got to go her own way, not as I want to see her have bad trouble ever come hard to her, only it ain't in me never Sam, after Melanctha did so, ever to say nothing more to her how she should be acting. You just see Sam like I tell you, what way Jem Richards will act to her, you see Sam I just am right like I always am when I knows it."

Melanctha Herbert never thought she could ever again be in trouble. Melanctha's joy had made her foolish.

And now Jem Richards had some bad trouble with his betting. Melanctha sometimes felt now when she was with him that there was something wrong inside him. Melanctha knew he had had trouble with his betting but Melanctha never felt that that could make any difference to them.

Melanctha once had told Jem, sure he knew she always would love to be with him, if he was in jail or only just a beggar. Now Melanctha said to him, "Sure you know Jem that it don't never make any kind of difference you're having any kind of trouble, you just try me Jem and be game, don't look so worried to me. Jem sure I know you love me like I love you always, and its all I ever could be wanting Jem to me, just your wanting me always to be with you. I get married Jem to you soon ever as you can want me, if you once say it Jem to me. It ain't nothing to me ever, anything like having any money Jem, why you look so worried to me."

Melanctha Herbert's love had surely made her mad and foolish. She thrust it always deep into Jem Richards and now that he had trouble with his betting, Jem had no way that he ever wanted to be made to feel it. Jem Richards never could want to marry any girl while he had trouble. That was no way a man like him should do it. Melanctha's love had made her mad and foolish, she should be silent now and let him do it. Jem Richards was not a kind of man to want a woman to be strong to him, when he was in trouble with his betting. That was not the kind of a time when a man like him needed to have it.

Melanctha needed so badly to have it, this love which she had always wanted, she did not know what she should do to save it. Melanctha saw now, Jem Richards always had something wrong inside him. Melanctha soon dared not ask him. Jem was busy now, he had to sell things and see men to raise money. Jem could not meet Melanctha now so often.

It was lucky for Melanctha Herbert that Rose Johnson was coming now to have her baby. It had always been understood between them, Rose should come and stay then in the house where Melanctha lived with an old colored woman, so that Rose could have the Doctor from the hospital near by to help her, and Melanctha there to take care of her the way Melanctha always used to do it.

Melanctha was very good now to Rose Johnson. Melanctha did everything that any woman could, she tended Rose, and she was patient, submissive, soothing and untiring, while the sullen, childish, cowardly, black Rosie grumbled, and fussed, and howled, and made herself to be an abomination and like a simple beast.

All this time Melanctha was always being every now and then with Jem Richards. Melanctha was beginning to be stronger with Jem Richards. Melanctha was never so strong and sweet and in her nature as when she was deep in trouble, when she was fighting so with all she had, she could not do any foolish thing with her nature.

Always now Melanctha Herbert came back again to be nearer to Rose Johnson. Always now Melanctha would tell all about her troubles to Rose Johnson. Rose had begun now a little again to advise her.

Melanctha always told Rose now about the talks she had with Jem Richards, talks where they neither of them liked very well what the other one was saying. Melanctha did not know what it was Jem Richards wanted. All Melanctha knew was, he did not like it when she wanted to be good friends and get really married, and then when Melanctha would say, "all right, I never wear your ring no more Jem, we ain't not any more to meet ever like we ever going to get really regular married," then Jem did not like it either. What was it Jem Richards really wanted?

Melanctha stopped wearing Jem's ring on her finger. Poor Melanctha, she wore it on a string she tied around her neck so that she could always feel it, but Melanctha was strong now with Jem Richards, and he never saw it. And sometimes Jem seemed to be awful sorry for it, and sometimes he seemed kind of glad of it. Melanctha never could make out really what it was Jem Richards wanted.

There was no other woman yet to Jem, that Melanctha knew, and so she always trusted that Jem would come back to her, deep in his love, the way once he had had it and had made all the world like she once had never believed anybody could really make it. But Jem Richards was more game than Melanctha Herbert. He knew how to fight to win out, better. Melanctha really had already lost it, in not keeping quiet and waiting for Jem to do it.

Jem Richards was not yet having better luck in his betting. He never before had had such a long time without some good coming to him in his betting. Sometimes Jem talked as if he wanted to go off on a trip somewhere and try some other place for luck with his betting. Jem Richards never talked as if he wanted to take Melanctha with him.

And so Melanctha sometimes was really trusting, and sometimes she was all sick inside her with her doubting. What was it Jem really wanted to do with her? He did not have any other woman, in that Melanctha could be really trusting and when she said no to him, no she never would come near him, now he did not want to have her, then Jem would change and swear, yes sure he did want her, now and always right here near him, but he never now any more said he wanted to be married soon to her. But then Jem Richards never would marry a girl, he said that very often, when he was in this kind of trouble, and now he did not see any way he could get out of his trouble. But Melanctha ought to wear his ring, sure she knew he never had loved any kind of woman like he loved her. Melanctha would wear the ring a little while, and then they would have some more trouble, and then she would say to him, no she certainly never would any more wear anything he gave her, and then she would wear it on the string so nobody could see it but she could always feel it on her.

Poor Melanctha, surely her love had made her mad and foolish.

And now Melanctha needed always more and more to be with Rose Johnson, and Rose had commenced again to advise her, but Rose could not help her. There was no way now that anybody could advise her. The time when Melanctha could have changed it with Jem Richards was now all past for her. Rose knew it, and Melanctha too, she knew it, and it almost killed her to let herself believe it.

The only comfort Melanctha ever had now was waiting on Rose till she was so tired she could hardly stand it. Always Melanctha did everything Rose ever wanted. Sam Johnson began now to be very gentle and a little tender to Melanctha. She was so good to Rose and Sam was so glad to have her there to help Rose and to do things and to be a comfort to her.

Rose had a hard time to bring her baby to its birth and Melanctha did everything that any woman could.

The baby though it was healthy after it was born did not live long. Rose Johnson was careless and negligent and selfish and when Melanctha had to leave for a few days the baby died. Rose Johnson had liked her baby well enough and perhaps she just forgot it for a while, anyway the child was dead and Rose and Sam were very sorry, but then these things came so often in the negro world in Bridgepoint that they neither of them thought about it very long. When Rose had become strong again she went back to her house with Sam. And Sam Johnson was always now very gentle and kind and good to Melanctha who had been so good to Rose in her bad trouble.

Melanctha Herbert's troubles with Jem Richards were never getting any better. Jem always now had less and less time to be with her. When Jem was with Melanctha now he was good enough to her. Jem Richards was worried with his betting. Never since Jem had first begun to make a living had he ever had so much trouble for such a long time together with his betting. Jem Richards was good enough now to Melanctha but he had not much strength to give her. Melanctha could never any more now make him quarrel with her. Melanctha never now could complain of his treatment of her, for surely, he said it always by his actions to her, surely she must know how a man was when he had trouble on his mind with trying to make things go a little better.

Sometimes Jem and Melanctha had long talks when they neither of them liked very well what the other one was saying, but mostly now Melanctha could not make Jem Richards quarrel with her, and more and more, Melanctha could not find any way to make it right to blame him for the trouble she now always had inside her. Jem was good to her, and she knew, for he told her, that he had trouble all the time now with his betting. Melanctha knew very well that for her it was all wrong inside Jem Richards, but Melanctha had now no way that she could really reach him.

Things between Melanctha and Jem Richards were now never getting any better. Melanctha now more and more needed to be with Rose Johnson. Rose still liked to have Melanctha come to her house and do things for her, and Rose liked to grumble to her and to scold her and to tell Melanctha what was the way Melanctha always should be doing so she could make things come out better and not always be so much in trouble. Sam Johnson in these days was always very good and gentle to Melanctha. Sam was now beginning to be very sorry for her.

Jem Richards never made things any better for Melanctha. Often Jem would talk so as to make Melanctha almost certain that he never any more wanted to have her. Then Melanctha would get very blue, and she would say to Rose, sure she would kill herself, for that certainly now was the best way she could do.

Rose Johnson never saw it the least bit that way. "I don't see Melanctha why you should talk like you would kill yourself just because you're blue. I'd never kill myself Melanctha cause I was blue. I'd maybe kill somebody else but I'd never kill myself. If I ever killed myself, Melanctha it'd be by accident and if I ever killed myself by accident, Melanctha, I'd be awful sorry. And that certainly is the way you should feel it Melanctha, now you hear me, not just talking foolish like you always do. It certainly is only your way just always being foolish makes you all that trouble to come to you always now, Melanctha, and I certainly right well knows that. You certainly never can learn no way Melanctha ever with all I certainly been telling to you, ever since I know you good, that it ain't never no way like you do always is the right way you be acting ever and talking, the way I certainly always have seen you do so Melanctha always. I certainly am right Melanctha about them ways you have to do it, and I knows it; but you certainly never can noways learn to act right Melanctha, I certainly do know that, I certainly do my best Melanctha to help you with it only you certainly never do act right Melanctha, not to nobody ever, I can see it. You never act right by me Melanctha no more than by everybody. I never say nothing to you Melanctha when you do so, for I certainly never do like it when I just got to say it to you, but you just certainly done with that Jem Richards you always say wanted real bad to be married to you, just like I always said to Sam you certainly was going to do it. And I certainly am real kind of sorry like for you Melanctha, but you certainly had ought to have come to see me to talk to you, when you first was engaged to him so I could show you, and now you got all this trouble come to you Melanctha like I certainly know you always catch it. It certainly ain't never

Melanctha I ain't real sorry to see trouble come so hard to you, but I certainly can see Melanctha it all is always just the way you always be having it in you not never to do right. And now you always talk like you just kill yourself because you are so blue, that certainly never is Melanctha, no kind of a way for any decent kind of a girl to do."

Rose had begun to be strong now to scold Melanctha and she was impatient very often with her, but Rose could now never any more be a help to her. Melanctha Herbert never could know now what it was right she should do. Melanctha always wanted to have Jem Richards with her and now he never seemed to want her, and what could Melanctha do. Surely she was right now when she said she would just kill herself, for that was the only way now she could do.

Sam Johnson always, more and more, was good and gentle to Melanctha. Poor Melanctha, she was so good and sweet to do anything anybody ever wanted, and Melanctha always liked it if she could have peace and quiet, and always she could only find new ways to be in trouble. Sam often said this now to Rose about Melanctha.

"I certainly don't never want Sam to say bad things about Melanctha, for she certainly always do have most awful kind of trouble come hard to her, but I never can say I like it real right Sam the way Melanctha always has to do it. Its now just the same with her like it is always she has got to do it, now the way she is with that Jem Richards. He certainly now don't never want to have her but Melanctha she ain't got no right kind of spirit. No Sam I don't never like the way any more Melanctha is acting to him, and then Sam, she ain't never real right honest, the way she always should do it. She certainly just don't kind of never Sam tell right what way she is doing with it. I don't never like to say nothing Sam no more to her about the way she always has to be acting. She always say, yes all right Rose, I do the way you say it, and then Sam she don't never noways do it. She certainly is right sweet and good, Sam, is Melanctha, nobody ever can hear me say she ain't always ready to do things for everybody in any way she ever can see to do it, only Sam some ways she never does act real right ever, and some ways, Sam, she ain't ever real honest with it. And Sam sometimes I hear awful kind of things she been doing, some girls know about her how she does it, and sometimes they tell me what kind of ways she has to do it, and Sam it certainly do seem to me like more and more I certainly am awful afraid Melanctha never will come to any good. And then Sam, sometimes, you hear it, she always talk like she kill herself all the time she is so blue, and Sam that certainly never is no kind of way any decent girl ever had ought to do. You see Sam, how I am right like I always is when I knows it. You just be careful, Sam, now you hear me, you be careful Sam sure, I tell you, Melanctha more and more I see her I certainly do feel Melanctha no way is really honest. You be careful, Sam now, like I tell you, for I knows it, now you hear to me, Sam, what I tell you, for I certainly always is right, Sam, when I knows it."

At first Sam tried a little to defend Melanctha, and Sam always was good and gentle to her, and Sam liked the ways Melanctha had to be quiet to him, and to always listen as if she was learning, when she was there and heard him talking, and then Sam liked the sweet way she always did everything so nicely for him; but Sam never liked to fight with anybody ever, and surely Rose knew best about Melanctha and anyway Sam never did really care much about Melanctha. Her mystery never had had any interest for him. Sam liked it that she was sweet to him and that she always did everything Rose ever wanted that she should be doing, but Melanctha never could be important to him. All Sam ever wanted was to have a little house and to live regular and to work hard and to come home to his dinner, when he was tired with his working and by and by he wanted to have some children all his own to be good to, and so Sam was real sorry for Melanctha, she was so good and so sweet always to them, and Jem Richards was a bad man to behave so to her, but that was always the way a girl got it when she liked that kind of a fast fellow. Anyhow Melanctha was Rose's friend, and Sam never cared to have anything to do with the kind of trouble always came to women, when they wanted to have men, who never could know how to behave good and steady to their women.

And so Sam never said much to Rose about Melanctha. Sam was always very gentle to her, but now he began less and less to see her. Soon Melanctha never came any more to the house to see Rose and Sam never asked Rose anything about her.

Melanctha Herbert was beginning now to come less and less to the house to be with Rose Johnson. This was because Rose seemed always less and less now to want her, and Rose would not let Melanctha now do things for her. Melanctha was always humble to her and Melanctha always wanted in every way she could to do things for her. Rose said no, she guessed she do that herself like she likes to have it better. Melanctha is real good to stay so long to help her, but Rose guessed perhaps Melanctha better go home now, Rose don't need nobody to help her now, she is feeling real strong, not like just after she had all that trouble with the baby, and then Sam, when he comes home for his dinner he likes it when Rose is all alone there just to give him his dinner. Sam always is so tired now, like he always is in the summer, so many people always on the steamer, and they make so much work so Sam is real tired now, and he likes just to eat his dinner and never have people in the house to be a trouble to him.

Each day Rose treated Melanctha more and more as if she never wanted Melanctha any more to come there to the house to see her. Melanctha dared not ask Rose why she acted in this way to her. Melanctha badly needed to have Rose always there to save her. Melanctha wanted badly to cling to her and Rose had always been so solid for her. Melanctha did not dare to ask Rose if she now no longer wanted her to come and see her.

Melanctha now never any more had Sam to be gentle to her. Rose always sent Melanctha away from her before it was time for Sam to come home to her. One day Melanctha had stayed a little longer, for Rose that day had been good to let Melanctha begin to do things for her. Melanctha then left her and Melanctha met Sam Johnson who stopped a minute to speak kindly to her.

The next day Rose Johnson would not let Melanctha come in to her. Rose stood on the steps, and there she told Melanctha what she thought now of her.

"I guess Melanctha it certainly ain't no ways right for you to come here no more just to see me. I certainly don't Melanctha no ways like to be a trouble to you. I certainly think Melanctha I get along better now when I don't have nobody like you are, always here to help me, and Sam he do so good now with his working, he pay a little girl something to come every day to help me. I certainly do think Melanctha I don't never want you no more to come here just to see me." "Why Rose, what I ever done to you, I certainly don't think you is right Rose to be so bad now to me." "I certainly don't no ways Melanctha

Herbert think you got any right ever to be complaining the way I been acting to you. I certainly never do think Melanctha Herbert, you hear to me, nobody ever been more patient to you than I always been to like you, only Melanctha, I hear more things now so awful bad about you, everybody always is telling to me what kind of a way you always have been doing so much, and me always so good to you, and you never no ways, knowing how to be honest to me. No Melanctha it ain't ever in me, not to want you to have good luck come to you, and I like it real well Melanctha when you some time learn how to act the way it is decent and right for a girl to be doing, but I don't no ways ever like it the kind of things everybody tell me now about you. No Melanctha, I can't never any more trust you. I certainly am real sorry to have never any more to see you, but there ain't no other way, I ever can be acting to you. That's all I ever got any more to say to you now Melanctha." "But Rose, deed; I certainly don't know, no more than the dead, nothing I ever done to make you act so to me. Anybody say anything bad about me Rose, to you, they just a pack of liars to you, they certainly is Rose, I tell you true. I certainly never done nothing I ever been ashamed to tell you. Why you act so bad to me Rose. Sam he certainly don't think ever like you do, and Rose I always do everything I can, you ever want me to do for you." "It ain't never no use standing there talking, Melanctha Herbert. I just can tell it to you, and Sam, he don't know nothing about women ever the way they can be acting. I certainly am very sorry Melanctha, to have to act so now to you, but I certainly can't do no other way with you, when you do things always so bad, and everybody is talking so about you. It ain't no use to you to stand there and say it different to me Melanctha. I certainly am always right Melanctha Herbert, the way I certainly always have been when I knows it, to you. No Melanctha, it just is, you never can have no kind of a way to act right, the way a decent girl has to do, and I done my best always to be telling it to you Melanctha Herbert, but it don't never do no good to tell nobody how to act right; they certainly never can learn when they ain't got no sense right to know it, and you never have no sense right Melanctha to be honest, and I ain't never wishing no harm to you ever Melanctha Herbert, only I don't never want any more to see you come here. I just say to you now, like I always been saying to you, you don't know never the right way, any kind of decent girl has to be acting, and so Melanctha Herbert, me and Sam, we don't never any more want you to be setting your foot in my house here Melanctha Herbert, I just tell you. And so you just go along now, Melanctha Herbert, you hear me, and I don't never wish no harm to come to you."

Rose Johnson went into her house and closed the door behind her. Melanctha stood like one dazed, she did not know how to bear this blow that almost killed her. Slowly then Melanctha went away without even turning to look behind her.

Melanctha Herbert was all sore and bruised inside her. Melanctha had needed Rose always to believe her, Melanctha needed Rose always to let her cling to her, Melanctha wanted badly to have somebody who could make her always feel a little safe inside her, and now Rose had sent her from her. Melanctha wanted Rose more than she had ever wanted all the others. Rose always was so simple, solid, decent, for her. And now Rose had cast her from her. Melanctha was lost, and all the world went whirling in a mad weary dance around her.

Melanctha Herbert never had any strength alone ever to feel safe inside her. And now Rose Johnson had cast her from her, and Melanctha could never any more be near her. Melanctha Herbert knew now, way inside her, that she was lost, and nothing any more could ever help her.

Melanctha went that night to meet Jem Richards who had promised to be at the old place to meet her. Jem Richards was absent in his manner to her. By and by he began to talk to her, about the trip he was going to take soon, to see if he could get some luck back in his betting. Melanctha trembled, was Jem too now going to leave her. Jem Richards talked some more then to her, about the bad luck he always had now, and how he needed to go away to see if he could make it come out any better.

Then Jem stopped, and then he looked straight at Melanctha.

"Tell me Melanctha right and true, you don't care really nothing more about me now Melanctha," he said to her.

"Why you ask me that, Jem Richards," said Melanctha.

"Why I ask you that Melanctha, God Almighty, because I just don't give a damn now for you any more Melanctha. That the reason I was asking."

Melanctha never could have for this an answer. Jem Richards waited and then he went away and left her.

Melanctha Herbert never again saw Jem Richards. Melanctha never again saw Rose Johnson, and it was hard to Melanctha never any more to see her. Rose Johnson had worked in to be the deepest of all Melanctha's emotions.

"No, I don't never see Melanctha Herbert no more now," Rose would say to anybody who asked her about Melanctha. "No, Melanctha she never comes here no more now, after we had all that trouble with her acting so bad with them kind of men she liked so much to be with. She don't never come to no good Melanctha Herbert don't, and me and Sam don't want no more to see her. She didn't do right ever the way I told her. Melanctha just wouldn't, and I always said it to her, if she don't be more kind of careful, the way she always had to be acting, I never did want no more she should come here in my house no more to see me. I ain't no ways ever against any girl having any kind of a way, to have a good time like she wants it, but not that kind of a way Melanctha always had to do it. I expect some day Melanctha kill herself, when she act so bad like she do always, and then she get so awful blue. Melanctha always says that's the only way she ever can think it a easy way for her to do. No, I always am real sorry for Melanctha, she never was no just common kind of nigger, but she don't never know not with all the time I always was telling it to her, no she never no way could learn, what was the right way she should do. I certainly don't never want no kind of harm to come bad to Melanctha, but I certainly do think she will most kill herself some time, the way she always say it would be easy way for her to do. I never see nobody ever could be so awful blue."

But Melanctha Herbert never really killed herself because she was so blue, though often she thought this would be really the best way for her to do. Melanctha never killed herself, she only got a bad fever and went into the hospital where they took good care of her and cured her.

When Melanctha was well again, she took a place and began to work and to live regular. Then Melanctha got very sick again, she began to cough and sweat and be so weak she could not stand to do her work.

Melanctha went back to the hospital, and there the Doctor told her she had the consumption, and before long she would surely die. They sent her where she would be taken care of, a home for poor consumptives, and there Melanctha stayed until she died.

William Carlos Williams

✻ 1883—

Williams was born in Rutherford Park, New Jersey, and has spent most of his life there, practicing medicine. He was educated at a preparatory school in Geneva, Switzerland, and at the University of Pennsylvania, where he was a friend of Ezra Pound. He took an M.D. at Pennsylvania, interned a year in New York, and did a postgraduate year in pediatrics at the University of Leipzig. Williams' ancestry is mixed; he knows of English, Jewish, Martinique, and Danish strains in his blood. Williams has said that he felt a strong and persistent urge to discover the American quality and the American idiom because of the diversity of his own heritage. He has been writing since his days in medical school—mostly poetry, but also fiction and plays. The Great American Novel, *which so clearly reflects Williams' preoccupation with things American, was published in Paris in 1923.*

The Great American Novel

1

THE FOG

If there is progress then there is a novel. Without progress there is nothing. Everything exists from the beginning. I existed in the beginning. I was a slobbering infant. Today I saw nameless grasses—I tapped the earth with my knuckle. It sounded hollow. It was dry as rubber. Eons of drought. No rain for fifteen days. No rain. It has never rained. It will never rain. Heat and no wind all day long better say hot September. The year has progressed. Up one street down another. It is still September. Down one street, up another. Still September. Yesterday was the twenty second. Today is the twenty first. Impossible. Not if it was last year. But then it wouldn't be yesterday. A year is not as yesterday in his eyes. Besides last year it rained in the early part of the month. That makes a difference. It rained on the white goldenrod. Today being misplaced as against last year makes it seem better to have white—Such is progress. Yet if there is to be a novel one must begin somewhere.

Words are not permanent unless the graphite be scraped up and put in a tube or the ink lifted. Words progress into the ground. One must begin with words if one is to write. But what then of smell? What then of the hair on the trees or the golden brown cherries under the black cliffs. What of the weakness of smiles that leaves dimples as much as to say: forgive me—I am slipping, slipping, slipping into nothing at all. Now I am not what I was when the word was forming to say what I am. I sit so on my bicycle and look at you greyly, dimpling because it is September and I am older than I was. I have nothing to say this minute. I shall never have anything to do unless there is progress, unless you write a novel. But if you take me in your arms —why the bicycle will fall and it will not be what it is now to smile greyly and a dimple is so deep—you might fall in and never, never remember to write a word to say good-bye to your cherries.

For it is September. Begin with September.

To progress from word to word is to suck a nipple. Imagine saying: My dear, I am thirsty, will you let me have a little milk—This to love at first sight. But who do you think I am, says white goldenrod? Of course there is progress. Of course there are words. But I am thirsty, one might add. Yes but I love you and besides I have no milk. Oh yes, that is right. I forgot that we were speaking of words. Yet you cannot deny that to have a novel one must have milk. Not at the beginning. Granted, but at the end at least. Yes, yes, at the end. Progress from the mere form to the substance. Yes, yes, in other words: milk. Milk is the answer.

But how have milk out of white goldenrod? Why, that was what the Indians said. The bosom of the earth sprays up a girl balancing, balancing on a bicycle. Rapidly she passes through the first—the second eight years. Progress, you note. But September was rainy last year and how can it ever be dry again unless one go back to the year before that. There are no words. It cannot be any otherwise than as this is built the bosom of the earth shrinks back; phosphates. Yet to have a novel—Oh catch up a dozen good smelly names and find some reason for murder, it will do. But can you not see, can you not taste, can you not smell, can you not hear, can you not touch—words? It is words that must progress. Words, white goldenrod, it is words you are made out of—THAT is why you want what you haven't got.

Progress is to get. But how can words get.—Let them get drunk. Bah. Words are words. Fog of words. The car runs through it. The words take up the smell of the car. Petrol. Face powder, arm pits, food-grease in the hair, foul breath, clean musk. Words. Words cannot progress. There cannot be a novel. Break the words. Words are indivisible crystals. One cannot break them—Awu tsst grang splith gra pragh og bm—Yes, one can break them. One can make words. Progress? If I make a word I make myself into a word. Such is progress. I shall make myself into a word. One big word. One big union. Such is progress. It is a novel. I begin small and make myself into a big splurging word: I take life and make it into one big blurb. I begin at my childhood. I begin at the beginning and make one big—Bah.

What difference is it whether I make the words or take the words. It makes no difference whatever.

There cannot be a novel. There can only be pyramids, pyramids of words, tombs. Their warm breasts heave up and down calling for a head to progress toward them, to fly onward, upon a word that was a pumpkin, now a fairy chariot, and all the time the thing was rolling backward to the time when one believed. Hans Anderson didn't believe. He had to pretend to believe. It is a conspiracy against childhood. It runs backward. Words are the reverse motion. Words are the flesh of yesterday. Words roll, spin, flare up, rumble, trickle, foam—Slowly they lose momentum. Slowly they cease to stir. At last they break up into their letters—Out of them jumps the worm that was—His hairy feet tremble upon them.

Leaving the meeting room where the Mosquito Extermination Commission had been holding an important fall conference they walked out on to the portico of the County Court House Annex where for a moment they remained in the shadow cast by the moon. A fog had arisen in which the egg-shaped white moon was fixed—so it seemed. They walked around the side of the old-fashioned wooden building—constructed in the style of the fine residences of sixty years ago and coming to the car he said: Go around that side as I will have to get in here by the wheel. The seat was wet with dew and cold—after the exceptionally hot day. They sat on it nevertheless. The windshield was opaque with the water in minute droplets on it—through which the moon shone with its inadequate light. That is, our eyes being used to the sun the moon's light is inadequate for us to see by. But certain bats and owls find it even too strong, preferring the starlight. The stars also were out.

Turning into the exit of the parking space he stopped the car and began to wipe the wind-shield with his hand. Take this rag said the other, with one hand already in his trowser pocket. So the glass was wiped on both sides, the top and the bottom pane and the cloth—which looked a good deal like a handkerchief—was returned to the owner—who put it back where it came from not seeming to mind that it was wet and dirty. But of course the man is a mechanic in a certain sense and doesn't care.

On the highway they began to encounter fog. It seemed in the rush of the car to come and meet them. It came suddenly, with a rush and in a moment nothing could be seen but the white billows of water crossed in front by the flares of the headlights. And so it went all the way home, sometimes clearer, sometimes so thick he had to stop, nearly—ending in his own bed-room with his wife's head on the pillow in the perfectly clear electric light. The light shone brightest on the corner of her right eye, which was nearest it, also on the prominences of her face.

Her right arm was under her head. She had been reading. The magazine Vanity Fair, which he had bought thinking of her, lay open on the coverlet. He looked at her and she at him. He smiled and she, from long practice, began to read to him, progressing rapidly until she said: You can't fool me.

He became very angry but understood at once that she had penetrated his mystery, that she saw he was stealing in order to write words. She smiled again knowingly. He became furious.

2

I'm new, said she, I don't think you'll find my card here. You're new; how interesting. Can you read the letters on that chart? Open your mouth. Breathe. Do you have headaches? No. Ah, yes, you are new. I'm new, said the oval moon at the bottom of the mist funnel, brightening and paling. I don't think you'll find my card there. Open your mouth—Breathe—A crater big enough to hold the land from New York to Philadelphia. New! I'm new, said the quartz crystal on the parlor table—like glass—Mr. Tiffany bought a car load of them Like water or white rock candy—I'm new, said the mist rising from the duck pond, rising, curling, turning under the moon—Unknown grasses asleep in the level mists, pieces of the fog. Last night it was an ocean. Tonight trees. Already it is yesterday. Turned into the wrong street seeking to pass the power house from which the hum, hmmmmmmmmmmmmmm—sprang. Electricity has been discovered for ever. I'm new, says the great dynamo. I am progress. I make a word. Listen! UMMMMMMMMMMMM—

Ummmmmmmmmm—Turned into the wrong street at three A.M. lost in the fog, listening, searching—Waaaa! said the baby. I'm new. A boy! A what? Boy. Shit, said the father of two other sons. Listen here. This is no place to talk that way. What a word to use. I'm new, said the sudden word.

The fog lay in deep masses on the roads at three A.M. Into the wrong street turned the car seeking the high pitched singing tone of the dynamos endlessly spinning in the high banquet hall, filling the house and the room where the bed of pain stood with progress. Ow, ow! Oh help me somebody! said she. UMMMMMM sang the dynamo in the next street, UMMMM. With a terrible scream she drowned out its sound. He went to the window to see if his car was still there, pulled the curtain aside, green—Yes it was still there under the light where it would not be so likely to be struck by other cars coming in the fog. There it was as still as if it were asleep. Still as could be. Not a wheel moved. No sound came from the engine. It stood there under the purple arc-light, partly hidden by a pole which cast a shadow toward him in the masses of floating vapor. He could see the redtail-light still burning brightly with the electricity that came from the battery under the floor boards. No one had stolen the spare tire. It was very late.—Well, said he, dropping the shade and thinking that maybe when he was busy someone might easily come up from the meadows and take the spare tire—Well, I suppose I had better see how things have progressed.

And so he backed out into the main street and turned up another block. And there he saw. The great doors were open to full view of the world. A great amphitheatre of mist lighted from the interior of the power house. In rows sat the great black machines saying vrummmmmmmm-mmmmmm. Stately in the great hall they sat and generated electricity to light the cellar stairs with. To warm the pad on Mrs. Voorman's belly. To cook supper by and iron Abie's pyjamas. Here was democracy. Here is progress—here is the substance of words—UMMMMM: that is to say meat or linen or belly ache.—Three A.M. To be exact twenty-eight minutes past three.

And all this was yesterday—Yesterday and there at her window I saw her, the lady of my dreams her long and sallow face, held heavily near the glass, overlooking the street where the decayed-meat wagon passes and the ice-cream cart rumbles with its great power and the complicated affairs of the town twitter toward the open sewer in the meadows by the Button Factory. Orange peel, tomato peel floating in a whitish, soapy flow—Her face without expression, the lady I am dying for, her right shoulder as high as her ear, the line of the shoulder sloping down acutely to the neck, her left shoulder also raised so that her head seemed to lie loose in a kind of saddle.

Supreme in stupidity and a fog of waste, profit in what is left. Oh what delectable morsel is left. Blessed hunchback, scum of loves weekly praying in all churches—which by the way take up the very best sites in the town. There she sat, her body low down below the window frame, only her face showing, and looked at me dully, looked because I looked—and my heart leaped up to her in passionate appeal that she should be my queen and run with me over the foggy land—Forward—Onward and upward forever.

So saying the day had progressed toward the afternoon and under the poplars the dried leaves had begun to collect. It had been unbearably hot. September is a hot month. The leaves had fallen one by one. No wind. One by one pushed off by the buds which swollen by the heat had thought that winter was over. Off with you. You stand in the way of progress, say the young leaves. Sitting on his chair he seemed like any other man but to get to the bed he suddenly descended to the floor. On his long arms—he Apollo, and using the stumps of his legs, apelike on all fours and talking quietly he swung himself up over the edge of the bed and lay down.

Over the field—for the fog had left the grasses in the early morning when the sun came up with majestic progression, haughtily leaving the dropping city under him—over the field—for it was late in the afternoon and the sunlight shone in with his poor broken legs, crippled as he was—the sun shone in from the west. The car had turned in to the wrong street and he had gone into the store where the paralysed Scotchman whom he had never seen before put him on the way—climbing into his bed sent his rays almost level over a patch of red grass hot and blinding. Over the field the heat rose and in it even from a distance due to the blur of light on their wings a great swarm of gnats could be seen turning, twisting in the air, rising falling—over the grass, fringed with the progressing sun.

But with great sweeps and sudden turns a dozen dragon flies seeming twice as large as they really were, from the sun blurring their transparent wings, darted back and forth over the field catching and eating the gnats. Swiftly the gnats progressed into the dragon flies, swiftly coalescing—and from time to time a droplet of stuff fell from the vent of a feeding dragon fly,—and the little sound of this stuff striking the earth could not be heard with its true poetic force. Lost. Lost in a complicated world. Except in the eyes of God. But a word, a word rang true. Shit, said the father. With this name I thee christen: he added under his breath.

And yet—one must begin somewhere.

Deeply religious, he walked into the back yard and watching lest the children see him and want what they shouldn't have he approached the grape vines. Selecting a bunch of Delawares he picked it with some difficulty spilling a few of the fruit. Then he walked to the other side and found some blue ones. These too he ate. Then some white which he ate also one by one swallowing the pulp and the seeds and spitting out the skins. He continued to eat but no word came to satisfy.

Somehow a word must be found. He felt rather a weight in his belly from eating so many grapes. He, himself that must die someday, he the deeply religious friend of great men and women in incipience, he couldn't find a word. Only words and words. He ate another bunch of the grapes. More words. And never THE word.

A novel must progress toward a word. Any word that—Any word. There is an idea.

His brother was ill. He must go home. The sun will soon be on the Pacific coast. To bed, to bed—take off the clothes beginning on the outside and working in. How would it be to take off the underwear first, then the shirt—

Progress is dam foolishness—It is a game. Either I have or—a thieves' game. Hold me close, closer, close as you can. I can't hold you any closer. I have been stealing. I should never touch anything. I should never think of anything but you. I love another. It is a word. I have left you alone to run wild with a girl. I would be tame. Lies flicker in the sun. Visions beset noonday. Through the back window of the shoe-shine parlor a mass of golden glow flashes in the heat. Come into my heart while I am running—jumping from airplane to plane in mid-air. I cannot stop: the word I am seeking is in your mouth—I cannot stop. Hold me against—

You are wrong, wrong Alva N. Turner. It is deeper than you imagine. I perceive that it may be permissible for a poet to write about a poetic sweetheart but never about a wife—should have said possible. It is not possible. All men do the same. Dante be damned. Knew nothing at all. Lied to himself all his life. Profited by his luck and never said thanks. God pulled the lady up by the roots. Never even said thank you. Quite wrong. Look what he produced. Page after page. Helped the world to bread. Have another slice of bread Mr. Helseth. No thank you—Not hungry tonight? Something on his mind.

The word. Who.

Liberate the words. You tie them. Poetic sweet-heart. Ugh. Poetic sweetheart. My dear Miss Word let me hold your W. I love you. Of all the girls in school you alone are the one—

Dramatise myself make it sing together as if the world were a bird who married to the same mate five years understood in the end transmigration of souls.

Nonsense. I am a writer and will never be anything else. In which case it is impossible to find the word. But to have a novel one must progress with the words. The words must become real, they must take the place of wife and sweet-heart. They must be church—Wife. It must be your wife. It must be a thing adamant with the texture of wind. Wife.

Am I a word? Words, words, words—

And approaching the end of the novel in his mind as he sat there with his wife sleeping alone in the next room he could feel that something unusual had happened. Something had grown up in his life dearer than—It, as the end. The words from long practice had come to be leaves, trees, the corners of his house —such was the end. He had progressed leaving the others far behind him. Alone in that air with the words of his brain he had breathed again the pure mountain air of joy—there night after night in his poor room. And now he must leave her. She the—He had written the last word and getting up he understood the fog as it billowed before the lights.

That which had been impossible for him at first had become possible. Everything had been removed that other men had tied to the words to secure them to themselves. Clean, clean he had taken each word and made it new for himself so that at last it was new, free from the world for himself—never to touch it—dreams of his babyhood—poetic sweetheart. No. He went in to his wife with exalted mind, his breath coming in pleasant surges. I come to tell you that the book is finished.

I have added a new chapter to the art of writing. I feel sincerely that all they say of me is true, that I am truly a great man and a great poet.

What did you say, dear, I have been asleep?

3

It is Joyce with a difference. The difference being greater opacity, less erudition, reduced power of perception—Si la sol fa mi re do. Aside from that simple, rather stupid derivation, forced to a ridiculous extreme. No excuse for this sort of thing. Amounts to a total occlusion of intelligence. Substitution of something else. What? Well, nonsense. Since you drive me to it.

Take the improvisations: What the French reader would say is: *Oui, ça; j'ai déjà vu ça; ça c'est de Rimbaud.* Finis.

Representative American verse will be that which will appear new to the French . . . . prose the same.

Infertile Joyce laments the failure of his sterile pen. Siegfried Wagner runs to his Mama crying: Mutti, Mutti, listen, I have just composed a beautiful Cantata on a theme I discovered in one of father's operas.

In other words it comes after Joyce, therefore it is no good, of no use but a secondary local usefulness like the Madison Square Garden tower copied from Seville—It is of no absolute good. It is not NEW. It is not an invention.

Invention, I want to buy you some clothes. Now what would you really like to have? Let us pretend we have no intelligence whatever, that we have read ALL there is to read and that Rimbaud has taught us nothing, that Joyce has passed in a cloud, that, in short, we find nothing to do but begin with Macaulay or King James, that all writing is forbidden us save that which we recognise to be inadequate. NOW show your originality, *mon ami.* NOW let me see what you can do with your vaunted pen.

Nothing could be easier.

My invention this time, my dear, is that literature is a pure matter of words. The moon making a false star of the weather vane on the steeple makes also a word. You do not know the fine hairs on a hickory leaf? Try one in the woods some time. You will grasp at once what I mean.

But Joyce. He is misjudged, misunderstood. His vaunted invention is a fragile fog. His method escapes him. He has not the slightest notion what he is about. He is a priest, a roysterer of the spirit. He is an epicurean of romance. His true genius flickers and fails: there's the peak, there in the trees—For God's sake can't you see it! Not that tree but the mass of rocks, that reddish mass of rocks, granite, with the sun on it between that oak and the maple.—That is not an oak. Hell take it what's the use of arguing with a botanist.

But I will not have my toothpicks made of anything but maple. Mr. Joyce will you see to it that my toothpicks are not made of anything but maple? Irish maple. Damn it, it's for Ireland. Pick your teeth, God knows you need to. The trouble with writing of the old style is that the teeth don't fit. They were made for Irishmen—as a class.

Tell me now, of what in your opinion does Mr. Joyce's art consist, since you have gone so far as to criticise the teeth he makes?—Why, my dear, his art consists of words.

What then is his failure, O God.—His failure is when he mistakes his art to be something else.

What then does he mistake his art to be, Rosinante?—He mistakes it to be several things in more or less certain rotation from botany—Oh well it's a kind of botany you know—from botany to—to—litany. Do you know his poetry?

But you must not mistake his real, if hidden, service. He has in some measure liberated words, freed them for their proper uses. He has to a great measure destroyed what is known as "literature." For me as an American it is his only important service.

It would be a pity if the French failed to discover him for a decade or so. Now wouldn't it? Think how literature would suffer. Yes think—think how LITERATURE would suffer.

At that the car jumped forward like a live thing. Up the steep board incline into the garage it leaped—as well as a thing on four wheels could leap—But with great dexterity he threw out the clutch with a slight pressure of his left foot, just as the fore end of the car was about to careen against a mass of old window screens at the garage end. Then pressing with his right foot and grasping the hand-brake he brought the machine to a halt—just in time—though it was no trick to him, he having done it so often for the past ten years.

It seemed glad to be at home in its own little house, the trusty mechanism. The lights continued to flare intimately against the wooden wall as much to say:

And what is good poetry made of
And what is good poetry made of
Of rats and snails and puppy-dog's tails
And that is what good poetry is made of

And what is bad poetry made of
And what is bad poetry made of
Of sugar and spice and everything nice
That is what bad poetry is made of

Here I am back again. The engine sighed and stopped at the twist of the key governing the electric switch. Out went the lights with another twist of the wrist. The owner groped his way to the little door at the back and emerged into the moonlight, into the fog, leaving his idle car behind him to its own thoughts. There it must remain all night, requiring no food, no water to drink, nothing while he, being a man, must live. His wife was at the window holding the shade aside.

A Rebours: Huysman puts it. My dear let us free ourselves from this enslavement. We do not know how thoroughly we are bound. It must be a new definition, it must cut us off from the rest. It is in a different line. Good morning Boss said the old colored man working on the railroad and started to sing: Jesus, Jesus I love you. It was Sunday, he was working on the railroad on Sunday and had to put up some barrier. It is an end to art temporarily. That upstart Luther. My God don't talk to me of Luther, never changed his bed clothes for a year. Well, my dear, IT'S COMING just the same. To hell with art. To hell with literature. The old renaissance priests guarded art in their cloisters for three hundred years or more. Sunk their teeth in it. The ONE solid thing. Don't blame me if it went down with them. DOWN, you understand. Fist through the middle of the rose window. You are horror struck. One word: Bing! One accurate word and a shower of colored glass following it. Is it MY fault? Ask the French if that is literature.

Do you mean to say that art—O ha, ha. Do you mean to say that art—O ha, ha. Well spit it out. Do you mean to say that art is SERIOUS?—Yes. Do you mean to say that art does any WORK?—Yes. Do you mean—? Revolution. Russia. Kropotkin. Farm, Factory and Field.—CRRRRRRASH.—Down comes the world. There you are gentlemen, I am an artist.

What then would you say of the usual interpretation of the word "literature"?—Permanence. A great army with its tail in antiquity. Cliché of the soul: beauty.

But can you have literature without beauty? It all depends on what you mean by beauty.

There is beauty in the bellow of the BLAST, etc. from all previous significance.—To me beauty is purity. To me it is discovery, a race on the ground.

And for this you are willing to smash—

Yes, everything.—To go down into hell.—Well let's look.

4

That's all very fine about *le mot juste* but first the word must be free.—But is there not some other way? It must come about gradually. Why go down into hell when—Because words are not men, they have no adjustments that need to be made. They are words. They can not be anything but free or bound. Go about it any way you chose.

The word is the thing. If it is smeared with colors from right and left what can it amount to?

I'd hate to have to live up there, she said with a frown. It was the soul that spoke. In her words could be read the whole of democracy, the entire life of the planet. It fell by chance on his ear but he was ready, he was alert.

And the little dusty car: There drawn up at the gutter was a great truck painted green and red. Close to it passed the little runabout while conscious desire surged in its breast. Yes there he was the great powerful mechanism, all in his new paint against the gutter while she rolled by and saw—The Polish woman in the clinic, yellow hair slicked back. Neck, arms, breast, waist, hips, etc. This is THE thing—The small mechanism went swiftly by the great truck with fluttering heart in the hope, the secret hope that perhaps, somehow he would notice—HE, the great truck in his massiveness and paint, that somehow he would come to her. Oh I wouldn't like to live up there!

FOG HOLDS UP LINERS say the head lines. It is a blackness, a choking smother of dirty water in suspension.—You should have been here this morning. You could look out and see nothing but a sea of cloud below us. Right at our feet the fog began and stretched off as far as the eye could perceive.

Up out of the trees with a whirr started the sparrows. With a loud clatter the grouse got up at his feet. The ground was full of mushrooms. Everything, no matter what it is must be re-valuated.

The red grass will soon open into feathers.

Peter Broom, yes sah, my grandfather sah, the greatest man in Prince George County. He had three hundred children.

So many things, so many things: heat.

What then are you trying to say in THIS chapter? And what of your quest of THE word? What of A.N.T. ant?

Why someone has offended Wells. He has retorted with NEO-ACADEMICIAN: And: No new form of the novel required. Lack of substance always takes the form of novelty mongering. Empire must be saved! Saved for the proletariat.

On the side of the great machine it read: Standard Motor Gasoline, in capital letters. A great green tank was built upon the red chassis, FULL of gas. The little car looked and her heart leaped with shy wonder.

Save the words. Save the words from themselves. They are like children. Young Men's Hebrew Association. Save them while they're still young. Words must not be allowed to say, to do—Geld them. They are not REALLY words they are geldings. Save the words. Yes, I repeat SAVE THE WORDS. When Voronoff would have had words to transplant, interstitial words—he said save the words.

And what has anything Wells says to do with serious writing. FIRST let the words be free. The words are men, therefore they are not men. They cannot, must not, will not be mustered of the people, by the people, for the people. They are words. They will have their way.

Puh, puh, puh, puh! said the little car going up hill. But the great green and red truck said nothing but continued to discharge its gasolene into a tank buried in the ground near the gutter.

And the fog had coalesced into rain. Rain to soak the firewood the boys had left beside their old fire, like good scouts, for those to come after and the great car continued to discharge.

5

What then is a novel? *Un Novello,* pretty, pretty Baby. It is a thing of fixed form. It is pure English. Yes, she is of Massachusetts stock. Her great grandfather was thrown out of the Quaker church for joining the Continental army. Hates the English. Her life is a novel—almost too sensational.

The story of Miss Li—so well told.

Qu'avez-vous vu? Or they that write much and see little. Not much use to us.

Speak of old Sun Bow pacing his mesa instead of Felipe Segundo in the barren halls of El Escorial—or asleep in his hard bed at one corner of the griddle.

My mother would have a little nigger boy come with a brush and sit at her feet and brush her legs by the hour.

Expressionism is to express skilfully the seething reactions of the contemporary European consciousness. Cornucopia. In at the small end and—blui! Kandinsky.

But it's a fine thing. It is THE thing for the moment—in Europe. The same sort of thing, reversed, in America has a water attachment to be released with a button. That IS art. Everyone agrees that that IS art. Just as one uses a handkerchief.

It is the apotheosis of relief. Dadaism in one of its prettiest modes: *rien, rien, rien.*—But wait a bit. Maybe Dadaism is not so weak as one might imagine.—One takes it for granted almost without a thought that expressionism is the release of SOMETHING. Now then Aemilius, what is European consciousness composed of?—Tell me in one word.—*Rien, rien, rien!* It is at least very complicated. Oh very.

You damned jackass. What do you know about Europe? Yes, what in Christ's name do you know? Your mouth is a sewer, a cloaca.

Complicated consciousness quite aside from a possible revaluation. It has no value for ME. It is all very interesting and God knows we have enough to learn.

The swarming European consciousness. But there it is much simpler—No good to us.

Swarming European consciousness: Kreisler and Ysaye were the only ones with any value. They had a few pennies over and above expenses. They swarm here now for something to eat. But the funniest are the ones from Russia; each excoriates the playing of the other and calls the other a Sheeny. Wow!

Really you are too naive. They are merely reacting to the American atmosphere—It is their work that counts. And besides a virtuoso is not really creative in any serious sense. Would a great artist, say Kandinsky—? In any case it all seems to preoccupy you so, and in a book about America, really—

Take their work. I resent it all. I hate every symphony, every opera as much as a nigger should hate *Il Trovatore*. Not perhaps hate it in a purely aesthetic sense but from under. It is an impertinence. Where in God's name is our Alexander to cut, cut, cut, through this knot.

Europe is nothing to us. Simply nothing. Their music is death to us. We are starving—not dying—not dying mind you—but lean-bellied for words. God I would like to see some man, some one of the singers step out in the midst of some one of Aida's songs and scream like a puma.

But you poor fellow, you use such inept figures. Aida has been dead artistically in Munich for fifty years.

Wagner then—Strauss. It is no difference to me. Tear it all apart. Start with one note. One word. Chant it over and over forty different ways.

But it would be stupid—

It would, if it were what I mean—it would be accurate. It would articulate with something. It would signify relief. Release I mean. It would be the beginning.

Do not imagine I do not see the necessity of learning from Europe—or China but we will learn what we will, and never what they would teach us. America is a mass of pulp, a jelly, a sensitive plate ready to take whatever print you want to put on it—We have no art, no manners, no intellect—we have nothing. We water at the eyes at our own stupidity. We have only mass movement like a sea. But we are not a sea—

Europe we must—We have no words. Every word we get must be broken off from the European mass. Every word we get placed over again by some delicate hand. Piece by piece we must loosen what we want. What we will have. Will they let it go? Hugh.

I touch the words and they baffle me. I turn them over in my mind and look at them but they mean little that is clean. They are plastered with muck out of the cities.—

We must imitate the motivation and shun the result.

We are very few to your many—

But what is all this but waste energy.

No it is not. It is as near as I can come for the present to the word. What good to talk to me of Santayana and your later critics. I brush them aside. They do not apply. They do not reach me any more than a baby's hand reaches the moon. I am far under them. I am less, far less if you will. I am a beginner. I am an American. A United Stateser. Yes its ugly, there is no word to say it better. I do not believe in ugliness. I do not want to call myself a United Stateser but what in—but what else am I? Ugliness is a horror to me but it is less abhorrent than to be like you even in the most remote, the most minute particular. For the moment I hate you, I hate your orchestras, your libraries, your sciences, your yearly salons, your finely tuned intelligences of all sorts. My intelligence is as finely tuned as yours but it lives in hell, it is doomed to eternal—perhaps eternal—shiftings after what? Oh to hell with Masters and the rest of them. To hell with everything I have myself ever written.

Here's a man wants me to revise, to put in order. My God what I am doing means just the opposite from that. There is no revision, there can be no revision—

Down came the rain with a crash. For five days it had been pending. With a loud splash it seemed to strike the earth as if it were body meeting body. The poplar leaves swirled and swirled. The gutters were wedged with water.

Oh you fool you are thicker than rain drops.

Give me to Moussorgsky. I am tired. Take me to the opera tonight and let me see Nijinsky dance his *Til Eulenspiegel* for I am tired to death with looking for sense among American poets. Igor will retrieve my courage. I could sit and listen in his lap for ever. Were not the American Indians Mongols? Or they must have been. Why could they not have been Chinese? Why could not the early Emperors have discovered America? Tell me, wet streets, what we are coming to, we in this country? Are we doomed? Must we be another Europe or another Japan with our coats copied from China, another bastard country in a world of bastards? Is this our doom or will we ever amount to anything?

Drown me in pictures like Marsden, make me a radical artist in the conventional sense. Give me the intelligence of a Wells. God, Hueffer is so far beyond him that what Wells says really sounds sensible.

Must it be a civilisation of fatigued spirits? Then give me Hueffer. My God it is too disgusting.

Great men of America! O very great men of America please lend me a penny so I wont have to go to the opera.

Why not capitalise Barnum—?

Bravo, bravo mon vieux! A noble apostrophe to your country but don't you realise that it is not a matter of country but the time—The time.

For God's sake Charlie bring a lemon pie.

So they lay in the little brook and let the cold water run up their bare bellies.

6

In spite of the moon in mid sky and the plaster of dully shining leaves on the macadam and all the other signs of the approach of fine weather there rang in his head: Such a cuddle muddle: Is that modern German poetry? I never saw such a lot of things mixed together under one title. These are modern times, Pa, airships and automobiles; you cover space—

And that's all right—

O America! Turn your head a little to the left please. So. Now are you ready? Watch my hand. Now: *Lohengrin* in ITALIAN, SUNG AT MANHATTAN—San Carlo Company Revives Wagner Opera, with Anna Fitziu as Elsa.

Sweet kisses that come in the night—O argyrol!

Rain, rain, for three days and three nights.

In the night a cesura. Suddenly the fire bell begins to ring. I wake with a start and hear the small boy calling from the next room. Eight thousand people wake and count the strokes of the black bells. It is not our signal. Someone has been set afire. The engines pass with a crash and roar of the exhausts. Their siren whistles shriek with a fortissimo rise and fall. In a thousand beds men of forty, women of thirty eight, girls in their teens, boys tired from football practice and little boys and girls down to babyhood wake and think the same thoughts. They listen and count the number of strokes, and sink back saying to themselves: Fire! Presently all but the few who are immediately affected are again asleep. The fire has burnt itself out.

Slowly the sun has been crossing Europe and will soon appear fresh from the sea with his benison. The tie of that black thought in the night will be broken. The opportunity will be lost forever. Each will rise and dress and go out into the rain on whatever errand the day has chosen for him.

Rain all day long. The sun does not appear. The heat is suffocating. The rattle of the torrent fills the ears. Water is everywhere.

In the night a wind wakens. It comes from the south-west about midnight and takes the trees by their heavy leaves twisting them until they crack. With a roar the wind batters at the houses, shaking them as if it were a heavy hand. And again for the second night running eight thousand men and women and boys and girls wake and listen or get up to close windows and to look out at the trees leaning with snapping branches, tossing and seething with a sound of escaping steam. It has grown cold. Pull up the covers. It has grown cold. Sixteen thousand hands have drawn the covers closer about the bodies. The wind is cold.

The sun has come back. The air is washed clean. Leaves lie plastered upon the streets, against the tree trunks, upon the very house sides. The bird bath is filled to overflowing. A lame man is hurrying for the train.

They had talked for hours. The new project was beginning to take form. It was the evening of the second day. There stood the train puffing out great volumes of dense smoke which no sooner arose than it was caught in the wind and sent flying out ahead of the train. I wish to God I were on that train wherever it might be going. Oh well, remarked the younger man and said good-bye, which is what it is to be a man.

He was too old, remarked the voice in the room next to the one in which the woman was lying, he never should have gone out in that rain. Too cold! At times it seems possible, even now. She took the hair between her thumb and index finger of the right hand and using her left hand swiftly stroked the little hair strands back toward the head to make it stand out. Ratting it, I told her. It ruins the hair. Oh well I haven't much left, it might as well be broken.

She wore blue stockings under a very quiet dress but the world has not beheld a more maddening spectacle. Devoted to the art of writing, he read with his mind watching her and his mind in the sky seeking, seeking some earth to stand on when the boys were tearing up the soggy turf with their cleats. What to do? There it is. The wind hesitated whether or not to impregnate her. So many things were to be considered. In the years since his passage over Ponce de Leon's soldiers on the beach—the wind footloose, gnawing the leaves had witnessed flying footballs that it had blown out of bounds. He had not a word to stand on, yet he stood, not knowing why. Fear clutched his heart. Visions of uprooted trees passed over his heart as he shook her heavy skirt about her knees. But she, oblivious to it all, walked with downcast eyes—looking at her feet or smiling pleasantly at one here and there in the crowd that was shouting and pressing to see the players.

In the night all nature was asleep as she lay with her young cheek pressed against her pillow and slept. The boys tossed and turned from the stiffness in their joints and from the bruises received in the game. But she lay quiet and asleep, the breath coming slowly in regular flow from her hollow nostrils moving them slightly back and forth.

Under the covers her young form could be made out, the left shoulder, the hips and the legs and feet, the left knee slightly bent and fallen to the mattress before the other. Not a sound in the room for a million years. Still she lay there asleep.—The wind has turned into hail.

Spring flowers are blossoming in the wind. There is the tulip, the jonquil and the violet—for it is September and no man shall know his defeat. So there are spring flowers that grew up through the ice that will be present later. It is of ice that they have made the flowers.

Yet sometimes it seems that it would still be possible. And this is romance: to believe that which is unbelievable. This is faith: to desire that which is never to be obtained, to ride like a swallow on the wind—apparently for the pleasure of flight.

The swallow's bill is constructed in such a way that in flying with his mouth open tiny insects that enter are ensnared in hair-like gills so that he is fed.

Here are a pretty pair of legs in blue stockings, feed. Yet without the thought of a possible achievement that would make it possible to command the achievement of certain—The boys kick the ball and pay no attention. The boys kick the ball up into the wind and the wind hurriedly writes a love note upon it: Meet me tonight. Say you are going to the Library and I will have my car at the corner of Fern Street. I have something to tell you. There is one word you must hear: You.

There is one word you must hear. It will come out at my lips and enter in at your ears. It might be written with letters on white paper but it is a word that I want you to have out of the lips into your ear. And she answers: I will be there. So he does not keep his appointment. Off he goes in search of a word.

But she goes home and weeps her eyes out. Her pillow is wet with her tears—

What do you think! He has left his wife, and a child in the high school has been ill a week, weeping her eyes out and murmuring his name. Is it not terrible?

It is the wind! The wind is in the poplars twiddling the fading leaves between his fingers idly and thinking, thinking of the words he will make, new words to be written on white paper but never to be spoken by the lips to pass into her ear.

Quietly he goes home to his wife and taking her by the shoulder wakes her: Here I am.

7

Nuevo Mundo! shouted the sailors. The sea was rippling like the bottom of a woven grassrope chair. A new world! Taking out their finest satins and putting on new armor the commanders of the little party ordered boats to be made ready and the royal standards of Arragon and Castile to be taken into them. The men meanwhile feeling the balmy air and seeing green and a shore for the first time in two months were greedily talking of fresh fruit—after their monotonous and meager diet of meat—of milk, of a chance to walk free in the air, to escape their commanders, and of women. Yes perhaps there would be women, beautiful savages of manifold charms. But most of all they were filled with the wild joy of release from torment of the mind. For not one among them but expected to be eaten by a god or a monster long since or to have been boiled alive by a hypertropical sea. Excitedly they went down the ladders and took their places at the words of the boatswain spoken in the Castilian tongue.

Of Columbus' small talk on that occasion nothing remains but it could not have been of Eric the Discoverer. Nor of the parties of Asiatics and Islanders—Pacific Islanders who had in other ages peopled the continents from the east. No matter: *Nuevo Mundo!* had shouted the sailors and *Nuevo Mundo* it was sure enough as they found out as soon as they had set foot on it and Columbus had kneeled and said prayers and the priest had spoken his rigmarole in the name of Christ and the land was finally declared taken over for Ferdinand and Isabella the far distant king and queen.

Yes it was indeed a new world. They the product of an age-long civilization beginning in India, it is said, and growing through conquest and struggle of all imaginable sorts through periods of success and decline, through ages of walkings to and fro in the fields and woods and the streets of cities that were without walls and had walls and burst their walls and became ruins again; through the changes of speech: Sanscrit, Greek, Latin growing crooked in the mouths of peasants who would rise and impose their speech on their masters, and on divisions in the state and savage colonial influences, words accurate to the country, Italian, French and Spanish itself not to speak of Portuguese. Words! Yes this party of sailors, men of the sea, brothers of a most ancient guild, ambassadors of all the ages that had gone before them, had indeed found a new world, a world, that is, that knew nothing about them, on which the foot of a white man had never made a mark such as theirs were then making on the white sand under the palms. *Nuevo Mundo!*

The children released from school lay in the gutter and covered themselves with the fallen poplar leaves.—A new world! All summer the leaves had been thick on the branches but now after the heat and the rain and the wind the branches were beginning to be bare. More sky appeared to their eyes than ever before. With what relief the children had pranced in the wind! Now they lay half covered in the leaves and enjoying the warmth looked out on the new world.

And he was passing and saw them. And wondered if it were too late to be Eric. What a new world they had made of it with their Cortezes, their Pizarros yes and their Lord Howes, their Washingtons even. The Declaration of Independence. I wonder, he said, whether it could be possible that the influence of the climate—I wonder if the seed, the sperm of that, existed in Columbus. Was it authentic? Is there a word to be found there? Could it be that in those men who had crossed, in the Norse as well as the Mongols, something spontaneous could not have been implanted out of the air? Or was the declaration to be put to the credit of that German George? Was it only the result of local conditions?

"A new declaration of independence, signed by Columbus, found in Porto Rico."

Indians in any case, pale yellow and with lank black hair came to the edge of the bushes and stared: The Yaquis territory lay north of the river Fuertes. To the south was Carrancista territory. The valley was fertile, the Indians wanted it.

During the week of November 13th, 17th, 1916—word reached Los Mochis that Gen. Banderas and the Villistas from Chihuahua had been defeated by the Carrancistas near Fuertes and were in retreat. During this week two Indians were captured by Los Mochis police and hung on willow trees below the Jaula.

On Saturday November 13th, Col. Escobar and his Carrancistas of the Fifth regiment of Sinaloa were withdrawn from Los Mochis and Aguila and concentrated in San Blas. Banderas and his Villistas meanwhile had come down the Fuertes, effected a junction with Bachomo and his Mayo Indians, and Monday night crossed the river above Los Tastos, tore out the telephone at the pumps and started for Los Mochis. All gate keepers encountered on the road were killed as were their families. Mr. Wilcox estimated the combined forces participating in the raid and on the other side of the river at 6,000.

The first intimation of the raid was at

one o'clock in the morning of Tuesday when with a *"Villa! Vive Villa! Vive Villa!"* the raiders swarmed into Los Mochis from three sides, shooting cursing as they galloped into town. From all over the town came the sound of smashing doors and windows, shots, yells and screams.

When I came here the Indians all used bows and arrows. Conscripted during the many revolutions they had deserted with their rifles until at last, after 800 of them, in a body, went over they used the rifle extensively. Wilcox lived at the pumps with his wife and daughter. A cocky Englishman, he poopooed the danger. He had been in the habit of telephoning into the town, seven miles, whenever a raid was coming. It was agreed we Americans were to keep to our houses, take our animals off the roads and wait with more or less excitement until it was over. We never notified the Mexicans. Had we done so once we should not have escaped the next raid. This time the Villistas were with the Indians. As you saw the first thing they did was to rip out the wires. Washington had just accepted Carranza as the power in authority and the Villistas were angry.

Wilcox and his wife and daughter were locked in a room all the first night while Banderas and Bacomo argued over their fate. Banderas was for killing Wilcox and taking over his wife and daughter for camp women. But the Indian stood out against him. It seems Wilcox had at one time given the Indians some sacks of beans when they were hard up for food. They remembered this. It was a good thing for the three.

At a previous raid an American engineer living near Wilcox was found dead. He was supposed to have run. Looked just like a pin-cushion, with the feathered arrows that were in him. Funniest thing you ever saw in your life. There were four bullets in him also.

The Americans were too scattered to resist. It was decided to save the few guns by hiding them. Bacomo rode up to the house with his escort,—ordered to give up all guns and cartridges. At the last moment he turned back from the stairs, entered Mrs. Johnson's room where the ladies were sitting on the beds and ordered them to get up. Under the mattress a miscellaneous collection of riot guns, rifles, shot guns, automatics, pistols and cartridges were found. When all the guns and cartridges to the last shell had been loaded on the horses behind the drunken soldiers Bacomo refused C.'s request for one of the riot guns and with a polite bow and a *"Con permiso, senores,"* he rode off.

In Mr. Johnson's cellar they had found all sorts of bottles from Scotch to German *Scheiswasser* and had drunk it all indiscriminately.

Cattle had eaten the standing rice. The pigs had got loose and over-run everything. Returning there were corpses on all sides. About one of these a triple battle raged. The pigs were ranged on one side, the dogs on another and from a third a flock of vultures crept up from time to time. The pigs and dogs would make a united rush at the birds who would fly a few feet into the air and settle a yard or so away.

These pictures are of Bacomo taken a year later just as he was being taken from the train by his captors. He was a physical wreck at the time but at the time of the raid he was a magnificent specimen of a man. It seemed there was some silver buried near Los Mochis which they wanted. He would not disclose its whereabouts unless they freed him and they would not free him unless he spoke first.

The end is shown in this picture. Here he is with the pick and spade at his feet surrounded by the Carrancista soldiers. He dug his grave and was shot and they buried him there.

The Indians have made a local saint of him and every night you will see candles burning on the spot and little plates of rice and other food placed there for his spirit.—

For a moment Columbus stood as if spell-bound by the fact of this new country. Soon however he regained his self-possession and with Alonzo Pinzon ordered the trunks of trifles to be opened which, being opened, the Indians drew near in wonder and began to try to communicate with these gods.

It was indeed a new world.

8

No man can tell the truth and survive—save through prestige. And no child either. Aristocracy is license to tell the truth. And to hear it. Witness the man William in Henry Fifth, the camp incident. Fear clutched at his heart.

Agh-ha-ha! Shouted the *vaqueros* plunging their spurs into the bronchos' sides. Up with the heels. Buck, buck, buck. Agh-ha-ha! *Fortissimo.* The wild and unexpected cry out of the Mexican Indian country rang through the quiet house so that the pup leaped up and rushed to the door.

Someone had taken the apple. Both denied they had had a hand in it. Each accused the other. The truth did not appear. For an hour the man tried his best to arrive at a just decision. Joseph Smith shook where he stood and fell frothing at the mouth. He was of Vermont mountain stock. His birth among the poor white trash there had not even been thought worth recording. Yet a vision came to him of the marriage in Cana. Christ drank the wine and Martha and Mary her sister became his wives—so to speak. It is the truth. The world shall be saved anew, said Joseph Smith in the mountains of Vermont—where the mushrooms are so plentiful among the fir trees.

Who had given the boy the apple against the father's express orders? Had he taken it himself—which he denied or had the girl gone into the store room—as he asserted but which she denied—and selected it herself? Where was the truth?

In Illinois Brigham Young was recruited. Off they set with fifty oxen for the Promised Land away over the prairies and deserts—through the Sioux country, in search of Zion. The whole world they would leave behind and for the truth's sake they would live in that far country—to be discovered, to which the Lord would lead them.

Go upstairs sir and take your clothes off. You shall go to bed for this lie—I'll say I took the apple Daddy, said the boy sobbing violently, but she gave it to me. In minute detail he repeated the story of how the apple was picked out of the basket by the girl and handed to him to eat.

Lions of the Lord. The boy would not give up his bride to Brigham and was *altered,* as a rebel. She went mad. In '49 a party of gold seekers came by accident into the valley they had found. They were gently received. A warning was given of hostile Indians and a special guard was appointed to conduct them safely on their way. But Brigham had had a dream. Men must not wander into the valley of Zion to disturb the ways of God's holy ones. A blood sacrifice had been demanded of Brigham by the Lord. John D. Lee was selected as he who must lend himself to the Almighty will of God for the good of the church and state. Slowly the party of gold seekers departed for California. At the narrow defile at Mountain Meadow the treacherous business was performed. All but a child were killed and Brigham and the Lord were revenged. Later John D. Lee was convicted of murder by government authorities and shot. A poor ignorant tool in the hands of that most mighty Lion of the Lord.

And you my girl. You have lied to me before this. Did you or did you not take the apple? No one will be punished but I must have the truth. Tomorrow is Sunday. You shall go to church, and up to the minister you shall march, and he will ask you what I am asking you now. In the face of God you shall say to him that you did not take that apple, then I shall know. Did you or did you not take that apple? I will have the truth. And you my young sir, I shall not punish you but I must have the truth. You shall stay in bed all day tomorrow, all next week as long as it takes for one of you to change your story. I will have the truth.

The mountains are savage about the valley. The lake is bitter, scalding with the salt. They knew they had found the Dead Sea. At last the child confessed, with bitter and hard tears that he had taken the fruit himself. It was the truth.

Clear and cold the moon shone in the partly denuded poplars. It was midnight and the little fellow to whom he had determined to teach the meaning of the truth was snug in his bed. Years before that Utah had been admitted to the Union as a state and polygamy had been more or less abandoned. The young folk were beginning to be ashamed of the narrowness of their cult and the bones of the fathers were rotten.

The glassy half moon in the dark leaves cast a dull light over the world upon which a calm had descended. Suddenly the pleiades could be heard talking together in Phœnician. Their words were clear as dropping water: What things they do in this new world: they said. Let us from now on swear to each other that we will give up every thought of wisdom and seek no further for the truth—which is, after all a veritable moon.—At this the moon was overcast for a moment by a falling leaf. The answer that came from that clear but broken ball rose slowly toward the stars: The child is asleep. Let us warn him of the folly of words. Let us bless him only with words that change often and never stiffen nor remain to form sentences of seven parts. To him I send a message of words like running water.— At this the stars smiled for they were married to one—

Elena, yo soy un wonder, she would say. *Vu par le jury.* And who is the jury but myself. The boy had struck her with a stone. Come we shall go and apologise, said Brigham Young. Into the neighbour's kitchen they walked. An older sister was cleaning the gas range. Where is your sister? But the truth is that all the while he had been hoping that just what had happened would happen. His eye ran up and down the girl's form. Secretly he was happy to have found her alone. I'm sorry, I will never do it again, Never again. Never again. Oh never, never again.

And how can I, now that it is all over, and I am old? But at first I tell you I cried my eyes out. I had just been admitted to the Beaux Arts. All was as near perfect as could well be. I had the friendship of La Baronne d'Orsay and then the stars withdrew their aid. I had to go back to Porto Rico. I had to leave everything behind to go back to that country where there was nothing.

There life ended. But it is over now. I was just beginning to do things. I tell you I cried my eyes out. But I am old now. I wanted you to see these drawings, to show you it was not a bluff.

The Indians are gone. It is late now. It is cold. September is over. October is cold. Words should be—Words should be—I am tired to death.

But two enormous women, middle aged, dignified, with still broad backs came down the street just as the very dirty little boy was crossing over. The three arrived at the entrance to the path at the same moment. The women looked hard at the filthy little boy whose face was stickly from apple-juice and black, with a great circle of dirt around the mouth. The women looked and the little boy hung his head and stumbled off into the long grass, almost falling into the abandoned foundation.

And so the little company went on foot 20,000 miles along what later became known as Emigration Trail, overcoming incredible obstacles, eating the draught oxen, through savage mountains on, on to the Mountain Meadow Massacre. For they would worship the Lord their God in peace and in their own way. At last the Mayflower was in the harbor and the pilgrims had landed and dispersed.

Yes, it was a New World.

But they have prospered and today the Mormon Church is all for goodness and it is powerful and rich.

A favorite trick of the Mayo Indians is, if they meet a man with good clothes, to take what they want and let him go on in his drawers.

So it was with infinite satisfaction that on looking up the little boy saw those two terrible viragos suddenly as low as he. *Nuevo Mundo.*

9

Calang-glang! Calang-glang! went the bells of the little Episcopal Church at Allandale. It was eight o'clock in the evening. A row of cars stood along the curb, each with its headlights lit, but dimmed so as not to make too much of a glare on the road, at the same time to save the battery while complying with the law!

On sped the little family all crowded into one seat, the two children sleeping.

In the Dutch church on the old Paramus Road Aaron Burr was married to Mrs. Prevost, Jataqua! It is near Hohokus, cleft-in-the-rocks, where the Leni Lenapes of the Delaware nation had their village from time immemorial. Aaron, my darling, life begins anew! It is a new start. Let us look forward staunchly together—

The long, palm-like leaves of the ailanthus trees moved slowly up and down in the little wind, up and down.

And along this road came the British. Aaron, the youth from Princeton, gathered his command together and drove them back. Mother I cannot sleep in this bed, it is full of *British soldiers*. Why so it is! How horrid.

And he too, on his memorable retreat, that excellent judge of horseflesh, George Washington, he too had passed over this road; and these trees, the oldest of them, had witnessed him. And now the wind has torn the finest of them in half.

Nothing more wonderful than to see the pears attached by their stems to the trees. Earth, trunk, branch, twig and the fruit: a circle soon to be completed when the pear falls. They had left at eleven and soon they would be home. The little car purred pleasantly to itself at the thought of the long night. Oh, to be a woman, thought the speeding mechanism. For they had wrapped something or other in a piece of newspaper and placed it under the seat and there were pictures there of girls—or grown women it might be, in very short skirts. Steadily the wheels spun while on the paper were printed these words:

The Perfection of Pisek-designed Personality Modes: A distinctly forward move in the realm of fashion is suggested by the new personality modes, designed by Pisek . . . modes that are genuine inspirations of individual styling, created for meeting the personal preferences of a fastidiously fashionable clientèle, the woman and the miss who seek personality in dress in keeping with their charms, characteristics and station . . . Thus you can expect at Pisek's only those *tailleurs*, gowns, wraps and frocks that bear the unmistakable stamp of individuality—styles that encourage and inspire admiration for their splendid simplicity and differentness . . . come to Pisek's . . . (the more the better) . . . see the new ideas in fashions . . . You'll not be disappointed . . .

What chit of a girl could have appreciated you, my darling boy, as I do. A man of your personality, so fresh in wit, so brimming with vigor and new ideas. Aaron my dear, dear boy, life has not yet begun. All is new and untouched in the world waiting, like the pear on the tree, for you to pluck it. Everyone loves you and will wait on you. For you everything is possible. Bing! and Hamilton lies dead.

As old Mr. Goss, who lost his hearing from an explosion of fireworks in Philadelphia after Lee's defeat, has said in his high nasal twang: Quite right, quite right, I've seen the country saved 8 times in the last fifty years.

At any rate it was a new world to them; they two together would conquer and use, life had smiled upon them. *Nuevo Mundo.*

Along the road the Dutch settlers came out from their attractive brown stone houses as the happy and distinguished couple went by. It was a great day for the little colony of New Jersey. There over the misty meadows the lights of Weehawken were beginning to glimmer as the little car and its precious freight drew near the end of the journey. The pear fell to the earth and was eaten by the pigs.

I wonder if he'll recognise me in my Greenwich Village honkie-tonk bobbed hair. The hairdresser said: Don't you do it, when I said I'd like mine bobbed too. So many of the girls had theirs done a year ago and now its just at that impossible stage where you can't do a thing with it. Better go to Europe or California until it grows again. There's a reason for travel: As the hair progresses the days grow fewer.

But is South Africa after all the country of the future?

Over the great spaces of New Jersey, Pennsylvania, Ohio, Indiana he sped in the Pullman car. City after city swept up to him, paused awhile at his elbow and plunged away to the rear with the motion of a wheel whose hub was hidden in infinity. And such indeed was exactly the case. He was being ground between two wheels, one on either side of the car and it was their turning that thrust him forward at such speed. The wheat was up in the fields but a fellow passenger assured him that in Kansas, only two days before, he had seen wheat twice as high —which explains the cause of so many abandoned farms in Vermont, he remembered, and settled back to another hour of idle staring. A new country he kept saying to himself. On a siding were cars loaded with emigrants from Holland booked through to San Francisco.

Into the elevator stepped the young man in a petty officer's uniform. His Spanish was exquisite to hear. The first battleship since the Spanish-American war was anchored in New York harbor. How well he bears himself. The Spanish are the only people in Europe whom civilization has not ruined. Savage men, big bearded chins—but shaved clean. They know how to treat their women—better than the French for the French—after all are *blagueurs* to a man. The Spanish stand still. What an ass a man will make of himself in a strange country! In armor De Soto wandering haphazard over Alabama. The Seminoles for guides. Buried him in the Mississippi. It is my river, he said. Roll Jordan roll. It is *my* river for I discovered it and into it let my body, in full armor, be put to rest. The cat-fish ate it. So roll Jordan roll. Diada Daughter of Discord: read it.

In Illinois, far in the west, over that trackless waste of forest and mountain and river and lake they came at last to a valley that pleased them and there they determined to build. So they fell to hewing trees and building their houses, work to which they had been bred and trained for two generations since Plymouth and Salem days. Cornwallis had been beaten fifty years before and Pitt had rushed to see the King crying: All is lost. A new world had been born. Here in the primeval forest the little colony of New

Englanders hoped to realise success and plenty.

In Bonnie, Illinois, the Presbyterian minister is a very good man. He is as good a preacher as Bonnie can afford and if anybody said that Bonnie is made up of mad-men—He would be shot. *Nuevo Mundo,* shouted the sailors. But their cry was by now almost extinct.

In polite stories the world had been made acquainted with the picturesque lives of these commonplace but worthy people. In detail their story had been told. Over the precipice in Yosemite the Bridal Veil Falls had been launching its water for a thousand years and ignorance was fattening his belly apace.

Bonnie, Ill., October 22. Dear Bill: Am up to my ears in painting, and am preparing to go to Alton, Ill., to work in the State Hospital, if I get a call, so am too busy now to read your book but think I'm going to like it and will devour it later. Sincerely. A. N. Turner.

And the little boy crept into the great chest like Peppo into the Cardinal's tomb and began to pick up the mothballs that had been left there when the winter things were removed.

An Indian would sense the facts as he wished. A tree would speak to him with a definite identity. It would not at least seem endowed with human characteristics: a voice, that would be all.

10

Arnold, this wind is, the wise and sagacious captain. Henchman of the wind. The wind is a lion with hooked teeth. The saber-toothed tiger inhabited the region west of the Alleganies throughout the pleistocene age. With a snarl it wrenches the limbs of the trees from their places and tosses them to earth where they lie with the leaves still fluttering.

Vacuous; full of wind. Her whole pelvis is full of intestine but aside from the ptosis I find nothing really wrong. The uterus appears to be normal. The bleeding may come from a cyst. At least there is no good reason for removing—for a hysterectomy. There it is. It. Like some tropical fruit color of the skunk cabbage flower. There it is, that mystical pear, glistening with the peritoneum. Here the cavern of all caverns. Alpha if not omega. Talk politely and obey the law. But do not remove it.

Oh my country. Shall it be a hysterectomy? Arnold there is a wind with a knife's edge.

And Remy says the spring of curiosity is broken at thirty. Nothing left at fifty but the facts of bed and table. He has the lilt of Heine at his best and in places quite equals the work of the author of Danny Deever. The catgut had slipped out of the needle. The young interne held the point of the suture between his fingers and the nurse approached the needle as accurately as she could. But the man's hand trembled slightly. For a moment they tried to complete the connection but failing in their attempt the nurse took the end in her other hand and soon had the needle threaded. The young doctor looked up as much as to say thank you.

Such a wind. At fifteen they seem noble, desirable beyond dreams. In the winter the trees at least remain stems of wood that resist with a will, whose branches rebound against the impact of sleet. At thirty they are what they are. The boy rebels and she with her hair in distressed tangles about the disorderly boudoir cap, at mid-day, whines and snatches at him as he jerks and defies her. It is beyond her strength to control a boy of nine. Clutching her dressing sack—oh slobbery morsel—about her breastless form with one hand she rushes as far as she dares to the porch edge, glancing furtively about for chance gentlemen or neighbors and tries to overtake the youngster. No, the young man has really escaped. He goes to school filthy again and what will they think of his mother.

At fifteen they are slender and coquettish and they cry if you are rough with them. Great burly fellow, she seemed to him all that he was not, the quintessence of Ibsenism, the wind among the reeds. Or perhaps the reed in the wind. Something to love, to take into the arms, to protect—If you can find any reason for doing a hysterectomy doctor, do it. Her husband is good for nothing at all. She at least is a power in her family. She is not like the native American women of her class, she is a Polock. You never saw such courage.

The schooner left Southampton bound for New York with a cargo of rails—steel rails. But the English emigrants were not like these modern messes. Those round, expressionless peasant faces of today. See that one there with the little boy at her side. Castle Garden. At last we are to be in America, where gold is in the streets. Look at that face. That is the kind of immigration we want. Look at the power in that jaw. Look at that nose. She is one who will give two for every stroke she has to take. Look at the intensity of her gaze. Well, she's English, that's the reason. Nowadays they have no more of that sort. These Jews and Polocks, Sicilians and Greeks. Good-bye America!

The head nurse's legs under her practical short skirt were like mighty columns. They held the seriousness of her looks, her steady, able hands. A fine woman.

11

The American background is America. If there is to be a new world Europe must not invade us. It is not a matter of changing the y to i as in Chile. They are bound.

The background of America is not Europe but America.

Eh bien mon vieux coco, this stuff that you have been writing today, do you mean that you are attempting to set down the American background? You will go mad. Why? Because you are trying to do nothing at all. The American background? It is Europe. It can be nothing else. Your very method proves what I say. You have no notion what you are going to write from one word to the other. It is madness. You call this the background of American life? Madness?

As far as I have gone it is accurate.

It is painting the wind.

Ah, that would be something.

Mais ça, are you a plain imbecile? That is a game for children. Why do you not do as so many of your good writers do? Your Edgar Lee Masters, your Winesburg, Ohio. Have you not seen the photographs of men and women on your walls? They are type, as distinct as a Frenchman or a German. Study these men, know their lives. You have a real work to do, you have the talent, the opportunity even. This is your work in life. You Americans, you are wasteful, mad—

Our background.

You would paint the wind. Well, it has been tried—many times, and do you know where that leads?

I know where it has led.

But do you know? Have you seen, felt, heard what they have seen, felt, heard, our Villons—

Apollo was out of breath but the nymph was more tired than he. The chase must soon have ended when she falling to her knees half from the will to be there half from fatigue besought her mistress Diana to save her from the God's desire. And she was changed into a laurel bush.

All about the hills where they stood the hard waxen leaves of the laurel glistened above the dead leaves of the hardwood trees, the beech, the maple, the oak.

You imagine I am French because I

attack you from the continental viewpoint. You are wrong. I am from the country of your friends Moussorgsky, Dostoiefsky, Chekov. At least if you will not yield me the point that America cannot be new, cannot do anything unless she takes the great heritage which men of all nations and ages have left to the human race.

You mean that I should not be an American but—Turgenef, enjoy you more if, well, if you were more comprehensible, a little more particular, *vous comprenez?* You sweep out your arms, you—I see no faces, no details of the life, no new shape—

The druggist's boy cannot be distinguished from his master when he says, Hello, over the phone—Is that what you mean?

Well, you are very much children, you Americans.

It is not to be avoided as far as I can see.

Let us have now a beginning of composition. We have had enough of your improvisations.

I am consumed by my lusts. No American can imagine the hunger I have.

It is the itch, monsieur. It is neurasthenia. Desire is not a thing to speak of as if it were a matter of filling the stomach. It is wind, gas. You are empty my friend. 'Eat. Then and then only.

Like all men save perhaps the Chinese you are most transparent when you imagine yourself most protected.

Her bosom reached almost to her knees. That morning in the October garden she had picked a violet for him and placed it in his coat. Watching the feet of men and women as they touched the pavement a strong odor of violets crossed his path.

He turned and saw the massive Jewess waddling by. It had been good perfume too.

These Polocks. Their heads have no occiput. They are flat behind. It is why when they put on their American hats the things slip down about their ears. The nigger's head isn't that way. You know how the bump goes out behind in so many of them. The club sandwich on her plate kept sliding apart, the top slice of bread would slip. Then she took the pieces in her fingers and poked the lettuce in under the sheet. On her breast was a black pin. It formed a circle. She looked up with her mouth full of food and resting both elbows on the table chewed America thoughtfully while she held the state of Maryland in her firm fingers. The ends of each finger were stubby, the nails cut short and as clean as well manicured nails could well be. Clatter, clatter, clatter. He could see himself in the plate glass behind her. He was conscious of his hat which he had not removed. He was at this table with these five women—one of them young, ready—and he had not removed his hat. There was in fact no place to put it.

I am begging, frankly. Ten cents a ticket. I have to raise fifty dollars by the end of next week. We want to fit up a room in our hall where the colored working girls can come and rest. On Thursdays we serve tea. Then they go back to the office. When the impact is over the man must think. I tell you I do not contemplate with relish seeing my children bred out of all these girls. Is it wrong? Well, I thought you said you had an appetite. Impregnate eighty of them, right and left as you see them here in this room. It would not be impossible. I cannot think of my children running about in the environment in which these have to live. My dear sir, you are a fool. You are lying to yourself—As to the girls, I frankly desire them. I desire many, many, many.

There she sat on the bench of the subway car looking idly about, being rushed under the river at great speed to the kitchen of her mother's flat. Malodorous mother. Or wrinkled hard-put-to-it mother. Savior of the movies. After the impact his great heart had expanded so as to include the whole city, every woman young and old there he having impregnated with sons and daughters. For everyone loved him. And he knew how to look into their eyes with both passion and understanding. Each had taken him to her soul of souls where the walls were papered with editorials from the Journal and there he had made himself father to her future child. As they went upstairs he saw how her heels were worn—Who will understand the hugeness of my passion?

But he had understood. The truth lay under the surface. Why then not—No two can remain together without training. Who better than that one who is practiced. The faithful husband of the clothing store madam is used to her. They functionate well together. He puts his hat in the right place. His money in the right bank. His arm fitted in just the posture best suited to their mutual height and width. All their practices were mated.

But he was an outsider. He was new to all. Her shoes are stitched up the back.

Card-index minds, the judges have. Socialism, immorality and lunacy are about synonyms to the judge. Property is sacred and human liberty is bitter, bitter, bitter to their tongues.

Walk up the stairs there little girl. But she is naked! These are all doctors. So the little tot struggled up the very high clinic steps, naked as she was, and all the doctors looked at her. She had some spots on her body that had been there a year. Had I been her father I would know why I am a fool.

Naked and free, free to be damned in to hell by a chance vagrant to whom she had taken a fancy. Her father did not know her. Did not even know that she existed. Cared less. We will look after her said the head doctor.

12

That cat is funny. I think she'd be a good one for the circus. When she's hungry she bites your legs. Then she jumps at you as much as to say: *Carramba,* give me something.

America needs the flamboyant to save her soul—said Vachel Lindsay to the indifferent mountains.

He might have added that America tries to satisfy this need in strange and often uncatalogued ways. America, living an exemplary three-meals-a-day-and-bed-time life in a wall-papered home, goes now and then *en masse,* by Gosh, to the circus to see men, women and animals preform exquisite and impossible feats or daring. What could be more flamboyant than the trapeze-performer hurtling through the air, the tiger leaping through man-made hoops, or the elephant poising his mighty bulk on his two forelegs lifted to the top of bottles? What more flamboyant than the painted clown, timeless type of the race, laughing that he may not weep, grinning through a thousand tragic jests while little human beings perform their miraculous tricks around him?

Jazz, the Follies, the flapper in orange and green gown and war-paint of rouge —impossible frenzies of color in a world that refuses to be drab. Even the movies, devoid as they are of color in the physical sense, are gaudy in the imaginations of the people who watch them; gaudy with exaggerated romance, exaggerated comedy, exaggerated splendor of grotesqueness or passion. Human souls who are not living impassioned lives, not creating romance and splendor and grotesqueness —phases of beauty's infinite variety— such people wistfully try to find these things outside themselves; a futile, often a destructive quest.

The imagination will not down. If it is not a dance, a song, it becomes an outcry, a protest. If it is not flamboyance it becomes deformity; if it is not art, it becomes crime. Men and women cannot be content, any more than children, with the mere facts of a humdrum life—the imagination must adorn and exaggerate life, must give it splendor and grotesqueness, beauty and infinite depth. And the mere acceptance of these things from without is not enough—it is not enough to agree and assert when the imagination demands for satisfaction creative energy. Flamboyance expresses faith in that energy—it is a shout of delight, a declaration of richness. It is at least the beginning of art.

All right go ahead: A TEXAS PRIZE CONTEST—The Southern Methodist University at Dallas, Texas, recently emerged from a prize contest which had a strange *dénouement*—

Look here young man, after this you examine those girls in the cold weather.

Who is Warner Fabian? *Flaming Youth* is the story of the super-flapper, of her affairs at country clubs and cozy home-dances with all the accompaniments of prohibition stimulants. Warner Fabian believes that the youth of this country feeds on excitement and rushes to knowledge "heeled" by way of petting parties and the elemental stimulus of jazz. The barriers of convention are down. Youth makes its own standards and innocence, according to the author, has been superseded by omniscience.

It doesn't matter that Warner Fabian is a *nom de plume* which conceals the identity of one of the ablest scientists of this country who has dared to look facts in the face, facts physical, moral and emotional. He has written the truth about youth, the youth of today as he sees it.

FLAMING YOUTH by Warner Fabian is the writing on the wall. It is the *Quo Vadis?* of the present moment.

Those who are following in the Metropolitan Magazine the fortunes of Pat, the most sophisticated and yet at the same time one of the most deliciously lovely heroines of recent novels, and the fortunes of her two sisters, may protest that Mr. Fabian's portrayal of youth in this novel is outscotting Fitzgerald and overdancing in the Dark. We feel however that this story of three girls and their many men is one which may sufficiently frighten mothers and electrify fathers and hit the younger set hard enough between the eyes to help America's youth to, at least, a gradual return to sanity.

And so the beginning of art ends in a gradual return to sanity.

To-day Modern scientific research has provided the most efficient agent for the treatment of local inflammation: DIONAL applied locally over the affected area acts promptly with prolonged effect. Drugless. Non-irritant. Non-toxic. Indicated in Mastitis, Burns, Boil, Tonsilitis, Mastoiditis, Sprain, Abcess, Bronchitis, Mumps, Contusion, Ulcers, Pneumonia.

If a man died on a stretcher he simply said: Dump it out. And ordered us back for another load.

Intended to stop at the school but his mind waylaid him. Down the hill came the ash-cart—on the wrong side of the street. He, up the hill, perforce went wrong also and with great headway. Just as he was about to pass the cart another car swung out from behind it, headed down hill at full speed. It was too late for any of the three to stop. In three seconds there would be death for someone. Angels would be waiting for mother's little boy. Without the minutest loss of time, in time with the Boston Symphony Orchestra at its best he swung far to the left, up over the curb, between two trees, onto the sidewalk—by luck no one was passing—and going fifty feet came back between two trees, over the curb to the roadway and continued his empty progress, rather hot in the face, it must be confessed. He felt happy and proud.

But he had missed his street.

Well let it go. Far away in front of him a locomotive stood indifferently at the avenue end, emitting great clouds of smoke. It was autumn, clear and cold.

But you Scandinavians, said the Frenchman, it is impossible to live in this way. Why France, which is ten times as rich as your countries, could not do it. You do not know what money is for. You throw it away like a sickness. To drink champagne like this is madness, and it is every night, everywhere, in Christiania, Cophenhagen, everywhere.

And there she sits staring out, not at the sea, but over Long Island Sound. Dreaming of her sons—and of the money she will make next year by renting the better of her two little shacks.

When you have paid up the twenty shares you may, if you like, retain them as paid up shares in which case you will receive the 5% interest, or, if you feel that you would like to do so, you may increase your holding to thirty shares and receive the 6%. Of course everyone is not able to do that. Do not worry about it, we will notify you in plenty of time when your book is balanced at the end of the six months.

Let's see. What is the number of your house? Four eighty? I'll see that they send it right up.

You know last Sunday was my birthday. Seventy-three years old. I had a party, a surprise party—my relatives came from all sides. But I couldn't get her downstairs. She's afraid. We had a banister put on the stairs, cost me nine dollars but she will not do it. She's so fat you know, she's afraid of falling.

Re Commissions due—Amount $1.00. Dear Sir:—You will please take notice that unless we receive payment in full of your account within FIVE DAYS after receipt of this letter, we shall draw upon you for the amount due.

A collection agency draft notifies the banks—those great institutions of finance —that there is serious doubt regarding the way you pay your honest obligations. The bank will take note of it. From there the information quietly passes to the various Mercantile Agencies, Dun's, Bradstreet's, Martindale's. And this is ONLY ONE cog in the wheel of ARROW SERVICE. Our reports cover the whole field of credit reporting.

Your continued indifference to our requests for payment has forced us to consider this action. The draft, with a full history of the debt leaves our office in five days unless your check is received in the meantime.

Let your better judgement guide you, and pay this account without any more trouble or expense. Yours very truly—MEMBERS: Retail Credit Men's National Association. Commercial Law League of America. Rotary International. O Rotary International!

At this, De Soto, sick, after all the months of travel, stopped out of breath and looked about him. Hundreds of miles he had travelled through morass after morass, where the trees were so thick that one could scarcely get between them, over mountain and river but never did he come to the other side. The best he had done was to locate a river running across his path, the greatest he had ever seen or heard of, greater than the Nile, greater than the Euphrates, no less indeed than any. Here he had confronted the New World in all its mighty significance and something had penetrated his soul so that in the hour of need he had turned to this Mighty River rather than to do any other thing. Should it come to the worst he had decided what to do. Out of the tangle around him, out of the mess of his own past the river alone could give him rest. Should he die his body should be given to this last resting place. Into it Europe should pass as into a new world.

Near the shore he saw a school of small fish which seemed to look at him, rippling the water as they moved out in unison. Raising his heavy head De Soto gave the order to proceed. Four of the men lifted him on an improvised stretcher and the party, headed by the Indians, started again north along the bank.

The whole country was strange to them. But there at the edge of that mighty river he had seen those little fish who would soon be eating him, he, De Soto the mighty explorer—He smiled quietly to himself with a curious satisfaction.

13

It was a shock to discover that she, that most well built girl, so discreet, so comely, so able a thing in appearance, should be so stupid. There are things that she cannot learn. She will never finish school. Positively stupid. Why her little brother, no bigger than Hop o' my Thumb has caught up to her and will soon outstrip her. Her older brother is the brightest boy in the High School. She will I suppose breed stupid children. Plant wizards choose the best out of lots running into the millions. Choose here there everywhere for hybrids. A ten-pound white leghorn cockerel, hens that lay eggs big enough to spoil the career of any actor. She might though have bright children. What a pity that one so likely should be so stupid. Easier to work with but I should hate a child of mine to be that way. Excuses—Try first. Argue after. Excuses. Do not dare.

There sat the seven boys—nine years old and there-abouts—planning dire tortures for any that should seduce or touch in any way their sisters. Each strove to exceed the other. Tying his antagonist to a tree Apollo took out his knife and flayed him. For sweet as the flute had been yet no man can play the flute and sing at the same time. But the God had first played his harp and then sung to his own accompaniment—a thing manifestly unfair. No doubt, his sense of being in the wrong whetted his lust for the other's hide. In any case he got what he was after. He was the winner and that was all there was about it.

Each boy would think with a secret glow of a new torture: I would dip his hands in boiling lead—they often melted old pieces of lead in a plumber's pot over a field fire to make slugs for their bean shooters—then I would tie a rope to his feet and drag him on cinders etc. . . . each inventing a worse torture than that pictured before. And all for their sisters' virtue. So there under the east wall of the Episcopal Church they sat in a group on the grass and talked together for an hour.

The real empire builders of our colonial period were not the statesmen, the men of wealth, the great planters but the unknown pioneers who fought single-handed and at once both the primeval wilderness and the lurking savage. The hand crooked to the ploughtail was shaped to the trigger.

The Mesa Verde cliff dwellers—a much advanced race—formed a partnership with nature in the science of home building. Masterpieces of architecture, the survivals of the cliff dwellings tell the story of the ages.

On the top of a point high above the steep cliffs stood Sun Temple, so called, scene of the great ceremonial dramas of the clan. The building is in the form of the letter D and many of the stones which make up the thousand-odd feet of walls are highly decorated.

The corner stone of the building contains a fossil leaf of a palm tree. Influenced by anything which even in shape resembled the sun, the primitive people walled in the leaf on three sides and made a shrine.

The word *bayeta* is merely Spanish for *baize*. Great quantities of this were made in England for the Spanish and Mexican trade, the major part of which was of a brilliant red color. In this way English *baize* became Spanish *bayeta* to the

Indians of the American Southwest. Familiar with the art of weaving, these Indians unraveled the bayeta, retwisted it into one, two or three strands, and then rewove it into their blankets, which are now almost priceless. This old blanket was picked up by the author in a New Mexican corral, for the purpose of wiping his buggy axle. It was covered with filth and mud. A number of washings revealed this glorious specimen of the weaver's art.

Accepted by a cultured and talented belle, Lincoln, according to his law partner, had already been refused by Sarah Rickard, an obscure miss of sixteen, of whom apparently nothing further is known.

It was twelve feet from the rock into the water. As he stood looking down it seemed twenty. His eyes being five feet from his heels made it seem by that much higher than it was. He had never dived from such a height in his life. He had climbed up there to dive and he must dive or yield. What would he yield? At least it was something he did not intend to yield. He tried his best to imitate the others, he stood on the edge and plunged. It seemed to him that he plunged. As a matter of fact he dropped over the edge with his body bent almost double so that his thighs hit the water with a stinging impact, also the lower part of his belly, also the top of his head. He did not feel certain of himself for a moment or two after rising to the surface. That was about enough. Memory began to fill the blank of his mind.

There it was still, the men around Mrs. Chain's table on Locust St.: $3.50 a week. A week? Yes, three-fifty a week. And that place in Leipzig where they had only half cooked fresh pork. *Schwein schlacherei!* Bah. One week was enough there. Fraulein Dachs, *pflaumen suppe*. That purple and sweet soup. The white cakes they sold on the station platform near Malaga, what were they called? It seemed to be some native bake peculiar to the place. The devil fish in a black sauce in Seville. Big lumps of dough, big as snowballs, *sauer braten*. But Mrs. Chain's prunes were the most wonderful. Watery tidbits. It was prunes or applesauce. Her daughter was simple I guess. Did her best to land one of the students, kept it up for twenty years. At that table I met one of my dearest friends. Will you have some bread? Yes. That look. It was enough. Youth is so rich. It needs no stage setting. Out went my heart to that face. There was something soft there, a reticence, a welcome, a loneliness that called to me. And he, he must have seen it in me too. We looked, two young men, and at once the tie was cemented. It was gaged accurately at once and sealed for all time. The other faces are so many prunes.

Have you ever seen a dish of small birds all lying on their backs on the dish and with feet in the air, all roasted stiff but brown and savory? Rice birds I think they called them. Or snails or baked eggs?

The old man raked slowly. It took him all day to finish the small lawn. But it was autumn and the leaves had fallen thickly. The bird bath was full of leaves. It was a sentimental picture. But after all why? The leaves must fall into every corner. If they fall into the bird bath that is all there is to it. Still it calls many things to the mind that are not evoked by the twingling of waves on a lake shore in August.

Clark had taken a job as clerk at Pocono, and she was a Quakeress. They got to know each other very, very well. And this girl in the steamer chair, it was the cattle men who attracted her. Let her go then, he said tying the cord with a piece of gauze twisted into a rope. When you bathe the baby for the first time do not put him into a tub but sponge him off carefully before the fire with castile soap and warm water. Be careful not to get the soap into his eyes. Is it nitrate of silver they use for a baby's eyes?

I could not tell whether it was a baby or a doll the little girl was coddling. The Italians' babies are often so very small. They dress them up so grotesquely too. It must be a rigid custom with them.

Nothing at all. All at once it seemed that every ill word he had ever spoken struck his ear at the same moment. What a horrible roar it made. But there were other things, too many to record. Corners of rooms sacred to so many deeds. Here he had said so and so, done so and so. On that picnic he had dared to be happy. All the older women had watched him. With one girl under each arm he had let his spirit go. They had been closer than anything he could now imagine.

14

Particles of falling stars, coming to nothing. The air pits them, eating out the softer parts. Sometimes one strikes the earth or falls flaming into Lake Michigan with a great hiss and roar. And if the lawless mob that rules Ireland with its orderly courts and still more orderly minds will not desist it must be crushed by England. So that to realize the futility of American men intent upon that virtue to be found in literature, literature, that is, of the traditional sort as known in France and Prussia—to realize how each serious American writer in turn flares up for a moment and fizzles out, burnt out by the air leaving no literary monument, no Arc de Triomphe behind him, no India subdued—To realize this it is necessary to go back to the T'ang dynasty where responsibility rested solely on the heads of the poets—etc. . . . etc. . . . Or better still why not seek in Aleppo or Jerusalem for the strain to save us.

America is lost. Ah Christ, Ah Christ that night should come so soon.

And the reason is that no American poet, no American man of letters has taken the responsibility upon his own person. The responsibility for what? There is the fire. Rush into it. What is literature anyway but suffering recorded in palpitating syllables? It is the quiet after the attack. Picking a sliver of bone from his mangled and severed leg he dipped it in his own gore and wrote an immortal lyric. Richard Coeur de Lion shot through the chest with an iron bolt wrote the first English—no, French, poem of importance. What of democratic Chaucer? He was only a poet but Richard was a man, an adventurer, a king. The half mad women rushed to impregnate themselves against him. And this is literature. This is the great desirable. Soaked in passion, baba au rhum, the sheer proof of the spirit will do the trick and America will be King. Up America. Up Coeur de Lion. Up Countess Wynienski the queen of Ireland.

Polyphemus took first one shape then another but Odysseus, the wise and crafty, held firm. He did not let go but Polyphemus did. In fact the God could not exist without Odysseus to oppose him.

Why man, Europe is YEARNING to see something new come out of America.

In a soup of passion they would see a little clam. Let us smile. This is—

The danger is in forgetting that the good of the past is the same good of the present. That the power that lived then lives today. That we too possess it. That true novelty is in good work and that no matter how good work comes it is good when it possesses power over itself. Europe's enemy is the past. Our enemy is Europe, a thing unrelated to us in any way. Our lie that we must fight to the last breathe is that it is related to us.

We are deceived when they cry that negro music is the only true American creation. It IS the only true from the European point of view. Everything is judged from that point of view. But to us it is only new when we consider it from a traditional vantage. To us it means a thousand things it can never mean to a European. To us only can it be said to be alive. With us it integrates with our lives. That is what it teaches us. What in hell does it matter to us whether it is new or not when it IS to us. It exists. It is good solely because it is a part of us. It is good THEREFORE and therefore only is it new. Everything that is done in Europe is a repetition of the past with a difference. Everything we do must be a repetition of the past with a difference. I mean that if negro music is new in an absolute sense—which it is not by any means, if we are to consider the Ethiopian—the probable Ethiopian influence in Egypt—then it is new to Europe as it is to us.

It is not necessary for us to learn from anyone but ourselves—at least it would be a relief to discover a critic who looked at American work from the American viewpoint.

We are a young nation and have not had time or opportunity to catch up with nations that had ten centuries start of us. We still labor under the handicap of our Puritan lineage. . . .

We shall not be able to plead childhood any longer.

Eric the Red landed in Providence, Long Island, and was put in a cage so everyone could see him.

This sort of stupidity we have to combat. I am not talking of the mass of plumbers and carpenters. I am talking of the one thing that is permanent. Spirits. I am saying that America will screw whom it will screw and when and how it will screw. And that it will refrain from screwing when it will and that no amount of infiltration tactics from "superior civilizations" can possibly make us anything but bastards.

We are only children when we acknowledge ourselves to be children. Weight of culture, weight of learning, weight of everything such as abandon in any sense has nothing to do with it. We must first isolate ourselves. Free ourselves even more than we have. Let us learn the essentials of the American situation.

We who despise the blackguards in the old sense. We too are free. Free! We too, with paddles instead of turbines will discover the new world. We are able. We are kings in our own right.

We care nothing at all for the complacent Concordites? We can look at that imitative phase with its erudite Holmeses, Thoreaus, and Emersons. With one word we can damn it: England.

In Patagonia they kick up the skulls of the river men out of the dust after a flood. In Peru, in Michu Pichu the cyclopean wall on the top of the Andes remains to rival the pyramids which after all may have been built of blocks of some plaster stuff of which we have lost the combination.

I know not a land except ours that has not to some small extent made its title clear. Translate this into ancient Greek and offer it to Harvard engraved on copper to be hung in the waterclosets which freshmen use.

And why do they come to naught? these falling stars, etc.

It has been generally supposed that among the peoples of the earth the age of maturity comes earliest in the tropics and increases gradually as one goes northward. But in North America this rule has one striking exception. It is not rare among Esquimau women that they have their first child at 12 and children born before the mothers were 11 have been recorded. Point Barrow Alaska 300 miles north of the Arctic circle.

But the early maturity of the Esquimau girls is strictly in accord with the supposition that the hotter the environment the earlier the maturity. To all intents and purposes the typical Esquimau lives under tropical or subtropical conditions. The temperature of the Esquimau house indoors frequently rises to

90°. When they go out the cold air does not have a chance to come in contact with the body, except for a limited area of the face. When an Esquimau is well dressed his two layers of fur clothing imprison the body heat so effectively that the air in actual contact with his skin is always at the temperature of a tropical summer. He carries the climate about with him inside his clothes.

When an Esquimau comes inside such a house as the one I have been speaking of he strips off all clothing, immediately on entering, except his knee breeches, and sits naked from the waist up and from the knees down. Great streams of perspiration run down the face and body and are being continually mopped up with handfuls of moss.

The effect of the overheated houses is more direct upon the women than the men for they remain indoors a large part of the winter.

Otherwise in North America among the Indians as one goes north from Mexico toward the arctic sea the colder the average temperature of the air that is in contact with the body through the year, the later the maturity of the girls. The most northerly of the Atabasca Indians appear to suffer a great deal from the cold.

The Dog Rib and Yellow Knife Indians are often so poorly clad that they have to be continually moving, for if they stop for even half an hour at a time their hands become completely numb.

In the evenings their wigwams are cheerful with a roaring fire but while one's face is almost scorched with the heat of the roaring flames one's back has hoar-frost forming upon it. At night the Indians go to sleep under their blankets covering up their heads and shivering all night. The average age of maturity of the girls of these tribes is as high or higher than that of north European whites.

But north from the Slavey and Dog Rib Indians to the Esquimau country the conditions suddenly change. One comes in contact with a people that has a system of living almost perfectly adapted to a cold climate, while the northern Indians have a system almost unbelievably ill adapted to the conditions in which they live.

In Puritan New England they wrapped the lover and his lass in one blanket and left them before the dying hearth after the family retired. There was a name for it which I have forgotten.

15

It was another day ended. Another day added to the days that had gone before. Merest superstition. The eternal moment remained twining in its hair the flowers of yesterday and tomorrow. The newer street lights sparked in the dark. The uphill street which that morning had been filled at its far end with the enormous medal-with-rays of the sun was now flecked with sparkles. It was Carlstadt, established as a free thinker's corporation by Carl Weiss of Berne from which all churches had been excluded. Another day—any day—.

There lay that great frame of a man with his heavy features relaxed his loose jowls rising and falling with each breath while the busy surgeons tinkered at his elbow. Soon they struck gold and out spurted the red. Martha, who had not gone downstairs for over an hour caught it in a white porcelain bowl, an ounce, two ounces—she thought—estimating the amount swiftly. Then four ounces, eight. He was a large man. When will they check it! His breathing had grown easier. He was benefitted. A pint! He was white. In an hour men on horseback were riding north and south. Washington was dead. It was another day. Any day.

Davy Crockett had a literary style. Rather than blow his squirrel to bits he'd strike the tree just under its belly so that the concussion would stun it. Such was the country with the element of time subtracted. What is time but an impertinence?

Homesteading in the far western states was a struggle. Every child born there had a mother who is thrice a heroine. A woman in such a country approached motherhood at a time when her husband had to be away from home. Up to the day of her confinement she had to milk, churn, care for the chickens, work in the garden and carry water to the house from a well three hundred yards away . . . The day of her confinement she did a large washing then walked two miles to the home of a neighbor.

For that the brat seized her by the lug with his little sharp teeth and drew blood. We'll have to put him on the bottle.

Nothing, save for the moment! In the moment exists all the past and the future! Evolution—! Anti-peristalsis. Eighty-seven years ago I was born in a little village in the outskirts of Birmingham. The past is for those that lived in the past, the present is for today. Or—today! The little thing lay at the foot of the bed while the midwife—It was in England 1833. And now by the sea a new world death has come and left his chewing gum in an artery of her brain. But I'll pay you for this, she said as they were sliding her into the ambulance, I'll pay you for this. You young people think you are awfully smart, don't you. I don't want to see them again, those fuzzy things, what are they, trees?

Good gracious, do you call this making me comfortable? The two boys had her on the stretcher on the floor. Yes, stay here a week then I can do what I please but you want to do what you please first. I wonder how much she planned.

16

Another day, going evening foremost this time. Leaning above her baby in the carriage was Nettie Vogelman, grown heavier since we knew her in the sixth grade twenty-five years before and balancing great masses of prehistoric knowledge on her head in the shape of a purple ostrichplume hat.

But where is romance in all this—with the great-coat she was wearing hanging from the bulge of her paps to the sidewalk? Romance! When knighthood was in flower. Rome. Eliogabalus in a skirt married his man servant.

We struggle to comprehend an obscure evolution—opposed by the true and static church—when the compensatory involution so plainly marked escapes our notice. Living we fail to live but insist on impaling ourselves on fossil horns. But the church balanced like a glass ball where the jets of evolution and involution meet has always, in its prosperous periods, patronised the arts. What else could it do? Religion is the shell of beauty.

The fad of evolution is swept aside. It was only mildly interesting at the best. I'll give you a dollar my son for each of these books you read: Descent of Man and Origin of Species, reprinted by Dombie and Sons, Noodle Lane, Ken. W. London, England 1890.

Who will write the natural history of involution beginning with the stone razor age in Cornwall to the stone razor age in Papua? Oh China, China teach us! Ottoman, Magyar, Moor, teach us. Norse Eric the Discover teach us. Cœur de Lion, teach us. Great Catherine teach us. Phryne, Thaïs, Cleopatra, Brunehilde, Lucretia Borgia teach us. What was it, Demosthenes, that she said to you? Come again?

Borne on the foamy crest of involution, like Venus on her wave, stript as she but of all consequence—since it is the return: See they return! From savages in quest of a bear we are come upon rifles, cannon. From Chaldeans solving the stars we have fallen into the bellies of the telescopes. From great runners we have evolved into speeches sent over a wire.

But our spirits, our spirits have prospered! Boom, boom. Oh yes, our spirits have grown—

The corrosive of pity, Baroja says, giving up medicine to be a baker.

Marriage is of the church because it is the intersection of *loci* by which alone there is place for a church to stand. Beauty is an arrow. Diana launched her shaft into the air and where the deer and the arrow met a church was founded and there beauty had died.

So youth and youth meet and die and there the church sets up its ceremony.

Who will write the natural history of involution?

I have forgotten something important that I wanted to say. Thus having forgotten and remembered that it was important the folly of all thought is revealed.

The deer lay panting on the leaves while Diana leaned over it to stab it in the neck with her dagger.

I have forgotten what I wanted to say.

Venus and Adonis.

The second time I saw her it was in a room of a hotel in the city.

17

As the Southern mountains are not like other mountains, so the mountaineers are not like others. For all their beauty these mountains are treacherous and alien, and the people who must wring a livelihood from the sawmills or from the tiny perpendicular farms high up under the sky come to be wary and secret like their woodlands.

The Cumberland mountain mother, by nature sharp and sane, has studied the moods of the mountains and of the animals. Illiterate though she be, she is full of ripe wisdom. Many, superior to the mountain woman in, say, sanitation might learn from sitting on cabin doorsteps that they are most often inferior to her in sanity.

Yet, frankly, it is often better to sit on the cabin doorstep than to go inside. The mountain mother struggles bravely against dirt, but if you live in a lonely two-room cabin, if you are the sole caretaker of six children under ten, and two cows and a large stony garden, and must help in the cornfield besides, you are excusable if in the end you "quit struggling." The mountain mother does not make herself and her husband and her children slaves to the housekeeping arts.

A mountain woman dips snuff—surreptitiously if she is young, frankly if she is old.

We settle down on the doorstep probably on straight chairs with seats of cornhusks twisted into a rope and then interwoven. There is a sound to which the mountains have accustomed me—the sharp jolting thud when a mother, if she possesses neither cradle nor rocker, puts her baby to sleep by jerking forward and backward on two legs of a straight chair. There is usually some two-year-old lying fast asleep on the bed just inside the door; or on the porch floor, plump and brown as a bun and studded with flies thick as currants.

Mountain children are as vigorous as baby oaks until they reach their 'teens, and then over-work begins to tell on growing bodies. A reedy boy of thirteen, just beginning to stretch to the length of spine and limb that characterises the mountain air, often gets a stoop that he never afterward conquers. In the more remote lumber districts I have seen boys of ten and twelve work all day loading cars. There too, slim mountain girls of twelve and fourteen stand all day in the icy spray of the flume to stack bark on the cars.

Here where isolation makes people fiercely individualistic public opinion is as slow to deny a man's right to marry at the age he wishes as it is to deny his right to turn his corn into whisky. At the age when boys and girls first awake to the fact of sex they marry and the parents, although regretfully, let them.

The unmarried mother is most rare. A boy of sixteen sets himself to all the duties of fatherhood. A fourteen-year-old mother, with an ageless wisdom, enters without faltering on her future of a dozen children.

But here is Lory. But again a disgression—: In any account of the mountains one must remember that there are three distinct types: the people of the little villages, almost all remote from railroads; the itinerant lumber workers, wood-choppers and mill-hands who follow the fortunes of the portable sawmill as it exhausts first one remote cove then another; and the permanent farmers who have inherited their dwindling acres for generations. Yet at bottom the mountain mother is always the same.

Lory lives in a one-room lumber shack, and moves about once in three months. The walls are of planks with inch-wide cracks between them. There are two tiny windows with sliding wooden shutters and a door. All three must be closed when it is very cold. For better protection the walls are plastered over with newspapers, always peeling off and gnawed by woodrats. The plank floor does not prevent the red clay from oozing up. The shack is some fifteen feet square. It contains two stoves, two beds, two trunks, a table and two or three chairs. In it live six souls: two brothers, their wives and a baby apiece.

Lory is part Indian, one surmises from the straight hair dropping over her eyes and her slow squawlike movements. Her face is stolid except when it flashes into a smile of pure fun. Dark though she is her breast, bared from her dark purple dress, is statue white. She looks down on her first baby with a madonna's love and her words have in them a madonna's awe before a holy thing: "I ain't never a-goin' to whip him. He ain't never a-goin' to need it, for he won't get no meanness if I don't learn him none."

The setting is fairyland. Mountain folk go far toward living on beauty. The women may become too careless and inert even to scrape away the underbrush and plant a few sweet potatoes and cabbages. They may sit through lazy hours mumbling their snuff sticks, as does Mrs. Cole, while children and dogs and chickens swarm about them: but even Mrs. Cole can be roused by the call of beauty.

"My husband he's choppin' at the first clearin' two miles from here, and he's been plumb crazy over the yaller lady slippers up that-a-way. He's been sayin' I must take the two least kids, what ain't never seen sech, and go up there and see 'em 'fore they was gone. So yesterday we went. It sure was some climb over them old logs, but Gawd them lady slippers was worth it."

I shall never understand the mystery of a mountain woman's hair. No matter how old, how worn or ill she may be, her hair is always a wonder of color and abundance.

Ma Duncan at fifty-five is straight and sure-footed as an Indian; tall and slim and dark as a gypsy, with gypsy's passionate love of out-of-doors. Her neighbors send for Ma Duncan from far and near in time of need. Going forth from her big farm boarding-house on errands of mercy. Up wild ravines to tiny cabins that seem to bud out like lichens from grey boulders wet with mountain streams, over foot logs that sway crazily over rock creeks, through waist-high undergrowth Ma Duncan goes with her stout stick.

As we reach a little grassy clearing Ma Duncan drops down to stretch out happily: So as I can hear what the old earth has to say me . . . Reckon it says, "Quit your fussin' you old fool. Ain't God kept your gang a young uns all straight so fur? He ain't a-going back on you now, just because they're growd."

Presently Ma Duncan sits up, her hands about her knees, her hat fallen from her wealth of hair, her gun on the ground beside her—often she carries a gun in the hope of getting a gray squirrel to be done in inimitable brown cream gravy for breakfast.

She looks out sadly over much worn woodland, with the great stumps remaining:

"I wish you could have seen the great old trees that used to be here. If folks wasn't so mad for money they might be here and a preachin' the gospel of beauty. But folks is all for money and all for self. Some-day when they've cut off all the beauty that God planted to point us to him, folks will look round and wonder what us human bein's is here fur—"

The mountain woman lives untouched by all modern life. In two centuries mountain people have changed so little that they are in many ways the typical Americans.

"The Lord sent me back" former pastor tells men in session at the church. With tears in his eyes, he enters meeting, escorted by two sons. Dramatic scene follows as he asks forgiveness for mistake he has made. Was in Canada and Buffalo. His explanation of absence is satisfactory to family and members he met last night.

Miss Hannen in seclusion at home. Her family declines to give statement.

Dominie Cornelius Densel, forty eight years old, former pastor, etc. . . . who left his wife and eight children etc. came home last night.

Miss T. Hannen, twenty-six years old, etc . . . who disappeared from her home, etc. . . . on the same afternoon that the dominie was numbered among the missing also came to her home the same evening.

Pictures of the missing dominie and member of his church who are home again.

18

Commodius renamed the tenth month Amazonius. But he died a violent death and the old name was returned.

I had five cents in my pocket and a piece of apple pie in my hand, said Prof. M. I. Pupin, of Columbia University, describing the circumstances of his arrival in America in the steerage of the steamship Westphalie from Hamburg half a century ago.

Today that American scholar of Serbian birth holds the chair in electromechanics at Columbia University.

Prof. Pupin is merely one of a host of former immigrants whose names are linked with the great strides in science, commerce, finance and industry and whose careers furnish living proof that America, besides breeding great men, imports them.

Claude Monet was born in Columbia, Ohio.

In industry and commerce the stories of many of the successful immigrants read like romances.

There is C. C. A. Baldi of Philadelphia who began with nothing and who is now one of America's foremost citizens of foreign birth. When he landed in this country thirty years ago he had only a few pennies in the pockets of his ragged trowsers. He knew no English and knew nothing of American customs, but he had heard of the opportunities which America offers to a wide-awake, ambitious immigrant willing to work.

Mr. Baldi bought thirty lemons with his pennies. He peddled them and with the proceeds of sales bought more lemons and peddled them. Before long he had a cart loaded with hundreds of lemons. In time the push-cart became a store and the store grew into a great business.

Other spectacular instances of success are furnished by the careers of Louis J. Horowitz, one of America's greatest builders and S. M. Schatzkin, who came to this country twenty-five years ago with 3 dollars carefully tucked away in his clothes and began peddling coal in the East side of New York. To-day Schatzkin has large sums invested in many big American enterprises.

Horowitz, who came here thirty years ago, built the Woolworth and Equitable buildings, one the tallest and the other the largest office building in point of floor space in the world. His first job was that of an errand boy. Later he worked as a parcel wrapper, then as a stock boy and then as a shoe salesman. After selling shoes he started selling real estate.

Witness, oh witness these lives my dainty cousins. Dear Madam: —It has often been said that one of the most interesting spots in America is the small space covered by the desk of the editor of the Atlantic Monthly.

All the qualities which make up the interest of life,—joy, sorrow, romance, ambition, experience,—seem to center in this spot in turn, radiating from every nook and corner of the world.

"Adventures," remarked the talented Mr. Disraeli, "are for the adventurous," and it is to those who think of life as the supreme adventure that the Atlantic is most confidently addressed.

If you care for a magazine that satisfies, vexes and delights by turn, you can safely subscribe to the Atlantic Monthly for the coming year.

Public Service Railway Company, Newark, N. J. Amazonius 10, 1920.—To our Patrons: As a fair minded citizen, your impartial consideration of the facts set forth in subjoined letter, written by me to the Board of Public Utility Commissioners under date of Amazonius 7th. 1920, is respectfully requested. Very truly yours, Thomas N. McCarter, President.

To the Board of Public Utility Commissioners of the State of New Jersey, Trenton, New Jersey. Dear Sirs: The rate of fare of 7 cents, with one cent for a transfer, etc. . . . , etc. . . . Such large cities as Boston, New Haven, Hartford and Pittsburg already have a 10c. flat rate. Etc. . . . etc. . . . Under the foregoing statement of facts the company is forced to file herewith a flat rate of 10c. where 7c. is now charged. Etc. . . . etc. . . .

Now when Christmas bells ring clear
Telling us that love is here
And children sing
Gifts that speak of thoughtful love
Just like angels from above
Glad tidings bring.

Rugs, mirrors, chairs, tables, W. & J. Sloane, N.Y., Wash., San F. Christmas Gifts Sure to be Appreciated.: Standing lamps, table lamps, book ends, Sheffield ware, desk sets, framed prints, porcelains, soft pillows, foot rests (D-2968 Rocking foot rest in Mahogany. Formerly $45.00. Sale Price $30.00!) sconces, mantel clocks, wall clocks, tall clocks, small tables, smoking stands, occasional chairs, screens, oriental rugs, Chinese embroideries, vacuum cleaners—Mirrors. Small Oriental Rugs: Mossouls, Pergames, Beloochistans, Lilehennas, Sarouks and Kirmanshahs.

California was peopled by the Indians first and then by the Padres who brought with them their sprigs of vine and of orange and of fig and also the art of irrigation. So that you will find today from the very northernmost part, from Klamath Lake down to the Imperial Valley in the South, the lands of California watered and made as fertile as the valley of the Nile.

That's all right. Yes Sir. But I come from the Eastern shore of Maryland. I'm an East Sho' man. Have you ever been on the Eastern Sho'? No? Well sir, we're a strange people and we have some strange legends on the East Sho'. When Adam and Eve lived in the Garden of Eden they fell sick and the Lord was very much disturbed over them, so he called a council of his angels and wanted to know where they should be taken for a change of air.

Gabriel suggested the Eastern Sho' of Maryland but the Lord said, No, No; that wouldn't be sufficient change.

Yes sir, down at Chincoteague they

have the biggest and the finest oysters in the world. Big as your hand and when you get a half dozen of them a couple of hours out of the water you know you have something.

It was at Chincoteague two Spanish galleons went ashore in the old days and some ponies swam ashore. To this day they have a yearly round-up on the island where the breed of these ponies is coralled, a short special breed of horse.

Tangier Island is another place. That's where the sheriff shot the boy who wouldn't go in off his front porch on Sunday morning during church service. Either in church or in the house during that hour. He shot him all right. They have little individual canals up to their back doors from the bay.

And the native, coming up to him suddenly with a knife as long as your arm, said, *Yo soy mas hombre que tu!* and started a swing at him. Had he not been so quick to seize a chair and bring it down on the man's head—What would have happened?

19

Sometimes the men would come in and say there was a turkey nest down in the meadow and they'd send me to look for it.

Once I fell in the mireage up to my waist. My, they was mad at me. "Can't tramp a meadow without falling in the mireage?" they said.

I miss it often. At nine they let me drive the hay-hoist with one horse and later with two. One morning I had the young team out. It was Allie's team of greys, they was only just no more than colts. They shied at a piece of paper. I could hear the men up in the barn yelling. "Hey, what's the matter down there!" But it was no use. I tried to get to their heads. I wasn't afraid of them. Allie said afterward he wouldn't have been surprised to have seen me killed.

One of the women stood in the road waving a broom. I can see her yet. I might have been able to manage them if it hadn't been for her but they simply jumped over a wagon and smashed the hay-fork and ran down the road two miles. Then they came back again. My but the old man was mad at me. All the black looks I got!

I used to hate the Old Man. Sometimes I'd be getting wood and he'd ask me why I hadn't done something. I'd say I hadn't gotten round to it yet. Maybe he'd throw a piece of wood at me.

I can remember the churning. I wouldn't exactly like to go back to it all but sometimes I miss it terribly. Sometimes it wouldn't take you more than five minutes to get to the butter and sometimes you'd churn for 45 or two hours and sometimes it would never come. We'd get four or five pounds or more at a churning. Then it would have to be washed and salted and packed in jars in the cellar.

So now that it is raining. So now that it is Amazonius—we go to buy a metal syringe at the factory because we know the men who live on our street who own the bricks that make the walls that hold the floors that hold the girls who make mistakes in the inventories:

Every order that comes in is copied. You must rely on your help. As the orders come in they are handled by a girl who puts them on our own uniform order sheets. So right there it begins. You have to rely on a young flyaway who has perhaps been up dancing the night before. It's easy enough for her to write "with" for "without" and—that's the sort of thing that happens. There is a certain minimum of error that you must count on and no reputable house will fail to make good promptly.

The glass blowers have never in my entire experience of 17 years suffered any harm from their trade. Why we had a boy in the old factory, a cripple, a withered leg, the weakest, scrawniest lad you ever saw. He's been blowing for us for 15 or 17 years and you should see him today. Why the fat fairly hangs down over his collar.

In our thermometer work they blow the bulb then fill it with mercury which is in a special container like the cups you get at Child's restaurant say. They never have to touch the stuff. When the bulb is full they seal it. Then the mercury in the bulb is warmed by passing the bulb through a flame. This is to drive it up the capillary tube. There can be no volatilization since the mercury is in the tube and this is the only time the stuff is heated. Then when the metal rises from the heat the other end of the glass is dipped in the stuff so that as the bulb now cools the mercury is sucked up filling the thermometer completely.

Sometimes, of course, a bulb breaks in heating so that the floor is full of the stuff.

The hydrofluoric acid for marking is used under a hood with a special exhaust-blower that has nothing else to do but exhaust that hood. There is not the slightest odor of fumes in the room. The air is as good there as here.

And what is your business?

Rag merchant.

Ah yes. And what does that mean?

Our main specialty is shoddy.

Ah yes. Shoddy is made from—

From woolen rags. The whole mass is put into a vat and the cotton dissolved out. It comes out in a great wet heap of stuff that has to be washed and dried.

Sometimes they burn the cotton out with gas. For instance you'll see a piece of cloth, grey cloth. The gas will take out the black cotton and leave the wool fibres all running in one direction. One of the secrets of the trade is the selection of the colors. That is red shoddy is made from red rags and so on. But they even take the dyes out of the cloth and use it over again.

You know the army coats the boys wore. They were 70% shoddy. It's all wool but the fibre has been broken. It makes a hard material not like the soft new woven woolens but it's wool, all of it.

After the stuff from the vats is dry they put it on the donkeys which turn it into loose skeins. From that stage it goes on to the making of the yarn for weaving when any quantity of fresh wool can be mixed that you desire.

The shortest fibre, that can't be used for anything else, is made into these workingmen's shirts you see. The wool is held in a container in the loosest state possible. This is connected up with a blower in front of which a loom is set for weaving a fairly tight cotton mesh. Then as the loom is working the wool is BLOWN IN! Where the cotton warp and woof cross the shoddy is caught.

Recently a Jew came in to complain of the lightness of the shirts he was getting. All we did was to yell out, "George turn on the blower a little stronger." One washing and the wool is gone. But the Jews are the smart ones. You got to hand it to them. They invent machinery to do anything with that stuff. Why one man made a million before the government stopped him by making cheap quilts.

He took any kind of rags just as they were collected, filth or grease right on them the way they were and teased them up into a fluffy stuff which he put through a rolling process and made into sheets of wadding. These sheets were fed mechanically between two layers of silkolene and a girl simply sat there with an electric sewing device which she guided with her hand and drew in the designs you see on those quilts, you know.

You've seen this fake oilcloth they are advertising now. Congoleum. Nothing but building paper with a coating of enamel.

¡O vida tan dulce!

Elinor Wylie

✻ 1885-1928

Elinor Wylie was born Elinor Hoyt in Somerville, New Jersey. She spent her childhood and youth near Philadelphia and in Washington, D.C. With her first husband she lived in Washington; with her second she lived in England and on the Continent for five years, then in Georgia and Maine, and then again in Washington. In 1919 the couple moved to New York. Mrs. Wylie was extraordinarily beautiful, with exquisite features and figure; she was also frail and perilously high-strung. Her appearance was only the outward expression of great power both in poetry and prose. In 1921 she published a volume of poems, Nets to Catch the Wind, *which was awarded a prize by the Poetry Society of America. In 1923 she was married to her third husband, William Rose Benét, the poet and editor. The couple lived in New York, though Mrs. Wylie (as she was always called) visited England often. In the last seven years of her life she worked unceasingly, and both her poetry and her prose grew markedly in brilliance and power. Exquisiteness and erudition characterize her four novels. For subjects she turned from the materialist 1920's to distant lands and cultures, and to romance and fantasy. In 1928 a stroke caused her instant death.*

The Venetian Glass Nephew

CONTENTS

BOOK ONE: PETER INNOCENT

And then he wept a little, and fell to talking of magic and macaroni.

PRINCE DE LIGNE

1 BLUE BALLOON

Peter Innocent Bon was about to return to the Republic of Venice; although he had that very day entered upon the eighty-first year of his age, his eyes, blue as veronica flowers, were even now full of a child's tears. His heart was lighter than a flower; indeed, it danced so high and airily, and teased the tenuous cord of his mortality with such persistent malice, that he conceived of it as a toy balloon, an azure plaything in a pantomime, caught by a thread of gold to stable earth, and germane to the sky.

It will be unnecessary to explain to minds versed in such matters that Peter Innocent Bon must by no means be confounded with John Bona of Mondovi, a misapprehension imaginable in the ignorant, since both were cardinals and both distinguished scholars. But wider far than the mere century of time separating the lives of these holy men is the gulph that sunders their natures and their activities. Consanguinity there may have been, in reason, but the two were never spiritually akin. Peter Innocent undoubtedly possessed the Antwerp edition of his cousin's works, published in 1777, and the devotional treatise "De Sacrificio Missæ" was often in his hands; a few marginal notes attest to application saddened by bewilderment. To those desiring to achieve a better comprehension of the character of Peter Innocent Bon, cardinal priest and cardinal prefect of the Congregation of the Propaganda, the historian recommends a careful study of his poetical writings (Venice, 1790) and his notes upon liturgical subjects (Parma, 1794). His memoirs, surveying as they did almost the entire length of the eighteenth century with a bland and illuminative eye, must have contained matter of the highest interest; this valuable document was unfortunately destroyed by Madame de Staël in a passing fit of temper during the composition of "Corinne," merely because it contained a simple unadorned account of the coronation of Corilla Olimpica.

On this eighth of May, 1782, Peter Innocent, clad in the grey-brown garb of the Franciscan Friars Minor, stood dreaming among delicate grotesques in the porch of his titulary church of St. Bonaventura. It was evening; the Roman sun had lost its imperial savagery, and tempered light lay tenderly upon the cardinal's brow. His face, that had beheld the secular world for eighty years, was lifted to the more transparent heaven; forgetting Rome and even the Vatican, he regarded the Holy City above the horns of the new moon. He looked affectionately yet familiarly into the little loopholes of the stars, with none of the bitter hunger of the returning exile; to Peter Innocent the bread of earth was never salty, nor the stairs of heaven too steep. As a boy may see at evening the lighted windows of his mother's kitchen, he saw without surprise celestial preparation for his home-coming through a bright chink that may have been Aldebaran. Tugging at its gilded thread, his heart danced over him, a blue balloon in deeper aërial blue.

Above the chiselled silver of his head, his heart danced, expanded by happiness and an exquisite gratitude towards all humanity and the Son of God made man. In particular, his heart blessed the new pope, Pius VI, for although Giovanni Angelo Braschi had ruled Christendom for some seven years, Peter Innocent never thought of him save as a handsome innovation, superseding with the suavest courtesy the cardinal's dead patron and beloved friend, the Franciscan Clement XIV. Now this same Pius, whom Peter Innocent a little feared, the more that he was beautiful and brilliant and vain, proposed for reasons of his own to visit the green lagoons and golden palaces of Venice, having among his suite, again for reasons of his own, Peter Innocent Bon, cardinal prefect of the Congregation of the Propaganda.

The cardinal did not concern himself with reasons; he thought of Venice, and the bright thread pulled hard upon his heart. He had not seen that city for nearly thirty years; not since his brother

Nicholas Bon was banished to the monastery of Venda by the Council of Ten and the Inquisitors of the Holy Office. In that same year Paul Dona was confined in the fortress of Palma, and five years later the noble Angelo Querini was imprisoned in the castle of St. Felice at Verona.

For a time the spirit of Peter Innocent suffered a faint infusion of bitterness throughout its milk and honey; he began to believe in spies and politics, and found himself disliking the Dominicans without feeling any particular love for the Jesuits. But he managed with admirable tact to hold himself aloof from all dissension, and it is certain that his veined patrician hand was not among those which upheld the fainting resolution of Lorenzo Ganganelli as the pontiff traced the momentous syllables of the brief, *Dominus ac redemptor* and signed it Clement, servant of the servants of God.

But this was years, and happy years, ago, and to-day Peter Innocent could remember that all these brave and liberal senators had been set free either by death or by the reforms of '63, and that Querini had travelled in Switzerland and become a valued friend of Voltaire's. The cardinal had long ago forgiven Venice, and upon this Ascension Eve his heart was a blue balloon because it was going home.

He thought of himself as a child upon other Ascension eves and morrows, in a past not dim at all, but radiant as a double dawn in sky and water. He saw the *Bucintoro* setting forth from Santa Lucia, a gilded barge arrayed in cloth of gold, with winged lions, tritons, nereids, painted with gold and burnished by the sun, with the great standard of the republic crackling like lightning overhead. He thought of the ancient glory of Venice, and of the Lion of the Evangelist. His grey habit of the Seraphic Order fell from his shoulders, and he was a child again, in a coat of sapphire velvet, with a silver feather in his cap.

Softly, very softly, the supple folds of dun-colour descended once more over this remembered magnificence, and Peter Innocent felt the worn, warm fabric about his fragile bones. Here, too, was cause for gratitude, for the new pope had permitted him to continue in this ingenuous disguise, first granted him by the generosity of Clement, so that he alone of the pontifical family went comfortably impoverished, clad in the mystic tatters of Assisi. Within a remote wing of the Vatican a wardrobe of ebony and figured brass guarded vestments of white and red and green, of violet and black and the more curious sheen of metal, with robes and rochets of a less sacral character and rich liturgical gloves and stockings, intermixed with honorific decorations.

Peter Innocent loved best to drift, elusive as a skeleton leaf, along the streets of Rome, recognized by all, but accosted by none save an occasional German traveller or English milord; the legerity of the French mind made the Gallic visitor quick to comprehend his desire for solitude, and the very transparency of the masking rendered it invulnerable. Whether or not he believed himself effectively disguised remained a mystery to the last. He spoke but little; indeed it was a common saying at the time that Clement had forgotten to unseal his mouth; his smile, however, impressed even the most impious as a small flame burning perpetually within the silver shadow of his countenance.

At the conclusion of Vespers, he often knelt in a sculptured recess of the Church of St. Bonaventura, while the words *O salutaris hostia* were borne upon the wings of ancient music towards the benediction. As the priest, his shoulders wrapped in the humeral veil, lifted the monstrance from the lighted altar and with it described in that already consecrated air the sign of the cross, the tears of Peter Innocent aspersed like holy water whatever evil might survive within those walls, beneath that vaulted nave.

2 CONSIDER THE LILIES

Near St. George in Alga, upon an irridescent morning of mid-May, the Doge and Signory of Venice received the pontiff and his suite, conveying them thence to the monastery of St. John and St. Paul, where they were sumptuously lodged. As the lacquered barge imposed its fan of ripples, like a peacock's tail, upon lagoon and narrowing canal, the visitors vied with one another in expressions of awe and contentment; they moved in the heart of a pearl whose orient skin was outer space. Peter Innocent alone was silent; his youth overwhelmed him as though every immemorial wave of the Adriatic were poured upon his pensive head. He bowed his face upon his folded hands; when he lifted his eyes again, they were dazzled by the great palaces of the Venetian patriciate, all arabesqued in marble and embossed by emblems. Here burned the silver torch of the Morosini; the silver ladder of the Gradenigo scaled the heavens; the five-leaved roses of the house of Loredan endured in frosted stone so delicate that it appeared to spread a perfume on the air.

The gondolas were black, but all their canopies were coloured like the parterres of a prince's garden. The sunlight smelled of musk and peppermint; although the day was warm, a lady carried a muff of panther-fur; she was followed by an Ethiopian in scarlet livery, bearing a letter sealed with Spanish wax. A naked child, an Eros cast in gilded bronze, drank from the sea-green shell of a melon, held high above his lips. Peter Innocent remembered that the Italians of an elder day, while yet that day was young, made melancholy synonymous with wickedness, and gave to the verb to "think" the sense of to "be sad." He took the meaning, but without a heavy mind; his heart's indulgence was poured like a libation over Venice and absorbed in her waters.

He remembered his old friend, the priest called Testa, the Diogenes of the spiders' webs, who shared his straw pallet with a familiar rat, and lived on mouldy bread and lentils. And he remembered, also, that other eccentric, the ancient with the iron bell, who was used to stand upon the quays and bridges, crying out with his own outlandish tongue and the bell's clapper, crying upon all men to be happy, in the name of God. And although this person was a Moor and an infidel, he was nevertheless a philosopher and a lover of humanity. Peter Innocent thought of him with kindness, preferring him, perhaps, for a reprehensible moment, to the Christian priest, and wondering if he were not the wiser man. For Peter Innocent, flying through sunlight followed by a peacock's tail of foam, attired for once in all the splendour relative to his spiritual and temporal state, had not forgotten that long before he had assumed this purple he had fared very happily as one of the jongleurs of God. So, like the Moor, he rang continually a little bell whose tongue was not of iron, but of gold, and bright and silent as a flame.

The cardinal Peter Innocent was at all times silent, since Pope Clement had neglected to unseal his mouth; now he was hushed into a profounder stillness by his private felicity, and by the high and rapid speech of those about him. The Doge and the Procurator Manin were engaged in conversation with the illustrious visitor Pius VI; although preserving every indication of reverence for his Holiness, the Venetian nobles did not hesitate to address him with fluency and animation. The pope's nephew, the blond and arrogant Braschi Onesti, grandee of Spain and prince or the Holy Empire, stared somewhat haughtily upon these self-possessed patricians; he wore a coat of carnation velvet, and the little finger of his left hand was all but hidden by an emerald of fabulous value. At his knee the Abate Monti crouched like a beaten hound. "Consider the lilies—" and the pope's device, cut on a hundred monuments in Rome, was an heraldic wind, blowing down lilies like waves of the sea! This, too, was inscribed on marbles by Canova and the recovered classical remains of Herculaneum; yet Solomon in all his glory had no finer coat than young Braschi Onesti, nor could his seal have utterly outshone that green intaglio graved with the head of Agrippina. So thought Peter Innocent, and as the thought was, for him, faintly malicious, his smile flickered for a moment like a flame that has had a pinch of salt sprinkled upon its clarity.

For here, and suddenly, a small regret, an obscure discomfort, touched the cardinal with a pain no more important than may be inflicted by a kitten's ivory claw. So slight a blow it was that his mind scarcely recorded it; the glancing scratch cut the thin skin of his soul a little, as always, and if this same skin had been a visible thing, the closest scrutiny might have revealed a vast number of similar punctures, microscopically bleeding. This was the recurrent thorn in the clean flesh of Peter Innocent; this was his cross: he had no nephew.

So far as he knew, he was the only cardinal suffering under a like deprivation. He could not but consider the circumstance as a direct chastisement at the hand of God, yet he could not for the life of him decide wherefore the divine anger had so visited him; he examined his conscience, and found no really adequate sin. Nieces he had in plenty, the pretty flowering of Nicholas's romantic marriage; his sisters, having entered convents in early youth, might not, according to his code, be expected to serve him save by the efficacy of prayer. So far prayer had proved singularly inefficacious.

For his own part, he had prayed and fasted and made pilgrimages; there had been a period of hair shirts, but these had been forbidden by Pope Clement and his physician as merely a protracted form of torture of dubious virtue under the peculiar conditions.

Sometimes Peter Innocent wondered very vaguely and benignantly at the number of nephews possessed by some of the more powerful cardinals; it did not occur to his charity, however, to regard these youths as a commodity procurable by other means than the help of God and the wedded happiness of one's brothers and sisters. Of late he had been pricked to a certain reverential envy by the pope's very evident satisfaction in the society of the magnificent Braschi Onesti, haughty, negligently handsome, a prince of nephews indeed, and, more lately, a prince of the Holy Empire. Peter Innocent might himself have preferred a gentler nephew, a creature malleable and engaging to the affections of a mild old man, but at this moment he was immensely taken by the carnation velvet coat and Cæsar's signet-ring.

It is conceivable that he may have permitted himself a passing dream of parenthood—conceivable, but unlikely. The extreme chasity of his body extended to his spirit, or perhaps it were juster to say that the body and spirit of Peter Innocent was in this eighty-first year of his age a single amalgam, made from two substances of equal purity. This much is probable; that returning at a jocund season to a home of such miraculous loveliness as flowed and floated in the waves and clouds of Venice, he felt within the stiff and sanctified chrysalis of his flesh a lively movement as of uncurling wings, such exquisite and painted films as a moth hangs down to dry from the under side of a linden leaf. And he would have provided with joyous gratitude an opportunity to any saint to slit him down the back like a locust, if thereby might be freed a younger, fairer, and, to his humility, more perfect being than Peter Innocent Bon, perishing for this mystical offspring with all the fervour of the elder phœnix.

So thinking, or, more precisely, feeling, Peter Innocent passed into the monastery of St. John and St. Paul, whose venerable porch was a cavern dripping with refreshment after the full and golden glare of noon.

3 RITORNO DI TOBIA

The next day dawned like a crocus, and all the lilies of the pontiff's suite arose in green and silver and vermilion.

Peter Innocent breakfasted on a large bowl of chocolate and a very small piece of *marzipan,* of which he was inordinately fond. The other cardinals sprinkled spices in their cups, or drank coffee sweet with sugar and brandy; they ate a great many little birds, roasted with bacon and red pepper, and they had strawberries from Passeriano and peaches from Algiers. Every one ate what he preferred; Braschi Onesti had candied chestnuts and champagne.

Presently the pope called Peter Innocent into his particular chamber. Pius was sitting up in bed; his beautiful ivory face had been grieved and weary under a canopy the colour of pot-pourri, heavy with a like perfume. Across his knees lay Sanazzaro's *Arcadia,* stamped with the dolphin of the first Manutius. At his elbow stood an engraved goblet of clear water.

"Peter," he said in a soft voice, "after I have received the Doge and the assembled signory and granted audience both public and private to various bishops of the Venetian territory, I shall be very tired. Yet, even so, I must assist, together with the Patriarch Giovanelli, at a *Te Deum* rendered by the voices of the ducal choir, accompanied by fivescore instruments under the baton of Pasquale Galuppi. I am ill; the journey has exhausted and the republic's arrogance annoyed a mind already languid with affairs. May I count upon your friendship to support me in this hour of trial?"

Peter Innocent was overcome by pity and amaze at the pope's condescension. He fell rustlingly to his knees, and picking up the pontifical slipper, which reposed upon a silken drugget by the bed, he kissed it with reverence. Pius smiled indulgently, extending his fine hand in a gesture of release to indicate a comfortable armchair plumped by pigeon-down. The cardinal regained his feet rather shakily and sank among these cushions, breathless.

"Holiness," he whispered, "what singular good fortune makes me capable of serving you, and in what essential does such service lie?" Privately, he prayed the business might not be connected with the Inquisition or the liberal opinions of his brother Nicholas.

"Merely this and thus," replied the pope, closing his eyes with an air of elegant fatigue. "This respectable choirmaster, Galuppi, has composed a cantata for five voices in my especial honour, and on the words of Gaspare Gozzi; it will be performed at the Incurabili this afternoon. Ludovico Manin pays for it, and it will be a very pretty compliment, but of course I cannot attend in person; the *Te Deum* will consume my extremest energies; my vitality can support no further burden. As the eldest prelate in my suite, you will make an acceptable substitute for the father of Christendom; as a Venetian, your presence will confer satisfaction, as, I trust, your sensibilities will receive pleasure; these men are your compatriots. May I rely upon you, my kind Peter?"

The cardinal was deeply touched by these proofs of confidence; he was also overjoyed at the prospect of hearing the musical result of a collaboration between two beloved friends of his early manhood; he fancied he might meet them again and kiss their frosty cheeks. He had heard news of this cantata; its subject, the Return of Tobias, impressed him as being even more appropriate to his own obscure instance than to that of the sovereign pontiff. And he thought of the fresh virginal voices of the Incurabili, which had been taught to weave vocal harmonies as painstakingly as the fingers of less fortunate orphans are instructed in the intricacies of lace-making.

"Yes," he contrived to breathe, and "Gratitude," and "Holiness," and so was about to depart, when Pius stayed him with a gesture of white hands.

"Peter," he said affectionately, "if you are wearied by this ceremony, I will permit you to absent yourself from the festivities of the evening. Do as you please, my dear good fellow; you must have youthful affiliations to rebind, old memories to renew and cherish. I shall understand; this night is your own, unhampered by any duty to me. And, you know,—" he smiled very sweetly,—"a higher power is vested in my unworthy person; you may do as you like, Peter, for to-night, without fear of the consequences." His smile grew more indulgent, and he laughed with a peculiar tenderness as Peter Innocent kissed his scented ring and left him.

4 CRYSTAL MONSTERS

Blue dusk, thicker than fog and tinted with expressed essence of heaven along the falling colour of the dew, enveloped Peter Innocent as he slipped from the lighted doorway of the Incurabili; the music prolonged itself through other channels than his ears, and seemed to influence the hue of the most distant star and the perfume of the nearest pomegranate flower. He was happy, but a little loneliness, even a little fear, tinctured his mood. He had been unable to identify either of his old friends, and had found himself too shy to ask for them among the brocaded crowd of notables. Unobserved, he had sought the consolation of the twilight; he loved to be alone, but to-night his tranquillity had somehow failed him. He felt cold and rather tremulous as a touch fell upon his shoulder.

It was Alvise Luna, the glass-blower of Murano. He had grown very old, and his pale eyes were sunken in a face blank and dusty as a bag of yellow meal. Peter Innocent was shocked by the man's appearance, and greeted him sympathetically.

"Eminence," said Luna in a voice threaded by a whine, "I had not hoped to be recognized, nor, if recognized, acknowledged as an acquaintance by your Eminence. I have fallen upon evil times. I, whose ancestors worked in crystal for the great Duke of Buckingham and visited Tuscany at the invitation of the munificent Cosimo Second, I have not, to be frank with you, one copper coin wherewith to brighten another, I have drunk water for a fortnight, and the things I have eaten are not fit to be mentioned in your eminent presence. I am reduced to working for the infamous Giorgio Barbaria, who wishes to manufacture black glass bottles on the English lines; I have, as you may remember, considerable knowledge of foreign factories, and he pays me a dog's wages to instruct him. I am starving; my wife and children are starving; my little grandchildren are already dead from malnutrition. May I humbly beg your Eminence to aid me in my undeserved and dreadful trouble?"

This Luna was a liar and a sorcerer, and the Holy Office was already upon his path, which led through some of the most unsavoury cellars of Venice, marked out by a slimy brilliance like the track of a snail. But Peter Innocent did not know this, and had he known, he would not have understood it. He saw that the man was frightened, and he believed that he was hungry. As a matter of fact, Luna had plenty of money and merely wanted more; at the moment an enormous supper of polenta was distending his greasy waistcoat. But he was a dyspeptic, and his wry neck and hollow eyes looked wretched enough to move a more obdurate heart than Peter Innocent's.

"Of course," said the gentle old man, "of course, my poor friend, I will do what I can to help you."

An hour later, Peter Innocent was picking his slow, uncertain way down a damp and noisome corridor; Luna followed him, holding a candle as high as the dripping ceiling would permit. They descended a worn flight of stone stairs, and found themselves in a low-vaulted chamber whose debased Byzantine arches were dimly illuminated by a pair of ship's lanterns dependent therefrom.

This apartment was but too evidently a cellar, for a good three inches of water, cold and ambiguous, polluted the embroidered clocks upon the cardinal's stockings. Nevertheless, certain portions of the walls were covered by tapestries smouldering with the rich fancies of the Renaissance, and a number of carved cabinets and tables showed surfaces inlaid with brass or panelled in exotic lacquer. At one end of the chamber's secretive length, a small furnace filled with wood ashes made a spot of expiring rose-amber in the gloom.

Luna walked to the centre of the room, and, rapidly waving his guttering tallow back and forth, ignited in a flash a score of white wax candles cupped in coloured glass. Peter Innocent saw that a superb chandelier hung from the highest vaulting of the roof, a fantastic thing of flowers and icicles and silver bells, tinkling in the midst of squalor. And now, with a tinted radiance flooding every corner of the cobwebbed cellar, a hundred graceful and preposterous shapes sprang into the enchanted view: winged and maned and dolphin-finned, griffins and lions, stags and peacocks, and monsters fabulously horned and taloned.

The cardinal perceived in addition to these savage and exquisite creatures the accustomed implements of the glassblower's trade: pontils and blowpipes, pincers and wooden battledores. Upon a platform, raised above the pervasive dampness of the stone-flagged floor, stood the workman's chair, with its rigid parallel arms suggesting some rude instrument of torture. Seated within this strange machine was a mysterious stranger, wrapped in a black cloak, and wearing a small mask of black velvet.

Peter Innocent at once became aware of an element of masquerade in the appearance of this person. Having himself long ago assumed a disguise, albeit an holy one, he readily observed the same quality in the dress of others, and as readily ascribed it to the most innocuous desire for privacy. He took the gentleman to be a person of simple and retiring disposition, and acknowleged courteously and at once Luna's gesture of introduction. The stranger rose, displaying an impressive figure, tall and muscular. He wore a quantity of beautiful lace, and his rings were diamonds of the first brilliance; save for these elegant details, his clothes were of a uniform sable hue. His head was covered by a short chestnut peruke, and through the slits of his mask his eyes glinted very dark and bright. The skin of his face and hands was swarthy and faintly lined; the cardinal judged him to be past his first youth.

"Your Eminence," said Luna in French, which he spoke fluently, having, for several disgraceful reasons, been much in Paris, "permit me to present M. de Chastelneuf, Chevalier de Langeist." The latter title was pronounced in the German manner, and the cardinal was at a loss to conjecture the stranger's nationality until he spoke. His manners were courtly, if a little antiquated and florid, but he conversed with a strong Venetian accent, and Peter Innocent had no doubt that he was a native of the republic.

The chevalier kissed the cardinal's hand with immense politeness, and began at once to speak of the prelate's poetical works, displaying a quite remarkable knowledge and acumen. In this way, and through the use of copious quotation from the classics, the gentleman contrived to convey an impression of learning and respectability, and Peter Innocent felt sure he must be a person of consequence.

Such, in a measure, was indeed the case, for M. de Chastelneuf, as this narrative must continue to call him, had at one time or another attracted the attention of almost every court of Europe, and on this very evening no less a notable than Messer Grand himself had given our gentleman much good advice not unconnected with the miasmic quality of the Venetian air, and the superior salubriety of Munich or Vienna. And since it was the chevalier's invariable habit to travel in a superb English carriage, emblazoned with the arms of a ruined lord, and as, moreover, he seldom travelled alone, he had been faced with the disagreeable necessity of selling his diamonds and his point d'Alençon without delay. Save for the fortunate intervention of Luna, who knew the cardinal's simplicity was good for at least a thousand sequins, M. de Chastelneuf might have been forced to part with his cross of the Order of the Golden Spur. It is not surprising that his happiness in greeting Peter Innocent was unfeigned and infectious.

Presently the cardinal found himself ensconced within the glass-blower's misshapen armchair, with dry slippers upon his feet, and a couple of hot bricks under these. A glass of excellent Levantine Muscat warmed his vitals; the long room appeared less cavernous, and the crystal apparitions which filled it glowed like jewels in the renewed stream of his own vivacity. His two companions were persons of wit and esoteric learning, and his admiration for Luna increased as he examined one by one the marvellous progeny of the workman's art. As for the chevalier, the delicacy of his mind was equalled only by its ascetic and fastidious grace: Peter Innocent was soothed and enraptured by this refined society.

The Chevalier removed his mask, and his face showed handsome and aquiline, almost Oriental in its dusky tints, yet all Venetian in the liveliness and valour which informed its every smile. He had a nose like a falcon, and his deep-set eyes were black and gold. He told Peter Innocent that he had, in his youth, been honoured by the friendship of Benedict XIV, who had once taken his advice upon some little matters of no importance.

Suddenly M. de Chastelneuf rose to his very considerable height, at the same time making, for the benefit of Luna's eyes alone, an enigmatical sign whose nature it is impossible to describe. Luna also rose; the pair appeared to move in unison to some unheard and rhythmical injunction; salt and spices were destroyed upon the fire, and their smoke premitted to dim the purer radiance of the candle-flames. Then, at an unintelligible word pronounced by the altered voice of Chastelneuf, the incredible came to pass

Peter Innocent beheld a golden griffin lift his wings to fan the air; a stag, of azure glass dappled with the same gold, stepped with a fairy pride across the expanse of Chinese lacquer which separated him from his mate, and the two, meeting, caressed each other with delicate gestures of affection. A humming-bird, with feathers blown in pearl-colour and crimson, flew from his perch, alighting on the leafy chandelier; the spray that received him bent and swayed, and from its largest rose a petal drifted to the floor.

There is not the slightest use in pretending that Peter Innocent was shocked or even very greatly surprised. His mind moved happily in an atmosphere of miracles, and the charming nature of these phenomena precluded any suspicion of evil. He felt like a child who perceives at his first carnival a blue sky flowering with confetti, or who is presented at Christmas-time with one of those delightful German toys called Christbaum, bright with silver foil and tiny scarlet candles. So, without uncomfortable amazement, he stared enchanted at the delicious marvel of awakened life.

5 PIAVOLA DE FRANZA

It was Luna who finally crossed himself surreptitiously before addressing the cardinal in hoarse and lowered tones.

"Eminence," he whispered, "you have seen what our combined skill can accomplish; this, however, is only the beginning. It is very pretty to watch these insects and atomies, but what would you say to a flying horse able to transport your Eminence to Ecbatana; or a Cameroonian gorilla, blown in the best *mille fiori* and capable of strangling, with thumb and finger, persons inimical to your Eminence's peace of mind? I have, too, an extremely practical Indian serpent, the poison fang ingeniously supplied with *aqua tofana*." And he laid his hand upon the lock of a great chest, bound with copper, which occupied one corner of the room.

Peter Innocent turned pale as milk; in another moment he would have been constrained to believe evil of Alvise Luna. But Chastelneuf observed the old man's uneasiness, and stepping forward with an air of well-bred piety, he refilled the cardinal's empty glass and reverentially saluted his cold hand. Then he spoke very softly and persuasively.

"Monseigneur," he said, for despite his marked Italian accent he continued to employ the French language, "you must not be offended by the rough jests of my poor friend Luna; he is a stupid fellow, but good as bread, and of a simplicity truly pitiable in these wicked times. See how he has been persecuted by the Three, those sinister officials who deprived your noble brother of his liberty, and who have been the death of innumerable worthy citizens of Venice. Consider his industry, and talent, and then reflect upon his wretched circumstances and the sufferings of his devoted wife and children. I am sure you will consent to help him, Monseigneur; he asks no charity, but merely that you will patronize and encourage his beautiful craft by the purchase of one or two little articles of undoubted utilitarian and æsthetic value. This, for example—"

He made as if to open the iron-studded door of an inner chamber, but Luna stopped him with a clutch upon the arm and an imprecation. Chastelneuf smiled imperturbably and proceeded, flicking invisible dust grains from his satin sleeve:

"Your Eminence will graciously refrain from considering me presumptuous when I make clear the extent of our success in manipulating Murano glass; we are able to vitalize not only dumb animals, but even, with God's help, creatures formed in the divine image. It is a great responsibility, but I trust we acquit ourselves worthily as custodians of this sacred mystery. Monseigneur, you are ever in the company of the elect, but I, who am like your Eminence of a certain age, know all too well that the pangs of loneliness sometimes invade the most profoundly religious heart, and that our declining years, in their hallowed progression towards our Father's house, must needs require now and then the pitiful grace of human companionship, in salutation and farewell. If, then, the presence of a little being compact of modesty and sweetness, at once a daughter and a loving friend, blonde and ethereal as the ivory ladies of Carriera, could solace some spiritual hunger—"

He broke off, and silencing Luna by an imperious movement of the hand, walked firmly to the iron-studded door and opened it. Within, stiffly disposed upon a small gilt chair of French design, Peter Innocent could discern, though dimly, something like a large doll or a little girl; the creature appeared about sixteen years old, and wore a pale pink dress, trimmed with feather flowers in the best possible taste. A quantity of silvery-yellow hair fell to her shoulders, and her fair complexion was transparent and tinted like a shell. Her eyes were closed, her face tranquil and pretty. The cardinal was forcibly reminded of the Poupée de France in the Merceria, and, less vividly, of his sisters attired for their first ball, which was that given by the Morosini for Count Oldenburg in 1708, when he himself was six years of age. Since that time he had not particularly observed female clothing, except now and then in shop windows, and always rather to admire than to approve. He felt obscurely ill at ease, and although his heart was wrung by a certain air of pathos conveyed by the little figure propped on its gilded chair, he did not want to look at it any longer. He was distinctly relieved when Chastelneuf closed the closet door, which swung to with a ponderous clang of metal. Yet he was aware of a slight sense of cruelty towards the curious doll; it must be very lonely in the dark, behind the iron door.

"I should have no use, I am afraid, for this interesting example of your art," he said somewhat timidly to the two men, who regarded him with scarcely concealed disgust in their veiled and greedy gaze. "I should really find myself at a loss to care for so complicated a piece of mechanism. The—ah—the young lady looks so alarmingly fragile, and I fear I do not understand the requirements of such—ah—such rarities. But I trust you will be careful to find a purchaser in whose kindness you can confide this poor —ah, child; she seems a mere child." He paused, interrogating them with his anxious blue eyes; they nodded in gloomy affirmation.

It is said by adepts, who may or may not be fitted to pronounce upon the subject, that when a man relinquishes the love of women from his infancy he condemns his predestined virgin to eternal violence wrought upon her by the demons of debauch. It is hardly reasonable to suppose that this young person artificially formed from Venetian glass can have suffered a like fate, but it is an unfortunate fact that Alvise Luna sold her, within the next fortnight, to an elderly senator of atrocious morals and immense wealth. He did not find her fabric durable, and perhaps she had no soul.

The chevalier was the first to break the uncomfortable silence; he was at once his suave and animated self. The cardinal felt better immediately.

"I quite understand your scruples, Monseigneur," he cried with enthusiasm, "and oh, how rare it is, in this material age, to discover virtue so sensitive or sympathies so warm as yours are proved to be! But surely, surely, there is some elegant trifle, some elfin toy, which might serve to remind you of Venice and of your youth within her occult circle of lagoons. A little greyhound, perhaps, or a talking parakeet; we have been particularly successful with parakeets."

At this instant the stupendous plan struck Peter Innocent like a falling star. He was dizzied by the glittering impact, and swayed in his chair, but his gentle voice was perfectly clear and steady as he answered: "Monsieur de Chastelneuf," he said, "and you, my old friend Luna, there is indeed something which I have long wished to possess, and with which your truly admirable skill may be able to supply me. Do you think, by any fortunate chance, that you could make me a nephew?"

Luna, who know Chastelneuf to a hair's-breadth of precise disillusion, started in alarm as the other parted his smiling lips to reply; the glass-blower could have informed you to a semi-colon of the exact witticism fluttering upon the chevalier's tongue. To his overwhelming relief, the pungent butterfly was swallowed without the faintest grimace, and the words which actually emerged were models of chaste sobriety. A perfumed handkerchief passed across the mouth, the ghost of a sigh, and Chastelneuf's expression matched his speech. He was decorous, and only Luna knew the measure of his stoical abstention.

"Your Eminence," said the chevalier, bowing, "does us too much honour thus to admit us into a consultation on family affairs. But, happily, we are most excellently fitted to advise and aid you in this respect; we have, I may say, made a specialty of nephews." And he reminded Luna, with the toe of his buckled shoe, that a cheerful demeanour was indicated for this occasion.

Alvise Luna was more than a little troubled; he had not bargained for so extensive an order, and would have preferred to undertake a contract for a dragon or a Hyrcanean tiger any day. He was a religious man at heart, and although he was strongly predisposed by nature and inheritance towards chicanery and murder he viewed with profound distrust the extra-natural and Hermetic practices of his companion. To him there was something infinitely alarming in the idea of pre-empting the power of Deity to shape a being human at least in semblance, if not in soul, and he would rather have made a dozen manticores than one small baby. Nevertheless, he fixed his mind upon the heavenly shimmer of a thousand sequins, and entered with tolerable good grace into the current discussion.

6 AVEEVA VADELILITH

Peter Innocent had no difficulty whatever in obtaining from the pope full permission to absent himself for an indefinite number of hours upon the third night after the strange adventure just related. This latter night was that of May nineteenth, the date of official departure for the pontifical suite, but Pius bade the cardinal do as he pleased, and if he chanced to be too late to join the other prelates upon their leaving Venice, he might easily overtake them, said the Holy Father, during the journey of the following day, which must be made by water, and slowly, as befitted so illustrious a progress. He conferred his blessing upon the grateful old man, and, with the same indulgent smile, embraced him.

The season was Pentecost, and the water running in the veins of Venice appeared like wine under the transmutation of the sun. Pius VI, attired in the extreme of liturgical splendour, celebrated mass at the church of St. John and St. Paul. Passing out into the Campo he imparted his benediction to the multitude from a high platform whose timbers were heavily overlaid with varnishes of gold. No sooner was this ceremony accomplished than Peter Innocent, his heart no longer a blue balloon, but a swinging censer of holy and aspiring prayer, hastened towards that equivocal quarter of the town in whose bowels the mysterious cellar lay concealed. He wore once more the indistinguished dress of a Franciscan friar, and as he walked, his eyes were fixed upon the pages of a little book whose covers bore the cruciform symbol of his faith.

Meanwhile Alvise and the Chevalier de

Langeist awaited him in the vaulted chamber of their secret activities; Luna was observably nervous, but Chastelneuf was calm and majestic, the very picture of courtly self-possession in his coat of gold brocade and black velvet breeches, with a jewelled order tangled in the rich laces upon his breast.

"Rely upon my diplomacy," said this personage to his shivering companion. "I have learned much since the days of Mme. von Wulfe and the grand operation. I alone of all the adepts of my acquaintance have survived the wretched effects of Balsamo's petty larcenies. Saint-Germain is dying in Hesse, under the unpleasant pseudonym of Zaraski. Cagliostro has incurred the rigours of imprisonment and poverty; he has abundantly deserved a severer punishment. I saw him first at Aix, in Provence, a mere boy, sewing cockleshells on his black oilcloth coat, while his young wife stood at his elbow, holding a great crucifix of some base metal coloured to resemble gold. She was adorably pretty, but depraved. That was twenty years ago, and I am wiser now; if my peculiar talents have languished, my judgement has ripened and matured. I am entirely satisfied with our preparations for to-night."

"That is all very well," sneered Luna, "but I have had all the hard work. My lips are cracked, and my hands flayed by such unexampled labours; I have performed prodigies; my lungs are old leather, and my windpipe scorched macaroni, yet you grudge me a glass of your precious *monte pulciano,* and I suppose I am to have a very dog's share of the money compared with your lion's portion. So it always is. Poor honest fellow that I am, I never manage to look out for my own interests, and yet I am the best glass-blower in the known world." And he began to weep in sincere self-pity.

"Quite true," said Chastelneuf, with careless good-nature, "and a lovely bit of work you've done to-day; your masterpiece, I cordially assure you. We could get an enormous sum for this juvenile Apollo from the director of the opera; he would make an ideal soprano, and both sexes would go into indiscriminate ecstasies over him if he appeared, shall we say, in the latest production of Cimarosa or Mozart? Of course I should have to alter my plans a little, but he should have a golden voice, I promise you. Only, I think our ingenuous prelate is, in the vernacular, the lucky draw in the lottery; he will not talk, and as he is by nature close-mouthed, he will have to pay through the nose."

"Are you determined upon waiting until after midnight to perform the undertaking?" asked Luna, with an anxious scowl. "I should have thought Thursday the more suitable date, and Thursday has yet three hours to run. Surely the thing you are about to do may be described as a political and religious operation; I have been reading your copy of Paracelsus, with its interesting marginal notes, and Paracelsus says very plainly that Friday is a day exclusively reserved for amorous works. I cannot see the connection, although it is quite like you to try to turn the most serious occasion into a common love-affair."

"Common, do you say?" cried the chevalier, indignantly. "*Cospetto!—Che bella cosa!* Is it a common occurrence in my life, I ask you, to refrain for three entire days from all human enjoyments, to confine myself to a vegetarian diet, and to eschew intoxicating liquors? A pretty regimen for a gentleman of my faculties! Then, too, I have had the trouble of burning, upon rising and retiring, a costly perfume composed of the juice of laurels, salt, camphor, white resin, and sulphur, repeating at the same time the four sacred words. I beg to remind you that I am no longer an amateur, as in the past; *Paralis* has advanced. As for the matter of the amorous operation, of course it is precisely that. Do you imagine

I could send his poor innocent forth into the world improperly equipped to deal with his fellows? Friday it must be, or I'm a Turk!"

"As you please, as you please," grumbled Luna, resignedly. "I merely thought you might look very fine in a scarlet vestment, with a wreath of oak, poplar, fig, and pomegranate leaves; also I happen to have some ambergris, balm, grain of paradise, macis, and saffron lying idle about the place, which I understand are the correct perfumes for Thursday. But I was purely altruistic; for my own part I wish sincerely it were Tuesday, so that we might inaugurate an appalling work of vengeance. I fancy the blood-coloured robe and the magical sword and dagger. There is a beautiful picture of them in Paracelsus."

His face was alight with eager satisfaction, but Chastelneuf silenced him with a haughty sign of disapproval.

"Nonsense!" he said impatiently. "You know nothing whatever about it, and I advise you to keep your long nose out of such dangerous matters; these instruments of precision in the hands of the ignorant are lethal to the soul. Now, if you have prepared the inner chamber according to my directions, all is ready; but first let us have a look at the boy."

Luna could not suppress a grin of pride as he led the way to a heavily carved cupboard in the farthest corner of the room; the thing was a veritable cathedral in miniature, gothic and grotesque, with a hundred saints and gargoyles leaning from among its wreaths of fruit and flowers. He opened the door of this piece of furniture to a cautious crack; Chastelneuf peered over his shoulder. The two smiled joyously at each other as Luna closed the cupboard door with care.

"Miraculous!" shouted the chevalier, slapping Luna on the back in a transport of enthusiasm. "Divine! And even now he seems to live: Alvise, do you know you have given him a distinct look of his reverend uncle: a sweet touch that; and oh, the delicacy of the thing! The hair, the eyelashes, the very finger-nails! O marvellous Luna!"

"It was a good thought that, to patronize your own tailor, though it has cost us a pretty penny," began Luna, handsomely, when a timid knock upon the outer door apprised the friends of Peter Innocent's proximity.

While Luna engaged the cardinal in more or less agreeable conversation, Chastelneuf disappeared into the inner apartment. The time passed rapidly, and Peter Innocent had just finished his third glass of wine and persuaded a pair of coral-coloured crystal love-birds to perch upon his forefinger, when the all but inaudible strains of a flute or violin recalled him from a waking dream. Guided by Luna, he passed into the other chamber, whence these sounds proceeded, and there beheld a scene of ceremonial enchantment.

Let it be clearly understood at once that the chevalier, whatever his peccadillos, practised only the higher forms of transcendental and divine magic, as opposed to nigromancy and goetia; otherwise he could have done nothing in the presence of such holiness as Peter Innocent's; the cardinal moreover carried upon his person a crucifix and a Book of Prayer, infallible talismans against the evil one. Here was no place for the Ahriman of the Persians, the Typhon of the Egyptians, the Python of the Greeks, the Croquemitaine, the obscene deity of the Sabbath. Let it be remembered that Isis was impeccable in her widowhood, that Diana Panthea was a virgin; that Apollonius of Tyana never yielded to the seductions of pleasure; that Plotinus of Alexandria was ascetic in the manner of his life; and that Raymond Lully was the victim of a hopeless passion which made him chaste forever. Vesper, not Lucifer, blazed now in the pentagram upon the marble pavement, and Peter Innocent stepped forward without fear.

The chamber, which was both larger and higher than the anteroom, was hung with charming tapestries of rose and green, and the chevalier was robed in vestments of sky-blue silk; a crown of violets encircled his chestnut peruke. His ring was enriched by a magnificent turquoise, and his clasps and tiara were of lapis-lazuli and beryl. The walls were covered with festoons of roses, myrtle, and olive, and the atmosphere quivered with the emanations of innumerable spices.

Upon the Parian floor there stood an altar of perfumes, and upon this altar there lay an unblemished lambskin, and upon this lambskin was traced in pure vermilion a pentagram with one point in the ascendant. It had been sprinkled with holy water, and dried by the smoke of myrrh and aloes, and over it Chastelneuf had uttered the names of the five genii, which are Gabriel, Raphael, Anael, Samael, and Oriphiel.

The adept towered above the tripod of evocation; he bore in the centre of his breast a copper talisman with the character of Anael traced thereon, together with the words: "Aveeva Vadelilith."

Luna withdrew into the shadows, where he waved slowly an enormous fan of swan's feathers.

7 CONJURATION OF THE POOR

Peter Innocent came forward into the light, which fell with an effect of moonshine from the sacred lamp. He had no sense of fear and, what is more singular, no sense of sin; this appears to be indisputable proof of the beneficent quality of the ritual employed by Chastelneuf, upon this occasion at least. The cardinal never told of that night's wonders, and had he done so he would certainly have been burnt by the Holy Office; but his conscience remained immaculate throughout. He had his private theories, however, concerning the Christian and supplementary ceremonies proper to the undertaking, and he held his book and his crucifix very firmly in his two hands as he confronted the chevalier.

Chastelneuf lifted in the air the true and absolute magic wand, which must not be confounded with the simple divining-rod, or the trident of Paracelsus. This was composed of a single perfectly straight branch of the almond-tree, cut with a golden pruning-knife at the exact moment of its flowering; one of the extremities was fitted with a triangular prism, and the other with a similar figure of black resin; this end of the wand was gilded, and that silvered. A long needle of magnetized iron pierced the entire length of this consecrated instrument, which was the verendum of the magus, too occult to be shown to uninitiate eyes, the chevalier was probably unwise to employ it in the presence of the cardinal and Luna, but he was a brave man, and very vain of his attainments.

"As this creature to whom we are about to impart the privilege of living is composed of natural elements, I purpose to invoke the spirits of these components, which are the Four: air, water, fire, and earth. He who is about to be born was formed from sand and holy water, fused in extremest heat and shaped by human breath. Through the agency of these powers, a spirit shall enter into this bodily image, but whether mortal or elemental I cannot tell, nor does it greatly matter."

Chastelneuf spoke thus with an authentic dignity, which deepened as he proceeded with the exorcisms. And now the cardinal perceived behind the altar an object of funereal character, resembling a bier; it was covered by a white cloth whose folds conformed in some measure to the outlines of a corpse decently disposed for burial. The thing had been invisible a moment since; now the rays of the lamp were concentrated upon its ominous quiescence.

Tracing their symbol upon the air with an eagle's quill, the adept now intoned the prayer of the sylphs; he exorcized the water by the imposition of the hands, and by mingling with it a little consecrated salt and the ash of incense. The aspergillum used was formed of twigs of vervain, periwinkle, sage, mint, and basil, tied by a thread expertly abstracted from a virgin's distaff and provided with a handle of hazelwood from a tree which had not yet fruited. The prayer of the undines was then recited with proper solemnity, and afterward the prayer of the salamanders, so soon as the fire had been suitably exorcized by the sprinkling of salt, white resin, camphor, and sulphur, and by calling upon the kings of the sun and lightning, the volcanoes, and the great astral light. Lastly, the earth was exorcized by efficacious means, and the gnomic prayer pronounced. The chevalier then lifted successively the sword, the rod, and the cup, and proclaimed, in a loud voice, the conjuration of the Four.

"Caput mortuum, the Lord command thee by the living and votive serpent! Cherub, the Lord command thee by Adam Jotchavah! Wandering Eagle, the Lord command thee by the wings of the Bull! Serpent, the Lord Tetragrammaton command thee by the angel and the lion! Michael, Gabriel, Raphael, and Anael! Flow, moisture, by the spirit of Eloim! Earth, be established by Adam Jotchavah! Spread, firmament, by Jahuvehu, Zebaoth! Fulfil, judgement, by fire in the virtue of Michael! Angel of the blind eyes, obey, or pass away with this holy water! Work, winged Bull, or revert to the earth, unless thou wouldst have me pierce thee with this sword! Chained Eagle, obey my sign, or fly before this breathing! This, by virtue of the Pentagram, which is the morning star, and by the name of the Tetragram, which is written in the centre of the cross of light! Amen."

At this moment the white cloth covering the body seemed to move of its own volition, rising slowly until it floated free of the bier; its corners were drawn apart, and the fabric violently divided into four quarters. Upon a narrow trestle Peter Innocent saw the figure of a young man; he appeared very tall and slender in his complete immobility. He was dressed in the fantastic extreme of fashion, and his costume was the more singular in that it was entirely white. He wore a white velvet coat embroidered with silver spangles, a velvet waistcoat to match, white satin breeches, white silk stockings, and shoes with diamond buckles. His linen and lace were exquisite, and on one hand was placed a curious ring consisting of a large crystal set over white satin.

The cardinal stared intently at the face of this elegant creature, but could distinguish little save the suggestion of a straight nose, arched eyebrows, and the glimmer of pale hair over a paler brow. The eyes were closed, the hands relaxed and quiet.

Meanwhile, above the tripod, the mystery thickened with the perfumed smoke; there came a loud command, a moon of radiance appeared, dissolved, and vanished, and with the most startling celerity the young man bounded from his couch and gracefully abased himself before the venerable prelate, in whom he seemed to recognize a father or a friend. At the same instant the chevalier stepped forward and affected an introduction between the two, mingling simplicity with polished ease of manner.

All were visibly moved by this happy consummation of their ritual, and even Luna permitted a few tears of relief and cupidity to trickle down his dusty cheeks. Chastelneuf was laughing, shaking hands, and offering choice wines in slim Murano goblets to the cardinal and his nephew. The boy smiled, bowed, and sipped with the most lifelike gestures of politeness; but Peter Innocent stood silent in a tranquillity like stone, bewitched and awed by his felicity, and gazing at his nephew with infinite love and wonder in his eyes.

8 CREATURE OF SALT

Upon the most minute examination, Peter Innocent failed to discover anything in the appearance of his young kinsman —for as such we must henceforward consider him—which could suggest an abhuman origin or composition. True, the boy's skin was so fair as to seem almost translucent, and the luminous flax of his abundant hair had the fragility of spun glass; but these details merely served to give distinction to his undoubted beauty. It is possible that Luna had employed, in weaving with his breath these miraculous lovelocks, a secret method by which his ancestors had produced *vitro de trina,* or crystal lace, of such spider-web delicacy that it shattered at the vibrations of an angry voice or the too poignant wailing of a violin. The long gold eyelashes matched the hair; the eyes themselves were the colour of sea water, the pure Venetian aquamarine.

As opposed to the very ornamental lightness of his physical equipment, the young man's manner was composed and firm, and his perfect self-possession might have contained a hint of patronage had its affability been less pronounced. He ignored Luna with charming good-humour, condescended to the chevalier without offending him, and put Peter Innocent at his ease with equal facility and despatch.

"My dearest uncle, my more than father," he cried with fastidiously restrained emotion, saluting the cardinal on both cheeks with the utmost tenderness, while two bright glassy tears, volatile as quicksilver, fell shining through the air. "Chevalier, that's a sound wine, though heavy to my particular fancy. You don't happen to have such a thing as a *viola de gamba* about, do you? A little music would not be amiss,—I am sure you sing, —that sweet duet of Cimarosa's, let us say." And he began to hum, in an enchanting tenor, the words:

Prima che spunti
In ciel l'aurora . . .

The cardinal put out his hand, and softly touched the white satin sleeve of his new nephew.

"Dear boy, it gives me the greatest satisfaction to witness your careless happiness," he said timidly, "but there is one thing, one slight precautionary measure, which I hesitate to omit, much as it grieves me to interrupt your singing. I wonder if I might trouble you for a little clear water?" he continued, turning to Luna with a courteous smile.

The chevalier bounded forward, eager to serve, with the stoup of holy water from the evocative altar; but Peter Innocent shrank hastily away as he shook his silver head in refusal.

"Not that, I think, my kind friend. Believe me, I am very grateful, but if I might have only a cupful from the spring which I observed in the adjoining cellar, I should prefer—Ah, you are goodness itself; I thank you."

Peter Innocent took the water which Luna brought him in a cracked china cup; holding it very carefully, he blessed it according to the Roman ritual, thus establishing its potency against evil spirits. This was a different consecration, indeed, from that surrounding the furniture of the chevalier's altar; this blessing, uttered in the old man's quiet voice, was spoken with another and an holier authority.

". . . that wherever thou art sprinkled every phantasy and wickedness and wile of diabolic deceit may flee and leave that place, and every unclean spirit. . . ." Thus was exorcized the creature of salt lurking invisible in the broken cup, and likewise the creature of water . . . "that thou mayst avail to uproot and expel this enemy with all his apostate angels, by the virtue of the same our Lord Jesus Christ."

Now was the water become a creature in the service of God's mysteries for the driving out of demons. In a whisper so low as to be well-nigh inaudible even to the boy, who at a sign had knelt upon the pavement with instinctive docility, Peter Innocent repeated certain formulæ of blessing especially efficacious against devils and invocative of divine protection. Clear drops of water fell upon the bowed and shining head.

Chastelneuf was secretly annoyed.

"That was quite unnecessary, I assure you," he said rather stiffly. "There is not an ounce of harm in the boy; the prescription calls for the purest ingredients, as Luna can tell you, and, for my own part, I have used the best magic known to the ancients. However, as you will. I suppose we all have our prejudices."

"I was sure you would understand an old man's anxiety," replied the cardinal, pacifically. "And now I will not trespass longer upon your kindness, save to give you this little wallet with my profoundest gratitude, and to wish you both a very good morning."

It was morning, and between the cracks in the jalousies pale blades of light were driven like angelic swords.

"Where are you taking the boy, Eminence?" asked the chevalier with renewed cheerfulness, playing a lively tune upon the jingling wallet, whose chorus was five thousand sequins. "Remember, he's scarcely used to a rough world as yet, and his fingernails may be brittle for a day or two."

"We are going to the Church of St. John and St. Paul, my friend, where this poor child must receive the sacrament of baptism," Peter Innocent said slowly. He looked with pity and something perilously near adoration into the smooth, transparent countenance of the boy, who clasped his arm and smiled in meek response.

Mounting a short flight of steps, M. de Chastelneuf flung open an iron-barred door, and suddenly dawn flooded the room like a river of golden water loosed upon it. Without, the canal still preserved a sleepy colour, neither grey nor blue, but the house-tops were painted in extravagant tints of rose and flame by a sun new-risen from the Adriatic.

"What name will you give the boy, Monseigneur?" inquired the chevalier. "I feel a certain proprietary interest in his fortunes, which under your auspices must be uniformly happy, and I should like to know his name."

The cardinal mused, considered, and replied.

"I believe I shall call him Virginio," he said, his eyes tracing the exquisite and ingenuous outlines of his nephew's half-averted face.

"A pretty name, but I trust it may not long be strictly appropriate; I have spared no pains to make our young friend a complete work of art, after the best natural patterns," answered the Chevalier de Langeist, with a not unpardonable pride, bowing deeply as Peter Innocent and his pale and luminous companion passed into the morning, and so were gone like a black pearl and a white, melting within a chalice of honeyed yellow wine.

END OF BOOK ONE

BOOK TWO: VIRGINIO

I had had an affair with the moon,
in which there was neither sin nor shame.
LAURENCE STERNE

9 OF SAPPHO LITTLE, BUT ALL ROSES

In Angelo Querini's classical garden at Altichiere there stood a summer-house dedicated to the goddess of Folly; this charming structure was, paradoxically enough, presided over by a bust of

Marcus Aurelius and decorated with a motto from Montaigne. A more apposite taste had graced the dovecote with a Grecian Venus, and raised an altar to the spirit of tranquillity in the midst of abundances of sweet basil, lavender, and thyme.

Midway between an Egyptian sarcophagus and an Etruscan monument, both heavily overgrown with deep viridian moss, a marble bench disclosed its rosy veining to the September sun, and seemed to invite a languorous repose in keeping with the season. From the door of the shadowed summer-house a young girl presently emerged; her lively glance surveyed the autumnal lawns and arbours, and instantly selected the carved and coral-coloured seat as most benignant to her mood. She carried an armful of books; these she disposed within reach, herself reclining in the sunnier corner of the bench. She was soft and inscrutable as a Persian kitten.

A black kitten among the bright and gilded trees, with hazel eyes transfused with gold, and hair so dark that only at the temples a darkening golden tinge survived in smoky black. Her dress was black as soot; such a dress, decent, and austere, as clothed Querini's admired and admirable young friend Fulvia Vivaldi in her Genevan retreat; too black, in spite of the clear muslin kerchief and the silver chain, for Rosalba Berni on her eighteenth birthday.

This was, then, the celebrated Rosalba, better known among the Arcadians of Italy as Sappho the Younger, or to the more affectionate few, the Infant Sappho. This child was an orphan by report, and by profoundly proven faith the ward and adoptive daughter of the noble and liberal Angelo Querini, ex-senator of the Venetian patriciate and valued comrade of Voltaire. It was openly declared that she was a descendant of Francesco Berni the poet, to whose sparkling blood she owed her marvellous wit and the inventive lightness of her mind; other more insinuating murmurs attributed these qualities to an equally effervescent source: the whispered name of the Cardinal de Bernis was a veritable Arcadian diploma of mental grace, and Rosalba's eyebrows were distinctly French.

She had these brows, arched forever in a delicate amazement, drawn upon a smooth forehead; her dark hair grew in a point; and her eyes were large between black lashes; their expression was calm, but impertinent. Her mouth was curled like a scarlet petal in some early frost of irony; her skin was white as the rose of her baptismal name. Across her slightly tilted nose a score of golden freckles made her human; for the rest, in form and elegance of gesture, she was Artemis.

Yet not the Artemis of ivory or of quarried stone, however exquisite. Rosalba was more vital than opening roses or ripened fruit; she lived and moved and burned within the chilly greenery with a palpable warmth; she was a flame whose consummation may be bitter, but whose promissory blooming is tenderer than apple blossoms. To the five senses of an observer she was indeed imagined flowers to breathe, as she must have been velvet to touch, cream to taste, the crescent moon to gaze upon, and, to the listening ear, a melody repeated by a mocking-bird.

It was all to the credit of M. de Chastelneuf that the five senses of this particular observer were so poetically acute; the young Virginio leaned upon a mossy column, while love for Rosalba Berni whirled over him like a fragrant wave, and left him drowned in those same waters from which the mother of such love arose.

"'O bianca Galatea!'" said Virginio, politely, quoting Metastasio.

"My name is Sappho," Rosalba replied rather crossly. "I do not care for Italian verse; I prefer the classics, and, above all, Ossian. I am at present busy, very busy, with a translation of the latter, for the benefit of those unfortunate people who are unable to read it in the original Gaelic."

"Is it not written in English?" Virginio inquired timidly. "And have I not heard that Signor Cesarotti—"

"Be silent, if you cannot converse intelligently."

Rosalba pronounced these words with perfect calm; she was imperial rather than rude.

"Precisely," Virginio returned, with a gentle smile; she was suddenly aware that he was far more beautiful than any Adonis in Querini's garden. He reminded her of marble. Or was it marble of which he reminded her? Something more translucent; crystal, perhaps.

"I am reading, as you see," she said more kindly, "but I can spare you a few moments; I dare say you would like me to show you the books I have this very morning received from my kind friend and guardian. Approach, young sir; the gate is unlocked, and if you will wear white shoes, you must expect the dew to spoil them."

Virginio drew near her as one who visits, in simple reverence and awe, the shrine of an immortal; she laughed, and made a place for him beside her on the bench, among the richly bound volumes which surrounded her.

"Here, my poor boy, are the 'Confessions' of Rousseau; I suppose you have never read them. For my part, I have been familiar with their pages for years; this rose-coloured levant is merely a new dress for an old and adored companion. Here, is the 'Cecilia' of Signorina Burney, published this same year in London; it will be so much Greek to you. Here is some real Greek; a manuscript copy of the Codex Palatinus, or Anthology of Cephalas; the original is unfortunately locked up in the Vatican library."

"Where could it be safer, or in the company of so many equally holy treasures?" asked Virginio in mild surprise, which turned to actual terror as Rosalba whirled upon him with the silken savagery of a little panther. It was now evident that, whoever her father, her mother must have been Italian.

"Are you a victim of superstition, and dare to enter these sacred shades?" she cried in honest indignation. Her eyes were burning amber, and the crisp tendrils of her hair appeared disturbed and shaken. Virginio trembled; a faint cracking sensation menaced his expanded heart.

"I am a Christian," he contrived to enunciate; he was very pale, and looked more than ever transparent. Rosalba was touched in spite of her convictions.

"Do not be distressed; I am myself a deist," she cried generously. Virginio put his cold hand over his sea-blue eyes; bright glassy tears fell into the air, and lay like silver on the yellow linden tassels at Rosalba's feet. "My poor boy, we have all made mistakes," she told him, seriously; she found his emotion curiously disturbing. "Look, I am often very silly myself; I have wasted half my birthday morning in re-reading a peculiarly childish novel by Carlo Gozzi. I am ashamed to admit that his fairy-stories have always had an attraction for my mind. Listen; it was this that I found so absorbing, this nonsense." And she proceeded to read the following passage from a shabby little book bound in coloured paper, and furnished with a marker of green silk ribbon.

" 'A lady, adorned in the Venetian fashion, with a Florentine petticoat, and a blue satin vest, apparently fresh from the mercer's, trimmed with sleeves of the finest lace; she wore rings and bracelets of the richest gold, and a necklace set with Indian diamonds.' "

10 POESY RING

Rosalba's voice died into quivering silence; she hung her supercilious head, and the contemptuous petals of her lips parted to sigh. "The 'Cecilia' was given me as a special concession to feminine frivolity; it may also serve to improve my English," she murmured with apparent irrelevance. "It is a delightful book, I am sure. And next year I am to have the Encyclopédie, if I am diligent. Has not my dear Jean-Jacques a beautiful new dress, the exact shade, would you say, of a pink geranium?"

Virginio's shining flaxen brows stirred faintly to a frown.

"Would you not prefer a beautiful new dress for the adornment of your own divine beauty?" he inquired with respectful interest. "I do not think a geranium pink coat particularly suitable to the charms of M. Rousseau."

"Oh, but I would rather have yellow," cried Rosalba, in spite of herself—"Pale yellow like a frosted leaf, or rosier, like the sunny side of peaches."

She stopped, sincerely sorry she had not been inventing pretty images for a poem about philosophy or the ringlets of a child. Shame tinted her cheek more delicately than imagination can contrive to colour it. Virginio's veins were molten with love and pity.

As a matter of stern, immutable fact, Rosalba was hardly a fit object for pity, although love enveloped her in a natural shower like sunlight. In the Venice of her time, and indeed throughout the whole of Arcadian Italy, she had from her precocious childhood been petted as a tenth and darling Muse; flattery had been her painted rattle, and early fame her skipping-rope. Yet since no visible laurel had enwreathed her hair, and since her dress was sombre with decorum, Virginio saw not Sappho, but Cinderella.

A blush suffused Virginio's face; the blood showed clearly, like wine that stains a pearly glass. From his hand he drew the curious ring which the Chevalier de Langeist had given him. It was a large crystal set over white satin; the band was gold, engraved with an English motto.

"Will you accept this trifling gift upon the fortunate occasion of your natal day?" he asked, with a graceful inclination of his luminous head.

"Yes, and most gratefully," Rosalba replied, with a smile of simple pleasure. "This is precisely what I have longed to possess; this must, I think, be an Indian diamond."

"Nearly, but not quite," Virginio admitted. "However, it is, as you see, very singular and charming; that is magic written on the gold. The words are possibly in cabalistic Hebrew; I know at least that they are secret and in the highest degree potent for conjuration."

"That is not Hebrew; that is English, I believe," said Rosalba, pondering the inscription. "It says—but this is extraordinary—it says, 'Fear God and love me.' The sentiment is elevated, and the language extremely choice; the whole forms an appropriate motto for a deist."

"The first words, yes; these are intended for the deist," explained Virginio, who did not have the slightest conception of the meaning of this mysterious term. "The rest—that enchanting phrase, if I may be permitted to repeat it; that legend, 'Love me,' this is addressed to the woman, the goddess, the eternal, unattainable Diana. Accept the prayer; put on the ring, O loveliest." He affixed the bauble, with a kiss upon her middle finger, where it hung a little loose; it had fitted his own slender ring finger to perfection.

"I shall give you a guard," he said, "a guard of Indian diamonds." Rosalba laughed for joy.

"Touching the comparatively unimportant matter of my presence here to-day," Virginio continued suavely, retaining, with an air of negligence, Rosalba's hand within his own, "I must explain that I bear a letter to the noble Angelo Querini; it is upon the part of my revered uncle and benefactor, Cardinal Bon. These two were comrades in their season of tender youth; their hearts preserve the innocence of that vanished aureate age. My uncle desires to intrust me to the occasional kindness of his friend; he hopes I may be now and then allowed to visit Querini in his hallowed seclusion. I require, it seems, a certain amount of rustic air; my constitution is unfortunately fragile." Virginio did his charming best to appear pathetic, and succeeded admirably in the attempt; against the light his lifted hand moved in a crystalline transparency.

Rosalba frowned at the name of cardinal, but Virginio had already learned to prefer a frown to a smile in such an instance; as a cardinal's nephew he was accustomed to many and repellent smiles upon inimical lips. He was rather grateful to the girl for her look of gravity; it was his profoundest wish to be taken seriously, and persons of both sexes were but too apt, in his brief experience, to credit him with a mental lightness commensurate with his physical mould.

"Why are you not in Rome?" Rosalba questioned somewhat accusingly. Her manner revealed fastidious distaste, and Virginio was deeply grieved by her intolerance.

"I am too ignorant as yet for Roman society," he said quietly. "My uncle has arranged for my education at the Academy of Nobles in Venice. The age of admission is only eleven, but I am very simple-minded, and, besides, nobody can be certain of my exact years. I have, for my own part, a strong conviction that I am not less than nineteen and not more than twenty."

"I should say you were tall for nineteen and remarkably silly for twenty," Rosalba answered cruelly. Then, as he stood silent and very pale, she put out her hand again and touched his fingers in impulsive pity. Her hand was warm and vibrating with life; Virginio's hand was cold and thin, and as she clasped it, an ominious cracking startled her with strangeness, she felt as if his fingers were so many brittle icicles.

"Be careful, Signorina; you may injure yourself," said Virginio, sadly, examining his hands with the minutest care.

Rosalba looked at her own palm, where a tiny scratch showed scarlet; she could have sworn that a splinter of glass still clung there. Suddenly she was afraid; she stared at the boy in an enchantment of horror. The sun shrank up into a savage polar star, and the heavens were another colour than blue. The trees had tongues, and when she shut her eyes, she could hear the shuffle of their heavy feet upon the protesting grass; its blades were presently to be reborn as serpents.

Then two bright glassy tears, volatile as quicksilver, fell shining through the disfigured day, and as they splashed upon Rosalba's little breast, she drew Virginio beyond her fear and comforted him in the security of innocence.

So, with the utmost simplicity, Rosalba Berni was constrained to fear God and love Virginio all in the space of five seconds, yet this thing, so quickly done, was not to be undone within the memory of that generation, and when the dark and the flaxen head were frost and silver, the event remained unchanged.

11 CALMON THE PHILOSOPHER

"I trust that the noble Angelo Querini will approve our engagement," said Virginio in a tone of practical good sense, after a brief and iridescent cloud of unreality had enveloped them for a time in silence, whose mist dispersed too soon. "I think we should hasten to make known to him the history of the past fifteen minutes; he has been as a father to your girlhood, and he should be told of our betrothal without delay."

"H-m," and "M-yes," replied Rosalba, doubtfully; she was not certain that she wished to be betrothed; still less did she desire to acquaint her noble guardian with a fact so subject to the alterations of fancy. "Oh—shall we?" she inquired with a notable lack of enthusiasm.

"It is our duty." Such was Virginio's obdurate opinion; Rosalba accepted it, to her own surprise and considerable indignation. Dimly, as an inauspicious providence perceived through wizard crystal, she began to be aware that her lover was incapable of bending, however cruelly a clumsy world might break the refinement of his substance. In a prophetic flash she realized that she must henceforward and always, as the ancient Venetian proverb has it, handle him with white suède gauntlets steeped in rosewater.

Gentle and grave, and by her footfall half reluctant, she passed from the sumptuous autumnal sunlight of the garden into the chilly corridors of Querini's country house; the floors were paved in lozenges of grey and yellow marble, and upon the walls a long procession was frozen in magical decay, which had once issued like a rainbow from the fresh and glittering palette of Carpaccio.

At her side Virginio stepped delicately and very proudly, in shining contrast to her austere black silk and bloodless lawn; he wore his white satin coat with silver spangles, and the lace upon his shirt might almost have purchased Constantinople from the Ottoman princes.

To Angelo Querini, in his pillared library, frescoed in faintly gilded russet and religious blue, and presided over by a bronze bust of Lord Verulam, the boy was an apparition from the fabulous other side of the moon.

This impression was the more amazing, in that Angelo Querini believed in neither apparitions not fables save as the results of an imperfect digestion and an inferior intellect. He was a mind so purely rational that it had long since demanded and received absolute divorce from his naturally impetuous heart, which was thereby set at liberty to be as affectionate and foolish as it pleased without disturbing in the slightest degree Querini's mental conviction as to the profound selfishness of all human action. In this way his head was enabled to breathe the invigorating airs of philosophic disgust, while his heart enjoyed to the full a lifelong orgy of benevolence; Minerva might have sprung from his reasonable brow, but the daughter of his breast was Charity.

Therefore it was a foregone conclusion that the liberal cynic would overlook the irregularity of Virginio's birth, and the kind old man receive him as a son. Rosalba, until this moment free as a humming-bird nourished at the Muses' hands, felt the meshes of a sudden net envelop her in its invisible gossamer. Being herself a philosopher, she reflected sagely that the disquieting fact of her capture being now quietly accomplished, there was no further wisdom in revolt. Besides, in her innermost soul she no longer desired a freedom vacuous of Virginio, and as she took her guardian's congratulatory kiss, she succumbed for the first time in her life to the warm, delightful luxury of complete unreason.

In this delicious mental condition, she listened ravished to Virginio's account of his supernatural origin; neither the boy's simple confession nor Querini's kindly satirical smiles disturbed her in the slightest degree. Personally, and counter to every conviction which had so far upheld her brilliant intellect, she was inclined to credit her lover; but the whole question appeared to her of trifling importance compared with the exquisite grace wherewith Virginio expounded it, and she cared very little whether he had emerged from an Arabian orange or flown to earth upon the wings of the celebrated Green Bird, so long as he had come to her at last.

"This is a romance worthy of the invention of your friend the Count," said Querini, answering her thought. He was benignant, he was even tender, but Rosalba recognized the sceptical amusement in his eyes. She blushed, then blushed again more vividly, ashamed of blushing.

"The Count must be right, after all; this story, of whose accuracy I can entertain no doubt, must prove him right," she said firmly, opening her own eyes very wide in a glance of calm and arrogant assurance. No longer need she conceal her predilection for fairy-tales, nor fear to admit that her favourite author was, after all, not M. Jean-Jacques Rousseau, but Count Carlo Gozzi. Magic was justified by experiment; it was become a verity, true, rational and possible, like mathematics or the rights of man.

It is regrettable to be obliged to confess that the noble Angelo Querini did not share Rosalba's belief in Virginio's narrative; he felt quite certain that the handsome youth was the blue-eyed flower of Peter Innocent's wild oats. It is to the credit of his heart, however, that he viewed the supposed offspring of the cardinal's folly with the most solicitous compassion and respect. His mind emitted a private spark of laughter, reflected in his eyes, perhaps, but admirably absent from his grave and courteous lips.

"Curious, curious indeed," he ruminated gently, while joining their hands with a logical deistic blessing. "These little ones are the children of superstition and vice, yet how powerless has been the error of their parents to infect their intrinsic loveliness! Oh, nature, virtue, reason, and Voltaire! Oh, excellent Helvetius! Philanthropically bestow upon these infants a ray of your own illumination! May their bodies remain pagan, their minds emancipated, and their moral qualities incorruptibly pure!" In his excitement he had almost pronounced "Amen," but caught himself in time to substitute a sentiment from the "Republic" of Plato.

12 UNCLES AND SONS

At this very moment, by one of those pleasing coincidences more common in romantic fiction than among the ineptitudes of moral life, the Cardinal Peter Innocent Bon, Count Carlo Gozzi, and the Chevalier de Langeist sat together within a turret chamber of the haunted palace of Saint Canziano; upon the countenance of each gentleman there brooded an expression of thoughtful melancholy. The lofty room, open to the four great azure winds of heaven, was festooned with cobwebs and dustily strewn with the count's famous collection of Arabian and Neapolitan fairy-tales. These volumes, in many instances richly bound in ancient levantine leathers, were fallen into a state of sad decay, repeated in the person of their owner, who had worn the same wig for twenty years, and whose silver shoe-buckles were broken. The door drooped upon its hinges, the window-panes were starred and splintered, and from the carven ceiling enormous spiders dangled mockingly above the absorbed faces of the three friends.

It can occasion no undue surprise to learn that Peter Innocent and Carlo Gozzi had been comrades since boyhood; the saintly and fastidious prelate and the aristocratic dreamer were spiritual kinsmen from their hereditary cradles. It is not generally known to history, however, that the patrician Gozzi and the adventurer Chastelneuf had even the slightest acquaintance with each other, and indeed it was the invariable care of both to conceal the circumstance; nevertheless, a sincere affection existed between them. It is possible that this mutual esteem was the result of a certain pamphlet, lampooning the Abbé Chiari, of which the chevalier was the reputed author. Such rumours had cost him dear in the opinion of the Council; they had, perhaps, rewarded him with the singular friendship of Carlo Gozzi.

Chastelneuf was splendidly attired in ashen-grey velvet; a silver-laced hat, a furred travelling-cloak, and a small white mask were flung upon a lamed and tattered chair at his elbow. Peter Innocent wore his severest habit; the slight disorder of its austerity suggested another journey, less luxurious than the chevalier's. Gozzi had wrapped his emaciated form in a ragged dressing-gown, apparently constructed from a bit of tapestry, in which the loves of Leda and her swan had been decently terminated by the sempstress; a virtuous pair of shears had shortened the fable with the garment, and left both the count and Leda colder for their loss. Two senatorial portraits by Titian and Tintoretto ignored the goblin chamber and its occupants with respective airs of proud detachment and opulent contempt.

"I had hardly expected to find my worthy—ahem—my interesting friend M. de Chastelneuf a member of our little company, Carlo," said Peter Innocent, timidly. He disliked very much the prospect of hurting any one's feelings, but he had come all the way from Rome on purpose to consult with the count upon matters of secrecy and importance; the chevalier's presence was a glittering blow to privacy, while his suave voice delicately divided silence, as one cuts a precious fruit. The cardinal, very kindly, wished him in Vienna.

Chastelneuf glanced at the count with smiling eyes beneath lifted brows; the latter answered the unspoken question at once.

"My dear Peter," he cried rather impatiently, "do you suppose the chevalier has travelled post from the Austrian frontier, and that at the gravest danger to his personal fortunes, for no better reason than to interrupt our consultation? On the contrary, it is he who shall resolve our difficulties; he has an excellent plan, and one which cannot fail to meet with your approval. But first let me ask you; did you furnish this vitreous young relative of yours with letters of introduction to Angelo Querini?"

"I did, without doubt," the cardinal assured him plaintively, "and at the cost, moreover, of several severe pangs of conscience. Querini is an estimable person in many respects, and my brother Nicholas was devoted to him. I cannot forget, however, that the man is an unbeliever and a Voltarian; he has insulted holy church upon various pretexts; he is a mocker and, I am afraid, a confirmed philosopher."

"'Mock on, mock on, Voltaire, Rousseau!'" muttered Carlo, who had seen the poem in manuscript among the papers of an eccentric English scholar of his acquaintance. "'And the wind blows it back again!' Where it listeth; true, very true. A detestable person, Querini; he cultivates plaster busts in his garden, which have devoured all the elves. But Chastelneuf says he has a pretty niece, a nymph by no means plaster."

The chevalier permitted himself to smile slightly in replying.

"Not a niece, my dear Count; a ward is surely another matter."

"Why?" demanded Peter Innocent with unwonted asperity; as an uncle, he resented the implied sneer without understanding it.

"Ah, Eminence, spare my blushes upon such a question!" Chastelneuf cried gaily; an impudent and evasive laugh puzzled the cardinal by its refined ribaldry.

"Do not quarrel, gentlemen," protested Gozzi, who was deriving a wicked satisfaction from this curious encounter between the powers of light and semi-darkness as represented by his friends. "We are all met to-day in order to discuss the future of two ingenuous young creatures in whom I, for my part, take the warmest and most fatherly interest."

"Two young creatures?" The cardinal looked pale with alarm. "Did I understand you to say two, my dear Carlo? Virginio has never been, so far as I know, anything in the least like twins."

"There is no question of twins, save in so far as the sweet affinity of lovers may simulate the natal bond," began Carlo Gozzi, but the chevalier interrupted him with something less than his customary politeness.

"Of course there can be no question of twins as yet," he said in a low, shocked voice, turning upon the cardinal a face congealed into dignified horror. "We are barely arrived at the point of arranging a match between Virginio and the niece of Cardinal de Bernis, and already your Eminence is talking of twins. The thought is perhaps a little indelicate, although we may all indulge such hopes in the intimacy of our devotions. But as to the match, is it not exquisitely suitable, and can you possibly withhold your approval when I explain—"

"Marriage! Virginio married!" exclaimed Peter Innocent, wildly; and, "Bernis! The niece of Cardinal de Bernis!" cried Carlo Gozzi with an almost comparable accession of surprise. "I thought he was going to study the Greek dramatists!" added the one, while the other ended, "And I, that she was the ward of Angelo Querini!"

13 SPIRITUAL FATHERS

"You were both quite correct in your conclusions," the chevalier reassured them.

"The divining crystal upon my watch-chain informs me that Virginio has this moment opened a folio of Sophocles, while the noble Querini is giving the best possible proof of his benevolent guardianship by conferring a double blessing and a modest competence upon the betrothed pair; his notary has but just entered the room; I believe he is about to draw up a new will. It is all very charming and idyllic, and I congratulate your Eminence most heartily upon a felicitous solution of your problems." He bowed, nor could the cardinal detect a look or gesture indicative of aught save urbanity and good humour.

"My problems were, after all, very simple, and you should not have come all the way from Vienna to solve them, Chevalier." Peter Innocent hoped he was not speaking too haughtily to this adventurous person; Carlo Gozzi healed whatever breach the gentle voice had made by laughing cynically and wiping his eyes upon a large bandana handkerchief. It was impossible to say whether he was merry or sad.

"It was all my fault, Peter my dear," said Carlo Gozzi. "I have been melancholy of late; I miss my poor Truffaldino and his company of masks. In parting, we embraced, weeping bitterly. I had not wept since that mischievous lunar moth, Teresa Ricci, flew away to the moon where she belonged, but now I cannot stay my tears. In vain have I attempted to be philosophical, which is merely to say heartless; my hopes have perished with the venerable comedy of Venice, which I must soon follow to undeserved oblivion. Meanwhile my one comfort has been the society of your delightful nephew; in him I have renewed my youth and experienced afresh the enchantment of fairy-tales and the ravishing pleasure of the impossible. I visited him in the sombre Academy of Nobles. In his black uniform, enveloped in a bright blue cloak, he was precisely like one of the disinherited princes of my own fancy; I loved him, and I longed to see him happy."

"I know you have been goodness itself to the boy, my Carlo; he wrote me of lessons in Arabic and antique Spanish. He cannot have been lonely in your edifying society, and now with these new excitements and adventures in the classics into which Querini is about to introduce him, his days will be overflowing with aureate dreams indeed. What more can the lad desire?"

"Don't you understand, Eminence?" asked the Chevalier. He gazed sternly at the cardinal, while true and generous indignation kindled within his smouldering golden eyes. His sinewy brown hand had sought and found his sword-hilt before it fell, still clenched, in recognition of Peter Innocent's silvered and benignant locks. "I beg your Eminence's pardon if I appear impetuous, but the boy, the poor boy, is, after all, very nearly human."

"Oh, I trust he is not merely human," interposed Gozzi. "There has been some talk of elementals, and I have always longed to meet an elemental. Virginio, with his translucent flesh, like flame made frost—Virginio is happily something better than human, or so I have believed."

"And is there something better on this inferior side of heaven?" Chastelneuf spoke with passion, and yet there was a perilous tenderness in his falcon look.

"We are all of us God's children, and fashioned in His image; we are moved by a breath of His divinity," said the cardinal, softly and somewhat fearfully; but Carlo Gozzi was not satisfied.

"Did you or did you not, M. de Chastelneuf, assure me, upon your honour as a gentleman, of this youth's supernatural origin?" he demanded hotly. "I have loved him like a son, because I conceived him to be magic incarnate; am I to learn now that he is a common mortal like myself, and perhaps of baser clay?" He stared significantly at the chevalier, and his words were a challenge.

"Oh, no! Oh, no!" said Chastelneuf, wearily. "Calm yourself, my dear Count; your suspicions are unfortunately unfounded. The boy is all that you could wish him to be; he is an exquisite monster, a celestial prodigy, blown from the very air itself, and captured in an earthy net so fragile that its meshes could not withstand the violence of a mortal soul. I do not know to a certainty what spirit informs this mutable fabric; whether it be a creature of the elder world, nourished in the heart of a sapling or fallen from between the breasts of a cloud; only I think it lacks the roughness and the pitifulness of humanity. Be content, both of you; the cardinal may have his angel and the count his elfin prince; Virginio will never disappoint you. I have given him a ring; the same was given me in my youth by a beloved friend, and its influence is infallibly benign. If it should chance to light a little fire in that hollow heart, and set true tears burning in those glassy eyes, such marvels are not harmful, but salutary and kind. I, too, have felt for Virginio an affection fatherly and apprehensive; I have come from Vienna for the express purpose of promoting his happiness, and it is my prayer—yes, my profoundest supplication to my Maker—that this happiness is about to be consummated."

He fell silent; to Gozzi, who knew him well, it was an amazement to perceive a veritable moisture dimming the vehement colour of his eyes.

Peter Innocent was moved; his countenance, placid and humane as a sacred effigy, was turned toward the Chevalier in lenient concern, as Chastelneuf sat down and covered his face with his hand, shaken by some curious fit of ardour or revolt.

"I will consent to any plan, within reason, which can promote my nephew's ultimate happiness," said Peter Innocent, gravely.

Chastelneuf still bit his lip in tormented silence, but Gozzi burst forth into voluble rejoicing as he wrung the cardinal's hand with warmth.

"Oh, good! very good indeed! This is the best news I have heard in a twelvemonth. Peter, I knew I could rely upon your merciful heart when you were made to realize the boy's loneliness and isolation; Chevalier, my compliments to your invariable sagacity. Oh, it will be an extremely charming little romance, a fairy-tale come true, not desiccated and compressed within the pages of a book, but alive and kicking its scarlet heels, as the ancient Bergamesque proverb puts it. And the lad is actually a fantasy in Murano glass instead of vulgar flesh and blood! I myself could not have invented a prettier conceit, or one more gracefully in accordance with the best magical traditions."

Peter Innocent observed this enthusiasm with indulgence, but a natural anxiety led him to seek further enlightenment from his friend.

"And who, pray, is the young lady whom I am about to embrace as the bride of Virginio and, consequently, my own child? If I am not mistaken, the chevalier described her as a niece of Monseigneur de Bernis."

"Oh, niece if you like; that title does as well as another," said Chastelneuf, with recovered sprightliness. "And, indeed, I honour your scruples; nothing is more lamentable than lascivious gossip and scandal-mongering. But in this case, it can do no harm to admit what your Eminence, as a man of the world, must already have suspected, in view of a certain prelate's profane reputation; the fact, in fine, and to make a long story short, that this lovely girl is a daughter of Cardinal de Bernis and . . ."

"But must you make it short, Chevalier?" interrupted Gozzi. He made no effort to conceal his eagerness, and his wintry eyes were bright with anticipation. "Your stories are always so entertaining, and never too good to be true; I am sure that Peter will join me in urging you to continue at your leisure with the recital of this mysterious amour. Eh, Peter, my boy, are you with me?"

14 NUNS AND LOVERS

Peter Innocent, whose eyes were blue as veronica flowers, and whose inmost soul was as a silver reliquary of chaste design, felt somewhat at a loss to conjecture whether or no he was, precisely, with Carlo Gozzi at the immediate moment. A doubt, insidious and sinister, as to the exact nature of the company filtered between the argent filigree of his reflections; he smelled brimstone as the count opened his tortoiseshell snuff-box, and observed with relief the normal outline of the chevalier's elegantly buckled shoes. When he replied, his speech was tempered by unaccustomed caution.

"Carlo, I cannot quite say that I am with you, but I hope I shall never be very far from such an old and trusted friend; no difference can sever us that may not be bridged by a clasp of the hand. Only I wonder a little. Is it, was it, entirely suitable for Cardinal de Bernis to have a daughter?"

Gozzi appeared slightly embarrassed, but Chastelneuf assumed the responsibility of answering without a trace of hesitation.

"Monseigneur, I feel your fears will be set at rest when I explain this affair; its complete suitability is perhaps its chief charm to a refined mind. The Cardinal de Bernis was possibly, in his youth, faintly inclined towards profligacy; he was brilliant and well bred, but flippant and occasionally unwise. Some of the ladies upon whom he bestowed his butterfly favours shared his weakness; one alone of all that rainbow number remained modest and virginal even under the intoxication of love. I knew her; it might have been my privilege to preserve her delicate illusions from maculation at the hands of beasts. She was unwavering in her faith, which, most unhappily for her, was pinned not upon the bosom of her God, but starrily, like a bright religious order, over the shifting heart of François-Joachim de Bernis."

"Proceed," said Gozzi. "This begins to be amusing."

"The tale is not truly amusing," said Chastelneuf, meditatively. "It is sad, I am afraid, and its only happy ending is Rosalba, who is herself not an end, but a beginning. For the French ambassador at Rome it is very sad; for a little Venetian widow it was, perhaps, sadder. I will tell it to you, if you like, but I cannot promise to make you laugh except at the ridiculous spectacle of my own tears."

"Go on, my friend," replied the inscrutable Gozzi. Peter Innocent was silent, but from an inner pocket he drew a fine cambric handkerchief, sweet with lavender.

"I am the villain of this piece, Eminence," the chevalier continued with a sort of melancholy pride. "When I have finished, you will find it impossible to condemn Bernis; your feelings towards the innocuous partner of his unwisdom can be no harsher than regret softened by commiseration. Ah, Caterina, if I had never led you into that select conclave of libertines, you might even now be a happy wife and mother, and I, content and honoured, the father of a lovelier creature than either Virginio or Rosalba! I may say without vanity," he added, "that in my youth I was not ill favoured."

"Proceed! proceed!" cried Gozzi, impatiently. "You were always as black as a Moor; Time has spilt no milk and roses from your leather cheek, over which you should waste your tears. Be good enough to stop crying, Jacques; tell your story."

"It is now nearly thirty years since I first saw Caterina," Chastelneuf went on. "She was but fourteen years old, and her little face had all the blameless brilliance of a child's. I loved her, but with a levity and cynicism incomprehensible to my maturer perceptions. I seduced her, but tenderly, for I had determined to make her mine legally and for life. We spent hours in the gardens at Saint Blaise, where we ran races together; the prize, which I permitted her to win, was a pair of blue garters. I was captivated; her candour, her ingenuousness, her vivacity, all contrived to make me her slave, for the union of beauty, intelligence, and innocence has ever swayed me.

"A parent, perhaps no crueller than her lover, but certainly for the moment more severe, immured Caterina within a convent at Murano; we were unable to meet, and had only the chilly comfort of smuggled letters, and the ambiguous tremors of hope, as sustenance for our reciprocal dreams. I gave her my portrait, commissioning a young Piedmontese to render it in the smallest miniature; he painted an exquisite Saint Catherine of the same dimensions, and a clever Venetian jeweller mounted them both in a ring. The patron saint concealed my countenance, but the expert craftsman had provided the fantastic setting with a hidden spring, and I fear that my pictured eyes often disturbed the devout eyelids of poor Caterina by hot and secular tears.

"This comedy continued for several months; I grew very thin and mournful, and lived miracles of faithfulness in the mere denial of my natural instincts. At last I made bold to enter the convent chapel; one of the novices was about to take the veil, and I knew I might pass unobserved among the crowd of visitors.

"After the investiture I walked into the convent parlour with the other pious spectators, and standing within four paces of my poor little love, I perceived her gazing at me in a species of ecstasy; happiness made wide her hazel eyes and parted her lips to suspire tenderness.

"Alas! I had no sooner conferred the fleeting joy of my smile upon this unfortunate child than I robbed her again, and forever; my heart, always elastic, rebounded from the small and shrinking form of Caterina, to fall with terrific violence at the feet of a tall nun beneath whose cool reserve a secret fire was visible, even as her coif disclosed an unlicensed curl of red-gold hair above a face fair to pallor and lovely to delirium. I was completely overcome; my head swam among singing clouds, and I should assuredly have fainted had not a kindly old lay sister led me into the sharp sea winds of the conventual garden.

"If ever I write my memoirs, which I shall refuse to call confessions, since that infamous rascal Rousseau has profaned the title, I may describe at leisured length the course of my infatuation for the nun, Mary Magdalen, and its legendary end; I may aspire to draw her portrait, more intimately even than my young Piedmontese drew it for me, naked upon a couch of black satin, demure and shameless behind an ivory medallion of the Annunciation fitted into the lid of a gold snuff-box.

"This refulgent lady was the friend of the Abbé de Bernis; she had taken the veil out of pure caprice, and had the discretion to conceal any unhappiness she may have felt. Her illustrious birth and her extravagant liberality procured innumerable privileges denied to the other nuns; the tale of her amorous adventures must not insult the laudable ears of your Eminence. Suffice it to say that she and I between us plotted to debauch the peaceable simplicity of poor Caterina; I gave my darling to the power of the dog, and in a room of mirrors, lighted by girandoles and candelabra of rock crystal and gilded bronze, Bernis took the child in his arms and drank her frightened tears with feverish avidity. I retired, laughing, to sup with Mary Magdalen in the adjoining chamber; the nun was disguised as a handsome youth in rose-coloured velvet and black satin, and we devoured oysters and truffles from silver chafing-dishes and fine Dresden china. The wines were burgundy and champagne; I remember that I was excessively thirsty. I was mixing a salad of anchovies and hard-boiled eggs when the door opened and Bernis entered, followed by Caterina.

"Bernis was a man of forty; to my intolerant eye he was already a little worn, a little thin; his good looks were faintly tainted by effeminacy. He was invariably dressed in the extreme of elegance; the beauty of his hands was proverbial.

"Now, with an air of the most polished courtesy, he offered one of these miraculous hands to Caterina; he bowed, and I saw nobility rise to his forehead, shaking back the perfumed flippancy of his thoughts as a lion shakes back his mane. So I knew that although I had abandoned my darling to the lion, the power of the dog was dead. I am ashamed to admit that I was furiously jealous of Bernis.

"I cannot tell you the truth of this matter because I have never known it. What I conceive to be the truth seemed inconceivable at that confounding moment; the room, with its vain and equivocal elegance, its exquisite depravity, its engravings by Meunius and Toletana, the lovely epicene figure of the nun, the perverse integrity of the ambassador's bearing, all conspired to render the scene incredible. Caterina, attired in a childish gown of green gauze, was composed and smiling; she looked up at Bernis, and her gaze was limpid with faith. I was very angry; knowing a portion of my loss, I raged inwardly, and longed to kill the two; the deeper significance of their mutual glances was hidden from my eyes by a curtain of blood."

15 CAME FORTH SWEETNESS

Peter Innocent had covered his face with the lavender-scented handkerchief, but Gozzi remained satirical and unmoved. The chevalier brushed the back of his hand across his shining and dilated eyes, as if to dissipate the remembered darkness of crimson. He continued to speak in a measured and deliberate voice:

"I did not see Caterina again; she returned to the convent at Murano, and within the year her parents had married her to an honest Venetian lawyer, who adored and tormented her youth with an intolerable devotion. Bernis, as you know, was soon afterwards recalled to France; the nun Mary Magdalen and I were left to console each other with meditations upon infidelity. Our natures were but too similar; each libertine despised the other, and we parted without regret or charitable illusion, without prejudice, and without compassion for each other's spirits, subdued to such resemblance by the unloving flesh."

"Peter, if you can make, as the peasants say at Chioggia, either dragon's head or mermaid's tail of this unholy rigamarole, you are a cleverer man than I, and that I should be sorry to believe!" exclaimed Gozzi in exasperation, as the chevalier's recital drew to an apparent close on a note of profound repentance.

Peter Innocent raised his seraphic and bewildered eyes, enlarged by tears too scorching to be cooled by a cambric handkerchief; he did not look at Gozzi or at Chastelneuf, but straight into the sky, a deep, blue pool reversed, suspended, spreading like a tree, like a shade, like the shadow of a sapphire rock.

"I can make neither head nor tail of this tragedy, Carlo," he answered, "yet, for my comfort, the chevalier has made me believe it has a heart, and that not chimærical or devilish, but vulnerably human. I cannot understand, and yet, beneath the covert and obscure, I can feel the beating of a heart."

"You are a cleverer man than I, Peter," said Carlo Gozzi, who believed in elves. He said it in humility, for sometimes he believed in angels.

"You are right, Eminence; it is the heart of poor mortality which beats in my story, and echoes in your ears; the sound is the sum of human hearts which still vibrate in unison because, though broken, they have mended each other with love."

Chastelneuf spoke solemnly, but Gozzi questioned him with a quizzical scorn.

"Do you say love, O melancholy Jacques?"

"I say it," replied the chevalier; the habitual visor of insolence masked his face upon the word. "To clarify the matter further for your Eminence's comprehension," he went on, in a light and cursive voice, "I must remind you that Bernis had no sooner become a power in France than he had the unfortunate honour of incurring the enmity of the royal favourite. He had the temerity to suggest that the Prince de Soubise was not a fit person to command the King's armies; the Pompadour was majestically offended, and when the pope presented Bernis with a cardinal's hat, Louis bestowed it upon him with his own hands and forthwith exiled him to Soissons, where he remained for six years, a broken and embittered man."

"Lorenzo Ganganelli loved that man," said Peter Innocent.

"I know he did, and therefore his successor hates him, Eminence; when you return to Rome, you may do a kindness to a dying lion."

"Chevalier, I think you are wrong; I am very old, and I should only weary the Cardinal de Bernis," Peter Innocent replied modestly.

"Your nephew's sweetheart will not weary him," Chastelneuf cried with a curiously happy laugh. "Wait; do not believe me a madman. I have more riddles to elucidate if you can spare me the patience."

"I have a fabulous appetite for old

wives' tales," Gozzi admitted rudely, and Peter Innocent was quiet and kind in his silence.

"Good," said the chevalier. "We were at Soissons, were we not? At Soissons in a cold December, with a northeast wind and seventy miles dividing it from the classic gaiety of Versailles. Here, among Gothic churches and darker mediæval memories of Saint Crispin the Shoemaker and Louis the Pious, here where Becket prayed and Abélard despaired, Bernis came alone and sorrowful, having put his trust in princes, and served his country better than his king's mistress.

"Imagine, if you are something kindlier than stone, the desolation of that Christmas season, when in Soissons the Gothic roses of Notre Dame were carved in snow, and the Cardinal de Bernis sat alone in his vast apartment. He had caused no fire to be lighted, no supper to be laid, and when the chimes, like stars made audible, began to pierce the midnight with rejoicing, he stopped his ears against their voices, and wept the burning tears of Lucifer fallen from heaven.

"At that moment, out of the darkness, upon the wings of the bells as it were, and feathered with snow like a little bird, Caterina came to him."

"Thank God!" said Carlo Gozzi, fervently. Peter Innocent said nothing.

"She folded him in her grey cloak, that was all feathered and furred with the snow, and she kissed his beautiful cold hands. It was the first kiss she had ever given him; she gave it to the lion who had delivered her from the power of the dog, at Venice, in the room of mirrors, on an evening of full carnival, when she was only fourteen years old."

"I am glad she came," said Carlo Gozzi, adding, after he had cleared his throat, "I suppose, then, that we are to understand that Rosalba Berni is the offspring of this interesting union!"

"Yes, you are to understand precisely that, my dear Count; I fear you are incapable of fully appreciating the poignancy of the situation, but the bare facts you are at liberty to understand," answered the chevalier with impudent urbanity. He finished the tale, turning his blazing eyes towards Peter Innocent, who continued to say nothing.

"When Caterina came to Soissons on Christmas eve, she was seventeen years old and a widow. At that time Bernis was past forty, and tired by the vanities of a Dead-Sea dream, an ashy-flavoured world. Six years later, when Rosalba was born in the South, her father could laugh very lightly as he sprinkled her with almond blossoms and peach blossoms and cherry blossoms or tickle her lips with a pigeon's feather. Perhaps he was happy because he had been recalled to court, where he had magnificently rejected the seals of office; perhaps he was happy because he was archbishop of Albi. Perhaps, on the other hand, he was happy because of Rosalba, who had been born in happiness in the South, in a farmhouse whose outer walls were covered with espaliered peach trees, and whose windows were fringed with climbing roses. Upon the day of her birth a golden peach knocked at the door and a white rose flew into the window. Bernis ate the peach and gave the rose to Caterina. To the child they gave the name Rosalba.

"At Albi, the archbishop's palace is a fortified castle of the Middle Ages, and perhaps it is not strange that Bernis loved better the farmhouse with the espaliered fruit-trees. Here for five years a golden age endured; a little world existed for a time, round and smooth and perfect as a peach. A bitter stone was hidden in its heart, but before Bernis set his teeth to that his felicity was absolute. Then, in the plenitude of summer, Caterina died.

"Bernis gave every rose in the garden to Caterina; she clasped them with gentle indifference. In this same manner she accepted his last kiss; he was glad enough to go to Rome, to assist at the conclave which elected Lorenzo Ganganelli. He had a chill conviction of her forgetfulness.

"Rosalba was conveyed to Paris in the care of an impoverished cousin of her father's; this gentlewoman was amiable, but frivolous and injudicious. Having acquired a little wealth through the generosity of her kinsman Bernis, she repaired to Versailles, taking the child with her. There, in the midst of that sumptuous, but effete, civilization, Rosalba was remarked by Madame Necker for her wit and beauty and selected as a playmate for that lady's precocious little daughter.

"Thus, while yet of tender years, the girl was made free of the best *philosophe* society; by the time she was twelve she was among the shining ornaments of Madame Necker's Friday receptions; the Mondays of Madame Geoffrin, the Tuesdays of Madame Helvétius, were incomplete without Rosalba's elfin grace. Her cousin desired above all else a fashionable marriage for her protégée but beneath brocaded petticoats the child's silk stockings, though gossamer and clocked with lace, were already obstinately blue. She refused, by impertinent implication, a round dozen of silver-gilded youths; Versailles was a blown Easter egg, excessively sugared, and she cared only for political reform and the awards of the Académie française."

16 DIVERSIONS AT FERNEY

"Intolerable imp!" exclaimed Count Carlo Gozzi in disgust. "It is this same horror, this unfeminine baggage, this most ungentle lady whom I have laughed to scorn in all my charming plays! She is the Princess Turandot, who utters riddles in the tone of an academician; she is Barberina, who has read Holbach while Carletti was dressing her hair. I had hardly realized the extent of her folly. However if you, Chevalier, say she is pretty—and you do say so, do you not?"

"And good? You have assured me of her virtue?" faltered Peter Innocent.

The chevalier regarded them with skilfully displayed contempt; he elevated his eyebrows the polite fraction of an inch.

"Eminence," he pronounced, "it is even possible, as the French pastry cooks have it, to put too many perfect ingredients into a pound cake. Enough, they remind us, is better than dyspepsia. Yourself and the count may live to regret the fact that Rosalba has never had a cold in the head or an illaudable impulse. Such things are, perhaps, disfiguring for the moment, but they humble the spirit of the young. Rosalba is not humble."

"Is she proud?" said Peter Innocent.

"Not in the least, Eminence," Chastelneuf replied. "She is merely perfect. You may be completely at ease in her company; she has the simplicity of the truly great."

Carlo Gozzi snorted indignantly, but Peter Innocent perceived no cause for annoyance. His simplicity excelled Rosalba's.

"And her friendship with Voltaire?" he went on a little nervously in spite of the chevalier's reassurances. "I have wondered, do you know, whether that were quite desirable. Of course its results were most fortunate; there can be no doubt that Querini has sheltered her from every tempered blast. But Voltaire as the intimate companion of a child of twelve —no, I confess the reflection has troubled me."

"Monseigneur, as I said to M. de Voltaire after reciting thirty-six stanzas of that divine twenty-third canto of 'Ariosto,' describing the madness of Roland with the most dreadful accuracy, —when I had finished, I assure you, the philosopher fell upon my neck, sobbing;

tears were in all eyes,—but, I repeat, as I said to him at this affecting moment, you are too satirical, *cher maitre;* be human, as now, and like Ariosto you will be sublime! Oh, I remember it very well! Your Eminence is right; there was a vein of irony in the man which I must be the first to deprecate. And yet, he had intelligence; I think Rosalba was attracted by his intelligence. Then, too, you would not have her guilty of ingratitude, and he was kind to her."

"He stole her from a convent, did he not?" inquired Gozzi, who was beginning to be bored by the continued amiability of his two friends. To his relief, Peter Innocent looked shocked; the chevalier remained incurably good-humoured.

"Oh, quite!" the imperturbable chevalier cried. "But such a convent! Really, I cannot, in your Eminence's presence, attempt to explain; there were, however, circumstances too distressing to recall. I should hardly go so far as to say he stole her; rescue is the appropriate word, surely. The affair was shrouded in mystery; some said she had been immured by her ambitious cousin for refusing to wed a one-eyed marquis; others that she had incurred the enmity of the Neckers by embracing the free-trade principles of Turgot. Still another version, and that which I am myself inclined to credit, ascribes her abduction to the machinations of a rich Englishman, Milord Camphor or Camphile, who returning widowed from the East, beheld and desired, within the chilly inspiration of a single breath, Rosalba's loveliness and warm vivacity. It is but natural that the squire of Ferney, who had heard all of these stories in their most exaggerated forms, should have hastened to free this adorable creature from the chains of tyranny and vile superstition."

"And the name of this convent?" asked Peter Innocent, rather apologetically.

"That, Eminence, I am not at liberty to divulge; another time, perhaps. You see," the chevalier added, "it was the same convent from which M. de Voltaire had previously rescued Philiberte de Varicourt."

"Oho! Belle et Bonne!" exclaimed the count, who evidently saw. Peter Innocent did not, but his modesty prevented him from demanding an explanation.

"Precisely. And here, very luckily for little Rosalba, our good friend Querini appeared upon the scene. He came to pay his last respects to Voltaire; the fatal journey to Paris had already been discussed; 'Irène' was well-nigh completed, and the patriarch experienced, within his venerable breast, a lively and determined longing to visit once more the country of his birth. The noble Angelo Querini found the household at Ferney more or less at sevens, elevens, and thirteens, as the school children say; Rosalba was crying in the boot closet under the stairs, and 'Belle et Bonne' was biting her nails in her boudoir. M. de Voltaire and the Marquis de Villette were locked in the study drinking English punch and suffering from profound depression."

"What had occurred to disturb their philosophical serenity?" asked Gozzi, with an air of quiet satisfaction.

"Nothing; nothing at all, save that the Sage of Ferney had committed the trifling indiscretion of addressing Rosalba as 'Plus Belle et Plus Bonne' in the fascinating presence of Philiberte. Our little friend had just completed a very creditable Horatian ode, entitled 'To My Heroic Champion'; this she recited, wearing a neat new frock of dark blue merino, with her hair arranged in becoming ringlets. The result was curious, and, to a man of eighty-four, disturbing. I have sometimes suspected that his decease was hastened—but, no, these ladies' dainty and frangible shoulder blades must not be burdened by so deplorable an event as the death of Voltaire! He perished of a surfeit of coffee and academic honours."

"Unrepentant," said Carlo Gozzi with intense and pleasurable conviction.

"Perhaps merely discourteous," said Chastelneuf, kindly.

Peter Innocent said nothing; he was absorbed in silent supplication for the immortal soul of François Arouet de Voltaire. The Deity's replying silence appeared to him an unconditional consent to his request for leniency. The softened airs and mistier hues of the Venetian afternoon surrounded this moment with a mild halo of salvation, and Peter Innocent felt sure that the sage was forgiven.

Far away, across the melancholy marshes of Altichieri, Virginio and Rosalba, fantastically cloaked and masked, had seized the same propitious moment to ascend the steps of the chevalier's elegant English carriage. They bore a large portmanteau and a couple of bandboxes, and the noble Angelo Querini, as he slammed the emblazoned door upon their smiles and blushes, wished them God-speed with all the prayerful emotion of his foolish heart, while his sagacious brow condemned them for a pair of young lunatics, whirling in spangled frenzy towards a riddle and a doom.

END OF BOOK TWO

BOOK THREE: ROSALBA

> But some, and these the elect among gardeners, will always prefer China Roses.
>
> CHRISTOPHER WARREN

17 GOLDEN BRIDE

"And now," murmured Chastelneuf with obvious regret, gazing dreamily over the housetops, which the descending day had diapered with a changed and more intricate design of shadow—"and now, I repeat, my patient friends, there is little left to tell. You have been indulgent; the hour grows older, and matures into a time more suited to adventure than to these vague reminiscences. In a word, Querini adopted Rosalba upon the spot; he conveyed her to Venice, and encouraged her in the study of the arts and sciences. Poetry was her natural voice; the Arcadian Academy received her with acclaim, and forthwith fell down and kissed the abbreviated hem of her schoolgirl's gown. The Infant Sappho was baptized in Castalia, and shaking the fountain drops from her juvenile curls, she lifted up her throat to sing. The rest you know; it cannot take me above five minutes to recount the principal events of Rosalba's Venetian career. You must remember—"

"But is it quite necessary, Chevalier?" Gozzi inquired with plaintive scorn. "We have all heard too much of the Infant Sappho; some of us, impelled no doubt by morbid curiosity, have even read her verses. We recall very vividly and with peculiar pain the ridiculous festivities which marked her coronation at Rome, and all the nauseating verbiage, which, with the bad luxuriance of a weed, has kept her reputation virulently green. If you desire to converse further about the past, I must beg you to confine yourself to your own memories; why not favour us with an account of your escape from the Leads?"

Chastelneuf smiled; he was well aware of the count's savage irony, but he turned to Peter Innocent with bland composure.

"If his Eminence wishes; I am always at his disposal."

"I should be charmed—" began the cardinal; but Gozzi interposed in sincere alarm.

"For God's sake, Peter, do not encourage the rascal; the story will be an affair of hours, and we have much to accomplish before nightfall. Did you succeed in procuring a suitable gown for the girl, Jacques? You are accustomed to these matters; you have seduced several milliners, and your taste is impeccable."

"I have arranged for everything; I have ordered the supper, and bespoke the best string quartet in the four hospitals. The casino is in readiness; I have not yet relinquished its key to the new tenant, and my own servant has seen to it that there are fresh fires on the hearths, fresh candles in the girandoles, and fresh white roses in the crystal urns. I considered jasmine, I mused on lilies of the valley, but I knew I was wrong; there must be only white roses for this wedding-night. Am I not wise, your Eminence?"

Peter Innocent was at a loss to reply; his blue eyes were clouded by fatigue and bewilderment.

"Wedding-night?" he faltered, suddenly afraid. "Is it Virginio's wedding-night?"

"That is for your Eminence to say," the chevalier replied with courtly mendacity. "Also, it were only proper to await Virginio's own decision as to this momentous business; having seen Rosalba, I cannot question its affirmative nature. Carlo Gozzi and I have been planning a little surprise for the young people; a fête, *un petit diner à deux*, quite simple, you comprehend, but complete in every detail. It is Rosalba's birthday; since the noble Angelo Querini adopted her, her garments have been fashioned with a severe disregard of the prevailing *mode*, and frivolity has been absent from her life. Even at her coronation she was permitted no greater magnificence than a Greek robe of virgin white; the material was velvet, I believe, but the cut was antiquated. The Arcadian Academy has adored her manner of dressing, so chaste, so austere, so truly classical; but Rosalba has been unhappy. 'This was well enough for Ferney,' she has said, 'but for Venice, no! I can be young only once; am I never to have a single little stitch *alla francese*, not even in a plain lemon-coloured Milordino with cloth of silver incisions, or a modest mantle of gold-green camelot lined with Canadian marten? I love my guardian with profound devotion, but I am, after all, a woman, and it is sad not to possess a robe of Holland *poussé*, trimmed with Spanish point!' Oh, she has wept, your Eminence; she has grieved in secret; we must endeavour to console her. What do you think; are you for flame or peach or girlish primrose? I am convinced it must be yellow. Tell me, do you agree?"

Around the cardinal's frosty and abstracted head a dozen rainbows seemed revolving in vertiginous arcs: colours of sun, of harvest moon, of comet's tail and hellfire streamed out upon the increasing violet of dusk, and lit all Venice with their fervency. He hesitated, and Gozzi answered for him.

"That is a problem for you and the milliner's apprentice to determine ecstatically between yourselves; it does not concern Cardinal Bon. Peter, we have indeed hoped that our little festival in honour of these children might result in a wedding; for me there must ever be the happy conclusion to my fairy-tales, and I think to-night's performance will be the ultimate fantasy which I shall prepare for any stage. I do not care for the girl save as the inevitable partner for the prince; it is sufficient that she is pretty and not too intolerably a fool. But for Virginio I desire happiness, and over and above that good measure, a little pleasure running down, like shining bubbles, like golden grains. I had thought, myself, that what with music and dancing and a small quantity of very light wine to enliven them, the babes might frolic until dawn, and then we could all hire a gondola—for mine is at the pawnbroker's—and, proceeding to the church of Saint John and Saint Paul, allow Peter to pronounce the blessing of holy church upon their union. Then, perhaps, another gondola, and an *al fresco* breakfast upon the sands of the sea or in some rustic grove. What do you say, Peter?"

This time Peter Innocent was at the trembling point of reply, but the chevalier sent him back into silence by an ejaculation of surprise.

"Good heavens! What an insanity is this, my dear Count! Surely the marriage must take place before supper; it is only right and *convenable* if the young people are to dance together all night. I could never countenance such indiscretion; I am sincerely shocked. 'Frolic until dawn' indeed! But of course his Eminence will not permit it even for a moment."

"Confound you!" cried Carlo Gozzi. "You know perfectly well, Jacques, that I did not mean—"

"What?" said the chevalier, demurely.

The count looked at the cardinal; then he sighed deeply, and returned to its decaying sheath the jewelled Florentine dagger which his hand had for a moment caressed.

"Never mind; nothing. I meant nothing, since Peter Innocent is here; but beware how you annoy me, Chastelneuf."

"Oh, I intended no harm!" the chevalier assured him gaily. "I am possibly a trifle over-scrupulous about the conventions, but you must contrive to forgive a finical old friend, Carlo. We must all be very kind to-night; as for the marriage, I leave its hour to the choice of Cardinal Bon, and its subsequent good fortune to the benevolence of Almighty God." Casting a triumphant glance at Carlo Gozzi, Chastelneuf bowed his head in double humility to higher powers.

"If Virginio must really be married, I do not think it matters very much whether I marry him before or after supper," said Peter Innocent, gently. His delicately chiselled face was worn by anxiety, but his voice was firm as he continued: "I had hoped, as Carlo understands, that my dear nephew might find a conclusive felicity in the charitable embrace of the church, as I have done. My earthly joy has so nearly approached the heavenly, I have so thirsted for the peace of God and have been so thankfully appeased, that I had prayed for him a like simplicity of rapture. But if Carlo here, who has seen much of the lad's expanding soul, concludes that the complications of the secular life are indispensable to his content, so be it. Further, if the chevalier's account of young Rosalba Berni is but half so veracious as his proven honour must guarantee, I am well satisfied of her worthiness to be Virginio's wife. Therefore I will not withhold my consent from these nuptials; my heart awaits the lovers. Only, since it is better to avoid a too precipitate deed, however valid, let us follow Carlo's advice; the wedding shall take place tomorrow morning at the Church of Saint John and Saint Paul, whose benisons be upon these children."

The tower room was trembling in the violet dusk, like an island pinnacle invaded by the tide; the tide was evening, which rose rather than descended, flowing softly, smoothly, and invincibly from the deep lagoons, without the lightest undulation of a wave, without a sound, yet influential as the sea itself. Blue-violet and grey, red-violet where the sun informed it, the evening drowned the room in tinted darkness, until the faces of the three friends floated like nebulous ocean monsters in the gloom: Peter Innocent's face was coloured like a dead pearl, Carlo Gozzi's gleamed phosphorescent yellow. The chevalier's nervous hands wavered, brown as water weeds; his countenance was obscured.

The stairs which mounted to the tower chamber were crumbled and hazardous, yet upon their peril some one climbed, a foot-fall tinkled suddenly, incredibly tiny, a scampering as of winged mice, a skimming as of swallows. The rumour neared; heels or hoofs clicked upon stone at a fawn's pace; feathers or gauzy fabrics rustled and flew. The rusty latch cried out, the leathern door creaked in a draft, and Rosalba was within the room.

By some perverse vagary of the evening clouds, the sun and moon crossed swords above her head; under this pointed arch of light she ran into the room. The sun's long final ray was rosy and dim; the moon's first ray was silvery green and poignant. But Rosalba was pure gold from head to foot; she was brighter than the swords of light. A chaplet of golden leaves confined the burnished shadow of her hair; her sandal thongs were gilded; her gown, an Arcadian travesty of Diana's, was cut from cloth of gold. Her face was clear and pale, and her little freckles powdered it tenderly, like grains of golden dust. Her eyes were gold made magically translucent.

Her quick glance swept the apartment in a single scintillation, then, uttering a wild and joyous cry, she rushed upon Peter Innocent with all the ardour and velocity of a shooting star.

He was afraid. She was throttling him with her slender arms, and yet her lips were soft upon his cheek, and somewhere, in the profoundest caverns of his heart, love moved and wondered, answering her from a dream.

"Darling, even if you are a cardinal!" she said, "and lovely, even if you are an Eminence! Oh, you are beautiful, and like Virginio; I knew you at once! I shall adore you, and obey you always!" And she fell to kissing his hand. The fragility of those unresponsive and chilly fingertips struck lightly yet insistently at her happiness, and she drew back in alarm, crying sadly:

"Oh, but you too, you too! You shiver and break when I touch you! Are you made of ice, that you cannot bear the little weight of my hand?"

Carlo Gozzi, to his own amazement, made a small sound of pity; the chevalier stepped forward and took the girl's hand between his own. He kissed it gravely and essayed to speak. At that precise instant the door swung open, and Virginio, sheathed in a silver cloak, came softly into the room; he entered like the twilight, and Rosalba was quenched within his arms.

18 TOO MANY PASTRY COOKS

"Inevitably ruin the meringue, as they say in Vienna!" the chevalier concluded lightly, closing his tortoise-shell snuffbox with a sharp click.

"Ah, you are right; the whole affair is whipped cream, and we are endeavouring to turn it into good solid butter." Carlo Gozzi agreed; his face was thoughtful and surprisingly humane upon the reflection. "What is man? A fantastical puff-paste, as Webster truly remarks."

"I implore you not to be forever quoting the English tragedians, my dear Count; it is disconcerting, to say the least, in this enlightened eighteenth century of ours. If Shakspere and his barbaric kin could have been gently licked into shape by the suave cat-tongue of Addison, they might have been endurable. As it is, I beg you to consider my earache, which is troublesome in November, and cannot brook a Gothic brutality of syllables. Touching the puff-paste, the simile is just enough, if Virginio is a man. I thought, however, we had determined him an elemental."

"H'm," said Gozzi, drily, "quite so, quite so. But, to my romantic fancy, an elemental moved among thunderstorms and whirlwinds; its least conceivable spirit was a snowfall. But Virginio is animated by the soul of an icicle or a small, pale skeleton leaf. I have no patience with him since he carries his arm in a sling."

"Come, come, my friend," cried Chastelneuf, "you are too hard on the boy. Rosalba is, after all, very impulsive; her dancing is hoydenish, and she is addicted to running races, like Atalanta gone mad. Look, there she is, at the end of the cypress alley; she seems to be indulging in a game of tag with his Eminence."

The scene, precisely etched in slender lines upon a clear green west of early winter, was the garden of a small casino near Venice; the hour was sunset. A delicate chill flavoured the atmosphere with a perfume of frost and fallen leaves; the chevalier wore his fur pelisse, and the count was wrapped in a Bedouin cape of camels' hair; his head was covered by a scarlet nightcap.

Over the lawn, powdered with blown yellow petals, the noble Angelo Querini approached; his grave and judicial garments reproved the perished flowers. He seated himself upon a marble bench by the side of the two friends, first spreading a shawl of Scottish plaid against the frigidity of the stone. His eyes sought the distant figure of Rosalba, which flitted unquietly along the vistas of the garden, exquisitely strange and savage in a cloak of tawny velvet lined with foxes' skins.

"She used never to be so wild a creature while she shared my roof," he said sadly. "She was always so studious, so docile, so domestic! God knows what possesses her poor little body; her tranquillity is turned to quicksilver. She runs like a rabbit, like a deer, to and fro within the confines of these walls, and at night she is very tired. I think she cries. She is afraid of Virginio."

"But Virginio is afraid of her!" cried Carlo Gozzi, rather angrily. "Rosalba is not afraid; she is a brave child. The boy is afraid; look at him now, leaning against the wall, as white as pumiced parchment, and as limp. He is a coward; how can he be afraid of a little woodland fawn like our Rosalba?"

It was true; the slim form of Virginio appeared crucified upon one of the stucco walls of the inclosure. His feet were crossed; his fair head drooped and fainted; one arm was outspread among the vines; the other hung in a black silk sling. There was an agony of weakness in the attitude; his transparent hand was clenched upon a broken tendril of vine.

"She is afraid of Virginio," Angelo Querini repeated obstinately.

"I believe you are both of you right; they are afraid of each other," said Chastelneuf. "Our experiment has not been wholly successful: two mild substances are, in the intimate fusion of marriage, beginning to effervesce; there are signs of an explosion. It is a pity, but the case is by no means hopeless."

Both Querini and Carlo Gozzi continued to stare indignantly at the pathetic spectacle of Virginio's despair. Querini felt a truly paternal solicitude for Rosalba, and Gozzi, upon learning that the girl was a confirmed admirer of his fairy drama, had quickly altered his opinion of her character and intellect. She appeared to him now the very embodiment of inner grace, and he reflected angrily that Virginio was a poor atomy to mate with this burning and spiritual child of love, who wore a wild beast's pelt above a heart more vulnerable than a little lamb's.

"The incident of the broken arm," drawled the chevalier, himself regarding Virginio through half-shut eyelids, "was, you comprehend, somewhat alarming to our young friend here. He is timid and fears to repeat the experience; his wife is impetuous and inclined to be careless. It is true that she did not actually touch him; they were running along the laurel alley, and he stumbled and fell. I was able to repair the damage, but it has shaken him seriously. Apparently he blames Rosalba; she, for her part, is proud, and in the consciousness of innocence, wounded to the soul by his implicit reproach. Neither will speak; their silence is like a darkness over them, in which suspicion flourishes."

"What does Peter say?"

"Nothing, in words; evidently he grieves, however, and I think he holds us responsible for the failure of his nephew's happiness. He feels certain that a monastery, rather than marriage is Virginio's natural haven. Rosalba he has forgiven, but he cannot look upon her without pain."

"Forgiven her! And for what fault, may I ask? Is it a crime on this unlucky infant's part that we have incontinently wedded her to a glass mannikin instead of decent blood and bone? God pardon us for our unholy meddling, for we have hurt the loveliest thing alive!"

Marvellous to relate, along the ancient leather of Carlo Gozzi's cheek a single glabrous tear moved slowly downward; the others observed it with awe, not attempting to answer until he had removed it with the sleeve of his burnous. Then the chevalier cleared his throat and spoke briskly.

"I share your indignation, my dear Count, but the fact remains. Peter has forgiven Rosalba; you know we cannot prevent Peter from forgiving people even when they have done no harm. He is incapable of harbouring resentment, but he must have the comfort of an occasional absolution to uphold him; he has remitted Rosalba's non-existent sins against Virginio. See how tenderly he addresses the elusive child. She shrinks, she starts like a doe transfixed by an arrow, yet Peter's shaft was feathered by compassion; he let fly from the strings of his heart. He is a saint whose silver niche should never know these invasive anxieties; I have erred in giving him a nephew."

Virginio stirred and wavered against the wall; languidly he straightened his slight limbs to glide across the grass toward his wife. He was very pale, and his beautiful face appeared mute, and blinded by mysterious sorrow; its smooth, pure contours were immobile as a mask of gauze over the countenance of one lately dead.

19 BURNING LEAF

"It is a pity Rosalba is late; she is always so fond of *perdrix au choux,* and François has surpassed himself this evening," Chastelneuf commented reflectively, emptying his champagne goblet for the twelfth time.

The salon of the little casino was brilliantly, yet softly, illuminated by innumerable candles, and the Murano mirrors which formed its walls steeped the repeated lights in cool sea-coloured distances. The pyramid of grapes upon the table seemed moulded from the same silvered glass, and the flowers themselves were a fountain of crystalline spray. Peter Innocent, Carlo Gozzi, and Angelo Querini stained the pale, bright chamber with their black and rusty-brown attire; the chevalier's crimson startled it like a blow; only Virginio, resigned and pallid in pearly satin, fitted into the settling like a clear jewel clasped by a ring. His air of fragility was heightened by a cold and fearful lucency upon his brow; he looked ill, refused all food, and drank nothing save iced soda-water. He did not speak, but occupied his visibly shaking hands in the manufacture of little bread pellets. These were not grimy, as are the bread pellets of ordinary mortals; they appeared to acquire an added whiteness from the touch of his delicate and listless fingers.

"I overheard her tell Lucietta to repair the grey and lemon lutestring for tonight; one of the silver tassels was amiss, I think. Without doubt, she intended to dine with us; her absence begins to be alarming." Chastelneuf frowned into his replenished wineglass.

"I will go search for her," cried Querini and Carlo Gozzi with simultaneous eagerness. Gozzi was already upon his feet; Querini was rising majestically from his carven chair. Peter Innocent said nothing; the silence of Virginio became appreciably more profound.

"Your pardon, gentlemen; I believe I am best fitted for this embassy." The chevalier's voice was authoritative, and he was at the door in three great strides. "There is a bonfire in the garden," he threw back over his shoulder, like an irrelevant glove, as he passed from the room. The challenge, if challenge it were, seemed flung directly into Virginio's bloodless and impassive face. The boy was whiter than white glass, more quiet than fallen snow; his long, fair eyelashes were lowered over his chill cerulean eyes.

Chastelneuf ran hastily from the lighted house into the obscurity of the dusk; behind him the windows made tall parallelograms of radiance, tinted by curtains of rainbow silk; in front a stranger colour tore the darkness into ribbons and flew upward in fringes of scarlet. "Merely the leaves, which the gardener is burning," the chevalier told himself in reassurance.

Nevertheless his buckled shoes leaped over the ground like the hoofs of a stallion, and he reached the end of the laurel alley three seconds in advance of Rosalba, who had danced into his vision on the instant, lighter, brighter, and more insensate than a burning leaf. Her cloak of fox skins opened into wings, the air upheld her, and she floated into the heart of the fire.

In another second she was safe; Chastelneuf stood over her on the smoking grass and stamped out the sparks with his buckled shoes; he knelt, and crushed between his sinewy hands the little ruffle of flame which scalloped the edges of her crumpled gown.

"Why were you so wicked, so cruelly wicked?" he cried. "Why did you not tell me that you wished to die? Do you understand that I am always here to give you whatever you want? Yes, even if it is death, I will give it to you; but sweetly flavoured and in a golden box. I will give you the death of these others if you desire it; I will give you life such as you have not imagined save in heaven.

"My child, my child, you have observed that I love you, but have you comprehended the quality of my love? It is such as you will never discover in the hollow veins of Virginio or among the noble ganglions of Querini's intellect; it is love, lust, passion, humility, and wonder; it is human, not divine, not animal, but the love of mortal for mortal; it is at your service. I love you; I have loved many times and in many fashions, but this love is all your own. Use it as you will; I have no expectation that you can return it in kind. I have done you an irreparable wrong; forgive me; I entreat your forgiveness, my darling. I believed that I loved Virginio, for he is the fair product of my ingenuity, but in attempting to provide him with those things needful to happiness I have sacrificed you, who are worth a million pale Virginios. You are the true child of my heart, and its ultimate affection; I will even love you with a father's love, if I may not love you with a lover's. I will subdue my spirit to your least command if you will promise me to live!"

The chevalier spoke with the most impassioned fervour, and Rosalba smiled among her tawny furs to see him so perturbed. In the midst of her own despair, she perceived nothing save cause for mirth in the agitation of one whom she had always regarded as a benevolent elderly gentleman, respectably conversant with the Italian classics and the court circulars of Europe.

Chastelneuf experienced a pang of extreme humiliation; he felt Rosalba's eyes, wild and acute as those of a trapped vixen, transfix his chestnut peruke and pierce to the silver stubble beneath it. The wrinkles upon his face were deepened as by acid, and his falcon look grew weary with the recollection of unrestful years. Rosalba, innocent alike of cruelty or compassion, shifted her gaze without speaking, and then cried aloud in the voice of a prisoned creature tardily released. Virginio, so veiled in twilight as to appear no more than a moving part of the invisible, now glided from the obscurity of the garden.

Rosalba shot upward like an impulsive flower nourished on subterranean flame; she ran, a pointed blossom of the dragon seed, straight to Virginio's heart. She might have been a dagger in that heart; the boy drew himself erect, closed his eyes, and stood swaying in an agony apparent as a wound. There was another and sharper cry, an echo and a confused murmuring; the two slim figures clung together for an instant. Then they were again divided; the blue translucent dusk flowed between them like a narrow river; they stretched their hands to each other, and their tears fell into the swift and narrow stream of time and were lost.

Chastelneuf forgot his own sorrowful anger in a sudden pity; he was intolerably saddened by the spectacle of the lovers' frustration. He wanted nothing half so much as to see them happy and at peace under the evening stars; their youth was darling to his senses, like the smell of flowers or the flavour of wine, and he observed it without envy. He relinquished the luxury of self-commiseration, and reminding his vanity how easily he might have been Rosalba's parent, he cleared his throat, straightened his chestnut peruke, and spoke.

"My children," he said in a tone admirably paternal and concerned, "I am inexpressibly grieved to witness your distress; I am forced to conclude that all is not well between you. Trust me to understand your reticences, but trust me yet again, and further, to resolve your problems in my larger experience. If you will confide in me, my dears, I can convince you of my ability to assist you in any dilemma."

Even as he pronounced the words with such judicial calm, his mind was troubled and his bowels wrung by a dreadful premonition; pity grew fierce as anger in his soul, and his heart gnawed at his ribs.

Dimly as he now discerned the two figures confronting each other across the profound spaces, coloured more ambiguously than twilight, of their mutual and mortal fear, he was yet aware of a difference in air and attitude, which made Rosalba, to the peculiar pattern of his own mind, the sadder by an infinity of pain.

Virginio stood silent and curiously withdrawn; his white satin shoes were rooted to the ground, but he swayed in the windless atmosphere, and the rustle of his garments and the glimmer of his flaxen hair made a faint music and a fainter illumination, like the stir of a sapling birch tree in the dark.

"Virginio?" said Rosalba, softly.

The rustle of silk and the glimmer of silvery gold appeared, to the chevalier's watchfulness, to assume a new quality; the one had the tinkle, the other the sheen, of something cold and glassy. The sapling birch tree wore no leaves; its slender branches were incased in crystal, and at the tip of every twig a smooth bright icicle hung tremulous.

"Virginio?" said Rosalba again, and again softly, but now she said it with despair.

The girl fluttered restlessly about; she was light as thistledown or dancing flame. Her little hands, emerging from the loose, voluminous wings of her mantle, were lifted continually towards Virginio in a gesture of supplication, mockery, and compassion. Although, in her brilliance, she was fire to Virginio's crackling ice, the chevalier remembered suddenly that the essential substance of that element is delicate and tender and more malleable than the very air, whereas ice is denser even than water, and often hard as stone. And he reflected truly that it was Rosalba's spirit that must inevitably be wounded in this unnatural warfare, however brittle Virginio's bones might prove.

"Have you no word to say to me, my children?" he entreated, and at last Rosalba answered him. She turned from Virginio with recovered composure, and faced Castelneuf with a look of great dignity and sedateness.

"I shall be most grateful for your support and guidance, Chevalier," she said politely. All tint or tremor of the fantastic had fallen from her aspect, and she was nothing stranger than a slight, elegant girl in a velvet cloak, who strove to appear haughty despite her evident fatigue, and whose pale and pretty countenance was wet with ingenuous human tears.

20 SPIDERWEB TANGLE

"I am willing," cried Rosalba, "to do anything; anything, everything, or nothing; I am the servant of the chevalier's advice."

"Anything within reason," amended Querini; his ward interrupted him with quite unfilial scorn.

"Oh, but anything, within or without, or far from reason as the moon from sirocco or I from Notre Dame de Paris! Reason is for old gentlemen, like you and M. de Voltaire; the chevalier understands my determination."

Chastelneuf, thus suddenly made free of the dedicated insanity of youth, smiled into the fire of cedar logs, pervaded by a sweeter, more scented warmth than theirs.

"Reason is not the goddess of emergencies." Carlo Gozzi spoke sententiously, ruffling his thin hair above a corrugated brow. Peter Innocent said nothing.

The little apartment was charming with its fawn-coloured *boiseries* and rose-garlanded carpet; the books behind their gilded lattices enriched the walls by a soft and variegated pattern of their own. The room was called the *study,* after an English fashion; its air was warm and intimate. Every one, with the exception of Virginio, preferred it to the pale and mirrored salon where he now sat alone, nibbling a long green strip of angelica and idly perusing the pages of Frederick Martens' "Natural History of Spitzbergen." "There grows an Arctic flower," he read; but his tranquillity was now and again shattered by the heat and hurry of voices from the open door.

"It is the only solution," pronounced the chevalier. His passing glow was fled, and melancholy possessed him, hollowing his eyes and parching the accustomed glibness of his speech. "I had forgotten my youth, I think," he continued, subdued to shame. "I remembered love, for that still lives in my breast, but I did not remember the races which I ran with Caterina in the gardens of Saint Blaise; my rheumatisms obscured my mind. Virginio can embrace his wife in comfort; his body is attuned to marital bliss. I arranged for that; it was in my opinion of the first importance. But I totally neglected to provide for the lighter contingencies of courtship; he cannot support the rigours of hide-and-seek or the excitement of a bout of blindman's-buff. A handspring would be the end of him. He is a perfect husband, I assure you, but he can never be a playmate for this poor child. When you are older, my dear, it will not grieve you; the domestic pleasures of the *foyer* will suffice."

He ceased; Rosalba was weeping uncontrollably.

"No! no!" she murmured through her

tears, "it is too difficult; I cannot bear it! Better a thousand times some violent change, some mad and excessive sacrifice! I lie in his arms at night; my breath is still because I love him, and his kisses close my lips over my laughter and my eyelids over my tears. But in the morning, when there is no more moonlight, and the sun is shining with the insistence of a golden trumpet made fire instead of sound, when all the red and yellow cockerels are crowing and the larks fly upward like particles of flame, then when I wake and look at him he is afraid. He trembles; when I spring up in the sunshine he trembles at my side; when I run to the window, he pulls the covers about his ears; when I fling the curtains apart to let the light rush in, he faints upon his pillow; the delicate vibration of the dawn afflicts him like a thunderstroke. I tell you, it is too difficult; I cannot bear it, and I would rather die than have it so."

"This is intolerably sad," said Peter Innocent. "The girl is not to blame, yet perhaps we shall have to put her into a convent."

But, "Never! never! never!" cried his three companions with an equal rage, and Rosalba fell upon her knees before him and anointed his hands with her despair.

"There is nothing for it, after all, but the magic," the chevalier repeated solemnly. With the utmost gentleness he raised Rosalba to her feet and conducted her to the shelter of a winged armchair near the hearth.

Reflected firelight rose and fell in rays upon her face, so that it shone unquietly between golden pallor and the colour of blushes; so also her ringlets were transformed from bright to dark and back again to brighter. The gauzes of her dress were disarranged, and among their folds hung here a pink and here a scarlet leaf, and here a frosty flake of ashes. Always she seemed to move and waver in the leaping light, stirred partly by its changes and partly by the shaking of her own heart, and although she was slight and shaken, her look was brave and vibrant and alive.

"Yes, the magic by all means," she said eagerly, quickened to fervour by a radiance above and beyond the cedar flames. "I am not afraid; it will not hurt me if I am not afraid."

"Non dolet!" cried Angelo Querini in a terrible voice, shielding his countenance from view.

"But you can assure us that it will be purely beneficent, or white magic, my dear friend?" asked Peter Innocent, with anxious concern; he was shocked by the violence of the chevalier's reply.

"I can assure you of nothing so absurd, your Eminence. The Deity may justly approve of the affair of Virginio; He cannot seriously object to the vivification of a few handfuls of harmless Murano sand and a pipkin of holy water. But it is another and a very different matter to deprive one of His creatures of the delights and powers bestowed upon her by Himself; we shall require the devil's aid in murdering Rosalba."

"Murder? Surely we are not talking of murder!" Peter Innocent made the sign of the cross, shivering visibly in the blast of horror invoked by the loud and bloody word.

"Ah, not officially, perhaps." The chevalier's bitterness was profound and quiet; absently he lifted Rosalba's warm, sunburnt little hand to his twisted lips. "We shall, indeed, leave her the privilege of living; possibly, in her new and chastened state, she may be duly grateful. But of this Rosalba, this child who sits before us clothed in light and eloquent with the breath of God—of this Rosalba nothing will remain. Yet, if you prefer, we need not call it murder."

"Remember that it is my own wish; the cardinal would have sent me to a convent."

The girl spoke gently and without irony, but Chastelneuf bowed his head as if a mill-stone hung upon his breast; what depth of water closed above that head, or whether tinged with salt or vinegar or gall, it were worse than useless to conjecture.

"It is your own wish; I will not dispute it," he said humbly. "I am, in point of fact, responsible for the plan; I myself proposed it, and, indeed, it appears to be the only unravelling, save the convent, of this deplorable tangle. Of course I could always rescue you from the convent," he added hopefully and under his breath to Rosalba. The girl did not heed him; her eyes were fixed upon Peter Innocent, and she addressed that venerable prelate with the desperate courage of a suppliant.

"I am no more afraid of black magic than of white, Eminence. In the whole world there is only one thing of which I am afraid, and that thing is Virginio's fear. Let me suffer this ordeal, whatever it may prove, and live thereafter in peace and contentment with my beloved husband; this is all I ask."

"A sacrifice proffered in such tenderness cannot come amiss to the mercy of God." Peter Innocent put forth his veined, transparent hand in a gesture of reassurance, and Rosalba thanked him with a pale, but valiant, smile.

"I shall have a word to interpose in this matter," said Angelo Querini. "I do not believe in magic, either black or white; it is not rational, logical, or decent. I do not wish Rosalba to be mixed up in necromancy and kindred follies."

"I believe in magic, and that so religiously that I cannot countenance such practices as the chevalier proposes; the danger to a simple child like Rosalba is appalling. It is well enough, when I write of it, for the negress Smeraldina to be dipped into a cauldron of flame, emerging whiter than a clay pipe, but for this little firebird to be caught and frozen into lifelessness, that is another story altogether, too tragic for my perusal. Let us turn her into a fawn or a vixen or a tawny panther, and set her free forever."

21 METHOD OF THE BROTHERS DUBOIS

"There is a villa at Strà, upon the banks of the Brenta, whose aviaries contain eagles from the Apennines, and whose fenced inclosures hold captive a hundred stags, wild roe, and mountain goats. Do you believe, because the hornbeam is green and the myrtle fragrant, that these creatures are happy? Rosalba, enchanted into some savage form, would wound her bosom against thorny walls, and find herself a prisoner among invisible labyrinths. She would still be bound fast to Virginio, to run like a hound at his heel, or flutter falconwise to his wrist. This were no freedom, but a strange refinement of pain. Rather let her shrink into a china doll and have done with feeling than that she should assume wings prematurely broken or a hind's fleetness without liberty of heart!"

"You are an orator, M. de Chastelneuf; allow me to congratulate you upon your eloquence." Thus spoke the noble Angelo Querini, one time senator of the Republic of Venice. "It might, however, be employed in some worthier cause than the wilful deception of a young girl. We have none of us forgotten Madame von Wulfe and the cruel farce of *Quérilinth*."

"I thank you for the compliment, my dear Querini; your approbation is ever welcome. For the insult I forgive you, even as I hope Madame von Wulfe has forgiven me. In the present matter I can have no motive other than altruism, and I assure you of my good faith. Nevertheless, it is for Rosalba to decide whether or no I now embark upon what must prove for all concerned a solemn and hazardous undertaking."

"I wish it; I demand it," Rosalba answered firmly. "Desperate as the means must be, it is my only remedy for torment. I am prepared to incur the equivalent of death in order to achieve peace for Virginio."

"The child is one of God's elected angels!" cried Peter Innocent in awe. "If she should unhappily perish in this dark adventure, she must in common fairness be canonized. Meanwhile I wish I had her safe among the Poor Clares of Assisi; she is too saintly for this secular arena of mortal life."

"Nonsense! She is nothing of the sort; she is merely a luckless girl who loves a glass manikin instead of kind, consoling flesh and blood!" the chevalier retorted with sardonic insolence. It was plain that his own flesh and blood were racked and poisoned by revolt.

M. de Chastelneuf was very pale. His eyes were sunken in his head, and his face was ravaged like a starving man's. Yet, worn and sharpened and intolerably wrung, he still maintained, despite this betrayal of his body, a certain victory of spirit, a simple affair of courage, perhaps, and accustomed coolness against heavy odds. And again, it was plain that he did not suffer for himself alone.

"Above all, we must be practical," he said, recovering perfectly his manner of impudent composure. "There is a method —not my own, I may say, but that of the celebrated Brothers Dubois, late of Vincennes—whereby young ladies are rendered harmless to the tranquillity of others and permanently deprived of their surplus emotions. Quite frankly, it is magic of a vehement and painful variety; the subject is ultimately transformed into fine porcelain, but the process is not agreeable, and the result, although miraculous, is somewhat inhuman. I have known fathers who submitted their daughters to the ordeal, husbands who forced it upon their wives, but never, until this hour, have I known a woman to desire the torture of her own free will. It is an agony more incisive than birth or dissolution; I dare not veil the circumstance with pity."

"And may a woman undergo this terrible ordeal and live?" Carlo Gozzi alone found voice, and that the thinnest whisper, to inquire.

"Yes, she may live, and flourish, and be fair and decorous and delightful." Chastelneuf ground his strong white teeth upon the words. "She may, to all appearances and outward seeming, remain a mortal woman; for aught I know to the contrary a purified soul may burn peacefully within the pretty fabric of her body. But—she will be porcelain; fine porcelain, remember, and no longer clay. In a porcelain vessel filled with clear water a rose may live for a little while, but out of clay a rose may rise alive and blooming, set on the roots of elder roses. There is a difference, but it does not matter."

"Nothing matters except Virginio," said Rosalba, softly.

Even as the chevalier drove sharp nails into his palms and bit his lip until he tasted blood, even as Peter Innocent bowed his lovely silver brow in sorrowful acquiscence, Virginio entered quietly and sadly, like the softer echo of Rosalba's voice.

None who looked upon him then wondered afterward at the fabulous chivalry of the girl's devotion; the lovers looked into each other's eyes, and their eyes were tender, pitiful, and afraid. Virginio wore a quality of pure translucent beauty, unwarmed by earth, the beauty of an element like sea or air, or that refined and rarefied sunlight mirrored by the moon. He wore this beauty meekly, and with a slight and delicate timidity he approached his wife and folded her within his arms. Felicity hovered above their bending heads, flying nearer, yet never alighting; the wings of felicity were so nearly visible that to Carlo Gozzi they appeared feathered like those of the pigeons of Saint Mark, and to Peter Innocent like the Holy Ghost itself in the shape of a silver dove.

Furthermore, to Peter Innocent, whose mind was a missal book of sacred images, Virginio figured as the young John Baptist, wandering immaculate in the desert, and Rosalba as a small golden lioness, of equal virtue and simplicity, but pagan and untamable and shy.

So, like a pair of legendary children, they came to the cardinal where he sat musing by the fire, and, moved by one impulse, sank upon their knees before him and inclined their bright locks to his blessing. The flaxen and the darkly burnished head bent side by side beneath his hand, and Peter Innocent's musings were made audible as prayer, and in the silence smoke rose like incense from the crumbling cedar logs, ascending through the chimney to the frosty night, and thence perhaps, to heaven.

22 PÂTE TENDRE

"If you were hard paste, we should have to send you to Meissen," said the chevalier, smiling and alert in an elegant new travelling-cloak of bottle-green broadcloth. The midday sun lay yellow along a vast map spread upon the writing-desk, and although it was November, the windows stood open to sweet and jocund breezes. An atmosphere of nervous gaiety pervaded the study; a strapped portmanteau and a Florentine dressing-case occupied the settee, and seven large bandboxes were piled in a corner.

Upon the mantelpiece two crystal vases exhaled a mist of jasmine, and between these were set a number of china figurines of exquisite workmanship. A fantastic bellarmine grimaced at a Bow cupid, and a delicious Chelsea group of the Four Seasons, modelled by Roubiliac, and glowing with every floral tint, contrasted curiously with a fine white Derby biscuit statuette of Queen Charlotte and her children.

"Yes, Meissen for hard paste," repeated Chastelneuf, cheerfully, "and from that grim fortress you might come forth with a rosy Saxon complexion and no sensibilities whatever."

"And no freckles?" asked Rosalba, with a pardonable feminine eagerness.

"No, my love; you would be as pink as a sugar-plum and as smooth as whipped cream. However, Meissen is far too Germanic for your peculiar mentality, and you could never survive its furnaces. It must be either Sèvres or Marseilles, since Hannong of Strasburg has been dead these two years, and you are averse to visiting England."

"I cannot forget that I am a Frenchwoman." Rosalba spoke with a faint trace of hauteur, gazing rather wistfully at the Chelsea figure of Spring, attired in a vernal dress of apple green and pearl colour.

"I should like to see you in white Marseilles faïence," said the chevalier. "I once beheld a shepherdess in biscuit-porcelain, made in the factory of the Duc de Villeroy at Mennecy, which was almost worthy of you. Nevertheless, I believe we shall be wise in selecting Sèvres. It was the scene of the Brothers Dubois's amazing discovery; they were subsequently dismissed for drunkenness and the practice of venomous magic. They came to me with letters from the Prince of Courland, whom they had greatly assisted in the search for the philosopher's stone. I was able to resolve the slight difficulties they had encountered by means of my infallible compound of Hungarian crystal and native cinnabar. Overcome with gratitude, they presented me with the secret recipe associated with their name. Since then I have ever been in a position to turn ladies into porcelain, but I have not often availed myself of the opportunity; the process is opposed to my principles and natural proclivities."

"Dear Chevalier, I am quite familiar with your sentiments," murmured Rosalba, sympathetically and a little shyly. "But you will surely not refuse to aid me, upon this occasion, in my search for happiness. I have understood you to say, have I not, that you are capable of complete and single-handed success in the absence of the Brothers Dubois?"

"But yes, and fortunately, since the Brothers Dubois are at present inaccessibly situated in purgatory or some even less salubrious region," Chastelneuf assured her. "I need no help in the matter, save that of such skilled workmen as are to be found in any porcelain factory, augmented by those supernatural agencies which I must not scruple to employ."

"I am glad it is to be Sèvres, when all is said and done." Rosalba gazed reflectively into a tortoise-shell mirror, comparing her image therein with the countenance of an enchanting china figure, sculptured by Clodion in the classic taste, which the chevalier, bowing, presented to her view, poised daintly upon the palm of his hand.

"Oh, it is undoubtedly your *genre!*" cried Chastelneuf with enthusiasm, touching the girl's pale cheek with a respectfully tentative forefinger. "The true Sèvres, the soft paste of the old régime, not this stony stuff they have derived from the Germans. You are the finest *porcelaine de France;* I know the ingredients." And he began to chant a medley of words, in which Rosalba was at some pains to distinguish syllables analogous to "Fountainebleau sand—pure sea salt—Aliante alum—and powdered alabaster." Certainly the chevalier was a gentleman of various and esoteric learning, whose knowledge of humanity was both profound and nice. Rosalba resigned her will to his, and faced the future with mingled fortitude and acute curiosity.

"It is decided, then, that the cardinal accompany us, while Virginio remains with Querini and Carlo Gozzi, perfecting himself in the study of Greek, Latin, Arabic, and antique Spanish. He will thus be enabled to compare philosophies with fairy-tales, and to contemplate life with the stoicism of the one and the insouciance of the other. I have also suggested that he become proficient upon the flute and engage a really good fencing-master," said the chevalier, divesting himself of his travelling cloak and taking a pinch of snuff.

"We depart in an hour's time," he continued lightly, consulting a sumptuous jewelled watch, "and you will doubtless prefer to make your adieus to Virginio unattended by the most affectionate friend. I withdraw, therefore, but shall await you, with restrained impatience, in the adjoining apartment. I am sure we shall have no cause to regret our decision in the matter of factories." His smile contrived a positive frivolity, and Rosalba experienced a thrill of gratitude.

"The cardinal makes me feel that I am setting forth upon a penitential pilgrimage," she said plaintively. "You are less alarming; allow it to remain a mere affair of millinery. I could almost believe that we were going to Paris to select a costume for the carnival."

"But that, in a way, is true enough, my child," cried Chastelneuf, retiring. As he went, he coughed thrice behind a fine lace handkerchief, and wiped his eyes.

Presently Virginio knocked gently upon the door, and entered like a cloud of cooler air.

"Adieu, Virginio, my darling," whispered Rosalba.

"Adieu, adieu, my heart's beloved," the boy replied. Their voices were too low for audible trembling, but their hands, clinging together in the final instant, shook like thin white petals in a hurricane.

"Virginio, good-bye."

"Good-bye, Rosalba."

"I am going."

"I know; good-bye, my love."

"Virginio—"

"My dear—"

"Good-bye."

They embraced; bright glassy tears fell upon Rosalba's breast, and upon Virginio's cold hands Rosalba's tears fell quick and glittering as sunshower drops, and warm almost as the kisses wherewith they were mingled.

The great door closed at last between the lovers, leaving no sound; its painted panels confronted them severally with Pan's cruel nonchalance and Medusa's uncomfortable stare.

Virginio examined his finger-nails; they were quite uninjured, but the least finger of his left hand appeared to have suffered a slight sprain.

Rosalba, drawing on her white suède gloves, observed without surprise that both her wrists were faintly flecked with blood, as though a bracelet of thorns had lately clasped them.

23 ORDEAL BY FIRE

Through a landscape lightly strewn with snow, and rendered graciously austere by long, converging lines of leafless poplars, the three strange travellers approached the neighbourhood of Paris.

The chevalier's English carriage was commodious and softly cushioned, and the discomforts of the journey had been negligible; nevertheless a ponderable sadness was bound upon the shoulders of the adventurers, as if indeed they carried ambiguous packs too heavy for their spirits. Their chins were sunk against their breasts, and even Chastelneuf strove quite in vain to dissipate this burden by companionable chatter.

"Paris must wait," he observed to Rosalba. "Afterward, when our affair is concluded, it will be time to think of the *trousseau,* which only Paris can fitly provide for a Frenchwoman. I consider you too fine for our Venetian barbarities of fashion, which tend ever to the extravagant and the capricious. You must see Bertin, of course; the queen swears by her, although the little Polignac, always so demure and so chic, is of another opinion entirely. But you will choose for yourself; it is the prerogative of Venus."

Rosalba raised her satirically penciled brows the least reproving shade, and the chevalier subsided into a conversation with Peter Innocent, who remained immersed in his breviary, vouchsafing now and again an absent-minded nod or a grieved monosyllable in response to the other's volubility.

"While I warmly second your decision as to the preservation of the strictest incognito, Eminence, I can assure you that no such peril attaches itself to our activities in this enlightened land of France as we should inevitably incur at home. In Venice we should have the Holy Office upon our tracks in a twinkling; here we need only fear the unfriendly attention of the Academy of Sciences.

"Instead of the Three and their spies, we must shun the associates of Bailly and Franklin. They are about to disturb the magnetic afflatus of Mesmer, but he, you know, is a charlatan."

"Yes?" said Peter Innocent, clutching his rosary.

They drove through the Forest of Meudon; beyond lay the park and the two châteaux. The sun was setting somewhere over their left shoulders.

"Have you heard that the duc de Chartres is cutting down the magnificent chestnut alleys in the Palais-Royal?" inquired the chevalier.

His companions preserved a silence unbroken save by sighs.

Presently they reached the outskirts of the ancient town of Sèvres; at a little distance from the factory, whose dark bulk rose upon the river-bank, a curious tower was conspicuous above a clump of nameless trees.

"Private workroom of the Brothers Dubois," the chevalier explained in hushed, oppressive accents.

"But they are dead, and the place is evidently deserted!" cried the cardinal, his voice vibrating to the chill along his spine.

"True; only too true," said Chastelneuf.

Perhaps the vitreous tiles which roofed the structure possessed a coppery glaze, perhaps the doors and windows were bound with this red metal, or perhaps the setting sun performed a sinister miracle of transmutation, and turned the tower into blood and flame. Its shape was very singular and menacing against the holy evening sky, where upon a field of violet a few small stars were visible. The carriage halted at a word from Chastelneuf, and came to a standstill at the mouth of a clearing in the clump of trees; feathery grasses, tipped with snow, had overgrown the path. The horses stamped their feet in the stillness; steam floated in thick clouds about their heads. The chevalier's Spanish servant, shrouded to the eyes in a sombre cloak, awaited his master's instructions with an air of taciturn complicity in some questionable design.

"Monseigneur, you will proceed to the inn at Versailles, where a fire, a feather bed, and a roasted fowl are in readiness," Chastelneuf declared, fixing the cardinal with an hypnotic eye. "Rosalba and I must now go on alone."

"On foot?" Peter Innocent asked in a weak voice.

"On foot, but not far; Rosalba will have ample opportunity to dry her slippers before the night is out." The words were significant and sharp; the cardinal shuddered.

"I am not afraid," said Rosalba, for the thousandth time, in a pitiful whisper. "They do not throw salt into the furnaces any more, nor use pulverized ox-bones, as they do in England."

"She need not suffer a second firing," said Chastelneuf. "I have concluded that no glaze is necessary, though, for that matter, the modern glaze is no longer by immersion, but by sprinkling, as in Christian baptism. But we shall leave Rosalba in the simple biscuit state. Console yourself, Eminence; your responsibility is heavy, but she shall be saved."

Peter Innocent found a slight support for his swooning spirit in the religious flavour of these final reassurances; he watched the pair depart through tears, and made his every breath a prayer as the trees met over the chevalier's haughty head and took Rosalba into their equivocal embrace.

For one brief instant the tower was split by a streak of brightness, and all the vehemence of fire outraged the tranquillity of the twilit wood; then the door closed, the smoke dispersed, the fumes faded in air, and with their going Peter Innocent was borne like thistledown, by the swift agency of two black horses, along the lonely road to Versailles.

24 SILVER CORD

In the ancient Satory quarter of Versailles, under the very shadow of the new cathedral of St. Louis, there lay a little tavern whose sign bore the symbol of the Silver Bowman. In the only parlour the narrow place afforded a clear fire had been kindled, before whose consolatory incandescence the Cardinal Peter Innocent Bon now warmed his hands and meditated upon the wonders of the world.

The eighth of these, to his enchanted thinking, and which had but this moment vanished in a visible smoke from between his fingers, was not the greater nor the smaller Trianon, nor yet the palace itself, nor the gardens nor the orangery. The thing had been more marvellous than these, both magic and geometric; a flower inclosed in a carven frame, a lovely formal pattern. A flake of snow, fallen from the dove-coloured skies of France, had melted in the heat of the fire.

Although Peter Innocent had often found the Roman winter of a severity too poignant for his anatomy to support without pain, he had rarely encountered the mysteries of frost and snow, and now his recollection wandered to the Christmas season of 1716, when he had seen Venice no longer blue and gold, but muffled and masked in whiteness. Oblivion like sleep had come at first upon the town, and then a bitter wind, and finally, when the sun shone again in the heavens, the palaces and church towers had flashed and scintillated beneath a covering of quicksilver. All this was memorable to Peter Innocent after many years, and he could picture the wine shop, even, where his father had taken him for a glass of malvasia from Epirus. He had been fourteen years old at the time, the malvasia had tasted warm as imagined Acroceraunian spring.

Since then, and so for uncounted Christmas seasons, Peter Innocent had forgotten the miracle of snow. Now he was enraptured, and opening the casement against a stubborn blast of the north, he filled his hands once more with the intricate crystals.

Yet all too soon the crystals dissolved again to icy moisture, and Peter Innocent considered beauty's evanescence as typified in those spilt drops of snow water.

A thin white wine of France stood in a green decanter by his elbow, but he foretasted it as cold astringent stuff; he wished Rosalba would return to brew him a glass of negus, with nutmeg in it, and the grated rind of a lemon.

A small volume bound in creamy vellum lay by the decanter, in a pool of green reflected light; he knew it for a copy of Rosalba's poems, printed at Pisa less than a year ago as a gift from Querini to his ward.

An absurd medley of quotation sprinkled the title-page with tags from Seneca and Catullus. Here cried the unchristian wastrel to his strumpet: "Remains to be slept the sleep of one unbroken night." Here the virtuous philosopher remarked, with equal gloom: "We are kindled and put out." Peter Innocent found the poems themselves hard to decipher in the failing light.

He picked up a fine Venetian edition of Theocritus, but the book fell open at an unknown line, and this is what he read: "The lamb is gone, the poor young thing is gone . . . a savage wolf has crunched her in his jaws, and the dogs bay; what profits it to weep, when of that lost creature not a bone nor a cinder is left?"

Peter Innocent poured out a measure of the thin white wine; the goblet was full to the brim, and a little wine was spilled upon the pages of the book, for the cardinal's hand was trembling. He shivered, huddled in his worn habit of the Friars Minor; he wished very heartily that he had indeed borrowed the chevalier's luxurious dressing-gown of quilted purple silk, as Rosalba had more than once suggested.

The streets of Versailles were veiled by falling snow, and the wheels of the few cabriolets and chariots which passed beneath the window of the inn were noiseless in their revolutions; only the occasional crack of a whip shattered the frosty silence. Peter Innocent was very lonely.

Almost, he believed, he would have welcomed the arrival of those visitors whom his shy secretiveness had so far avoided. His incognito had been studiously preserved; even the curious eye of Louis de Rohan Guéménée, Cardinal Grand Almoner and Archbishop of Strasburg, had failed to mark the elusive wearer of the grey-brown garb of St. Francis.

With the benediction of Assisi's name, there came into Peter Innocent's mind a sudden longing to be comforted, and he turned, like a bewildered child, to the dear protection of his patron saint. His fingers sought and found the leaves of another book, wherein his own scholarly Italian hand had traced certain passages from the life of Francis. His sight, under the encroaching dusk, grew dim; then he saw plainly what was written in the book.

"O brother fire, most beautiful of all creatures, be courteous to me at this hour, knowing how well I have always loved thee and ever will for His love Who created thee!"

Upon the instant, the fire upon the hearth appeared to lift its terrible head in anger and spring like a tiger at his throat; he put up his feeble arms in a defensive gesture, and dropped them again in despair. The portent was revenge from heaven.

For even now, at his advice, at his desire, Rosalba was giving her body to be burned. "Be courteous to me at this hour—" The hour was struck, and the jaws of the furnace had received the child.

He caught up the decanter of wine, and flung it, a bubble of green glass, into the burning fangs of the fire, where it was destroyed in a moment. Then he fell upon his knees, and would have beat out the flames with his hands; but his strength failed him, the monster leaped upward with a roar, and Peter Innocent felt its teeth fasten in his shoulder; then he fainted.

He was revived by the chevalier's voice and Rosalba's touch upon his temples. The window stood open to the snow, which blew inward, golden particles emerging strangely from an infinity of blue dusk; a handful of snow was sprinkled over his eyes, which throbbed with fever. The fire still raged within its bars, but as Rosalba stooped to tend it, he could have sworn that she spoke in a low, caressing tone, and perhaps admonished it by a sign; presently the flames sank down and seemed to slumber.

The chevalier's cloak was wet with snow, and his face confessed a weariness and lassitude most carefully excluded from his speech.

"All is well, Eminence," he said, flinging his laced hat upon the table with a long-drawn sigh of fatigue. "She has survived our ministrations; a diabolic ordeal has served its purpose, and she has returned to you alive. Of her courage I cannot speak; her present composure may speak for her, even in silence. Yet perhaps, of her charity, she has a word for those who have wronged her."

Rosalba leaned at ease against the window-frame, and the snow blew past her lifted head and powdered it with particles of gold. There was about her an air of perfect calm; she was poised, composed, and quiet, yet without stiffness; her attitude had the grace of a bird arrested in flight, a flower flexible, but unmoved by wind. Peter Innocent knew instinctively that her spirit was unstirred by any pang that may not be suffered by an exemplary child of seven.

Her face was exquisitely clear and fresh in every tilted line and smooth velvety surface; her hair was miraculously symmetrical, and its thick scallops had the quality of gilded bronze. Her mantle fell about her in delicate sculptured folds.

"God give you peace!" said Rosalba to Peter Innocent, with a gentle candour unaware of pity and its intolerable demands.

25 INTERIOR BY LONGHI

How delicate a contrivance of language must lull the imagination to repose before it may sing or picture to itself, while half-asleep, Rosalba's homecoming!

This must be spoken in a whisper, dreamed in a meditation, drawn in the palest colours of pearls, set to an accompaniment of reverential music, veiling silence with a silver veil.

In that hour when the shadows flow like clear blue water along the golden sands of day, in the mildness of afternoon, in a place profoundly quiet, Virginio and Rosalba met and kissed.

Their very garments were awed into submission, so that silk dared not rustle or flowers shed their fragrance; the heels of their shoes were dipped in magic, so that they made no sound, and a dimness like the smoke of incense obscured the shining of their hair.

Nothing else in the world was ever so soft as their lips and the clasp of their hands; these were softer than the wings of grey moths or the frosty feathers of dandelion seed.

A little brush, smoothing thin pigments on a polished cedar panel, may trace more lightly and precisely than any pen the figures of Virginio and Rosalba, the wedded lovers of a fairy-tale, who now live happy ever after, in Venice, in a world of porcelain and Murano mirrors.

It has been said, and that upon distinguished authority, that Pietro Longhi survived, in the amber peace of a mellowing century, until the age of eighty; the statement is difficult to refute.

For those who would believe it, there exists in support of this theory a small painting, bearing the artist's signature not only in the mere syllables of his name, but, more convincingly, in every curve and colour of the scene itself.

The hand of a very old man is evident in the fine performance; the lines waver, the colours are subdued and etherealized. The hand is the hand of Longhi, and he was an old man when Rosalba returned to Venice in the amber twilight of a dying century.

This twilight fills the picture, and is reflected from the mirrors of the background; the faces of the lovers emerge like stars from this profundity of twilight. The figure of Peter Innocent is there, quiet as a carven saint in his niche; he wears the grey-brown habit of the Friars Minor, and his veined and fragile hands are folded upon a cross. That noble brow and faint ironic smile can only be Querini's, and Count Carlo Gozzi looks impish and melancholy in a new periwig and the rich mantle of a patrician. The chevalier is absent; it is said he has retired to Bohemia.

The faces of the lovers are most beautiful and pure; the gentle and elegiac quality of their love appears unmarred by longing. Having forgotten fear and the requirements of pity, their tenderness becomes a placid looking-glass in which each beholds the other; the mercurial wildness which no longer moves them is fixed behind this transparent screen, lending brightness to the mirrored images.

At any moment they may awake; Virginio will put on his pearl-coloured greatcoat and wrap an ermine tippet about Rosalba's throat, and the season being winter and very clear and cold, they will hurry to a fashionable pastry cook's to eat whipped cream and wafers.

THE END

Bibliography

GENERAL

BREWSTER, DOROTHY, AND AGNES BURRELL. "The Short Story and the Novelette," *Modern Fiction.* New York: Columbia University Press, 1934.

CLARK, BARRETT H., AND MAXIM LIEBER, eds. *Great Short Stories of the World.* Cleveland: World Publishing Co., 1953.

CONNOLLY, CYRIL, ed. *Great English Short Novels.* New York: Dial Press, Inc., 1953.

LEWISOHN, LUDWIG. *Expression in America.* New York: Harper & Brothers, 1932.

SCHORER, MARK, ed. *The Story: A Critical Anthology.* New Jersey: Prentice-Hall, Inc., 1950.

SHIPLEY, JOESPH, ed. "Short Story," *Dictionary of World Literature.* New York: Philosophical Library Publisher, 1953.

HERMAN MELVILLE

FREEMAN, F. B. *Melville's Billy Budd.* Cambridge: Harvard University Press, 1948.

HOFFMAN, CHARLES G. "Short Fiction of Herman Melville," *South Atlantic Quarterly,* LII (July, 1953), 414–30.

WRIGHT, N. "Form as Function in Melville," *PMLA,* LXVII (June, 1952), 330–40.

MARK TWAIN

DE VOTO, BERNARD. *Mark Twain at Work.* Cambridge: Harvard University Press, 1942.

FEINSTEIN, GEORGE. "Mark Twain's Idea of Story Structure," *American Literature,* XVIII (May, 1946), 160–63.

GOOLD, EDGAR H. "Mark Twain on the Writing of Fiction," *American Literature,* XXVI (May, 1954), 141–53.

KRAUSE, S. J. "Twain's Method and Theory of Composition," *Modern Philology,* LVI (February, 1959), 167–77.

STEPHEN CRANE

BERRYMAN, JOHN. *Stephen Crane.* New York: William Sloane Associates, 1950.

FORD, FORD MADDOX. "Technique," *Southern Review,* I (1935), 20–35.

KWIAT, JOSEPH J. "Stephen Crane and Painting," *American Quarterly,* IV (Winter, 1952), 331–38.

STALLMAN, ROBERT W. "Stephen Crane's Revision of *Maggie: A Girl of the Streets,*" *American Literature,* XXVI (January, 1955), 528–36.

HENRY JAMES

BEACH, JOSEPH WARREN. *The Method of Henry James,* enlarged ed. Philadelphia: Albert Saifer, 1954.

BLACKMUR, RICHARD P., ed. *The Art of the Novel: Critical Prefaces.* New York: Charles Scribner's Sons, 1934.

HOFFMAN, CHARLES G. *The Short Novels of Henry James.* New York: Twayne Publishers, 1957.

MATTHIESSEN, F. O., AND KENNETH MURDOCK. *The Notebooks of Henry James,* rev. ed. New York: Oxford University Press, 1955.

Henry James, Special Number, Modern Fiction Studies, III (Spring, 1957), 73–96.

GERTRUDE STEIN

HOFFMAN, FREDERICK J. "The Color and Shape of the Thing Seen: Gertrude Stein," *The Twenties: American Writing in the Postwar Decade*. New York: Viking Press, 1955.

STEIN, GERTRUDE. *Three Lives* (contains *The Good Anna, Melanctha,* and *The Gentle Lena*). New York: New Directions, 1942.

WILSON, EDMUND. "Gertrude Stein," *Axel's Castle*. New York: Charles Scribner's Sons, 1931.

WILLIAM CARLOS WILLIAMS

BURKE, KENNETH. "The Methods of William Carlos Williams," *Dial,* LXXXII (1927), 94–98.

KOCH, VIVIENNE. *William Carlos Williams*. New York: New Directions, 1950.

POUND, EZRA. "Dr. Williams' Position," *Polite Essays*. 1937.

ROSENFELD, PAUL. "William Carlos Williams," *Port of New York*. 1924. Pp. 103–13.

WILLIAMS, WILLIAM CARLOS. *I Wanted to Write a Poem,* reported and edited by Edith Heal. Boston: Beacon Press, 1958.

ELINOR WYLIE

Collected Prose of Elinor Wylie (includes her best known pieces, with biographical and critical prefaces by Stephen Vincent Benét, William Rose Benét, Isabel Patterson, Carl Van Doren, and Carl Van Vechten). New York: Alfred A. Knopf, Inc., 1933.

CABELL, JAMES BRANCH. "Sanctuary in Porcelain: A Note on Elinor Wylie," *Virginia Quarterly Review,* VI (1930), 335–41.

KOHLER, DAYTON. "Elinor Wylie: Heroic Mask," *South Atlantic Quarterly,* XXXVI (1937), 218–28.

LÜDEKE, H. "Venetian Glass: The Poetry and Prose of Elinor Wylie," *English Studies,* XX (1938), 241–50.